I0797300

NONVIOLENT

DIRECT ACTION

NONVIOLENT

A Memoir of Resistance, Agitation, and Love

REVEREND
JAMES LAWSON JR.
and Emily Yellin

RANDOM HOUSE
NEW YORK

Random House
An imprint and division of Penguin Random House LLC
1745 Broadway, New York, NY 10019
randomhousebooks.com
penguinrandomhouse.com

Grateful acknowledgment is made to the following for permission to reprint previously published material:
People magazine: Excerpts from "Why Did a Nice Girl Like Anna Sandhu Wed James Earl Ray? 'I Love Him,' She Says" (October 30, 1978) © 2025 People Inc. All rights reserved. Reprinted from PEOPLE and published with permission of People Inc. Reproduction in any manner in any language in whole or in part without written permission is prohibited.
Time magazine: Excerpts from articles from *Time* magazine dated April 12, 1968; April 26, 1968; and August 16, 1968 © 1968 TIME USA LLC. All rights reserved. Used under license.

Hardcover ISBN 9780593596241
Ebook ISBN 9780593596258

Printed in the United States of America on acid-free paper

2nd Printing

BOOK TEAM: Managing editor: Rebecca Berlant • Production manager: Richard Elman • Copy editor: Bonnie Thompson • Proofreaders: Taylor Teague, Caryl Weintraub, Ruth Anne Phillips

Book design by Simon M. Sullivan

The authorized representative in the EU for product safety and compliance is Penguin Random House Ireland, Morrison Chambers, 32 Nassau Street, Dublin D02 YH68, Ireland.
https://eu-contact.penguin.ie

Dedicated to My Beloved Family

My wife, Dorothy Wood Lawson

My three sons, John, Morris, and Seth

My grandchildren, Raven, Devin, and James

My parents, siblings, and daughter-in-law Cima

and the entire Wood and Lawson tribes

I dream a world where all
Will know sweet freedom's way
Where greed no longer saps the soul
Nor avarice blights our day

—Langston Hughes

Contents

FOREWORD

An Exemplar for Our Time: James Lawson, Saintliness, and Nonviolence

by Eddie S. Glaude Jr.

James Morris Lawson Jr. stands as one of the towering figures of twentieth-century America. Dr. Martin Luther King Jr. described him as one of the "noble men" of the Black freedom struggle. I can imagine that, without his influence and powerful presence, the Civil Rights Movement would not have taken the shape that it did. A fervent believer in the spiritual and revolutionary power of nonviolence, Reverend Lawson dedicated his life to teaching its principles and its possibilities for life in this country.

His was a life full of transformative journeys and experiences. As a young college student in 1951, he was imprisoned for refusing to register with the armed forces. After serving his time, he traveled as a Methodist missionary to India only to find himself studying the nonviolent philosophy of Gandhi and its potential for igniting social and political change. He studied at the Oberlin School of Theology and at Vanderbilt Divinity School. He eventually met Dr. King in 1957, who urged him to come South, and there James Lawson began to teach a generation, young and old, about the power of nonviolent civil disobedience.

Reverend Lawson and Dr. King were the same age, born four months apart. We lost King at thirty-nine, but Reverend Lawson lived to the age of ninety-five, and he would dedicate the rest of his days to the work that they had begun together. In Memphis and then in Los Angeles, he fought for economic justice, and would coin the term "plantation capitalism" to define what the movement was fighting to dismantle.

To my mind, every young person in this country should know about Reverend Lawson—about his contributions to American democracy, his courage, and his unshakable faith in the capacity of human beings to be better, more decent, and committed to a more just world. Reverend

Lawson advised Dr. Martin Luther King Jr. and the Southern Christian Leadership Conference (SCLC), was critical to the development of the student movement in Nashville, Tennessee, later helped organize the Student Nonviolent Coordinating Committee (SNCC), and trained countless activists in the principles of nonviolence. In every way, he was an extraordinary man.

In his ministry, Reverend Lawson emphasized the love of God and the life of Jesus. He preached a Gospel that lifted up the least of these in a fallen world. Nonviolence stood as a radical enactment of that love in a world racked with violence. For him, such an approach was not simply a strategy or a tactic to end segregation. Nonviolence was more than a tool; it was a way of life. Until he took his last breath, Reverend Lawson urged us "to see nonviolence as an alternative to the chaos of violence," and to see it as a means to transform the country, the world, and ourselves. His life and witness helped make this country a better place, and he stands as an example for how we might live with conviction and courage in the face of the evils of our own time.

Too often we center the history of the Civil Rights Movement around the personalities of those who were in front of the cameras. Dr. Martin Luther King Jr. and John Lewis, for example, stand as heroic figures in a movement made up of ordinary people who dared to challenge Jim Crow segregation. Their actions and deeds are illustrative of the movement itself. With these men (and, more often than not, men are centered in the story) and an emphasis on the more dramatic events of the period (e.g., the March on Washington or Bloody Sunday or Dr. King's assassination), a too narrow and sometimes distorted understanding of the Civil Rights Movement emerges: a story that guides our eyes to particular people or specific moments where spectacle and heroism blur.

In some ways, this narrow approach is consistent with the "great men" theory of history. Here men who are divinely inspired, with distinctive attributes like courage and intelligence, change the course of history. Their biographies become the story of the moment. *They* are the agents of substantive change. But what is often obscured by this view are structural and social realities as well as the actions of lesser-known characters, who are no less inspired, that make the moment possible.

James Lawson is one of those critically important figures (and with him a host of other powerful, everyday people come into view). He dedicated his life to challenging not only white supremacy, but the underlying violence that organizes our way of life far beyond the question of legal rights. He insisted that we could live together differently and that we could respond to hate with an enveloping love. Attending to his life, especially now with this autobiography, reveals his presence and influence in most of the significant moments of the Civil Rights Movement (e.g., from the Freedom Ride to Memphis) and shows the radical power of his belief in nonviolence. He was there, often in the background by choice, in the shadows, prodding, training, and believing that nonviolent struggle could hasten the collapse of white supremacy and transform the country. He refused the gradualism of the legal approach of the NAACP. Segregation had to be challenged immediately and directly with "soul force."

To be honest, my own disposition does not lend itself to the kind of nonviolent, courageous action of the likes of Diane Nash, John Lewis, and Reverend Lawson. Perhaps I am too much like my father, who, when I was young, seemed angry and unwilling to tolerate the foolishness of white people. I guess I internalized the chaos. In me, rage simmers just beneath the surface. Smiles hide the wildness in the eyes. Years of disciplined restraint keep the tongue civil. As a young man growing up on the coast of Mississippi, I found the words and actions of Dr. King and those in the Civil Rights Movement inspiring. If not for them and their willingness to challenge what James Silver described as the closed society that was Mississippi, I would not be here. Nevertheless, I could not imagine myself facing down the hatred of white folk without lashing back. I believed they deserved my rage and hatred, not my love. Too many Black bodies sit at the bottom of Mississippi rivers for that. Too many places are haunted by the dead strung up on Spanish oak trees.

But I have come to learn that hatred turns on you and eats your insides. It darkens the eyes. Love, instead, nurtures the spirit and the imagination. It demands something more than the spittle of rage. Love can free you from *them* and *their* hatreds. I don't mean to be sentimental about love, nor am I referring to some abstract idea of *agape*. Loving people, tending to them close to the ground, demands something more from you—from me: that you see and feel the human being right in front of you and understand that life can call forth a kind of vulnerability *in you* that allows you to be fully human. Love enables the recognition that indifference to that life can easily make you monstrous. Yet the leap to the necessity of nonviolent struggle, of loving your enemies under all circumstances, remains a hard question for this country boy shaped by the raging ghosts of Mississippi.

I am a bit—and I suspect younger people are as well—leery of the constant badgering today by politicians and pundits to engage in nonviolent demonstrations. As if those in power can dictate the form and shape of the cries of the oppressed. Calls for nonviolence feel, at times, like an unseemly repetition (a nostalgic longing for that moment in the 1960s and that movement) and a desire on the part of some to discipline forms of political dissent. They would have us believe that the only legitimate form of protest is that of the nonviolent march animated by basic liberal demands. In this sense, the philosophy of nonviolence comes to younger generations often as a form of constraint or as a performative exercise that, at best, leads to tinkering around the edges of policy matters. One need think only of the marches against police violence in the Black Lives Matter movement to get a sense of the limitations of this form of protest. Police still rampage, and now with impunity. But that does not mean violent protest is the only viable alternative. Burning down the QuikTrip convenience store in Ferguson, Missouri, did not change the nature of policing either. I am aware of the pitfalls of violence, especially when challenging the state. No need to throw away lives with actions that will not fundamentally change circumstances. No need to risk hardening your heart, either. And it is here that the lessons abundant in the life and witness of James Lawson come into full view.

Reading his words, I was struck by how he introduced the methods of nonviolence, with each progressive step aimed at intensifying the tension with dramatic action to bring about substantive change.

1. Fact-finding: Study the situation, obtain all the facts.
2. Negotiation: Present the facts, and raise the moral issue.
3. Education: The entire community must be informed of the real issues; rumor and fear must be matched with facts. Dramatic forms of education can be used, such as marches, demonstrations, mass meeting.
4. Preparation for Satyagraha: When the other stages of nonviolence fail to bring the desired changes, then the nonviolent group must prepare for direct action.

And the fifth and final stage involved nonviolent direct action, which entailed a variety of tactics that included "the sit-in, the boycott, the vigil, and civil disobedience" (deliberately breaking an unjust law to expose it).

Marches alone are not sufficient. In fact, they stand as a dramatic form of education. They focus attention for just a moment. Demonstrations around the public lynching of George Floyd brought police violence to the attention of millions. In that sense, marches do a certain kind of work, but they cannot be the end in itself. We need only think about where the country is today *after* those massive demonstrations. Another step is required. For example, Reverend Lawson openly criticized the James Meredith march in *Concern* magazine in July 1966. Just a month earlier, Meredith had been shot the day after he embarked on his solitary march against fear. Civil rights organizations and leaders vowed to complete the march from Memphis, Tennessee, to Jackson, Mississippi. Here the tensions within the movement came into full view, particularly regarding the efficacy of nonviolence. Stokely Carmichael (who later changed his name to Kwame Ture) even called for "Black Power" over the standard chant of "Freedom now." Of course, Reverend Lawson disagreed with the slogan and the calls for violence, but more important, he wanted the leaders of the march to transform the demonstrations into radical direct action. Confront directly police brutality with civil disobedience. As he said, and his words matter in our own times, "Marches are not enough to break the hold of racism on the economic, social, political structures. . . . Somewhere along the line the Civil Rights Movement will have to become revolutionary."

The philosophy of nonviolence is more demanding than simple stories told about respectable forms of protest or demonstration. Nonviolence, as Reverend Lawson understood it, is *a revolutionary praxis* that forces one to see how violence has corrupted the world and has malformed each of us. We have internalized the chaos, he believed. That insight and insistence, it seems to me, whether one becomes a disciple of nonviolence or not, is a lesson we all desperately need to learn, because it is fundamentally right.

But there is more than strategy and tactics in these pages. Reading *Nonviolent* offers, at once, an insider account of the Civil Rights Movement and an inspiring spiritual autobiography of a life that, for all intents and purposes, was *saintly.* As a scholar of African American religion, I turn to the lives of these exemplars not simply for the history of the Black freedom movement, but for how they offer ethical and moral resources for living good lives. In other words, there is philosophical material to mine here. What might James Lawson's life teach us, for example, about the idea of saintliness? About the enactment of religious convictions in the world? And here I am thinking about William James's definition of saintliness in *The Varieties of Religious Experience*. Saintliness is a quality of character enacted in the world that is seen and felt deeply by others. It describes those persons whose characters have been fundamentally transformed by spiritual emotions that constitute "the habitual center of [their] personal energy." Everything about the individual exudes this quality; it sits at the heart of who the person is. James writes about the features of saintliness as "a feeling of being in a wider life than that of the world's selfish little interests." A willful self-surrender to God (or to some ideal that enlarges life) that offers a kind of freedom from the constraints of the world as it is. So much so that there is a shift in the emotional center of the person toward "more loving and harmonious affections" and away from the ugliness that saturates the world. A shift toward " 'yes, yes,' and away from 'no,' where the claims of the non-ego are concerned." An affirmation of the sanctity of life in a world rife with disposable people. James Lawson was more than a brilliant strategist. His embrace of nonviolence reordered how he inhabited the world. If William James could revise *Varieties,* and if he needed a more contemporary example of saintliness, James Lawson would fit in perfectly.

As a child of four years, Reverend Lawson punched a white boy in the jaw for calling him a n——r. He writes that the memory of that encounter has never faded. It was his first call of God: that no one should be denied dignity and standing because of the color of their skin, and that he must resist that kind of hatred in the world. In this moment, as a young boy, he felt the call of God to respond to racism (to injustice) but he turned to violence to defend his humanity. What oriented him, initially (at four years old or as he looks back), was the realization that he mattered and that no human being could determine his value. He was somebody, precisely because he was a child of God. But how would he fight a world that declared he was nobody because of the color of his skin, that he did not matter, and was disposable? Would he lash out and meet violence with violence?

His mother, Philane Cover Lawson, a devout Christian and an immigrant from St. Ann, Jamaica, thought differently. She urged her young son to see that there was a better way than violence. She asked the searing question, "What came of his lashing back?" And it is here that Lawson describes a second numinous experience. The first insisted on his value as a human being: that the call of God was heard in the context of a powerful realization that, no matter his color, he was loved, he belonged, and he mattered. The second experience shaped how he would respond to the world that sought to fix him and others in their place—a world that announced that it was "for white people only." As his mother talked, Reverend Lawson recalled, the room went silent, and he heard another voice. "It resounded from a vast depth beyond her and beyond me, and yet was in my body." That voice declared, "You will never fight in this way again. You will never do that again."

Nonviolence took its place in his soul alongside an unbreakable commitment to love and justice. In both accounts, the commitment to justice and to nonviolence was rooted in the presence of God. That encounter shifted the habitual center of his personal energy. It reoriented his heart and charged him to go forth with what, for him, became a proven truth: that violence destroys life and nonviolence sustains it. Violence serves those who seek to dominate. Nonviolence, he believed, serves justice.

I highlight the importance of these conversion experiences to underline what motivated Reverend Lawson's witness and why I attribute saintliness to his life. His commitment to justice and to nonviolence carried with it something more than the lessons, principles, and tactics learned from Mahatma Gandhi's execution of *satyagraha,* or the training he received under the tutelage of A. J. Muste, executive director of the Fellowship of Reconciliation, or the mentoring from James Farmer and Bayard Rustin. Both values, that of justice and nonviolence, were like fire shut up in his bones. William James notes that such an inner condition of saintliness has practical consequences that range from asceticism, strength of soul, a sense of purity, to a tenderness for one's fellows, even for one's enemies.

James describes in detail the ideal of Christian nonresistance in the testimony of Richard Weaver, a boxer who became a beloved evangelist. The example illustrates how the shift in a person's habitual center of gravity evidences itself in the life lived. Weaver refused to respond to violence with violence. He took seriously, even when he was guilty of backsliding, the moral precept to "love your enemies, bless them that curse you, do good to them that hate you, and pray for them which despitefully use you, and persecute you." One does so for the reason: "That ye may be the children of your Father which is in heaven: for he maketh his sun to rise on the evil and on the good, and sendeth rain on the just and on the unjust."

Reverend Lawson lived this commitment amid unimaginable cruelty, among white men and women who could be overrun with bloodlust in the blink of an eye and engage in that distinctive American ritual of burning or lynching or torturing that helped them evade what James Baldwin called "the bloodstained self." With the power of nonviolence, Lawson lived as if he knew intimately of this other kingdom close at hand that fortified his spirit to face such evil. In November of 1951, he wrote this in his journal: "I think God intends to use me in some special task. I know now that God bombards my heart and soul so persistently because He sees me as a potential God-force in a decadent world." With this faith, he walked into the belly of the beast and, without lifting a hand in violence, risked life and limb to challenge this country to leave behind the evils of racism, sexism, and greed for a world more just and loving. God bombarded his heart and soul so that the evils of men could not corrupt it.

Of course, William James notes the excesses of saintliness. That a certain fanaticism or madness may attend the actions of those so transformed by spiritual emotion. When reading Reverend Lawson, at times, one cannot help but wonder how he could be so comfortable asking people—young people in particular—to risk their lives on the assumption that white people (or those who hold the reins of power) might be moved by their sacrifice and love—especially when the evidence suggested that they were more inclined, more comfortable, with being monstrous. But one does not have to agree completely with the saint. If we look at this country today, violence abounds. Political forces aim to destroy the gains of the Civil Rights Movement and to dismantle its infrastructure. They attack diversity, equity, and inclusion. They traffic in the evils that have corrupted the soul of this nation since its founding. One could easily conclude, given the evidence, that Reverend Lawson failed in his mission. It might be better to say that the country has failed. But success of this sort is not the measure. The saint's example is "a leaven of righteousness in the world." The power of Reverend Lawson's witness has a gravitational pull that draws those who encounter him into the orbit of his convictions. His is an enveloping, transformative love. We need not believe in nonviolence like he did, we may not feel the call of God upon us like he did, but *through* his example, Reverend Lawson calls us to be leavens in our own time, to find our own voices to speak back to the evils that distort and disfigure our days, and to find the will to engage in that revolutionary act to say *no* to the violence that destroys and to shout *yes* to the love that affirms the dignity and standing of every human being—to shout yes to love!

Eddie S. Glaude Jr.
Princeton University

Author's Note

This memoir is based in part on documents, including sermons, diaries, articles, and letters, as well as on newspaper, radio, television, online, and magazine accounts of events—all of which added detail to my recollections and evoked the moment at critical junctures in my life. It is also based on countless interviews with my collaborator, Emily Yellin, starting in 2017, and interviews with various others through the years, as credited in the endnotes, including Emily's father and my friend David Yellin. He interviewed me about my life many times between 1968 and 1972 as part of an ambitious archival project documenting the Memphis sanitation strike.

Along with our editors, Emily and I made a few deeply considered choices about style and content I feel we should mention at the outset, since sensitive issues come up throughout the book.

- My own written work that was quoted was edited minimally for clarity and accuracy. The quoted words of others were not altered.

- The words "nonviolent" and "nonviolence" were never hyphenated when I used them—in line with how Mahatma Gandhi, who coined the terms, intended them. We maintained hyphens only when others used them in published writings.

- This book spans nearly a century. We decided to use the term "Negro" the way I and others used it in the context of the time until the late 1960s, when the term "Black" became the norm.

- Generally, we did not spell out the derogatory word that is most often used to degrade Black people, because I do not use the word myself.

We indicated it by writing it as "n——r" if I was using it in a story or if, in the course of my narrative, I was quoting someone else who had used it. When I quoted a document or other printed material written by others where it was used, as in hate mail I received, we did spell out the full word.

- According to current publishing style, we capitalized the initial letter in the words "Black" and "Brown" when referring to people. We did not capitalize the initial letter in "white." Similarly, we capitalized the initial letters in the term "Black Power," but not in the term "white supremacy." This kind of distinction is one that has evolved through the years, and we chose to respect the well-reasoned standards set in our own time. With writing from others, we preserved a lowercase initial letter when that was the style used in the original writing or publication.

PART ONE

1928–1957

RESISTANCE

A good person will resist an evil system with his whole soul.

—Mahatma Gandhi

ONE

Jimmy, There Must Be a Better Way

Seven years old in second grade (top row, middle), Lorin Andrews Elementary School, Massillon, Ohio, 1935. VANDERBILT LIBRARY

I smacked a white boy in his face when I was four years old. He lived a few houses down from me on Tremont Street in Massillon, Ohio. It was 1933. We were the same age, and I thought we were friends. Seconds before, the two of us had been having our usual kind of fun in the overgrown vacant lot on our block—throwing around stones we found in the dirt and shooting them from slingshots into the air. All of a sudden, he started calling me names, hurling racist words at me, words that were forbidden in my house, like "n——r." But it wasn't only that word. It was the harshness. He was rejecting me, and somewhere within my little-boy self I realized he was seeing me as not fully human, all because I was Black.

For the first time, racism had come at me directly. I was shocked. I felt betrayed. I thought, "Why would you say those things about me and call me those names? We're playmates." Before then, it had never occurred to me that a boy who was part of our neighborhood group of friends—we had run freely together countless times, along the shores of the shallow creek behind our houses, exploring, catching minnows, or just wading in—would harbor such hatred toward me. I wasn't angry, exactly. His turn on me happened so quickly, and I knew he was wrong. But he broke our bond. He was wielding an ugly, hostile force and hammering my life with it. He was hurting my spirit. I wanted him to stop.

So I balled up my fist, reached back as far as I could, swung my arm around with determination, and hit him in his jaw. Hard. Or as hard as a four-year-old could. He was startled. So was I. Then he hit me back. The whole thing could not have lasted more than a minute. Neither of us left with noticeable bruises or cuts. In the end, I suppose I won our tough-kid scuffle. I was a better fighter than he was. And he was the first one to back off. I believed I had taught him a lesson. And no one in our group of playmates ever called me those names again, including him. My punching worked. Or so I thought.

The memory of that moment has never left me. Although most of the boy's physical characteristics have faded away, and his name escaped me long ago, my mind held on to our clash, turning it over, hoping to divine some message I suspected it contained. Decades passed, and I grew more skilled at recognizing signs and heeding signals, until I realized why punching him had left such a lasting imprint on me. It was my first call of God.

As that boy began his tirade, I felt a force rising up from deep inside, stronger than the mean message in his words. It was an inkling, or an impulse, a spur, urging me to challenge the hate he was spewing. I couldn't resist it. If I could go back to my four-year-old self and explain that mysterious, astonishing, empowering force I sensed within me that day, I would tell my younger self that it was God's love. And I would assure him that it would always be there for him from that day forward—reminding him that no one has the right to deny, question, or assault the fact of his humanity, his character, his essence.

I use the word "reminding" because by the time I was four, my parents had already instilled that message in me. They cared about me, directed me, and provided for me. I was their oldest son, with five older sisters and three younger brothers. And even at that early age, I already knew I was Jimmy Lawson. I was a child of God. I was loved. I belonged. And I mattered.

It took me a while to understand how rare it was for a Black child growing up in such a racist nation to get the chance to internalize that kind of message. I see now how my family and my faith gave me that foundation and it became my armor and my refuge. It also cultivated a lifelong fortitude that would serve me well in the face of all the bullies and hatred I would encounter. And it tempered me with the love, compassion, and moral clarity I would need to help others do the same.

God's first call to me sparked another certainty that grew within me as I got older. I had a purpose. I now believe God gave me a task that day: to resist racism, to continually unmask it, along with any other efforts to diminish human beings. It was the beginning of a spiritual journey in which I would always—with every ounce of energy and life I had in me—challenge racist definitions of myself and of other people. Forever after that day in 1933, I would never accept such behavior from anyone, and I would spend my whole life helping others refuse that kind of degrading and devaluing treatment too.

That journey has taken me all over the world: to India and through Africa in the mid-1950s, and to the American South in the late 1950s and the 1960s, where I worked with my friend and colleague Martin Luther King Jr. We campaigned to desegregate Southern cities, including Little Rock and Birmingham, and strived to spread economic equity and racial justice throughout the South and the nation. Others who shared my convictions, our convictions, have called me a mentor, like John Lewis and Diane Nash. They turned into my lifelong friends after 1960, when we organized our first lunch counter sit-ins together and desegregated downtown Nashville. In 1961, I was arrested at a bus station in Jackson, Mississippi, on the Freedom Ride and was sent to Parchman Prison. I traveled to Vietnam in 1965, in the middle of the war, on a peace mission. And when James Meredith was shot on a highway in Mississippi in 1966, the church where I pastored in nearby Memphis became the staging area for the March Against Fear, during which Stokely Carmichael (who later became Kwame Ture) made the term "Black Power" famous.

In 1968, I headed up the strategy committee when thirteen hundred Black sanitation workers went on strike against the city of Memphis. They were the men who marched almost every day of the sixty-five-day strike with the iconic signs declaring, "I AM A MAN." They were the people Martin was in town supporting when he was assassinated. Grief at losing him has never left me. But his memory became a constant inspiration for me to carry on my conviction to my task, our task.

It followed me when my wife and children and I moved to Los Angeles in the mid-1970s, where I was assigned to be the pastor at one of the largest Methodist churches in the city. Ever since, I have advocated in California and beyond for workers' rights and the rights of immigrants, women, LGBTQ people, and many others on the margins of full citizenship in this country. In 1992, in the midst of the uprisings in L.A. after the not-guilty verdict for the police officers videotaped beating Rodney King, I rallied against police brutality—an issue I had begun addressing decades before. And I continued to live out my convictions into the twenty-first century, and into my nineties, including as a teacher and mentor to those in the immigrant student movement and as a voice in the Movement for Black Lives.

Mine has been a rich life. I have carried out God's original task for me faithfully, despite my flaws and missteps along the way. There is still so much more to do. But when I look back to that four-year-old's punch in the vacant lot in Massillon, Ohio, I also see seeds of another vital quest in my life, one related and equal to the task God gave me that day. This one has been more complicated and nuanced, and in many ways even harder to fulfill, than my unwavering conviction to stand up to racism and dehumanization wherever it appears. It is my quest for the most effective way to assert that conviction, to carry out my task. That search led me to embrace nonviolence.

In all the campaigns for human rights I have joined since the 1950s, I have conducted workshops on nonviolent direct action for thousands of people. For more than twenty years, I taught classes on nonviolent social change at UCLA and California State University, Northridge. I also conducted an ongoing nonviolence workshop once a month for most of my time in Los Angeles, just as I first did weekly in Nashville in the late 1950s. Through everything, I have helped many people affirm a proven truth, one I hold to be self-evident: commitment to violence ultimately destroys people, but commitment to nonviolence ultimately creates, sustains, and secures inalienable rights like life, liberty, and the pursuit of happiness for us all. Violence serves tyrants. Nonviolence serves justice, the common good—the forming of a more perfect union.

Still, nonviolence is mostly misunderstood, misinterpreted, ridiculed, and shunned. Most Americans believe that nonviolence merely involves being passive and is therefore weak—not doing anything in the face of threats. In fact, nonviolence is an active, durable, and infinitely powerful practice. It is an art and a science, and more effective and sustainable than violence has ever been or ever will be.

I came to nonviolence through an evolution, from my childhood and into adulthood—a practical choice for me, as the stakes got higher while I was growing up in the United States, where I learned early that racism's tyranny could be lurking around any corner or in any vacant lot. But it took much of my first decade for me to recognize that path before me. For the first nine years of my life, I trusted violence as the most effective way to stand up to racism and protect myself, as I once believed it had done in the face of that white kid's hateful words when I was four.

Our neighborhood in Massillon was racially mixed but largely white, with one Black family on just about every block. We were that family on our stretch of Tremont Street. That boy and I, and any of about twenty-five other boys from a roughly five-block radius, would gather whenever we could, not only at the creek behind my house but in the streets and nearby parks, on sidewalks, or along any stretch of open ground. We'd play war, or cops and robbers, or cowboys and Indians, or we'd put together a pickup game of baseball, football, or basketball. From age four on, I was a hard player, quite athletic, and I loved to run and have fun. Whether it was tackle football on asphalt or scrappy wrestling on concrete curbs, the scrapes and bruises didn't stop me. I got back up and kept going.

From almost as soon as we could walk, and talk, and play, our conditioning as American boys had taught us that violence was the only normal, acceptable way to cope with any attacks, hurts, or grievances. So at four, that boy lashed out at me because his whiteness had already trained him to hate Black people, which at its root is another form of violence. I punched him because while growing up in this country, I had already learned that physical fighting was the best remedy for incoming hostility. Anything else was spineless, or naïve, or worse. I bought into that myth at first. After all, physical violence handled his verbal ambush of me that day. And I won.

Looking back, I now see that starting in childhood, a dialogue persisted between me and violence. I was drawn into it—unwittingly, at first—because I was part of the larger, ongoing relationship between violence and untold generations of the Lawsons: between violence and my father, mother, sisters, and brothers, and between violence and my grandparents, and their ancestors, too. I can follow its links back to at least the day my great-grandfather murdered the man who enslaved him in Maryland, and liberated himself to Canada through the Underground Railroad. That's not a story I knew about until I was an adult.

But when I heard it, I began to trace a direct line from him—Dangerfield Lawson—to that day I hit the white boy in the face. With time, I also recognized a telling moment in my decision not to mention the fight to my parents. I kept my punch at him a secret—between my young self and violence. Of course, I might not have told my parents simply because I didn't want to get in trouble or I didn't want to risk having to give up fights on the playing fields. But I have come to believe that my reasons went deeper too, into my budding subconscious, where violence had found such a hospitable nesting place for a while.

Because even though I was four, I think I had already sensed the difference between my mother's and my father's relationship with violence, even if I couldn't have been operating from such awareness consciously. My parents agreed on many things, like the strong message that we children were not allowed to use bad language. We were not allowed to mistreat each other, even in our anger or fear. And in our house, they agreed, we didn't ever hit anyone. But the decision of whether to use violence out in the world was where they divided. Mom would say one thing and Dad would say another. My father did believe a punch was necessary in some circumstances, especially for us boys. My mother, however, would not have any of it, anywhere. Their differing attitudes were a recurring issue in our family throughout my childhood. So somewhere in me, I must have felt I shouldn't share the story of my encounter in the vacant lot, because my parents might ask me to choose a side in their debate. My childhood home was happy and peaceful. Why rock the boat?

Philane Cover Lawson, my mom, was no more than about five foot three. She could pass for white on the street, and did. A lot of folk in Massillon did not know that she considered herself Black, she was so light-skinned. She had children like me, who obviously had brown skin. But Mom often fronted for the family. I think it's why she was able to maneuver in the world back then as well as she did. And she was the central figure in our home, keeping everything running smoothly. Although

Mom was soft-spoken, she could be very firm. She was an excellent seamstress who made shirts and clothing for us, because stores were not well stocked in the 1930s. I fondly remember trying on a Christmas suit she made me as a little boy, and her examining the fit to be sure it was right.

Every Sunday morning, our house filled with smells of the most wonderful baking bread—rolls and loaves. Mom was an expert baker and cook. I can see her now, mixing her doughs on Saturday to let them sit overnight. She would make a batch of bread that would last our family two or three days. To wake up early Sunday morning with that bread aroma throughout the house was something else. We'd have it hot for breakfast, with butter and different kinds of jam.

My dad, Rev. James Morris Lawson, whose name I inherited, was dark-skinned, probably five foot eight, and somewhat husky-looking, but not rotund. He was bald on top, with hair only on the sides and the back of his head. Dad was active physically and introduced me to sports. He taught me to ride a bicycle, play ball, catch, and bat. My father also had tremendous social concern and compassion. He was a Methodist minister, like his father and grandfather before him. Every year or two, Methodist ministers were required to move. So, our family lived in a lot of places before settling in Massillon when I was four. Dad's bishop called him there to be the pastor at St. James AME Zion Church, three blocks away from the parsonage house the church provided us on Tremont Street.

One day, early in first grade, I wasn't able to avoid my parents' debate around violence any longer. It was September, and because my birthday came toward the end of the month, I hadn't yet turned six. Right from the start of school, some of the boys I didn't know had decided to pick on me for being a "PK," a preacher's kid. I think they were trying to see whether I could stand up for myself. So I knew I had to fight certain kids who insisted on fighting me. Otherwise they would pick on me forever.

During this particular lunchtime, some friends and I were heading to our homes to eat, since we lived only about five blocks away from the Lorin Andrews School. But a group of seven or so other first-grade boys followed me, making a lot of racket to try to provoke me. The majority of them were white, but a few were Black. They had encouraged a second-grade boy who was Black to follow us down the street, too. The boys were egging on me and him, trying to get us to fight. Because the kid was a second grader, I guess they figured he could whip me.

One of my friends began walking right beside me on the sidewalk to support me. We tried to ignore the boys taunting me. They were not cussing. But they called me yellow because I wouldn't fight the kid, who was a little bigger than I was. I never stopped walking toward home as they hit at me and pushed me, following closely on my heels. I wasn't afraid or intimidated. I was moving in the confidence that there was nothing wrong with me and I had done nothing wrong, which I now understand is a stance that makes it hard for bullies to keep on bullying.

When the noise from all the ruckus hit my house, Dad came to the door to find out what was going on. I turned from the sidewalk and headed up the steps. As I attempted to rush into the hallway, I told him they were trying to get me to fight that kid and I wasn't going to do it. But Dad said, "Well, no. You go back out there and fight him." My mother had moved up toward the front of the house by this time, because she'd heard the commotion, too. And she said, "Oh, Jacob, no. He should not go out there and fight. That is not what should happen." She called Dad Jacob, a name from his childhood, even though to everyone else he was James. But Dad insisted. So I went back out and fought the boy. We hit at each other's shoulders and faces. We got a little bloodied. But we fought to a draw.

Violence had reared up in my life again, this time right in front of my parents. And Dad was glad I met its challenge head-on. He would say, "Boys have to learn to fight to take care of themselves." And Mother would say, "No. You learn to do it another way. You don't have to do it that way."

She embraced Christian love fully: *Love thy neighbor as thyself.* Dad believed in the concept of Christian love, too, but he also could not get past certain harsh realities in the world outside our home, which stopped him from carrying the idea as far as my mother did. This conversation about how to reconcile our religion with the use of violence continued between them, mostly around our dinner table. Yet among my friends in the neighborhood and during my first years of grade school, sparring with each other—which my mother might have considered violence—was merely how we boys played.

Boxing, for me, was a sport, and an exciting one. It also played a pivotal role in my community. Our whole family, including my mom, would gather around the radio in the parlor to listen to heavyweight fights featuring Joe Louis, a hero in the Black community in the 1930s and 1940s. The violence of boxing wasn't the point. Living in a white world, in a white America—with racism and segregation very much alive in the North, and with Jim Crow dictating life in the South—we all wanted to see Joe Louis win. Everyone supported him and how he represented the Black community. He was a counter to the trauma inflicted upon Black people during those decades. It was trauma hardly noticed or addressed in the white world, where it originated—like the lynchings that were reported on the front pages of the Black press but rarely, if ever, on white newspapers' front pages. In 1937, when Louis knocked out James J. Braddock to become the heavyweight champion—he went on to defend his title twenty-five times and held the championship for a record twelve years—he reached a rare position of prominence for a Black man, all across the country. We felt more than a sense of pride. We knew he was working against the odds, and achieving the impossible. It showed us that maybe we could achieve what seemed impossible, too. The pageantries around Joe Louis fighting a boxing match, and Black folk identifying with that, helped prepare our minds in the middle of the twentieth century for the social changes we were convinced needed to happen. Soon thereafter, Sugar Ray Robinson would carry on in the same tradition, and he became another of my childhood heroes.

Black newspapers were our most reliable sources for information and inspiration about those bends toward change. My parents subscribed to a couple of them, including the *Pittsburgh Courier* and the *Call and Post* from Cleveland, which came to our house weekly. As soon as I was able, I tried to read them, even before the first grade. Those papers connected me with my family and to our community. I saw a world where Black people advocated for our own pursuits of happiness, and called out and stood up to the injustice that surrounded us.

As I navigated through grade school, my parents' disagreement about violence began playing out inside me. I grappled with which side I was on. At first, my father's side won, guiding me most strongly for the next few years. As a little kid, overt violence felt like the trustiest shield I could conjure against the racism I encountered in the neighborhood, at school, and around town.

Once, in Massillon, my sister Daisy and I walked over to a park in the eastern section of the city to play together on a Saturday or Sunday afternoon. I was in third grade and Daisy was in fourth. Daisy had been born sixteen months before me and was a year ahead of me in school. We were close. Most of the people at the park that day were white. Almost immediately, a white boy accosted us with racist words, calling us "n——r," and "jungle bunny" and "blackie." Daisy and I both jumped him at the same time. He was about a head taller than Daisy. She was kind of a husky girl, but we both attacked him. I came away from that fight with a terrible headache and a bloody nose. I remember that one. I don't think Daisy got hurt, but she hit him, too. And he fought back. We both struck him a few times. And then he was gone.

Any Negro kid in Massillon would have had this kind of experience a number of times. But not everyone reacted the way we did. When I read *The Autobiography of Malcolm X,* he told of growing up in Michigan, and how he and his brothers and sisters were called "n——r" and "coon" and other names so often that he thought it was normal. That was completely foreign to me. In my childhood view, being called names was a battle cry. My brothers and sisters felt exactly the same way. Instead of thinking it was normal, we took it as an affront to our race, as a signal that the harassers had been badly taught by their families. Our parents had trained us never to consider that kind of treatment as anything but unwarranted.

I do remember noticing, however, that those white kids expressed their fury only when no adults were around to see them do it. White kids never spoke to us that way in school or on the playground of the school. It happened only in the streets and at the park. I don't remember a lot of cursing or name-calling at school. But at the park, white boys and girls flung around their inherited racial prejudice with abandon.

Massillon, Ohio, was a town of about thirty thousand people. Some white families had come out of the South, because Massillon was a thriving steel town with a variety of factories, and good jobs were available in the mills. Segregation was in full effect in the South at the time. In southern Ohio around Cincinnati, across the river from Kentucky, there were segregated schools. But not in Massillon. Still, my town was not immune from the vicious structures and customs of racism, including all the kinds of casual bigotry that were alive and well throughout the country. Perhaps because of my task from God, I believed that those white kids who harassed us had to be corrected. And I thought my fists were still the best way to do it. Violence seemed to work in moments of conflict—although I was starting to notice that it didn't put an end to all the hatred around me once and for all. And the older I got, the more I was beginning to see the limited effectiveness of punching people who came at me.

One day when I was about seven or eight, my dad showed me one other option. He took me to his desk and opened the drawer where he kept a gun. He pointed to the .38 pistol and told me never to touch it. I had never seen a gun before, except in movies and pictures. Telling people never to touch something can make them especially curious, wanting to touch it more. I didn't feel that way. I kept my hands off. I wasn't sure why Dad showed it to me. But the moment felt important. It was also a little scary. Guns raised the bar on the consequences of violence. Still, Dad had his reasons.

After he had spent two years at St. James in Massillon, the Methodist Church moved him to a church in Anniston, Alabama. This time, we all stayed in Massillon rather than move down to Anniston, in the Jim Crow South of the 1930s. Dad took the train there on weekends, leaving on Friday night or Saturday and coming back on Monday or Tuesday. He said he always carried the gun whenever he traveled to the South. Because he was always going to be a man, regardless of the cost. He meant he was not going to take any racist guff from anyone. He wasn't going to take any junk. His fists weren't enough with Jim Crow. A gun was necessary. He trusted the gun to protect him.

He told me he had started carrying it when he was ministering in Sharon, South Carolina, in the 1920s. Once, he said, he saw a group of white men harassing, cursing, and verbally abusing a Black boy on the street there. He went into the middle of the pack, put his arm around the boy, and pulled him out. The two of them went back to the boy's house, where a woman whom Dad assumed was the boy's mother came to the door, grabbed the boy, and slammed the door, without saying a word to my father. She was afraid. Everyone was. This was about thirty years before white terrorists kidnapped and murdered fourteen-year-old Emmett Till in Mississippi. In fact, Dad told me his congregation became so fearful after he had protected the boy that they wanted him to leave. The retribution from enraged Southern white people was usually brutal. But nothing more happened. And Dad didn't leave. After that, though, he decided he needed to carry a weapon at all times down South.

In Massillon, despite fewer segregation laws and customs, Black people still had to deal with racial issues and injustices. My dad would get calls and go out at three or four A.M. to help deal with police mistreating

Black people or with racist threats. He was one of the founders of the National Urban League branch in Massillon. He was adamant that in every town where he was a pastor, if there was not already a chapter of the Urban League or the NAACP, he would start one. So he became the man people called when they had troubles with racial issues.

Dad feeling he had to arm himself fit with his belief that a little bit of violence was sometimes necessary. His strong moral commitment to the ongoing struggle against racial injustice in the United States drove him. A gun represented the power to survive in the fray, to defend yourself and your community. There I was, just starting to figure out who I would become and where I would fit into the world. The gun made sense to me. So many of Dad's stances at that time in my life became my stances. He might not have seen it this way, but he was my earliest model for how to navigate being a Black man in the United States, even though Dad had been born in Canada.

Our family roots in the United States go back at least six or seven generations, so I never saw my father as an immigrant. Our Black heritage in this country has always been much more a part of my view of myself than any idea that my family was not American, or not part of the continuum of Black people standing up to American white supremacy.

We know the names of our Lawson side only as far back as Dangerfield Lawson, Dad's grandfather, the one who escaped enslavement in Maryland. His story was passed down through the generations. Lately, we have been able to find some records that show he was born into enslavement in Virginia in 1806. By the time he was sixteen, he was living on a plantation in Hagerstown, Maryland. The story goes that he escaped with a horse and wagon from that plantation. But his enslaver went after him on horseback, caught him, and began whipping him. My great-grandfather rose up, wrestled the whip away from the man, and strangled him to death with it. Then he left the man lifeless on the ground and rode off again. Abolitionists helped my great-grandfather get to Pennsylvania and then into Canada.

A few years later he married my great-grandmother Elizabeth Harris, in Canada. And in 1837, my grandfather Henry Dangerfield Lawson was born in Caledon Township, Ontario, near Toronto. In 1842, my great-grandfather took the British Oath of Allegiance to become a Canadian citizen. Their family eventually settled in Guelph, Ontario, where my grandfather, and later my father, grew up.

In 1864, Henry Dangerfield Lawson married my grandmother Sophia Still, from Philadelphia. The story my father told me was that his mother, Sophia, my grandmother, was the daughter of William Still, the famous abolitionist in Philadelphia, often called the father of the Underground Railroad and the counterpart of Harriet Tubman. Both that story and the details about my great-grandfather liberating himself from enslavement were planted in me at a young age, forever connecting me to a tradition of resistance, a tradition of declaring my freedom in the midst of a hostile or oppressive environment.

My mother was born in Brown's Town, Jamaica, but my connection to the island didn't figure into my childhood much, either. Mom grew up in St. Ann Parish, on the north coast of the island. She immigrated to Jamestown, New York, when she was about twenty-five, as a nanny for a white English family from Jamaica. In Jamestown, she joined the only Black Methodist church in town. My father was the pastor. He was a widower then, with two small boys. My father's first wife, their mother, had been gravely ill and died by the time my mother came to his church. I never heard much about my parents' courtship. But when they married, my mother found herself living in the household with her stepsons, my older brothers, Mark and Edwin, until they left home, before I came along. Almost immediately after Mom and Dad married, they had five girls of their own, one right after the other: Dorothy first, then Betty, Ella, Frankie, and Daisy. I was born next, when they lived in Uniontown, Pennsylvania, where Dad was the pastor of a church that had been a part of the Underground Railroad. After me came three more boys, Bill, John, and Phillip.

I eventually learned that my mother appeared to be white because her father was a Scottish settler in Jamaica. I remember hearing that my grandfather on my mother's side was white. But I don't remember being told much, if anything, else about him, not even his name. All the relatives who knew this information were gone before I thought to ask, and the official records are scarce. From what I have been able to piece together, his family had owned sugar plantations in St. Ann. I assume that included a history of enslaving Black people, a practice that was finally outlawed in Jamaica in 1838. So the memory of enslavement would not have reached my mother or her parents. And since my mother never mentioned her father or told me much about Jamaica, I did not grow up feeling much identification with the Jamaican half of my heritage.

I never thought of myself as a first-generation American. In fact, I didn't realize Mom was an immigrant until later in my childhood. She was simply my mother, not an American or a Jamaican. By the time I came along, she had lost any trace of a Jamaican accent. And neither of my parents made references around us about being Jamaican-born or Canadian-born. Instead, I think they tried to conform, to fit in, to assimilate. And they wanted that for us. Fitting in with the dominant culture and standards of the United States was the only path most Black immigrants saw toward being able to live their lives and thrive. So I was definitely raised as an American boy from Ohio, one who believed I belonged in the world around me.

However, when I began to read and hear the stories of American history in school and in books, I could see that they left out Black people. My older sisters taught me to read, using the Bible, well before my school years. And I became a voracious reader who devoured everything and anything in print from then on. My mother often said that if I wasn't outside playing baseball or something, I always had a book in my hand. I read stories of Frederick Douglass and Harriet Tubman before first grade with my sisters and parents, and in church. So I knew about enslavement and that Black folk were around during the early years of this country's founding. But once I got to elementary school, no Black men or women appeared in the stories taught to me about early America.

I'll never forget my first day at the Lorin Andrews School. We were introduced to the library across the street, a branch of the city library. After school, I went over there and started pulling out books and looking at them. I was drawn to books about Daniel Boone and early settlement. That started my fascination with the American frontier, which continued throughout my life. I got a library card and read all the adventures of Daniel Boone, as well as books about the woodsmen's competitions against the Indians, the Indian Wars, and also about the mistreatment of the Indians. We hadn't learned how to use more respectful terms to refer to Indigenous people back then. Jim Bowie, out of Texas, was a character I read about. Men like him were the heroes of the American myths I consumed as a kid—bloody stories of white men gallantly portrayed robbing, abusing, and killing Native Americans. I saw that their violence was venerated.

I definitely had a sense from the start that parts of the American story were missing in those early books I checked out with my first library card, and those I read in my classes at school. I can't say I understood how wrong it was immediately. But as I got a little older, I certainly saw the disregard for my own heritage in what I was reading about and being taught.

My father's church was a refuge from the many omissions, dismissals, and outright dangers I faced in white America. The African Methodist Episcopal Zion Church (or AME Zion Church), where my father and grandfather pastored, is a denomination founded by free Black people in New York City in the late eighteenth century. AME Zion and AME were the two denominations Black people formed at that time to get away from the racial discrimination within the white-run Methodist Episcopal Church in North America. Harriet Tubman actively participated in the AME Zion Church, which served as an abolitionist church and supported the Underground Railroad. And Paul Robeson, the baritone singer, stage and screen actor, lawyer, and civil rights activist, grew up in the AME Zion Church.

One of my warmest childhood memories is of Dad conducting Bible study for adults in our parlor. I would sit on the floor at his knees when he had people over and he would ask me to deliver passages from the Bible to the group. I felt so proud. And during our family meals, I sometimes got to speak the prayer we always said at the table before we ate.

Dad also ignited my religious core through the music he loved. All of us kids were in the church choir at St. James. He got us singing old and contemporary anthems, Negro spirituals, and gospel songs at church and at home. I knew them by heart. Whenever I hear a hymn like "God So Loved," I think of that time. And we all sang Handel's "Messiah" in the choir every Christmas Eve. Singing these pieces over and over further instilled my sense of belonging to the continuum of liberation and love that God and Jesus represented in my family, and in my religion.

In Dad's religious background, and my mother's, ethical responsibilities dominated—especially the responsibility of caring for people who were hungry and poor. That defined my parents. There was less emphasis on what I now call the dogma of Jesus: religion that promotes a rigid belief system with a static set of rules that must be blindly followed, even if they don't resonate for everyone. My parents focused instead on how Jesus's life set an example for the way we treated each other in the family, in our church, in the neighborhood, and as we moved about the world. My parents taught us, "Treat others exactly as you want to be treated." *Do unto others as you would have them do unto you.*

Because of that, I mostly saw Jesus as a teacher and guide, not as some kind of religious icon. It's important to note that the AME Zion Church was not a church that used white images. So I never had an image of Jesus that was white. We didn't have a lot of pictures around the church at all. But the AME Zion Church Sunday school literature depicted Jesus as Black, not as white or European. He always appeared as an African throughout my childhood.

All of my parents' children were active in the church. My younger brother Bill and my older sisters Dorothy and Betty became skilled church musicians. My brother Phil became a pastor. And while I do not actually remember either of my parents ever telling me to go into the ministry, my parents showed me how to live my religion and my deepest convictions out in the world. From watching my father being a pastor and preaching every Sunday to seeing him working with the Urban League, I took in Dad's spirit of standing up for others who might not be able to do so for themselves. And I remember the thrill I felt when he sometimes pulled me into his work.

He always took me with him whenever he went up to Cleveland to be a guest preacher at the Reverend Dr. James Lincoln Black's church. Dr. Black was Dad's good friend and the pastor of St. Paul's AME Zion Church, a big congregation in a large building in the center of Cleveland. We would visit Dr. Black's church a few times a year, mostly because my dad's two adult sons from his first marriage both lived in Cleveland. Edwin was a chef on a ship on Lake Erie. And my oldest brother, Mark, who had his own family, was a member of Dr. Black's church and a soloist in the choir.

Rev. Dr. James Lincoln Black was tall and slender but strong physically, with an imposing presence. He had medium to dark brown skin. His hair was graying but well groomed. His distinctive-looking face showed character, warmth, and strength, with a narrow chin, high cheekbones, and a large nose. And he used his baritone voice well in the pulpit. He was loving like a father or grandfather figure, and regal like a godly figure. To me, he represented religion at its best. I wanted to be the kind of pastor Dr. Black was: intelligent, stately, a person of wisdom and grace. Besides my dad, Dr. Black was the one who inspired me most during my childhood to join the clergy, to want to preach, and to be a local pastor serving my congregation.

Dr. Black always treated me like someone special. Being my father's son was to be revered. He would not let me sit in the pews when he and my dad were preaching. One morning, a year or two before I started first grade, just as the service began and with my dad already in the pulpit, Dr. Black insisted that I come up and sit in a pulpit chair for the first time. I knew this was where the most important people in the church sat. The idea of going up there with those big men lit me up. I was so proud to do what Dr. Black asked. I walked up to the pulpit and climbed into the massive chair. It was so big and high, my feet couldn't touch the floor. My father, another pastor, and Dr. Black were all up there. And me. From that day on, every time I came with my father, Dr. Black expected me to sit up in the pulpit. That simple act bolstered my emerging sense of myself, and of the possibilities for me in the church.

Around 1939, my dad decided to leave the AME Zion Church and join the Methodist Episcopal Church, which had split into two main denominations in the United States in 1844: the anti-slavery Northern Methodist Episcopal Church and the pro-slavery Methodist Episcopal Church, South. It took nearly a century for the white-run denominations to merge again in 1939, into the Methodist Episcopal Church, and my father wanted to be part of helping them unite. But the only way the Southern denomination could be persuaded to merge was to separate out the Black congregations in the northern districts into their own unit, called the Central Jurisdiction. So, my father became a pastor in the still-segregated Central Jurisdiction of the Methodist Episcopal Church. We as a family, however, continued to attend St. James AME Church in Massillon.

My first decade on earth was lived during the Great Depression. To me, it was normal that my father would take us boys to the part of Main Street lined with retail stores—J. C. Penney, women's and men's shops—two or three blocks from our home. We would pick up cardboard boxes in the alleys, bundle them, load them onto a cart Dad had made, and pull them to a nearby paper mill, which bought them. It was how we made a little extra money. As a kid, I never saw my sisters scrubbing floors. Every Saturday night, when traffic in the house slowed down, my brothers and I always had to scrub the kitchen floor and the downstairs.

By my fourth-grade year, my parents had made the decision that our family was going to stay permanently in Massillon, even if my father had to travel elsewhere to preach. My mother put her foot down, saying, "We're not moving anymore." She felt we should stay where there was a good school system, to give all of us kids the chance for a solid high school education, and a good, supportive church community. Her decision held.

Then, somehow, during the height of the Depression my parents managed to buy a house at 33 Groose Avenue, by the Tuscarawas River. It was bigger than the Tremont Street house, with some land on the side where we could start a large garden. The neighborhood was quieter, in a more residential part of town. And our garden on Groose Avenue kept us from hunger during those lean years.

Until we moved there, I would have said that my father won the early rounds of my parents' disagreement about whether we should fight with people. My rumbles on the street and in the park verified that I had adopted violence as my chosen way. But one day after school, when I was nine years old, my mother's influence took over for good.

She and I greeted each other in the kitchen when I got home. "Jimmy," she said, "I have an errand you must run for me," and she sent me uptown, probably to get some groceries for the dinner she was cooking. It was a beautiful, warm spring day, and as I turned onto Main Street I noticed a child about my age all alone in the front seat of a car with its windows wide open. He saw me coming around the corner, too. As I was passing by, he stood up on the seat of the car, leaned his head over, and then pushed all but his bottom half out of the window and yelled at me, calling me "n——r." There was racism again. And right behind it came violence to cheer on my standard reaction, which I had down pat by then. I hauled off and slapped him in the face, and I went on my way to take care of my mother's errand.

Returning home, I came into the kitchen through the back door once more, gave her whatever the errand was about, and let her see I had paid for it. Then I sat down on a chair near her. She had her back to me and was facing the stove, preparing the evening meal. I was behind and to the side of her, sitting beside the kitchen door, which was closed. We proceeded to visit, talking about our day. That's when I told her about the incident up on Main Street. I had not told her about the many other times I had done the same thing. But for whatever reason, that was the day I decided to mention hitting the boy spouting racism.

Her response was plain and straight. I've never, ever forgotten it. She asked, "Jimmy, what good did that do?" Even-toned as usual, she didn't raise her voice at all. She accented the words in distinct places so that I knew it was a question. "Jimmy, what good did that do?" It was pointed at me, and challenged my fight behavior. She was calling out the violence in me.

I didn't respond. The question pushed me around. So, I was quiet. I listened. She said what I'd done was of no value. She reminded me who I was: Jimmy Lawson. She reminded me that my father was a pastor, and that we were deeply involved in the church, and that we worshipped God, and loved God. She said that we sought to do the right things, and to be the kind of people God wanted us to be. She reminded me that we were people of love, and we had to rely on ourselves to do right by other people, to do right with God, and to follow Jesus. I don't know exactly how long her soliloquy was, but I know she finished it with this sentence: "Jimmy, there must be a better way."

She meant there must be something more effective than punching, smacking, and kicking—there must be a better way than violence. She was always up-to-date on current events. I often saw her in the evening sitting in her favorite chair, reading the day's newspaper. So I knew she was an informed person. She didn't try to tell me what I must or must not do. She simply raised the question, "What good did that do?" Then she followed up with a promise wrapped inside a remedy.

Even in those little kid fights, there must be something better than the violence. And as she was talking, everything began to go silent all around me, with a kind of white silence. At least eleven people were living in our house at that time—my five older sisters and three younger brothers, and my father, mother, and I were all at home that day—but I didn't hear any noise. There was no radio. There was no piano playing. The house was dead silent. I was completely still—breathing, no doubt—but there was a blankness, a feel of nothing filling the air.

That's when I began to hear another voice. I heard my mother's voice at the same time. But the other voice rose up. I didn't know where it was coming from. It resounded from a vast depth beyond her and beyond me, and yet was in my body. It seemed to go all through me. I realized later that it was my voice, but it was also a voice beyond myself. It said, "You will never fight in this way again. You will never do that again." It didn't say, "You might do it again." It said, emphatically, "You will never do it again."

That experience has stayed with me for every day of my life. It dwelled in the back of my mind as I grew, worked, lived, and learned. I recognize it now as something called a numinous experience—a moment that speaks directly to the core of your being. In biblical and religious language, it is known as a *mysterium tremendum,* or mystical meeting—a transcendent encounter in which you sense the presence of God and you sense a call from God. In my mind, that sort of experience is always linked to moral and ethical decisions. It is never feeling the spirit for the sake of feeling the spirit. Instead, the spirit is suggesting some things that you have to do, going after you with full impact. You can try to describe it, but you can't explain it. You pay attention to it, though. Some people might also call it an aha moment.

I didn't know any of those definitions when I was nine. I only knew that it happened in our kitchen. And throughout it, I couldn't see or hear anything but my mother, white light, and that voice. My mother had her back to me the whole time, talking while facing the stove, cooking. She never turned around to look at me. I only heard what she was saying, along with the voice that I did not recognize, that was far bigger than I was. I don't remember any feelings in my body. I was more in a state of absolute stillness, a state of receiving.

In the end, as my mother finished talking, saying that there must be a better way, I heard that resounding voice one last time, within me and all about me. Once and for all, it firmly declared, "You will find a better way."

TWO

I Shall Always Love You

Longfellow Junior High School, Massillon, Ohio.
VANDERBILT LIBRARY

I stopped accepting invitations to fight. My playmates both in school and out of school soon recognized I was not in that business anymore. Some would mess with me anyway—trying to push me around. But I stopped taking the bait. I was beginning to see walking away as the most satisfying response to people who tried to provoke violence.

That didn't stop the bigoted name-calling. From about fourth or fifth grade on through junior high and high school, I lost count of the number of times I used nonviolence to parry yet more racist insults on the street and in parks—although I did not call it nonviolence then. I saw it as using my mother's approach, of tapping into the power of love and taking on the way of Jesus—loving my neighbor as myself.

One beautiful spring day, in almost the exact spot on Main Street where I had slapped the boy in the car a few years before, a different white boy yelled a racist name at me out of the window of his family's parked car. This time, I walked over to the child and asked him friendly questions. I found out his name and told him mine. We figured out that we were both twelve years old. I forced him to see me as a person and a potential playmate. Then I said to him, "You mustn't use that language on me." He had said his parents were in a store nearby, and I thought about waiting there to meet them, to let them know they were teaching their son the wrong things. But I decided I didn't have enough time to do that, because I was on an errand for my family. So I said goodbye and went on my way.

Even as I was beginning to commit myself to stopping all kinds of violence around me, including violent words that degrade people, World War II was breaking out in Europe. Hate was engulfing whole nations. Still, in my own life, I continued rejecting the reflex to use physical violence, and I banished hurtful language, too. I decided that was how I wanted to live as I was stepping from childhood into adolescence. My ideas were only beginning to form. The influences surrounding me at home, at school, around town, and in church exposed me to what seemed like a vast world of ideas, which I absorbed voraciously, as I continued imagining the person I wanted to become.

During the late 1930s and early 1940s, I spent a lot of time studying the Bible. Jesus became fascinating to me. I was particularly enthralled with the Sermon on the Mount, in Matthew. It included "turn the other cheek," which I practiced all through junior high and high school. I was forming a moral and theological core. I didn't necessarily see it that way then. I was merely following my curiosity and growing sense of purpose.

I listened to a lot of radio programs then, too, and read many newspapers and books, as I have ever since. And my whole childhood had a soundtrack, which resided with us in the home my parents created. That music was inside me by age four. *Wade in the water.* It grounded me within myself, my family, and my community. *God's gonna trouble the water.* It had been passed down to us for generations. *Go down, Moses.* Forming me. *Let my people go.* The joy in the music and the comfort in the words became my steady bulwarks. *Mary, don't you weep.*

Around the piano in our parlor, my family came together to sing spirituals and gospel songs. Between my sisters, my brothers, my parents, and me, we had altos, sopranos, tenors, and basses. My voice was always a large one that could sing tenor and bass, as well as baritone bass. *This little light of mine.* I hit the low notes and the high notes in my time. *I'm gonna let it shine.* Dad would sing with his rough, throaty voice. Dorothy and Betty played the piano. Bill picked the piano up on his own at age five. By the time he was seven or eight, he could play anything by ear. He went on to play saxophone in high school. And as the years went on, Phil, the youngest, played drums, and I played the tuba, as did John after me. The language, melodies, and harmonies sustained us through whatever came our way. I relied on them. *Steal away to Jesus.* At an early age, I was learning to care for my spirit. *Steal away home.*

The radio in our living room linked us to worlds beyond Massillon. There was no television in the 1930s and 1940s, and the internet's arrival was at least half a century away. The radio kept us up-to-date on everything that was happening in ways no other technology had ever done before. I learned to care about what was going on in the world since keeping up with it was something my family emphasized. We always gathered around our radio to hear Franklin Roosevelt address the nation. The radio also brought us cultural events, which helped us make sense of or find refuge from the disturbing parts of the news. On Saturday mornings, we listened to the Metropolitan Opera. Contralto Marian Anderson wasn't allowed to sing with the Metropolitan Opera until 1955 because she was Black. But I heard her on so many other programs growing up that I got to where I could recognize her voice on the radio after catching only a few notes—in the same way I could immediately identify Beethoven's Ninth or "Lift Every Voice and Sing." On Saturday nights, we listened to the big dance parties starring Artie Shaw, Duke Ellington, Glenn Miller, and Louis Armstrong. I loved music in all its forms.

Sunday mornings before church, we listened to a religious radio show that had started in nearby Cleveland but went national. Called *Wings Over Jordan*, it was one of the first American radio programs that Black people produced and hosted. Guests included distinguished religious and civic leaders, artists, and academics who rarely appeared anywhere else on the airwaves at the time. People like Langston Hughes, Adam Clayton Powell, and Mary McLeod Bethune would talk, preach, or give speeches. The show grew in popularity and continued for more than a decade, further helping till the ground and set the tone among Black people for coming change in the United States. All of this gave me a good grounding in my culture, the issues that were important for Black people, and some of the great minds and talents addressing and expressing them in the world.

My family life kept me steeped in love and care. I don't remember much conflict at home, even with all those siblings. The house we moved into on Groose Avenue was set back along the east bank of the Tuscarawas River, which ran through Massillon. It had wooden floors and four bedrooms upstairs, but only one bathroom for all of us, with a bathtub and no shower. One of the bedrooms was quite big. My sisters shared that room. My brothers and I lived in another, smaller room. Dad had his own office, and then there was my parents' bedroom. The yard on one side of the house was huge. We planted our large garden there. I learned how to use a hammer and helped build the chicken coop and the chicken yard, where we got our own eggs. We often sold some of the chickens for meat, along with the geese and ducks we also raised. Dad taught us how to plant and harvest, and how to build fences and maintain them, all of which he had learned during his childhood in Canada. In the spring, Dad would hire a farmer with a horse and plow to come work the soil. All of us would be out there, with my mother and father supervising—planting corn, peas, tomatoes, beans, and all kinds of other vegetables and fruits.

We took it for granted that we each had to pull our weight around the house. But it didn't feel like chores (even though it was) as much as a time to help keep the house and the family functioning well, with benefits for us all. I first learned the concept of how community and shared responsibility worked in my childhood home. During the summer and fall, Mom and Dad would lead us in the kitchen as we canned corn, beans, pears, and apples and made applesauce. We peeled and chopped, preparing the fruits and vegetables for Mom's cooking, before the canning. Dad would do the final twist on the Mason jars of food to make sure they were tight. Then we would store them on racks and shelves in the basement for the upcoming cold months.

My dad, my sisters, and I would each go grocery shopping or run errands for my mother. There was an A&P grocery store off Main Street, a few blocks away, where we got bread, meat, and basic goods. And the milkman delivered milk.

Then there was the reward for all our work. On Saturdays, my brothers and I made sure we got our chores done quickly, so we could catch the afternoon matinee at the movie theater on Main Street. For about ten cents, we watched westerns, and cops and robbers. I especially enjoyed the Tom Mix cowboy movies.

Looking back, I can see that growing up with five older sisters must have been part of why I had a fairly charmed childhood. As the oldest son of my mother and father, I think I rarely had to struggle for love or attention, and that gave me a quiet confidence. I also learned a lot from my sisters about the challenges women faced in the world, which helped me better understand the women in my life as an adult. But my older sisters started to move away when I got to seventh grade. Dorothy went to Philander Smith College, in Arkansas. Then Betty graduated. Next came Ella, and Frankie. Daisy was still home for most of my growing-up years, when she and my younger brothers, Bill, John, and Phillip, were my close companions. We shared the work of the family and at church and made it as fun as we could.

For instance, my little brothers came with me through all kinds of weather when I volunteered as a custodian at St. James Zion, beginning in junior high. Part of my job on Saturday evening was to prepare the building for the Sunday morning service. In winter, my brothers and I would light the furnace as soon as we arrived, bringing coal into the basement to get the fire roaring. Then we would go upstairs to sweep the floors and dust the place—the pews, the pulpits, the lecterns, and the choir seats—making certain everything was in place. As we worked, Bill, John, Phillip, and I would gleefully race up and down the aisles—laughing, talking, playing, and messing with each other. We felt a festive freedom as we took care of that sacred place.

Before we left the church on Saturday nights, we would bank the furnace, so the church would be warm enough the next morning. That meant smothering the fire with enough new coal that it would continue to burn slowly, smoldering, keeping the heat going through the night. In the morning, somebody else would come in early to stoke it, so the flames could rise again, adding the ideal flow of warmth to the whole building in time for the service. I loved contributing something that made our congregation feel comfort on Sunday morning.

When I was about twelve or thirteen, I began a practice of praying every day. I would try to read the Bible, meditate, and reflect, in both the morning and the evening. My initial prayer practice originated from my habit as a child of reciting the Lord's Prayer, which I memorized early and could call upon at any point in my life. I knew I was a little different from a lot of kids my age, for starting such spiritual practices so young. But I did it because I felt it, not because anyone was forcing me to comply with any religious requirements.

And I loved school. Again, I knew not all of my peers felt that way. But for me, junior high—seventh through ninth grades—was a thriving time as was almost all of my time in school. I got involved in school sports, theater, and speechmaking. I had only ever played sandlot sports—baseball, softball, football, and basketball. I also swam, and when I was eleven, my sister Dorothy, who was a good athlete, taught me to play tennis. But making the varsity football team in seventh grade was the first time I had formal coaching. I learned basic blocking and tackling techniques. I didn't have any problems with catching the ball or throwing the ball, but learning how to block and tackle properly was important. I liked running and carrying the ball, because I was fast and I could dodge. I liked receiving passes, and I did some quarterbacking. I loved playing on those teams. Learning the discipline it took to hone my athletic abilities and the strategy involved in team play gave me skills and training that would keep on benefitting me and my work for the rest of my life.

Speech and drama rounded out my education and helped me learn to speak and perform in front of audiences, skills a pastor needs. Every year of junior high, I was in the musicals we staged at the school. They were mostly Gilbert and Sullivan—*H.M.S. Pinafore* and *The Pirates of Penzance*. In nearly every one, I had a solo. A number of us with good voices got to sing solos.

All my teachers in Massillon were white. But I never felt they discriminated against me. My fourth-grade teacher, Miss Bender, noticed I was having some trouble in class and recommended getting my eyes checked. I didn't want to, but she sent home a note to my parents. It turned out I was nearsighted. I got glasses, and never had trouble seeing again thanks to her care. In eighth grade, I admired and loved my history teacher, William Rohr, an extraordinarily fine man who also coached the basketball team. He often came out on the football field to watch us practice and give us advice, too. His influence helped me realize that I wanted my life to count for something.

Even in what could be called my relatively carefree life as a kid, the turmoil of the outside world did invade. I was in eighth grade, on December 7, 1941, when Pearl Harbor was bombed. I remember listening to news reports on the radio late that Sunday night, and on into Monday and Tuesday. It rocked us all. Everyone in the country was almost as one in unanimous support of the United States joining the war, because we had been attacked. I was an enthusiastic supporter of World War II. I guess I was tapping into some form of patriotism. I knew from reading the newspapers that Hitler and his hate were overrunning Europe. People were saying it was an essential war, a just war. And the federal government quickly mobilized most people in the United States behind the war effort.

Three of my sisters went to work in an airplane production plant at Wright Field, just outside Dayton. And my father began work in a defense plant in Massillon to supplement his pastor's income. He was a guard at the gate of Tyson Roller Bearings, which produced small parts for the military. He worked the evening shift, from about three in the afternoon until eleven or twelve at night. The plant was gated, and his guard booth was right at the entrance. It wasn't that many blocks away from our house. Sometimes I would take his dinner to him, which mostly was a way to show Dad my love for him, but also made me feel I was doing something to help the war effort.

In ninth grade—the last year of junior high—I was all set to play on the football team again. But I had to have surgery for some sort of growth on my face, which meant I couldn't join the team. I was disappointed. After the surgery, part of my face was all bandaged up for a while. I could have gotten really down. But once again, I had my family to keep me grounded. My brother John, who was three years younger, told our friends in the neighborhood that the bandages were because he had hit me for messing with him. He thought it was funny. Secretly, I did too. Though I acted like it bothered me, just to play along. Of course, John and I continued an affectionate banter about that for a while. Soon, the surgery healed and I went on.

When ninth grade ended, I was quite certain I was being called to be a pastor in a local church. It wasn't only because I wanted to follow in my father's footsteps. My inward journey to becoming a clergy member had begun with that punch I threw at age four, and continued through the numinous moment when I was nine. It matured, until there was no doubt in my mind that God was speaking to me, calling me—directing me to embrace Jesus's insistence upon the way of love, not the way of violence, not the way of hatred. The call was deeper than an intellectual belief that hate was wrong. It was a calling to a higher purpose. It centered on demonstrating and imitating the love of God with myself, my family, in my congregation, on the street, and in the world. I was compelled to follow that path. I could not explain why. But I knew I had to follow it.

Still, I had begun to question certain parts of the Bible in junior high. By then, I was reading the New Testament on my own, the four books of Jesus—Matthew, Mark, Luke, and John. I had particular problems with the Apostles' Creed. I accepted the first part: *I believe in God, the Father Almighty, maker of heaven and earth.* My issues were with the second part: *And in Jesus Christ, his only Son, our Lord, who was conceived by the Holy Spirit and born of the Virgin Mary.* That's the part I thought was not true. John said that Jesus was born of woman. Mark had no story at all about his birth. Matthew and Luke, the other major writers of the New Testament, didn't say anything about it. Paul, who's the writer of most of the literature in the New Testament, denied it. Because, he said, Jesus was born of the flesh of a woman. So I concluded that the Apostles' Creed was not historical. According to the scriptures, it was not true. I decided to stop saying it. In the Methodist tradition, it is one of the earliest creeds that's repeated in church services. But as I came out of junior high and entered high school in tenth grade, I would no longer repeat it in church, because I didn't believe it was true.

Another thing I declared to God in junior high school was that I would obey no racist laws, no Jim Crow laws. To the best of my ability, I would always resist them. Say no. Say they are wrong. I knew from the Negro papers and from our family's discussions that Jim Crow laws had been deliberately enacted to dismantle the gains of the Reconstruction era. Racism was an evil I would always fight off.

At Longfellow Junior High School, I was Jimmy Lawson. But when I started at Washington High School, in tenth grade, I introduced myself to everyone as Jim Lawson. Jimmy disappeared. As I was just about to turn fifteen, I threw off my kid name and replaced it with the name I would go by as an adult. I told my family, and they began to call me Jim, too.

It was right around that moment—one of my first stabs at declaring the man I would become—when my father made his terrible mistake.

In the fall of 1943, the chaotic instability of the world at war was echoed in my own life, as the idyllic stability of my childhood days suddenly shattered. Dad decided to leave our home. Permanently.

He planned to split his time between Guelph, Ontario, his birthplace, and Cleveland, where his sons from his first marriage were living. He would not be living in our home any longer—the home on Groose Avenue, where his name was on the deed.

It's a bewilderment to me to this day just what was going on. The only way I can answer it is to assume that he had some sense that he should not be so settled in Massillon, Ohio. Maybe he was thinking he was too encumbered with family. I don't know. I am pretty sure it was not another woman. And none of us saw big problems between our parents. He did not hold the old line of masculinity that says the man dominates the woman. I never saw or heard any of that. He was supportive of us all. We had always managed to eat, and my parents had bought property together. Neither of our parents had big salaries at any point in their lives, but we managed. That could only have happened through getting along with each other and being cooperative.

If someone could have explained Dad's departure, then maybe I would have accepted it. But no comprehendible cause was given. I pored over my entire life, and couldn't find a reason for him to leave. I tried to discern a defect in his fatherhood. All my searching only led me to confusion. I couldn't complain about him as my father. I felt like he always did what we needed. In my first fourteen years of life, he was there. I couldn't dismiss that. I had a solid dad. My sisters, brothers, and I did not feel Dad had neglected us in any way. We loved him. I loved him. To me, my family life was ideal. It supported me. I looked up to my dad. Until the last days of my fourteenth year, I admired his example of being a family man, a man involved in his family's life, which he strongly molded in me.

Then he disappeared.

And he never told us why. All he said was "I'm leaving." He said he was going to preach somewhere.

He had been ordained in Canada in the British Methodist Church. Apparently, he was fairly well known and liked as a preacher there. Also, most of his brothers and sisters lived in Canada. Only two of his siblings had moved to the United States and become citizens. Dad's decision meant he was choosing to go back to his early ministry of the 1910s, '20s, and '30s. I think Dad had an idea that he was not fulfilling his calling as a minister, rationalizing that God wanted him to leave us, that he had to do it. But he was misled. It was a monumental error. He had no business doing it. He still had work to do with us.

Instead, his leaving almost destroyed our family, and almost killed my mother.

She sat in her big living room chair for days. She was quiet, almost totally still. We all knew she was deeply, profoundly hurt. I don't remember seeing any tears, but I could tell she was suffering pretty badly. Dr. Malloy, our family doctor, came by every morning on his way to the office to check on her, for two or three weeks. She didn't leave the house, and we all walked softly around her. Ella and Frankie were still living there then. And so was Daisy.

I was furious. My father leaving our home was traumatic. It was my first crisis. How could I be in the house with my mother during those first days and not feel angry? We all hurt. At one point, I was in the living room with my mom, talking about my father. I started prancing around, yelling. I was not cussing, because I didn't know how to cuss. But I was fussing in a football voice, booming and noisy. My whole body was tense with rage. I was even making threats about Dad. I wanted to pretend he was not my father. If I could disown him, I figured, maybe the hurt would leave me too. I was not controlling myself.

My mother spoke quietly, and told me to stop talking that way. She forced me to calm down. She could see that his abandonment of us was starting to break me, but she would not allow it. She was emphatic that my clamoring was no way to handle my anger, because it would not help me, or him, or her. She was speaking very, very quietly, so I had to stop prancing and marching in order to listen, to hear her. There was my mother, once more, making space for my anger, not asking me to suppress it. Instead, she was acknowledging it, but encouraging me to express and frame it in a more constructive way. Of course we didn't have the word for it then, but I can see now, Mom was pushing me toward what would become my dedicated practice of nonviolence.

Even in the midst of her own searing pain, my mother absolutely forbid us from breaking with our father. She stressed to me that he was still my father, and I had to care about him and deal with him directly. I had to see him as a full, worthy human being. She talked to me about my feelings and told me that if I was going to express them, I needed to do so to him. She wanted us to write him letters, telling him why we were angry. But she insisted we stay connected to him. That was the phenomenon that was my mother.

So, I wrote him letters. I told him I thought his leaving us and our home was a bad decision to have made—as a father, as a man, and as a pastor. I don't remember if he ever responded. When he came back to the United States, he stayed in Cleveland. He could have come back to the big Groose Avenue house and his small office there. He could have easily traveled between Massillon and Ontario, as he did between Cleveland and Ontario. But my father never returned to Massillon while I was living at home. Not even to visit.

Of course, when a man deserts his family like that, the scars never heal completely. I'm not sure any of us ever fully got over it. But all my first lessons from my mother in managing my feelings differently would eventually allow me to let my anger, hurt, and bewilderment around my father's absence be what it was for him, without crushing my spirit. And now, my longtime application of nonviolence in my life and work has transformed me so fully that I can talk calmly and think rationally about that most horrible time, which could very well have ruined my life. It is still rather extraordinary to me that my mother had started priming me when I was a teenager in a crisis—informally, and without knowing where she was leading me—for the ideas and practices we would use years later to foster a revolution in this country.

A few weeks after Dad left us, Mom came out of her depression and reorganized herself to become the major support of our family. She was the embodiment of endurance, which I also learned a lot about from her. She taught me that as a human being I might face all sorts of challenges and situations, but basically I was supposed to endure. She would teach us not to let ourselves be turned into something we were not, when facing the episodes of life. "Don't let yourself act in ways you'll be sorry for later on," she said. Mom's way was to live fully in each day, in each moment, in each task, and in each challenge. She would sum up her approach by saying, "Be natural." She always said that. She taught me to see people and care about the people in front of me in the moment, no matter where I was. "Don't make your life something other than what it is." *Be natural.*

Facing this episode in her life meant Mom started working away from our home. She had been a seamstress in Jamaica, and so she found seamstress work at a store in Massillon. Eventually, she became a cook in a downtown ice cream shop called Isaly's. They had the best ice cream in Ohio, along with sandwiches and lunch. The name Isaly's stood for "I Shall Always Love You." We stopped by there all the time to get ice cream after school and then walk Mom home from work. Isaly's ice cream tasted like pure happiness. My favorite was the chocolate and vanilla mixed cone.

One of the most enriching things I did throughout high school was participate in speech and debate tournaments. Our teams traveled all across the state of Ohio, and into Pennsylvania and New York, to compete. As preparation, we had daily assignments to go to the library and read all the newspapers and magazines. That's when I began a discipline that has remained a part of my life ever since: regular, extensive readings about current events, and interest and concern for what goes on in society.

My debate partner in high school, Chuck Sohner, became a lifelong friend. When we traveled to tournaments, we stayed in the same hotel room. Because I was Black and he was white, whenever we went to a hotel, our caring teachers made it clear to the hotel that Black students were going to be treated the same way as the white debaters, that we would not be insulted in any way. They saw to it that we stayed at hotels where all of us were met with dignity and respect.

Continuing my love of music, I was also in the marching band in high school, for all three years. I learned to play the tuba to earn my spot. One of my favorite songs to march to was "When the Saints Go Marching In," which we played with a jazz arrangement. For a while during my sophomore year of high school, I worked part-time at night in the Woolworth's on Main Street to help earn money for the family. The manager thought he was making a breakthrough, hiring his first Negro employee as a porter. Soon after, I was promoted to stock boy and earned a little bit more money. Fairly quickly, though, a white boy came in, and without any warning to me, the manager named him the stock boy and made me a porter again. I spent about a week talking to him about this inequity, and to other officials of the store. Clearly it was about race. When the manager finally said he wasn't able to reverse it, I told him I wouldn't work there anymore, and I quit.

I got to know a mixture of kids at Washington High, many of them with religious beliefs that were different from mine. There were Jewish students, Roman Catholic students, and Lutherans in my high school. In my ongoing study of the Bible, I rejected the anti-Judaism I saw wrapped up in Christian stories. In my reading of the four books about Jesus, I recognized a clear anti-Jewish theme in the Gospel of John. I did not accept it. It was during that time in high school that—alongside my determination to obliterate racism—I made a commitment that religious bigotry had to go, too.

But all my convictions didn't stop me from receiving some of that prejudice. On several occasions the police would stop me when I was walking home by myself late at night after a band rehearsal, drama class, debate, or some kind of meeting at the school. They would call me "boy." The town was small enough for these men to know who I was, and to know my family, and where I lived. Their stopping and questioning me was so unnecessary. I felt frustrated. So I leaned on my budding practice of remaining calm even as I let myself feel my own anger within, and of staying collected in the face of other people's antagonism. I didn't suppress the deep rage that welled up in me. I felt it. Yet, instead of directing it back toward them, I channeled it into a kind of internal resistance.

I refused to feel insulted or assaulted by those men. I saw the situation for what it was: racism. I did not let it threaten the way I felt about myself as a person. I was using my mother's approach. *Be natural.* I knew they were wrong. I didn't know the term "police brutality" yet. But I realized the police officers were abusing their authority to put me in my place because I was a Negro. Still, I was who I was. I was a child of God. And I understood that this kind of treatment of Black people had to be changed. I was starting to foster these survival skills as a teenager—of cultivating composure and not losing my sense of self in the face of racial hostility. That practice would serve me well throughout my life when, like most Black people in the United States, I faced many more encounters with racist officers. Those experiences ignited my passion for the work I would do as an adult on social justice campaigns to rid the country of abusive policing.

My sister Dorothy got back from college around 1944 and began a job at the local Urban League. All of my brothers and sisters were raised to be part of that kind of work in the community. I was about sixteen when

Dorothy and I joined Massillon's NAACP youth chapter together and went to all the meetings. Not only was I finding out the rewards of activism, but I also learned during that time that I probably didn't want to go into a career in sales. Because one of my tasks with the NAACP youth group was to go out and knock on Black people's doors to sign them up for memberships. I was an absolute failure at it. I didn't get the NAACP a single membership. At least I got to spend lots of time with my big sister Dorothy at all those meetings. She taught me so much about a woman's perspective on human rights and equality, and how even as a Black male I still had more status in our society than a Black woman.

My worldview was expanding just as a reckoning with the toll of war was beginning around the globe. In the spring of 1945, a month after FDR died, Germany surrendered and the war ended in Europe. The horror of the Nazi death camps was revealed—an ultimate expression of violent cruelty and hatred. A few months later, the United States flexed its own capacity for violent destruction as our country dropped two atomic bombs: one on Hiroshima, Japan, on August 6, and the other on Nagasaki, on August 9. World War II officially ended a few weeks later with Japan's surrender.

No one was exempt from grappling with the implications of those literal earth-shattering events. When we entered our senior year in the early autumn of 1945, the National Forensic League changed the topic of the debate we were preparing for the coming season to something like: "Does the atomic bomb make mass armies obsolete?" We had to find out all we could about the atomic bomb. There was not much material because it had all been secret information up until then. We had not even heard about the Manhattan Project until August 6.

We were the championship debate team in the state of Ohio. So we were compelled to do thorough research on the bomb. I tried to read just about every document that had been written, up to that time, about atomic energy and the Manhattan Project. I particularly remember reading what Norman Cousins wrote. He vehemently opposed atomic bombs. Still, since I was a dutiful American kid, my conclusion was that we needed what was called a preventive war, to forestall attacks on us in the future. I believed we should take the bombs and drop them on Russia to obliterate it. I did not yet see a better way.

A few months later though, by the end of my high school years in the spring of 1946, I was beginning to have a change of heart. I started to realize that all the Bible verses I had learned and practiced growing up—*walk the second mile, turn the other cheek, pray for the enemy, see the enemy as a fellow human being*—contained the seeds of a resistance movement. They were not acquiescent or passive. Through those ideas, my own life expanded, and my inner strength grew. I had actually seen people changed because I responded with the other cheek, or I went the second mile with them.

It was only after I graduated from high school that my critiques of war and violence evolved more fully, as I continued my study of Jesus's life. I knew I would be required by law to register for the draft when I turned eighteen in September. Yet, growing opposition to violence and war was brewing within me. I was divided. I was not a conscientious objector, but neither was I a soldier. I saw that a lot of people took the early part of the Old Testament and used it to justify war, because of the battles with the Philistines. But I was beginning to realize that they ignored the fact that by the time of the great prophets, like Jeremiah and Isaiah, there were stringent denunciations of war and violence in the Bible. I was questioning violence in any form, and that included participation in the military. I did not know for certain what I would do.

My options were both wide and quite limited. I had considered a lot of places for college. My grades were good and I had many activities to show for my time in high school. I ended up getting a couple of scholarship offers. But I soon saw that we didn't have enough money for me to go. So, I decided to stay out of school for a year and work to make money myself. Almost immediately, I got a job at the J. C. Penney on Main Street as a stock clerk. I did everything from janitorial work and washing the front windows to stocking inventory on the shelves and anything else that was needed.

In September 1946, I turned eighteen. I was required to go down to the draft board in Massillon to register. I knew that war was absolutely counter to finding a better way, as my mother and God had charged me to do. But on the appointed day, I walked into the draft board office and made my way to the table where I was supposed to fill out the form to register for the draft. A middle-aged white woman from Massillon was sitting there. I said to her, "I don't think my religion will let me go to war." She didn't seem to know how to respond.

She gave me the form. I think she figured that if she ignored what I had said, maybe I would just fill it out and move on. I told her I wasn't going to sign anything that would take away my right *not* to join the military. Again, she didn't seem equipped to handle my concerns. All she seemed to know was she had to get me to fill out the form and register for the draft, like every other man in the town when he turned eighteen years old. She did her best to urge me to do what the law required me to do.

I sat down with the form and answered all the questions. Then, in the margins I wrote, "I'm filling this out now. I'm not sure I should, because I'm not sure I can support the war in light of my religion. I'm going ahead and obeying the law and registering. But I recognize I may well conclude one day that I should not have registered." I wrote more around the edges warning that I might not be able to carry out the soldier's life.

I didn't want to sign away my life or join an organization that was counter to all I believed. Just a year or two earlier, I had been in favor of war. But as I faced the prospect of giving up my life and therefore supporting the killing of others, I was not sure I would do it. My convictions were leading me to another path.

I took the form back to her. Again I emphasized my point: "I want to be sure I am not signing anything that obligates me to join in a war." Just to be sure, I persuaded her to write on the card, "This man thinks he is a conscientious objector." I hoped that if someone else wrote that, along with what I had written, it meant I would maintain the option to decline military service, if it ever became necessary. Then I left that place and put it all out of my mind. I had a year before college, and I was determined not to waste it.

I took time to read a lot, including older, popular re-creations of the life of Jesus, such as *In His Steps* and *Ben-Hur*. I was able to do some traveling for the Methodist Church, too. In 1946 and 1947, I attended several church conferences for young people, such as district meetings at the Methodist camp in Clear Lake, Iowa, which I had visited several times in high school and would continue to visit often after that year. I became president of my conference of the Methodist Youth Fellowship, meaning I went to the national conference on Methodist youth, which was a meeting for the state presidents and conference presidents of Methodist youth organizations. We worked with professionals in the church on what these agencies should be doing and how to improve youth and student ministry. I knew I was headed for the ministry, so I took the first step and became what was called a "local pastor" in August 1947. That meant I was a layperson who was qualified to lead worship and to preach in Methodist churches, but not to lead a church.

In that year after high school, as the terrible harms of World War II became more and more apparent in the world, I was growing keenly aware of the contradiction between the meaning of love as I saw it in the life of Jesus and the consequences of war. I was grappling with how to reconcile the two in my own life. How can a nation that proclaims to stand for the rights of everyone to live, be free, and pursue happiness also cause so many to suffer? I was finding I couldn't justify the devastation in Hiroshima and Nagasaki anymore. And I certainly couldn't ever support the use of atomic bombs, under any circumstances.

In the spring of 1947, after applying and giving much consideration to which college I would attend, I decided that Baldwin-Wallace College in Berea, Ohio, was my soundest option. It was a Methodist school, and it had offered me the best scholarship. Also, it was only sixty miles from Massillon. I would start there in the fall of 1947. The soldiers were home, and the GI Bill was going strong, providing them with free education. A boom in college attendance had begun. I would be entering a mostly white college, with a newly diverse wave of postwar students.

THREE

Concealed Battle

Baldwin-Wallace College, 1947–1951.
VANDERBILT LIBRARY

I began to write in a journal just before I entered college, establishing a practice that served me well then and in the years to come.

Aug. 28, 1947

Every time college enters my mind I start thinking of the great expenses it's going to take. Every time I think of college finances I think that Jim will not be entering college this fall. . . . It's alright when the time for decision is far away, but get closer to the crisis and watch me squirm. But I can't afford to lose faith. God is my only help. I don't have a lot of money, but God can help in some way.

Sept. 22, 1947

Today, on my nineteenth birthday, I was very pleasantly surprised with a wrist watch. I needed one very badly. To me, the gift was just another blessing from God. I owe Him a lot. Whether I'll ever repay him will depend on my ability to put my life in his hands. . . . Sunday, Sept. 28th I leave for college, my first year. There I must work hard to learn. There I must . . . put what I learn to the Christian advantage. At Baldwin-Wallace I must develop a belief in Christ that will overcome all difficulties.

Sept. 26, 1947

Forty-eight hours from tonight I'll be in bed at Baldwin-Wallace. . . .

God, give me strength to lead and faith to follow so that at Baldwin-Wallace I'll be a Christian Example.

As soon as I arrived on campus, I began to see people I knew from regional Methodist youth meetings and camps, and from debate and speech tournaments around Ohio during junior high and high school. And since we were all new to college, we began to plan freshman gatherings every week so we could meet other students and get oriented to college life. Our class was active from the start.

Within the first month, we elected class officers at a freshman class meeting. To my great surprise, longtime friends like Jim Cox, Bob Farkas, and Arlene Alison nominated me for president. And I ended up winning. Bob was from just outside of Cleveland. Jim was from Akron. Both had been in Methodist youth groups with me for years. Arlene and I went to Washington High School in Massillon together. She was Methodist and we were solid friends because we participated alongside each other in many high school speech and debate programs.

Immediately, I presided over the election of the other officers in our first meeting. I was the only Black student in the room, and as far as I knew, I was the first Black class president at Baldwin-Wallace. But I didn't feel that my friends chose me with the intention of breaking that kind of barrier. Instead, I think they did it because I was Jim Lawson, who they knew well from various high school and church activities.

In 1947, Baldwin-Wallace had some seventeen hundred students, and about one hundred and fifty were Black, with forty-five or fifty of us in the freshman class. The school had been founded by a Methodist educator and businessman in Berea, Ohio, on the principle of access to education regardless of race, gender, or ability to pay. Its first Black graduate, the Reverend Dr. Daniel Webster Shaw, who had been born into enslavement, was the class of 1883 valedictorian. By 1947, our class had a larger and more visible group of Black students than previous years, partly due to increased recruitment of Black athletes. And more than half of us were living in the dorms on campus. Add to that the influx of World War II veterans, who were older and more mature, and our freshman class was ready to break some campus traditions.

Establishing me as freshman class president shook the whole college, and especially the fraternity system. A part of their bailiwick had always been to see to it that only their potential pledges became officers of the freshman and sophomore classes. However, Greek organization rules did not allow Black people, Jewish people, or anyone except white, Protestant students into their clubs. So when my class made the move of electing me, it unsettled long-standing campus conventions.

And then there were the Wednesday evening dances we started. Unlike fraternity and sorority functions, our events welcomed everyone. A lot of popular records were played, from Glenn Miller, Artie Shaw, Duke Ellington, and Louis Armstrong. We did the two-step, swing dances, and waltzes. It was cheek to cheek, as I had learned at home with my sisters and at high school dances. I thought I was a pretty good dancer. The events were mixed, Black and white, male and female. To me, the girls were not white girls or Black girls. They were fellow students. We were all friends, getting acquainted and having fun. I remember dancing with white Southern women and asking about their lives and why they were at Baldwin-Wallace. All of us talked and visited a lot in those first months, coming together, becoming college friends.

Freshman year, I also joined a Baldwin-Wallace program that sent students to local Methodist churches around Berea on Sunday afternoons or evenings to meet with junior and senior high youth groups. We went to white congregations. The other BW students in the program were all white, and mostly men. Oftentimes, I would easily recognize that people in some of those local churches and youth ministries had never been near a Black person. They had never been in the same meeting, in the same church room, or fellowship hall, or sanctuary. In those instances, I did not view myself as a Black man giving them that experience. I saw their discomfort in those situations as their problem, because they hadn't been exposed to more of life.

In high school and college, at conferences and different events around the Midwest, I actually had young white people come up and ask me if they could touch me and rub my arm. Apparently, they thought my pigmentation might rub off. When it didn't, they were surprised. Such requests did not alarm me, because I recognized that these people had been brought up without seeing themselves as being like me, a human. They hadn't reached a point in their own humanity, as I had, where they understood that they belonged everywhere and were alive right along with everyone else on earth.

This sense of belonging in my own life grew steelier on campus in that first quarter of college, even after it was dented. One night, I asked where everyone was and heard that some of my guy friends were in one of the dorm rooms at the end of our residence hall. So, I knocked on the door. Someone said, "Come in." I saw two of my best friends, Jim Cox and Bob Farkas, as I entered. And about fifteen other guys I knew were sitting on double bunks, and on the floor, and on the table. It was a barracks-type dorm, and we were a noisy lot. We felt fairly close to one another and often had these kinds of bull sessions, discussing topics of the day. Jim Cox greeted me saying, "Come on in, Jim, we were just talking about you."

They had been talking about race. Everyone in the room was white. And all but Jim Cox, Bob Farkas, and maybe another guy or two were saying, "Negroes stink." This was the topic of the bull session that night. These were guys who had elected me president of the freshman class. I had double-dated with them. Some of us who were the same size had exchanged clothing to wear on dates. I walked into the room uneasily as they talked. Jim and Bob, disagreeing with the idea, mentioned me, another freshman, named Bill Ross, and Harrison Dillard, a junior, who was an Olympic gold medal winner and in 1948 would be called the "world's fastest man." They were challenging the premise of inferiority. I was too stunned to say much. Jim and Bob asked, "What about Jim, and Harrison, and Bill?" Someone answered, "Oh, we aren't talking about them. They don't stink." Apparently, we were the exceptions. As Jim and

Bob continued to challenge them, the rest of the guys never let go of their original idea. It turned out that when they thought about it, they had to admit to Jim and Bob that all the Negroes on campus were exceptions.

It was ridiculous. I stayed in that room, but my sense of being one with these guys was shaken. I felt betrayed. One kid in particular and I were extremely close. We often visited and talked, and were very much like each other temperamentally. When he got a care package from home, I was probably the first guy he came after to help him eat the food. We had almost the same classes. And yet, he persisted in repeating, "Negroes stink." I was astounded. The small dorm room felt like a den of lions. But they weren't scary lions, lounging on bunk beds and sitting on the floor, casually spouting their inherited ideas. They looked sad and confused to me. Somehow, however, they also had a smug confidence. It did not give me any kind of a good feeling to have them say that I was an exception, and Bill was an exception, and every other Negro they knew on campus was an exception. I didn't say much as the talk continued for almost three hours. But I felt I had to stay. As I listened and watched, the room became more like a hospital ward to me, because of the sickness I could see all around me.

Many times, in the face of such racist talk, I had to fight a concealed battle within myself, which always reminded me of the whole iceberg character of that struggle lurking just below the surface. I took our friendships at face value, and our equality as a given. But the myth of white supremacy was so deeply ingrained that it was almost impossible for many of them to do the same. In the end, their discussion substantiated for me the idea that it is very difficult for a white person in America not to be a racist.

Because I lived and operated in a lot of predominantly white circles at college and in the church, I continued to encounter directly many of the complicated patterns of racism that permeated society. During those college years, and because of the awareness in my family before that, I was coming into adulthood having no illusions about the perplexities—the strangeness, the utter weird weirdness—of racism. I could never ignore its unwelcome omnipresence in our society. So I stayed on guard against its bizarre distortions, making sure they didn't pierce my spirit.

One Sunday afternoon, my friend Arlene and I went to a concert together. On our way, she told me that junior and senior fraternity and sorority members were issuing warnings to white freshman girls who went to freshman functions and had friendships with me. They told these girls that they would be ostracized if they continued the friendships. Soon after that, I went for a walk to the park with another friend, Ruth Chafee, who was white. I had known her from Methodist circles before college. She told me that fraternities were putting pressure on white freshmen women, saying that the Black men at BW were not to be dated. She told me they were saying, "If you're friends with Jim Lawson or Bill Ross, then you cannot be our friends, and you won't be recruited into sororities, and you won't come to any fraternity parties." After that, a number of the girls who had been responsive and friendly to me at parties pulled out of our activities.

A couple of white freshmen women made it clear to me directly that they could no longer associate with me. Another said her older brother had told her in no uncertain terms that she had to stop being friends with me immediately. He said his fraternity brothers had had bull sessions about getting these white girls to stop being friends with Black people, and of reeducating the freshman white boys about their friendships with us, too. My first reaction to such targeting was just plain hurt—and isolation. I felt alienated and rejected. In their admonitions to white freshmen, I was told, they had discussed me. I wondered how many other folk they had influenced. I suspected there were more than I realized. Still, the ones who had told me about it were not influenced. Arlene and Ruth and a few other white classmates, including Bob Farkas and Jim Cox, remained friends of mine throughout college and beyond.

I had already learned that childhood punches never stopped the sickness infecting so many white people. My deep, unshakable sense that I belonged in the worlds I was inhabiting didn't seem to help them imagine a way out of their illnesses either. This was bigger than any of these people. It was an outbreak of evil. During the first half of my freshman year, it came for the adult forming in me.

Around that time, I was introduced to a small book of poetry called *There Is a Spirit Which I Feel*, by James Nayler, a seventeenth-century English Quaker. He was persecuted for his religion, and was badly beaten and left for dead in a field beside a country road. He wrote the title poem in his dying hours, and it became part of my daily devotional readings in college.

> There is a Spirit which I feel that delights to do no evil, nor to revenge any wrong. . . . Its hope is to outlive all wrath and contention and to weary out all exaltation and cruelty. . . . I found it alone, being forsaken; I have fellowship therein with them who lived in dens and desolate places in the earth. . . . Bring me forth a rock before all the world . . . present me to the world in thy strength, in which I stand and cannot be moved.

Instead of retaliating against the cruelty, I used it to propel me. I found the will to redouble my earliest conviction. I was never going to accept racism as the way of the world. I knew I might not cure it. But I became more committed than ever to putting an end to the conditions in which it thrived and metastasized.

A fortuitous milestone on that quest happened in the late fall of 1947, when the history department invited a man named A. J. Muste to campus for a series of lectures. He was the leading pacifist in the United States at the time, a Dutch-born Presbyterian minister and elder, and the executive director of the Fellowship of Reconciliation (FOR). His mild manner belied the fact that he was one of the boldest and most courageous men I would ever know.

I attended all of his talks on campus. Muste discussed the same issues I was living. He opened the door for me to a way of thinking that upheld where I was going, and what I was studying and discovering. He introduced me to an intellectual, spiritual, artistic, and moral fermentation that was taking place in the United States. His visit showed me that there were people who were critics of the status quo. I got names for ideas I couldn't define before. I discovered there was more than the NAACP and the Urban League fighting racism. There was the Fellowship of Reconciliation. There was the Congress of Racial Equality (CORE). There was John Swomley, a FOR board member, peace activist, and Methodist ethicist. There was George Houser, a Methodist minister and civil rights advocate. And there was Bayard Rustin. Both Houser and Rustin had resisted the Selective Service draft in 1940 and had gone to prison for it, and they organized nonviolent direct action campaigns to challenge segregation in the 1940s and 1950s.

I went up and spoke to A. J. Muste right after his first afternoon lecture. I followed him around that evening and for the next day he was on campus, and talked to him whenever I could. I joined FOR immediately.

From then on, I looked to Muste's thinking, his intellect, his spirituality, and his work for guidance and inspiration. In that first meeting he also saw me, and the potential I had for the struggles in which he was engaged.

Exploring the practice of a spiritual life sustained me through the ups and downs of freshman year. I continued to study the Bible on my own. And almost every morning I was up by six, sometimes earlier. I would take an hour or so to read the scriptures, systematically over time, cover to cover, back and forth, but concentrating on the books about Jesus. The Psalms was a book of music and poetry that was always a must, too. I went through those, not just reading but examining, studying, and thinking about what I read, and praying. I was coming to a deeper understanding of the fact that I was a child of life, not death, and not hatred. I was a child of love. I was seeing that I was never alone. I could live in my own skin. This self-knowledge provided me a firm structure—I don't like to use the military terms "fortress" or "citadel"—from which I could withstand a lot of incoming vitriol. And my spiritual life meant I didn't get floored or overwhelmed easily, or for long.

In my college work, I kept on studying politics and religion. I read theologian Reinhold Niebuhr's *The Children of Light and the Children of Darkness*. He wrote: "Man's capacity for justice makes democracy possible; but man's inclination to injustice makes democracy necessary." Niebuhr's influence helped me see the unrealized promise of democracy in the United States of America. It increased my growing sense that nonviolence added to democracy could dismantle racism. From then on, throughout college, I made it a practice in every term paper and class project to focus on race, war and peace, and nonviolence. I wrote about Gandhi in sociology, Thoreau in English. And in world literature, I did a study of Tolstoy, who had become one of my favorite writers.

Another reckoning slowly began during my college years. Cleveland was only about fifteen miles away from BW. Since my father was living there part-time, pastoring at some churches, I would take the bus to see him quite often, on the weekends. My sister Ella was also living and working in Cleveland, and I would travel in on Sundays and go to church with her. Then she'd cook a big dinner. So the college boy ate well, because she was a really good cook. And in the bargain I got reacquainted with my father.

I still felt regret at his abrupt exit from our home when I was growing up. But over time, the emotions and pain dissipated. By my college years, we had a spirit between us of going forward in the now. I went to church with Dad a few times to hear him preach. Other times, if he wasn't preaching, we attended a service together and we had conversations. We never talked about why he left us. I accepted I would probably never know for sure. But we talked about our lives then and there in the moment. I had to find forgiveness. I saw him from an adult point of view for the first time. Despite his mistake, I felt that the example he set for me was basically a good one. Gradually, we built a basis for an ongoing relationship.

During college, Ella married an extraordinary man named Roosevelt King, and I was his best man. My dad officiated at the ceremony, which was held at Ella's home in Cleveland. Dad also finally came back to Massillon for a day, to officiate at Frankie's wedding to a fine man named Joe Reed. My mother was there, too. My parents never divorced, but they never lived together again. These were moments of good cheer and celebration. Healing came, as Dad shared in the joy and gladness of everyone in the family again.

A few weeks before the first quarter of freshman year was over, I got a package from my younger brother John, still in Massillon. He was a few years behind me in school. But we were about the same size. Inside was a note he had scribbled to me saying, "I like this sweater. I bought one for myself and I bought one for you." It struck me as a wonderful brotherly gesture, unsolicited. He had thought of me and figured I would like what he liked, so he had bought two. Whenever I wore that sweater I would think of my funny, caring little brother, and it seemed to keep me just a bit warmer. My family members were my foundation of love, and continued to be my touchstone.

Another foundation growing in my life was the influence of Mahatma Gandhi, whom I had already met in print, before college, through the Black newspapers, which closely covered his anti-colonial, nonviolent resistance to British rule. He impressed me with his insistence that the world was nowhere near the kind of world God wanted, nor the kind of world we human beings were capable of having. I read his autobiography as soon as a U.S. edition was published, during my freshman year. He was becoming one of my greatest mentors from afar. Gandhi led the way when India gained independence as a democracy in August 1947. But religious violence broke out that fall, and Gandhi was shot and killed after a prayer vigil in January 1948.

Assassination was a new brand of violence to me, a hollow deed. Of course, I had no idea then how many more times it would echo through our struggle for justice.

Gandhi embodied nonviolence—the practice I was increasingly seeing as the best way to resolve our world's most pressing problems, including racism. Gandhi taught that violence was a misuse of power, an abuse of power. It failed all the time, and set us back all the time. About the only thing that violence produced was some unjustly powerful people.

I came to find out midway through freshman year that I had enemies among the faculty and administration. The main offender was the chair of the religion department.

Dr. Ernest Knautz, a German Methodist Old Testament scholar, was a preacher, like I was. I took one of his classes on the Old Testament freshman year. Hearing the material, I wanted to know more. Throughout my education, in almost all of my theology classes, including his, I raised the issue of religions supporting violence and war. I realized Dr. Knautz was a supporter of war. I was no longer a supporter of war. Initially, I underestimated how much my inquisitiveness in his class upset him. It turned out that he was also vehemently opposed to any kind of interracial dancing or dating. A few of the guys had challenged him on that belief in class, and they told me that their contrariness made him visibly angry. He never discussed it when I was in his class, but he discussed it at other times, and it got back to me.

So, there I was, a Black student. I didn't have an athletic scholarship, which was a more acceptable role for a Black man at the time. I had arrived on a scholarship based on my academic achievement. I was known by faculty people as a leader in campus religious activities. I was already a national Methodist student conference officer. I had taken my first steps to becoming a Methodist minister. Baldwin-Wallace was connected to the Methodist Church, and many professors were Methodists. My major was sociology, and I was a good student. I used the library. I asked questions in class and spoke with conviction. Apparently, I wrote good papers. But Dr. Knautz thought I was too militant. And he decided to tell me so himself.

Toward the end of the second quarter of my freshman year, he called me into his office for a meeting. I had no idea what it was about, but

I sensed that his office wouldn't be a friendly place for me. He didn't greet me warmly. Instead, he looked at me like I was a problem. Then he started in.

"The school is receiving criticism," he said. "People say you are dating a white girl on campus."

He did not stop to hear my reaction. "That is wrong. Friendship is okay. But friendship should not lead to dancing. It should not lead to dating. And it absolutely should not lead to marriage."

I corrected him. I knew he was talking about Arlene. I tried to tell him that he was mistaken: "Professor Knautz, the girl you are referring to is just a good friend. We went to high school together in Massillon and have been going to Methodist camps together for years. We both came from families that taught us that it was a good friendship. We are not dating."

He looked at me with doubt and a little disgust. I said, "I don't think it would be right to break off a friendship just because a few people can't understand it as a normal, healthy kind of socializing."

He took on an air of concern, layered over his contempt. "You could go far in the Methodist Church and in the United States, if you change your ways. You are talking like a radical, extremist, misbehaving militant."

He saw me as all of that, and I wasn't any of that. I sat there staring at him as he ranted. Another lion's den. Another cowardly lion. I was just being myself. However, he believed that I should not be who I was. He didn't use those words.

"You need to change your ways," he said. He wanted me to be someone else as I walked the campus and went into cafeterias and ate like I belonged there. He wanted me to stop the way I was part of the Methodist student movement on campus, and the way I got in fraternities' and sororities' business, pointing out their discrimination.

"You should not be going to freshman social events and dancing with the girls—the white girls," he said. There were some Black women in classes, but almost all of them lived at home in the Cleveland area, not on campus, and so they didn't come to the on-campus socials. The women there were white. And I danced with some of the white women who were my friends.

"You ask too many questions in class," Dr. Knautz said. "You talk too much."

Along comes this older white man warning me—a young Black man who was sincerely exploring the possibilities of life—that I was on the wrong course. He had no model for me. I was Black, and taking part fully in my college, my community, and my church. He was basically telling me to stop being Jim Lawson.

But I would not back down. *Be natural.*

I did not yield and agree that I was militant. I said, "I did not elect myself freshman class president. I was nominated by folks who knew me in the freshman class, Methodist white guys, mostly. I am a student on this campus. I like the university. I will be continuing to live my life as I think I need to live it."

He fell silent.

"My motto," I continued, "the major spiritual rule in my life, is to follow Jesus—intellectually, spiritually, and otherwise—to gain what I can from that pursuit, and let my life be shaped by it. How other people see me is their problem."

Quietly but firmly, I made myself clear: "I will be fighting racism and bigotry for the rest of my life, because they are sins and evils." I added, "And the church needs to be rid of them, just as much as universities do."

That was about all he could take. We ended our conversation in a draw. His racist suspicions lived on. I left and continued as before.

My first year at college confirmed that I was not going to contort myself into someone else. Also, I learned even more clearly than before that racism was not solely a thorn in the Southern side of the United States. It was all over the place, even in a Methodist college in Ohio.

Still, I knew that the South had laws that encoded racist customs. The North just enforced the racist customs with the kind of sideways attacks I had endured freshman year. If I was experiencing those in Ohio, I knew others had it much worse in Georgia or Mississippi. So it was during my freshman year that I decided I wanted to work in the South after college. I wanted to go where the problem of race was most acute and needed to be confronted most directly. Wrong doesn't change unless people move to confront it. I felt that if we could go into the heart of the enemy camp and address racism head-on, we could address it anywhere. I kept that ambition to myself, but it was definitely planted during that first year of college.

By the start of sophomore year in 1948, a group of friends from my class and I had declared ourselves to be "anti-fraternity." The idea sprang from some of my white friends, like Bob Farkas and Jim Cox, who had stuck with me through so much of the racism I'd encountered as a freshman. Knowing that I wasn't invited to the fraternity parties they were invited to, they decided not to go to them, either. We talked about it, and they recognized it for the bigotry that it was. But then we got to know a group of World War II veterans who had formed their own fraternity, which cut out all the hazing, the blackballing, and the exclusion based on race or religion. Black, white, Jewish, Catholic, and any other men were welcome in Beta Sigma Tau, which had a high scholarship standard. Among those founders was Harrison Dillard, the Olympic medalist. Before the war, he was a Cleveland track and field star who had enrolled at Baldwin-Wallace in 1941, just as the United States joined the war. In 1943, the army had drafted him into the segregated all-Black 92nd Infantry Division, better known as the Buffalo Soldiers. He returned to Baldwin-Wallace in 1946 and resumed his track career. He won two gold medals in the 1948 Summer Olympics, and two more in the 1952 Olympics.

The men of Beta Sigma Tau at Baldwin-Wallace were rather remarkable and especially sharp. A lot of them were pre-ministerial students, pre-law students, English majors, or musicians. I hadn't planned to become a fraternity person, but Beta Sigma Tau was an effort at reform and change, so I pledged in my sophomore year. We were a pretty talkative bunch, holding a lot of bull sessions into the wee hours of the morning on every conceivable subject.

My close friend Jim Cox also joined Beta Sigma Tau. We were both pre-ministerial students. We decided to become roommates sophomore year, and together we witnessed clearly some of the real weaknesses and hypocrisies of the church. At Baldwin-Wallace, even though it was a church-related college, Negro and white men and women had never been roommates until I came to campus. It just so happened that in our particular dorm, the housemother was a good friend, and she asked everyone whom we wanted to room with. Right away, Jim Cox and I picked each other. Our housemother did not go to anyone for permission. She just gave us and everyone else our first choices, to the best of her abilities. That broke the ice, but not everywhere. When some other Black and white students across campus decided they wanted to room together, they ran up against not only reluctant housemothers but administrators—all of whom were big Methodists, of course—who interfered, and even intimidated and harassed students to prevent them from rooming together.

I was glad Jim and I could be roommates. I knew I could rely on him. A few months into sophomore year, some of the Black men on campus complained to me and to Jim that they had nowhere to get a haircut. One student from Ethiopia, in particular, said barbers in town would not cut his hair. So Jim and I decided we would check it out and report back.

Berea's typical old town square was surrounded by stores, with four or five barbershops in a five-block area. Jim and I went to test them, to see if they would cut a Negro's hair. Our tactic was very simple: I would walk in first and take a seat, and then Jim would walk in behind me, soon enough after I entered that it would be clear to everyone there that I was ahead of him and then he was next. If I was not asked to move to a chair by the barber but Jim was asked, then Jim would decline, saying I had gotten there ahead of him. The first shop we went into, we were physically thrown out. When Jim insisted that I be served, the barber would not talk to us. He went into an absolute rage, roughly ousting us from his shop. Since we were just testing, we brushed ourselves off and went on to the next establishment. In the next two shops, the barbers were adamant that they would not cut my hair. They were going to serve Jim Cox, but not me. In each case, though, Jim said, "Well, if you're not going to cut his hair, I'm going to leave, too."

In the fourth shop, we recognized the owner. He was an usher at the First Congregational Church. It was a one-seat shop. Only one barber worked there. I walked into that shop when it was empty. Jim followed me shortly thereafter. The barber motioned me to the chair to cut my hair, while Jim waited to have his hair cut next. There was no rejection. The owner had spoken to me on many Sunday mornings when I had gone to his church. He recognized me, and I think he found it impossible to say that he would not cut the hair of this person whom he had ushered into church on Sunday. I think it was a simple, moral confrontation for him, and he answered it positively.

So, we went back to campus and told the Black students that his was the shop to go to. We told the Ethiopian fellow he could go there and his hair would be cut. And we encouraged our white friends who we knew were good guys in the Christian movement on campus to go to that shop, too, because the owner would cut a Black student's hair, while the other shops would not. On any number of occasions, I would quietly test places like that, so that I learned something of the dimensions of racism in public spaces. I didn't see it as the proprietor's issue as much as our society's issue. The owners who refused service to any paying customer, for whatever reason, were participating in society's disease.

I was becoming even more deeply committed to changing this terribly broken society, to getting rid of the monkeys on the backs of myself, my fellow Negroes, poor people, and so many others. I was in favor of a radical overturning of the systems with built-in cruelties that oppress, and hurt, and cripple people.

By the end of my sophomore year, I was also wrestling with whether to follow all the official Selective Service processes and declare myself as a conscientious objector or to refuse to cooperate at all. The world and life I wanted had at its center the law of love as Jesus tried to live it, and teach it, and demonstrate it. It permitted a man to lay down his life for another person. But it did not permit anyone to make the choice to take someone else's life. Therefore, I was not going into anyone's army under any circumstances.

My friend and debate partner from high school, Chuck Sohner, had applied to be a conscientious objector, or CO, when he'd registered for the draft. But he never got approved, because he was not a member of a church. I testified for him and was with him through that whole appeal process, which involved hearings before the draft board, with witnesses and lawyers. He was judged insincere by his local draft board, partly because he didn't have all of the traditional religious trappings—for example, he couldn't say that he had been baptized. The verdict that he didn't qualify and had to go to war made a very deep impression on me. Chuck's case showed me how the state was unjustly defining sincerity and conscience. I thought it had no business doing so.

The main people who would get that conscientious objector designation belonged to the "peace churches" such as the Quakers, the Amish, and members of the Church of the Brethren. A lot of Methodist men could not get conscientious objector status. I probably could have gotten a CO exemption as a pre-ministerial student. But my position was that the Selective Service Act was another unjust law, like Jim Crow laws. I didn't want to participate in an unjust system in any way. Becoming a CO would have been working within that system. And I made the decision that I would never take a ministerial deferment, which I saw as discriminatory and elitist—giving preachers a chance to opt out when so many others didn't get that chance. That's why when filling out the forms, I did not mention that I was a pre-ministerial student.

Eventually, I decided to take a "noncooperative position." I simply was not going to go through with any of the steps required to participate in the draft, including trying to be a CO. I didn't believe a person should break laws, such as the traffic laws, which are there to protect us all. But certain laws were absolutely contrary to the meaning of freedom and justice, such as segregation laws and military conscription. I would never obey a segregation law. The conscription laws were similar. Therefore, I could not cooperate. Not many people on campus saw it my way, even those who were potential conscientious objectors. I was an oddball.

My acts of nonviolent resistance to the draft were not about being a spectator. My evolving nonviolence practice required active, aggressive, strategic engagement—confronting human struggles and advancing the world toward justice. In 1949, I sent my draft card back to the draft board in Massillon without filling it out, effectively announcing my intention to become a non-registrant for the draft. Defying the Selective Service marked the first time I so publicly applied the law of love to my life, my country, and the world.

FOUR

Unimaginable Warfare

Reverend Lawson's speech "Alternative to Destruction" was the state of Ohio winner and placed third in the National Intercollegiate Oratorical Contest, Northwestern University, 1950. VANDERBILT LIBRARY

On Monday, January 8, 1951, I was arrested for refusing to report for military service. An FBI agent came to my home in Massillon to take me into federal custody. We went before a U.S. commissioner in Cleveland that day. I was told of the charges and released on $1,000 bond. A trial was set for a few months later. I had known arrest would be likely as soon as I sent my Selective Service card back in the fall of 1949. But nothing happened immediately. The draft board did not bother to respond. So for more than a year, I was able to go on enjoying college, staying involved in my church and family life, and planning for my future.

I had earned my license to be a pastor in the summer of 1949, which was the next step toward becoming ordained. It was one of many paths that came to fruition during my junior year at Baldwin-Wallace from 1949 to 1950. I thrived, becoming president of our campus Beta Sigma Tau chapter and taking on multiple leadership positions in Methodist youth groups in Ohio and nationally. Also, Berea's active Fellowship of Reconciliation branch evolved into my home away from home.

I was constantly reading Fellowship of Reconciliation and Congress of Racial Equality publications throughout college. I learned how Bayard Rustin and a fellow founding member of CORE, James Farmer, and others used nonviolent direct action to organize sit-ins at Chicago restaurants in the early 1940s. They also took bus rides to integrate public transportation on the East Coast. I had joined the active CORE branch in Cleveland during freshman year. As I got to know A. J. Muste, Bayard Rustin, and James Farmer better, each of them influenced my thinking and development and I became more and more involved in FOR and CORE.

Both my world of ideas and my realm of possibilities were expanding. For instance, I began to realize there was such a thing as language that was symbolic, not literal. So, I reconsidered my teenage rejection of the Apostles' Creed and started repeating it again in church services. I started my work as a pastor around that time in 1950, during my junior year, when I took my first church appointment, in Canton, Ohio, at Turner Chapel Methodist Church, a small congregation about sixty miles from BW. Since it was only eight miles from Massillon, I would go home on weekends to be near the church.

All through junior year, the prospect of arrest was in the back of my mind. But I focused on making the most of college. One way I did that was through intramural sports. It was an outlet for me to enjoy the practice and the play, without the pressures of anything varsity. Yet I was on the varsity speech and debate team at BW, and we placed in many tournaments. That mix allowed me to cultivate my intellectual rigor while still nurturing my love of sports.

In the spring of 1950, I won the Ohio state intercollegiate oratorical contest. That meant I went on to the national contest at Northwestern University, in Evanston, Illinois, at the end of April. My speech was entitled "Alternative to Destruction," about how Gandhian nonviolent direct action could foster world peace. I was telling big rooms full of students from Ohio, and then, at Northwestern, from all over the country, how applying Gandhian philosophy and tactics to current world issues could change the whole equation.

I started with my basic premise that global harmony was based on two antagonistic nations, the USSR and the United States, which both said they wanted peace but behaved in a way that induced war and disharmony.

> America makes an atomic bomb. Thereupon, Russia enslaves European scientists until they, too, have the bomb. Then the United States talks about super-atomic bombs and the hydrogen bomb. . . .
>
> The inevitable result of the present struggle is unimaginable warfare, for there is a law of life, "whatsoever ye sow, that shall ye also reap." Therefore, if man continues to sow the seeds of armaments, hatred, and suspicion, then man must reap those results.

The conflicts between the Soviet Union and the United States were all over the news. The idea that a cold war was taking place scared everyone. And no one could see any way out that didn't involve military might.

> Cold war may bring hot war. . . . But there is an alternative which has worked before . . . nonviolent direct action. . . . Gandhi began to teach four hundred million people that the way to achieve Indian independence was through nonviolence and truth. He taught them that they could hate the actions of the British, but must never hate the British soldier or British people. He said, "You are fighting a system, not an individual, not a race, or not the people of another country, but a system."

This lesson would start to become accepted only decades later. The force of the truth in Gandhi's simple message opened some minds, even if it didn't penetrate much beyond the gathered group of student public speakers.

> War and nonviolent direct action are modes of social action, aimed at the solving of social conflict. . . . But nonviolent direct action is also superior to war because it does not necessitate wholesale murder, bloodshed, and devastation of property and natural resources. Furthermore, it breaks the vicious circle of hatred and revenge, and is consonant with democracy and Christianity by exalting and respecting people, while protesting their actions and institutions.

I placed third in the national contest.

Two months later, during the summer after junior year, I attended an annual ten-day, Midwest-region Methodist conference that brought together youth leaders from local churches, high schools, and colleges. I had always enjoyed my time at the big Methodist-owned campground in Clear Lake, Iowa, where that year I was the chair of the conference. About 120 people attended, including my brother Phillip, who was four years younger and still in high school, but he was an officer in the conference, too.

A few days into the event, on Tuesday, June 27, 1950, we got the news that President Harry S. Truman had announced the United States was joining the growing conflict on the Korean Peninsula, to defend the South from the invading North. The United States was entering into another bloody war. Right away, I figured the draft would pick up greatly, and the Selective Service would take care of its backlog.

As chair of the conference, I served as presiding officer for many of the sessions. I decided to tell everyone there that war meant I was likely to be arrested sometime soon. Clergy members and a few friends around the conference knew I had declined to register for the draft. And, of course, my brother Phillip knew. When I made the announcement during a session with the whole group, almost everyone understood I had done it not only for the sake of conscience but for the sake of civil disobedience to an unjust law.

I wasn't part of any movement. I had simply determined that I should not cooperate. The Selective Service law created two classes of men, an elite class, whose members could get out of being drafted, and an underclass, including many who were from racial minorities or living in poverty. Men with fewer loopholes were forced to go to war. Thus, military conscription was akin to racial injustice.

Later that summer, in August 1950, I received a notice in the mail from the Selective Service classifying me as 1-A, which meant "available for military service." I also received a questionnaire to fill out to become a conscientious objector. I wrote the draft board, saying I still could not participate in the process. I sent back the classification card along with the unopened questionnaire. In September, after I started my senior year of college, I was sent an order to report for a physical, and I did not show up. In October, I received a notice to report for induction on October 31, 1950. In response, I wrote another letter reiterating my intention not to be a part of the military system.

Every time I got a notice, I always responded with an explanatory letter saying why I was returning it. I also went in person to the draft board from time to time. A couple of the people I met with there thought I was a coward. They said I was "yellow." That was their simple dismissal of my stance. They didn't want to engage in conversation with me about it. There was a Black draft board member too, and he felt the same way about me as everyone else.

In early December 1950, I was an official delegate of the Methodist Church to a White House conference President Truman had convened on children and youths. When I got to the D.C. hotel with my reservation, I presented whatever was necessary to show I was a participant in the White House conference. The person at the front desk affirmed that the documentation was correct. "But," he said, "we're sorry, the hotel is full. There are no more rooms tonight." I went outside and walked around for a few moments to calm down. I then stepped into a public phone booth on the sidewalk and called the hotel. I said I had just arrived at Union Station, only to find out that I was not going to be able to leave until the next evening. The clerk said, "We have rooms tonight. Do you want a room?" This hotel had just told me it was all full up. So I made the reservation. When I went back inside, the front desk again refused me.

This affront had happened to me two or three times before in other places. I would always have to find other accommodation. I had not devised a good method to confirm the rejection was because I was Black. In my study of nonviolence, I was learning that one of the first steps was to gather information about the suspected injustice. So that time, I had checked out what I had always suspected: racism drove them to tell me lies. Yet, while I had the evidence, I knew of no official way to hold the hotel accountable, no channel to right the wrong in that moment. Such discrimination had not yet been made illegal or even shameful for most hotel owners. I ended up staying elsewhere.

Around Christmastime, it became clearer that my arrest was imminent. When some of my brothers had reached draft age, they had decided to declare as conscientious objectors. At first, my father said, "Well, it's how we have raised them." My mother said, "It's because we have taught them to love." It wasn't until I was facing prison that it became a family crisis. One night, my brothers and I were pacing back and forth between the living room and dining room, along with my mother, who was upset. She did not want us to go to war. But she did not want me to go to prison. We tried to reason with her. Finally, we said, "If you had not expected us to take this to heart, why did you teach us that love is the law of God, and the law of God is our guide?"

She paused for a very long time. She had heard us. From that moment on, never again did our mother question our stances on the draft or on war. Ultimately, her approach to violence had won with the boys in our family. We were finding that better way.

I was at home in Massillon that Friday in the winter of 1951 when I was arrested. I had received a call the Friday before from an FBI officer with whom I was acquainted. We had arranged for him to come to my home, since I would be there for my pastor duties in Canton. When he arrived, he explained that he had a warrant for my arrest. He said he wanted to arrest me himself at my home, because he did not want an agent who didn't know me to come out to Baldwin-Wallace and do it there. I thought that was a fine gesture.

When I went back to school the following week, everyone on campus knew about my arrest. And the administration said I could no longer represent the school in speech or athletic activities. The president of Baldwin-Wallace, John Knight, made that decision. I went and talked to him about it, but I couldn't prevail on him to change his mind. Several faculty members who were my friends also talked to him, but they couldn't shake him, either.

In contrast, my bishop and my conference highly supported me. My church was still part of the segregated Central Jurisdiction. And I had a Black bishop, Matthew W. Clair Jr., who had served as a chaplain in World War I. However, after that, he had become a strong pacifist. Any number of preachers made clear their support for me. And some of the bishops of the Methodist Church got together and organized a defense committee for me, to help defray my legal costs. My attorney, an American Civil Liberties Union (ACLU) lawyer in Cleveland, had been a CO in World War II. I felt well-supported.

In March, I was indicted and arraigned. I pleaded not guilty, and my bond was continued. The trial was held on April 24 and 25, 1951, in Cleveland, at the Northern District of the Ohio Federal District Court. I waived my right to a jury trial. Two professors from Baldwin-Wallace testified on my behalf, along with a fellow student and the minister from the Methodist church I attended in Berea. My case was pretty cut-and-dried.

We didn't really have a defense. We tried to challenge on constitutional grounds, but the judge rejected our logic. The Board of Missions of the Methodist Church and a number of bishops of the church spoke out in my favor, because I was so active within the church. The Board of Missions asked the judge to grant probation or suspend any sentence, to let me go to Africa as a missionary. Because by this time I had been accepted by the board to travel to a high school in Harare, Zimbabwe (called Rhodesia then, before independence from the British government), as soon as I graduated in June.

But the judge rejected it all. He said my being so active in the youth conference of the church was why he had to sentence me to three years in prison. He was establishing a precedent to show other young men that they could not defy the Selective Service.

I went immediately from the courtroom to the Cleveland city jail. I was supposed to graduate and, a few weeks later, to march with my class. Of course, I didn't get to do either. The president of Baldwin-Wallace stayed quiet through it all. He did nothing except to decide that I would not graduate. He was a Methodist preacher and a college president. But he didn't know how to handle me. The challenge my decision posed seemed to be simply beyond his spiritual grasp.

A few days later I was transported to Mill Point Federal Prison, which was called an honor penal institution of the federal system. It sat in the hills of West Virginia, surrounded by thick forests, through which no one had ever escaped.

FIVE

Troublemakers

Judgment and Commitment — Cr. Form No. 25

District Court of the United States

FOR THE

NORTHERN DISTRICT OF OHIO

EASTERN DIVISION

United States of America
v.
JAMES MORRIS LAWSON

No. 20286 Criminal

On this 25 day of April, 19 51 came the attorney for the government and the defendant appeared in person and[1] by counsel.

It Is Adjudged that the defendant has been convicted upon a finding of guilty of the offense of knowingly failing and refusing to report for induction into the armed forces of the United States, under the provisions of the Selective Service Act of 1948, as charged[2] in one count of the Indictment and the court having asked the defendant whether he has anything to say why judgment should not be pronounced, and no sufficient cause to the contrary being shown or appearing to the Court,

It Is Adjudged that the defendant is guilty as charged and convicted.

It Is Adjudged that the defendant is hereby committed to the custody of the Attorney General or his authorized representative for imprisonment for a period of[4] three (3) years. No costs assessed.

It Is Ordered that the Clerk deliver a certified copy of this judgment and commitment to the United States Marshal or other qualified officer and that the copy serve as the commitment of the defendant.

Charles J. McNamee, United States District Judge.

The Court recommends commitment to:[6]

(Signed) ______ Clerk. (By) ______ Deputy Clerk.

[1] Insert "by counsel" or "without counsel; the court advised the defendant of his right to counsel and asked him whether he desired to have counsel appointed by the court, and the defendant thereupon stated that he waived the right to the assistance of counsel." [2] Insert (1) "guilty," (2) "not guilty, and a verdict of guilty," (3) "not guilty, and a finding of guilty," or (4) "nolo contendre," as the case may be. [3] Insert "in count(s) number ______" if required. [4] Enter (1) sentence or sentences, specifying counts if any; (2) whether sentences are to run concurrently or consecutively and, if consecutively, when each term is to begin with reference to termination of preceding term or to any other outstanding or unserved sentence; (3) whether defendant is to be further imprisoned until payment of the fine or fine and costs, or until he is otherwise discharged as provided by law. [5] Enter any order with respect to suspension and probation. [6] For use of Court wishing to recommend a particular institution.

Sentenced to three years in federal prison for not cooperating with the Selective Service Act of 1948. NATIONAL ARCHIVES

When I was preparing to serve my prison sentence, I was a little surprised to find that there were more Methodists who supported me than I'd realized—bishops, preachers, and teachers. During World War II, the Methodist Church had more conscientious objectors in prison than any other denomination. I already knew I wasn't a pioneer in standing up against the draft. I was a latecomer. Two early mentors who became my friends,

Bayard Rustin and George Houser, had refused to cooperate with the Selective Service during World War II in much the same way I was doing a decade later. And they had spent time in federal prison for the offense. Bayard had been excused from military service because he was a Quaker, but he was sent to prison for refusing to do the alternative civilian community service that the Selective Service required. He saw it all as part of the machinery of war that went against his religious beliefs. George was a Methodist minister who could have gotten a dismissal from service because he was a member of the clergy, but he chose not to claim that status and was also sent to prison.

As I was going through the arrest and conviction process, I spoke to both of them. I also spoke to A. J. Muste. All three had become my mentors and continued to influence my thinking and development as a student and my embrace of nonviolence. These people were thinking and going in the same direction as I was. I was welcomed into this other community, beyond my own family, that became integral to shaping my spirituality, my character, and my development and learning. So, I could never feel lonely or out of place when I took a stand. Their support helped sustain me not only through prison but throughout my life.

In the months leading up to my trial, I read all I could to prepare for the probability of time in prison. One of the main things I learned from all my inquiry was that in prison, for your own sanity, you had to accept the routine imposed on you. But you could not lose your sense of self and free will to that routine. You had to use the discipline of the routine to work on your own goals and needs. For instance, meals were served when they were served. And you either ate or you didn't eat until the next meal. I would begin fasting in prison, as a spiritual practice. So I didn't always have to eat just because the prison said it was time to eat. I developed my own scheme of where to focus my mind and energy, and worked to make use of my time in prison on my own terms.

One of the ways I did that began on the day I entered Mill Point prison camp, when I made a commitment to try to write in a notebook every day—a kind of journal, to chronicle my internal life in prison and find meaning in the isolation and challenges I would face.

May 11, 1951 (Friday)

Arrived at Mill Point, W. Va. to begin 3 yr prison sentence.

Well, this is the payoff after 4 years of Christian objection to war. . . . My emotions are mixed. My only real concern is that I, directed by God's voice, discover His discipline for the prison experience. If I am willing to yield every desire to Him, certainly prison will be a testing ground for future Kingdom building.

I went to prison confident in the fact that I was doing what I needed to do, following the course God wanted me to follow. God's voice was within me. It was my voice, enhanced and molded by a loving voice from Eternity. The inspiration during my prison term—the compass that moved me in prison—was from the past. It was the path of Jesus, even though his path was in the first century and mine was in 1951.

My family and friends and I exchanged letters. But there was one close friend who was on my mind more than just a little, and who I hoped would become more than just a friend. Her name was Carol Hamilton. She was from Columbus, Ohio, and attended Ohio Wesleyan University. We had met through Methodist youth groups. When I met her, I said to myself, "That's who I'm going to marry." By the time I went to prison, I had known her for four years. We never really dated. I had never even kissed her. But I had met her parents and saw her whenever I was in Columbus. I kept in touch with her throughout my time in prison.

In the middle of my first letter to Carol from prison, in May 1951, I expressed my feelings about our relationship.

Dear Carol,

. . . Since my incarceration I've received a ton of mail and my folks have received another ton. But the other afternoon a special delivery letter came which I've waited for for several days. It was your letter! Each day that it didn't come, I wondered why. As I read your letter, Roger (just one of the fellows I met in jail), said, "You like her quite a bit, don't you?" All he knew was that the letter was from a girl. Rog was right. I consider you one of my most dearest and cherished friends. And if there ever arises a chance for me to make it more than a friendship, you ought to let me know . . .

As Ever,
Jim

In the early mornings at Mill Point, we were supposed to stay in our dorms until breakfast. We called them dorms because Mill Point was a minimum-security prison and didn't really have cellblocks. There were no fences around the prison, just remote, deep woods, which meant that no one who tried to escape got far. The doors were not locked, and the guards did not carry guns or sticks. That meant I did not get any objection when I began a routine of waking up earlier than the bell and going over to the library to read and write in my journal for a while. I was finding some freedom for my mind, if not in my circumstances.

Mill Point Federal Prison was supposed to be an enlightened place at the time. Set in the Allegheny Mountains of West Virginia, it was called an "honor camp," intended for first-time offenders with crimes that were not considered violent. Most of the white prisoners were Southern moonshiners from Virginia, West Virginia, Kentucky, North Carolina, and South Carolina, along with some Jehovah's Witnesses, who were in prison because their religion barred them from participating in a military draft. The Northern white men were usually there for white-collar crimes. And the Black men were mostly college graduates. A few of the inmates at Mill Point were there for refusing to name names or otherwise cooperate with the House Un-American Activities Committee.

The food was pretty bad—no flavor or variety and few fresh vegetables. There were bells, and bed counts, and you were given some kind of job, which often added little value to your mind or life and paid little or nothing. I was assigned to be the clerk in the garage. I did the bookkeeping and manual labor. Mill Point prison camp produced and milled lumber, so it used a lot of vehicles and needed a full-time garage. I was what they called a "grease monkey," a term used among mechanics and applied equally to white and non-white people in that job. I had to get down in a grease pit, after which a car or truck was rolled over me. From the pit, I did the greasing and changed the oil.

May 12, 1951 (Saturday)

Many of the men here feel that I'm totally out of place. That I ought not to be in prison. . . . Certainly if I am concerned about my personal kinship to all men, then no man in prison belongs in prison if I am not also in prison. Eugene Debs made this so very clear in At-

> lanta, as long as there is a criminal class I am of it; as long as there is one soul in prison, I am not free. . . . Every man is my brother. . . . If I cannot go to prison for what is right, then how do I expect right to ultimately triumph?

At Mill Point, there was a group of us that I called COs (conscientious objectors), even though we weren't all officially recognized as that. Each of us felt the government had no right to order its citizens into war. In addition, I believed the Selective Service was set up to send a higher percentage of Black men into wars. Eventually, these other COs at Mill Point joined me each day in coming to the library for a kind of disciplined study routine.

I think at least four or five of us in our group probably could have gotten official CO status and avoided prison altogether. But avoiding prison was not our purpose. Three of our group were Quakers or Mennonites who also—even though they came out of the peace church traditions—took the position of noncooperation. Jim Pierce was a white Methodist who took the same noncooperative stance that I did. We met early each morning before the sun came up to meditate, pray, and talk together. We would meet again in the prison library in the evenings, after dinner. The same group of us would talk about current events and discuss what we were each reading. It made the summer quite stimulating and provocative.

Also, I worked with the warden to plant the idea that as soon as a prison librarian position opened up, I would be given the job. Almost all federal prisons had established good libraries by that time, as every prison where COs had served their time had gained a good library by the time they left. It is a little-known story how COs got their families and congregations, their acquaintances, and other organizations, like the American Friends Service Committee, to send books. That's how Mill Point ended up with such a fine library.

May 16, 1951 (Wednesday)

> One of the tasks which confronts me in prison is the Christian discipline of my life. . . . Many men serving prison sentences in righteous causes use the time to emerge as greater defenders of the right. I must do the same.

May 19, 1951 (Saturday)

One inmate who has already become a strong friend and will in the future become still closer is Art Dossie, formerly from Birmingham, Ala. But now from Washington D.C. Art is a graduate of Howard University, with an engineering degree. He is serving a 3yr. sentence.

I liked Art Dossie so much. He was a kind, scholarly man. He was sent to Mill Point during the later part of the Red Scare because he wouldn't give congressional investigators the names of people the government suspected of being Communists. He would rather go to prison than betray people with whom he had served on committees around Washington, D.C. On principle, he did not cooperate with the innuendo-filled, anti-Communist waves of alarm during that era. Not all of us in prison were there for violating someone's rights. Some of us were there for refusing to do so.

As I settled into my sentence, I used my journal and letters to close confidants to share some of my deepest notions of what I believed and of what I saw as my life's purpose. I look back at these musings of an idealistic young man—inexperienced in most ways and mercifully unaware of the trials that life would hold—with patience and affection. At the beginning, I worked out my thinking about the goals and machinations of military systems that set people against each other.

June 5, 1951 (Tuesday)

Joe Stalin is merely a reflection of ourselves. The same is true of Hitler! A nation like a man reaps what it sows. . . . A civilization that adopts war, hatred, violence, immorality, fear . . . reaps violence hatred, etc. Rome, Greece, Genghis Khan, Napoleon, Czarist Russia, Hitler, British Empire, Europe, Spain, Mussolini, Japan. Soviet Russia? U.S.? So it means that our America continuing to use the above methods is inevitably headed toward its own downfall.

I articulated what would become a central tenet of my opposition to oppression.

July 11, 51 (Wednesday)

The adherent of nonviolence does not say anything about not getting injured or hurt, he merely sticks to the desire not to inflict injury on others.

And in a letter to Carol, I not only bragged about my baseball triumphs, I also envisioned (and described for the first time) the nonviolent revolution I saw coming in America, led by Black people, who I likened to the "untouchables" of India. It was a vision that had been forming in my mind of how this country could be transformed, in order to live up to its original ideals.

July 16, 1951

Dear Carol,

I just received your letter so I decided to answer immediately. Again, it was very good to hear from you, or need I tell you this? Today was a pretty good day. Two of the garage men were sent on tasks outside the camp. . . . So, I kept busy under trucks most of the time. This doesn't imply that I can fix a truck only that some bolt was loose that any moron like myself could tighten.

Yesterday we played the toughest ball team we've had in so far. An all-Negro team from Denmar, they were supposed to beat us. In fact, most of the inmates were betting that the outside team would win. . . . But . . . in the last inning . . . not bragging, but it was one of the best games I've ever pitched, and the tying run plus the winning run were made by the pitcher. We wanted to win chiefly because so many wanted us to lose.

Another reason for writing you so soon is to gain your opinion about a couple of matters which have been quite a bit on my mind. You know of Gandhi's nonviolence, his efforts in South Africa and India. You may also know of the nonviolence used by CORE in race relations in the US. Such a method of social action stresses: God at the very core of life; love for all men, most of all the opponents; truth, in plan and action; refusing to be a part of evil social patterns; redeeming the opponents rather than condemning them. . . .

> Well, the big question which has been constantly turning in my mind is: why can't a mass nonviolent revolution be staged throughout the South where the segregation pattern is much like the "untouchables" of India? Such a movement would have to start with one person who has the Christian vision to make such a revolution a reality in his own life. It could begin as a project of self-improvement, getting rid of hatred for the dominant group, getting rid of self-impurities. At the same time, co-operative economics could be introduced to encourage both poor whites and poor Negroes to break economic chains which bind them. Then, finally after much negotiation and talk failed to move those who could remove segregation then, staging a mass breaking of segregation laws and immediately packing the jails with both groups who want to live in harmony with each other. . . . Are there any reasons why we should not have such a revolution in our country for such purposes? Let me have your ideas, Carol.

In 1948, President Truman had issued executive orders desegregating the United States military and the federal workforce. But upon my arrival at Mill Point in 1951, the inmate population was still segregated. The COs and I decided that something ought to be done. We started by talking to the administration and asking for a meeting of inmates on the matter. They agreed to it. The parole officer of the place and one of the lieutenants of the guards met with those of us who were interested.

We realized we could use the one blessing of segregation under this system: Negro inmates had the "A dorm" all to ourselves. There were only about forty of us, and we lived at one end of it, with the other end completely empty. Each of us had our own double bunk. We had lots of air. The white dorms—B and C—were jam-packed, housing more than a hundred people each. So some white guys besides the COs came to this meeting in the administration building to say that they wanted to move into the Negro dorm. They said, "I am willing to move up there—let's integrate that way."

That meeting caused outrage among the white Southern moonshiners. They were especially angry at the four white conscientious objectors and the three or four other white men who said they would move to the A dorm to live with us, and they accused all the conscientious objectors, including me, of being troublemakers.

My friendships with white people from before prison also upset some of the prison administration. My friend Bob Farkas—one of my circle of college friends that included my roommate Jim Cox—visited me at Mill Point a few times, along with other friends from Baldwin-Wallace, church youth groups, and home. It always caused some turmoil.

August 25, 1951 (Saturday)

Well, Lawson, old boy, if certain officers were peeved with you before for having visitors of a much lighter complexion, today they're really burning. First Harper and Marynell, now Farkas. Jim couldn't come down, so Bob drove the 400 miles himself, a long trip, and another strong sign of our friendship. He leaves for the army this Tuesday, thus further splitting up the circle. Frankly, I hope his heart keeps him out. I'm never fighting for any country. Bob is too fine a lad to waste his energy and talent in the army. But like millions of men throughout our world, a government's call is stronger than personal religion's ties. That doesn't affect our deep friendship.

The Sunday after our Tuesday meeting with the administration, a rumor was circulating that a bunch of the hillbillies were out to get me. They said I was stirring up trouble on this "integration business." And they were focused on the other "conscies," calling all of us unpatriotic. After lunch that Sunday, a vicious fight broke out down in the white dorms. And some guys unmercifully beat up a fellow. A couple of us ran down and tried to break it up, but the lines were drawn, and the hate toward us was unbendable. The slightest trigger could result in even worse violence.

Later that Sunday afternoon, I went over to the garage where I worked, to get some records I needed. The garage was set apart from the dorms and the main part of the camp. Soon after I arrived, I heard a great trampling of feet. It was a group of Negro guys, including Art Dossie, charging over there, yelling for me. I stepped outside, and they said that some of the hillbillies were on their way to get me, and they urged me to close the garage up and come on back where they could keep an eye on me.

That evening after supper, I went to the lieutenant, the chief man on duty that day, and told him he needed to keep his eyes open, because there could be some real trouble. I told him about the moonshiners' drinking and the threats they were making. I told him Negro fellows were arming themselves in response. He laughed it off.

> **August 26, 1951 (Sunday—written on Wednesday, August 29th, 1951)**
>
> After another visit from Mom, Daisy, Paul, Christie, Berlya. . . . In the afternoon, against a weak Marlington team, I smashed a homer the 1st time up, then the next time switched to left-handed and drove another homer far into right center field. But the afternoon and evening events quickly clouded the day. . . .
>
> About 6 PM, the five COs got together for our study period. At 8 we broke up for count, at which time Dossie warned me first that at least 3 men came from "B" to tell him of definite plans to get me. I was, therefore, to stay undercover. . . .

After eight o'clock that night, three of the white conscientious objectors who were in the other two dorms, B and C, were pounced on and thrown out of the dorms by a group of the whites. All of the guards came out and put the white COs in the infirmary for the night, and then kept watch. Early the next morning, they came and got me and put me in the infirmary, too. That afternoon, we were all driven from Mill Point to a federal prison two hundred miles away in Ashland, Kentucky. They told us it was for our own safety because some of these whites were stirred up. But on our arrival at Ashland, the word was that *we* had been the "troublemakers, trying to ruin the prison."

Five of us had been transferred to Ashland. I was the only Black man. Ashland was much more of a prison than Mill Point. It had some dorms, but also maximum- and minimum-security cell houses.

On the second or third day at Ashland, the assistant warden called all five of us in together. Instead of talking quietly, he sat behind his desk and screeched at us about how he'd heard we were troublemakers from Mill Point. He wanted us to know that he ran Ashland and that they had a "hole" to take care of smart guys. He said, "I am the boss. I run this place. If you've got any problems, you come to me. If you don't come to me, you'll find yourself in the hole." Then he called us in separately, one by one, and gave us the same routine.

Apparently, he had gotten a report on me from Mill Point, because when I met with him, he said, "I know you're the ringleader." Then he assigned me to a maximum-security cell house where the robbers and murderers and professional criminals were held—the people who were considered dangerous.

In orientation, I learned that this prison had a sizable library and educational department, with daily classes in the evenings where people learned to read and write, and there was an inmate newspaper, too. When I told the vice warden that that's where I should be because I almost had a degree from college and I was a Methodist minister with my own congregation, he hit the ceiling. He said it couldn't be done, there was no opening. But within days, I was assigned to the library.

Ashland's library was larger than the one at Mill Point, as large as many branch libraries in the country. It had a fine collection of books, especially in the fields of religion, psychology, and the social sciences. Because the COs were all now separated into different cellblocks, we wouldn't be able to convene in the Ashland library for our daily meetings. The only times we all saw one another were when we would sit together at movies and during church services. Gone was the kind of uninterrupted time together that we had in the library at Mill Point, when we would talk regularly about what was happening in the world and share our ideas about how to address the dilemmas of the day.

The increased isolation at Ashland led to a lot of time for introspection. I wrestled in my journal with some issues of politics, religion, and sexuality that were shaking my spiritual core.

September 3, 1951 (Labor Day)

We drop the bomb on Japan, and for this we ought to be repentant. For my part in that massacre I pray God will forgive me and that the people of Japan will not hold it against me. But now, we mean to use the bomb again, only a bomb 250 times more terrible.

Once again our feelings are against Russian Communists with little or no affinal feelings for the persons involved. We are preparing for atomic warfare, but regardless of the potency of these weapons for victory, what about the people? Are we again utterly relegating persons to the level of buildings? Are we again completely ignoring people as our brethren with essentially similar drives, and desires? Are we again temporarily invalidating Divine Right to "life, liberty, and the pursuit of happiness" for every man? Atomic bombing necessitates just that.

September 9, 1951 (Sunday)

The greatest struggle of my life is still raging. My opponent for some reason is unremitting; he offers me no quarter . . . won't let me rest—day or night. He doesn't lose patience with me, nor show His anger, and yet He's made it plain to me, that the chase will last for many days. He's asking me to surrender all—no feeble proclamation to serve, no firm resolves—no part way religious living—but an unconditional . . . surrender of life, voice, hands, feet, brain, possessions, energy everything. . . . If I try to escape into the land of imagination, like a panther charge He attacks more vigorously. . . .

Such a life means immeasurable hardship . . . insurmountable tasks, heartache, days, weeks, years of tears; the giving up of success, home, family, career. . . . Such a life demands the denial of self, the acceptance of God.

I'm afraid God, Jesus and Gandhi were different from me. I can't surrender like that. I'm afraid to suffer, to carry the wear and tear of heartache, to face beatings, jail, and final death. Can't I just be a comfortable minister, acclaimed as a social prophet, supporter of many good causes? I'm weak God, afraid, unwilling to trust that much—it's too hard for me—won't you let me go—find someone else—I can't—I can't God—you don't want me—I'll fail Thee at every turn—I'm afraid of such a life. It means giving up too much—friends will scoff and scorn—people will call me fanatic, fool, mad—They'll say it's . . . aggressive ego—martyr complex.

My internal wrestling was punctuated during the next week with a return to grace and gratitude, and then some more reckoning with myself and God's will.

September 11, 1951 (Tuesday)

Thoughts drift back in a sweet spirit of memory, days, at home, in school, and church and traveling. I need to be quite thankful that my life was nurtured in such a rich background. Rich, not financially even though this has never been a worry. But rich spiritually, morally, rich in growth experiences, and friendships, and exposure to the Christian vision of life, and opportunities to witness for Christ. I'm here in prison, not because of a drought behind me, but because God provided the courage and spirit which make me willing to endure death for His Kingdom. Of course, too often, I've failed to be thankful in terms of real living. The number of years that God has hounded me, I want to be further along the path of Christian discipline. Many mistakes and failures on my part have hindered His Will in my life.

Superficial pretensions often covered my real life. My desire to be a lady-killer; to appear well-off; to be a popular leader; to be surrounded by friends; to dominate a local situation; to be brilliant; to be the athletic star; to be "successful" in every area possible. Such a personal veneer, unfortunately, has been an effective blockade against God completely sweeping thru me. Fortunately, God, knowing the real person, refused to give up and so the last 6 years have been a personal chase with the Eternal, Never-tiring Hound of Heaven. God continues to stand at the door and knock. I haven't surrendered my all yet, but just as sure as the sun rises and sets, so the day is inevitable when God knocks away the last bit of veneer to possess me entirely. I look forward to that day with joyful anticipation.

September 14, 1951 (Friday)

At the core of most religions is the thought of self-giving for others, self-sacrifice for others, redeeming others through love. When two members of Gandhi's Ashram committed an evil act, Gandhi fasted for 3 days, not to intimidate them, but rather to intercede to God for them. For the two, this Gandhian act was an act of love, and they immediately repented in tears and asked for forgiveness. Such intercession is central to the life of Jesus. Jesus understood the necessity of intercession. For him, no other method was available. So he gave his life as an act of intercession. To show men that they could return to God's ways; to reveal love as the "Spirit of God."

The process of intercession is hard to understand and explain; yet, it works. The reason: God.

I was about to turn twenty-three, and my sexual self was still emerging. Being in prison and so removed from the outside world during that time was a particular challenge. And being a member of the clergy set me apart from most of the men around me there. I was trying to deal with all of this at once, and my earnestness in that pursuit came through in my journal.

September 17, 1951 (Monday)

One of my deepest concerns right now is sex. Naturally, when men are locked up away from feminine company, the topic of unique interest is women. This in itself is understandable, as long as the conversations don't distort inter-sex relations. Most men in prison consider sexual intercourse of prime importance outside of money. For one to insist that sexual intercourse ought to remain within marriage is unheard of. The average inmate does consider sexual intercourse as the "natural" thing with women. This usually means with as many different women as possible. Thus, in prison, masturbation takes the place. No one considers masturbation out of place or wrong, just as sexual intercourse with as many women as possible is perfectly natural.

Now I arrive from an entirely different atmosphere. My family is poor, but religious, and we therefore refuse to hold money and sex as Babylonian idols. I've, therefore, been taught that the social and psychological disadvantages of sexual intercourse outside marriage could ruin future happiness. So, even though, sexual intercourse has been possible, I've never yielded because of a personal belief that intercourse ought to remain as a part of marriage.

But most fellows in adolescence masturbate. I've been no exception, and masturbation has been and is still a major problem. It is not a steady habit, but off and on. I think it's wrong. Wrong because I feel it's an unnatural process (and I don't think sexual promiscuity is the natural). Wrong because, it wastes energy which is actually a creative potential. Wrong because during the process, God is forgotten. Wrong, because it's a practice I can't do with God's sanction. Wrong because it disorganizes the mind and continues the frustration. Wrong because of the evil thoughts about other persons. In jail the practice is easier because of the social atmosphere. And yet the atmosphere also produces, in me, a greater reaction against it. So, here, we make or break the habit. Well many persons will say you are only going thru a natural stage, I insist it's an unnecessary stage and must therefore go from my life. And with God's help all habits which often separate us will end.

September 20, 1951 (Thursday)

Birthday proclamation

Whereas: September 22, 1951 is the 23rd birthday of James M. Lawson, Jr;

Whereas: past birthdays have been observed as special days of Christian dedication;

Whereas: the goals of self-denial and Christian discipline are still to be acquired in Lawson's life;

Whereas: fasting helps one to keep in mind spiritual purposes and goals;

Whereas: fasting can be a self-giving process;

Whereas: Lawson desires and needs this kind of spiritual discipline,

Be it therefore resolved that:

On Friday, September 21, 1951, said James M Lawson will recognize said birthday with 34 hours of fasting to be ended Sat. morning, Spt. 22th. The fast is primarily for self-purification and dedication. But this day of prayer will also greatly consider the suffering and toil of millions of others in our world and endeavor to become more compassionately aware of human kinship. And finally James M Lawson, Jr. takes upon himself the terrible sins committed today and carries them to God as His Agent of reconciliation. Among these are: (1) Fear, hatred, suspicion of the cold war; (2) Korean War, the forces as persons on both sides; (3) the starving, pestilent-ridden of China, India, Africa; (4) Ruth Reynolds and Puerto Rican independence; (5) racial prejudice thru out the world; (6) people under physical and spiritual tyranny!

This proclamation is issued with the loving guidance of God and fulfilled by His Love and Grace in me! That His Kingdom May Yet Reign!

James M. Lawson, Jr.

The earnestness of that journal entry makes me laugh. It was a youthful tactic I devised to reaffirm my devotion to the lifelong, imperfect quest of following Jesus's example.

September 21, 1951 (Friday)

Someone has said that Francis of Assisi came closest to wholly imitating the life of Jesus on earth. A comfortable Italian lad with a naturally sensitive spirit rejected the revelries of youth, the glory of war, the right to property, to live a life of absolute love for all men, especially the "unfortunate" of the world. Here was no apologist for love, but one who recognized a divine affiliation with all living things especially those who had to suffer.

Today the world is clasped in the stringent arms of suffering. There are people who face daily the apparent utter futility of life; Korean orphans, starving Chinese, pestilent ridden Indians, persecuted South Africans, segregated Americans, wounded soldiers, enslaved Russians, disinherited Europeans, diseased lepers; men and women of all climates, every nationality, of all religious faiths, all breeds, various shades of color; but who with one accord belong to the Human Race and are ordained by God as his children. But few recognize this relationship, and fewer, yet, share this relationship. In this day of fasting, I want to become poignantly conscious of these my brethren, near and far. I want God to breathe through me, His compassionate care for them, until their suffering is, my suffering; their enslavement my enslavement; their pain, my pain; their joy, my joy.

. . . Our world has gone mad with the intense battle between "Russian communism," and American capitalism, for these are essentially the opponents. And circling all combatants, whether physical or mental, is a dark tremendous psychological cloud of fear, hatred and suspicion. Consequently, each move is directed very largely by this cloud. The foes fear each other. . . . Each gov't intensely hates the other and this hatred is rapidly passing on to the people. Each move by one is met suspiciously by the other. Internal affairs soon subordinate themselves to the psychological aspects of "cold war." . . . Liberties are by-passed; a few men are granted amazing powers over all; all good causes revert to the motive of stopping the enemy. Economies are disrupted; welfare and service programs are pigeon-holed; military authorities dictate foreign policy and domestic activities. And the cloud increases.

. . . For many persons, the present encounter is fate or destiny, beyond their influence or control but in reality the one right chance to avert such adversity rests on individuals who reject the motives, attitudes, and actions of the "cold war" and instead adopt the spirit of reconciliation; burst the cloud with the power of love, courage and trust, withdraw from supporting the struggle of doom.

Fasting, for me, reemphasizes my role as an "instrument of peace." During this day, I again bring to bear the spiritual forces of God in combat with the evils of the "cold war." Only His Spirit in men can save our generation.

Dispel the cloud of hatred, O Lord. Draw men unto Thyself and call us to be representatives of your Reconciliation.

The Korean War started as a struggle of liberation, police action to liberate the South Koreans, from their brethren the North Koreans. I'm not certain that the present condition is an improvement over the results of non-intervention from the U.S. The War of Liberation has failed. For who or what has been liberated; the thousand in their graves?

We certainly didn't liberate the Koreans from communism, for now the soil is enriched for a bumper crop of communists. We didn't liberate them from starvation, economic bankruptcy! We didn't liberate them from lack of clothing, or homes. Where or what are the fruits of this liberation?

One of the most valuable things I learned throughout my time in prison was that people who were called bad people were just people, human like myself, men like me. I could not look down on them, because we were all equal. These guys in this close-custody cell house were in there for murder, manslaughter, mugging. But I came to trust completely a fellow who at that time was probably forty years of age, hard-nosed, respected throughout the prison as being a real tough, a genuine crook, a criminal. His name was Liberty, and he was a mugger from Washington, D.C. He was hard as nails. We had a number of real talks. Liberty was a Black man, and he insisted that his vocation was as honorable as mine. He told me of his persistent effort to find work when he was much younger, and how he had never been able to find any job that paid enough to enable him to live halfway decently. He told me he became a mugger because crime was the only business where he could get enough to support himself and his family.

To the outside world, Liberty was just another criminal who needed to be locked up. To me, he was perhaps my greatest teacher in prison. I saw a strong moral thread in Liberty that I didn't always see in people considered more virtuous in our society. I believe our society had failed him and then, in turn, saw him as the failure. And in the middle of that predicament, the incongruity of his name was not lost on me. I felt lucky to have met Liberty and gotten to know him as a friend. I think the fact that I was a minister helped him open up to me in a way he might not have done with many others. I was able to listen to him with compassion and that seemed to affirm his value to himself even as it strengthened our bond. We each widened our views of the world through our friendship.

I found a number of friends like Liberty in prison, a number of men who I knew full well were real men. I found them genuinely human, with the same fears, and doubts, and problems that we all have. I heard about the circumstances under which many of them grew up and lived as adults, being born into poverty and living in poverty. And I was sure that anyone born or living under the same circumstances would become the same. If I ever had prejudices up to that time that a person should be counted down and out, prison eliminated such feelings in me. Since that time, I have absolutely refused to count out people and say that they're too corrupt or that the way they are is the way they were born to be.

If I had blinded myself to the goodness in us all, or didn't believe in everyone's capacity for transformation, I probably should have found a different line of work. Yet I only had to look at more of my own journal entries from 1951 to confirm this faith, as the solitude of prison was bringing on a storm of change within me.

October 8, 1951 (Monday)

It is rather unfortunate for me that ever since I've been in jail, certain men have felt it their obligation to become my protectors. In Cleveland, in Mill Point and now at Ashland. These men are well-meaning in that they respect me for my views and feel as though I ought not to be in prison. And yet, they also disarm me. For at an instance of violence against myself, I'll first have to persuade them not to fight. What I really must do is to rise to every opportunity to help them to see the rightness of nonviolence. It is very interesting to note that Buddha was an adherent of nonviolence. He said to treat conquerors as sick children. Overcome their conquest with kindliness. Muhammed was also originally a proponent of nonviolent love. But like the later followers of Christianity, Muhammed later took to the sword because he felt that love would never win people to his religion.

October 9, 1951 (Tuesday)

There is a spirit I feel deep within which would possess me wholly. A spirit which constantly chides me for every mistake and would now purify me to perfection. Its goal for me is goodness. Its method, unreserved love for men. I would pray for those who hate me, and do good to those who do evil. Against tasks impossible, all things become possible. Amid hanging clouds, this spirit is my one guide. I know that this is God.

October 10, 1951 (Wednesday)

I am only 23. In 23 years, few men have surrendered themselves wholly to God. Such a divine process is long and hard. The men must re-learn stimuli and responses. Worldly desires must be flushed from the system. Youthful self-confidence must evolve to God-confidence. Early habits must yield to Christian disciplines. I began hard in 1945 to so surrender. Since that time I've caught a clear vision of this God-intoxicated life and I desire it more. But the way is narrow, and I must be patient. Trusting in God's power to ultimately live in me completely. This patient faith must not become an appeasement for or of sin. Nor can my conscience now rest. But rather I need to be ever conscious of my responsibility.

I fail Thee often, Lord. But have patience with me. Especially must Thou be merciful unto me. Cleanse me of all selfish desires. Remold my life by the power of your spirit within me.

I felt that some of my fellow inmates had ambivalence toward me. On the one hand, there was respect. Some of them believed religion was unconcerned about their lives. But many of them seemed to sense that mine was not a sham religion, and that I was genuine. Some of the guys brought their problems to me, and trusted me with their confidences all the time. And a few men asked for my help in navigating prison operations or their families' concerns. I counseled some of my fellow inmates on how to talk to or write letters to family members about what they were experiencing in prison. And I sometimes helped men figure out how to approach administrators about their needs.

But there was also a good, humorous picking at me. Liberty and some of the former military guys teased me all the time. They could not believe I was there, when I didn't have to be. We also had long and serious conversations about why I chose to go to prison. Some still could not understand me. That distance between us carried into the things I tried to steer away from during discussions with my fellow inmates.

November 1, 1951 (Thursday)

Last evening we finally reached the subject of sex and my opinions towards sex. Up to this time I've tried to avoid the subject (perhaps cowardice) because I realized how far apart we would be on the subject. They asked about whether I've had sexual intercourse. Unlike at Mill Point, I replied that the subject was very personal, but that my religious beliefs certainly didn't permit sexual intercourse. Then the usual emotions arose. "Well, if God didn't want you to 'love,' why did He make men." "What's any better than making love?" "If God made anything better, He didn't show it to men." I think the subject was constructive in that these fellows became exposed to another concept. I don't want to sound pious, but I think the discussion went far better than at Mill Point.

We then strayed to "dope," for several of the inmates used dope, morphine, heroin, cocaine! An educational process for me.

At Ashland, I had my first encounter with men propositioning me for sex. It was the one period in prison where I was of a fearful mind. I had not knowingly encountered people with differing sexual orientations, and the way some of the men approached me made me feel physically threatened and unsure about how to handle myself. At that time in our society, only sex between a man and a woman was considered normal. Being of that era, I had some incorrect social conditioning myself, which, I see now, amplified my fears. My journal reveals that limited view—in my attitude, and in my use of language that I later learned was harmful and stopped using.

November 2, 1951 (Friday)

Well, I invited an inmate to join me after 11:30 for a talk until he gets tired. Perhaps I should say that he invited himself. . . . I hope that he doesn't expect any alleviations of frustrations. Perhaps I ought to plan what we'll do and discuss. Perhaps I could use the time to counsel the man. In any case, no misunderstandings must arise from the visit. I am again treading on dangerous ground. I don't want to create the wrong impressions. I do want to help when I can in a way which will advance true values.

November 3, 1951 (Saturday)

The chap last night didn't wish to stop. He wanted me to "relieve him of his sexual charge." In other words, carry on a homosexual affair. Puts one in a hard spot. He's in a bad way for his asking turned to pleading.

He said that no one need know except he and I. That up to the time of my arrival he was okay. But now he has a hard time. We talked about an hour. He trying to convince me and I trying to really help him. When I turned to God as his real help he decided to leave. . . .

Such an experience is personally revolting to me. It's a sad state of affairs when the only response I gather is one of homosexual interest. I will not allow this to happen again.

My Christian upbringing had never specifically taught me to have such a strong reaction to sexual orientation that was different from mine. In fact, the Bible never condemns the fluidity of sexuality, as some have tried to claim. But the misguided culture of the time had infected me. Later, I grew to understand that what I had absorbed was hurtful and hypocritical. Fear had directed my reactions. I *was* afraid. Some of the men began to say that if I did not select a partner among them, I would be gang-raped. That conversation went on almost daily, out in the yard and elsewhere. That talk had been building up for almost two months. I wasn't sure what to do or what to say. At first, I mostly tried to avoid or ignore the situation and the talk and the men who were taunting me. Then, as it became more constant, I didn't think I could tell anyone what was happening, because I believed that exposing the people harassing me would only make the threats worse. Even I knew that a tattletale would not fare well in prison. But I wasn't faring well when I felt there was nowhere to turn, either.

November 9, 1951 (Friday)

> What a day! A day accentuated by another proposition to be a partner in another love affair. The third such proposition. This time the approach was different and hardly to be ignored. . . . The notion is that I am a "girl" and that some inmates are having me. But that I'm a dignified whore and not a common whore. Only certain men are allowed. (Who these men are, remained a mystery.) The fact is that I'm effeminate, I look like a "woman." I have certain mannerisms which are effeminate. I don't fight or curse which, of course, means that I'm a clean "girl." I've got good hair and very smooth skin. Since I've been here, two men have come in my room with intent to "make love."
>
> According to the 3rd propositioner, on two other occasions persons wanted to enter my room with razor blades or blankets and force me to submit. The only way to take the pressure off me is for the propositioner to assume the weight and I to become his "girl." Then he would call the other men off, and do any little tasks which I need. This is the only solution for the propositioner. My athletic characteristics have little to do with it. "You could be forced into the affair. If you were in a penitentiary with hardened criminals, and didn't give in, you'd be dead long ago." The propositioner then went on to state that he had no intent to force me unless I wanted to. Then he would not be in my room after hours unless I wanted him in my room. . . . He goes for me. Maybe I don't go for him. In any case, I might as well face the reality that inmates think of me as a prison girl.
>
> The men in the institution want to know the score with me. When do I give out. I was greatly troubled over what I could do, (1) to stop the idea that I was a girl; (2) to prevent any attack on myself.

This was the first time in my life I felt so physically and emotionally scared. I had no idea what any of the things that they threatened to do to me would feel like. I didn't want to know. The fear began to consume me day and night.

Eventually, these men told me that my cell was accessible. They could get into it. And one night, I thought it was going to happen. I was even ready to fight physically against any of them who broke into my cell. I walked around the cell, picking up the steel chair, seeing whether I could swing it and use it as a weapon. I was afraid and didn't sleep—being awake felt safer.

November 10, 1951 (Saturday)

Most of last night was spent wide awake. I opened the window and sat for I don't know how long. I put my head against the back wall and sat on the bed. I laid there with my eyes partly closed, but alert to the slightest noise in the cell block. Needless to say I feared going to sleep. No peace or cessation of fear came. It wasn't until the moon had gone down that I finally crawled into bed. I didn't hear the morning whistles. I woke up feeling as though I had a hangover.

The issue has to be faced. I must find a course of action then follow through.

I felt fear outside the cell too, in the yard, where the harassment and intimidation were most intense. Then, without bidding during this time of almost constant tumult and menace, I had another one of my numinous experiences.

On one of the nights when I felt scared to go to sleep, I was walking the floor with my shoes, socks, pants, and shirt on. I kept picking the chair up and putting it down—for exercise and to practice fighting off any harm. I heard a voice saying steadily, "Jim, Jim, what are you doing? So afraid? You did not come here because you wanted to come. You are in prison because I sent you there. So why are you fearful?" I walked the cell, hearing this voice, and finally I knelt down to pray by the window. Suddenly, I felt every vestige of my fear disappear. It was as though the panic and alarm just flowed out of my body, down through my feet and was gone. I became totally unafraid. I felt the Lord vanish the fright's energy out of my system, never to return. I became poised, calm, and at ease. A few days later, the harassment stopped. Never again did I worry about being attacked in my cell.

I am fairly sure that Liberty took on the role of my protector in our cellblock—although I never tried to get his help. I sensed it right around the time I had heard that voice telling me "You have no business being fearful." Liberty and I never discussed the threats I had gotten directly, but I'm sure he knew about them. And I believe that because of our respect for each other and our friendship, he stepped in and stood up to the men threatening to assault me. Liberty taught me a lot about the innate worth in all human beings. I would sometimes return to the lessons of our friendship, especially as my life became more and more centered on advocating for recognition of everyone's shared humanity and respect for basic human rights.

November 16, 1951 (Friday)

I know now, more than ever before, I think God intends to use me in some special task. I know now that God bombards my heart and soul so persistently because He sees me as a potential God-force in a decadent world. This is not egotism, for I also know that it will be God not Jim Lawson. . . . I also know that all my life, I'll make human errors but that God will truly make His way known through me.

I think the special task is a visitation of God in the United States as the answer to the plight of the Negro and poor whites and also as a hope for the industrial and scientific tangle. God's calling me to move among the poor with His Light of Peace and good-will. It will be a religious revival.

I do not yet know whether the task goes to the South or to some slum area. Both are ripe unto harvest. I have a hunch, however, that it's the South for here the lines are more clearly drawn and the issues and sides more solidified. In the South, God would try to bring love and good-will as motivations and means to break segregation in the socio-economic chains on Negroes and whites. Such effort has never been made. God now wants me to surrender so that He can make the effort.

A vision for my future was emerging. The purpose and direction of my work was on my mind—and so were my personal needs and wants.

November 23, 1951 (Friday)

One of my deepest fears is that despite God's constant hounding of my soul for complete surrender, I'll refuse to surrender and then become a middle class, "successful" preacher rather than a lower class mystic failure. The failure is what I want. The success is the easier and more conducive to American society.

So often, young men set out with the "fire of the Spirit" burning high within. Nothing seems to quench the flame. Then as age creeps in, the "fire" begins to dim. And smoke becomes more apparent than flame. This is the pitfall for so many young men. We desire to settle down with families, achieve social and economic security and experience a comfortable Parish. The demand for social conformity pours water on the "fire" for Christian perfection.

I feel these forces also in me. God knows that I don't want to yield to this spirit. I want rather to grow more radical for Christ as the years pass by. A true disciple bucks conformity more as conformity pressures increase.

O Lord, root out all desire for comfortableness. Rather instill within me a driving fire of Christian adventure and daring. In this way lies life-eternal and victory over the grave.

Some of my fellow Black inmates were thinking and talking about dealing with the segregated world we knew awaited us on release from prison. And like Black people everywhere, we agreed on the need for change, although we didn't always agree on the leaders or the tactics.

December 12, 1951 (Wednesday)

I'm convinced that O'Neil really believes in a Machiavellian approach to race relations, any means to achieve the end of "1st class citizenship." He suggests a small army of Negro men to change things. . . . With him this is serious business. So now, we have two, Dossie and O'Neil, who feel very strongly that violence is necessary to make the dominant group yield privileges to the Negro. I hope that this remains in the talking stage. But for all I know, some group may be planning a violent effort. . . . As the hate for the whites increases, the possibility of violence being used increases. Once violence is used in any area, the situation will call for martial law, for the violence will be like a chain in which acts of violence by one side or the other will continue.

Real hope is to tackle the conscience of decent people in the North and South. If the goodness that is in most persons can't be tapped and used in the racial question, then no amount of violence will succeed. I can't help O'Neil or Dossie to see this, for they simply believe that violence hasn't been used for the right cause. And yet, the fact remains that I've got to gain not only their support but the loyalty and love of Negroes all over the United States. And not only Negroes, but others as well. If God be willing, then He'll use me for just such a mission. Or perhaps I should say, if I be willing—God will use me.

Spending Christmas apart from my family for the first time was hard. I wasn't sure how many Christmases would pass before I could be with them again.

December 25, 1951 (Tuesday—Christmas Day)

What can I say to describe this experience of Christmas? It has been like none I've ever experienced. For the 1st time I've been away from home, away from immediate family. And in this awayness comes a greater near-ness to the real essence of Christmas. Perhaps in such social isolation the sensitive soul can gain far more than any loss. At least, that's my feeling now.

December 27, 1951 (Thursday)

Today I gave a pint of blood to the Red Cross. Much of the blood now used will be used in Korea for saving American men, then sending them back to the front. I wish this were not true! I wish that after being saved, they would return to the U.S. to fight no more. The rest of the blood will go for other emergencies and possibly to a North Korean fighter. I would hope that my blood could be used for the latter. However, I gave the blood in the spirit of good-will, hoping that whoever gets this blood may somehow feel obliged to save others, not destroy. It is becoming increasingly obvious to me that my country, the United States of America, is the real threat to world peace.

I say this with deep sadness, for the U.S. is still my country and still offers the greatest opportunities to all men.

Throughout my first year in prison, I had some hopes for parole. The Methodist Church kept trying. They said they would take full responsibility for me if I was released. Other clergy members and friends tried to write letters and circulate petitions. It was all to no avail. Repeatedly, I was reminded that the federal government was using me as a cautionary tale for anyone coming after me, to illustrate what happens if you don't cooperate with the Selective Service.

At the start of 1952 they told us that paroles were not being granted. So I decided not to bother applying anymore. But my lawyers kept pushing, along with the church people who had supported me all my life. I was fairly well surprised when I was called into the prison office in early spring and told I was being placed on the parole list. And a few weeks later, to my further amazement, I was released from prison on probation to the Methodist Church and the Board of Missions. My church had promised the parole board that I would be sent out of the country on a mission as soon as I graduated from college. Those were the same conditions the Methodist Board of Missions had offered to the federal judge and federal prosecutor at my trial in Cleveland the year before. The court had rejected the offer then. To my great delight, this time the federal government accepted the terms, and I got out of prison after thirteen months in custody, in May 1952. I wrote Carol one more letter from prison to tell her the good news.

May 11, 1952

Dear Carol,

Don't be at all surprised if I should sudden-like pop in on you sometime this week. I was granted parole on Tues. May 6th, and will probably be released on May 13th. We are only waiting on the release papers from Washington.

I told her my plans to spend the summer in Hartford, Connecticut, for training to be an international missionary. I said I would go back to Baldwin-Wallace in the autumn to finish my degree. And at the start of the year, I would "sail for India where I plan to remain for around 5 years. In the process I hope to teach and direct athletics, but also become acquainted with Eastern philosophy, Gandhi, Africa, and other opinions toward the Western world." I ended the letter saying:

> If and when I arrive "outside" I'll drop a note or call you. . . . Hoping to see you soon.
>
> Jim

Writing letters back and forth with Carol helped me through my time in prison. She was a good friend. Unfortunately, our lives never brought us together into any other kind of relationship after that. But I have always been grateful for our friendship.

When I was released, a federal parole officer in Cleveland had to make sure I followed my prescribed plan of going back to Baldwin-Wallace and finishing my degree and then leaving for India. Even though I still wanted to go to Africa, the Methodist Board of Missions had told me before I left Ashland that the next available spot was with a group they were sending to India in 1953. It sounded like a great opportunity, and I found a good work situation because I had a friend in Nagpur, India, who knew of a school there that needed a physical education teacher and coach. Soon, the principal of the Hislop school wrote and invited me, and I accepted. My years of athletic play and training were paying off.

First, I had to spend that one more quarter at Baldwin-Wallace. When I had left for prison in April 1951, some of the faculty had urged the president to grant me my degree without having to complete another term since I was weeks away from the end of my last quarter, and was in good standing with the school. But my enemies on campus disagreed, including the chair of the religion department, Dr. Knautz, who had spoken to me so harshly in his office during my freshman year, telling me to stop befriending or dating white girls on campus and "talking like a radical, extremist, misbehaving militant."

After life in prison, it was jarring to be back on campus. Not only had I gained a clearer sense of my purpose on earth but I had forged a deeper commitment to fulfilling it. Also, my view of other people had transformed. I no longer believed, even secretly, that anyone was unworthy of the same love and respect as anyone else. I had known before prison that love and equality were foundational values that my religion taught, and my country espoused. But it wasn't until after my time in prison that I truly believed in the deepest parts of my heart that all humans were created equal and endowed with inalienable rights, and that loving my neighbor was the way to live.

Prison was supposed to chasten me. It was supposed to scare me into compliance with an unjust system. Happily, the effect was almost wholly the opposite. I found a fearlessness that would endure. And I saw and felt the urgency of resistance to injustice even more strongly than I had when I did what got me in there—refusing to participate in the Selective Service.

SIX

Soul Force

Nagpur, India, 1953–1956. VANDERBILT LIBRARY

John

I was only five months free from a prison term for refusing to participate in the Selective Service process when my little brother John was being sent into the fray. We had all gathered for Thanksgiving in 1952, back home at 33 Groose Avenue. That week, John would receive his orders to go overseas. I felt wary. He was to report to Vandenberg Air Force Base in Southern California, and from there, he would fly off to Korea on December 1 or 2.

Coming home to Massillon and my family for Thanksgiving felt like an escape for me. Just the year before I had been in prison, and had imagined I would still be there for a few more Thanksgivings. Yet, it was a foreboding time for all of my younger brothers, because they were each dealing with their own decisions about the draft and war. Bill, John, Phillip, and I—as people of the Christian faith, and as people of the Methodist tradition—were all convinced that war was sinful and wrong. We had conversations about it with our parents. My mother, in particular, wanted her sons to work, play, and mature without taking part in a war.

Bill had been the first to face the situation after me, since we were approximately a year apart. He had applied for non-combatant status when he turned eighteen, which, if approved, meant he would have joined the army but not serve in any position where he would have to harm or kill anyone. The local draft board had refused his application. From then on, he did not participate in the Selective Service process any further. A few years later, in September 1952, a U.S. marshal arrested him and the U.S. attorney in Cleveland indicted him. Our mother and I went with him to his court appearance. The judge challenged the U.S. attorney about the difference between being a non-combatant, as identified by the draft board, and a conscientious objector. The U.S. attorney couldn't answer the judge's questions. The judge called him on it, essentially telling the prosecutor that he would have to answer that question before the case could proceed. In the following months, we waited to hear more. But the U.S. attorney had quietly dropped the case and never bothered to inform Bill. We were pleased that for the rest of his life, the draft board never contacted him again.

Next up was the third son, my brother John, who was about three years younger than I was. When John was still in high school he told me that he was planning to start his own business. In 1950, after he turned eighteen, he volunteered to go into the armed forces because some people told him he would need to be a veteran if he wanted to start a business. So, he went directly into the U.S. Air Force after high school. I was arrested and sent to prison during the first years of his service, when he was still based in the United States. But we remained connected, and I knew why he was doing what he did. I might not have agreed that it was the only way for him to be able to start a business, but I supported his first big decision as an adult.

Our youngest brother, Phillip, had become a conscientious objector when his time came to deal with the draft. So, John was the only one of us heading to war.

On the Saturday after Thanksgiving, more than twenty inches of snow fell in Massillon, and I drove John through it to Akron, about thirty miles away. I saw him off at the snow-covered air force base, where he boarded a plane to the West Coast, and to war.

I got back to Baldwin-Wallace for classes on the following Monday. Soon after I had made my way to campus, as I was settling in for my last few weeks of college life, my mother called. She told me that the air force plane transporting John to Korea had gone down in the mountains northwest of Los Angeles during a snowstorm. We didn't know if he was missing or dead. I tried to remain strong for her while we were talking on the phone. But the news cut at my heart.

We heard nothing for a few days. My sweet little brother was on my mind every minute. Living with the uncertainty was a kind of purgatory for us all. And then came confirmation: John's plane had crashed in the Sierra Madre in California. All on board were presumed dead. The harsh conditions made a search impossible.

I wept when I heard that John had died. I was mostly in shock. He was a fine man, and such a loving brother.

My enduring memory from that time of searing pain was my mother's great sadness and deep grief. It is the kind of loss that never leaves you. Our family continued to believe that war was immoral. And I continued to oppose the very war machine that had just claimed my caring, kind younger brother.

Gathering myself in the midst of such a heartbreaking loss, I managed to finish college, finally, at the end of 1952.

India

During my five years at Baldwin-Wallace and in prison, I had studied Gandhi and learned about how nonviolent opposition to oppression had been applied in Africa, Europe, Asia, and India, as well as in parts of the United States. My determined pursuit of the tactics and strategies of nonviolence had been spurred when my mother had charged me with finding a better way, and that search became embedded in my spiritual journey and directed me as I navigated a world where Jim Crow persisted. I ended up convinced that Black people were going to shake off the nightmares of racism with nonviolent direct action. Deep inside, I knew there was going to be a massive nonviolent movement in the United States. Black people would create it, and I would be a part of it. I didn't know where it was going to happen. I didn't know how. I just knew there was going to be a campaign, and for the past five years I had gone about studying nonviolence so intently because I was sure it was going to be integral to triumph in the struggle. My upcoming move to India would allow me to continue that quest.

In late March 1953, my visa came through and I left for a three-year assignment in India, setting sail from New York City to Southampton, England, on the *Queen Elizabeth*. The journey was long but allowed me some time to prepare for the transition to life abroad. Everything was new. And I was ready for the opening up of my life, especially since a year before I had been in prison. I spent a few days in London. It wasn't lost on me that I was in the capital of colonialism in the English-speaking world. We then sailed on to India from Southampton. That ship, the *Canton,* went through the Strait of Gibraltar to Cairo and the Suez Canal. Not being able to linger was my only regret. Within days of leaving Britain, we arrived in Bombay. I had reached India.

Someone from the Methodist Church was there to greet me and see me through customs. We went directly to the Bombay train station and headed to Nagpur, a city of more than five hundred thousand people. It was the biggest city I had ever lived in, and unlike American cities, it was not dominated by automobiles. Walking, bicycles, and buses were the primary modes of transport. I had been told this in orientation, so I had a bicycle on order. Up to then, except for trips out of town, I had mostly been a walking person anyway. During the summer orientation in Hartford the year before, I had decided not to buy a car while in India. A bicycle would be better for me physically. And to own an automobile back then in Nagpur meant you belonged to a certain elite segment of society. I did not want to be identified in that way.

I was received warmly in Nagpur's intellectual, social, and religious communities. Everyone made me feel at home. Almost immediately, I was a part of a Methodist Church congregation, and I worshipped there on Sundays. I also had a football team to cultivate and coach. And I was building friendships with a number of faculty at Hislop. So, I belonged. I lived in a big compound, in a small but satisfactory apartment, with a bedroom, a living room, and an adequate bathroom, shower, and kitchen.

I did not see India as a foreign country. I saw it as a country of people like myself. I especially liked David Moses, who was the president of Hislop College (what Americans would call a high school is essentially what is called a college in India, as it is in the British education system). My apartment was attached to his bungalow. He was a good man—born and raised in South India. He had majored in philosophy, then moved to the United States to get a PhD from Harvard. He liked the fact I was a Black man, a colored person like he was, and not a white British or American person. To David, my being an athlete was an asset. He said I could teach his teams scientific ways of training and preparing for sports, which he wanted to help model in India. He appreciated that I knew what colonialism was, and that therefore I understood a little about what India had come through with gaining independence from Britain in 1947.

Great Britain had founded Hislop College as a state institution in 1883. My missionary assignment there was teaching the Bible and coaching. Three languages were spoken at the college: English, Marathi, and the national language, Hindi. I was teaching the Bible in English and coaching football (what Americans think of as soccer but the rest of the world calls football) in English, too. About fifty players joined our two teams each year, and we won many regular-season games and a few tournament championships. In addition to football, I ended up coaching basketball, track and field, cricket, and tennis, too. I had never played or followed soccer or cricket, but I studied them and was able to apply general principles of coaching to two sports that were new to me.

For instance, as many athletes and coaches know, on any given day, the best team can be defeated by a lower-ranked team. A single athlete is rarely the reason a game is won. The winning team is usually the team that has more of its players in sync with one another, making the group move as one, in unity. The players don't compete with each other. They collaborate. Those principles for coaching aligned nicely with the principles of nonviolent social change, which I was continuing to study and starting to teach.

I began to date in India more than I ever had before. When I arrived, I was dating an American named Jean, whom I met at the summer missionary orientation in Hartford. We stayed together for a while in India. At one point, we said that we were engaged, but I soon realized she wasn't right for me, and I broke up with her. Then I started dating another American woman, Naomi. I broke it off with her, too, because I concluded that I could not marry a white woman. Jean and Naomi both were white. They both were good people. But I was having an awakening about who I wanted as a wife. At that time, the affinity, collaboration, and support I felt a marriage would need, especially as I tried to do the work I was hoping to do in life, seemed as if it would be exponentially harder, if not impossible, with a white woman as my wife.

Being away from your home country gives you a valuable perspective on it and yourself. Living in India was a major event in my life adventure. Since I had ended up there, I made a point of getting the chance to meet some of the people who were with Gandhi in the independence movement, and to learn from them about nonviolence and its applications in changing a nation. I was also eager to be in the Indian scene during the leadership of the first prime minister of India after independence, Jawaharlal Nehru. He had nonviolently fought against colonial rule alongside Gandhi. Spending a few years in India while it was finding its way as a democracy taught me about the aftermath of winning against oppression. I saw the pressures that come with shouldering responsibility for making and navigating change.

So, I doubled down on my study and reading in India, including keeping up with what was happening in the United States. The *New York Herald Tribune* came to me, along with *Newsweek, Time,* and *The Progressive* magazine. It took six weeks for them to arrive, so I was always six weeks behind. But I read about the Supreme Court's *Brown v. Board of Education* decision in the United States in 1954, overturning separate but equal public schools, and about the horrific lynching of fourteen-year-old Emmett Till in Mississippi in 1955. I heard how the photos of his mangled body, which his mother demanded be shown, shocked so many white Americans into realizing the immorality and brutality of Jim Crow, seemingly like nothing else before. My sense that an inevitable racial awakening would happen in my home country increased as news of these kinds of developments reached me in the mid-1950s. Progress and awareness appeared to be inching along.

In U.S. progressive and liberal politics during the twentieth century, the notion predominated that violent revolutions were the most effective ones. Strong debates took place on any number of college campuses. I had been a supporter of World War II in high school, and of guerrilla warfare, until I realized that any violence was an abusive use of power. It really does not give us what we hope for or what we think it promises us.

And violence fails all the time. For me, a far more effective premise—nonviolence—had revealed itself through studying Jesus's life, and then again when I encountered Gandhi in my reading during high school and college. In India, I saw firsthand the fruits of a successful nonviolent movement against colonialism taking root.

Gandhi introduced the concept in 1906 when he was living in South Africa. He said he deliberately chose the word "nonviolence" from Jainism—one of the three ancient religions of India, along with Buddhism and Hinduism. At the core of Jainism is the word *ahimsa,* often translated as "Do no harm. Do no injury." Some people carried this idea to the extreme, wearing masks to keep gnats from flying into their mouths, so they wouldn't hurt the insects. But Gandhi translated *ahimsa* into English as one word, "nonviolence," with no hyphen. He wanted the English term to convey the deeper concept of *ahimsa*—as a mystical sense that life is beyond description but must be held as sacred, that life is a massive gift and you have to relish it, cherish it, and cultivate it. *Ahimsa* is not hate or disrespect, both of which are violence. It's the opposite. It is nonviolence.

Before Gandhi coined the term "nonviolence," *ahimsa* was often translated into English as "passive resistance." But that was a British phrase that grew out of the British women's suffrage movement. Gandhi rejected that translation, not only because it was British, but also because it didn't capture the action that is inherent in *ahimsa,* in nonviolence. Gandhi saw nonviolence as using power for creation, building community, and enriching life. To him, the word "nonviolence" did not mean merely "no violence." It also meant being active in creating change and fostering hope, instead of being weak and merely sowing destruction. Violence, he believed, was exercising power in the wrong way, for decimation, domination, and destruction. Nonviolence was exercising power for the mutual benefit, fulfillment, and prosperity of everyone.

Another Sanskrit term, *satyagraha,* is the practical application of *ahimsa,* or nonviolence, to situations of conflict. In its simplest form, *satyagraha* overcomes evil with good, hate with love, deception with truth, and inflicts no harm to living beings in the process. In English, *satyagraha* is most often translated as "soul force."

The concept of *satyagraha* had been around for centuries. The word comes from a combination of two Sanskrit words: *satya,* meaning truth or love, and *graha,* meaning tenacity or force. So *satyagraha* is the force of truth, the force of love, the force of the soul. But it can only be *satyagraha* if *ahimsa* or nonviolence is at its dynamic, active core. Nonviolence is the power and spirit that drives soul force.

Gandhi and the independence movement in India applied soul force to politics in a way that had never been done before. That was the inspiration for what we later called nonviolent direct action. Trained in the techniques of nonviolence, they exposed the cruelty, injustice, and untruths of oppressive British rule, eventually transforming the power structure in their country. Some of the soul force methods Gandhi used were fasting, non-cooperation, picketing, and civil disobedience. Their long, successful campaign of steady, sustained, and strategic nonviolent action led to Indian independence.

But *satyagraha* required training. Nonviolent soul force preparation was even more rigorous than training for violent military action. In fact, Gandhi's soul force would not have succeeded without extensive practice, deep commitment, and strategic planning. There was a fairly active Christian student movement on university campuses in India during Gandhi's time that focused on using soul force to eliminate poverty and advocate for economic equality and access to education in the new democracy.

Nonviolence was a science to Gandhi, that he said had rules and outcomes as exacting as any other scientific process. I adopted that scientific approach to nonviolence during my first year in India, as the best way to transform injustice. Soon, I began to be invited to speak to student groups on nonviolence and soul force. My approach was to present it as a kind of scientific equation. For instance, you cannot overcome evil with evil. You can't imitate evil and expect to get something different. If you do that, you simply multiply the wrong. Instead, a goodness of some kind must be used to combat evil.

My Christian upbringing melded naturally with the equations I saw in nonviolence. The scriptures insist that wrong can be transformed only by doing right. So it never felt foreign to me to teach Gandhian concepts, even in Gandhi's own country.

When I first began to study his teachings in the United States in the 1940s and early 1950s, Gandhi had impressed me with his insistence that the world must be better, that it was nowhere near to being the kind of world God wanted, or the kind of world we human beings were capable of creating for ourselves. Gandhi's work was covered fairly closely in Black newspapers as he was campaigning for independence in the 1930s and 1940s. Black people saw his work as having applications to their struggles and gained inspiration from his successes. Gandhi had inspired the work of Howard Thurman, the great Black American theologian and Baptist minister. Thurman was the first dean of Rankin Chapel at Howard University and in 1935 and 1936 had led a six-month delegation of Black Americans to India to study nonviolence and soul force, *ahimsa* and *satyagraha*. When Thurman asked Gandhi what message he had for Black people in the United States, he said, "It may be through the Negroes that the unadulterated message of nonviolence will be delivered to the world."

Living abroad continued to help me see the United States more clearly, especially its relationship to violence. The Western assessment that nonviolence meant lying down and doing nothing in the face of violence overlooked and dismissed its essence as an active, disciplined practice. Only preparation for military violence was seen as legitimate and worth pursuing in my country. We were never taught about the extent to which many of the laws and core principles of the United States came about because people engaged in creative nonviolent civil disobedience, which included creative and innovative public demonstrations. The religious liberty we have in America came about primarily because people like Roger Williams, the staunch proponent of the separation of church and state, took aggressive, nonviolent action. American society has been shaped as well by the nonviolent campaigns of the Underground Railroad, the labor movement, and the movements for women's and Black suffrage. Ordinary citizens have effected and stimulated necessary change for centuries using soul force, even if it wasn't called that. But we always tended to frame the history of American power in terms of violence: pushing back Native Americans, taming the wilderness, and warring against nations we saw as threats to us.

Most people in Western nations didn't understand what nonviolence and soul force were, much less that they were such effective options for resolving conflict. And Christians in India bewildered me with their disdain for Gandhi because he was not a Christian. But Gandhi read the Sermon on the Mount from the Gospel of Matthew as part of his meditations every day. Back in the 1940s and 1950s, missionaries knew that. They also knew that a European missionary had attempted to convert him to Christianity—an offer he of course declined. Gandhi thought that religions could enrich each other, but that it was wrong for missionaries to seek to convert anyone from one religion to another. A lot of Indian Christian people disagreed.

During my time in India, I too became a critic of the conversion business of missionaries. The twentieth century missionary movement from Europe and the United States in Asia and Africa was also mostly conservative. Missionary groups were generally comprised of Christian white men and women who were both clergy and laypeople. They usually did not see colonization or white supremacy as a harm. They did not see segregation as a wrong to be rejected, or as a wrong that Jesus would not have tolerated. In fact, many missionaries viewed the rising independence movements as Communist fronts rather than as the efforts of people who wanted to be free, to decolonize, and were expressing that, usually through nonviolent resistance. This was another way I found myself breaking with the missionary movement of my own church.

Gandhi had read the Bible from cover to cover, and appreciated the tenets of Christianity. He was especially drawn to the statements by Jesus about love: "You've heard it said, 'Love your neighbor and hate your enemies.' I say, 'Love your enemies.'" The more I studied Gandhi, the more I came to see Jesus as one of the earliest practitioners of what Gandhi dubbed nonviolence.

Until I became enmeshed as a missionary in India—and this was reinforced later, during my travels through Africa—I did not know the extent to which the church's missionary system was so very wrong. But when I got to India, I found that most missionaries were isolated from the reality of the people they were trying to convert. The missionary movement had done some good things early on—before the European governments and empires took over in so many countries. Missionaries started education programs focused on children and literacy, with special emphasis on schooling for girls. They established medical schools and agricultural schools. But by the time I arrived in India, all they had was their terrible dogma, which told them that only the Bible was right, only Jesus was right. To me, bigotry was at the heart of their work.

That was part of why I gravitated toward many of the Africans I met who were studying in India. I was regularly invited to their African Students Association meetings. They were from all over the continent, but chiefly from East and West African countries that had been taken over and ruled as British colonies. Those meetings gave rise to intense and exhilarating discussions among us about the revolution then happening across Africa, about independence from European nations, and about nonviolent tactics to achieve independence.

Africa

My three-year term as a missionary would be coming to an end in the spring of 1956. So in the year before that, I began to plan a long summer journey through Africa. My parents helped me map out and finance the trip. They knew I had always had an interest in spending time in Africa. I especially wanted to meet with the many people committed to those nonviolent independence campaigns taking hold across the continent. I saw their work as aligned with what I would do when I returned to the United States.

By then, I also had a recurring sense that there would be a person who would emerge to lead such a campaign in the United States, and who would become, truly and unfailingly, my Moses. I had brief glimpses in my mind that this person would be someone I would work with to make a movement of Black people flower and grow. It might sound like a fleeting notion I could have dismissed as fantasy. But I knew—in my bones, my heart, and my soul—it was something much more.

Then early one morning in December 1955, I came in from our team's practice on the football field. I showered and had my breakfast as I usually did. The *Nagpur Times* was on my desk, and the first thing I saw was a headline about a new movement in the United States among Negroes. The article told of a bus boycott in Montgomery, Alabama, and it mentioned a young minister named Martin Luther King Jr.

I was so elated to read the news that I started clapping my hands, and jumping, and shouting. I was alone in the room. But my next-door neighbor, another professor at the school, Chris Theophilos, came running in to find out what was wrong. I showed him the paper and told him how important this was, because I had been hoping and dreaming that such a movement could be possible in America and would start one day soon. I had never heard of Martin Luther King. Nobody had. He was fresh out of Boston University and had taken up pastoring in Montgomery about three months before the bus boycott started.

But now I knew his name. And I knew my role. Because of my eight or ten years of experience openly practicing nonviolent struggle with a Christian biblical sense, I knew I would be one of those helping him encourage our movement to be nonviolent. I would be teaching nonviolence as an effective, alternative, intelligent, spiritual way of handling and managing conflict and injustice. I began looking forward to meeting him when I got back to the United States. But first: my trip to Africa, which had suddenly taken on a new urgency and relevance.

Right after I finished my tour of duty in India, in May 1956, I headed to Bombay. I sailed from there in early June on a ship called the *Amra,* across the Indian Ocean, to Mombasa, Kenya. I had arranged the meetings I would have on the trip myself, with help from some of the people I met in India and from American church officials. I had written ahead to various people, saying I was coming. I was to spend two months traveling in Kenya, Uganda, Tanzania, Rwanda, and Burundi, then head west across the Congo to Angola. After that, I would continue up to Nigeria, Ghana, Liberia, and Sierra Leone.

Everyone welcomed me with great joy and enthusiasm, because back then not many American Negroes made their way to Africa. I made notes during my travels in a beautiful little blue notebook I'd found somewhere in India. It fit in my coat pocket.

June 28, 1956—Mombasa

> Arrived at 2 p.m. Mombasa harbor is very pretty, and clean. . . . The Africans who came aboard with immigration met me immediately and talked freely—welcoming me to Kenya, asking me to stay longer—wanting to know why the American Negro did not take a bigger interest in Africa.

My arrival amplified my long-standing emotional affinity with Africa. Everywhere I went, I was received as an American brother. Black people were taught in America that we had no past. But in my home, we didn't accept that erasing of our past. Early on, we learned that my great-grandfather was enslaved and had escaped to Canada, and that my grandmother's family had a whole history of involvement with the Underground Railroad in Philadelphia. For us, our history was a point of great pride.

One of my first and most vivid memories of my time in Africa involves the Indian Ocean beaches in and around Mombasa, where the fishermen worked. They had huge nets, stretching out into the ocean, way beyond the shore. Between fifty and a hundred men and boys would line up on one net to haul it in. It was no small operation. At the right moment, all the men and boys would pull at the same time. And when they began to pull, they would use this chant: *Harambee.* They drew out each syllable. *Har-am-bee.* It means "all pull together," but that isn't an exact translation. *Har-am-bee.* Fundamentally, it meant that everyone bent their bodies forward and back in sync with one another, and used all their strength at the same time to haul in the net filled with fish from the ocean.

I saw and heard this marvel more than once at the Mombasa shore. Hundreds of men, from young to much older and gray-haired, would chant *"Harambee!"* as they dragged in the nets heavy with fish for the markets. The chant enabled them to move as one, almost as if they were performing a dance, in harmony. A man or two could not pull it in alone, and there was only one big net at a time. *Harambee* became a key word for me in my pastoring from then on, and it would become the motto of Kenya after the country gained independence in the 1960s.

I spent five weeks in Kenya. For about three of those weeks, I stayed in Nairobi, at the home of the brother of one of my African student friends from Nagpur. John Ndisi and I had become remarkably close in India. John's brother Meshach was the first African labor officer in the British Kenyan government, and a founder of the Kenyan trade union movement. Meshach had degrees in industrial relations from Oxford University and the London School of Economics.

July 1, 1956

Trip to Nairobi. Segregated train—all Africans in coach No. 1. Indians in charge! All Africans are always in the same coach. And this is persisted in by the Indians who carry out the policy. The travel agent told the railway reservation clerk that we were Africans. This clerk carried out the segregation.

Later I asked the Sikh conductor, who told me he could do nothing. Said that the system was a part of Kenya. Then remarked how he did not receive the same pay as a European in a similar post with similar experience.

Equal pay for equal work is a burning issue with Kenya. Meshach Ndisi tells me that it started with the government which has been advising private businesses to adopt it. But so far no European or Indian business has adopted it.

Even in government the European officer often receives an additional allowance which keeps him ahead of the Indian or African counterpart.

Met the secretary of the Typographical Workers Union, G. J. J. Olula—1,475 members working in presses owned by Indians. He says that equal wages for equal work is one of their goals, but should they strike for it and win, the Indians would simply stop hiring Africans and use only Indians.

A few years before, in 1952, a movement to overthrow British rule in Kenya had started, called the Mau Mau rebellion. As it became more and more violent, the government labeled it the Kenya Emergency. Part of what triggered the worst violence was colonial appropriation of Kenyan land. African people killed thirty-two white settlers and more than two thousand Africans who were suspected of complicity. White colonists, including the British government, then went all out to destroy the Mau Mau by death and imprisonment. By the time I arrived, the rebellion had been put down in many places. Jomo Kenyatta was the rebel leader, and he had been imprisoned. Many others were killed in prison, while awaiting a fair hearing. In addition to putting down opposition to colonial rule by force, there were many other ways in which the British tried to undermine the decolonization process. Meshach Ndisi, my host, introduced me to the beer parlors the British had built all over East Africa, stocked with cheap beer. This was one of the ways. Get them drunk.

During my time in Nairobi, I met others in the labor and independence movements. I also met businesspeople, like Norbert Charles, who helped me understand the underlying issues at the root of the Mau Mau uprising, even though neither he nor Meshach Ndisi supported the violence of the rebellion.

Charles was an impressive Kenyan businessman who, despite his success, understood well the hardships faced by Africans wishing to participate in the economy. The system made Europeans rich and kept Africans underpaid—the Europeans in his firm earned much more money than Charles did. Likewise, the system automatically favored Europeans, lavishing on them every opportunity and perk, making sure that no such considerations went to Africans.

July 3, 1956

Charles blames plight of African on lack of capital—if he had money he could capture the African consumer. European standard of living bankrupts Kenya. Africans cannot have same standard, economically impossible. European is extravagant, lives in luxury. Most Americans join the typical European. Members of govt. do little.

Charles explained how the rebellion had forced the British-run government to pay some attention to issues of inequity for Africans. He pointed to new housing and school projects that would have taken years to come to fruition without the rebellion. I also met an African lawyer in Nairobi named Charles NjoNjo. He was educated in England and returned to Kenya, where he got involved in politics. He asked me, "How can you as a colored man be a Christian in our kind of world? What can you do as a Christian? My faith is shattered. Until power is in my hands, I'll be like them—Europeans. Once the reins are in our hands, we can then be Christian."

Throughout my travels in Africa, almost everyone I met with asked me to stay, or to come back and bring more American Negroes. Meshach and I had long talks about that when I was a guest in his home.

Tuesday, July 10, evening

Ndisi: "You should return to Kenya. We need more American Negroes over here. We see Europeans and Indians here as technicians. We wonder why the American Negro does not come. I don't think the African would mind seeing his country flooded with American Negroes."

Why?

"They would be sincere. They will not have forgotten their old ancestry. We would prefer being exploited by the American Negro."

I also met with church leaders and missionaries. One who stood out was Rev. David Steel, the minister of St. Andrews Presbyterian Church in Nairobi and the Parish of East Africa, which included Uganda and Tanzania. He was a voice for independence in response to the emergency, and worked to gain the freedom of Africans who had been detained in prison camps without trials.

Thursday, July 12, 1956

Amazing how conversation with one of God's men always lifts my whole life. Such a person is the Rev. David Steel—minister of St. Andrews, Nairobi—prophet of God. He was the prophetic voice of the church during the days of the emergency—using his pulpit, the radio, his church bulletin and direct talks with the government to make God's voice heard above the clamour of hate.

Gov't. often as violent as Mau Mau. Both sides were violent beyond any justification. Many innocent Africans suffered. People were detained without use of the law—innocent as well as guilty—again this was protested by the church.

When my friend John Ndisi in India first heard I was going to Kenya, he not only got me in touch with his brother Meshach in Nairobi, but said he wanted me to be sure to visit his parents at their family home. So Meshach Ndisi took me from Nairobi out into the highlands, to where their parents lived. I spent an unforgettable four days in the village of Manywanda, Uyoma, on the shore of Lake Victoria. Their father was a parson of the Church of England. I was welcomed like a king. Everyone had heard that an American Negro missionary was visiting Pastor Ndisi. They organized a gathering of about two hundred people, mostly Christians, who came from all over the area on foot or by bicycle to meet me.

Friday, July 20, 1956

Reception at Manywanda

Rev. Ndisi: Tell your people that our girls and boys have not got education. We thirst. We thirst for education. We have no doctors, no good farmers, we need teachers.

At that reception, Reverend Ndisi presented me with an *aguata*, a hollowed gourd used in every village home for drinking and eating. He said, "Brother Jim, we want you to take this with you wherever you go to remind you always that in Africa, we thirst, our children thirst. Go to America and tell your Christian people to come over here and help us." I have kept it with me, and hung it on the wall. It always reminds me that people in Africa, and all over the earth, thirst to know the fullness of life. I was beginning to see that the constant questions I heard about why more American Negroes didn't come to Africa and help were not so much questions as pleas, from people who were living under the same evils of white supremacy as we were in the United States. Our heritage was stolen from us when white enslavers kidnapped us from Africa and brought us to Europe and the Americas. In Africa, European colonizers stole the people's land and effectively enslaved them in their own countries. The same evil had to be fought wherever it existed.

From Manywanda, I traveled not too far away to the home of Jaramogi Oginga Odinga, who in 1964 would become the first vice president of Kenya, after independence. I stayed with him for a few days. Odinga was a labor man and a small contractor in business, actively engaged in politics and in the effort to get the British out. We visited and talked politics. I met his family. I walked with him through the jungle and rode with him to his home place, which was deep in the jungle, close to Lake Victoria.

I also visited a nearby school in Maseno and spoke to more than two hundred students. Then I spoke at a community gathering in Kisumu, where two European government officials frowned and stared at me throughout the meeting. But the Kenyans who attended were excited and enthusiastic about my being there.

In each country I visited, I met with missionaries, as well as with people active in the struggle to gain independence in central Africa. I visited schools, hospitals, and businesspeople in large companies. After Kenya, I went to Uganda, Tanzania, Rwanda, and Burundi. I arranged for meetings through missionaries or Americans who the Methodist Board of Missions put me in contact with. But I didn't always stay with the Methodist missionaries. In Kampala, I met the former editor of the English-language newspaper *The Uganda Herald*, A. C. Duffield, a British man, who spoke to me about the "savages" of Africa. In my notes, I described him as "paternalistic," which is perhaps too polite for what he was.

July 28, 1956

Mr. Duffield, elderly journalist, is not liked in Uganda. Duffield talking: "You must remember that only 50 years ago these people were naked little savages in the jungle. We have done marvels in that time. But we cannot expect too much now. They will not have the standard which your people (the Negroes) in America have. You have been in

> America for 150 years. What these people have acquired is only veneer—the culture does not go deep. The education is only on the surface. When some social situations arise—these people can easily go back to the jungle (Mau Mau as an example)." Duffield is typical "father of the people" who simply loves the "little savages."

In the Belgian Congo (now the Democratic Republic of the Congo), I met Patrice Lumumba, who was on the verge of leading his country's independence movement. He would go on to be the first elected prime minister of the Congo when it gained independence from Belgium in 1960. We spoke through interpreters, as he communicated in French and his Indigenous languages. He was a good man who was never given a chance to realize a fully independent Congo. Long a target of the United States, shortly after his country's independence, he was executed by a Belgian-supported faction during a coup. Belgium was the Congo's colonial oppressor and wished to maintain control of the country's mineral wealth. The assassins were proven to have had the tacit support of the CIA, which saw the Congo only as a pawn in the Cold War, and feared Soviet influence there. The aspirations of Africans yearning for independence mattered not at all to officials in Washington.

I got a feeling for the isolation and insulation of the white man in Kenya, Uganda, and the Congo. The white missionaries and businessmen all lived together in compounds, and I found them unaware, even then, of the great agitation of spirit rising in the breasts of Africans. In the Congo, for example, the Europeans I met were pointing to Kenya and saying that such a rebellion couldn't happen in the Congo. I found it fascinating how on several days I would be in a meeting with Europeans, and I would hear some variation of these ideas of impermeability. Then, on the very same day, I could step into an African home or a café and hear exactly the opposite.

The same held true out in the bush. On a Sunday afternoon I was invited to Léopoldville, the capital of the Congo (now Kinshasa), where a tea was being given at a school with a fair number of westerners. On the way to the city, my host and I stopped at a little café in a small town. I walked into the place, and as soon as they found out I was an American minister, I was immediately approached by a couple of Congolese civil servants who were working at some menial job. They took me off to the corner and proceeded to talk to me about their efforts to organize a union, and the things they were trying to do to get people out of the country for education. So it became obvious to me that agitating forces in the Congo were already at work among the Africans—expectations were there. But I did not find any awareness of those forces on the part of either the European or American missionaries or businessmen I met anywhere in Africa. They had a moral blindness, a seemingly willful insensitivity to the history and the soul of African nations.

However, I also saw firsthand that the European governments that were ruling countries in Africa were already in some turmoil over the more vocal people they knew about in their colonies who were advocating for self-determination, calling for the British or the Belgians or the French to go home and let them have their country. The white Christian governments of America and Europe were all of the same mind: their superior culture represented civilization in these countries, and these people could not govern themselves. It was a paternalistic racism: *We can govern you, but you can't govern yourselves.* Gandhi was told the same thing, outright. The British said, "You Indians can't govern—you'll make all kinds of mistakes." And Gandhi told the British negotiators, "Yes. But they'll be our mistakes."

From the Congo I traveled to Lobito and Dondi in Angola, which was ruled as a province of Portugal. And then I went into Nigeria, to Lagos and Calabar; to the Gold Coast (now Ghana), to Accra; to Monrovia in Liberia; and to Freetown in Sierra Leone. Nigeria's population was the largest in Africa. Sierra Leone, Ghana, and Liberia were all relatively small countries.

Africa in the 1950s was in a great fermentation. Kwame Nkrumah was organizing in Ghana around what he called "nonviolent Positive Action" against British rule, using demonstrations and strikes, inspired by Gandhi's success with nonviolence in India. He was, of course, dismissed by the British government as a radical and by U.S. foreign policymakers. But in 1952, he was elected as prime minister of the Gold Coast and, later, as prime minister and then president, after leading the country to independence in 1957. I did not get to talk with him, although I met others involved in the struggle there.

I also went to the departure places in Ghana. I saw the dark dungeons where people laid when they were kidnapped and about to be sent into slavery in North and South America. It was not much of a tourist area back then. But I did visit and I remember feeling the darkness there.

When it was time to get back to the United States, the Board of Missions travel people advised me that the best route was from Lagos to Lisbon, and then from Lisbon to New York City. On the flight from Lagos to Lisbon, I saw something I had never seen before: a Black pilot and a Black co-pilot. I cannot adequately describe my elation. Those two men would fly me toward my home. It was a last profound revelation for me, in an African journey that had been filled with such moments. My months in Africa had changed me, and I was ready to put the lessons of my experience there to work back home.

Martin

I returned to New York on September 1, 1956. My mother picked me up with Bill and Phillip, after driving across Ohio and Pennsylvania. I spent about three weeks at home in Massillon and then was off to Oberlin Graduate School of Theology. I picked Oberlin because I wanted to be in Ohio again, where I could rejoin my family and become acquainted with my new nephews and nieces—my sisters' children. Oberlin had accepted me before I had left India. I figured that after getting a master's degree there, I would go on to Yale or somewhere on the East Coast to pursue a doctorate. Then, I believed, I would be ready for my calling as a pastor at a local parish, and eventually in the South.

Oberlin was the most supportive place I had ever lived. It had always been known for its progressive student activism and as a pioneer in equality, as one of the first colleges to admit Black people, in 1835, and as the first to admit women, in 1837. Back in the 1930s and 1940s, when most college towns looked upon Black and international students with some hesitation, Oberlin was one of the few places where a Black man could get his hair cut anywhere in town. The students and faculty of Oberlin, and the city itself, had worked over the years to ensure that there was an openness to the whole place.

I lived in a room on campus, right next to the library. Many friendly faces welcomed me, both in the graduate school and in the church community. It was a smooth transition. I jumped into my courses and studies and experienced an invigorating intellectual climate. Oberlin gave me a period of looking inward, and of provocative theological study in subject after subject.

Also, I had a courtship at Oberlin with a Japanese graduate student named Aiko Yokoya, a very fine person. She was studying Christian religious education. The United Methodist women were financing her master's degree, and as part of their program, she was committed to going back to Japan and working in the Methodist Church there after she finished at Oberlin. We were not sure what would happen. But Aiko and I had a lovely kinship.

Early on at Oberlin, I also became friends with Harvey Cox, who was fresh out of seminary and was the YMCA chaplain there. One day, he called me to tell me that Martin Luther King Jr. was coming to speak at a convocation on campus, and that I should plan to eat lunch with him and about a dozen others after the talk. At noon on February 7, 1957, I heard his speech, called "The Montgomery Story," in which he recounted his experiences during the thirteen-month boycott, that had just ended two months before, when the city began to desegregate its bus system.

The twelve-hundred-seat Finney Chapel was packed. The largest venue on campus, it had been named after a nineteenth-century American evangelist, Charles Grandison Finney, who had advocated for abolition, the Underground Railroad, and equal access to education for women and Black people. Finney was an early professor at Oberlin and its second president. The chapel was just a block away from the graduate school complex. Afterward, I walked directly to a small meeting room that people in Oberlin used for all kinds of gatherings. Two tables were set up for a meal. I was surprised to find nobody else there yet.

Then I heard someone following me into the room. It turned out to be Martin King. He had walked over by himself. In those days, he did not travel with an entourage of any kind. I quickly shook his hand and introduced myself. I said I was a student in the Graduate School of Theology and had just returned from three years in India as a Methodist missionary. He became immediately interested in hearing more about me. We sat down at a table facing each other and talked for a while before everyone else arrived for lunch. He wanted to know all about my experience in India. He said, "Oh, I would love to do that one day." We talked about Gandhi and nonviolence, and I expressed my support for all he had done in Montgomery. I also recounted for him my exuberant reaction when I first read about the Montgomery bus boycott in the *Nagpur Times*. I told him that I had been expecting something like that to happen in the United States, and said I knew I would be involved in it when it did. I told him that I saw him as the spokesperson for nonviolence and I was going to do whatever I could to support him.

He asked about my plans. I said I would be finishing my graduate degree at Oberlin and then might get a PhD. But, I added, in any case, I expected to move to the South and work in the struggle when I was done with school, because I thought Black people in the segregated South needed a minister like me the most.

He listened intently. Then he said, "Come now. Don't wait. Come as quickly as you can. We need you now." He said they didn't have anyone with my background and my knowledge of nonviolent change. Here was this man, who was doing the most important work in the country, telling me that he needed me right now. I sat for a moment. I heard the man, and I heard also the voice of destiny and of God. *Don't wait.* I wanted to finish my degree. But I understood that this call was more important. This wasn't just idle lunch-table conversation. This was a fateful moment that would change the course of my life. I looked him in the eye and quietly said, "I will come as fast as I can."

I was still—very still—as I pondered. I was a graduate student without income at that time, thinking, "How is this going to happen? How am I going to do this?" It would take me a while to find a way.

While at Oberlin, I was pastoring a small church in Norwalk, Ohio. Every Sunday, I preached there. Also, I had committed myself to working as a temporary assistant pastor in Detroit during the summer of 1957. St. Luke's Methodist Church was in an area where whites had fled and Blacks had moved in. The church was trying to reorganize itself for the new community, adjusting to what was called "white flight." It could also be called racism.

During my Detroit summer, I was becoming more creative in my thinking about how to resist. A friend of mine who visited a couple times was trying to persuade a barbershop in the city's Greyhound bus station to serve Black people. So I went to test the waters. I sat for a time, and then the barber, who was a relatively small, rotund white man, came in. He was the owner, and he started fuming. He wanted me to leave immediately. I stayed. He called me racist names, and yet I stayed. Then he came for me. He attacked me and dragged me out of the shop. As I was analyzing the situation afterward, I thought it might have been funny to have gotten up and moved around from chair to chair, staying out of his reach and not letting him touch me. I knew I could move pretty fast, and chances were he couldn't, because he was kind of heavyset. I thought I would have laughed as he was doing it, highlighting the absurdity of his racism. Sometimes, you just have to laugh.

Through that summer, Aiko and I were dating seriously. And immediately after I got back to Oberlin from Detroit, in late August, I had to have my appendix removed. So I wasn't considering my future or moving South right then. I don't remember talking to Martin King during those months either, about when I was coming. But I had told him to his face I would get there soon. So early in November 1957, I talked to A. J. Muste, my great mentor and executive director of the Fellowship of Reconciliation in New York. I said to him, "I'm dropping out of school and moving South." A.J.'s response to me was "Don't make any decisions until I call you back."

A couple of weeks later, we talked again and he told me that one of the people who was working in the South for FOR had recently resigned. He asked me, "Will you come and be our Southern secretary?" Immediately, I said, "Yes." I didn't hesitate. It meant I would have a job and therefore a salary, which would make my move possible. Also, the kind of organizing and training in nonviolent direct action I would be doing with FOR was exactly what I envisioned was needed in the South.

The next step was to negotiate with Glenn Smiley, who was the staff person in charge of the field operations for FOR, based in Nashville. Glenn had been deeply involved in the Montgomery bus boycott the year before. He had to step in after Bayard Rustin, who also worked for FOR, was forced to leave Montgomery or risk being exposed as gay by white people opposed to the goals of the campaign there.

I could have chosen any city in the South as my base. I considered Atlanta, as well as a few other places with divinity schools where I could continue my studies. But I had already stayed in Nashville a few times before, including for a week-long meeting of national leadership of the Methodist Youth Fellowship, which was based there. It was through the MYF and FOR that I had met and worked with Bayard Rustin, Charles Walker, John Swomley, Jim Farmer, and George Houser, back at Baldwin-Wallace. Howard Thurman had worked with FOR as well, in the 1940s. They were all kindred spirits and guides to me as I evolved. Every time I had gone to Nashville, I had stayed in the homes of professional staffers, laypeople, and clergy members, because segregation meant there were no hotels for Black people there.

So Glenn and I agreed that I would move to Nashville and he would help me get set up there. He had convinced me that Vanderbilt was a better school for me than Emory, Duke, or Southern Methodist University.

What became Vanderbilt University originally had been founded as a training ground for Methodist ministers in the 1850s. Its founders were part of the Methodist Episcopal Church, South, the group that had broken off from the main church in 1844 because the Southerners couldn't support the main church's pro-abolitionist stance. It wasn't lost on me that Vanderbilt's founders and their successors into the mid-twentieth century were Southern, white Methodist men of their time: enslavers and later segregationists.

Vanderbilt wasn't the most inviting place. But I knew I was coming to a region where racism was the most overt of anywhere in the country at the time. Facing this nation's continual racist legacy head-on, in its harshest form, was my intent. I knew I would have found such heritage anywhere I tried to settle in the South. But Glenn strongly persuaded me to choose Nashville as my landing spot, saying it was the best city for me "because you'll have friends there who know you and who will support you." He was right. And Glenn was a good, commonsense man. I had never met him before I moved to Nashville. But I came to admire his wisdom, and became so grateful for the life-changing work we would do there and throughout the South in the late 1950s and early 1960s.

PART TWO

1958–1967

AGITATION

Those who profess to favor freedom, and yet deprecate agitation, are men who want crops without plowing up the ground. . . . Power concedes nothing without a demand. It never did and it never will.

—Frederick Douglass

SEVEN

Nashville Symphony

James and Dorothy Wood Lawson wedding, Charleston, Tennessee, July 3, 1959. VANDERBILT LIBRARY

A few weeks before Christmas in 1957, all my nieces and nephews spent the holiday with us on Groose Avenue. Since I had been away for a few years, that visit gave me time to get better acquainted with them. Betty brought her girl. Frankie's kids came. Ella and Daisy didn't have any children yet. Dorothy brought her sons, Robert, David, and Anthony, and her daughter, Roberta.

We had a good time, playing touch football, baseball, softball, and even a little basketball. At one point, my mother and I were in the kitchen, talking. The kids were all down in the basement, running around, playing, and trying out new toys. Suddenly, we heard Dorothy's oldest boy, Robert, who was nine, screaming at the top of his lungs, maybe in some pain, but also with some indignation. He was yelling in anger at David, who was eight. "Just wait till I get you, David!" he shouted. "I'm going to get you, David!" I went to the top of the basement staircase and demanded that Robert come up to talk. He stomped up nearer to me, and I walked down a few steps toward him. I asked what happened. He said that David had pushed his head into the basement's concrete wall.

He was tearful, crying. His face was all wet. But he continued insisting loudly, "Just wait, I'm going to get that David." I tried to calm Robert down. But he was not letting go. Eventually, he sat still long enough that I thought he had gotten out all of his anger. So I said, "Robert, why don't you forgive David now? You know what forgiveness is. You learned about it in Sunday school." He looked at me, a little bit more composed than he had been, and said, "Uncle Jim, I am going to forgive him." I smiled, thinking I had negotiated the peace. He had resolved his feelings and chosen his higher self. Then he added, "Uncle Jim, I will forgive—just as soon as I get done doing what I'm going to do to him."

I burst out laughing. Robert laughed, too. And we continued laughing together for a while. It was a very human moment. He was saying what a lot of people say: "I'm going to forgive him, when I get good and ready—after I settle it." I went back to the kitchen, told my mother, and we also laughed about that one. It's still one of my favorite family stories.

The whole holiday was joyous. Wherever else I was, until that Christmas—including prison and India—33 Groose Avenue in Massillon, Ohio, was always where I returned, where I laid my head, my homestead, my home. But I was packing up my stuff. In January, I closed out my work at the Norwalk, Ohio, church where I had been pastoring. Then, a few weeks into 1958, I boarded a bus and headed to the South.

Almost immediately after I arrived in Nashville, on February 2, I began to travel the region as FOR's Southern secretary in support of the nonviolent struggle for human rights beginning to take hold in this country. Within that first week, Glenn Smiley and I drove more than three hundred miles to Little Rock, where nine Black high school students had integrated Little Rock Central High School a few months earlier, in the fall of 1957. Glenn had been there once before. We both stayed at the home of a white University of Arkansas medical school doctor and faculty member, G. R. Lewis, who was a FOR member.

We met with all of the Little Rock Nine on our very first day in town, visiting with them for about three hours in Daisy Bates's living room. She was president of the Arkansas chapter of the NAACP. We sat and talked—essentially doing our first impromptu nonviolence workshop that day.

They had already been in an ongoing battle with many of the white students at the high school, whose parents were members of the White Citizens' Council and the Ku Klux Klan. Those groups recruited white students and persuaded them not to rest until the Black students were thrown out of the school. At their meetings, the adults would plan ways for white student recruits to harass and hurt the Black students. Little Rock businesspeople and conservative elected officials were also members of those white supremacist groups. And the constituents of Arkansas's segregationist governor, Orval Faubus, was a segregationist whose constituents appreciated living in a segregated city. Any change to that established order threatened them.

Of the 517 Black students who lived in the Central High School district, eighty had expressed interest in going there. But the all-white Little Rock school board had decided that only a fraction of that number—nine Black students—would be authorized to integrate the school. In a fifteen-hundred-student school, more than eighty would have been best. But if even the eighty students who had volunteered could have gone, at least they might have shared the burden and pressure. Instead, each of those nine brave teenagers ventured forth, representing multitudes, into an unrelenting barrage of American racial hatred and cruelty that almost broke them all.

Six of the Little Rock Nine were girls, and three were boys. At our first meeting, one of my early questions for them was: What hurts the most? How do they try to harm you the most physically? The girls said that white boys and girls kicked them, tried to trip them, tried to push them down the stairs, and roughed them up all over school. The boys told of being struck in the face with rocks and fists and kicked. In gym class, the boys' clothes were stolen while they were in the shower, and stuffed into the girls' bathroom toilets. Their lockers were urinated on. White students threw eggs or tomatoes at them and splattered ink and glue on them. All nine of them were called "n——r" repeatedly, along with other verbal harassment, humiliations, and attacks—all day, every day. White kids would walk behind some of the Black girls in the hallways between classes, stepping on their heels as they walked, until they bled. The stories were horrible. And one of the girls told me about what they called "bombing." Some of the Black students' family homes had received bomb threats, and their parents got harassing phone calls all through the night. But this kind of bombing was different.

A white kid would wrap up a rock, golf ball, or marble in a piece of paper or plastic and throw it at one of the Black students in class, or the hall, or the cafeteria. These bombs would hit them in the head or other parts of their bodies. She said it hurt and stung badly. And since the bombs usually came from behind, it wasn't always clear who had thrown them.

After hearing a few of these stories, I asked the students what they were told about this kind of violence when they agreed to go to Little Rock Central. They said the NAACP and their parents had told them, above all, "You can't fight back. Because that will blow up the whole experiment. They'll kick you out of the school. So, no matter what, do not fight back." Hearing that, I was personally outraged, inwardly angry, and hurt that this group of nine Black high school students was told they could not fight back and then were given no other guidance. I think when a child is being threatened with hurt or harm, you cannot legitimately tell them, "Don't fight back" without also giving them alternate strategies, ideas, and support around how they can best deal with such terrifying violence and threats.

I never directed my anger toward the local NAACP. However, I felt it had not done enough heart searching on how the students themselves would get through this ordeal and hadn't fully considered how not fighting back would help or hurt them. What would be the cost to them of not fighting back? These students and their parents had been sent into a highly dangerous situation and not been properly equipped to deal with the relentless violence they would inevitably encounter. We needed to help them see the power they already possessed, and to teach them to fight back in a more effective way than imitating the ways of their tormentors. We should, I thought, be telling the students: Fight back with love and nonviolence. Resist, because you are on the front lines of helping to change Little Rock and this country.

I listened, tried to interpret and transform the messages they had gotten, and then to present a more constructive one that I thought would benefit them. "Look," I said, "your parents and the lawyers and the NAACP do not actually mean you don't fight back. Because they want you to grow up as healthy people. So in that kind of hostile climate, you have to resist."

I told them, "You cannot fight back in the same way your enemies are fighting—the way of the white students and their parents, or the governor and the hate organizations. But you do have to fight back, for your own safety and value. Because if you don't fight back, you're apt to get into real trouble inside yourself. You may do great harm to your entire life. You could even become sick, because a person doesn't go through the kinds of abuse you have gone through without being terribly upset. You are facing a great wrong, and a wrong that you do not deserve."

I shared the story of Jackie Robinson in 1947, when he desegregated baseball. He was told, "If a guy spikes you, get up and go back and play ball. Don't spike him, or rush out and try to swat him with the bat." In fact, according to a Robinson biography, Branch Rickey, the manager of the Dodgers, asked Jackie if he thought he could, for one year, get up and play the best ball anyone had ever seen, and not retaliate. They talked about that being the best way to let the desegregation happen. Let the nation see a Black ballplayer playing good ball. Don't let the enemy stop him. The Little Rock Nine were not playing a game. But I was trying to show them they could use a different kind of bravery, the kind it takes not to retaliate.

Glenn and I gently explained ways the students could resist using their minds, wits, and courage. We said such a fight would be more effective than swinging their fists at their tormentors. We reminded them of Martin King and the Montgomery bus boycott, which had ended successfully a year before. No one had been physically violent, but they had exposed to the world the great wrong they were facing, through their strategic, persistent, creative illustrations of it in public. I encouraged them to use their imaginations as a weapon, to imagine different ways of responding.

We tried to convey how violence is not just physical but can also be structural, ideological, spiritual, and moral. I was drawing upon what I had learned about racism and sexism and verbal abuse as forms of violence, and why in the early twentieth century Gandhi had introduced the concept of nonviolence. Because nonviolence was a way of translating the word "love" into resistance.

Early on, my parents and sisters and brothers had taught me that love was quite powerful. And that moments of illness or crisis, or moments when you are under threat, are the moments when you should practice love. Because that's the best way through whatever the crisis is. We have so thoroughly convinced ourselves of the powers of violence that we have in many ways sabotaged or cast out of our system the powers of love and truth. But we are armed as human beings with creativity, with love, and with truth, and these things have abundant powers.

Glenn and I spent some time asking the students and their parents to commit to the idea that a new situation is possible without the sin of violent racism—that the segregated city of the present is not locked in eternity. It can be changed.

After those five meaningful days in Little Rock, I could see we would likely need to return to Little Rock to continue the work. Glenn and I headed back to Nashville. And a few days later, we began a drive from Nashville through Kentucky, West Virginia, Virginia, North Carolina, and South Carolina. His wife, Helen, went with us for part of the trip. He was acquainting me with the South. Until then, Nashville had been the farthest into the South I had ever traveled. Glenn was also introducing me to FOR members and staff, and some of the activists around the region. I was getting acquainted with my clientele.

In early March 1958, Glenn and I began organizing our first conferences in the South on nonviolence and social change. Martin Luther King Jr. was the featured speaker at one of our earliest conferences that spring for clergy and community members in Columbia, South Carolina. It was the first time he and I were on the ground together since I had arrived in the South. He was delighted that I had made the move, and I felt I was exactly where I was meant to be.

When I conducted a nonviolence workshop at that conference, Martin sat in the front row. He listened carefully. And when we opened it up to questions at the end, he stood up before anyone else. He asked about how to use the power of love in nonviolent direct action.

I answered, saying that confrontation had to be a part of nonviolent resistance. Nonviolence had a spiritual, moral, and political power, something a lot of people did not recognize at that time. I said the love at the core of nonviolent resistance was an active force that could change and overcome evil. It was what Gandhi had called "soul force," and it was the driver of nonviolent resistance and direct action. Violence, on the other hand, was driven by forces antithetical to love. Nonviolence built up a beloved community. While violence tore down and destroyed communities, nonviolence went beyond the idea of a lack of conflict to the level of using love to address conflict and to resolve it without destruction.

Martin had never seen me conduct a nonviolence workshop before that day. It solidified not only our work together but our friendship. And for the rest of his life, he had me lead a major nonviolence workshop on the very first day of every Southern Christian Leadership Conference (SCLC) annual convention. He made a big deal of my work in his opening speeches at the SCLC meetings, and would insist that everyone come back after lunch for the nonviolence session. And he would always be there himself in one of the front rows. Leading with love was our shared ethic and always at the heart of our friendship.

Next, Glenn and I began to work with the newly formed group called the Nashville Christian Leadership Council (NCLC). Rev. Kelly Miller Smith, pastor of the First Baptist Church in downtown Nashville, participated in Martin Luther King's first SCLC event in Atlanta, in late 1957. In early 1958, he gathered local members of the clergy to start the NCLC. Their stated goal was to "apply the central tenets of our faith to the problems of injustice and persecution and segregation." The NCLC invited Glenn and me to conduct a three-day workshop on Christian nonviolence for a small group of interested people in the spring of 1958.

By then, I had written up a handout for the workshops. It included definitions of nonviolence as Gandhi and Jesus had practiced it. I passed out the information sheet which also discussed ways of training for nonviolence—such as meditation, prayer, study (I included a bibliography of books and articles), practices (speak the truth, forgive, restrain from any form of violence in your personal relations at home, at church, or in the community), and experimenting with "nonviolent resistance to certain customs of discrimination and segregation—bus travel, waiting rooms, drinking fountains and restrooms." I told them, "Do this quietly, without announcement. As one begins to practice this, courage will increase for bigger efforts."

I then got to what I called "virtues of nonviolence," such as "speak softly without excitement; if possible, smile, indicate that you neither hate nor fear the other party; do not get involved in an argument; discover a way to take the attention of the party away from the situation; stress the spiritual issue."

Next, I introduced methods of nonviolence, which I presented as stages. "One moves progressively from step to step," I said.

1. Fact-finding: Study the situation, obtain all the facts.
2. Negotiation: Present the facts, and raise the moral issue. . . .
3. Education: The entire community must be informed of the real issues; rumor and fear must be matched with facts. Dramatic forms of education can be used, such as marches, picketing, demonstrations, mass meetings.
4. Preparation for Satyagraha: When the other stages of nonviolence fail to bring the desired changes, then the nonviolent group must prepare for direct action.

As examples, I mentioned how Gandhi created "an army of nonviolence which went through regular physical and spiritual training," and how in Montgomery people were prepared through "continuous mass meetings and workshops on nonviolence." The fifth stage we listed was nonviolent direct action, or *satyagraha,* and we explained five of its tactics: the sit-in, the boycott, the vigil, the strike, and civil disobedience (deliberately breaking an unjust law to expose it).

It was mostly adult members of FOR who attended that first Nashville workshop for the NCLC. But at least one student was there: John Lewis, a bright young undergraduate from American Baptist Theological Seminary. He was on board with us right from the start. He and I made our connection that day. It lasted forever. And John was vital as we began recruiting other college students into nonviolent direct action training. Both the NCLC and our workshops were initially slow to take off. I was also still finding my way with FOR.

After two months of almost nonstop travels around the South, in early April, I went home to Ohio for a few days. I saw Aiko one afternoon during that trip, and we talked about continuing our relationship. We wanted to try to make it work, but it wasn't clear how we could, since I was becoming increasingly committed to my work in the South and had applied to attend Vanderbilt Divinity School in the fall. And she was obligated to go back to Japan after her studies. She agreed that FOR was the right fit for me. So we kept it open and we kept in touch. I did not date anyone else, and neither did she.

In between my other travels and appearances that winter and spring, I repeatedly returned to Little Rock by myself for one, two, or three days at a time, because of the Little Rock Nine. I wanted to be sure that the students made up their own minds, had their own ideas, and operated out of their best character. We had small get-togethers, as well as gatherings in a church after school, where the nine students met with seventy-five to 125 supporters, including Black pastors, other Black students and parents, and some white students, too.

During one of my visits with the nine students, one of the girls, Carlotta Walls, told us about a white boy in her eight A.M. class who had "bombed" her again. She said that this bomb had whizzed by her ear, missing her, but had hit the wall beside her and dropped to the floor. Her legs became shaky as an idea came to her: She walked to the wall, stooped down to the floor, and picked up that rock and took it over to the boy's desk. She didn't say how she knew it was him, but he had always been a major tormentor. She gently put the rock on his desk, in front of him. And with her best energy, she simply looked him in the eye and smiled. According to her report, that changed the boy so much that his name came off the list they were keeping of the people who were trying to hurt them the most. The next morning when she walked into the classroom, he was standing by the door. He said, "Good morning," and smiled at her. And he was never again one of those doing the tormenting.

The fact that she had responded calmly, no matter the fear churning inside her, was extraordinary. The Little Rock Nine were surrounded by our nation's culture of violence: segregation, the governor, the school board, and the parents of white kids. But Carlotta, in the highest moment of torment, had reflected back to the world not her agony but her humanity, the inward awareness that she was a human being and was acting out of human goodness.

That is what I was trying to share with the Little Rock Nine. I told them, "Do not let yourselves get sick. You must fight back, but do it without anger. And do it without imitating the folk who are fighting you. They're wrong, so don't copy their wrong." I didn't tell the students what to do. Rather, I urged them to resist from within themselves. "Use your imagination," I would say. "Be creative. Be courageous. Figure out how you can say no to what they're doing to you and not let them drive you out of that school."

We talked about how their opponents were living with a sense that Black people must know their place, and how that place involved not competing with white people. That place did not come with good wages or a medical degree. We discussed how racism doesn't only damage the targets. It also damages the perpetrators. Although the perpetrators are usually unaware of how their behavior has damaged them.

The students' best defense against racism, I said, was in their character, in what they were seeking to do in joining the struggle to end segregation.

For instance, the Black high school in Little Rock, Dunbar High, had no sufficient science laboratory. Central had any number of good labs. I pointed out that all of their Dunbar classmates deserved a good biology lab and a good chemistry lab. But segregation prevented them from having access to one. So, they were fighting this fight for things like getting good labs at Dunbar. Sometimes, articulating a simple, material goal clarifies the mission.

Of course, as I went from place to place in the South, I ran into violence and harassment myself. I was in and out of Little Rock a lot during 1958. Once, early on, at the Little Rock Continental bus station, I went up to the magazine counter to buy a package of gum. I was also looking for a magazine. The man behind the counter said, "I won't serve you unless you walk around to the colored waiting area." I didn't move. I never used the "colored" waiting room, because I would not obey segregation rules. I just stood there as he finished with a customer in front of me. He said again, "I'm not going to serve you." I stood there a little while longer. Then I changed the subject on him, striking up a friendly conversation by asking him something about Little Rock, or about his family. I never felt any rage during this incident. I just tried to engage him in a cordial exchange. He eventually talked to me, and we had a nice visit. Then he served me. I had become a human being to him, and it had challenged him to treat me another way. After that, every time I came back through there, we talked and were friendly and he served me.

Another time early on, I was driving with Glenn Smiley in Maryland, heading back to Nashville. It was midmorning, and we had been to a meeting in Baltimore. We decided to stop for coffee at a Howard Johnson's restaurant along the highway. We went in and waited for a few minutes, but no one seated us. Finally, a waitress said that she couldn't serve us because of a Maryland law that required a public restaurant to have two restrooms, one for white and one for Black people, if Black people were going to be customers. We asked to talk to the manager, who was a youngish guy in this thirties.

Standing near the restaurant's counter, we sort of jokingly pointed out to him that we hadn't asked for a restroom. We only wanted coffee, so the law didn't apply to us. He sort of smiled at that. He could see the point. Then we said, "No one has walked out since we have been standing here talking to you. What do you think would happen if we had gone ahead and sat down and you had served us?" He said, "I don't know." We said, "Why don't you try." He said, "Well, I'll try anything once."

Then the waitress who had refused us the first time said, "I won't serve them." But another waitress spoke up and said, "I will." So we sat down and had coffee. Nothing happened. And the manager said goodbye as we were leaving. I don't remember any rage in that situation, either.

Whenever someone refused me service, I never let it end there. I would always either try to talk to the manager or to take action right then and there, on the spot. I felt fearful some of the time. Other times, I was quite indignant and outraged. But generally it was not when I was personally being threatened. I would get most angry and outraged over the treatment of others. I think that's because for most of my days I have had a fairly deep sense of personal identity and security, and a sense of who I am and what I am. Very few things on the outside can threaten that.

Sometimes members of my congregations and other people have said to me that you need to get mad and angry, and cuss a few times. But that's never been a part of my way of thinking or relating to people. When I face hostility, it's more of a challenge to me, an opportunity to see what can happen, rather than a time to feel angry or threatened.

In early May, I went back to Ohio once more to visit my mother. I also saw Aiko. That was when we decided we could not make our relationship work. We were good friends. But I had a revelation in that moment that I needed to marry a Black American woman. In India, I had realized that marrying a white woman in the 1950s was not a challenge I wanted. My strong feelings for Aiko had taught me that I definitely could fall for a woman who wasn't Black. But when it came to making a decision of whether to take the next step, I realized marrying a woman who wasn't Black would create too many problems for any relationship because of the work I had to do in the South and in the movement with Martin Luther King. Growing up with five older sisters and a strong mother gave me a huge respect and some glimpses of what Black woman experienced in our nation. That affinity and familiarity, and a shared understanding of the challenges of Black people that we would be addressing in our movement, all pointed me to the decision that I wanted to marry a Black woman. Aiko and I broke up in the first week of May. We were sad, but we felt sure of our decision.

The next week, I participated in a weekend retreat on high school integration at the Highlander Folk School in Monteagle, Tennessee. Leaders from around the South attended, including Rev. Will Campbell, a Baptist from Nashville, and Rev. Andrew Young from Atlanta, who was in the Congregational Church, which became the United Church of Christ. I knew his family, since his younger brother Walter Young was attending Baldwin-Wallace when I got back there for my last semester in 1952. At Highlander Folk School, humanistic, integrated groups could meet, talk, and visit. Almost always, they tried to recruit a handful of Black folk. But since Highlander had originally been created for the purpose of fortifying unionism, and unions were mostly white then, its main purpose was not to address segregation. For all its virtues, Highlander was still considered pretty white.

The most momentous part of that retreat by far was meeting Will Campbell. He was the head of the racial justice program at the National Council of Churches, based in Nashville. The minute we met, we connected, related, and engaged. So much so that he offered me a ride back to Nashville on the Monday after the retreat was over. Will's view of theology came closer to my own biblical position than that of anyone else I had ever met in the white community. We didn't always agree about the efficacies of nonviolence. But he at least clearly understood the nonviolent demand that I tried to preach, practice, and teach.

Meeting Will also led me to the most important connection I would ever make in my life.

When he and I arrived back in Nashville, we stopped off at his office at the Scarritt College campus, adjacent to Vanderbilt. We walked in, and I was delighted to see that Will's secretary was a Black woman. In that moment, my appreciation of Will Campbell went up even further. That a white man would hire a Black woman as his secretary—this was never done. It would never have been done in Ohio at that time, much less in Tennessee. And when I turned to meet her, I immediately recognized how extraordinary she was to have taken such a job. I mean, being a Black secretary in a white office just wasn't something many Black women did anywhere in the country at that time, especially in the South. I thought she must have had an exceptional character to withstand the pressure of such a situation in Nashville.

Of course, I also noticed right away that she was quite attractive. When our eyes first met, I grinned. She smiled, too. Will introduced us. Her name was Dorothy Wood. I recognized that the important work she was doing with Will was in line with my principles and goals. And even in our brief visit in Will's office that day, there was no doubt that Dorothy and I clicked and were attracted to each other. So I asked for her phone number. And I called her later that evening. It was Monday, May 19, when I met Dorothy at her job. We went on our first date on the following Saturday, May 24. I took her to a movie at the Ritz, a Black-owned theater across the street from Fisk University, on North Jefferson Street in Nashville.

When Aiko and I broke it off, I had made the decision that I wanted to marry a Black American woman. I had also decided then that I would date only people I was attracted to for marriage. Within a week of those decisions, I met my Dorothy.

In the first weeks of dating, I didn't tell her I was studying to become a minister in the Methodist Church, because women often said they would never marry a pastor. The life of a clergyman meant a lot of sacrifice on the wife's part. So I didn't bring that into the picture until a few weeks later. Instead, on that first date, I told her about my work in FOR and how I had met Will, and about some of the experiences I was having with the Little Rock Nine. And we talked about Martin King. I liked her immediately for who she was, and was so pleased that she clearly had a steadfast, well-thought-out Christian faith.

Three days after that first date with Dorothy, on May 27, 1958, I was in Arkansas again, with Martin. Early in the day, I attended his commencement speech at Arkansas AM&N, a historically Black college in Pine Bluff. Then we drove together to Little Rock for Ernest Green's graduation from Central High School. He was the only senior among the Little Rock Nine. And at that ceremony, Martin and I were probably the only two "outside agitators." That's what white conservative Southerners called anyone who wasn't local and was in town working for racial justice.

I was beginning to establish relationships with activists in key Southern cities, including Birmingham, Memphis, and Little Rock, and working hard to find other connections in multiple places around the South. In July, I got word that I had been accepted at Vanderbilt Divinity School. For part of July and much of August, I traveled through the South, as well as to Ohio and the East Coast. As the summer went on, my relationship with Dorothy grew more serious. We wrote letters to each other when we were apart.

On July 22, she wrote to me:

> This separation has been good in the sense that I am still conscious of your presence and am becoming increasingly aware of how much you mean to me. You must know that I miss you—the moments we shared in many fine and dear ways.
>
> I know you are busy but don't be so aloof in your next letter (just a suggestion, I am keeping the right thought-process). I must close for now but just remember that Dorothy thinks of you often and misses you and awaits your return. Hurry home.

Classes began at the end of September, just as I turned thirty. I was the fourth Black student ever to be accepted at Vanderbilt. The trustees had decided to admit only Black graduate students and no undergraduates. They had accepted two Black men from Nashville as law students, without announcing it to anyone. And they had accepted me as a graduate student. The divinity school and the law school at Vanderbilt wanted to be ahead of the other large universities with Methodist origins—Duke, Emory, and Southern Methodist—in terms of desegregation. In 1953, the divinity school had admitted the university's first Black student, Joseph A. Johnson Jr., who went on to be a professor of theology and a bishop in the CME Church. But four years later, the university only wanted to admit a few more of us quietly and slowly. They expected colored students to come to Vanderbilt and be largely invisible—go to classes and go home. We were not supposed to participate in life on the campus. No one told me that directly. But I knew. I was not expected to eat in the university cafeterias. And I was not offered a place to live on campus. Rather, I lived about five blocks away from the Vanderbilt Divinity School, on Twenty-First Avenue.

Since I loved sports, I joined the university's touch football league. And I joined the divinity school's basketball team. I was the only Black player on those teams. It was a first for the university. At lunchtime on the very first day of classes, a group of students in the divinity school who knew me from Methodist circles said, "Jim, let's go to lunch." So I ate with them on campus at Rand Hall, in the main cafeteria. I was the only Black person there. At Vanderbilt, I was challenging the segregation on campus while studying Christian teachings for my degree work.

I was not following the pattern white people at Vanderbilt and in Nashville had envisioned for me. During registration, for instance, while standing in a line to sign up for classes, I learned that Vanderbilt discounted tickets to the symphony downtown for their faculty members and students. Pleased to hear this since I loved music, I took advantage of that perk. I invited Dorothy, and she agreed to go with me.

When we arrived at the auditorium, we were reflexively ushered to a Negroes-only section of the balcony. But another usher looked at our tickets and told us our seats were on the concert hall's first floor. So we went back downstairs and showed our tickets to the usher there, who seemed a little surprised. Still, we were led to our seats, and we sat down to enjoy the performance. And that is how Dorothy and I desegregated the Nashville Symphony Hall in 1958.

Martin was in New York City in September for the publication of his first book, *Stride Toward Freedom*. It was his first-person account of the Montgomery campaign and also touched on influences in his early life. The book had gotten very good reviews, and he was beginning a tour to promote it. Three days after the release, he was signing books at Blumstein's department store in Harlem, when a forty-two-year-old woman stabbed him with a letter opener. She was reported to be mentally ill. The wound was almost fatal. But thankfully, he was taken to Harlem Hospital and saved.

I was stunned. We all were. Violence was chasing the leader of our budding nonviolent movement not in the South but in Harlem, where life was supposed to be safer for Black people than almost anywhere else in the country. Real fear of losing him hit me. Everyone around him knew the stakes were getting higher as he and our work got more attention. The rest of Martin's book tour was postponed. Slowly he grew stronger, and in late October he returned to Montgomery to recover further.

Even as I was immersed in my graduate studies, I was also continuing to conduct workshops, and to speak and work with FOR around the South. I had been focusing a portion of my energies specifically on both Birmingham and Memphis for a few months. In Memphis, I had a couple of meetings in 1958 and 1959 with Black clergy and community leaders interested in bringing nonviolence training to the city. We planned a conference, "Christian Nonviolence and Racial Tensions," for early November.

In Birmingham, issues were at a boiling point by that fall. For years, racist terrorism had gripped the city. The leading local advocate for desegregation, Rev. Fred Shuttlesworth, had survived a Ku Klux Klan bombing of his church and his home—the Bethel Baptist Church parsonage—on Christmas in 1956, the night before a planned demonstration to protest bus segregation laws in Birmingham. In 1957, white segregationists brutally beat Shuttlesworth and stabbed his wife, Ruby, when they tried to enroll their children in an all-white public school. They survived another bombing of Fred's church in 1958. Klansmen in collusion with local police officers were responsible for these attacks, but they were never convicted of any of them. Shuttlesworth had been one of the founders of the SCLC in 1957, and an active member of the Alabama NAACP. When the state of Alabama had outlawed the NAACP in 1956, he had founded the Alabama Christian Movement for Human Rights (ACMHR), which carried on the NAACP's work.

On October 20, 1958, dozens of Black demonstrators boarded city buses and took seats in the front to resist segregation, as had been done successfully in Montgomery almost two years before. In the end, thirteen local ministers who had boarded buses were arrested and held in jail for violating the Jim Crow bus policies. Fred Shuttlesworth was not among them, but he was arrested in the aftermath, accused of organizing the demonstration.

The next week, three Montgomery ministers involved in the Montgomery boycott arrived in Birmingham for an emergency ACMHR board meeting at Reverend Shuttlesworth's home. He was still in jail. At noon, four police detectives entered the house without warrants and arrested the three ministers and put them in jail, too, for planning a bus boycott in Birmingham.

I arrived later that afternoon and spoke to a mass meeting that night. By the end of the week, leaders had decided that a boycott of the bus system would begin on November 1. But the lack of organization and planning among the people who opposed segregation troubled me. And there was deep division between Shuttlesworth and other ministers leading the movement in Birmingham. I especially did not feel that the leadership had a handle on how to proceed nonviolently. I saw a need for nonviolence training among the leaders and then among the supporters of desegregation. I wrote to Will Campbell, saying I feared that Birmingham might become "a bloody battlefield," and "could well prove to be a tragic city" if there was not unity among the Black ministerial leadership there.

On November 3, I also wrote to Martin to express my best wishes for his recovery and to update him on my experience in Birmingham.

> Dear Martin,
>
> It is good to know that you are back in Montgomery again and see from your statement from the early part of this month that your recent experience in New York has served only to strengthen your Christian life and understanding. I, like everyone else, was quite shocked to suddenly hear of this incident. The more I thought of it, however, the more it seemed to me somehow that this was God's way of speaking to you. It convinced me further that he has great plans for you in the achieving of a beloved community in our time. Rest assured of my continuing prayer and high regard for you.
>
> I have just returned from Birmingham. . . . We may be on the threshold of a major breakthrough. However, so much of this is dependent upon the unity of the leadership. I suspect that Fred Shuttlesworth, in spite of his great courage and drive, is in real need of personal counseling which probably can only come from you.

I also reiterated to him my long-held vision of the movement we were creating:

> I have been convinced for nearly 12 years now that the only hope for the Negro in this country is a genuine movement of nonviolence

> which reflects many of the characteristics of the Montgomery boycott and which strikes not only at the fear of the Negro but also at the power structure of the nation which continues to perpetuate social injustice. If this is to happen it will be because of the ministry uniting as one body and giving initiative leadership to the countless number of Negroes who urgently want such leadership.

Martin and I were becoming trusted friends as well as partners in the movement. I was making another significant personal and professional connection in Birmingham in 1958, with Rev. Nelson Smith and his wife, Leslie. He had helped found the ACMHR and was the pastor of New Pilgrim Baptist Church in Birmingham, where many mass meetings were held. I got to know him and his family during my visits in 1958 and I would stay with the Nelsons when I came in and out of Birmingham through the years that followed. They became dear friends to me and Dorothy. And the SCLC greatly relied on Nelson as a leader in Birmingham as the movement continued, even as Fred Shuttlesworth left the city in 1961 but remained involved with the movement there.

A few weeks after my time in Birmingham in the fall of 1958, I spent Thanksgiving at Dorothy's family home in Charleston, Tennessee, about three hours east of Nashville. But during the long holiday weekend, a popular white evangelist and faith healer at the time, Oral Roberts, brought his Million Souls for Christ crusade to Nashville. He held large gatherings at the Nashville Fairgrounds Coliseum, where he preached of healing the sick by laying on of hands. The NCLC got word that the five-day event was to be segregated. Black people would be allowed only in a designated area in a balcony off the main floor. So I came back to town to attend the event with some other Black clergy members.

We went into the coliseum and about five of us found seats on the floor, despite threats of arrest and physical violence. Some people were asked to go to the balcony but did not, and instead we asked to speak to those responsible for making the event segregated. We got no resolution and ended up leaving.

I wrote Oral Roberts a letter telling him about our experience at the event and questioning his policy. He sent me back a less than adequate response. So I replied to his letter, calling out the segregation he supported:

Dear Brother Roberts,

> Many thanks for the response of your letter of last week. I, likewise, send you brotherly greetings in the name of Christ. May I say, however, in love, that your letter does not answer the basic issue I tried to raise with you. . . .
>
> . . . I have reached the place where I no longer am able to accept pious statements about integration or about race. The only thing I can accept is the authentic witness of a life which no longer participates in the social sins of our time. This is to say, as frankly as I dare, and yet as one who has nothing but Christian regard for you, that you cannot remain a consistent disciple if . . . meetings you conduct shall be segregated. It might be a hard decision for one in your position to have to make but it is these radical decisions that Christ calls each of us to make.

That was the kind of letter I wrote many times over as we began our all-out challenges to segregation wherever we saw it or experienced it.

After Thanksgiving with Dorothy and her family at their home, it became clearer and clearer to me that she was the one, and that we were going to marry. We had dated exclusively since May 24. She was becoming more involved in my work. Our interests aligned naturally as she continued her work with Will Campbell, which had been her first job after graduating from Tennessee State University. For Christmas 1958, Dorothy and I agreed I would return to Charleston and spend it with her family.

I greatly admired her father, Curtis Wood. He was one of this country's unheralded pioneers: Black men who did the best they could with their families but very often were shunted aside and ignored professionally. They did not have a job like a pastor or a teacher, but they were the leaders of their communities, forward-looking people who stood their ground. Her dad was the clerk for the Second Presbyterian Church in Charleston, which was part of an all-Black Presbyterian denomination. By the time I met him, he was known across both Black and white groups of Presbyterians. He hated racism and segregation, and he would often speak up in their area of East Tennessee, which included Charleston, the county seat of Cleveland, and the rest of Bradley County. Although he was a high school graduate, he could never get a decent job. So he opened two or three of his own businesses and drove a bus. With that, he managed to get all three of his kids through college. Dorothy's two brothers also graduated from Tennessee State.

I was impressed by her father's character and also by her mother. And I know her father and mother were both impressed by the work I did with the Southern Christian Leadership Conference and the Fellowship of Reconciliation, and because I was a colleague of Martin Luther King Jr.'s. That was all a plus for any number of people in her family's circle.

Of course, according to her brothers, nobody was good enough for her. But her brothers and I got along very well. She had a sizable extended family in Charleston too, all of whom accepted me from the start, and adopted me. Also, the Black community that surrounded her and her family was solid.

I had bought a ring, and I proposed to her on Christmas Day. But I pulled a trick on her, which I believe upset her, even though she never admitted it. I put the ring in the box it came in, and then I wrapped the ring box in a slightly larger box, and then I wrapped that second box in an even larger box.

We were at her parents' house, but it was just the two of us when I gave her my Christmas gift for her from under the tree. The box was much larger than a ring box. I don't think she knew for sure, but it frustrated her that in the first unwrapping there was another box, and then *another* box. I thought it was funny. I remember proposing to Dorothy as a good experience. But I think that she was a little perturbed by all those boxes.

Still, she said yes.

EIGHT

Let My People Go

Nonviolence training for sit-ins, Clark Memorial Methodist Church, Nashville, 1959. SCLC

In Nashville at the end of 1958 and coming into 1959, the big issue for Martin, Kelly Miller Smith, me, and about a hundred others in the movement was where the next Montgomery would be. When and how could such a successful campaign occur again? After more than a year of touring in the South, I talked with Glenn Smiley and A. J. Muste at FOR and we agreed that I should give a major portion of my time to making the second campaign of the current movement happen.

Almost immediately, I realized this new campaign was going to have to be in Nashville. We had a good start there with the Nashville Christian Leadership Council—already established as an early affiliate of the SCLC. It had a strong director in Rev. Kelly Miller Smith, and leaders like AME minister Rev. Andrew White, a doctor named Charles Walker, and an activist named Johnetta Hayes. Agitation and protest had happened in other places. But I had found no other local group engaged in the struggle at that time with the depth and commitment of the NCLC.

It would help that Nashville's segregation was not enforced by law. It was a custom or policy throughout the city, so we wouldn't have to go to court to challenge laws. And the city had a newspaper, *The Nashville Tennessean,* that was somewhat more open to covering racial injustice and our movement than most others in the South. Also, Nashville was home to three Black colleges (Fisk, American Baptist Theological Seminary, and Meharry Medical College), a Black state university (Tennessee A&I), and a major white university (Vanderbilt), all with groups of students and professors open to new ideas and change. It was the state capital too, with a political life beyond the city government and with statehouse workers and the governor living in town. Our impact could potentially be multiplied beyond one city. Furthermore, the Black community in Nashville had already begun to organize, with Black lawyers and clergy members leading the way. Nashville clearly provided just the right setting to ignite and sustain a campaign.

I went to Kelly with the idea of launching a major campaign in Nashville to confirm the effectiveness of the desegregation strategies used in Montgomery and to show that they could be repeated locally. He agreed. The NCLC board agreed, too. By January 1959, we began planning our nonviolent direct action campaign, and I was to be the primary organizer and strategist. Kelly and I began holding Saturday morning meetings, following a Gandhian methodology.

First, we would do the fact-finding: investigate and make a sort of laundry list of the plights and tortures Black people faced in Nashville. For almost six months, we simply sought out descriptions of all the separate manifestations of racism and segregation that were hurting Black people and the community. From March through May, we held a series of discussions at Kelly's church, the First Baptist Church, located downtown, to hear from as many Black Nashville residents as possible. We listened to what they were up against. We examined everything anyone brought forth and tried to get a detailed account of it.

Some of the big problems were segregation in the schools, police violence against the Black community, and even the fact that Black people couldn't be tellers in banks. People also told us of hostile treatment in the banks where they were customers. As the investigation process progressed, we heard more and more stories about downtown, which was the center of business, of the economy. Downtown was where many people worked, but almost all of the jobs for Black people were as maids and janitors. No white-collar jobs were open to Black people in Nashville in 1959, including being a cashier in a department store or a grocery store. In the places where Black people bought groceries, clothing, or shoes, there were no Black folk clerking or waiting on customers.

By the end of May we had a list that shook us, of the indignities and threats Black people had to endure merely to survive day to day in Nashville in 1959. It included the separate water fountains marked "Colored," white people of all ages calling adult men and women "boy" and "girl," and workplaces where no Black people could advance beyond menial work. Yet the more we heard from Black mothers, the more we were particularly moved.

One woman, whose account I will never forget, said, "You men don't really know what life is like in segregation. We are the ones who shop. When we go into downtown Nashville, there is no place we can stop with dignity and rest our feet. There's no place we can sit down and have a cup of coffee." She said there were no restrooms that were not marked either "Colored Ladies" or "Colored" period, which usually meant Black women and their children were relegated to a toilet in the basement of a store, if they were lucky, because they were not allowed to use the customer restrooms that white women and their children used.

A few women described how at Harveys, a major downtown department store, there was a beautiful children's area on the third or fourth floor where white mothers and their children could stop, and their children could play on nice swings and sit in animal-shaped seats. The white mothers could have a cup of tea or coffee or a cold drink and relax for a few moments before they went on and finished their business. The Black mothers told us about having to explain to their children why they could not play on the merry-go-round or with the toy cars, as the white kids did at Harveys. Then one woman said to us directly, "You preachers and our husbands do not know the pain of having to shop downtown for our family. We do your shopping for you, so we're the ones who bear the brunt of the racism, of the segregation in Nashville."

We heard many stories of how Black women had to brace themselves every day, to find the courage and confidence they needed merely to shop for groceries in a downtown with "Whites Only" signs all around them, degrading them, and enforcing hostility toward their very existence.

Another woman told us about buying shoes for her three-year-old boy: "We could not try on the shoes in the store. I had to buy the shoes and go home to find that the shoes were a little bit too wide or long for my small son. Then I had to go back to the store." If her son had simply been allowed to try on the shoes in the store before she bought them, she would have found the right fit immediately. There would have been no going back with her receipt to get a new pair of shoes that also might not fit, forcing her to go through the same process yet again.

Those two or three unnecessary trips back and forth meant riding on public transportation that was not designed for the comfort of Black people or the service of their needs. By 1959, Nashville's bus company had pulled its segregation signs down. Yet there was still an understanding that Black people would sit in the back, and white people would sit in the front. The system was still patently racist, and still segregated. These wrongs had gone on for years without change. But our generation was no longer willing to tolerate the intolerable.

The Black women proposed a large target: to desegregate downtown Nashville. Until that time, no group of Negroes in any city, including Montgomery, had made the decision to desegregate their entire downtown and succeeded. That is, no one had gotten the segregation signs pulled down, changed the restroom language, integrated segregated waiting rooms, demanded service in a restaurant or at a lunch counter, and insisted that Black children could play on the carousel in a department store.

But the Black women of Nashville, many of whom were activists in the community already, impressed upon us their urgent need at that exact moment in 1959. Voting in elections and engaging in long legal battles would not soon enough change the psychological, spiritual, and moral toll they had shouldered for years. They were prepared for and committed to standing up against the abuse then and there. Those Saturday morning community workshops gave us our spiritual and moral target.

As I grasped how large our ambition was to be, I was astonished, and I was anxious. I realized I had to put up or shut up, although I never said that to myself. I do remember thinking, "Good Lord, what are you putting me into?" I was concerned that I did not know enough or have enough experience to deal with such a large, powerful goal. I had never done something like this before, nor had anybody else. It was too late to turn back. I had no choice but to commit myself to making it happen.

Before anything else though, Dorothy and I had a wedding planned. On July 3, 1959, after fourteen months of dating, we got married in Charleston, Tennessee, at Dorothy's home church, Green's Chapel Second Presbyterian Church. Both my mother and my father came to the wedding. It was a glorious family celebration. I had found the love of my life. Marrying Dorothy Wood helped to affirm and stabilize my purpose and path. There have been three significant women named Dorothy in my life: my aunt who was my mother's sister, my oldest sister, and then my wife. Committing to her not only brought us both deep joy and everlasting love but also strengthened our shared quest for justice. I had a wife in the same field, working with the National Council of Churches, who both understood and was prepared to continue that work alongside me. We took a little time to enjoy our marriage. But our life's work was beginning right away.

The plans for a Nashville campaign were coming along, while my FOR work continued. Later in July, the SCLC and FOR organized an institute at Spelman College in Atlanta on nonviolence and the dismantling of segregation. Martin and Glenn gave the keynote addresses. Martin had finally gotten to go to India earlier in the year, where he met with numerous people who had worked with Gandhi and carried out nonviolent direct action during India's struggle for independence from Great Britain. The trip deepened Martin's commitment to nonviolence.

Various discussion groups and panels took place during the three-day gathering. Martin, Bayard Rustin, and I led a session on the process of nonviolent resistance. Glenn Smiley and John Lewis ran other sessions, as did Ella Baker, who was working as the executive director of the SCLC at the time. It was an exciting event in the early days of our work. We were kindred spirits coming together to foster a nonviolent revolution.

In mid-August, I made my first venture into Mississippi, a place that had always seemed to be at the heart of American racial terrorism. I was a featured speaker at the Southern Christian Ministers Conference in Jackson, Mississippi, along with Martin and Ella Baker. Then, in September, Glenn and I presented a workshop on nonviolence at the SCLC national convention in Columbia, South Carolina. Those conventions each year reminded us of our larger struggle and included major figures like Thurgood Marshall; Roy Wilkins; Whitney Young, the head of the Urban League; and Dorothy Height, president of the National Council of Negro Women. Afterward, we would all go back to the tasks at hand.

The next step in our campaign to desegregate downtown Nashville was deep preparation and planning. We decided to start with the restaurants inside department stores, as a symbol of the entire problem. Even though he still spent time engaged in the work in the South, Glenn Smiley had moved back to FOR headquarters in Nyack, New York. But from afar, he still provided good leadership and gave me useful advice about Nashville. Kelly, the NCLC, and I began to recruit people to our cause that summer, inviting them to join our nonviolence training workshops in the fall.

I knew we had to find and cultivate young people, high school and college students, because they could be shaped and formed. That's why the military goes after eighteen-year-olds. And I felt, in a sense, that we were building a nonviolent army. Young people would be the ones most available to go through constructive training in nonviolent direct action. Young people would bring the right amount of enthusiasm and physical energy. They would also bring mental idealism and spiritual curiosity. They would *be natural* at it.

Kelly had already recruited John Lewis the year before, when John was his student at American Baptist Theological Seminary. Kelly knew John wanted to beat up on the racism and economic injustice he had lived through growing up in Troy, Alabama. John in turn recruited Bernard Lafayette, another student at American Baptist. Bernard had grown up in poverty in Tampa, Florida. One of his earliest memories was of trying to travel to downtown Tampa with his grandmother in a streetcar where segregation meant they had to pay the driver at the front and then exit the streetcar and walk around to the back door to enter and find a seat. But drivers would start driving off before they could reboard, taking their money and leaving them without a ride. Rev. C. T. Vivian, who had been involved in the founding of the SCLC and was a member of the NCLC executive committee, also recruited some people. Marion Barry, from Memphis, was in that first group. He was starting graduate work in organic chemistry at Fisk, having graduated the previous spring from LeMoyne-Owen College in Memphis, where he had been president of the student NAACP. Marion had nearly been expelled in his junior year there after criticizing a white trustee of the college for racist public comments.

I recruited a white exchange student named Paul LaPrad, who had come to Fisk from Indiana. He was a member of the Church of the Brethren, one of the three historic peace churches. Along with the Quakers and Mennonites, the Brethren believed in Christian pacifism. Before coming to Fisk, Paul asked people he knew who he should meet in Nashville and was told, "You call Jim Lawson. He will help you through." Soon after he arrived, he called, and I invited him to join the campaign. Paul became one of our recruiters, and told me about Diane Nash, a Fisk student from Chicago. Paul said Diane was alarmed and upset walking around segregated downtown Nashville, being exposed for the first time to the physical signs of segregation and the embedded inequalities of the Jim Crow South. I told Paul, "Recruit her, and recruit anyone else."

I called Dorothy's brother Phillip Wood, who was a first-year student at Tennessee Agricultural & Industrial, also called Tennessee State, the Black state university in Nashville, and told him what we were doing. I asked him to join us. He said no very emphatically. At eighteen or nineteen, he felt that being involved in the movement was just not where he was in his life. But he said his roommate, Curtis Murphy, might be interested. Curtis had grown up in rural West Tennessee. He was so smart that he had outgrown the schooling there. So he moved in with his aunt, sixty miles away in Memphis, where the Black schools were better, and attended Booker T. Washington High School. When Curtis headed to Tennessee A&I, his father told him, "Don't you join any of that stuff that's going on in civil rights. Don't get kicked out." Despite his father's fears, Curtis agreed to be at the workshops. His name is not as well known as those of some of the other people who emerged from this group, but Curtis became one of our finest leaders.

Each time we recruited one person, we asked them to recruit other people. We wanted as many people as possible to come to the workshop because it would be preparation for the downtown campaign. In the end, we had somewhere between twenty and thirty participants at the first fall workshop on a Tuesday night at Clark Memorial Methodist Church, a small church near the Fisk campus.

I had no idea how many people would be there. Who knew if everyone who said they were coming would show up? When I walked in and saw the small group, I said to myself, "This is an insufficient group—not enough people." My doubts were confirmed that first night. Yet I knew this was a long-term campaign, and such things often start small.

Clark Memorial Methodist Church's fellowship hall was rectangular, at least fifteen by forty feet. It was in the basement, so the windows were along the tops of the walls. We met in the evenings, which meant there wasn't much light down there, especially in the wintertime. Few people knew the others there. They were from four different Black colleges in proximity to one another on the north side of Nashville. Clark was the perfect place for us to meet and feel safe—near Jefferson Street, within blocks of the Fisk and Meharry campuses, and about a mile away from Tennessee A&I. This meant that most students could walk there. Community members parked in the church parking lot, and students from American Baptist Theological Seminary got rides.

At the beginning, we introduced ourselves and said why we each had come. In those early workshops, there was no one from predominantly white schools in Nashville, like Vanderbilt or Belmont College. Paul LaPrad was the only white person in that original core group. Other students who were with us from the start included Dolores Wilkerson, Rodney Powell, and Gloria Johnson. C. T. Vivian was one of the adults in the core group.

I began the workshop with an explanation of nonviolence and why it works. I introduced the participants to Gandhi, and some of the other people I had learned about in college. I brought up some of the Black folk in the United States who had adopted nonviolence, including Bayard Rustin and author and theologian Howard Thurman, who met Gandhi and brought his teachings back to the social justice movement in the United States in the 1930s. I also spoke about Europeans like those involved in the underground, nonviolent Danish resistance in World War II as well as the Norwegian teachers who had resisted Nazi occupation, an account that was circulating quite a bit back then. And I introduced them to the story of William Penn and the settlement of Pennsylvania, which was a nonviolent Quaker experiment.

We hadn't been meeting long when another American Baptist Theological student, James Bevel, joined the group. At first, he was only giving John Lewis and Bernard Lafayette rides from Fisk and going on about his business. He was reluctant to join. He was from a large family in Mississippi, where he had picked cotton as a child and later joined the military before coming to the seminary. Others told me that James thought I was a fool. After he finally came to one of the workshops, James said, he went to the library and found books on some of the things I had talked about to see whether I was speaking the truth. He was a good critic. He eventually came around and became part of the group. John Lewis said he also went to the library to find books from some of the people and events from history I mentioned. But I did not assign any reading or give the participants a syllabus. We were not in a classroom. I was organizing people to launch a campaign.

Among people who called themselves progressive, there was an idea that young people would make everything better. But successful movements have to recruit intergenerationally to achieve justice goals. The whole community must be engaged. The wisdom and experience from people of all ages are essential for opening hearts and minds within a movement, and among the opposition. So C. T. Vivian was not the only community member in those workshops. In fact, Black women activists shaped our mission. And at the beginning of the Nashville campaign, the NCLC, which launched the campaign and recruited people to join, did not have a student in it.

Once you include young people, though, they have to be equal partners. They can't be brought in and told what to do. I understood that young people in our country, as well as adults, were steeped in the conventional status quo of our violent American culture. Accepting the supremacy of violence was a seemingly immutable effect of being born in the United States. Such trust in violence as the ultimate power meant resistance to nonviolence was ingrained in most of us. I couldn't change anyone's immersion in U.S. culture. I only asked everyone who joined us to be willing to consider other options, including practices people from other places lived by—alternatives to violence that made life better and helped to cast off oppression. People had to be encouraged in the workshops to see nonviolence as an alternative to the chaos of violence they knew and had internalized. They had to come at their own pace to seeing it as a tool to change the status quo, to dismantle the racist structures of segregation and allow justice to emerge.

One of the ways I presented nonviolence in the workshops was to say: "We have not yet become a democratic society. So, a lot of dismantling of the wrong still must be carried out. Nonviolent direct action is an effective way to go about doing that work—on your own behalf and on behalf of your families."

I told everyone in the very first workshop, "United States culture has conditioned us all to the absolute validity of violence—leading most people to think guns, bombs, and nightsticks are the greatest sources of power. But guns and wars don't transform hearts and minds—yours or anyone else's. Violence violates the human spirit, the will to be fully alive, and to build communities of justice and love." It was 1959, and Dwight Eisenhower was president, so I reminded them that he once said, "I hate war as only a soldier who has lived it can . . . its brutality, its futility, its stupidity." From day one, I pushed hard on that idea, and on the famous Civil War quotation from U.S. General Tecumseh Sherman: "War is hell."

My point was to drive that home, so nobody mistook the gravity of what we were attempting. And to emphasize our nonviolent intent, I added: "You cannot use hell to create heaven. You cannot overcome evil with evil. You overcome evil with good. Violence only increases dangers—seen and unseen. Only nonviolence, which is love and justice in action, can resolve conflict and dissipate danger in a way that is not destructive."

I asked them to commit themselves during our campaign of using nonviolent responses to aggression. Because for any insult or injury, nonviolence has an answer. The idea was to teach them to see the incident clearly, and prepare themselves in heart, mind, and feelings to handle antagonism fearlessly and without violence.

From the first workshop and throughout the training process, I lifted up Jesus as a nonviolent practitioner. I knew that Diane Nash was agnostic but had grown up as a Roman Catholic in Chicago. I knew that John Lewis was a Baptist who'd been immersed in the water in Alabama. I knew that 99 percent of the workshop participants were members of Christian churches in their youth, if not in college. I felt the literature of the Bible was the place to begin to teach them what the science of nonviolence was about, and to inspire them to see its effectiveness throughout history.

I turned to Jesus of Nazareth and the Book of Exodus in the Hebrew Bible. It is the first written account we have of a people's movement that allowed those who were enslaved to escape and start on their own development. Then I talked about how enslaved Black people in the United States were forced to sing when working in the fields, so that the enslavers knew where their captives were at all times. As they sang they composed a magnificent body of musical literature with major themes about escaping captivity in Egypt. The music enabled them to redefine slavery for themselves, assume a measure of control over their lives, and recognize that they had to get rid of enslavement as quickly as possible. We don't know all the songs, because they weren't written down or recorded. But they were passed down. So we still have a whole lot of poetic lines.

I brought up "Go Down, Moses" as one of the songs Black people had composed. It illustrated how Black Christianity in the United States developed differently from mainline, white Christianity—because we aimed our stories of Jesus and Moses at emancipating ourselves from our circumstances.

Go down, Moses
Way down in Egypt's land
Tell old Pharaoh
To let my people go

I mentioned how we saw ourselves in the enslaved people escaping Egypt.

No more shall they in bondage toil
Let my people go

And we saw ourselves escaping enslavement in America.

We need not always weep and mourn
Let my people go
And wear those slavery chains forlorn
Let my people go

Those of us who grew up with the Negro spiritual knew it was mythological music. We also realized that its messages were disguised but that it consistently said: We are not slaves. We are people of God. We've been given life for our own purposes, and for God's purposes, and not for the purposes of enslavement.

Oh let us all from bondage flee
Let my people go

Then I connected this heritage to the relatively simple goal of our Nashville campaign: segregation will end. It was direct, but difficult. And the effort to make such a demand known, and see it through, required significant fortitude. Everyone in our workshops was asked to take a hard look at themselves and be willing to say, "I'm not going to hit back. Just because you threw that stone at me and I saw you, I'm not going to let my anger flood over me." We had to discipline ourselves not to allow anger to take precedence in this movement. For instance, we wouldn't have people in the movement who said, "No. I am going to throw that stone back at them" or "I am not going to let that person call me that name."

My experience as an athlete and a coach came into play. I talked about how a football team practices endlessly to develop a game plan, along with the personal power and discipline to get through the toughest moments. "It's not going to be easy," I said. "You may get hit. You may get beaten up. You may get jailed." I used my story of being in prison. I used my story of sending my draft cards back, because in following Jesus I could not commit violence against people. I could not become a member of anybody's army.

This movement, and each campaign in it, intended to push our country to live up to its founding promises from the U.S. Constitution and the Declaration of Independence: "We the people" are all "created equal," with "certain unalienable rights," such as "life, liberty, and the pursuit of happiness."

I put forth the idea that I was deeply patriotic. I would never kill for my country, but I was prepared to die for my country, for our movement.

In those first weeks of the workshops, we did role-playing exercises to prepare for the violence that was sure to be committed against us. One of the early scenes we played out was based on a story from Martin King's childhood. He was about eleven years old and standing on a street corner in downtown Atlanta, waiting for his mother or father. All of a sudden, a white woman hurried across the street. He saw her coming. She rushed up to him and slapped him, saying, "You are the dirty little n——r who stepped on my shoes." He had never seen the woman in his life.

In our role-playing I asked the participants to partner up with one other person. One partner was to be a Black person sitting on a park bench doing nothing, and the other partner was to be the white aggressor, coming up to them on the street or in a park and hitting them and calling them racist names. The response had to be nonviolent. We would set up confrontations in workshops where a person might get slapped or hit or knocked down. And we would experiment and help the person walk through how to respond to the kinds of hostile situations likely to come up as they did this work. The point of the role-playing was to think about how to respond to the violence. People would talk about it and evaluate their experiences. They were to figure out, "If this happens to me on Church Street in Nashville, how will I react? If that happens to me when I'm at a sit-in, what does it mean? How do I respond?" The exercises gave them space to think through an incident in the abstract before it became reality, where they might be blindsided and not know what to do.

There were varied reactions in the room. And understandably, there were skeptics. Diane Nash was skeptical. But she was bitterly disgusted with the segregation she encountered in Nashville and she wanted to do something about it, so she kept coming to the workshops. She stayed because she didn't know of anybody or anything else in town working to make changes. All of the Black people in the group lived with the racist things that happened to them every day. And they knew the history of the United States. They didn't need education about that. The objective was to bring their feelings about those nonstop assaults on their spirits to bear, in a mental, spiritual, and moral attitude of nonviolence instead of violence. The practice of nonviolence was the skill we needed to cultivate, so we could challenge the status quo and change it in a concerted, disciplined way.

Of course, people brought up the issue of self-defense. Our conditioning makes us believe violence is our only tool for self-defense—that violence will protect us. But nonviolence includes essential tools for self-defense that can protect us more effectively than violence. For instance, in a tough situation, one of the first things you have to do is keep your cool. No matter how frightened you are, how ruffled you are by the attack or hostility, you must try to keep your head. Self-defense, therefore, requires wit, courage, poise under duress, and being able to see all the available options. These techniques are at the core of nonviolence strategy.

Among the nonviolent tactics we suggested in the workshops was one that came from the Bible: turn the other cheek. And if they slap the other cheek, you turn it back again. This was an idea a lot of people resisted most strongly. People said it was giving the enemy what they wanted. It is perhaps the hardest part of nonviolence to accept at first. The practicality of it is that when violence is used against you, there is power in your response. Meeting violence with violence does not work when one side is outmatched physically. So turning the other cheek is about other forms of power against evil, including taking the blows and not wavering in your goals. In the moment, nonviolence can appear to be weak and passive. But it actually is an active, steely, radical response that confuses evil, not giving it the reaction it seeks. Not imitating the evil of the oppressor ruins the goal of oppression, which is to rob people of their dignity, agency, and humanity.

Still, I was not asking these people to go blindly, disregarding their own safety. I emphasized in those workshops that commitment to this campaign included the possibility that any one of us might get severely hurt. That was steadily in people's minds—how this form of resistance would likely cost us something. They had to be prepared to sacrifice their lives for the sake of changing the place and customs we were trying to change. It was a similar to the commitment any violent organization asks of its troops. We did not play games about the sacrifice any of us might have to make. Part of a commitment to nonviolence included saying, "No matter what happens, I'm going to live this kind of life, and I'm going to change the scene in which I live."

We never pretended that if you tried one of these options in a conflict situation, you wouldn't get clobbered. We never avoided the possibility, because nonviolence and violence have a similarity. Those who practice either must be prepared to do some suffering. The army recruitment posters don't tell you that. But the reality is that you not only learn to kill, you also have to learn to expect that you may get wounded or killed yourself. Both violence and nonviolence share suffering.

In conventional versions of patriotism, people are always talking about getting hurt, injured, crippled, or killed in wartime. All sorts of people and their families accepted the premise: "If I'm in this war, I might get hurt. I might have to sacrifice my life." So one of the things I continually emphasized in the Nashville workshops was that we call upon people to make all kinds of sacrifices in wartime and pretend that's the only way they can get things done. We are calling on you, I said, to make sacrifices in nonviolent direct action too, and in the long run the result will be more effective and less destructive than violence.

Because at the end of this battle, we expected to live side by side with white people. We expected our children to go to the same schools. We expected Black people to have the kinds of jobs they wanted, everywhere and anywhere, and to live wherever they wanted to live, to be what they wanted to be. We had to be able to live with one another, which, pragmatically, could not happen with hating, killing, torturing, and lynching. From a practical point of view, we didn't want to blow up downtown Nashville. We simply wanted to open it up, so that everybody had a chance to participate in life there fully, as human beings, without any obstacles due to creed, color, class, gender, or anything else. Going past any theoretical tenets of nonviolence, the practical issue was how to create a community where all people are people with a fair chance at the gift of life.

Early on, some people dropped out of the workshops. Others joined as we went along, including a few more white students. But by November 1959, there was unanimity in the core workshop group that everyone was committed and it was time to desegregate Nashville. We all went forth with faith in nonviolent direct action as the way to do it. Following Gandhian principles, we were to have no one leader, but leadership was to be shared among men and women in the group.

My strategy in each demonstration was to have someone designated as the spokesperson for the group. That was done as a safety tool, to prevent our people from getting involved in back-and-forth arguing with the spectators while they were sitting at a lunch counter. Instead, they would sit silently or talk quietly to each other. But if there was a need for a spokesperson, it would be a Diane Nash or a Pauline Knight, who had become two of my favorite people in the student group. Again, growing up with five older sisters made the idea obvious to me that women would be at the forefront with men. The spokesperson might have also been Curtis Murphy, John Lewis, Bernard Lafayette, Julian Scruggs, Angeline Butler, Paul Brooks, or Kenneth Frazier—he was another fine leader who emerged.

We settled on a name for the group—the Nashville Nonviolent Movement—and we put out a statement of purpose, ending with these nine guidelines:

1. Remain nonviolent under all circumstances.
2. Be courteous and kind even against discourtesy.
3. Follow the decisions of the spokesman.
4. Return a smile for an expression of hate.

5. Look forgivingly upon our opponents who are their own worst enemies.
6. Resist violence with both the spirit and action of nonviolence.
7. Remember that we work for the creation of a new community which benefits all people.
8. Meditate upon the teachings of Jesus, Gandhi and Martin Luther King Jr.
9. Take our purpose with all due seriousness.

We decided that two days after Thanksgiving 1959 was a good day for a test run of our sit-in strategies. It was partly to acclimate the students but also to verify that the segregation was taking place, and where, and how. A small integrated team of students was to enter a store and buy something. Then, as a group, they would go sit at the lunch counter in the store and order something. There was to be one spokesperson who did all the talking. If they were refused service, the spokesperson was to politely ask why, then ask to speak to the manager to understand the policies further. Once they heard the responses, they were to get up as a group and leave, quietly, without anger, and come back to the church to report on what they had found.

On Saturday, November 28, we met at Kelly's church downtown. A group including John Lewis, Diane Nash, and a few other students was ready to go. The men wore coats and ties. The women wore skirts and blouses. Diane was to be the spokesperson that day. We saw them leave, with members of the First Baptist Church acting as their drivers, planning to drop them off at Harveys department store and pick them up later.

A little more than an hour later, they returned to First Baptist, and we heard how it went. They said they bought a few small things, such as a handkerchief or two, and then sat at the counter, waiting to be served. A waitress said she could not serve them but was polite. Diane asked to speak to the manager. A middle-aged white man named Greenfield Pitts eventually came out and said the store policy was not to serve colored people. When Diane asked if the white people among them could be served, he said no, because they were with Black people. He was not hostile and seemed a little embarrassed. Diane thanked the manager, and then the team got up and left without any harsh words or actions.

I was pleased and congratulated them all on such a successful outing. We agreed to do it again the next week. On Saturday, December 5, John

Lewis was the spokesperson of the team that went to test the Cain-Sloan department store, an upscale competitor to Harveys. More Black people shopped at Harveys than at Cain-Sloan, so there were fewer Black people in the store daily. This time, a waitress met the group before they could sit down and told them the restaurant did not serve colored people. John spoke to a manager, who was polite but a little less patient than Mr. Pitts at Harveys had been. The group left quietly and returned to First Baptist, where we debriefed again. The two test runs had gone perfectly. We had facts upon which to base our next moves. And the process excited and energized the group.

As Christmas 1959 approached, everyone left for the holidays, inspired to come back and go ahead with our plan to take on the greatest challenge most of us had ever faced. We believed 1960 would be our chance to begin dismantling the racial status quo keeping Black people down in one American city. And many of us hoped our success there would further fuel the movement to continue doing the same all over the South, and eventually the entire country. We headed into the promising new decade before us with determination, courage, and cautious optimism.

NINE

The Myth Has Exploded

Reverend Lawson's arrest for sit-in organizing work. Dorothy Lawson and Rev. Metz Rollins are right behind him, at First Baptist Church, downtown Nashville, March 4, 1960.
GETTY IMAGES

By early 1960, I was almost entirely focused on planning the downtown Nashville sit-ins. Our Tuesday night workshops were growing steadily, with more students joining each week, and we even added Thursday sessions. In the early workshops, everyone had felt they were up against a monumental force—segregation. But I emphasized that targeting specific, manageable goals was the way to succeed. Excitement mounted as we progressed, fueled by the test runs in November and December. What had started as practice in the workshops was now becoming real. By January, it was clear the sit-ins could and must happen.

Theoretical discussion gave way to action. I saw the students beginning to tap into their own courage. Fear was lessening, morale was rising, and we knew the time was near. However, we delayed the launch. Part of the reason was my own schedule, as I was finishing the semester at Vanderbilt and couldn't fully dedicate myself to the massive task ahead.

Then, on Monday, February 1, four Black men who were students at North Carolina Agricultural and Technical College, in Greensboro, went into their local Woolworth's, sat at the lunch counter, and asked to be served coffee and doughnuts. They were refused because of their race but stayed there until the store closed. After that, they returned, and the number of students joining them increased. They kept coming back each day, and also initiated sit-ins at Kress and Walgreens lunch counters, as well as several restaurants in Greensboro. Of course, we were paying attention, and Greensboro lit a fire in our group. Within a week, college student sit-ins had spread across North Carolina, to Charlotte, Durham, and other cities. Then they spread to other Southern states. On Wednesday, February 10, students led sit-ins in Hampton, Virginia, and sit-ins were brewing for that coming Friday, February 12, in Rock Hill, South Carolina.

I got a call on the morning of February 10 from my good friend Rev. Douglas Moore, a Methodist campus minister who had worked with the students who started the Durham sit-ins. He knew about our Nashville workshops, and he asked when we would start our sit-ins. With that, I immediately called Kelly Miller Smith, and we agreed it was time to move. We might not have been the first to demonstrate, but I was sure we were the most prepared to sustain a nonviolent campaign. I called Paul LaPrad, and we started to organize a meeting for six-thirty the next evening at Fisk. We reached out to Diane Nash at Fisk, John Lewis and Bernard Lafayette at American Baptist, Curtis Murphy at Tennessee A&I, and to all of the steady workshop participants.

We also lined up some Vanderbilt Divinity students as observers. They would be in each store ready to work, watching the scene. And if we needed them as witnesses in a trial after any arrests, they had to be prepared to testify. The observers were all white, because nobody would realize a white person was working with us in a store. I also pushed this choice because in a racist society, white observers would have more legal weight in any court processes. Will Campbell helped recruit other observers from Church Women United and similar groups. Nashville was the headquarters for the Baptists, the Methodists, and the Church of Christ. And it was the headquarters for *The Upper Room,* a popular Methodist devotional magazine, which had become popular worldwide by then. So there were some white people in Nashville who were dedicated to eradicating racism and segregation through their religious commitment.

On Thursday, February 11, about seventy-five of us met at the Fisk University chemistry building, because it was easily accessible. Our plan was simple. We agreed to begin our campaign that Saturday, February 13. We already had a strong core of people prepared, all of whom understood how to do the sit-ins. We decided we would start with three lunch counters on Fifth Avenue, one of the main downtown shopping streets: Woolworth's, Kress, and McLellan's.

The students had formed a central committee, with representatives from each of the five major participating campuses—Fisk, Tennessee A&I, American Baptist, Meharry, and Vanderbilt—and adults from the executive board of the NCLC. All the central committee members had been equipped from the beginning to assume leadership in any categories of the struggle, including as spokespeople—Diane Nash, John Lewis, C. T. Vivian, James Bevel, Pauline Knight, Angeline Butler, Marion Barry, Curtis Murphy, Bernard Lafayette, Paul Lee, Delores Wilkerson, and others. They were all ready.

All decisions were reached through consensus. When division persisted, we had long meetings until we could act in accord. All public statements were completed and accepted by the whole committee, no matter who was asked to make a first draft. Usually, Diane Nash and Kelly Miller Smith were our chief spokespeople. What one spokesperson said was meant to represent the entire movement. We tried to think, speak, and act in the spirit of nonviolence.

I was an organizer on the ground and behind the scenes, but not out front. I deliberately refrained from being visible publicly. The chief reason was that I was an adult and was perceived as an outsider, having come South and to Nashville only two years before. Plus, I was not the story. What the local people were doing was the story.

In fact, I wasn't even in Nashville on February 13, the first day of the sit-ins. I had to be in Chattanooga that Saturday, because I had promised a group of Black students there, at Howard High School, that I would return to conduct a workshop on nonviolence and help them plan their sit-in.

Chattanooga had no Black colleges, so it was the high school students who led that action. They were committed. They ended up beginning their sit-in campaign the next week.

Back in Nashville, on Saturday, February 13, about 250 people gathered at Kelly Miller Smith's church in the morning, despite a heavy snowstorm. We had drawn up a set of ten points and printed them on cards that were handed out to the 124 students who would trudge through half a foot of snow to Kress, McLellan's, and Woolworth's. Most of the students who sat at the counters were Black, but a few white students also sat with them instead of being observers, so that the counters would be truly integrated.

LUNCH COUNTER SIT-IN SUGGESTIONS

DO NOT:

1. Strike back nor curse back if so abused.
2. Laugh out.
3. Hold conversations with floor walker. Be quiet.
4. Leave your seat until your leader has given permission to do so.
5. Block entrances to stores outside; nor the aisles inside.

DO:

1. Show yourself friendly and courteous at all times.
2. Sit straight; always face the counter.
3. Report all serious incidents to your leader.
4. Refer information seekers to your leader in a polite manner.
5. Remember the teachings of Jesus Christ, Mahatma Gandhi, and Martin Luther King. Love and nonviolence is the way.

"MAY GOD BLESS EACH OF YOU"

Just as in the December test runs, all the men wore suits and ties and the women wore skirts and blouses. They left the First Baptist Church and walked in an orderly way to the downtown shopping area.

We had notified the police that we were coming. A couple of students had consulted with local NAACP lawyers, and notably with Z. Alexander Looby, a city councilman and probably the most prominent Black lawyer in Nashville. Kelly Miller Smith had made initial overtures to two or three of the managers of the variety stores to ensure we were abiding by any relevant laws and for the safety of our people. At around twelve-thirty P.M., the three groups entered the stores, made small purchases, and took their seats at the lunch counters as planned. All the groups had similar experiences. Each of the lunch counters closed down, rather than serve Black students. At Woolworth's, John Lewis was the spokesperson of the group. He reported that they encountered some taunts from white customers, and that some of the staff looked scared. The white customers and workers referred to Lewis's group as "n——rs" and used other derogatory language. At each lunch counter, the students stayed, reading and sitting quietly until later that day, when the word was passed that it was time to leave.

The day after the first sit-in, *The Nashville Tennessean* reported that the students "went on a two-hour sit-down strike at lunch counters in three Nashville variety stores yesterday after waitresses refused to serve them." Diane Nash, who was the spokesperson for the group at McLellan's, told the reporter, "We just got tired of having no place to eat when we shop downtown. So we decided to do something about it."

After the first sit-in, everyone in our group believed our campaign was going to work. Nothing in our strategic plan had failed. The students, the clergy members, and the women activists who made it happen were working together interracially and intergenerationally.

The following Thursday, February 18, we had another lunchtime sit-in downtown. About two hundred demonstrators went in groups to the three stores we had gone to the Saturday before, and we added another five-and-dime, called Grant's. No one was served, the counters were shut down again, and the students stayed on their stools. A short article in the *Tennessean* on Friday, February 19, was headlined, "Negroes 'Strike' Counters Again," but it focused particularly on the white people in our group: "The students, a number of them white, remained seated quietly, some of them reading, for about 30 minutes. One white student among them, Carol Ann Anderson of Rosemead, Calif., a junior art major at Fisk University, read a copy of Booker T. Washington's *Up from Slavery*."

My role was to walk around and see how things were going at each location as we demonstrated. If we heard of a trouble spot, I went there. That Thursday, I moved around the four places where we were conducting sit-ins. I talked to a couple of police officers who were helping to keep white boys from congregating in a store or at a nearby corner. I came to understand that the official police attitude was that there would be no violence. They would not let others attack us.

Even as our Nashville campaign continued, other college and high school students were initiating more sit-ins all around the South. About two hundred of the high school students I had been working with in Chattanooga had gone into variety stores in one block of downtown Chattanooga on Friday, February 19, and peacefully sat in at the segregated lunch counters. They came back each day after that, despite verbal and physical harassment and worse from young white segregationists. On the third day, Chattanooga's mayor instructed the police to use fire hoses to break up demonstrations on the city's streets. The next day, as three thousand white students attacked the Black demonstrators, Chattanooga became the first city in the South where the nation witnessed the spectacle of a city government using high-pressure water hoses against its own citizens to put down demonstrations.

Back in Nashville, on Saturday, February 20, some 350 students went in groups to the four lunch counters we had visited before, as well as Walgreens drugstore. Again, as soon as our people asked for food service, the counters were shut down. At Walgreens, it took only two minutes for the counter to shut down, and management put up a sign that read, "Counter closed in the interest of public safety." Just as before, our groups remained sitting at the counters for a few more hours, doing homework or reading books or magazines. The *Tennessean* reported that, "John Lewis, a ministerial student at American Baptist seminary, worked on a sermon." Luther Harris, a Fisk student, was a spokesperson that day. He told the reporters about the students' commitment to nonviolent direct action to change segregation. "As long as we obey these principles we are bound to succeed," he said. "It took Gandhi 36 years in India, but I don't think it will take us that long here."

At first, there was the general feeling in the city that an unusual form of student fever had hit Nashville: let the kids have their kicks, many white residents figured, and it will flit away. Also, white academics, political progressives, and the news media interpreted the sit-in campaign as simply an off-the-cuff affair. But in every instance, the demonstrations were planned and strategized—including in Greensboro, where the students were coached and encouraged by local NAACP leadership and ministers. Still, the demonstrations were viewed as if their actions had all happened spontaneously. In fact, some in the media compared the sit-ins to "panty raids," which were considered harmless pranks in the 1950s, when male entitlement ran especially rampant.

But in Richmond, Virginia, the segregationist *Richmond News Leader* seemed to feel a deeper threat. The newspaper's editor, James J. Kilpatrick, a well-known, ultraconservative white supremacist columnist, published an editorial on Monday, February 22, after observing the sit-ins there, that ultimately criticized the student demonstrators. But he started his piece with an inkling of what, in retrospect, might be considered self-awareness:

> Many a Virginian must have felt a tinge of wry regret at the state of things as they are, in reading of Saturday's "sitdowns" by Negro students in Richmond stores. Here were the colored students, in coats, white shirts, ties, and one of them was reading Goethe and one was taking notes from a biology text. And here, on the sidewalk outside, was a gang of white boys come to heckle, a ragtail rabble, slack-jawed, black-jacketed, grinning fit to kill, and some of them, God save the mark, were waving the proud and honored flag of the Southern States in the last war fought by gentlemen. Eheu! It gives one pause.

A main goal of the nonviolent practitioner is to dramatize an issue by creating a public display, to educate people about a particular injustice. They show, or demonstrate, that the wrong exists.

Here was Kilpatrick, a well-known segregationist editor from Richmond, Virginia, pausing and thinking about the issue of race in a way he might never have done before. Without fully acknowledging it, and despite his reverence for the Confederacy, he was questioning the morality of his own worldview. He was essentially saying: "What is this? The quality people are supposed to be the white mob. But it's the Black students who are sitting calmly in the midst of a storm of hatred, and sitting bravely self-possessed." It made him reflect. The Black people were supposedly disorderly, but they presented a picture of human dignity and courage. The white people were supposed to be the guardians of decorum, yet they attacked Black students who were not attacking them and were, instead, quietly but firmly asking for peaceful change.

We heard frequently in those days that Nashville was a moderate city and had the best working relationships with Black people in the South. The mayor, Ben West, had been elected as a moderate, with much of the Black community's vote. But in the South generally, those white people who counted themselves as moderate also felt they understood best how race relations should proceed. They presumed to know more about what was hurting Black people than we knew ourselves. And they presumed to know more about how we ought to make changes than anybody else. They believed that the people doing the sit-ins were going at it all wrong. They said it could be done better through calm, quiet negotiation and dialogue. So those of us organizing movements and events were counted as very radical people, as if we were the ones upsetting race relations in the community. Even the powers that be at the *Tennessean* did not seem to think we knew what we were doing, or that we had much to offer in any effort to lead Nashville's downtown desegregation.

The young white hecklers also didn't think we had much to offer. But during the first three public demonstrations in Nashville, the police and store management were fairly helpful in controlling the rage of the white people who harassed us. A deceptive calm prevailed. Initially, there were no violent incidents. However, the potential troublemakers kept up a steady barrage of threats and curses. Their rage gradually increased in those first two weeks, and it became evident that explosions of violence could and would occur.

A group from our central committee and I went to speak with the police chief. We came away quite convinced that we would have violence and arrests at the next big demonstration, which was planned for the last Saturday in February.

Downtown merchants pressed Mayor West to do something to stop us, not through negotiation and settlement but through a show of force. The mayor, in turn, consulted his legal department for advice on how to use the machinery of the city against our movement. City lawyers began searching for laws they could use to make what we were doing into a crime. We figured out the city's strategy. They were hoping to use disorderly conduct codes to arrest us. In response, the NCLC and a group of white ministers who were aligned with our goals unsuccessfully tried to arrange a meeting with Mayor West.

The city leadership was so confident that they could make us disappear that, we realized, they were about to rescind the basic police and store-management protections we had received during our first three sit-ins. The police would start to become the enemy, instead of keeping white supremacist young people out of the stores and off the streets. We adapted our strategy accordingly.

Instead of arriving all at once and packing each of the lunch counters, we would send out small, compact groups to each counter. Then when the first group was arrested, the next small group would arrive. I was using the example of Gandhi's 1930 Salt March to plan that day. The colonial British government did not allow Indian people to collect and produce their own salt from their seashores, where salt was gathered from waters evaporating along the shore. British-run facilities stationed themselves near the sea and began running all the salt distribution networks throughout India. On top of that, they taxed salt when Indians went to buy it. Gandhi picked this issue to illustrate the tyranny and exploitation of colonialism and the need for Indian self-rule. He knew salt was essential to the everyday lives of Indians and that the British monopoly on it deeply affected all Indians.

So he started a 240-mile march to the Arabian Sea and was joined by tens of thousands along the way. He informed the police that he would be coming to protest the government's salt tax. When he and his followers reached the shoreline to break the British ban by gathering their own salt, police officers met them there. That day, the British had kicked down all the salt deposits that formed along the shore, scattering them in the mud. Gandhi's response was to pick up some mud with salt lodged in it, thereby violating the British bans on salt collection. Nonviolently, he was violating an unjust law. As expected, Gandhi was arrested.

From jail, he appointed one of my favorite people, Sarojini Naidu, as the Salt Satyagraha leader. She took over, marking the first time Gandhi had accepted a woman as his equal in the struggle for Indian independence. Thousands of people had been trained and prepared in nonviolence, and they converged on a government saltworks site. But instead of everyone going all at once to the gates of the saltworks, where they knew the police would beat them with their steel-tipped lathis, Naidu sent in smaller units of one to two hundred protesters. Broken bones and bloody heads came out of it. Yet there was no physical retaliation from the demonstrators. As soon as the first group got beaten, another group moved in and took those people away from the gate to attend to their wounds. And then the third group quickly moved up, and those people were also beaten and bloodied. They just kept coming like that.

The police were overwhelmed. These demonstrations spread along the coast at salt-collection sites, and more than sixty thousand were arrested in small groups during the campaign. News reports and photos of British police brutally beating nonviolent Indians spread around the globe, as did the outrage against the British. The Salt March was compared to the Boston Tea Party in the American Revolution. The Salt Satyagraha is considered one of the most successful nonviolent campaigns of the Indian independence movement.

The Salt March example inspired our plan to get arrested in small groups that Saturday, February 27, in Nashville—the day that came to be known as "Big Saturday." We agreed that when the first team of five or ten got arrested, we would send in another team to take their place at the lunch counters. And we would keep sending people in and they would keep getting arrested, until the police were overwhelmed.

The central committee asked me to do the briefing in the sanctuary of the First Baptist Church as the initial three hundred or so people began to show up. Many had been in the workshops, but not all of them. I spoke about nonviolence and the necessity of not retaliating during the sit-ins. I spoke of how at their site they had to follow the spokesperson on their team. And I warned them that there would probably be violence and they would likely be arrested. Everyone who went out that day had to be prepared to face both. I tried my best to do what the central committee asked—be certain that every demonstrator saw personally what we were facing and was committed to the need for strict nonviolent discipline. We all further agreed that if arrests came, we should stay in jail indefinitely. The prospect of jail or violence did not deter anyone. In the end, we had about five hundred people ready for whatever might occur.

As I was speaking, I noticed that a couple of police officers had come into the church. And I realized there were also reporters there. That's the moment when they first seemed to understand that our sit-in movement was not some spontaneous college student fad. It was scrupulously planned, with a strategic method behind it.

As expected, Saturday, February 27, 1960, was when the earliest incidents of physical violence against our people began, and when the police began to do disappearing acts. The first horrible incident of the day was at McLellan's, and it contained much symbolism. Paul LaPrad, the white

Fisk student and our spokesman at McLellan's, was the victim. By this time, he had become a special target. One white sit-in participant ignited more anguish and violence than did any of the Negro participants.

Young white men entered the store and went straight to Paul, yelling at him, calling him names. They pulled him off his stool and relentlessly beat and kicked him. Photographers took stirring pictures of the violent bloody attack and of the assailants. Then the police came in and arrested Paul and the other students who had remained quietly at the counter. Despite the clear documentation of those white boys beating Paul, not one of them was arrested or publicly identified. Only Paul and the rest of the students sitting in were taken into custody. But we kept going.

As soon as one group was arrested, we had a second wave poised to step in and take their seats. The police moved from McLellan's, over to Woolworth's, back to McLellan's, and again to Woolworth's. In the space of one hour, officers cleared the lunch counters three times, arresting dozens of people, only to find that many more were quite ready to be sent to jail as well. The police were bewildered and a little demoralized when they realized the students wanted to be arrested. Officers became increasingly hostile and rough in handling them. But the students met that with calm and reason.

One student spokesperson told us what happened when he said to a police officer, "We have nothing against you. We know you're merely trying to do your duty. And we intend to cooperate fully with you. We will not resist in any way." The officer's attitude melted. He became a kind teacher assisting a bunch of greenhorns, rather than a tough cop.

But soon, our observers reported, the police began leaving the stores. They let the white mobs take over. That day in Woolworth's was when we faced the worst violence of the entire campaign. Young white men lined up three and four deep in the aisles of the store. Taunts, cursing, and racist name-calling jammed the air. Merchandise was thrown. Cigarettes became weapons used to burn another human being. Young white men threw tobacco, salt, and dirt into the hair of young Black women. Their elbows and fists struck many blows at the demonstrators from behind. Several of our men were pulled off their stools, kicked, and beaten. At least one demonstrator was rolled down the stairway from the second floor to the first. Only after an hour or more of that did the police, urged by us, finally return and stop the attack.

Having expected to end the "nonsense" with a few arrests, the police and their superiors did not know what to do. The city was entirely unprepared to handle our Salt March–inspired strategy.

Early the next morning, Sunday, February 28, about seventy-five ministers sent a telegram to Mayor West, asking him to meet with us the next morning at the First Baptist Church. He agreed, and showed up on Monday, February 29, to face more than two hundred clergy members of all denominations waiting for him at Kelly Miller Smith's church. Several reporters also appeared.

Most of the ministers had supported West's campaigns. But now they were angry and discontent. Who made the decision to arrest? Why did the police arrest students and not their attackers? How could the mob take over the stores with police standing by and doing nothing? The mayor was pointedly questioned about his private attitudes toward segregation and his responsibility for the events of Saturday. Mayor West knew he was on the spot. Rarely if ever has a mayor of the South been so strongly confronted. He didn't have answers. He talked about segregation and affirmed his belief in Christian faith and democracy, and said that he had urged the merchants not to discriminate. But he also said he felt that they had property rights, which the students violated.

I pointed out to the mayor that the arrests on Saturday were made on charges not of trespassing but of disorderly conduct, which could be interpreted any way the authorities wished. Furthermore, I suggested that human rights took precedence over property rights. Then I reiterated how we had seen the power of the city aligned with the power of the mob and downtown merchants, those trying to discredit and crush our effort. This was a deliberate attempt to ignore our message about the immorality of segregation.

I further pointed out how laws in the South were being used to keep the Negro in his place. Recently, the Virginia General Assembly had taken just fourteen minutes to pass three "emergency" anti-trespass bills designed to prohibit sit-ins. I said that every step by the Negro was met by a new law designed for tyranny, and not as a law of a democratic society. I said that when law became a "gimmick" to manipulate and intimidate a movement, we had no choice but to continue. We had to be willing to face both violence and arrest, but there could not be fear of such unjust laws.

At that, the mayor exclaimed that I was calling for a "bath of blood" and insisted that he would preserve law and order (although law and order on that Saturday had meant allowing white supremacists to try to crush a nonviolent movement). Several ministers immediately jumped up to tell the mayor that he had misunderstood. But the politician's dramatic show prevailed. The newspapers ignored the significance of our message and focused on labeling me as an "organizer," "chief agitator," and "anarchist" who was trying to destroy law and order.

One specific newspaper that ran with that angle was the ultra-segregationist afternoon paper, the *Nashville Banner*. Big Saturday was a watershed moment, forcing Nashville to take note of our campaign. Big Saturday was also when my name and involvement were revealed to the public. On Tuesday, March 1, the *Banner* published an editorial about me titled "No Place in Nashville for Inciters of Strife."

> In that inflammatory role . . . as the ramrod of strife directed from the outside, is the Rev. James Morris Lawson, Jr., of Massillon, Ohio, a Negro divinity student at Vanderbilt University, field representative of the Fellowship of Reconciliation.
>
> His capacity for mischief shows in the crisis he has brought on race relations not only in this city, but at other points in the South which he has visited on that mission of incitement. His arrogance is that of the agent of strife, employed for just such assignment. His effrontery was demonstrated yesterday in contemptuous challenge of civil authority, terming the law a "gimmick," and declaring in substance the intention of riding rough-shod over the city's avowed purpose of law enforcement.
>
> He is, in short, continuing to advise the element behind him to violate the law. That is the incitation to anarchy.
>
> There is no place in Nashville for flannel-mouth agitaters [*sic*], white or colored—under whatever sponsorship, imported for preachment of mass disorder; self-supported, vagrants, or the paid agents of strife-breeding organizations.

Contrary to all my best efforts at avoiding it, I was becoming the story, which could only distract from the issue of segregation we were attempting to address. And as it happened, the executive committee of the Board of Trust of Vanderbilt met that Monday, February 29, as well. On the executive committee were two of the university's most outspoken segregationists: John Sloan, the president of the Cain-Sloan department store, one of the sites where we conducted sit-ins, and James G. Stahlman, the publisher of the *Nashville Banner*. They wanted me expelled immediately. They were adamant and used the *Banner*'s ultra-right-wing editorial page to push their point of view.

The dean of the divinity school at Vanderbilt, Bob Nelson, became the go-between, relaying messages to me from the university administration and trustees. Neither the Board of Trust's executive committee nor the chancellor, Harvie Branscomb, ever spoke to me directly. On Monday, February 29, Nelson told me the trustees were demanding that I be expelled, but they would be willing for me to withdraw, so that I could return to school later. Through Nelson, the administration asked me to issue a statement to contradict the news reports. I did so, reluctantly, on Wednesday, March 2, saying, in part,

> Under no circumstances have I ever made or will ever make the categorical statement that students should violate the law. These are not my words. Defiant violation of the law is a contradiction of my entire understanding of and loyalty to Christian nonviolence.
>
> . . . Throughout the demonstrations, particularly and foremost the last on Saturday, the students remained wholly loving and non-violent even though the violence directed against them was beyond anyone's imagination. The press failed to effectively communicate that . . .
>
> In saying that "the law has been a gimmick to manipulate the Negro," I do not say that I have disrespect for the law as such.
>
> . . . The intention of the sit-in was to invite the genuine concern of the community for a large element of the community which is deprived of normal services by custom. The sit-in has never intended to invite riot or the breakdown of public order and, for my part, will never do so.

But my statement did little to quell the fury. On Wednesday, March 2, the *Banner* published another editorial aimed at me. In this one they described me as "lacking in intelligence" and an "overgrown juvenile delinquent." The editorial said, "To plead his cause in the name of 'Christian reconciliation' . . . is so much hogwash. And his use of the Divinity School of Vanderbilt University as a base and screen for his nefarious operations is as detestable as his effort to cloak his racial deviltry in clerical garb."

The paper went on to say, "The sooner both Nashville and Vanderbilt are rid of the presence and the baneful influence and tactics of Mr. Lawson, the better. He has forfeited his privilege to further education at Vanderbilt, if that were his real purpose in enrollment there. And he certainly has worn out any possible welcome or imagined usefulness he might have had as a Nashville resident, temporary or otherwise."

The *Banner* had published a news article about my missionary work in India the day before, under the headline "Lawson Said Trained in India for Mission Here." Of course I never said that. The headline writer twisted my words to imply that my work with the Methodist mission in India had been insincere and that I had brought destructive foreign influences back to America.

At the end of the March 2 editorial, the paper's editors had picked up that theme in calling for me to leave town:

> His departure for other fields for his "Christian missionary" endeavors couldn't come too soon for the good of Vanderbilt University and the general welfare of Nashville, Davidson County, and the state of Tennessee.

The piece ended with dog whistles for its segregationist audience:

> Harlem might be a good spot to cultivate, Mr. Lawson. Or would the Rev. Adam Clayton Powell consider that "unfair competition?"

I contemplated leaving the school voluntarily. But Dorothy adamantly opposed it, as did Will Campbell. They thought I should make the administration take the action of ousting me—one of the first and few Black students at the university—if that's what they wanted. The divinity school faculty got wind of what was going on, and they organized and started notifying the administration of their opposition to expelling me. The law school faculty, the medical school faculty, and many other faculty members also demanded that the trustees not do it.

Meanwhile, I went to my classes on Tuesday. On Wednesday, another 350 demonstrators resumed the sit-ins, adding some stores and the two bus stations in Nashville. Another 63 people were arrested.

I went to classes on Wednesday. I did not withdraw. Then on Thursday morning, March 3, Vanderbilt's chancellor, Harvie Branscomb, came to the divinity school and announced my expulsion to a sizable crowd of people gathered in one of the large rooms there. I entered through the back door and heard him say that I was expelled. He never notified me directly.

Being a student at Vanderbilt, I was more visible and vulnerable to attack from the white part of Nashville who supported segregation than were students at Fisk, Tennessee A&I, and American Baptist. Most of the editorials and press reports were trying to isolate me from the movement and our "core leadership" concept: that we had no one leader but led by consensus.

A large number of Vanderbilt faculty members had their letters of resignation written. The only reason they did not immediately resign in protest was that the chair of Vanderbilt's board and the chancellor had agreed that I could return at some point.

Of course, as soon as I was kicked out, the Christian world knew about it. Theological school faculty members and bishops from around the country barraged the university with criticism for even considering expelling me. And many schools sent invitations for me to go there right away and finish my studies—Yale, Harvard, and the University of Chicago among them.

To understand my reaction to all of this is to understand my own spirituality, as well as Dorothy's. Our unshakable sense of purpose came from our deep, shared commitment to defeating the evils of racism and injustice. I don't remember either one of us being nervous or frightened or upset by any of what was happening. We both recognized that there would be some costs to the work we did. And Dorothy and I knew that we had done nothing wrong. We were being maligned, not because we had committed a crime but because society had committed a crime against us and against all Black people. Therefore, if expulsion happened, it happened. And because of the offers that poured in, we knew I would finish my degree somewhere. Intellectually and spiritually, we had the upper hand.

It is important to also note that we felt no sense of animosity toward anyone. The first year of our marriage, when I was a student at Vanderbilt, we had friends and neighbors there. I was quite pleased and excited by the curriculum and the faculty. We liked the place. We were always going to address social justice issues together, and the idea that our marriage could be sacrificial was part of our relationship from the start. We had deliberately selected each other. We knew almost from the moment we met that we were going to date, and that it was probably going to be the last time of dating for either one of us. From the first day of our courtship, we talked about the struggle for racial justice. We knew that these sorts of ups and downs were possible. We were partners in this life and in this love.

Dorothy and I had heard during that eventful first week in March that an arrest warrant was being issued for me. We believed there was a connection between my expulsion from Vanderbilt and my impending arrest. I had even told colleagues that if Vanderbilt expelled me, I would be arrested soon after. And sure enough, just minutes after I overheard that I'd been expelled, I got a call from someone at First Baptist telling me they'd heard the arrest would happen the next day. This prior warning allowed Dorothy and me to stage how it would happen. We agreed that forcing them to arrest me in the church was a good idea. We decided to meet up with supporters at First Baptist. We brought my Bible and some books I wanted from home. At least I would have some work to keep me occupied, in case I had to stay in a while.

Four officers arrived at the First Baptist Church, on Capitol Hill. They had to walk through the church to arrest me. We were sitting in the front row of the sanctuary. Kelly Miller Smith was right in front of the pulpit, down in the chancel. And the church was full of people. In the pictures of my arrest, you can see Dorothy's shoes, the lower part of her legs, her coat. And then in some of the pictures, her face is right behind me. In most of the pictures of my arrest, she is there.

The police didn't put handcuffs on me. But all four were hostile to us. And Dorothy told them again and again, "He's not resisting you, so why are you trying to rough him up? He's trying to walk with you." I didn't hear her, but she told me later she said that all the way up the church aisle. They were pretending, feeling they had to appear tough. They understood this was a public event. But in front of everyone I had told them I was not resisting, so they couldn't really manhandle me too much.

People from the church kept shaking my hands as we walked by. In a number of the pictures, Metz Rollins, a Presbyterian minister with his collar on, is right there with me. He's a tall, slender guy. Also, Kelly Miller Smith had made sure the title of his upcoming sermon was posted on the marquee sign outside the church, so it would appear in the photos of the police taking me down the front steps. It read, "Father, Forgive Them." It was from the Bible verse in Luke that says, "Father, forgive them, for they do not know what they are doing."

We were told at the time of my arrest that a couple of these police officers were extremely racist. But Dorothy and I were calm, and I smiled through it all. I had on a coat and tie—my costume. I planned to stay in jail, as Dorothy and I had agreed. I even felt a certain sense of relief and thought I could use the time in my cell for reflection and rest. But the central committee didn't want me in jail. And the Vanderbilt Divinity School faculty would not hear of it. So faculty members bailed me out that evening, and I was home by about one A.M.

In two days, I had been expelled, arrested, jailed, and bailed out. I was physically exhausted but intellectually and spiritually very much alive. I had been teaching everybody else that there were risks in this work. You can be arrested. You can get hurt. So while I didn't know the exact day or week it would happen, neither Dorothy nor I were surprised by the roller coaster that week. Our default response was to continue to do the work we were doing.

The divinity school faculty had begun negotiating to get me back in at Vanderbilt. And the calls kept coming in for Dorothy and me from other theological schools, inviting us to relocate to their campus immediately so that I might finish my courses. We were negotiating. In the meantime, I went back to work full-time for FOR, continuing my work around the South. Dorothy continued at the National Council of Churches.

And one of the nicest stories I ever heard came from my mother in a note she wrote me after I was expelled and arrested. It had been in the news all over the world, and everyone in Massillon knew what had happened. My mother said she had met "sister so-and-so" on the street when she was shopping uptown. It would have been someone from the church who had known our family for a while. Mom said the woman expressed sympathy, saying something like "Too bad about Jim." And my mother said she told her, "Oh, I do not have to worry about Jim. Because Jim always seeks to do God's will. So, I never worry about him." That was one of the kindest things anyone could ever say. I have never forgotten it.

The sit-in campaign was going strong, and we were having meetings of the central committee more than once a week. I used the meetings as a kind of practical laboratory for our continuing preparation, and for analysis of what we were doing. John Lewis, Diane Nash, and a whole slew of us were getting together, assessing what happened, breaking it down, and planning our next steps. More and more people became involved in our work, and more of our central committee people began teaching nonviolent direct action. The compounding numbers of people being trained in nonviolence was an invisible but lasting impact that our Nashville campaign had on the entire movement.

The day I was arrested, Mayor West announced that he was appointing what he called a "biracial committee" to try to resolve the student sit-ins. It was biracial because there were two Black men on it—the presidents of Fisk and of Tennessee A&I. There were also five white men and no women. Two men were lawyers, and two were businessmen. The chairman was a former chancellor of Vanderbilt. But as a result of the mayor's attention, the students agreed to pause the sit-ins, in good faith, while the committee did its work.

All along the way, we had been having informal conversations with downtown merchants. We had consistently found Greenfield Pitts, the head of Harveys department store, to be easy to talk with and quite cordial. He was from Chicago and recognized the problems, and had been prepared to desegregate from day one. He told us, "Black people make up twenty or thirty percent of our annual income. Yet we have to prevent them from sitting down at the counter and eating." He said, "We're losing money over the deal." We knew that at least the manager at Harveys did not want to tell Black people they couldn't go to certain places in the store. But the culture and customs of white Nashville prevented him from acting on his inclinations.

By the end of March, the biracial committee had been meeting for several weeks but still had not issued its report. We began to feel that pausing the sit-ins was a mistake. On Wednesday, March 30, we held a prayer vigil outside Mayor West's office. More than two hundred people joined us at city hall to pray for his support in eliminating segregation. And the national media was visiting Nashville more and more, to pick up the stories of the sit-ins. A reporter from the *Tennessean,* David Halberstam, who had been covering us from the beginning, began writing some articles for national outlets as well. In *The Reporter*—one of the American magazines I had subscribed to and read in India—Halberstam wrote an excellent piece for the March 31, 1960 issue that portrayed where we were, and where Nashville was, six weeks after our first sit-ins. He started by saying our campaign had "turned Nashville into one of the South's most explosive racial areas." He told how we had decided to halt our demonstrations to allow the biracial committee to do its work.

> But the damage is already staggering: city court trials have been a farce; seventy-seven Negro and three white college students were convicted and fined fifty dollars each for (non-violent) disorderly conduct; sixty-three more will soon be tried; the original eighty have been rearrested on state charges; mass meeting of Negroes follows mass meeting; rumor follows bomb threats. And the end is not in sight.
>
> . . . Nashville is not Little Rock. The struggles over integration in schools and buses were settled years ago. Ironically, however, that may be part of the trouble now. The battle, in the view of the white community, was over. Discussion stopped; white consciences were cleansed.

David Halberstam interviewed me, and I was able to speak about the ways in which the approach to eliminating segregation was changing from solely legal avenues, or what we traditionally call "civil rights," to a new strategic kind of demonstration in public that directly confronted the customs, institutions, and culture which maintained racial disparities and worse. We were calling it "nonviolent direct action," or "nonviolence" for short. Our Nashville campaign, I told him, was on the cutting edge of proving the efficacy of nonviolence. Because as important as it was, the 1954 Supreme Court decision in *Brown v. Board of Education* had not ended the many problems Black people in the United States faced in 1960. Halberstam quoted me talking about how the confrontational nonviolent tactics of the Nashville campaign marked a dramatic break with some of the more docile-seeming compromises of past decades:

> "Nashville was ripe for this. Sure, the people of Nashville thought they were making good progress. But to a lot of us, to the young Negroes, this talk of good progress is sheer hypocrisy. . . .
>
> "Progress has come," said Lawson, . . . "but it hasn't begun to touch some of the commonplaces of life that affect the Negro deeply, the normal but subtle things that bite at his internal life, that he feels make him subhuman."

> . . . The Negroes, Lawson went on, "are tired of middle-class methods of seeking our rights. The legal redress, the civil-rights redress, are far too slow for the demands of the time. The sit-in is a break with the accepted tradition of change, of legislation and the courts. It is the use of a dramatic act to gain redress."

Halberstam was a white reporter who worked for a white newspaper. But he was the reporter we trusted the most to convey our story. I was pleased with him from the first time I met him. He was a young reporter then, having graduated from Harvard a few years earlier. He spent a year reporting in Mississippi before coming to Nashville. He was close in age to many in our student group, and they loved him and treated him as an equal. His reporting in the *Tennessean* was fair. We couldn't have asked for more than that. And his age allowed him to relax and be at home with lots of our people, several of whom—John Lewis, Diane Nash, Bernard Lafayette, Gloria Johnson, and others—saw David as a friend. He often ended up with the inside track on us. We considered his reporting on our campaigns in 1960 and 1961 to be the best of any in the South.

In that piece he wrote for *The Reporter*, he came closer to an accurate portrayal of our situation than anyone else in the white media landscape at the time. For instance, he perfectly summed up the attitudes we were facing in Nashville and the South with this passage:

> The Negro, according to the Southern myth, is content. Even the young ones. The myth has exploded with their sit-ins.

In the time he had spent with us, he caught on to our intentions and our effect, and reported on how we were evolving.

> For a week, I have watched the Negroes at their meetings, watched them growing more determined and confident all the time, surprised by their own strength.
>
> . . . City officials had calculated that the demonstrations would collapse because of the fear of arrest. But the Negro students . . . stand up to the police. When eighty were arrested, older Negroes tried to post bond. The students refused. "It was a revelation to us," said Z. Alexander Looby, a veteran attorney and patriarch among Negro leaders here. "Those kids didn't want to get out of jail. They

didn't want to make their bond. They felt their cause and wanted to prove it. A revelation."

A Republican city councilman and NAACP attorney, Alexander Looby was a devoted, courageous pioneer for social justice in the South. He had become one of us, a vital part of our campaign. He organized ten lawyers to represent our people for free during the trials of the first eighty students arrested, and of all the others of us who followed.

What I was saying to David Halberstam about older leaders at that time didn't pertain to Alexander Looby. I was talking about conventional Black leadership in general, which I believed had become too comfortable. Therefore, many younger people saw them as too removed from much of the nitty-gritty pains and dehumanization most Black folk felt living under segregation, particularly in the South. In fact, even though some local NAACP chapters were involved in the sit-ins, the national office of the NAACP told student chapters in Nashville, Knoxville, and Richmond, Virginia, not to participate. And in 1960, the NAACP national office made non-participation in the sit-ins an official policy for all its chapters. Also, right straight across the South, all sorts of people in the Black community were saying sit-ins weren't the way to go.

That's one of the reasons I had said, from the very beginning, that the Montgomery bus boycott and the sit-ins were as much of an awakening for Black leadership and many Black Americans as they were for white people. A lot of Black people had adjusted to the evil, while white society as a whole had ignored it. The sit-in movement and the whole nonviolent movement for social change was a statement to the Black community that we did not have to settle for this evil. We were exhibiting how each of us had a responsibility to get liberated and to organize together.

There had been a lot of restlessness in the Black church in the 1940s and 1950s, and even earlier. Many of us growing up in those days, including Martin Luther King Jr., said, essentially, "Segregation is wrong and I'm gonna do everything I can to fight it." It was true in my own life. I don't think any of that fierce undercurrent of saying, "This stuff has to stop, and we're not gonna put up with it" was ever captured by the NAACP or anybody else during that time. They were focused on changing laws, which was important. But it left a gap.

By the time 1960 came around, the national sit-ins had begun to fill the gap. Students in almost every state in the country, and certainly in every Southern state, were sitting in. More people than in previous decades were willing to experiment with new ways of trying to transform this country. Students were often freer than anybody else in the Black community in that regard. They were young. They had campus responsibilities, but for the most part their families supported them or they supported themselves with scholarships and by working. As with pastors in the Black church, students were among the freest people in the community, and therefore more able to take risks.

Halberstam's *Reporter* article began to show the nation how those risks manifested when he described the white harassment and violence he witnessed from "the punks" at that Woolworth's store during our Big Saturday sit-in. He said "almost 350 people," including "a press gallery of reporters and photographers," all watched the lunch counter "like spectators at a boxing match":

> First it was the usual name calling, then spitting, then cuffing; now bolder, punching, banging their heads against the counter, hitting them, stuffing cigarette butts down the backs of their collars. The slow buildup of hate was somehow worse than the actual violence. The violence came quickly enough, however—two or three white boys finally pulled three Negro boys from the counter and started beating them. The three Negroes did not fight back, but stumbled and ran out of the store; the whites, their faces red with anger, screamed at them to stop and fight, to please goddam stop and fight. None of the other Negroes at the counter ever looked around. It was over in a minute.

To add to the pressure from the sit-ins, we initiated a boycott of the downtown Nashville businesses that maintained segregationist policies—in early April, just before the Easter shopping season.

During all of this work, I was traveling for FOR again, which meant going to different places where there were sit-ins, to help, advise, and consult. I went to Greensboro and Raleigh in North Carolina; Columbia, South Carolina; and Millsaps College and Tougaloo College in Jackson, Mississippi. I met with students from all over the South who were starting their own sit-ins. The SCLC was paying attention to the sit-ins, too. Ella Baker, who was serving as the executive director of the SCLC at the time, also had close contact with many of the students leading the sit-ins in the South. She saw the energy and enthusiasm, so she proposed to Martin King a gathering of student demonstrators at Shaw University in Raleigh, North Carolina, on Easter weekend. Shaw was the first historically Black university in the South, founded in 1865, and it was Ella's alma mater. Martin liked the idea. They approached me, and the three of us planned the gathering together. Ella persuaded the SCLC to put up the first $800 to make it happen. I called people who were organizing in different parts of the South. I invited students and clergy members to participate, and asked them to send other people who would be interested in coordinating student actions. I said we wanted to come together and share conversations about what we were doing, discuss the sit-in campaign, and see where it led.

During Easter weekend, in mid-April, about 120 people came to Raleigh for the conference, almost all of them Black students. Doug Moore, the pastor from Durham who had called me in early February, Rev. Matthew McCollom from South Carolina, and a few other pastors active in the sit-ins were there. The National Student Association, a network of American college student governments, had sent a small group. It was the primary white and the primary Northern delegation. Otherwise, everyone was from centers in the South where there had been strong sit-in campaigns. The Southern sit-ins were largely Black-run campaigns, while in the North they were primarily white. Our Nashville movement had the largest delegation at the conference. Julian Bond was there representing the other large delegation, from Atlanta, even though he had been born in Nashville. Later, he would write that of all the groups represented, it was the Nashville group that most seemed to know what it was doing.

We didn't structure the gathering with lots of speeches and panels and separate groups talking. I used my experience from student conferences around the world to organize the program so that all the participants contributed. We called it a working conference. Everyone who had come would discuss the same issue, at the same time, in the same room. We did not divide into small groups.

As a student worker and a student minister, I was able to get Ella Baker and Martin King to agree that there would be no preconceived ideas and no preconceived plans. However, Ella did ask me to give a keynote address on April 15, the first night of the conference—which was also Good Friday.

My talk got a lot of attention from outside the conference, because I said that many people in Black leadership, including those in the NAACP, were more engaged in conventional conversations than in working on how we could change our society. But I was focused on the audience in the conference. My challenge in that moment was to bring together a wide range of students and speak to them about working together and using nonviolence as a key to our success. I called the speech "From a Lunch-Counter Stool," and in it I echoed something Ella Baker had said in her opening speech earlier that day. She had asked, "Is it just a lot of nonsense over a hamburger? Or is it far more?" I would address the gap I knew existed and that Martin and Ella knew existed, too.

> At the beginning of this decade, the student generation was "silent," "uncommitted," or "beatnik." But after only four months, these analogies largely used by adults appear as hasty clichés which should not have been used in the first place. The rapidity and drive of the movement indicates that all the while American students were simply waiting in suspension; waiting for that cause, that ideal, that event, that "actualizing of their faith" which would catapult their right to speak powerfully to their nation and world. . . .
>
> . . . Eventually our society must abide by the Constitution and not permit any local law or custom to hinder freedom or justice. But such a society lives by more than law. . . .
>
> . . . We who are demonstrators are trying to raise what we call the "moral issue." . . . We are pointing to the viciousness of racial segregation and prejudice and calling it evil or sin. . . . Until America (South and North) honestly accepts the sinful nature of racism, this cancerous disease will continue. . . .
>
> . . . The nonviolent movement is asserting: Get moving. The pace of change is too slow. At this rate it will be at least another generation before the major forms of segregation disappear. All of Africa will be free before the American Negro attains first-class citizenship. Most of us will be grandparents before we can live normal, human lives.
>
> The choice of the nonviolent method, "the sit-in," symbolizes both judgment and promise. It is a judgment upon middle-class conventional, halfway efforts to deal with radical social evil. . . . As one high school student from Chattanooga exclaimed, "We started because we were tired of waiting for you adults to act."

I then gave my opinion that traditional Black leadership—in groups like the NAACP and its magazine, called *The Crisis*—was really not engaged in fighting the current conditions harassing and destroying Black folk.

> After many court decisions, the deeper South we go, the more token integration (and that only in the public schools) we achieve. *Crisis* magazine becomes known as a "Black bourgeois" club organ, rather than a forceful instrument for justice. Inter-racial agencies expect to end segregation with discussions and teas. Our best agency (the NAACP) accents fundraising and court action rather than developing our greatest resource, a people no longer the victims of racial evil who can act in a disciplined manner to implement the Constitution. . . .
>
> But the sit-in is likewise a sign of promise: God's promise that if radically Christian methods are adopted, the rate of change can be vastly increased. This is why nonviolence dominates the movement's perspective. . . . Nonviolence strips the segregationist power structure of its major weapon: the manipulation of law or law enforcement to keep the Negro in his place. . . .
>
> Nonviolence in the Negro's struggle gains a fresh maturity. And the Negro gains a new sense of his role in molding a redeemed society.

The part about the NAACP and afternoon fundraising teas was a smart-aleck dig. I supported that organization and always had, ever since my sister Dorothy and I had joined the NAACP youth chapter in Massillon when I was a junior in high school. But at Shaw, I called the sit-in campaign what it was in part: a critique of traditional Black leadership.

The speech reached our audience and resonated deeply. Still, the few papers covering our gathering picked up on my NAACP criticism and not much else, and then portrayed it as indicating a rift between the SCLC and the NAACP. *The New York Times* coverage of the event was headlined "Negro Criticizes N.A.A.C.P. Tactics."

But we were focused on the work at hand. As the talks during the conference progressed, it became clear that we needed some kind of continued organization. I was asked to chair a steering committee for the conference, and we were charged with coming up with a vehicle to continue coordinating and promoting the nonviolent direct action movement, particularly among the young. We brought back a proposal. It began with the idea that we call ourselves the Temporary Student Nonviolent Coordinating Committee. I insisted that the word "nonviolent" be part of the name. And we put forth the idea that each state would have one person on the committee. Plus, there would be one person on the committee from each of the two most supportive white organizations: the National Student Association and the World Student Christian Federation, which was the multidenominational Protestant movement in the United States. Also, we were to have three or four at-large members.

Then we started to draw up the founding statement. But instead of all of us doing it together, through a task force, as I suggested, the group asked me to write it. This sort of irritated me at the time, so I remember it well. I had to spend Friday and Saturday after the evening sessions working on that statement of purpose. The committee members would not put together a task force for doing the work they demanded. The task force was Jim Lawson.

On Easter Sunday, April 17, Marion Barry was elected the first president of what came to be called the Student Nonviolent Coordinating Committee, or SNCC, pronounced "Snick." And the founding statement I wrote was approved at the end of the conference that afternoon.

Even as we were organizing SNCC, Martin, Doug Moore, and I had some fruitful conversations that weekend about the future of the SCLC. We discussed the idea of Doug and me becoming the staff for the SCLC, to help it and the movement develop. Up to then, Ella Baker had been the only staff member of the SCLC, serving as its interim executive director. Martin King was fumbling a little on how to create a staff structure. But with the sit-ins mobilizing so many communities across the South, he saw roles for me and for Doug.

Martin and Doug had been classmates at the Boston University School of Theology. Doug was considered much more radical than Martin, even then, so they had not been particularly close in school. In 1957, Doug had organized a sit-in at Royal Ice Cream in Durham, North Carolina. It was a model for the Greensboro sit-ins. For a while—since well before 1960—he had been organizing students in much the same way I had. Martin now wanted to harness the impatience we all felt, which had spurred our new direct action approach. We all knew we were in the early stages of a momentous movement, and we all felt hopeful as the SNCC conference wrapped up on that Easter Sunday evening. About two thousand people came to a closing mass meeting at the Municipal Auditorium in Raleigh, where Martin spoke. He echoed some of what I had said on Good Friday, calling the sit-in movement "a revolt against those Negroes in the middle class who have indulged themselves in big cars and ranch-style homes rather than in joining a movement for freedom."

After Easter weekend, I went right back to Nashville. The mayor's biracial committee had released its plan recommending an unacceptable solution of segregated and desegregated sections in restaurants. We were not on board. It was becoming clear that the biracial committee was not going to spur significant change. We would have to keep doing the pushing.

We decided we would accept only direct negotiations between our group and the merchants, not through second or third parties like the biracial committee. Our central committee created a negotiating subcommittee co-chaired by Diane Nash and Kelly Miller Smith. Some downtown businesspeople had already been talking with us, telling us they thought segregation was wrong and that they ought to desegregate. But they didn't know how to do it. And no businessperson wanted to lead the way. So we set out to create a plan.

The Easter season boycott we had initiated earlier in April had been a success. Accompanying it, by the middle of April, were daily sit-ins and poster walks—which were similar to labor union picketing. Participants marched in circles or back and forth in front of businesses, carrying handmade posters with slogans and messages. *The New York Times* was now covering our movement closely. On Monday, April 18, Harrison Salisbury wrote a front-page article headlined "Nashville Issue Is Full Equality":

> Backing up the sit-in, the Negro community in the week before Easter conducted a massive "withdrawal of patronage" or boycott of the downtown retail area where the struggle has been concentrated. In the later part of the week hardly a Negro entered the stores involved in the struggle. In fact, there were few even on the sidewalks of the central shopping area.
>
> This brought into play an economic weapon of importance. . . .
>
> It is estimated that Negroes spend about $7,500,000 annually in the downtown stores. The volume is enough to make the difference

> between red ink and black ink on the ledgers of many establishments.
>
> Unlike business men in some communities farther South, Nashville's merchants do not view integrated lunch service to Negroes in terms of morality. They say it is just a matter of dollars and cents. They are afraid they might lose business from the country folk they have attracted to the old city area at great effort. . . .
>
> But Negroes believe the Easter boycott may cause some business men to recalculate the costs of their present policy.

On Tuesday, April 19, our attorney, Z. Alexander Looby, and his wife, Grafta, were shocked from their sleep at five A.M. when a bomb virtually destroyed their home near Fisk University. Miraculously, no one was injured.

I heard the boom. Diane Nash heard the boom. A number of us heard the loud boom—because it was near where most of us lived in North Nashville. We were all up early, getting dressed for our six A.M. central committee meeting. Only later did we find out that the cause was a bomb at our lawyer's house. Our offices on Jefferson Street were one block over from his home.

Of course, that bombing became the subject of our meeting. We immediately decided that we would not exercise our anger by trying to do violent or hateful things in return. Instead, we would direct our energy and anger toward what would strengthen the movement. Quickly organizing ourselves, we unanimously agreed on a silent march that day, from Tennessee A&I down Jefferson Street past Fisk, and on to city hall. We put out the word, asking people who were mad about the bombing to join us in a massive march to city hall. We aimed to confront the mayor with his own statements that encouraged the terrorism, and with our demands that the police defend the right of every citizen of Nashville to protest publicly.

Mayor Ben West had been evasive with us. He was not talking to Kelly, our chief spokesperson, or any delegations of the Black preachers who had supported him when he first ran for office. He seemed not to know how to deal with this crisis—or to want to. We sent Mayor West four telegrams that morning from different people, saying that we had been trying unsuccessfully to get ahold of him before the bombing. But in the aftermath of the bombing, we said, we were marching to city hall.

We added, "We hope you'll meet us there." C. T. Vivian drafted a statement, which we edited. Diane Nash and he were asked to be the spokespeople who would read the statement to the mayor.

At 11:55 A.M., several hundred of us set out on the three-mile walk. It was the first time I had ever participated in a march in Nashville. All along the route we took on hundreds more people, especially as we passed Fisk and Meharry Medical College. Then we took on a large delegation of students from Pearl High School. Because it was a silent march, we told people that if they had to talk, they could only whisper. We handed out small papers for the march, which many people carried. They read, "We shall let our complete silence be our only speech." We had no megaphones. We did no shouting. We could hear all the noise from our feet, from our shoes on the sidewalk up and down the ranks. The silence was stirring.

I was up front, moving between the third and fourth rows. Diane Nash was in the first row of the group, along with John Lewis and Bernard Lafayette. Rodney Powell and Gloria Johnson were there. They were both studying at Meharry Medical College and later married. Curtis Murphy and a number of other people were in those first five or ten rows of marchers. We came straight down Jefferson, then moved toward downtown, walking among the state and city buildings. This march was one of the largest the South or even the nation had seen up to that moment. And it was a nonviolent, orderly march. By the time we got to the square at city hall, we numbered three thousand people. The mayor had come out onto the stairs and was waiting for us when we arrived. C. T. Vivian and Diane Nash spoke with him. We hadn't given them instructions as to what to say in that exchange.

But C.T. began with the statement we had written earlier in the day.

> We have come from every part of the city. We are those of all races. Together we have come to urgently beseech the mayor. . . .
>
> . . . The citizenry is outraged and must speak when one of Nashville's most honored citizens and city councilmen's home is bombed and injustice is visited upon many. We feel that this bomb can silence decency in Nashville or cause decent men to speak more loudly than the bomb. The mayor has steadfastly ignored the moral issues involved in segregation. . . . He has not used the moral weight of his office to speak out against violence and hate mongers. . . . By his lack

> of decision he has encouraged violence by permitting the police to use their authority with partiality. They have from the beginning arrested the wrong people and allowed hoodlum elements the freedom of violent action against peaceful demonstrators. . . . He has continued to ignore the realities of the pressing need for full citizenship for all of our citizens.

As C.T. ended his remarks, asking the mayor "to act sanely," the crowd erupted in applause. Mayor Ben West was visibly angry with C.T.'s statement and its critique of his leadership. He did not seem to like a Black preacher talking to him that way. He gave a counterstatement, saying, "I deny and resent to the bottom of my soul the implications you have read in that statement. I intend to see that order is maintained in this city." He spoke about desegregating the schools. Then he said, "I am doing my best to find the person who bombed the home of my friend Councilman Looby."

After a few more words from West, Diane spoke up. We had not, as far as I knew, given her any instructions. But she simply asked him, "Is it wrong to discriminate solely because of race?"

He replied, "I appeal to all citizens to have no discrimination, no hatred, no bias, no bigotry."

Diane asked, "Do you mean that to include lunch counters?"

He said, "Little lady, one of my first acts as mayor was to desegregate the lunch counter at the Nashville Municipal Airport. And there has been no trouble since."

Diane replied simply, "Then, Mayor, do you recommend desegregation of the lunch counters in the stores?"

Mayor West replied, "Yes. Yes. But that is up to the store owners, of course. I can't tell a man how to run his business."

The crowd cheered when the mayor confirmed that he had indeed just said he supported ending segregated lunch counters. The next day, the huge banner headline across the front page of the *Tennessean* read, "INTEGRATE COUNTERS—MAYOR."

I have said that Mayor West counted himself as a moderate. When we made our first demands to desegregate in February of that year, he felt it couldn't be done at that time, and he opposed many of the other measures we put forth. But with that march and confrontation on the steps of city hall, we forced him to say publicly that everybody should be served downtown. Diane skillfully backed him into a corner. Finally, Ben West had the courage to say what was right, and what was wrong, and that the right way needed to be followed.

We knew what we were doing when we selected our spokespeople for that event—a Black preacher who was angry and a Black student with simple questions. Those were the two. What they accomplished, together with the largest crowd we had ever had, was no small feat.

People came away from that moment with a real sense that we all had done something to make a difference, to change Nashville. Everyone in the mass meetings afterward also expressed how successful the whole march felt.

Martin Luther King was already scheduled to speak in Nashville the next evening, Wednesday, April 20, at Fisk University. Kelly Miller Smith had invited Martin, who was happy to come support our campaign. After the march the day before, his visit turned out to be our largest mass meeting to date, with more than four thousand people inside the Fisk gymnasium. The start was delayed when everyone had to evacuate because of a bomb threat.

About an hour later, we finally got started. Alexander Looby, still shaken from the bombing the day before, stood up before the crowd and waved. The cheers overwhelmed him and he began to cry, and so he sat back down as the loving applause continued. Martin stepped onto the stage with Kelly Miller Smith, me, and C. T. Vivian accompanying him, and he took a seat next to Mr. Looby. The *Tennessean* reported on the bomb scare and the speech in the next day's paper:

> Referring to the threat and to the Tuesday morning bombing . . . King said: "The diehards should know by now that bombs will not stop us."
>
> The statement drew thunderous cheers from the audience that packed the bleachers and crowded the floor of the huge gymnasium and overflowed outside where other thousands stood and sat to hear the talk by loudspeaker.
>
> King praised the Nashville sit-in movement as "the best organized and the most disciplined in the Southland."
>
> "I came to Nashville not to bring inspiration but to gain inspiration from the great movement that has taken place in this community," he said.

> The leaders and the students of the Nashville sit-ins, King said, "have gained a better understanding of the philosophy of the movement (non-violence) than any other group."

In two days, the tide had turned. Even so, we still did nonviolent sit-ins and poster walks to keep the pressure on for a little longer. With our effective economic boycott we knew we were on our way to achieving our goal of starting the desegregation of downtown Nashville. Our negotiating committee had drafted a plan for the businesses we had targeted. And the merchants had agreed to it.

The course of action was straightforward. We would stop the demonstrations, but we would not announce it. The merchants would make sure their people were ready to treat Black folk with total equality. They would take down the "Whites Only" signs, without announcements. And they would start remodeling their restrooms. All their segregationist policies would be dropped. There were no laws to change. We were simply ending the entrenched policies that had perpetuated centuries-old segregation customs in one city in the American South. A Black woman who couldn't even try on a hat or a dress in a downtown Nashville store up to then, finally could. And there would be no more buying shoes and taking them home to see if they fit, only to have to bring them back and try again if they did not. All that was over.

We agreed to an experimental phase for two weeks, in which several Black couples we selected would come in and be among the first to be served. We promised we would not make any announcements about it. Police officers would not be around. And we all agreed on Tuesday, May 10, as the start date. We began to send in people, but the "experiment" was so successful in the first week that the negotiating committee and the merchants said, "Forget it. It's working. We don't have to experiment any longer."

That was it. The first sit-ins were completed. We had won.

But as our negotiating committee made clear, to the merchants and to the city, our efforts were not done. In fact, we were only just beginning. Our goal was full desegregation of all businesses in Nashville. We planned to talk to merchants about Black employment in the stores and access to all jobs at all levels. We let them know to expect us again. We told them, "We're coming back for more."

TEN

Such Starry-Eyed Men

The first Freedom Ride bus headed into Mississippi, May 24, 1961. First row, left, Julia Aaron Humbles and David Dennis Sr. Second row, left, Joseph Carter, and Bernard Lafayette, Reverend Lawson behind them. On the right side of the bus behind the national guard troops is Rev. Andrew White. PAUL SCHUTZER, LIFE MAGAZINE, SHUTTERSTOCK

We were so engrossed in our campaign to get rid of segregation in downtown Nashville that it sometimes seemed as if our movement was the only thing happening in the world. Of course, world events had continued. And the world was watching us, too. In May 1960, just a few days before we succeeded in desegregating the six downtown stores we had targeted, a Black independence leader from what was then called Northern Rhodesia visited Nashville. Kenneth Kaunda was on a tour organized by the pro-independence American Committee on Africa (ACOA). A few weeks before, he had been released from prison after serving several years for his nonviolent resistance to the British-run government. He had started his American visit in April in New York City, where he had given the keynote speech at ACOA's annual Africa Freedom Day. In May, he traveled around the country visiting leaders of our movement to end racial segregation in the United States. He came to Nashville and we spent a morning and afternoon together.

Time magazine covered his trip and described him as one of the African leaders determined "to destroy the Central African Federation, a nation tacked together by Britain in 1953 in a desperate effort to make a stable, viable country out of three dissimilar territories carved out of the bush by empire builder Cecil Rhodes." The article went on to say that the Central African Federation was aligned with South Africa's apartheid policies, which were what Kaunda and others were fighting to end. Four years later, in 1964, his country finally shook off the British government and formed the nation of Zambia. He would be elected as its first president.

Time described Mr. Kaunda's tour as "a month-long schedule of visits to Washington, the Mid-West, and the South. High point: a meeting with some young U.S. Negro leaders of the lunch-counter campaign in the South, to compare notes on tactics."

That day in Nashville, Kaunda and I toured the Tennessee Valley Authority—one of President Roosevelt's New Deal projects, envisioned as a regional economic development agency and federally funded utility company. Kaunda was a good man, thirty-six years old and committed to nonviolence. Our tactics were his tactics. We were aligned. He gave a talk at Fisk that Tuesday night, May 3, sponsored by the NCLC and FOR. After Nashville, he went to Atlanta to meet with Martin.

I was supposed to have gotten my master's degree with my Vanderbilt class in June 1960. Instead, I was expelled in April. After Dorothy and I fielded the countless offers from universities around the country, we chose Boston University, where Martin had finished divinity school. They accepted all of my courses from Vanderbilt and said I could finish by August 10. I only had to take one class. The rest of my work there was through reading courses with professors in the fields that I had been working on at Vanderbilt, such as social gospel, and a course on Karl Barth, one of the best-known twentieth-century theologians. I also did a reading course in theology with Harold DeWolf, who was one of Martin's advisers when he was at BU. We moved to Boston for the rest of the summer. Briefly, Dorothy and I thought about staying there so that I might get a PhD in sociology. But events would steer my life in a different direction.

Going back to the South to work for the SCLC after finishing my degree at BU kept looking like the best option. The conversations that had started a few months before at the SNCC founding conference in Raleigh, about Doug and me going on staff at the SCLC, had continued. However, Roy Wilkins, the head of the NAACP, had taken umbrage at my speech in Raleigh and had written to me and then to Martin, who sent the letter to me. We talked about it and both Martin and I responded to Roy, saying my remarks were not a criticism of the NAACP as an organization but a critique of the slow pace of change when working only through legal channels.

Around June 10, I got a call in Boston from A. J. Muste saying he was coming up from New York to take me to lunch. When he arrived he told me that leaders of the NAACP, upset at my criticism, had informed the SCLC and Martin King that if I joined the staff of the SCLC, the NAACP would no longer work with the SCLC. Martin wanted me to hear this news in person, and he asked A.J. to deliver it. Of course I was upset. It felt like a slight to what I saw as my contribution to the deepest goals of our movement. I was learning that the strength of my fierce commitment to radical nonviolence meant there would be certain limits to the roles I could play publicly in the movement. I would adjust and find the advantages in that later. But in that moment, Roy Wilkins effectively barring me from joining the staff of the SCLC was a hard blow to absorb.

Soon after that bitter news came from A. J. Muste, I heard that the outgoing Methodist bishop of Nashville had appointed me to become pastor of a church in Shelbyville, Tennessee, a small town an hour south of Nashville. At first, I was disappointed because the bishop had promised Dorothy and me there would be an appointment in a city. The bishop was responsible only for Tennessee. That would have meant Memphis, Nashville, Chattanooga, Knoxville, or possibly, with some finagling, Little Rock, in Arkansas. But Shelbyville was a rural community. Dorothy and I would have to do some serious thinking.

Ever since junior high school, "Reverend" had been the title I most felt called to embrace—I wanted to be pastor of a local church. I talked to Charles Golden, the incoming bishop of the Nashville-Birmingham area, to tell him that I wasn't sure yet about coming back to the South and had considered remaining in Boston to get a PhD. After the news about the

SCLC not panning out, I was uncertain. I had known Bishop Golden for several years by that time and liked him. He wrote me back, asking me to "please take the appointment." He wanted me to be in the Nashville area. "Jim, you need to come back," he said. "I'm a new bishop and this is new territory to me, I don't know it. I need you to be part of the leadership in this new conference in Tennessee." I couldn't tell him no. It wouldn't be the last time Bishop Golden would steer my path in a fruitful direction in the clergy, and in life.

Shortly after graduating with my master's degree from BU on August 14, 1960, Dorothy and I returned to Nashville so I could accept the appointment at Scott Memorial Methodist Church, in Shelbyville. Dorothy resumed her work at the National Council of Churches racial justice office, working with Will Campbell.

Scott Memorial Methodist Church was halfway between Nashville and Chattanooga, in Bedford County, the national center of the Tennessee walking horse industry. Every August and September in Shelbyville, a big event called "The Celebration" took place, with walking horses from around the country. I was told through my district supervisor that some people in the Methodist Church administration thought I would probably flunk the appointment to Scott Church, given that it was a rural assignment and I had become famous—or infamous—for the sit-ins. Some folk in the Black community in Nashville and in the Black church saw me as a dangerous person. Other pastors in Tennessee were saying I would never make it as a rural pastor because I was a Northerner, or because the Black community in Shelbyville would be afraid of me. Of course, none of that was true.

What they did not understand was what I knew from my warm embrace in the rural Tennessee community of Charleston, Dorothy's hometown, which was similar to Shelbyville. Dorothy's family looked forward to the changes that needed to come in the 1960s. I never heard a critical word about me or my work from them or from anyone in Charleston, Tennessee. Nor did Dorothy.

My appointment did give a few people at Scott Memorial Methodist Church pause, but it gave many others hope. Here was this guy who had been kicked out of Vanderbilt for his work with Martin King, and he was coming to Scott Church. The congregation became responsive to my preaching, my teaching, and my leadership. For Dorothy and me, it turned out to be a great experience.

As I was pastoring in Shelbyville, Dorothy and I continued to live in Nashville. I resigned from the Fellowship of Reconciliation in the fall of 1960 to focus on my new appointment. But I kept up my work in the movement in Nashville, and continued to travel to other hot spots around the South.

That year, the student sit-in campaign would spread to include nonviolent demonstrations in just about every state. Many thought of Nashville as the epicenter of the sit-ins. High school, college, and university students from all over the country reached out to us with moral support, mostly through letters. Many picketed in their own communities. Even though Woolworth's and some of the other national five-and-ten-cent stores around the country had segregation policies only in the South, our national supporters picketed those chain stores in their own communities to show solidarity with us in the South. Their support also included demanding that universities around the country desegregate and make life easier for students of color and for international students.

Dorothy and I also continued to receive a large volume of white hate mail at our home in Nashville. Even during the summer we spent in Boston, we had gotten letters addressed to me through the divinity school at Boston University:

> *Listen Nigger—*
>
> *90% of ALL white people, the nation and WORLD OVER, support the SOUTH and segregation, 100%!!*
>
> *The only white people who support HEINOUS integration, are communists, the leadership of the Bolshevik national council of churches, and fools!!*
>
> *We don't want to EAT next to you coons, nor do we desire, that our children attend school with jigs, nor do white people wish to in any way, to socialize with you shines!!*
>
> *Nothing, but NOTHING, smells as bad, as a perspiring, FAT lipped, kinky haired nigger.*
>
> *Boogie, you and other niggers, should go BACK to Africa, where you be long!*
>
> *white people, will NEVER "amalgamate," with you filthy black savages!*

While that kind of taunting became commonplace, it never was normal. The people who spoke like that were such weak models of their beliefs, and inept agents of their cause. To me, they were merely misguided people who tried to stand in the way of everyone's freedom from oppression.

On the other hand, students and adults kept joining our movement. I attended monthly meetings with SNCC, and staff meetings with the SCLC. I was included, even though I was not officially on the SCLC staff. I had become a sort of consultant. Also, I was going to meetings of the NCLC and to meetings of the Nashville Student Movement's central committee. All of those meetings, retreats, and gatherings of staff members were in the service of planning what to do next, and were part of the fermentation of our young movement.

After the first sit-ins, some of the signs in Nashville began to change. But it would take several years of work before public life was fully desegregated in Nashville. In November 1960, we continued that work with another series of sit-ins at seven more lunch counters, led by Bernard Lafayette, John Lewis, and James Bevel. The fact that I participated in some of those sit-ins was pointed out in the local as well as the national press, including in *The New York Times.*

The sit-in movement had become national news. On Saturday, November 26, 1960, Martin debated James J. Kilpatrick, the same segregationist Richmond newspaper editor and columnist who had written the editorial in his paper in February attacking the sit-ins. The thirty-minute debate about the efficacy of desegregation, and in particular the sit-ins, took place in New York City and was entitled "Our Nation's Future." It aired on NBC.

Martin was being pulled further into becoming the spokesperson for the entire movement, whether he wanted to be or not. He and his wife Coretta were expecting their third child in January, and he was juggling family, his church, and the movement, as I was. In fact, Dorothy and I were beginning to revel in our own growing family. By Christmas 1960, we had found out that Dorothy was pregnant. It was such a joyous time in our lives, even as it was a crucial time in the life of the movement. Dexter King was born right after the start of 1961, and our first child was expected in the summer.

Early 1961 was also when our Nashville campaign expanded to include demonstrations against segregated movie theaters. We conducted what came to be called "stand-ins" at movie theaters from February through April of that year. Black people were not allowed to sit on the ground level of any movie theater with white moviegoers. Instead, the balconies of the movie theaters were designated for Negroes. To get to the balconies, we would have to buy a ticket at the box office and then go outside and around the side of the building to the alley and climb the fire escape to a separate entrance for the balcony seats.

On Wednesday, February 1, more than one hundred students demonstrated at four downtown Nashville movie theaters on Church Street: the Paramount, the Tennessee, the Crescent, and Loew's. They wore lapel pins that read, "Remember Freedom Day—February 1," commemorating the one-year anniversary of the Greensboro, North Carolina, lunch counter sit-in. Through SNCC, we coordinated with students in other Southern cities using the same tactics. We would try to buy tickets for the downstairs, and when refused we would go to the back of the line and try again. That would slow down ticket sales for the box office. White demonstrators would buy downstairs tickets and give them to Black demonstrators to enter the theater. When we were denied entry, we would stand silently outside the theater. Sometimes we would sing.

All of the Nashville theaters closed that first day, rather than sell us downstairs tickets. *The Nashville Tennessean* reported:

> Harold Stark, manager of the Crescent, said the Negroes appeared between 6:30 and 7:30 p.m., and stood in the line quietly outside the box office after the cashier refused to take their money.
>
> "We told them that it is a community policy to have segregation in the movies," said Stark. "Then we turned out the lights and closed down."

The next day we went back, and three of the four theaters closed. The Loew's theater stayed open. An assistant manager at the theater told a reporter for the *Tennessean,* "We are not going to close and we are not going to let them in." The paper said Loew's had a sign in its box office window that read, "No, we are not integrated."

We continued to demonstrate at the four movie theaters. Over the next days, young white people began to heckle and harass us on the street outside the theaters. The police offered little protection, and there were no arrests of the hostile white people.

On Monday, February 20, 1961, twenty-eight students standing quietly outside one theater were arrested on the fraudulent charge of blocking a fire exit. The officers gave the students the option of moving on or being arrested. They all chose to be arrested. Lester McKinney and John Lewis were among them. More students who had been demonstrating at other theaters on Church Street joined McKinney and Lewis and asked to be arrested, but the paddy wagon was full, so the officers turned them away. Of the twenty-eight arrested, only one was not yet in college—a fifteen-year-old high school student—and only one was white, a woman who attended Tennessee A&I. All the students refused bail and instead stayed in jail until their trial the next day, when the charges were dismissed because the codes the police used to justify the arrests were outdated.

The next evening, a larger group of young white people stood across from the demonstrators on Church Street, shouting obscenities and throwing rocks. When it was time to leave, we marched back to the First Baptist Church, which was nearby. The crowd of white people followed, screaming at us with the military marching chant "Hup, two, three, four." They jumped some of our students from behind and began to beat them. The police were not around. Most of us made it back to the church. But two of our people were hospitalized with injuries. Again, not one of the violent white people was arrested.

Each of the next two days brought more hostility from white people. On Wednesday, February 22, about one hundred people stood-in at the four theaters. The *Tennessean* reported, "A group of white youths led by a blond man with a high-pitched voice, cursed, kicked and threatened to knife Negro stand-in demonstrators downtown last night."

We stood quietly in front of the theaters after trying to enter and being refused. We sang hymns. The hecklers grew increasingly agitated. The *Tennessean* described the scene:

> Police allowed a group of white youths, standing four-deep, to form, opposite the Tennessee Theater. Two hours later, officers decided to break up the jeering group, which whistled "Dixie" through rolled-up newspapers and hurled verbal insults across the street at the demonstrators, particularly the white girl students standing-in.

As we left to head back to First Baptist, the mob of whites again followed. The paper said they were "throwing rocks, kicking the students, and hitting them with sticks and umbrellas." Reporters and photographers were attacked. Rev. Metz Rollins, a steadfast and determined member of the NCLC, was hit by one of the rocks. The paper reported, "He was wearing the white collar and black vestment of a minister." A white person drew a knife on a Black student. Only then did the police step in. But no one was arrested.

On Friday, February 24, the crowds formed across the street from the theaters again and threw rocks and eggs. "During the stand-in," the *Tennessean* reported, "theater personnel ushered white persons into the theaters, but held back the demonstrators." When we finished that night, James Bevel led the demonstrators back to First Baptist. The paper said:

> Following at the end of a long, singing line of students was the Rev. James M. Lawson Jr. . . . And close behind him was a group of 25 white boys who kicked and cursed the Negroes until an officer chased them off.

I remember the scene well. I was at the back of the march, because that's where the worst of the harassers gathered, throwing Coke bottles at us, spitting on us, yelling and screaming at us, hitting and kicking us. As often as I could, I tried to turn around and face one of the loudest white boys who wanted to do us in. He kept cussing me out. Finally, I looked him in the eye and said, "Did your church teach you to talk like this?" He said, "They taught us segregation." I replied, "But did they teach you to hit and spit and kick and cuss other human beings?" He responded as though I were hitting him over the head with my fist. Then I turned around to get my bearings and keep moving in the right direction. When I next pivoted to face him one more time, he had disappeared through the crowd. I never saw him again at a movie theater demonstration.

Nonviolence creates a moral jujitsu. Violent forces expect either a hostile response or cowering and fear. It knocks them upside down when they don't get any of that. If I am faced with a hostile assailant, my practice has been to obey Jesus and turn the other cheek. Psychologically, it is a very extreme weapon. Now, it's true, the assailant might then sock me on that cheek as well. But the assailant might also do something else, because he is so upset that instead of using my fist against him I turned the other cheek, as happened with that young white man on the march that night. He ran away.

It took another two months, but by the end of April, we had succeeded once more. The downtown theaters lifted their segregation policies. As we had the year before with the stores, we negotiated a transition period with the theater owners. Quietly and without announcing it, our people went in pairs to the movie theaters and sat wherever they wanted to sit, instead of in the segregated balconies.

We had desegregated another aspect of daily life in the city. And once again, we put the city on notice. We were not stopping. During our stand-ins, we passed out leaflets to passersby, signed by the Nashville Nonviolent Movement, that said: "Do not be deceived, we do not simply intend to integrate a few counters or theaters. We want better jobs and housing; more educational and vocational opportunities; and expanded social and recreational facilities."

Sometime in the spring of 1961, as John Lewis was participating in the stand-ins and finishing up his degree at American Baptist Theological Seminary, he saw an announcement in *The Student Voice,* SNCC's newsletter:

> Freedom Ride, 1961, sponsored by CORE, will be a dramatic move to complete the integration of bus service and accommodations in the deep South. The ride will begin in Washington, D.C. about May 1 and end in New Orleans on May 17. Traveling via Greyhound and Trailways, the Ride will test the recent Supreme Court decision banning segregation of interstate passengers in lunch room facilities operated as an integral part of a bus terminal. Cost for Freedom Ride, 1961, will be borne by CORE. Participants will need to pay only incidental expenses. For further information write Gordon R. Carey, Field Director, Congress of Racial Equality, 38 Park Row, New York 38, N.Y.

John decided he wanted to go on the Freedom Ride. He came to me, and we discussed it. I encouraged him to do it. Then he asked me to write a letter of reference for him to send along with his application to CORE, which I did. He was one of the original interracial group of riders selected, and became the youngest member in the initial part of the Freedom Ride in 1961.

Of course, John's participation meant our Nashville central committee had an automatic kinship with the Freedom Ride. We also had a kinship with Jim Farmer, a co-founder of the Congress of Racial Equality and an organizer of the Freedom Ride. I knew Jim had been thinking about it for a while. I first met him in the late-1940s when I was in college and he and Bayard Rustin worked for the Fellowship of Reconciliation. That's when FOR and the Congress of Racial Equality used sit-ins to desegregate lunch counters in Chicago, Boston, Los Angeles, and Washington, D.C. I had closely followed that effort and learned a lot from it.

In 1946, a case in Virginia had reached the Supreme Court. The ruling in *Morgan v. Virginia* outlawed segregation in interstate travel. To test that ruling, in 1947, FOR's George Houser and Bayard Rustin organized the Journey of Reconciliation. Sixteen men, eight white and eight Black, boarded buses scheduled to travel from Washington, D.C., through Virginia, North Carolina, Tennessee, and Kentucky, to affirm that segregation in interstate travel had indeed been eliminated. The group got as far as North Carolina, where a white mob attacked them, and two of the men on the bus were arrested. They eventually turned around and did not complete the trip.

While the 1946 *Morgan* ruling meant that segregation on the buses and trains themselves would eventually be lifted, it did not do away with segregation inside the stations or in their dining areas. All across the South, those were still segregated. But in 1960, another Supreme Court ruling on another Virginia case, *Boynton v. Virginia,* finally outlawed segregation in all facilities related to public transportation, which meant there should not be any whites-only areas in any bus or train station in the United States. The *Boynton* ruling inspired Jim Farmer and George Houser to organize the 1961 Freedom Ride, which itself had been inspired by the unfinished 1947 Journey of Reconciliation.

But this time, women would be on board. Washington, D.C., would again be the starting point. From there, the riders would be testing bus stations deeper into the segregationist-ruled South, along the coast to Georgia, across to Alabama and Mississippi, and then into Louisiana. Just as the Journey of Reconciliation meant to test the *Morgan* ruling, the Freedom Riders were intent on calling attention to whether the *Boynton* ruling had really desegregated interstate travel, or if Deep South segregation still prevailed in bus and railway stations.

In Nashville we were watching the Freedom Ride closely and supporting the riders wholeheartedly. There was some tension during the first few days of the ride through Virginia and North Carolina. But the worst violence came when they reached Rock Hill, South Carolina.

Rock Hill is where, despite active lunch counter sit-ins the year before, the whole town remained staunchly segregated. And a year later, on February 1, 1961—the day we all commemorated the initial sit-in the year before in Greensboro—nine students from nearby colleges sat in again. They were arrested for trespassing and offered two options: either pay the $100 bail or work for thirty days on a chain gang. They adopted the "jail, no bail" stance we at SNCC had pushed, and went to York County Prison Farm on February 2, 1961. There, they became known as the Rock Hill Nine. When SNCC leaders heard of their arrest, four of them, including Diane Nash, decided to go to Rock Hill and join their campaign. On February 6, the SNCC group sat in at Good's Drug Store, on Main Street. They were immediately arrested. Of course, they also refused bail. The two men, Charles Sherrod and Charles Jones, were sent to the chain gang, and Diane and Ruby Doris Smith, a student from Spelman, were sent to the York County jail. Soon after that, about forty more Nashville students went to Rock Hill and staged demonstrations against their arrests.

So Rock Hill was known as a place of deep resistance to desegregation. When the first Freedom Ride bus pulled into the Greyhound terminal there, John Lewis and Al Bigelow, a white Freedom Rider, were designated as the two who would enter the white waiting room. Al was a Harvard graduate and already an anti-nuclear activist. They got off the bus together and went inside. As they headed to the white waiting room, a gang of young white men in leather jackets confronted them, beat them, and cracked open their heads. They were lying in their own blood when the police finally stepped in and stopped the attack. The bus had arrived in the Deep South, and for the first time on the Freedom Ride, two riders were bloodied.

We received news of the attack with deep concern, but we all knew that the Freedom Ride had to keep going. As it turned out, John's head wound still allowed him to keep his plans to fly to Philadelphia that night and be interviewed the next day for foreign service work in Africa. He intended to rejoin the Freedom Ride in Montgomery. The other riders made their way into Georgia after he left, where they spent time with Martin King in Atlanta.

On Sunday, May 14, Mother's Day, their two buses left Atlanta—one group riding on the Greyhound bus line and the other on the Trailways line, as usual. They entered Alabama, which was known as one of the two most brutally segregationist states in the country. The other state was Mississippi, where they were scheduled to go after Alabama. It was always a toss-up about which state was worse.

Anniston, Alabama, was the first stop in the state for the first bus, the Greyhound. The Trailways bus followed. After that, their next stop was to be Birmingham. Anniston was where my father was a pastor in the 1930s and felt the need to carry a gun because of the danger to Black people in that city. Thirty years later, when that first Freedom Ride Greyhound bus arrived in Anniston, the bus station was locked. A mob of fifty Ku Klux Klansmen armed with clubs, metal pipes, and chains was waiting for the Freedom Riders, and began to bash the bus, cutting its tires and smashing the windows. The police had been warned of an attack, but officers hung back, arriving well after the mob had begun its assault. The cops then promised to escort the hobbled but still functioning bus out of town, so that it could safely continue on its way. Instead, they abandoned the bus soon after it left the station. Another mob attacked, and one of the Klansmen threw a firebomb into the bus through a shattered window. The mob blocked the bus exits. The Freedom Riders and other passengers frantically escaped through the windows, and once they were out, they were then beaten savagely. Walter Bergman, a retired white college professor, was beaten so badly that he had a stroke and was never able to walk again. He would use a wheelchair for the rest of his life. His wife, Frances Bergman, another Freedom Rider, was also badly beaten in Anniston. Years later, Bergman successfully sued the federal government when an FBI informant who had infiltrated the KKK said he told the agency about the impending attack in Anniston, and they deliberately ignored it, suggesting ties between the Klan and local law enforcement.

Once the Anniston police finally stepped in and stopped the attack, passengers received limited medical care or no care at all, because both the ambulance and the hospital workers in Anniston, who were white, refused to transport or treat Freedom Riders. Finally, Rev. Fred Shuttlesworth, from Birmingham, arrived. He had organized a volunteer caravan to take the riders into Birmingham, so that they could be treated there.

When the riders on the Trailways bus arrived at the Anniston station, they had heard about what had happened to the Greyhound riders and so didn't get out of the bus. A few white men boarded. The driver told the Black Freedom Riders he wouldn't drive the bus to Birmingham unless they moved to the back of the bus, in accordance with a state segregation policy that had been against the law since 1946 but was still upheld by most bus companies in the South. The Black riders did not move. The white men then forced them to the back of the bus, beating, kicking, and cursing them. Only then did the driver agree to proceed to Birmingham.

Upon their arrival at the Birmingham Trailways station, another mob of Klansmen attacked them with bats and lead pipes. News reporters and camerapeople who were covering the arrival were also attacked. Once again, there was no sign of the local police at the terminal that day. It was later discovered that Birmingham's notorious head of public safety, Eugene "Bull" Connor, had made a deal with the KKK, agreeing that his officers would stay away so the attackers could have free reign on the Freedom Riders. White Freedom Riders were treated especially brutally that day. Jim Peck, a white Freedom Rider who had also been one of the men on the 1947 Journey of Reconciliation, was beaten so badly he had to have fifty-three stitches in his head and face.

All the Freedom Riders were so abused and weary by the time they got to Birmingham that they made the decision to end the ride and fly into New Orleans, their original destination, bypassing the rest of Alabama and all of Mississippi. John Seigenthaler, a Nashville native working for Attorney General Robert Kennedy's Justice Department, was dispatched to Birmingham to try to deal with the rogue white Southern officials and to get the Freedom Riders safely out of town.

As the violence escalated, President Kennedy and his brother Robert, the attorney general, tried in vain to reach Alabama Governor John Patterson, who was a Democrat and had supported President Kennedy in the 1960 election. Patterson, an enthusiastic segregationist who had also served as the state's attorney general, had defeated a circuit court judge named George Wallace in the 1958 governor's race, and prided himself on having "run the NAACP out of Alabama."

Just before the violence erupted in Alabama, the country had cast its eyes to the heavens, becoming obsessed with the then very novel idea of space travel. On May 5, Alan Shepard had sparked the public imagination when he became the first American ever to be launched into space, in his capsule called *Freedom 7*. For several days that May his expedition was the biggest news story in the world. But as the photos and TV coverage from Anniston and Birmingham of burned-out buses and badly beaten riders began to circulate, national attention returned to the harsh realities of life on the ground beneath our feet, and to the Freedom Ride. The *New York Post* ran an editorial entitled "Battle in Alabama," which connected the two events.

> The country has been properly reverential about the valor exhibited by Commander Shepard in his conquest of space. But the best in the democratic character is also exhibited by such men . . . who are seeking to lead us beyond the boundaries of bigotry and know-nothingism, and who have stoically taken so many beatings in their quest for a new world. A bus ride across Alabama under the banner of the Congress of Racial Equality (CORE) may be as daring an exploit as any ride in a space ship. We need more such starry-eyed men on earth.

I was in Ohio in early May, at my mother's bedside as she was having major surgery. But I spoke on the phone two or three times a day with Diane Nash and John Lewis during that time. When the riders decided against completing the ride through Alabama and Mississippi, I told John and Diane, "We can't let the Freedom Ride die by white mob." Part of the commitment we all made in the workshops I conducted in Nashville was not to let violent people get away with their violence, and not to allow them to stop our fair and just petition for justice. So our central committee—always made up of a majority of students from the participating campuses in Nashville, as well as a minority contingent of community people from the NCLC—debated how the Nashville campaign should respond to the Freedom Ride coming to a stop in Birmingham.

Although I was with my mother, and Dorothy was two months away from giving birth to our first child, I told Diane that I was in favor of going on. And I made it known to her that as soon as I could leave Ohio, I would join the Freedom Ride. Dorothy and I agreed it was something I needed to do. But I had promised her that no matter what, I would be home for our child's birth.

Our movement in Nashville became determined not to let the KKK violence stop our nonviolent campaign. And we knew we had to notify others in the movement that we were going to continue the journey. First we called Jim Farmer and Martin King. Then we informed everyone at CORE, the SCLC, FOR, and the NAACP. Diane Nash and John Lewis informed SNCC.

Then Diane and I agreed on the next step: we would contact Attorney General Robert Kennedy and tell him we would not back down and that it was vital that the Freedom Ride continue on to Jackson, Mississippi, and from there on to New Orleans. Diane made the phone call to our Justice Department contacts and got as far as RFK's deputy Burke Marshall. Then she called Fred Shuttlesworth, in Birmingham, to let him know we were coming.

We talked about all the dangers, but at every turn we affirmed together that we had to go anyway. The NCLC board was reluctant. Then they saw the resolve of the students, and they agreed to provide money for expenses on the road. The decision to continue the Freedom Ride was not impulsive, and included the kind of careful behind-the-scenes work we did throughout the movement: organizing, strategizing, getting done what needed to be done.

Early on the morning of Wednesday, May 17, 1961 (the seventh anniversary of the Supreme Court's *Brown v. Board of Education* ruling), our Nashville group of ten boarded a Greyhound bus headed to Birmingham. There were six Black men—John Lewis, Paul Brooks, William Barbee, Allen Cason, Charles Butler, and William Harbour—and two Black women—Lucretia Collins and Catherine Burks Brooks—as well as one white man, Jim Zwerg, and one white woman, Salynn McCollum. It was agreed that Diane would stay off the buses and coordinate and manage the ride from Nashville, so that there would be someone to call for support as needed, and someone to call if things went wrong. Diane decided to have a separate phone line installed at the student movement office for incoming calls only, and to keep the office open twenty-four hours a day, so anyone who needed help could always get through.

A few hours after the bus left for Birmingham, Diane got a call from John Seigenthaler. Apparently, Burke Marshall had told Robert Kennedy that the Nashville students were heading down to Alabama to complete the ride and that their spokesperson was a young Fisk student named Diane Nash, who had forcefully conveyed that she wasn't willing to stop their efforts. John Seigenthaler had then gotten a call from Robert Kennedy, famously asking, "Who the hell is Diane Nash?" Kennedy told Seigenthaler to call her and tell her to stop the Nashville group from going to Birmingham. Seigenthaler tried to tell Diane that the riders might be beaten or killed. She told him she understood. She also said he should know that everyone on the bus had signed their last will and testament the night before leaving for Birmingham. There was no stopping them.

When they arrived at the Birmingham city line, police officers boarded the bus and immediately arrested Jim Zwerg, who was white, and Paul Brooks, who was Black, for sitting together at the front of the bus. Then the police escorted the bus to the terminal. When they got there, the police began taping paper over the windows so the press members who had gathered to cover their arrival could not see what was happening on board and the riders couldn't see outside. The police ordered all non–Freedom Riders off the bus. Salynn McCollum got off. Leo Lillard had driven her to Pulaski to board the bus so she wouldn't have the same kind of ticket as the others, and because she was white, she was able to leave. She was under strict orders not to get arrested, so that she could tell Diane what was happening. She exited the bus and called Diane. The others were kept on the bus for a few hours. When they got off, they entered the bus station, where Bull Connor was there to arrest them for their "own protection," he said. Fred Shuttlesworth objected and was arrested too, along with Salynn, who had waited for them and had been identified as a Freedom Rider.

At the jail, they were separated by race and gender. Fred Shuttlesworth was taken to a different part of the jail and released fairly quickly. The other Black male riders were held for two days in the jail without the city filing any charges against them. John Lewis described how they handled their jail time using nonviolent resistance tactics from our Nashville workshops.

> We men were put in a cell that looked like a dungeon. It had no mattresses or beds, nothing to sit on at all, just a concrete floor.
>
> We went on singing, both to keep our spirits up and—to be honest—because we knew that neither Bull Connor nor his guards could stand it. Later on Connor would tell reporters that was one of the worst things about this experience for him—listening to the sound of our singing.
>
> We refused to eat or drink. Our noncooperation extended to the food and water we were offered. We hadn't eaten since leaving Nashville that morning. We didn't eat that night, or the next day. We sang.

The jailed riders were cut off from us all. Late at night on the second day, Bull Connor came to the jail and took the Nashville Freedom Riders away in a caravan. No one knew where they were headed. As it turned out, Connor took them to the Tennessee state line and left them in the dark by the side of a rural road after midnight. They found their way to a phone and called the number Diane had set up. Leo Lillard was again pressed into action. He drove down and picked them up. But instead of going to Nashville, they headed back to Birmingham, to Fred Shuttlesworth's home, where they slept that night. They were determined to start the ride the next day.

I was keeping up with their movements through Diane. And I was trying to make my way back to the South. On Friday, May 19, eleven more Nashville riders traveled to Birmingham and met at Fred Shuttlesworth's home. That afternoon, twenty-one Nashville Freedom Riders headed to the bus station to catch the three P.M. bus to Montgomery. The trip was canceled. No drivers were willing to operate that vehicle. It took hours of negotiating, involving the bus company, the city, the governor, the U.S. attorney general, and the president. Finally, on Saturday morning, May 20, a Greyhound bus carrying only Freedom Riders left Birmingham, with state troopers escorting them to Montgomery.

All was quiet until the bus got to Montgomery's city line. The state troopers quit their escort as planned, but there was no evidence of the city police, who were supposed to take up the guard. So the bus headed on to the station unescorted. When it arrived, the Montgomery Greyhound station looked deserted. But as soon as the Freedom Riders began to get off the bus, it became clear that Klansmen had been lying in wait again. The Klansmen, along with Klanswomen and even their children, went on the attack. They first targeted the national news reporters and camera crews who were at the station to cover the bus's arrival. Several reporters were seriously injured. The next target was Jim Zwerg, the only white man among the riders. They called him a "n——r-lover," dragged him off, and beat him with his own suitcase until he was lying unconscious in the parking lot. Next, they held his head still to give access to the white women and children, who scratched and clawed at his face, calling him a "race traitor" and worse.

After that, they turned their attention to the rest of the riders. The Black men riders had managed to get the five Black women riders into a cab. They had also tried to include the two white women riders. But the

Black driver would not drive them, as segregation laws in Montgomery forbade integrated cabs. So the two white women were left behind. Just as they were about to be brutally attacked, John Seigenthaler, who was there to represent the U.S. government, tried to intervene. Siegenthaler himself was beaten with a steel pipe, knocked out, and left bleeding in the parking lot. The two women were beaten until they eventually escaped. Then the massive crowd, armed with baseball bats, pipes, chains, bricks, and garden tools, and shouting "Git them n——rs," went after John Lewis, Bernard Lafayette, and all the other Black men there, attacking and beating them with glee and celebration.

Once it was over, most of the riders were taken to local doctors who people on the ground knew, because ambulances wouldn't pick them up. Jim Zwerg was taken to the hospital by the only Black cabdriver they found who was willing to break the segregation laws and transport him. One of our group, nineteen-year-old William Barbee, was the most severely injured. A Klansman had punched him repeatedly and knocked him to the ground. Then a second Klansman had held him down while a third drove a section of pipe into his ear and beat him with a baseball bat. Barbee was a student at Tennessee A&I, a member of CORE, and a bright, committed participant in the sit-ins and the stand-ins. Somehow he survived the attack, but he was paralyzed for the rest of his life. The vicious beating he endured that day led to his early death after he barely reached the age of forty. Everyone in our Nashville movement had been prepared to give their lives for the cause of ending racism. William Barbee did so.

The terror of the Montgomery attack alarmed everyone. That afternoon, those who were able gathered at the home of Rev. Solomon Seay. He was an AME Zion pastor who had fought injustice for decades and was a leader of the Montgomery Improvement Association, which had formed in late 1955 during the bus boycott there. Some of the riders also went to Ralph Abernathy's church, where there was to be a rally the next night. Martin interrupted a speaking tour in Chicago and flew into Montgomery to join them. The Kennedy administration was enraged. At this point, one of their own, John Seigenthaler, had been injured in the attack. From there on out, Bobby Kennedy became more engaged in our struggle, even if he was not always supportive.

On Sunday, May 21, some fifteen hundred people attended the rally at Ralph's church, First Baptist, where Martin spoke. Approximately three thousand Klansmen stormed the area—throwing rocks through the church windows and burning cars outside, as six hundred U.S. marshals assigned to Montgomery tried to hold them back. There were no local police officers to stop the KKK violence. Finally, after pressure from the Kennedy administration, Governor Patterson sent in the Alabama National Guard to disperse the mob. But it was a tense night, and while some people were able to leave the church, the National Guard troops prevented others from getting out. The troops had Confederate flag patches on their uniforms, and many, if not all of them, sympathized with the KKK. So even as they acted to disperse the mobs, they were hardly offering protection.

The troops forced people to remain in the hot church building all night, with tear gas lingering in the air. Martin, John Lewis, and others had gotten out and gone to the home of a local pharmacist, Dr. Richard Harris, who had opened his house to the people who were on the bus as they recuperated. He had been a Tuskegee Airman in World War II, and his grandfather had been an Alabama state senator during Reconstruction. Dr. Harris lived down the street from where Martin used to live in Montgomery, and his house and the drugstore he owned were the hubs of meetings and activity during the bus boycott.

On Tuesday, May 23, 1961, Governor Patterson spoke to the press and accused Martin of coming to Montgomery to create a riot. The governor said that Martin "was helped to get here and escorted by the federal government." Patterson called King the worst of all the "outside agitators," the term Southerners had been using for a few years whenever anyone stood up against segregation or any form of racism. He said, "The best thing for King, and all of the so-called 'Freedom Riders,' is to return to their homes, go back to their books, and mind their own business."

The Kennedy administration also continued to urge an end to the Freedom Ride. The president was set to meet with Soviet Union leader Nikita Khrushchev on June 4 in Vienna, and most in the white community who considered themselves moderates and who thought they supported some form of desegregation believed the Freedom Ride was too extreme. The idea was that our demonstrations were damaging the image of the United States abroad. Not many mentioned what the extreme and brutal nature of racial inequality was doing to the image of the United States. Robert Kennedy called for a "cooling-off period," which got applause from moderates and some liberals but was met with angry replies from many in our movement, with multiple people pointing out that Black people had been cooling off for hundreds of years.

A few hours after the governor spoke on that Tuesday, Martin, John Lewis, and Ralph Abernathy held a press conference of their own to announce that the Freedom Ride would continue. "It is not only impractical," Martin said, "but it is immoral to urge people to accept injustices, oppression, and second-class citizenship in an attempt to wait until the so-called 'opportune time.' The time is always right to do right. We cannot wait. We cannot continue to accept these conditions of oppression in order to satisfy the whims and caprices of a few people who would say that this is hurting us in international affairs. The thing that is hurting us most is the continued existence of segregation and discrimination. And we think we are rendering a great service to our nation. For this is not a struggle for ourselves alone. It is a struggle to save the soul of America."

Late that Tuesday night, C. T. Vivian and I and a few others headed to Montgomery from Nashville. Diane had gone there, too. We drove all night and arrived at the Trailways station in Montgomery early on Wednesday morning. We freshened up and had some food at the bus station restaurant. It was the first time the restaurant had allowed Black people to eat at the lunch counters there. So, we had inadvertently integrated the Montgomery bus station restaurant as we were heading on our way to Jackson.

Then we boarded the first of the two buses headed to Jackson that day. Many had been urging Martin to come with us, but during the meeting the night before at Dr. Harris's house, he and those closest to him had decided it was best for him not to join us. Still, he was at the bus station to see us off, along with a large contingent of journalists, about twenty of whom were going to ride on the bus with us. Also, hundreds of Alabama National Guard troops were there and positioned along the route, to escort us to the state line. Then, presumably, Mississippi National Guard troops were going to pick up the escort and take us to the Jackson bus station.

Seven of the twelve on our Trailways bus were from Nashville: Bernard Lafayette, Alexander Anderson, James Bevel, C. T. Vivian, Matthew Walker, Joseph Carter, and me. Three more were student CORE members from New Orleans: Julia Aaron, Jean C. Thompson, and David Dennis. The other two on the bus were Harold Andrews, a SNCC member and student at Morehouse, in Atlanta, and Paul Dietrich, a SNCC member, Howard University divinity student, and the only white rider on that bus. The National Guard troops boarded carrying their guns and gear. We left the terminal just after seven A.M. and headed west toward Jackson.

All on board recognized that this leg of the ride could end as badly as the previous ones, and maybe worse—with more vicious attacks, firebombing, even death. But I do not remember an ounce of anxiety or fear on that journey. I cannot explain it easily. I once heard Bernard Lafayette, in a discussion, say that from early on in the movement fear was no longer a part of his feelings. And I cannot remember any demonstration of fear from my fellow riders on that leg, either. This is a phenomenon people don't often recognize. When you're engaged in the struggle against injustice, if you carry an authentic understanding of what you're doing, you have resources of human spirit that are phenomenal. During my time later in the movement, I drove into Mississippi by myself on any number of occasions, and did not experience a bit of fear.

We did have some reservations about the way our journey was unfolding. It was announced that the bus would not make any regular stops between Montgomery and Jackson. C. T. Vivian took exception to that with one of the national guardsmen because we would not get a restroom break. But the only time the bus stopped was at the Alabama-Mississippi state line.

I was designated as the spokesperson for the group. At one point, people on the bus said, "We don't like all these National Guard around here." I don't know who instigated that discussion on the bus, but I became the mouthpiece for it. When we stopped at the state line to switch to Mississippi troops, I was the one to tell the press that we felt the government should call off the National Guard and the state highway patrol. We knew we were going into a dangerous situation. But if all those escorts were what was necessary for us simply to ride a regularly scheduled bus and go into public bus terminals, then we would rather take the risk of doing it without all the troops surrounding us, to illustrate what we were up against as Black people.

I spoke to an Associated Press reporter, Hugh Mulligan, who was on the bus with us and quoted me in a story about the Freedom Ride. I said we were prepared to bear the white rage and violence we might face as we headed farther into the Deep South, adding, "Only when this hostility comes to the surface, as it did in Montgomery and Birmingham, will we begin to see that the system of segregation is an evil which destroys people and teaches them a contempt for life. We are trying to reach the conscience of the South. Brutality must be suffered to show the true character of segregation." Exposing the issue to the public until they can no longer ignore it is the point of nonviolent direct action. That was our paramount goal with the Freedom Ride. The organized racist terrorism we were unmasking was nothing new to Black people in the South. Facing up to it was new and especially unnerving to much of white America.

Claude Sitton, one of the other reporters on the first bus with us that day, also wrote about the ride between Montgomery and Jackson. His reporting for *The New York Times* showed both the growing exasperation at our tactics among some elements of the American establishment and a growing resolve within our movement to continue at all costs.

> The convoy snaked across the gently rolling plains of the Alabama Black Belt like an armored battalion penetrating into enemy territory.

Sitton reported there were forty-two vehicles that accompanied our one bus through Alabama and into Mississippi, along with aircraft monitoring us from above. As national guardsmen lined the aisles inside the bus, we sang songs to keep our spirits bolstered, like "Down Freedom's Mainline."

> Considerable doubt has been expressed over whether those involved in the latest assault on segregation in the Deep South have advanced the Negro's cause.
>
> . . . Many persons believe that the riders have dissipated much of the sympathy that they attracted initially.

He quoted me objecting to all the escorts and asking that the bus travel without guards, come what may. "Only through nonviolent demonstrations," I said, "in which we accept violence without returning it in kind can we accomplish our purpose. . . . The chances are that without people being hurt we cannot solve the problem."

Most of the rest of the article emphasized the points of view of the people who did not support us. It said, "White moderates and many liberals of both races have objected to the continuation of the protest." The article predicted we would keep going anyway, and said we were "the most active and militant Negro faction today." It added that Dr. King called us "misunderstood pioneers in a holy cause."

The New York Times then said it was "doubtful" that we would "accomplish any striking progress in the Deep South in the near future." And the article declared, "Negroes exerting pressure within their own communities through established methods of protest and legal action will continue to be the principal force for change."

The report ended by subtly mocking us, saying: "In the opinion of many observers," those Negroes who use conventional methods, "rather than the roving demonstrators, may be the first to reach the end of 'freedom's mainline.'"

But we were not thinking of naysayers that day. We also were not deterred when we saw some of our more menacing opponents out of the bus windows along our route. They held derogatory signs, nooses, and shotguns, and shouted slurs as we rode by. And we paid little attention to the National Guard and state highway patrols of Alabama and Mississippi, other than being concerned about their presence and how it was not letting us ride at our own risk to draw attention to the terrorism Black people routinely faced in Jim Crow's America. Mostly, we concentrated on our task.

We gathered in the back of the bus to hold a workshop on nonviolence and on the decision not to allow mob violence to stop the Freedom Ride. We used the bus ride from Montgomery to Jackson to analyze, first of all, the situation in which we were engaged, and, secondly, to organize our strategy for getting off the bus in Jackson. We wanted to make sure everyone in our group knew precisely what to do and how to behave when we arrived.

We anticipated that as the first bus going in, we would either get attacked by a mob in Jackson or be arrested. To meet either contingency, we organized in twos, with the idea that each pair would stay together no matter what happened. Partners were not to lose sight of each other and were to stick to each other like glue, even if we faced violence. As duos, we would get off the bus together and proceed together into the bus station. We would be courteous and nonviolent. Even if we got mad or afraid, we would maintain a spirit of outward calm. We were to manage our courage from the inside of our hearts and souls. Resistance from within and among ourselves would give us our armor.

My partner was Alexander Anderson. We were already good friends. He was the pastor at Clark Memorial Methodist Church, in Nashville, where we held all our nonviolence workshops. As we arrived at the Trailways station in Jackson, Alex and I moved very quickly down the steps of the bus, into the station. In Jackson that day, we paid no attention to the segregation signs. We headed straight to the main, white-designated areas of the bus station. Alex and I immediately found the restroom marked "White Men" and went in there, as we had agreed during the group meeting. Other pairs walked into the general waiting room that had "Whites Only" signs and sat down. Others targeted the lunch counter and tried to order.

At first, we met no opposition. But there were police officers everywhere—in the restroom, in the waiting room—and almost immediately, we were arrested. We were not put in handcuffs. Rather, we were simply escorted past a line of troops and reporters to waiting paddy wagons, which were standing ready to transport us to the city jail. This was before the Supreme Court's *Miranda* ruling, so we were not read our rights. In Mississippi in 1961, the police were free to do whatever they wanted to do or say whatever they wanted to say. They had little to no restraints.

Alex and I stayed together. We were arrested together. We were put into the paddy wagon together. We were processed in the city jail together. And we were cellmates in the city jail.

On the television news that evening, NBC anchorman David Brinkley spoke out against us. We didn't see his report in jail, of course. But I now know that his words that night reflected the national attitude of most white people who considered themselves not to be part of the "race problem." He seemed more aligned with the segregationist governor of Alabama than with his obligations as a journalist when he referred to the Freedom Ride as "accomplishing nothing whatsoever. On the contrary," he said, it was "doing positive harm." He went on: "The results of these expeditions are of no benefit to anyone, white or Negro, the North or the South, nor the United States in general. We think they should stop it."

I can only imagine what so many of those white male journalists at the time might have predicted about Gandhi's Salt March if thirty years earlier they had been reporting on it as it was happening in the same way they were reporting on the Freedom Ride. We were using the same successful organizing principles as Gandhi to achieve change, and ultimately, we would prove them wrong.

As debates on the efficacy of our actions were unfolding outside, on the inside a second group of riders would join us shortly. There were twenty-seven of us altogether. John Lewis, James Farmer, and thirteen other riders were on the second bus from Montgomery. They arrived later in the afternoon on Wednesday and were arrested as soon as they entered the Greyhound station. From our cells, we could see some of them coming into the jail. And we could hear all their voices as they arrived.

As Alex and I were first put in our cell, the jailer said, "You can stay in there and rot, as far as I'm concerned." He didn't cuss. But with a great deal of vitriol he said that we were not human beings like he was. We were criminals in his mind, and he would have nothing to do with us.

Alex and I decided that for as long as we were in that cell and that man was one of our jailers, we would work on him. He was mean-faced. He was angry. He clearly had never talked about or thought about a Black man as a human being. He believed that being a white man and a jailer meant that he could mistreat people, especially Black people.

We made a decision together that we were going to try to use the powers of nonviolence, of care, and of love for him, and see what happened. We started by telling him that we were pastors of Methodist churches and we preached every Sunday. We said we both had congregations for which we were responsible. I think that might have been part of why he started to thaw. We told him we planned to be pastors toward him. After that, we simply did not respond to his fears, or hatreds, or posturing. We responded to the fact of his humanity instead.

In spirit, language, and behavior, Alex and I reflected love, truth, beauty, and the best of humanity and creation. We never matched his hostility. We faced his ideological and spiritual position in support of segregation with our own sense that he was a child of God to be respected and loved in spite of the way he had treated us. It was the power of love, the power of nonviolence. Whenever he said something hostile, we didn't return that attitude. Instead, we would change the subject and ask him about himself: "How long have you been a jailer?" and "What are some of the experiences you've had as a jailer?" Or we asked, "What kind of family do you have?" "Do you have children?" "How are you and your family doing?" I don't remember ever directly exploring racism or segregation with him. But we found a way to confront him that made him come to terms with himself and his relationship to us.

He didn't change in the first couple of days. But we kept responding to him as a person. Within a few more days, that man was talking to us like a parishioner—telling us about his issues, about his family, himself, and his struggles. His attitude toward us changed, utterly. He began to treat us with equanimity. With the meanness gone, his spirit changed to gentleness. On two or three occasions, he stood in the little narrow hallway in front of our bars and talked to me as I helped him gently reaffirm himself as a man. I also helped him recognize that I was a fellow human being. I had looked him in the face and tried to see him for who he was, rather than for his misbehavior. I had responded to him with compassion and gentle, kind resistance—resistance that did not imitate his hostility.

Being treated with care while he was lashing out changed him. I had learned this face-to-face tactic of nonviolence in high school, in the Methodist Church, and I have applied it over the years in my own struggles and in the movement. That jailer became our friend. Instead of our jailer, he became someone who was sympathetic with our humanity and with what we were doing. He ran errands for us. He brought us messages. In fact, on at least one occasion, he brought us ice cream for dessert in the jail.

On Friday, May 26, the twenty-seven of us from the first two buses into Jackson were put on trial, as a group. Meanwhile, more groups of Freedom Riders from the South and a few from the Northeast were coming into Montgomery and Jackson and being arrested.

By this time, our presence and tactics were known not only to the Ku Klux Klan, Southern governors, sheriffs, police departments, and the executive branch of the federal government, but also to the Federal Bureau of Investigation, which was following us closely. In the years since then, many FBI records from the 1960s have been released, revealing the extent of its surveillance of our movement. The agency watched, kept records, and made reports on many of us. It also kept documents from our arrests and convictions.

In a report from the New Orleans field office, an FBI officer described our trial in the Jackson courthouse:

> James M. Lawson, Jr., was the first witness for the defense. He stated he was a Methodist minister from Nashville, Tennessee. He stated he bought a ticket from Montgomery, Alabama, to Jackson, Mississippi, and at the time he boarded the bus, he thought that it would make scheduled stops. . . . He advised the bus made no rest stops . . . he reportedly requested rest stops of the bus driver.

The report described our arrival at the Jackson bus station:

> Lawson stated that he went into the white men's rest room and again was told to move on.
>
> Lawson admitted that he did not move on, stating "it would have been rather embarrassing to move at that time." Lawson stated that he was actually placed under arrest in the rest room. . . . He was taken from the rest room to the paddy wagon.
>
> . . . Lawson testified that as a Christian and a minister, he felt that a sad state of affairs had arisen when a person could not travel without the necessity of calling out the National Guard. He stated he was trying to make certain the country was democratic as to all persons. He advised the reason he made the trip to Jackson was a "private call from God."

The judge found us guilty of disobeying a police officer. We received a suspended sentence: sixty days in prison and a $200 fine. Only the four New Orleans riders paid the fine and got out, along with one of the Nashville riders who had to return to campus to take a final exam. The rest of us chose jail, no bail—refusing to pay the fine as long as segregation existed. We wanted to break the threatening power of arrest and prison. When you are not afraid of the state's power to enforce injustice, then you can find nonviolent ways to stand up to its methods of keeping injustice in place.

We were sent to serve our sixty days. As the wave of riders from around the country came to Jackson by bus and by train, they also got arrested. The Jackson jail couldn't hold us all. First, we were sent to the county jail for a few days, and finally they sent us to the notorious Parchman Prison, in the Mississippi Delta. We were all herded into vans, trucks, or buses. Initially, they didn't send any women there. A handful of the white men who were on the Freedom Ride might have been sent to Parchman, too, but we would remain segregated from them.

Parchman was a highly security-minded state penitentiary. I saw more harshness, racism, and brutality of the spirit from the all-white officers and guards in Mississippi state jails and prisons than in the federal prisons where I had been held. Yet, perhaps oddly, I don't remember a white prison official in Mississippi referring to us by racist names. I assume we scared them. We were people resisting and breaking racist laws in a spirit of courage and confidence that probably caused them more fear of us than we had of them. We were Black men who faced them, and looked them in the eyes, and insisted on being who we were. Most likely, those white officials never had seen such a thing before.

Racism and the white terrorism that accompanied it caused a lot of Black folk to blink and hide. In Mississippi in the 1940s, if a white person walked toward you, you had to step off the sidewalk and let them pass by, or you could get beaten. The many Mississippi corrections officers and managers at Parchman had rarely if ever been challenged like this in their white supremacy, or in treating inmates who were mostly Black and poor whites with such disdain. We Freedom Ride people had been arrested for riding a bus and not obeying racial segregation. That in itself would have been perpendicular to their experience, and hard for them to process. Also, we were mostly soft-spoken people who simply but firmly would not submit ourselves to the indignity of racism. We asked questions. We talked with one another and we built a community. We were human beings of a type they had not known existed. Our very presence, in a way, shocked some of them. They had never imagined that such people were possible.

The Freedom Riders were put in a separate cellblock in Parchman, away from the general prison population. Sometimes four, five, even seven men would be in the same area, which meant that we had companionship all the time. So we carried on an almost continuous conversation about the movement up to that time, the Freedom Ride, and our present situation in Mississippi and in Parchman. One of the things I had pushed hard in my work across the South was that if you got jailed, you should rejoice. I taught that jail time should be time for study and learning together, and that we should use it as an opportunity for personal reflection and improvement, and to experiment with evaluating our behavior in the movement. And each of us could compare our actions to our understanding of nonviolence. We might not have many books, but we could share with one another where we had been and what we had done up to that moment, for the purpose of trying to figure out what our next steps would be.

When we first arrived at Parchman, the superintendent had introduced himself and told us what was expected. New prisoners in any prison were always briefed about what they could and could not do, and about the harsh punishment for failure or disobedience. In Parchman, sometimes some of our people made jokes about the rules, and some laughed. But the levity was part of bolstering a firmness we always had in us, an insistence we were not going to be intimidated. In all we did, we said, in effect, "We are on a crusade for truth and justice. If you let me out that door today, I will go back to the Freedom Ride." Two or three of us tried to explain to the superintendent why we were there, which I suspect really confused him. I don't think he or anyone else in that prison office was able to understand it.

After the superintendent met us all, he then took us out of the cellblock one by one, into an area where he and a group of officers questioned each of us alone. It was close enough to our block that we could all hear each man as he was being interrogated. Plus, we had agreed ahead of time to talk loud enough so that everyone else in the cellblock could catch what we said. I don't know if they recognized what we were doing, but we heard their pattern of trying to intimidate every Black person who came into that prison.

I was the first or second person they called in. The superintendent questioned me from behind a desk as anywhere from seven to ten officers stood and walked around me. I calmly told them that they could not expect us to comply with their dehumanizing, antebellum systems and customs, because we were engaged in a struggle to end segregation and racism, and we were doing it through the spirit of love. I said, "No matter how you treat us, we're not going to yield. You cannot stop us from doing what we're doing to save our nation, to save our people."

When C. T. Vivian was called in to be questioned, one of the officers standing behind him hit him over the head with a hard club. C.T. jumped up to his feet and, without rage, asked the man, "Why'd you hit me?" I think that shocked the officer. C.T. was expected to cower. But Reverend Vivian was not a person who backed down.

As the days went on, more of the liberal people who said they were sympathetic to our cause criticized our tactics and agreed with the Kennedy administration's call for that "cooling-off period." *The New York Times* published a scolding opinion piece on Sunday, May 28, 1961, saying, "The Freedom Riders, for all their idealism, now may be overreaching themselves." The paper ended the editorial with advice for us: "We repeat: the Freedom Riders have made their point. Now is the time for restraint, relaxation of tension and a cessation of a courageous, legal, peaceful but nonetheless provocative action in the South."

A Gallup Poll of public opinion conducted between May 28 and June 2, 1961, asked, "Do you approve or disapprove of what the 'Freedom Riders' are doing?"

22% Approve
61% Disapprove
18% No opinion

The more pertinent question instead should have been, "Do you believe this country should continue to deny Black Americans the basic human rights and dignity the Freedom Riders are demanding?" We did not worry about the national polls. We kept going. More students and adults from all over the country rode into Jackson to integrate the buses and bus terminals. They were arrested and joined us in jail. Eventually, Mississippi sent as many as four hundred of us, from all over the country, to Parchman Prison. About seventy-five people came from California, organized by CORE on the UCLA campus. It's quite possible we had more white people on the Freedom Ride than we did Black people. I've never made a final accounting, but that is how it seemed in the end.

One of the important things about that time was the sizable group of Nashville people who used prison as a time for enacting what we had envisioned in those first days and ran what some called the University of Nonviolence at Parchman. There was an around-the-clock conversation. The depth of commitment was different for each person who went on the Freedom Ride, which is one reason why we Nashville people tried to turn the jails into schools for understanding nonviolent struggle. We taught others about where we had come from, and where we were hoping to go.

Early in June, I honored the promise I had made to Dorothy, who was in the last weeks of her pregnancy. She was able to call me twice while I was in jail in Mississippi. She got me once in the Jackson city jail, and once at Parchman. When I received the second call from my wife, I decided it was time to bail out. I knew the Nashville Student Movement people were doing the good work in the prison. And they supported my leaving, because I was about to become a father.

Arriving back in Nashville, I also got back to the people who were carrying on our efforts there. Picking up the Freedom Ride and continuing the plan was only part of what we did in the summer and fall of 1961. We were also expanding the sit-ins, picket lines, and boycotts. Throughout April, May, and the summer of 1961, we talked to reluctant grocery store managers and owners about employment for Black people. In Nashville, Black people couldn't even be cashiers, clerks, or office workers at the very stores where we spent our money. So we decided to picket and boycott the grocery stores until they changed.

Just after I left Mississippi, seven of us were invited to the White House for a private meeting with Robert Kennedy. Diane Nash and I would represent the Nashville movement. She was also representing SNCC at the meeting, along with Charles Sherrod. In addition, Diane had become the chair of the small executive committee that ran the Freedom Ride. Wyatt Tee Walker would represent the SCLC, as its executive director. Gordon Carey, the only white person in the group, represented CORE. Two lawyers were also invited. One from Washington was Belford Lawson (no relation, as far as I know), the first Black attorney to win a case before the Supreme Court—a ruling in favor of the New Negro Alliance, which he had founded in 1933, and its right to organize boycotts of businesses in Black neighborhoods that did not hire Black employees. The second lawyer at the meeting was Lolis Elie, from New Orleans, who had a long history in the effort to desegregate New Orleans, having represented many CORE members there.

For both John and Robert Kennedy, the Freedom Ride was their first active engagement with our emerging movement. Before our meeting, both Kennedys were vocal in saying to Martin King, and to Roy Wilkins, and to Jim Farmer, "These demonstrations do not help us." They said to all Black folk, "Give us a chance to get good and established in office, and to learn what we're doing, and figure out what we ought to be doing."

David Halberstam reported on our meeting with the attorney general. By 1961, he had left *The Nashville Tennessean* to write for *The New York Times.*

> The Attorney General, it was learned, told the group of six Negroes and one white person that he felt the bus riders had made their point on travel facilities and there was no further advantage to be gained in continuing them as a protest against segregation.
>
> . . . Meanwhile, the Attorney General told a Senate subcommittee that it had cost $225,000 to send United States marshals into Mont-

gomery, Ala., during Freedom Ride disorders. Mr. Kennedy defended the action in the face of sharp criticism by two Southern Senators.

At the meeting on Friday, June 16, Robert Kennedy urged us to focus on registering voters in the South instead of the Freedom Ride. David Halberstam reported that I was designated as the spokesperson for the group and made it clear to the attorney general that "the Freedom Ride and demonstrations will not end. We will continue to build what we are building." In fact, the Freedom Ride was still going on during our meeting. I didn't leave jail just to go see Robert Kennedy. We in the movement felt these kinds of conversations with people like the attorney general and the president, who had just been elected the year before, were necessary to inform them of our goals and enlist support from them.

Most of us in the movement had affection for John and Robert Kennedy, because they were wise and courageous enough to recognize that they had to talk to people like Martin King and others who were demanding an end to racism and segregation. And I think they both knew our actions were unique in the history of the country: people going to jail for sitting in, ignoring segregation signs, and boycotting. As they took office, people were in jail for challenging the laws and practices of segregation. I had a good feeling about them. They were part of my generation, and were curious and willing to hear from all kinds of people.

A few weeks later, on July 17, 1961, our first child, John Clifford Lawson II was born at Meharry Medical College hospital, right near Fisk University and a few blocks from Tennessee A&I. We named him after my little brother John, who had died nine years before, in the crash of a military transport on his way to the Korean War.

I went to pick up Dorothy and the baby after they'd spent two or three days in the hospital. Dorothy had John on the bed and was getting dressed to go home when I discovered that she had never handled a newborn baby before and didn't know how to change a diaper or how important it was to take care with a newborn's head and neck. It made me laugh. Growing up, I often helped to care for my younger brothers. That's where I learned how to hold a newborn, bathe a baby, and change diapers.

I took the hospital blanket off John and dressed him in the clothing I had brought from home. I put his diaper on as Dorothy watched me and assisted me. A new mother is exhausted and sleep-deprived, but I was able to be useful, gently helping her learn to diaper our baby.

When we got home that first evening with John, I prepared to bathe him before putting him in the bed. I made the decision that instead of using a special pan, I would bathe him in the bathtub. I did that with each of our boys. The water was warm and ready, and I kept my left hand spread across his neck, head, and back as I bathed him with my right hand. I was now a father. Dorothy and I were parents. What a sweet time it was.

Dorothy's mother came up to Nashville from Charleston and spent a few days with us after the birth, as she had before John was born. Both of Dorothy's parents accepted me fully. She called them Mom and Dad, and I did, too. Dorothy and I had known each other for only fourteen months when we got married. So in those early years, we were very much still discovering each other, which made it an especially satisfying time.

Late in August 1961, Stokely Carmichael and a Howard University classmate of his who had been on the Freedom Ride, Dion Diamond, were released from Parchman and stopped to spend a little time with us in Nashville. There is a kind of funny story about them, from when we were picketing grocery stores over the issues of racism and jobs. They joined a couple of our picket lines. And a day or two into their visit, I got an urgent call from one of our most committed people, Delores Wilkerson, saying, "Reverend Lawson, you're going to have to do something about Stokely and Dion."

I said, "What do you mean?"

"Well," she said, "I was on a picket line in front of the A&P, and they swaggered so much and taunted the white people so much that I wanted to take them out of the line." She said, "Reverend Lawson, you're going to have to talk to them. Or they're going to have to leave, because we don't have that kind of behavior in our struggle in Nashville."

That was one of the many times I had a talk with Stokely Carmichael about how nonviolence is a disciplined method. We do not repeat the antics of our opponents. We maintain a decorum that allows our humanity to confront them. I don't know if Stokely and Dion ever really got the message.

Stokely and I discussed these things almost everywhere, from 1960 to when he changed his name to Kwame Ture and went to live in Africa, a decade later. Stokely was something of an intellectual who was profoundly influenced by some of the reading he did at Howard University on politics and revolution. He was also deeply enmeshed in the culture of the United States, which meant that nonviolence was an affront to his sensibility. In probably the most violent society in human history, we in the States cannot even discuss nonviolent solutions for mass killings or police brutality. To even suggest there are other ways of living that ought to be brought into play is considered either naïve or foolhardy. Nonviolence proved too difficult for Stokely to embrace.

But it was working. In September 1961, some of the main goals of the Freedom Ride were realized. The Interstate Commerce Commission ruled unanimously to prohibit racial discrimination in interstate bus transportation and terminal facilities. "The time has come," Robert Kennedy said in the petition he filed asking for the ruling, "for the commission to declare unequivocally by regulation that a Negro passenger is free to travel the length and breadth of this country in the same manner as any other passenger." Beginning on November 1, 1961, all interstate buses had to display signs saying, "Seating aboard this vehicle is without regard to race, color, creed, or national origin, by order of the Interstate Commerce Commission." Also, terminals for interstate buses had to post the commission's new regulations, and bus companies were forbidden from using terminals that segregated passengers by race.

Although an editorial in *The New York Times* praised what it called the ICC's "long-overdue but still welcome decision," it also took the opportunity to scold us for our efforts one more time: "Much of the credit for overcoming the inertia and political resistance which hamstrung the I.C.C. before on this issue must obviously go to the Freedom Rider movement of last spring. Though, as we argued at the time, the movement raised dangers when it continued beyond the realization of its point of focusing attention on the need for integrated interstate bus transportation, nevertheless that demonstration started the chain of events which resulted in the new I.C.C. order."

Backhanded compliments aside, the editorial did end with this gratifying sentence: "Now it is absolutely and unmistakably clear that those who oppose this freedom with respect to interstate bus travel are the law breakers, subject to the full force and severity of the law on which this nation stands."

A few days after that ruling, the SCLC annual conference was held in Nashville, with the theme "The Deep South in Social Revolution." I was the keynote speaker. My speech was entitled "The Womb of Revolution," and I spoke about the road ahead:

> We are merely in the prelude to revolution, the beginning, not the end, not even the middle. . . . I do not wish to minimize the gains we have made thus far either through the courts or through our growing enterprise. . . . Since 1954, we have seen steady gains made. Since 1955, we have seen three major nonviolent campaigns, the last two involving many throughout the nation.

The three campaigns were the Montgomery bus boycott, the sit-in campaign, and the Freedom Ride. And I went on to say that while being free to sit anywhere on a bus, or at any lunch counter, or in any transportation terminal waiting room were necessary first steps, they were not the structural changes necessary for real change. Toward the end of my speech, I pointed to where many of us envisioned the movement going in the coming years:

> But it would be well to recognize that we have been receiving concessions, not real changes—sit-in concessions . . . Freedom Ride concessions.
>
> Notice that still too few Negroes are in either managerial positions where they can earn the real money of business or in positions where they can make basic policy decisions about American life.
>
> . . . Remember that the way to get revolution off the ground is to forge the moral, spiritual and political pressure which the President, nation, and world cannot ignore.

ELEVEN

Which Side Are You On?

Reverend Lawson, center, confers with James Bevel, right, during the Birmingham campaign, May 6, 1963.

BILL PRESTON, NASHVILLE TENNESSEAN VIA IMAGN

Ideology, strategy, and keeping our eyes on the prize drove each of our campaigns. We were striving to move the nation, which meant not only stirring minds but also reaching people's hearts. Speeches, demonstrations, and even legal actions were essential—but so were those songs. Each and every one we sang together—in mass meetings, on marches, and in prison—uplifted our spirits, conveyed our purpose, and infused the movement we were creating with a vital sense of unity.

"We Shall Overcome" became our most famous anthem. Guy Carawan was the first person I remember singing it in Nashville, in February 1960, during the sit-ins. A musician and folklore scholar, and the director of music at the Highlander Folk School, in East Tennessee, Guy came to some of our meetings and would usually bring his guitar. He began dating Carol Ann Anderson, one of the exchange students at Fisk. During the first days of the sit-ins, she was the white student who *The Nashville Tennessean* had reported was reading Booker T. Washington's *Up from Slavery* while sitting in at a downtown Nashville lunch counter. Guy and

Candie, as she was called, eventually married. In Raleigh, at the founding of SNCC in April 1960, Guy got up and began singing the song, and by the end of the meeting, everyone there was singing it together. A few days after the Raleigh conference, when Martin spoke at Fisk just after Alexander Looby's house was bombed, Guy and a number of SNCC people, including John Lewis, got up on the stage and began singing "We Shall Overcome."

Guy and folk singer Pete Seeger introduced a number of white folk songs from labor movements to our students, who then rearranged them with a cappella elements from the Black church. Many of those labor songs, including "We Shall Overcome," had also evolved from religious spirituals. One song that stood out for me was "Which Side Are You On?" It had been written in 1931 by an activist named Florence Reece, the wife of a mine worker and union organizer in Harlan County, Kentucky.

Some of the original lyrics from Kentucky involved the sheriff there, J. H. Blair:

If you go to Harlan County
There is no neutral there.
You'll either be a union man
Or a thug for J. H. Blair.

Which side are you on?

With a lot of the songs we sang, people could make up verses as they went along. In Parchman, a lot of songs were spread and created in that way. One of our Mississippi versions of "Which Side Are You On?" was about the state's segregationist governor, Ross Barnett. The "Tom" in the lyrics is the title character in Harriet Beecher Stowe's 1852 novel *Uncle Tom's Cabin*. It is a deep insult when Black people call each other "Uncle Tom."

Down in Mississippi
No neutrals have we met.
You're either for the Freedom Ride
Or you Tom for Ross Barnett.

Which side are you on? . . .

After Parchman, many of the Freedom Riders went to other places in the South and put nonviolence into practice. In the fall of 1961, around the time of my SCLC keynote speech, an internal discussion had begun at SNCC about strategy. Many of our Nashville people were pushing for more direct action campaigns, particularly in Mississippi. But others within SNCC were advocating the importance of voter registration across the South, particularly in Mississippi and Alabama. The consensus was that SNCC could do both direct action and voter registration. Diane Nash, James Bevel, Bernard Lafayette, Catherine Burks Brooks, and Paul Brooks stayed in Jackson after the Freedom Ride and began working on organizing through SNCC for direct action campaigns with residents, CORE, and the local NAACP. Catherine Burks and Paul Brooks met during the Freedom Ride and had married in August 1961.

Another outstanding nonviolence practitioner, Charles Sherrod, was one of the four SNCC people (including Diane Nash) arrested in February 1961 in Rock Hill, South Carolina, for joining the sit-ins there. He then went on the Freedom Ride into Mississippi and was part of our meeting with Robert Kennedy. Afterward, he traveled to McComb, Mississippi, and worked on SNCC desegregation demonstrations and voter registration efforts, alongside a teenager who had grown up in Nashville and joined our movement there, Cordell Reagon. The two of them eventually went to Albany, Georgia, with SNCC, and began organizing and teaching nonviolent direct action. They led a major public desegregation campaign in Albany in 1961 and 1962 that included both direct action and voter registration. Hundreds of Black folk marched there, and hundreds of Black people went to jail, including Martin King and Ralph Abernathy.

In the Albany campaign, music was confirmed yet again as an important element of the movement. Cordell Reagon assembled a quartet called the Freedom Singers, consisting of himself, Rutha Mae Harris, Charles Neblett, and Bernice Johnson. They made some of the songs we had been singing their own including, "Ain't Gonna Let Nobody Turn Me 'Round," "Woke Up This Morning with My Mind on Freedom," and "Keep Your Eyes on the Prize." A few years before, in Nashville during the sit-ins, Bernard Lafayette, James Bevel, and two other American Baptist Theological Seminary students, Joseph Carter and Samuel Collier, had formed a quartet and had written and recorded some freedom songs. But the Freedom Singers took off from Albany and began touring the country, with proceeds from their concerts and appearances going to fund SNCC. They even performed with Harry Belafonte at Carnegie Hall.

Although I talked to people in Albany as the campaign progressed, I never went there. Martin King wanted me to come, but I was tending to my new son, John, my family, my church in Shelbyville—the congregation had to leave its location, find land, and build a whole new church site—and the continued movement in Nashville. In November 1961, when the Albany campaign had just begun, I traveled to India. The executive committee of the World Council of Churches had invited me to their assembly in New Delhi, to brief and advise them about what I had learned from my role in the nonviolent movement in the American South.

Ultimately, the Albany campaign did not result in all the segregation signs coming down, or in eliminating other external signs of segregation. So the news media called it King's failure. But a man like Martin wasn't afraid of failing, because even his failures tended to be rather magnificent. People engaged in direct action are haunted by the responsibility and audacity of what they are doing when they launch a campaign. You have to get over the fear of failure. Martin had, in his lifetime, many, many dark moments where he thought that everything was lost, but he kept pressing on.

The newspeople who called Albany a failure were looking in the wrong places and through the wrong eyes. *The New York Times,* NBC News, CBS News, and a few others didn't allow themselves to see the breakthrough in the fact that Black folk in a Southern city had organized with a common mind and decided that in their town, all segregation had to end. In a small community like Albany, when hundreds of oppressed people are willing to go to jail in a nonviolent fight against a system they know is causing their subjection, that can never be called a failure. In fact, with more than one thousand Black people getting themselves arrested in Albany, there is no way anyone sensible can talk about failure.

Once a person sees the lie in racism and works to counter it with truth and action, their sense of personal agency is bolstered. Their inward spiritual patterns and visions alter, which ultimately goes on to affect their outward actions. Nonviolence calls this "the awakening," or the spiritual transformation. When a group of people who have gone through this join together in the goal of eliminating such oppression, change is inevitable. The Black people of Albany were inspired. The drive to end segregation sprang from them. As I remember it, one captain of the Albany, Georgia, police department said during the campaign, "We know things have changed, and are going to keep on changing. The Negroes have lost their fear."

Another facet of the Albany campaign the news media dismissed at the time was the importance of the number of students who came to a town in Georgia from all over the country that summer to register voters and get involved. The Albany campaign was a direct result of the Freedom Ride. Students nationwide were seeing the wrong in segregation and how their peers had gotten involved in our nonviolent effort to end it. Albany was our first illustration after the Freedom Ride of how much young Americans, through SNCC and CORE and other organizations, wanted to continue the work. Albany was a bellwether of the changes in the hearts and minds of Black people and almost all young people in the United States in the early 1960s. It was interracial and intergenerational, with students and adults working together for the same goal. So I didn't see any of that as failure. I saw it as a triumph. The failure was among the powers that be in Albany, who refused to seize the opportunity presented to them of eliminating their racist systems once and for all.

In January 1962, Bishop Golden called me into his office and asked me how the building was going at my Shelbyville church. I told him it was on schedule, in the construction phase. He said, "Well, you need to finish it before June, because in June I'm moving you." In the Methodist tradition, a pastor is not a permanent fixture, and pastors are regularly moved around. At that time in the Methodist Church, a lot of appointments were political. That meant a kid like me, in his early thirties, would never have been appointed to a big church. You had to earn your shoes. But Bishop Charles Golden was a different kind of bishop, one who liked to mix things up. He made assignments based upon the gifts of the pastor and the needs of the church and the conference. He was more strategic in his appointments. He did not tell me at that time where he was sending me, because he hadn't decided. But in his office that day, he bluntly said, "We need your leadership in the conference, Jim." He and many others in the Methodist Church generally supported my work in the movement and within the church. Bishop Golden told me, "Be ready in June to be reappointed to the place where I think the church most needs you."

In the meantime, I continued to conduct workshops on nonviolence for the SCLC, and in the process, I scouted out where we might conduct our next direct action campaign. We were talking about Augusta, Georgia, and Birmingham, or possibly somewhere in Mississippi.

In 1961, we had opened a SNCC office in Jackson, Mississippi, when Diane Nash was coordinating the Freedom Ride from there. Bob Moses had already come down to Mississippi from New York and was spearheading SNCC's voter registration work, which went on for the next several years. Jim Bevel and Lester McKinney helped further the operation in Mississippi in the fall of 1961. That was also when Diane Nash and James Bevel got married. I went to Jackson in February 1962 for the SCLC, and Diane was four months pregnant. I was there to meet with her and others from the Nashville movement who were in Jackson working with SNCC.

In April 1962, Diane decided to drop her appeal of the Freedom Ride charges against her. She had been charged with contributing to the delinquency of minors because she trained students who had been arrested on the Freedom Ride in Mississippi. At six months pregnant, she faced two and a half years in a Mississippi prison. She wrote an open letter to the public and the press under the auspices of her position with SNCC on April 30, 1962, describing her reasoning:

> To appeal further would necessitate my sitting through another trial in a Mississippi court, and I have reached the conclusion that I can no longer cooperate with the evil and unjust court system of this state. I subscribe to the philosophy of nonviolence; this is one of the basic tenets of nonviolence—that you refuse to cooperate with evil. The only condition under which I will leave jail will be if the unjust and untrue charges against me are completely dropped.
>
> . . . In the long run this will be the best thing I can do for my child. This will be a black child born in Mississippi and thus wherever he is born he will be in prison. I believe that if I go to jail now it may help hasten that day when my child and all children will be free—not only on the day of their birth but for all of their lives.

> . . . In following nonviolence, we have been experimenting with a new and revolutionary method that can bring about a redeemed society. But we have faltered and hesitated—and made many mistakes—because it is new and we are feeling our way. Now I think each of us—regardless of what others may do—must make our own decision. . . . I have made mine.

When she showed up for the hearing, she took a seat in the front of the segregated courtroom and wouldn't move to the back when asked. So she was given a contempt of court charge and sentenced to ten days in prison. Instead of posting bail, she served her time. When she was released, her other state charges were dropped. Mississippi's power brokers had figured out that further imprisoning a pregnant woman was not good for their already tarnished image. So her case was dismissed.

As Diane was navigating all of that, sometime in April, Bishop Golden phoned me to tell me that he was sending me to Memphis, to become the pastor of Centenary Methodist Church, which at that time was the largest church in his territory of Tennessee and Kentucky. The Methodist Church was still segregated in 1962, and there was talk in the Lexington Conference that, being a Northerner, I wouldn't succeed in Memphis. Of course, that was nonsensical. Some also felt I was too young and hadn't been around long enough to lead the largest church in the province. A lot of people were upset, because the bishop had made a number of appointments like mine—promoting people ahead of their position in line for a particular place. In our official *Book of Discipline,* it says that when a pastor is appointed to a church and a congregation, it is understood that the community where that church is located also becomes part of his ministry. In this case, Bishop Golden said, "Jim, Centenary is a church that needs you, and Memphis is a city that needs you. You need to be a leader in Memphis."

By 1962, Martin and Coretta, Andrew Young, Wyatt Walker, Diane Nash, James Bevel, Metz Rollins, and a whole slew of people were involved in direct action. We represented what might have been called a different wing of the struggle. There was a tension between the older, conventional, centrist leadership in the movement and our emerging group of younger people who were demanding an immediate end to segregation. We felt centrism was an inadequate approach. What is centrism in relation to the evil of segregation? There is no such thing as being a moderate when it comes to sins like racism or sexism.

Another verse from the Freedom Ride version of the song "Which Side Are You On?" expressed it simply:

Come all you Negro people
Lift up your voices and sing.
Will you join the Ku Klux Klan
Or Martin Luther King?

Which side are you on?

But moderation and centrism were what I found among Black people in many parts of Memphis in 1962. I had visited the city a few times in the years before we moved there. A group of Memphis lawyers and clergy members had invited me to speak at some mass meetings, and I had done a workshop or two in Memphis on nonviolence as well. I knew of Centenary Methodist Church, but I had never visited the church. Dorothy and I were committed to going where we felt I needed to go as a pastor, and where the bishop needed me to be. So we began our move in mid-June. Dorothy and John remained in Nashville for a time, and I drove to Memphis by myself. I gave my first sermons at Centenary with Dorothy still in Nashville.

Even though Memphis was officially part of Tennessee, which is considered an Upper South state, it felt more like a Deep South city than Nashville did. The southern border of Memphis's city limits is Mississippi. The border to the west is the Mississippi River, with Arkansas on the other side. That proximity was evident among Black people in the city, many of whom had come to Memphis for refuge from sharecropping, an economic system that enforced the firm grip of racism and poverty in Mississippi and Arkansas. Memphis had a much larger Black population than any of the large cities in Tennessee, but wariness of defying brutal systems of white supremacy was common among Black residents. The idea that Memphis was more a part of Mississippi than Tennessee was a quip everyone in Memphis repeated—usually as a slight to both Tennessee and Mississippi. Yet in terms of Mississippi's nearly peerless oppression of Black people, the quip cut especially close to the truth. In a letter to Glenn Smiley that summer about my new home, I even joked that Centenary gave me "a good platform in the capital city of Mississippi."

I found Memphis to be much further behind a number of other Southern cities in terms of the movement. I came to find out that it was an NAACP town, which meant many of its Black leaders in business and in the clergy were more conservative than in other towns. Gains had been made in 1960, in terms of desegregation through a sit-in movement. But the Memphis sit-ins had been reined in soon after they began. Consequently, little momentum had been created, which meant subsequent picketing downtown only drew a handful of people.

Picketing was not any good unless it could create some kind of nonviolent confrontation. You had to have hundreds, even thousands, of people. And you had to be prepared to escalate from picketing to sitting in, or some other strategy. You mixed your weapons and made certain the nonviolence weapon you used was appropriate for the kind of confrontation or chaos needed to get your ends accomplished. If you didn't, that was a loss. Since Memphis hadn't had sit-ins inside the department stores, the picketing at those stores did not create much of a confrontation. And so when a boycott of the stores did eventually occur, it was never really effective. That was one of the mistakes many groups around the country made. They used picketing without the numbers needed or without making it part of a larger strategy, and it didn't work. Then they gave up on direct action altogether.

On the other hand, I was aware, before I arrived, that Memphis had some of the most visionary Black leadership in the state, both in the church and in politics. For example, I had already met A. W. Willis, who was a member of Centenary. He was a prominent lawyer and later became the first Black member of the Tennessee legislature since Reconstruction. I also knew one of his future law firm partners, Russell Sugarmon, who was a brilliant lawyer and later a judge, too, educated at Morehouse and Harvard. And I knew Ben Hooks, who was a Baptist minister, a lawyer, and one of the founders of the SCLC. He later became not only the first Black criminal court judge in Tennessee but also the first Black commissioner of the Federal Communications Commission and, after that, the executive director of the national NAACP. All three of these men—A. W. Willis, Russell Sugarmon, and Ben Hooks—had expressed how delighted they were that I was coming. They welcomed me wholeheartedly. Their involvement in the NAACP chapter in Memphis gave me confidence in it. And when I joined, their support from within led me to my first connections in the Memphis movement.

Centenary was an urban church, with members from both Black areas of the city. Most were from South Memphis, where the church was located, but some were from North Memphis, too. It was a cross section, with about eight hundred members, some of whom were on welfare or had small retirement stipends. But probably a couple of the best-paid Negroes in the city were members, too. Besides teachers, we did not have too many other professional people, like businesspeople or doctors. We had only one dentist and one lawyer.

I proceeded to get acquainted with the church and found a nucleus of people at Centenary who were all for my being active in the city, right away. For instance, A. W. Willis was definitely in favor of the kind of outreach I was attempting, and was becoming a pillar of the Memphis movement himself. He had represented the Black students who had integrated Memphis State University in 1959 and would go on to represent James Meredith, who would do the same at the University of Mississippi a few months after I arrived in Memphis. Soon after that, he would become a partner in the first integrated law firm in Memphis.

By September 1962, Dorothy, John, and I were all in Memphis. I still traveled and worked in the movement with Martin King. I saw those commitments as a part of my work as a pastor. I stayed involved in the Southern Christian Leadership Conference and continued to conduct workshops on nonviolence around the South. Through the fall of 1962, I was reaching out to places across the South that we thought might be fertile ground for our work, under the auspices of the SCLC. I led workshops in Somerville, Tennessee, and Danville, Virginia. In October 1962, I taught a three-day nonviolence workshop in Clarksdale, Mississippi, at the invitation of the National Council of Churches and the respected Clarksdale activist Aaron Henry. I also conducted a workshop at Duke University, in Durham, North Carolina. And I led a three-day nonviolence workshop with students at Miles College, an HBCU just outside Birmingham. The demand for help in organizing was coming from all corners of the South—where it seemed as if even the land itself was swelling with resistance to segregation.

I conducted some sessions on nonviolence at the 1962 SCLC annual conference in Birmingham in September. Within weeks, we made a consensus choice to confront that city—one of the most violent in the country—as our next target for a nonviolent direct action campaign. We had a strong movement in Birmingham—led by Rev. Fred Shuttlesworth, along with several SCLC people, including my good friend Rev. Nelson Smith, who believed desegregation of the staunchly white-dominated city would be a decisive accomplishment. First, though, we would have to contend yet again with the city's formidable commissioner of public safety, Bull Connor, the rabid segregationist who oversaw the police and fire departments and had treated the Freedom Riders so roughly in 1961.

Birmingham's virulent reputation sprang from the KKK and other white terrorist groups that were firmly planted there. People determined to enforce and defend separation of the races forever, at all costs, ran the city's government and almost all of its other most prominent power structures. Among the many examples of their rampant, unchecked vigilantism were the bloody beatings and lifelong injuries so many Freedom Riders endured—with no consequences whatsoever for the perpetrators.

White Birmingham would not change willingly. But the Black people of Birmingham had their own movement. Their goal, and ours, was not just to bring down segregation but to get Black folk hired in lots of new capacities and to stop police brutality. Any push for those sorts of changes would surely cause the city's establishment to foment yet more violence against us and the local people in the movement. But we were ambitious, committed, and ready to organize for the fray.

Of course, the state of Alabama was in league with Klansmen, too. In the gubernatorial election of 1962, Alabama had replaced John Patterson with an even more ardent segregationist, George Wallace. If Patterson had disgraced his state with his callow indifference to the mob violence that savaged the Freedom Riders in Anniston, Birmingham, and Montgomery, Wallace left no doubt during his January 1963 inauguration that he was ready to defy decency even further. With the governor of Mississippi, Ross Barnett, standing nearby in solidarity, along with many other segregationist Southern politicians in the crowd, Wallace spoke at the rebel-flag-festooned statehouse in Montgomery. It was the same building—as he proudly reminded those gathered around him—that had once housed the first capital of the Confederacy. With all the world watching, he proclaimed: "Segregation now. Segregation tomorrow. Segregation forever."

As white Birmingham cheered such declarations, Martin Luther King would denounce Birmingham as "the most thoroughly segregated city in the South." Black people who lived there referred to their hometown as "Bombingham." Between 1957 and 1963, everyone knew that the Ku Klux Klan and the White Citizens' Council were behind at least seventeen of the bombings of Black homes and churches. But the cases went unsolved, and the bombers were never prosecuted. Alabama law enforcement shielded them, instead of protecting the Black citizens who paid the taxes that paid their salaries and were the peaceful ones, not in the business of bombing homes and churches. Racists had used bombs occasionally in other places, including Nashville. But by 1963 in Birmingham, bombs were the weapon of choice, and targeting Black people with explosives was almost like a plague.

In the first five years after I met Fred Shuttlesworth we had gotten to know each other well and were firm colleagues in the struggle. I had gone in and out of Birmingham at his behest a number of times between 1958 and 1963. Three or four of those visits were after incidents of violence. Once, white thugs attacked Fred on a main street in Birmingham. Another time, his church was bombed. In yet another assault, his home was bombed. After each of those incidents, I would drop everything and head to town.

In those early years, I almost always stayed with my friends Rev. Nelson Smith and his wife, Leslie. Nelson was a well-known Baptist preacher, and his home was my home in Birmingham. I also met a fellow there early on named Charles Billups. He was a labor activist who joined our struggle, too. Very often, Charles would pick me up at a bus station or the airport and serve as my driver. He was an active participant in Fred Shuttlesworth's organization, the Alabama Christian Movement for Human Rights (ACMHR), which had promptly been formed in 1956 after the state banned the NAACP for its participation in the Montgomery bus boycott.

In Birmingham, a small group gathered weekly under the auspices of the ACMHR, which was an affiliate of the SCLC. The participants were mostly clergy, although there were a number of laypeople, like Charles Billups. We affectionately called those gatherings "the meetings of the Fred Shuttlesworth movement," and they often included a Sunday school class in the church. There would be preaching. We would fortify one another, talk about why our work was necessary, and envision the changes we could bring to our society. Fred planted the seeds of change in that city and was determined not to stop at concessions from white moderates.

I formed some deep relationships in Birmingham. My intention in going there so often through the years was to help lay the framework for exactly the kind of direct action campaign we decided to set in motion in 1963. I spent much of February, March, and April leading workshops and conducting advance work there for the SCLC as a strategist and troubleshooter.

In January of 1963, Martin asked about a dozen of us who were his close advisers to meet at the Dorchester Academy in Georgia, where we planned the Birmingham campaign. That's when Martin King made it clear to me that I could not be arrested in Birmingham. My role was to be the one who stayed on the outside to do the work of recruiting people, persuading more people to participate. I would deliberately keep a low profile so I could be most effective, and that is why my work did not appear in many accounts of that campaign. Of course I had tried to do that in Nashville, until the *Nashville Banner* and Vanderbilt made my work public, and I became a part of the story. In Birmingham, I was more easily able to stay behind the scenes, since by then so many other leaders were taking part in the campaign, including several in the movement who had become quite recognizable, and were there drawing attention.

Wyatt Walker, who was the executive director of the SCLC at the time, had a strategic plan for the weeks of demonstrations that would start in early April. He called it Project C, for "Confrontation," and the plan included direct action and economic pressure through a boycott of segregated businesses. There were three main goals in Birmingham: to abolish segregation in the city that perhaps most symbolized oppression; to raise enough national awareness of Southern racial injustice that the Kennedy administration would be forced to defend our civil rights, as they had not done in places like Albany; and to get enough support from Northerners to pass a national civil rights act in Congress that would overturn all segregation laws everywhere.

One of our first steps was to launch a boycott on the cusp of the 1963 Easter buying season, as we had done successfully in 1960 in Nashville. Then we would start the most visible part of the campaign with sit-ins, followed by mass marches.

On Tuesday, April 2, Martin arrived in Birmingham and checked into room 30, his second-floor suite at the A. G. Gaston Motel—one of the few nice places where Black people could stay back then in the segregated city. The Gaston is where we all stayed once the campaign was underway. We planned most of the Birmingham strategy in the front room of Martin's suite, which everybody called "the war room"—a consciously sardonic name, given that our campaign was strictly nonviolent.

On April 3, 1963, the Birmingham campaign started. Fred Shuttlesworth and Nelson Smith issued what was called the "Birmingham Manifesto" through the ACMHR. The pamphlets they distributed announced our campaign by saying, "The patience of an oppressed people cannot endure forever." It went on:

> The Negro citizens of Birmingham . . . have been segregated racially, exploited economically, and dominated politically. . . . For years, while our homes and churches were being bombed, we heard nothing but the rantings and ravings of racist city officials.
>
> . . . The absence of justice and progress in Birmingham demands that we make a moral witness to give our community a chance to survive. We . . . believe that The Beloved Community can come to Birmingham.
>
> We appeal to the citizenry of Birmingham, Negro and white, to join us in this witness for decency, morality, self-respect and human dignity. . . . This is Birmingham's moment of truth in which every citizen can play his part in her larger destiny.

That morning, Martin, Wyatt Tee Walker, and I spoke to the approximately sixty-five sit-in volunteers who had arrived at our training and assembly point—the Sixteenth Street Baptist Church—for the first afternoon of sit-ins at the five businesses we had chosen. They had all signed their commitment cards, which I had composed. The cards started with these words: "I hereby pledge myself—my person and body—to the nonviolent movement." And they listed ten points to remember. One of the points was "Remember always that the nonviolent movement in Birmingham seeks justice and reconciliation—not victory."

Everyone there had gone through some or all of our training sessions. So no one was caught off guard about the seriousness of our task. Everyone was excited, united, and ready to go. My purpose was to remind them of the commitment this campaign required while they still had time to quit. No one did. We spoke to everyone about the presence of our lawyers and the process of going to and being in jail. Everything was so similar to what we had done in Nashville that I needed only a word or two in my own notes to prompt me for each part of the briefing.

Next, we outlined the strategy. We would go out in "squads" or "teams," and everyone would have mutual responsibility for one another. There would be a spokesperson for each squad. We would employ varied approaches to the different lunch counter sites—some protesters arriving in cars and others on foot, as free people living their lives would do.

We made a point of emphasizing how everyone had to be willing to stay in jail for a while. We had asked for a commitment of six days. We also talked about maintaining morale, telling the volunteers what we had learned in Parchman about how singing freedom songs was a surprisingly helpful way to keep one another's spirits up, to bolster a sense of purpose and togetherness.

The volunteers fanned out to the downtown lunch counters. Two sites were at national variety store chains, Woolworth's and Kress; one was at a national department store, Britt's; and two were at Alabama-based department stores, Loveman's and Pizitz. Four of the lunch counters shut down immediately. But one, Britt's, stayed open, and the staff called in the police, who arrested twenty-one people. The story of the arrests was shunted to the back pages of the Birmingham papers, and the manifesto was published in only one local Black newspaper. *The New York Times* covered the events with one reporter, and those stories were also buried away from the main pages. For the next three days, more sit-ins led to more arrests. We were slowly building our campaign.

By Saturday, April 6, thirty-five people had been arrested. That day, Fred Shuttlesworth and Charles Billups led a march from the Gaston Motel to city hall. It was modeled on what we had done in Nashville. Marchers walked in pairs, quietly, in orderly lines. Bull Connor, unmoved by quiet and orderly, was there to cut them off before they could get near city hall. Twice, the police ordered the marchers to turn around, saying they did not have a permit to "parade," even though a few days before our people had tried to obtain a permit, only to be refused one by Connor himself. Then the police cut off the access street to city hall. So Reverend Shuttlesworth, Charles Billups, and the rest of the marchers stopped and knelt and began to pray in the street, as they had planned to do if they had reached the steps of city hall. It was what we called a "kneel-in." Usually we did it on the steps of white churches that refused to admit Black people to their services. But doing it in the streets of Birmingham was what was called for in that moment. As expected, the marchers were all arrested, including Shuttlesworth and Billups. There was no violence, but the police did have attack dogs present.

We got messages from some of the people who had been arrested. One member of Fred's church called to tell us, "It's not so bad here. We're ready to stay here for the duration." And one of the volunteers, who I knew only as Miss Brown from Birmingham, told us, "I'm ready to go to jail for as long as necessary to change segregation."

During all the activity of those first days of the campaign, I was often in the war room at the Gaston Motel, working on strategy or monitoring the demonstrations with Wyatt, Ralph Abernathy, Andy Young, Martin, and others. Other times, I was nearby at the Sixteenth Street Baptist Church or at Kelly Ingram Park, directly across the street from the church, working to coordinate the volunteers and conduct training. We kept up steady action.

On Palm Sunday, April 7, a march that started at the Sixteenth Street Baptist Church turned violent when the police ordered their dogs to attack marchers. In Birmingham, Bull Connor and his police used dogs and huge firefighters' water hoses more vehemently than anyone did in any other campaign we had seen up to that point. Their goal was both to provoke us and to shut us down. Of course, there were always some from the Black community who came to our demonstrations to stir up violence in reaction to the police provocations. The white community, including most newspapers and the police, characterized our nonviolent resistance as "unruly," although it was really the police who were unruly.

Many Black people who would not take part in the demonstrations still supported our efforts, and a few of them came out to observe, keeping their distance. An Associated Press photo from that Palm Sunday showed a police dog attacking a young man who was there to watch. He was not someone we had trained in nonviolence. But that photo made papers all over the world, causing outrage at the disproportionate violence directed against us, and reflecting badly on Bull Connor and his overzealous police force.

As the situation developed, our strategy changed. *The New York Times* reported on a diversion tactic we used on Wednesday, April 10. It was a "decoy march," and it worked so well that we would deploy it a few more times in Birmingham, to divert resources away from the main action.

The paper went on to make clear that there would be no retreat in our campaign, and it gave a glimpse into our organizing structure.

> The desegregation effort here is organized like a military campaign. Strategy is planned by a "strategy committee" of twenty-five, headed by Dr. King and the Rev. Fred L. Shuttlesworth. . . . Several hundred volunteers have enlisted to picket, demonstrate or do anything else they are told. They know they may go to jail. . . .
>
> More than 150 persons . . . have been arrested here in eight days.

What they didn't know was that our planning and preparation went well beyond the on-the-ground, in-the-moment strategy committee. During the months and weeks leading up to the start of the Birmingham campaign, Martin had met with other key people outside the South, who helped us in various ways, including with fundraising. Martin's great friend and a great member of the movement, the actor and singer Harry Belafonte, was perhaps the most active in that respect. His apartment in New York City was the setting for many meetings of supporters. Also, he had provided bail-fund money for us a few times—when circumstances called for us to get out of jail instead of staying in, or when anyone who had committed to spend time in jail needed to leave for personal reasons.

Other performers, too, would hold benefits so that our work could continue. A Black folk singer from Ohio named Len Chandler was very involved and active, and later became a presence on the front lines in the South. He lived and played music in New York, in the same circles as Bob Dylan, Pete Seeger, and other folk musicians. Len wrote his own songs for and about the movement. And, of course, he occasionally came up with new lyrics to some of our standards. He said he always added this verse to "Which Side Are You On?" whenever he played at benefits in the North:

Come all you northern liberals
Take a Klansman out to lunch
But when you dine, instead of wine,
You should serve nonviolent punch.

Late at night on Wednesday, April 10, Bull Connor got an injunction issued against our campaign and its leaders, prohibiting all of the actions we had already taken, including sit-ins, boycotts, parades, picketing, and kneel-ins. The new mayor, Albert Boutwell, who had just defeated Connor in the mayoral election a few days before with some backing from the Black community, supported the injunction too. The formal order was delivered to Martin at the Gaston Motel around one-thirty A.M. Issuing injunctions had become a tactic used against us many times throughout the South. It could sometimes take years before any resolution was reached in the resulting court case after an injunction. So it was an effective strategy.

To counter them, we were considering marching in defiance of the injunction on Friday, April 12, which was Good Friday. But late on Thursday, the city informed us that our bail fund had run out. Many of our people were still in jail. They had committed to only six days. Their stay looked like it might be prolonged indefinitely. We had a hard time seeing how we could get them out and still continue with the campaign. It was a discouraging development. Where were all the white folks who had spoken of supporting us, now that we needed them?

Among my handwritten notes from that moment I had jotted down a biting joke that circulated among us then, as we talked ruefully about how unreliable white moderates could be.

> A Negro goes to Heaven and knocks at the gate.
>
> St. Peter comes and opens it, and says: You'll have to go to the back door.
>
> N: The back door?
>
> P: You're colored, aren't you? Back door.
>
> N: But I've come from the U.S. We have been changing segregation from 1954 to 1963. We had the Freedom Ride. And since a housing order came through, I've lived in an integrated neighborhood in Mississippi. My children went to an integrated school. We belong to a white church with a white pastor. In fact, last Sunday, my white pastor took me to the river for a baptism and put me under the water. That's funny—the last thing I remember is going under the water.

Dark humor helped as we grappled with finding a way past that Thursday night's bad news about our funds. A few hours later, the sun had not yet risen on Good Friday when all twenty-five of us on the strategy committee began packing into the war room at the Gaston Motel.

The mid-twentieth-century decor of the Gaston's only suite was considered luxurious. Our lively core group—most of us in our early thirties—filled the yellow- and green-upholstered couches and chairs, leaned against the wood-paneled walls, and sat on the brown-carpeted floor. Room 30 also featured a rotary dial phone and a black-and-white TV. This was a meeting of our inner circle, something we held early every morning of the Birmingham campaign to refine and revise our plans and find consensus. While talk volleyed around the room, Martin didn't call me "Reverend Lawson." He called me Jim. I called him Martin. We didn't call Martin's closest confidant and adviser "Reverend Abernathy." He was Ralph. The born diplomat among us, Andrew Young, was Andy. And Dorothy Cotton, one of the most powerful women in the mostly male-run movement, was Dorothy. We were all brothers and sisters.

Bayard Rustin, James Bevel, and all the others in that room were infuriated at the latest injunction tactics of the new mayor and of Bull Connor. The city's action meant that anyone who marched in Birmingham from then on would be taken to jail after only a few steps.

We were debating new ideas about what Martin should do. What if he violated the injunction and marched with everyone that day, joining those already in jail, showing our resolve, and drawing more attention to our efforts? Or would his time and fame be better spent traveling the country, raising much-needed money to keep this campaign going?

Intense talk flowed freely as options were weighed. I looked to Fred Shuttlesworth, who had just been released from jail himself after his arrest the previous Saturday in the march to city hall. I could see in his face that even for Fred, this was a new low. He was incensed that the injunction had been deployed to restrict our freedom and power, and was intended to crush us.

Our strategic considerations that day showed the extent of our care and planning during the Birmingham campaign. At one point, Martin left the front room of the suite to go into his bedroom alone. He later said he was in there struggling with whether or not to go to jail. He felt the burden of all our hopes, and the hopes of so many Black people in Birmingham and the nation. His father, who was in the room with us at the time, had urged him not to go to jail.

A while later, Martin emerged from his bedroom. He usually wore a suit and tie to demonstrations, but he had changed into work clothes. It signaled to us all he had decided to defy the injunction, and was going to jail. He said, "I don't know what will happen. I don't know where the money will come from. But I have to make a faith act."

Martin wrote about the decision to defy the injunction in his 1963 book on the Birmingham campaign, *Why We Can't Wait:*

> The time had now come for us to counter their legal maneuver with a strategy of our own. . . . Two days later, we did an audacious thing, something we had never done in any other crusade. We disobeyed a court order.

Ralph Abernathy and about fifty others joined Martin and were arrested soon after they ventured out. Martin and Ralph were separated from the rest of our people and put in solitary confinement. They were not allowed to speak to anyone inside or outside the jail. Cutting them off from the rest of us and from their families was yet another tactic designed to break them and us. In his lifetime, Martin had many, many dark moments, where he thought all was lost. He said later that this was one of the worst of those times. Anxious moments crept into his heart during his solitary confinement in Bull Connor's jail. He knew that he was there with hundreds of our people and that there was no money for bail. Without bail on hand for when and if anyone was scheduled to leave, we could not keep asking people to get arrested. Our tactic of flooding the jails was in jeopardy. Martin was worried about the movement and about the morale among Black people in Birmingham. Also, he was concerned that he was not able to be out raising more money. It was one of the more severe tests of the movement to date. But Martin kept pressing on.

A few days later, on April 16, 1963, Martin's lawyers and Coretta were finally able to break his solitary confinement and talk to him. He gave the lawyers scraps of paper he had written on in his cell, in longhand. He had even jotted some of his thoughts in the margins of a copy of the daily paper, *The Birmingham News*. The lawyers smuggled out the writings without any of the jail officials noticing. They were his reaction to a letter condemning our actions that had appeared in the newspaper, signed by a group of Birmingham Christian and Jewish clergymen. Martin had written enough in response to make an essay, which would come to be known simply as "Letter from a Birmingham Jail." It would eventually be recognized as one of the most important pleas for justice against tyranny in American history, even though at the time it was published to little fanfare. In the brilliant essay, he countered his fellow clergymen's criticism with fierce words expressing what we all felt, saying, "I am in Birmingham because injustice is here" and "Injustice anywhere is a threat to justice everywhere."

At one point he turned the local criticism back on those who had voiced it, saying,

> You deplore the demonstrations taking place in Birmingham. But your statement, I am sorry to say, fails to express a similar concern for the conditions that brought about the demonstrations.

A few paragraphs later, he took the opportunity to identify our purpose:

> Nonviolent direct action seeks to create such a crisis and foster such a tension that a community which has constantly refused to negotiate is forced to confront the issue. It seeks to dramatize the issue that it can no longer be ignored. . . .
>
> We know through painful experience that freedom is never voluntarily given by the oppressor; it must be demanded by the oppressed. Frankly, I have yet to engage in a direct action movement that was "well timed," according to the timetable of those who have not suffered unduly from the disease of segregation.

Toward the end of the long letter, as a way to prod the city and the nation urgently into complete desegregation, he appealed to America's belief in its superiority.

> We have waited for more than 340 years for our constitutional and God-given rights. . . . The nations of Asia and Africa are moving with jet-like speed toward the goal of political independence, and we still creep at horse and buggy pace toward the gaining of a cup of coffee at a lunch counter.

"Letter from a Birmingham Jail" was published in *The Christian Century* magazine in June, then excerpted in a few other publications that summer, garnering scant reaction.

A few days after Easter Sunday, while Martin and Ralph were still in jail, we heard that Harry Belafonte had raised $50,000 for our bail fund and had sent word that he would continue to raise money for as long as we needed. Martin got that heartening news from his lawyers.

═

There was only one small Black college in the Birmingham area, Miles College, unlike in Nashville, where we had a few Black colleges with a large number of students willing to join our campaigns. Some of the SCLC staffers had been pushing, even before 1963, for us to work with Black high school students as well. A number of times during the SCLC conference in Birmingham in the fall of 1962, we had that conversation in staff meetings. There was, of course, much discussion among us about whether it was right to involve people younger than college age in the campaign. Our general consensus was that high school students were on the threshold of adulthood, old enough to make decisions and old enough to do the work.

After Martin and Ralph left the jail, on Saturday, April 20, we had to regroup. In Birmingham, we decided, we needed to engage certain Black high schools—including Parker, Ullman, and others—and talk with students about joining our movement there. Jim Bevel was on the SCLC staff and had arrived from Mississippi the day Martin went to jail. Ella Baker was in Birmingham by then, too. They were the ones who ended up recruiting hundreds of the younger students. We set up workshops where the students were trained in nonviolence. And they all signed the same nonviolence pledge as the college students and adults.

On Wednesday, April 24, a youth rally was set for the Sixteenth Street Baptist Church, in downtown Birmingham, which continued to be our main staging area for the demonstrations and marches. Jim Bevel inspired the students who packed the church. He even showed them an NBC documentary about the Nashville sit-ins, featuring the silent march to city hall and Diane Nash's brilliant questions for Mayor Ben West, which first broke the stranglehold of segregation in Nashville. The students were ready to march. The word went out that on Thursday, May 2, there would be a major march of Birmingham's children. With help from two sympathetic and popular local radio DJs, Bevel used coded words to tell the young people where to meet for the "party" and other details.

By eight A.M. that Thursday, more than eight hundred Black students, as young as six and as old as twenty, had filled the Sixteenth Street Baptist Church. Around one P.M. the students began leaving the church in groups, all taking different routes to make it hard on the police, heading toward city hall and the shopping district. They were singing "We Shall Overcome" and "Ain't Gonna Let Nobody Turn Me 'Round." They also sang "Which Side Are You On?" with at least one new line: "Will you join us, or will you Tom for the big, bad Bull." The various groups of students were arrested in waves. Most didn't get too far from the church. A few others managed to make it all the way to the shopping district and to city hall. At first, police cars were used to pick up the protesters. But there were so many young people that the police needed to bring out school buses to carry them all to jail or to the juvenile detention center. In the end, at least six hundred were arrested. One girl taken into police custody was only six years old. It was by far the largest march in the Birmingham campaign.

The following day, as many as fifteen hundred students stayed out of school to join the next march. As the marchers began to leave the church around one P.M., the police decided to meet them with a degree of brutality that would shock the world. They brought out their trusty fire hoses and police dogs. Three young marchers were bitten, and many more were knocked down by the powerful blasts of water. The police locked the doors of the church so more than five hundred of the children could not leave to march. By the end of the second day, 250 more demonstrators were arrested, mostly people under the age of eighteen.

Jet magazine covered the demonstration, which became known as the Children's Crusade, focusing on a seven-year-old girl, Jennifer Denise Fancher, whom a police dog had bitten. Her mother, proud of her bold daughter, took her in for a rabies shot and said that Jennifer Denise wanted to go back out the next day. In a photo of her in the magazine, she was carrying a sign that said, "I'll Die to Make This Land My Home."

> Jennifer Denise already feels dead inside, because every ounce of air she's ever breathed has been poisoned with segregation. But partial freedom envelops her now, since she's made her freedom commitment—her defiant decision that all of Bull's (Police Commissioner Eugene "Bull" Connor) dogs and all of Bull's men can't force segregation on her again.

Martin did not march with the children. Neither did Ralph Abernathy. I did not march in Birmingham at all. I was always training demonstrators and organizing behind the scenes at the Gaston Motel or at various churches, and making sure we knew who was arrested and when, and where they were afterward. We were also plotting our next moves at every point in a day and through each week. I usually stayed at Nelson Smith's home. Because he was so deeply connected in Birmingham, I was able to reach out through him to many people locally who coordinated with those of us from out of town.

By Sunday, May 5, the nation and the world had seen photos and television footage of children being forced back with fire hoses and police dogs. It stirred many to call for the federal government to intervene. The marches continued, with many more adults joining in than ever before. Estimates were that anywhere from one thousand to three thousand people marched that Sunday, with Charles Billups leading the way. Folk singer Joan Baez, who was twenty-two at the time but already famous, came to Birmingham to play at a benefit concert at Miles College. She had been raised as a Quaker. Her father was a Mexican-born physicist and her mother was of Scottish descent. Growing up in the U.S., she had experienced racial slurs because of her Mexican heritage. With that background, she gravitated toward nonviolence and civil rights and came to Birmingham to join our efforts. When she tried to attend a mass meeting at Nelson Smith's New Pilgrim Baptist Church, she was blocked from entering because she was considered white and segregation laws prohibited her from meeting in public with Black people. Guy and Candie Carawan had been invited to join us too, and sing with us. But they were barred from entering the church as well, and were arrested outside on the steps of the church. Black comedian Dick Gregory came to Birmingham from Mississippi, where he had been registering voters.

The marches continued. The arrests continued.

By Tuesday, May 7, when another several thousand adults marched, they could not all be arrested because the jails of Birmingham were full. It was the first time during the movement that we had accomplished what Gandhi did in India.

That evening, as Fred Shuttlesworth was returning to the Sixteenth Street Baptist Church after marching, firemen deliberately used the hose on him alone as he was heading down some stairs. The force of the water threw Fred against a wall, and they kept the water coming at him. He was knocked unconscious and had to be taken away in an ambulance. Bull Connor was reported to have said that he wished Fred had been taken away in a hearse instead.

But the tide was turning, despite—or perhaps because of—Bull Connor's fire hoses and attack dogs. By Friday, May 10, white merchants, industrial leaders, and city leaders had finally realized that we would not stop. They had gotten pressure from President Kennedy and Robert Kennedy. They had seen the damage the demonstrations and Bull Connor were doing to Birmingham's image. It dawned on them that desegregation was inevitable.

Around two P.M. that day, Martin, Wyatt Tee Walker, Ralph Abernathy, and Fred Shuttlesworth held a press conference in the Gaston Motel parking lot to announce that a settlement had been reached. I was in the crowd watching. Fred was just out of the hospital and not at his full strength. But he had insisted on being there. Desegregation of lunch counters, restrooms, department store fitting rooms, and other public facilities would occur during the next ninety days. Negroes would begin to be hired for higher-level jobs throughout Birmingham. People held in jail for demonstrations would be released. And a biracial committee would be established to open communication between Blacks and whites to avert the need for further demonstrations.

Most people in Birmingham and the nation were relieved. Martin went back to Atlanta. I returned to Memphis. But the local KKK was in a fury. They held a major rally the next night on the outskirts of town, and around ten P.M. that Saturday, May 11, they also firebombed the house of A. D. King, Martin's brother. No one was hurt, physically. Then just before midnight, Klansmen also threw a bomb from a car, aiming for room 30 of the Gaston Motel. They missed, hitting the room below. The older woman in that room was hurt but not killed. No one was in room 30 at the time. In Bombingham, white fury was not gone. It was a wounded animal, dangerous and out for violent revenge.

There were definitely costs to our work in Birmingham. But from the point of view of being an organizer, I have a lot of confidence in what I did there. And almost immediately after Birmingham, I saw the fruition of some of my other work. Sit-ins began in Durham, North Carolina, where I had conducted a workshop in 1962. One thousand people were arrested. Duke University workers came out publicly in favor of desegregation, and within months the city outlawed segregation. In Danville, Virginia, where I had worked with activists, a campaign was launched in late May to push for better jobs and working conditions for Black people. Police responded with violence, and the city government issued an injunction and arrested the local leaders of the campaign. Some gains were made, but the white power structure there prevailed for a while. The SCLC and SNCC were both involved in Danville, and continued to work there throughout 1963.

Also in late May, sit-ins began in Jackson, Mississippi. A few months before, in January 1963, I had gone to Tougaloo College, an HBCU in Jackson, to work with students there on direct action techniques. In May, they started a sit-in at the downtown Woolworth's. Segregationists attacked the Tougaloo students and some adults as they sat at the lunch counter. The Jackson police did not intervene, and the white mob grew bolder. First, it was racial cursing. Then, it was dousing the demonstrators with ketchup, mustard, and sugar and throwing a mixture of water and pepper in their eyes. In the nearly two hours of this attack, the violence progressed to dragging demonstrators from stools, beating and kicking them, and stomping on their heads, until at least one student was unconscious. Still, no police intervention. FBI agents observed but also did nothing to stop the attacks. By 1963, everyone knew the FBI was watching every event of every campaign.

The students and the Tougaloo faculty and local clergy members who joined them managed to remain nonviolent during the whole ordeal. They conducted other sit-ins through the next week and a half, in which more than six hundred high school and college students participated. The city ended up holding many of the demonstrators in cobbled-together cells at the state fairgrounds, because, again, the jails were full. Of course, the segregationist mayor issued an injunction against any more demonstrations.

I was asked to travel to Jackson in early June, during the height of the campaign, to work with local leaders, including the president of Tougaloo, Rev. Adam Beittel, whom I had collaborated with on earlier workshops for the students. I also met with the NAACP field secretary in Jackson, Medgar Evers, who had helped us in Jackson during the Freedom Ride two years before, when we were sent to Parchman Prison. Doing his job in the middle of Mississippi took tremendous courage and commitment. The hostility he and his family faced on a minute-to-minute basis was intense. I never worked with him very closely, but I did admire his resolve and commitment. On that visit, I talked with him, Reverend Beittel, and others in Jackson about the virulent opposition they faced and how to address it with nonviolence. We decided to change their strategy to a more nimble one with smaller targeted demonstrations.

I was back in Memphis by Tuesday, June 11, 1963, when George Wallace vowed to "stand in the schoolhouse door" to block the enrollment of two Black students at the University of Alabama, in Tuscaloosa. President Kennedy, moved by this wave of our movement and angered by the spectacle of Wallace's defiance, nationalized the Alabama National Guard to force the integration of the university. That night, Kennedy would make his first speech to the nation that solely focused on racial justice, and on desegregation in particular. It was an era when presidents were just learning to use the power of live television, and the nation was learning to tune in for such an event. Kennedy called for a federal law to outlaw segregation throughout the country.

> If an American, because his skin is dark, cannot eat lunch in a restaurant open to the public, if he cannot send his children to the best public school available, if he cannot vote for the public officials who will represent him . . . then who among us would be content to have the color of his skin changed and stand in his place? Who among us would then be content with the counsels of patience and delay?
>
> . . . We preach freedom around the world, and we mean it, and we cherish our freedom here at home, but are we to say to the world, and much more importantly, to each other that this is the land of the free except for the Negroes; that we have no second-class citizens except Negroes; that we have no class or caste system, no ghettoes, no master race except with respect to Negroes?
>
> Now is the time for the Nation to fulfill its promise. The events in Birmingham and elsewhere have so increased the cries for equality that no city or state or legislative body can prudently choose to ignore them.

The president said he would ask Congress to enact legislation ridding the country of segregation. He also spoke of expanding the federal government's role in desegregating education, to live up to the Supreme Court's 1954 *Brown v. Board of Education* decision. And he said he would seek greater protection for the right to vote.

That was when we knew the Kennedys were choosing our cause. It was a heroic speech. For the first time ever, a president of the United States appealed to the moral conscience of the country and emphatically called for an end to segregation in America. He was the first president to publicly insist that the crisis Black people were trying to reverse was a crisis for the whole country. It was a very presidential statement—and one of the great moments in the presidency of the United States. The courage and common sense it took could only be compared to Lincoln's. But no American president had ever committed himself so completely to a program of civil rights for Black people.

The very next day, we would be reminded of just how far we still had to go. A segregationist vigilante murdered Medgar Evers, the NAACP leader in Jackson, Mississippi, in the driveway of his home as he returned late at night after another long day of organizing. Evers was only thirty-seven years old, he had a young family, and he represented everything Mississippi white supremacists reviled, which was everything we were trying to do to create justice and equity in the state and the nation. Medgar was a dedicated colleague and a vital touchstone in a brutal place. His murder left a great void. His wife, Myrlie Evers, would carry on with his work in many heroic ways. But she had lost her husband, and his children had lost their father. With Medgar's death, we all reckoned yet again with the fact that the terror was nowhere near over. The more we accomplished, the more brutal the backlash. We faced death and mayhem—family, friends, and colleagues beaten severely or killed, and the mass arrests. In the movement, all of that was seen as part of what we had to walk through if the work was going to get done. Many of us lived with the constant prospect that any one of us might have to pay a supreme price.

The president had just praised our patriotism in his televised speech. But the FBI did not seem nearly as concerned, if at all, with those violent segregationists who were terrorizing Black Americans all over the South, or those who had killed one of our leaders, Medgar Evers. Instead, they refocused on us as the threats.

All through the 1960s, there was never a time when I was not aware that J. Edgar Hoover was our enemy. I expected that my phones were tapped, in Nashville and in Memphis, during the sit-ins, the Freedom

Ride, and the Birmingham campaign. But I never paid much attention to it, and didn't let any of that interfere with what I was doing. Part of the attitude of those of us in the struggle was that we had nothing to hide. We were doing what was right. It was our enemy doing what was wrong.

Eventually, I would learn for sure that an agent in Memphis was keeping an eye on me. The FBI had approached one of my friends for information about me at the time, and he told me. Years later, I saw some records showing the extent of their surveillance of me, as part of investigations into supposed Communist infiltration of the SCLC. A report from the Memphis field office of the FBI in July 1963 called me "a possible racial 'thorn in the side' of the Negro conservative movement and white community of Memphis." The report went on to say, "James M. Lawson is in favor of as many mass racial demonstrations as possible, despite the fact that the local NAACP leadership is more conservative and is generally averse to demonstrations." It said I had "traveled all over the South putting on" what they called "racial demonstration 'workshops.'" That the word "workshops" was in quotation marks meant that they were not only questioning my motives but also mocking them.

The truth, by that time, was that I had been asked to join the board of the Memphis NAACP soon after I'd arrived in Memphis. I had been involved with the NAACP for decades. My criticism of the organization had been out of love, not enmity. And the same month that FBI report was written, I had traveled to Fayette County, Tennessee, about forty miles east of Memphis, with other members of the Memphis NAACP to help some students who had participated in a few of my workshops there. That trip was the first time I was ever shot at.

On Saturday, July 20, 1963, around twenty students held Fayette County's first sit-in, at a Rexall drugstore in Somerville, and were arrested. After the arrests, John McFerren, a great activist in Fayette County, called A. W. Willis to ask for help because he was afraid the students were in danger in the county jail. A.W. conveyed his concern to Ben Hooks, Russell Sugarmon, and me, and along with A.W., we drove there from Memphis. The three of them were already lawyers for the movement in Fayette County, because it was likely there were no Black lawyers in that county, or any who could risk taking on the case. We went in Ben's station wagon, first to John McFerren's store, and then to the courthouse in Somerville, the county seat, to try to get a hearing for the demonstrators, and to let the town see we were watching.

I had known John McFerren for many years. In the late 1950s and early 1960s, he and others had begun voter registration campaigns in Fayette County and had registered 257 Black sharecroppers who were living in poverty working on cotton plantations. But when they registered, the landowners retaliated and evicted the sharecroppers and their families from their homes. White merchants wouldn't sell to the Black people who registered to vote, and Black merchants who did sell to them were cut off from their suppliers. John and his wife, Viola, along with one or two of the few Black landowners in the area, set up tents on their property for the families that had been evicted. The settlement became known as Tent City and got national attention. Then they took legal action against the white landlords who had evicted the sharecropper families.

Fayette and neighboring Haywood County were the only majority-Black counties in Tennessee at that time. They were also high on the list of counties in the entire United States for residents living in poverty. If Black people had truly been represented in government there, they would have dismantled segregation. Fayette County's southern border was the Mississippi state line, and the threat of majority-Black voting blocs there were similar to the threat they posed white supremacists in the state of Mississippi.

When I moved to Nashville, in 1958, FOR supported the voter registration drive in Fayette County. When Tent City was set up, in 1960, a steady part of our work in the NCLC was raising money and sending clothing and food to the people there, as white store owners in their own town refused to sell them food. We helped keep the people of Tent City alive. In 1961, President Kennedy got involved and signed an executive order to send surplus food from U.S. farms to Tent City. Meanwhile, the white governing forces, many of whose members were also members of the KKK, made deals with major oil companies not to sell gasoline to the filling station John McFerren owned. That meant Black farmers in the area who depended on his gasoline could not run their trucks or tractors for work. Robert Kennedy's Justice Department investigated the discrimination, which led to a federal consent decree in 1962 outlawing the practice of landowners using economic pressure to suppress people from registering to vote. In the summers of 1962 and 1963, groups of Northern college students came to Fayette County to help with voter registration.

On that Saturday, July 20, 1963, after local high school students in the county joined the college students at the Rexall drugstore sit-in and they were all arrested and taken to jail, a large mob of white men gathered outside the courthouse. When we arrived, they were hanging out of their pickup trucks with their rifles, and perched in windows and in trees. They had torches to light up the town square. They were ready to assault the jail and likely lynch the students. We were there to ensure their protection. The harassers knew we were watching them and, therefore, that the whole world was watching. While in town we got the court to set hearings for those arrested on the following Monday. We stayed until almost midnight, when the mob had finally gone and we felt the students weren't in danger any longer. The sheriff said he would escort us out of town, and appeared to understand the importance of keeping us and them safe. Once we got to the Somerville city limits, he told us his deputy would see us to the border with Shelby County, the county that included Memphis. But he only directed us to a road he said led to Memphis, and then he left. His deputy was ahead of us on that dark, deserted road when we noticed a whole platoon of white men in a caravan of dozens of cars and trucks coming up behind us, their rifles jutting out of their windows.

Ben Hooks turned to me and somehow mustered some gallows humor: "Jim, you've been preaching all this creative suffering to gain redemption. Do you think we should let them beat the hell out of us?" I said, "No. Redemption through creative suffering requires witnesses. There are no witnesses back there, just participants. Drive faster." Ben was already speeding toward Memphis. The deputy was not around anymore, and the caravan seemed to be all around us by then. We were doing our best to navigate the situation when a bullet flew into the front windshield. It cracked the windshield but didn't break all the way through. Yet shards of glass hit Ben and A.W. in the front seat.

We all crunched down in our seats. Ben drove as fast as he could with his head ducked. I snuck a couple of glances at him. He was peering at the road through the steering wheel, with his head way down in the car. Any conversation we had after the shot was intent on getting us out of that county. We didn't feel safe until we arrived back at the Memphis city limits.

The whole power structure in those rural counties was aimed at stopping the movement in West Tennessee. The white supremacists were extremely volatile and venomous about our organizing work, which made all the sheriffs and the state police into our enemies. They did not want Black folk in the western part of the state to get involved in the political process at all. Despite the ideological differences the year before about whether the movement should focus more on voter registration or on nonviolent direct action, by July 1963 we had all come to see that in practical application in the rural South, voter registration *was* nonviolent direct action. Registering voters in places like Fayette County, Tennessee, or anywhere in Mississippi was likely to bring out the brutality of segregationist terrorism in the same way that a sit-in or a march might. So, it turned out that the choice to focus on both simultaneously had been correct. With the way 1963 was playing out, it was clear that the dangers of being aligned with our work in any way were compounding. And the year wasn't over yet.

Throughout the summer, everyone in the movement was busy preparing for the March on Washington. In August 1963, *The Atlantic Monthly* finally published "Letter from a Birmingham Jail." It got the widespread attention it had always deserved, and went on to become a classic treatise of the movement. What many people didn't realize was that the idea for the March on Washington had sprung from the Good Friday morning meeting at the Gaston Motel in Birmingham a few months before, where Martin made the decision to violate Bull Connor's injunction and go to jail.

Even though we were engulfed in the Birmingham campaign that morning, at one point the talk took a heated, emotional detour, to a discussion about the national implications of our work and the federal government's neglect of our cause. A major question emerged in that moment: "Why aren't we doing something about Washington, D.C.?" I think it was Hosea Williams who spoke up loudly, saying we ought to be going after the president and Congress. Others chimed in, too. Congress was filled with white segregationist men who seemed to like things just the way they were. At that time, we still felt President Kennedy was not doing enough to deal with the blatant terrorism we were experiencing in places like Birmingham.

A charged tone of outrage filled the room. "Why isn't the national government doing more to combat the brutal forces against us?" Soon a passionate, urgent demand arose: "We have to do more—take some action." That's when someone said, "We should storm the Capitol." I remember those words precisely.

There was some other wild talk, like "Let's go invade Washington. Let's put a million people around the walls of Washington, D.C., and refuse to move until changes begin." The sentiments kept going like that for a while. But we did not act on those first angry and potentially violent impulses.

We came back to nonviolence, and picked up on an idea that had started with an earlier generation. In 1941, A. Philip Randolph, as head of the Brotherhood of Sleeping Car Porters, had used the threat of a massive march on Washington to demand desegregation of the defense production industry just as the United States was getting involved in World War II. When President Roosevelt signed a bill meeting the union's demands, Randolph called off the march. Then, in 1948, he again threatened a march on Washington, demanding the integration of the United States armed forces. And when President Truman signed the bill that did that, Randolph called off that march. Just a threat to march was enough to change things then. By 1963, our goals were larger, and we knew we would need more than threats.

But we also knew we needed widespread support to pull off such an ambitious march. So, in the Good Friday meeting, we had made this plan: Once the Birmingham campaign was over, Martin would be meticulous in making a series of phone calls, in just the right order. First, he was to call Roy Wilkins, the head of the NAACP, and get him on board. Then he would call Whitney Young of the Urban League, because those were the two most established civil rights organizations. After that, Martin would call A. Philip Randolph.

Martin made those first calls because we knew he had to address the fact that he was a newcomer, nearly thirty years younger than Wilkins and forty years Randolph's junior. The young whippersnapper, Martin King, had emerged as a major advocate of truth and justice in our country. Many conventional leaders were having a hard time with his notoriety. In 1963, he was thirty-four—my age. Deference to those who had come before us was an important part of the dynamic that shaped the Washington March plan from the beginning.

After those three men signed on, as we planned that morning, Martin then would reach out to our contemporaries: James Farmer of the Congress of Racial Equality and John Lewis, who was chair of the Student Nonviolent Coordinating Committee at that time. Along with the SCLC, those groups were called "the Big Six" in the movement. In all of the phone calls, Martin was to say to those men that they must form—along with himself—a committee to plan every facet of a march on Washington as quickly as possible. Of course, A. Philip Randolph was delighted. It made sense that Randolph would immediately become the chair of the 1963 march, and he appointed Bayard Rustin as his executive to organize it.

Bayard, the tall, thin, brilliant strategist of numerous campaigns, including the Montgomery bus boycott, was in the room with us that Good Friday morning, having come down to Birmingham from New York to help us strategize the Birmingham campaign. He could have headed back home right then and planned the whole march on his own. But he often had to work behind the scenes, because he was gay. At the time, the threat of being exposed was thought to be too big a vulnerability for the movement. I know this caused him great distress. But that morning, he helped us think through the call strategy, and began to engineer how to make the march a success. And Bayard's painstaking work is the primary reason that the march went off so well.

Born out of our fury that Good Friday morning, in our Birmingham "war room," the August 1963 March on Washington for Jobs and Freedom was the biggest march ever, up to that time, in Washington, D.C. More than 250,000 people from all over the country marched peacefully to the steps of the Lincoln Memorial to demand our full rights as citizens, including the right to vote. No one was arrested or killed. And Martin Luther King gave his most enduring speech, the "I Have a Dream" speech—invoking the preamble to the Declaration of Independence with "We hold these truths to be self-evident, that all are created equal" and the preamble of the U.S. Constitution, which promised "to form a more perfect Union, establish Justice, insure domestic Tranquility." He called the words in those founding documents "a promissory note to which every American was to fall heir."

> It is obvious today that America has defaulted on this promissory note insofar as her citizens of color are concerned. Instead of honoring this sacred obligation, America has given the Negro people a bad check, a check which has come back marked "insufficient funds."
>
> But we refuse to believe that the bank of justice is bankrupt.

I did not go to the March on Washington. I had committed long before to be an organizer and teacher at a ten-day regional meeting of

Methodist students in upstate New York that August. These were the young campus leaders of the Methodist student movement. We had about 130 students, with a few adults as faculty. But we decided to interrupt the conference so that people who wanted to could go to the march. We were able to get two or three buses for people from our camp to make the trip from New York to Washington that day. From our point of view, it was a learning experience. I had planned to go too, but we didn't have enough room for every student who wanted to attend. I decided to give up my seat on the bus so that a student could go instead.

I watched on television as Martin expressed to the world the hope for real change in the American system. Our fervor on Good Friday in Birmingham had sparked a concrete, constructive, nonviolent plan that undergirded one of the most famous, effective demonstrations in our movement. Never had a demand for Black rights and dignity been made more eloquently or before a larger audience.

August flowed into September, and it seemed as if our successes were beginning to catch up with our tragic losses. We couldn't have known that the darkest season of terrorism yet was upon us.

On a Sunday morning, September 15, 1963, in Birmingham, at least three KKK members planted a dynamite bomb outside the basement of the Sixteenth Street Baptist Church, the place we had used as the training and staging ground of the Birmingham campaign and the Children's Crusade. It exploded and instantly killed four girls inside as they were there preparing for the congregation's Youth Day: eleven-year-old Denise McNair, fourteen-year-old Addie Mae Collins, fourteen-year-old Cynthia Wesley, and fourteen-year-old Carole Robertson. Everyone in Birmingham knew one of those girls or their families, including Condoleezza Rice, who was eight at the time and went on to become the first Black woman to serve as U.S. secretary of state. She and Denise McNair had played with dolls together. The great freedom fighter Angela Davis was also from Birmingham and a college student at the time. Her mother and Carole Robertson's mother were close friends.

I will never forget the devastating sadness and the anger we felt, all around the country. Among my movement colleagues, we had to lean on one another—as we had all through that year. I had to do a lot of work to help bolster the faith of my congregation, too. For me there was no doubt about continuing. But as our moral movement was penetrating the public consciousness, the stakes were getting higher, and the violence even more evil.

Then came November 1963. Dorothy and I were at a Methodist bishops' conference in Nashville, on Friday, November 22, at a large United Methodist church across the street from Vanderbilt University.

After lunch, we got the news that President Kennedy had been shot and killed in Dallas. I remember sitting there and quietly weeping. Dorothy and I both wept.

John Kennedy represented a new style of president. He was the youngest president ever elected, and a person who was willing to actually figure out what was going on in his country. He addressed issues like civil rights and poverty directly, in ways his predecessors had never dared to do. He saw our country's mix of people from different backgrounds as our strength, not as something to fear. And he understood that fear of people who are different leads to injustice and discrimination and would ruin our nation. I was very much aware that he died for talking about how we could have a different kind of nation and a different kind of world, and acting on it. I believe his assassination was not merely an isolated incident.

I knew that what many saw as his alliance with us was also a factor in his assassination. He had talked to Martin King, and listened to him to find out what we were expressing about this country. But a lot of people did not want a president who addressed racism and segregation—a president who acknowledged that those ailments weren't a Negro problem, they were everybody's problem.

Forces of spiritual wickedness in our nation were involved in the assassinations of the 1960s, and that included the assassination of John F. Kennedy.

Two days after JFK's death, on Sunday, November 24, I gave a sermon to my congregation at Centenary Methodist Church in Memphis.

> Dorothy and I were at the bishops' conference in Nashville when the news came. Neither of us could believe it at first. The meeting stopped, with everyone pretty well shaken by the suddenness of death coming to the young President of the United States. . . . When Bishop Golden opened the meeting again, we sat in silence, then in prayer. I could only weep. . . . I was weeping for my people—the American people, and my land, America.

> Almost every sensitive American knows deeply that the bullets which cut down the president . . . have somehow altered our lives.

I understood that my congregation was feeling the same despair that was having its way with so many across the nation who had invested their hopes in President Kennedy.

> Signs of our shock and grief are everywhere. . . . Literally everything has come to a grinding halt—the wheels of diplomacy, business, politics . . . the cancellation of all regular programs on TV and on many radio stations until after the funeral, the great rush to churches because only eternity can console the nation. . . . Many hearts today are in mourning. . . . The entire world has been hushed by the sound of rifle fire.

I tried to provide some context or perspective that would remind us of the forces we were up against at that time. The losses were mounting. I knew I had to mention them, so we could grieve properly, and so we could redouble our campaigns for a better world.

> Consider for a moment what our society . . . does, cruelly: Medgar Evers; four little girls murdered while attending Sunday school; Christians ostracized by their friends simply because they spoke up for justice; little children who do not have enough to eat in America; sharecroppers exploited all their lives and then threatened with death if they dare register to vote; peaceful nonviolent demonstrators throughout the land beaten and jailed merely because they are striving to fulfill the American ideals for which Kennedy stood; Congress standing still while poverty goes on. . . .
>
> This day requires from us more than mourning or pity. . . . We will labor that this honored man will not have died in vain. But from his death, we shall discover new measures of devotion to God; strive to build a just and redeemed society; beat back the citadels of prejudice and fear and hate; encourage the forces of truth and love, lift the weak.

In the end, I tried to help us all remember to keep our eyes on the prize.

> In this spirit, I have decided that God wants me to press all the more for peace, freedom, justice. . . . This is no time for considering

anything but how we Christians hasten the effort to heal the hate, end the strife, construct justice, create the new society where our land will have that fresh impulse of freedom and human dignity.

We must not mourn for JFK. We must not allow the voices of hate to preach revenge, or ridicule of Oswald. We must instead . . . let God use us in this mortal moment.

TWELVE

Quagmires

Reverend Lawson and Stokely Carmichael walking with students to a Freedom Summer training session, Oxford, Ohio, June 1964. ASSOCIATED PRESS

For centuries, it was illegal to teach an enslaved person to read in most Southern states. Taking away your mind's freedom was just as integral to enforcing enslavement as taking away your body's liberty. Suppressing Black literacy upheld slavery—a perfect complement to chains, whips, and sexual assault. Black people whose minds were as free to think, read, and write as white people's would inevitably unseat the common justification for white supremacy and slavery in this country: the myth that Black people were intellectually inferior to white people and, therefore, less than human and, therefore, not deserving of white

America's inalienable rights. In the eighteenth and nineteenth centuries, keeping Black folk illiterate was so essential to the economic and social status quo that most slaveholding states enacted anti-literacy laws as stringent as all the other laws designed to encode enslavement and prevent uprisings against that cherished institution.

By the mid-1960s, most of those laws were gone. But to dismantle the Jim Crow practices that replaced them, we had to address the enduring myths and legacies that remained. In 1964, Black people in Mississippi had one of the lowest literacy rates in the nation. Of course, the segregationists realized the benefits they reaped from keeping Black people illiterate. One hundred years before, teaching a Black Mississippian to read would have resulted in ruinous fines and years of prison time. By the twentieth century, instead of laws enforcing illiteracy, the state enacted somewhat subtler laws that called for complicated voting tests and poll taxes to enforce their inherited traditions of racial oppression.

Black response to Jim Crow spurred justice movements before we came along, focused on voting rights as a key to Black empowerment at the local and national levels. In the 1960s, the SCLC knew that continuing those efforts to enable voter representation had to include teaching literacy in states like Mississippi, where more than 40 percent of the population was Black, but Black people were less than 5 percent of registered voters. In the 1950s, the great Septima Clark had created Citizenship Schools in South Carolina, developed them further working at the Highlander Center, and then brought the concept with her when she began working at the SCLC in 1961, and became its director of education and teaching. Citizenship Schools taught Black people to read, write, and understand their rights—a powerful act of resistance.

During that time, I began to notice another form of illiteracy, one afflicting most Southern sheriffs and all the other segregationist white people whose interests they protected. Those men and women were illiterate when it came to democracy and the common good that true democracy promotes. Their ignorance propelled them to commit brutal, angry, destructive acts that made everything worse for everyone and left them in a spiritual bankruptcy.

Despite them, our struggle began to bear some fruit by 1964. On January 23, Congress passed the Twenty-Fourth Amendment to the U.S. Constitution, prohibiting poll taxes for voting. Of course, there were still the literacy tests and other obstacles we had to eliminate. Then, in

February, the Civil Rights Act, which President Kennedy had initiated the summer before his death, passed in the House of Representatives. Yet we knew it would face a serious fight in the all-white Senate.

One day in late March, both Martin and Malcolm X went to Washington, D.C., to observe the Senate debate on the bill, using their celebrity to underscore the gravity of the legislation. Just outside the Senate gallery, they crossed paths. Photographers caught the famous moment when they shook hands and greeted each other cordially. It became famous because it was the only time in their lives that they met in person. What wasn't discussed much at the time they met was that Malcolm, who had just announced his break with the Nation of Islam, was beginning to call for those of us with the same goals to align more closely. *The Washington Post* reported that Malcolm said to Martin when they met that day, "I am throwing myself into the heart of the civil rights struggle and will be in it from now on."

That was a heartening thing to hear as the Civil Rights Act made its way through Congress and the 1964 presidential campaign intensified. We needed all the solidarity we could muster because the segregationists were doubling down. In Mississippi, the state Democratic Party had neglected to select even one Black delegate to go to the national convention in August, in a state that was about 41 percent Black. With support from the leadership of SNCC, Mississippi organizers formed a new party as an alternative to the state's Democratic Party, called the Mississippi Freedom Democratic Party. Another key partner with SNCC in that new party was the Council of Federated Organizations (COFO), which had been established in 1961 after the Freedom Ride to coordinate the activities of local and national groups working for civil rights in Mississippi. COFO included SNCC, CORE, the SCLC, the NAACP, and local groups all over the state. Bob Moses was the leader of COFO. He had been working steadily in the South after arriving from New York City in 1961 to work as director of SNCC's Mississippi Project, which was centered on voting rights and literacy. Bob was involved in COFO from the start. His adamant challenges to the Mississippi Democratic Party's racial ban, along with those of Fannie Lou Hamer and Ella Baker, led to the founding of the Mississippi Freedom Democratic Party.

Just as enforced illiteracy had impeded full citizenship for Black people in Mississippi, decades of Jim Crow tyranny meant that very few Black people in the state had ever registered to vote. So in the spring of

1964, Bob Moses and John Lewis, who had become the chairman of SNCC in 1963, began planning a summer project to increase voter registration and education campaigns across Mississippi. They called it "Freedom Summer" and recruited college students nationally—from the Ivy League, from HBCUs, and from other prestigious colleges and universities in the Northeast and on the West Coast. The students were asked to come to Mississippi and work with local activists in registering Black voters and taking them to the polls, as well as setting up and staffing "Freedom Schools" throughout the state. Those schools—located in churches and community centers—taught literacy, Black history and culture, and voter education to young people. They were inspired by the idea of Citizenship Schools for adults.

I would conduct a session on nonviolence for the Freedom Summer volunteers before they headed down to the South. That was just one endeavor I took on during a period when our movement was evolving with great purpose, and initiating a flurry of desegregation campaigns and other events in the spring and summer of 1964. My personal strategy to handle it all was to focus intently on the moment, as I navigated from one place to another and between my roles as father, husband, and son, and as special adviser to the SCLC, as well as a pastor in the Methodist Church.

In late April and early May, the decades-long effort to desegregate the Methodist Church came to a head. Working for desegregation in the South when segregation still stood firm in my own denomination had never been tenable. I was at the forefront of a long campaign for Black Methodist churches to become part of the larger church infrastructure without the separate, segregated Central Jurisdiction. But our moves closer to that in 1964 were not successful. We were told to wait. It felt like a slap in the face. Our impatience with such deferrals in the South was driving our movement there. And here was my own church using similar delay tactics nationally. The indignity was hard to bear. So I redoubled my efforts and kept going.

Around the same time, the Civil Rights Act was stalling in the Senate, because Southern Democrats were leading a sustained filibuster against a vote on it. So the SCLC decided to search for a place to join a campaign that would illustrate the issues the bill was meant to address. We wanted to call attention to the urgency of those issues as the bill's fate hung in the balance.

It became clear to us that an ongoing effort to desegregate the city of

St. Augustine, Florida, was the right campaign to join. Established in 1565, and considered the oldest town founded by Europeans in the United States, St. Augustine was about to celebrate its four hundredth anniversary. Yet Black people had been excluded from planning the celebration, which had received money from the federal government because of the anniversary's importance in American history. A local Black dentist, Dr. Robert Hayling, had led a long, vigorous movement for desegregation in St. Augustine, and in March 1963 he and local activists began a forceful series of sit-ins and marches, to call attention to the city's failure to include Black people in its commemorations.

That brought out the Ku Klux Klan, which had been menacing Black people in St. Augustine for decades. In the fall of 1963, Hayling was driving with three friends—all active in the local NAACP—when they came upon a large Klan rally. Before they could get away, the Klansmen viciously beat him and his friends with tire irons and lug wrenches. As was the routine at the time, the men who had attacked Hayling were acquitted of any crime, while Hayling was tried and convicted because the Klansmen testified that he had a gun on him when they attacked him. Hayling never carried a gun. In early 1964, Klansmen also drove by and fired their weapons into Dr. Hayling's home, killing his dog. At that, Hayling sent his wife and kids to live with his parents in another town, then urgently called Martin King, asking him and the SCLC to come to St. Augustine. Martin agreed, and in May, after the KKK had escalated attacks on local activists, Martin arrived in St. Augustine to publicly join the campaign and bring attention to the conditions.

Martin rented a beach house for three weeks and took part in marches and mass meetings, which the SCLC helped organize. At the end of May, Klan members drove by and fired shots into Martin's cottage. No one was home at the time.

I was in St. Augustine frequently in May and June 1964. Martin specifically asked me to come and help with strategy and nonviolence training. We marched at night to give working people a chance to march with us. That was quite unusual for our movement, and it distinguished the campaign in St. Augustine from our actions in so many other places.

Every one of those nights, mobs of angry white people would gather along our routes to throw bottles, cans, and stones. I was alarmed, walking down the street as stones kept coming at us through the darkness of night. It was terrifying. How do you protect yourself from a stone hurled at your head at night? I would hold up my hands to protect my eyes and my head as much as I could. I was lucky, but others were badly injured. Segregationist terrorists beat Andy Young with a crowbar one night as he was leading a march. The air in St. Augustine crackled with the risk of impending violence. But neither violence nor the threat of violence stopped us. Every night for more than a month our movement marched. And every night we had to contend with the harassment from white mobs as mounted sheriff's deputies sat atop their horses like statues, doing nothing to help us. The sheriff there, L. O. Davis, called those mounted police "the posse." Throughout the St. Augustine campaign, we all knew how vulnerable we were in that city.

The June 6, 1964, *New York Times* quoted Martin calling out St. Augustine's extreme white violence and asking the city to change.

> Dr. King told white leaders that they could prevent a resumption of widespread demonstrations next week by making a "good faith" move toward ending discrimination.
>
> There was no indication that the whites would make such a move. . . .

The article said he had asked the federal government to do more to protect our demonstrations in St. Augustine. And he was quoted commenting on the threats made to his life that the SCLC had received during our campaign there.

> "Well, if physical death is the price that I must pay to free my white brothers and sisters from permanent death of the spirit, then nothing can be more redemptive. . . . We have worked in some difficult communities, but we have never worked in one as lawless as this," Dr. King said.

The article also mentioned that SCLC attorneys had filed charges in federal court that week accusing the sherrif of the county with recruiting "special deputies to handle racial trouble from the ranks of the Ku Klux Klan."

Three days later, the cottage Martin had rented a few weeks before was vandalized and set on fire.

June 1964 had us operating at full force on so many fronts across the

South and even in the Midwest. The SCLC was supporting the St. Augustine campaign, and I was there helping lead and manage marches, demonstrations, and strategy sessions. Freedom Summer was getting underway in Mississippi, led by SNCC. Bob Moses and John Lewis held their two-week training session that month in Oxford, Ohio, where I taught nonviolent resistance to the mostly white Freedom Summer student volunteers before they headed south to Mississippi. And while Lyndon Johnson was campaigning for reelection across the country, in Washington, D.C., Congress was deciding the fate of former President Kennedy's Civil Rights Act.

The House had approved the bill in February 1964. But on March 30, segregationists in the Senate started filibustering the bill. The obstruction was spearheaded by Richard Russell, a Democrat from Georgia, who led what was called the Southern bloc of senators. He had been a staunch segregationist for years. In 1946, when a fair employment and education bill came before the Senate, he was part of a filibuster then, too, and said on the Senate floor, "We will resist to the bitter end, whatever the consequences, any measure of any movement which would have a tendency to bring about social equality and intermingling and amalgamation of the races in our States." Russell was especially passionate about preserving school segregation. In 1946, he also said in the Senate, "Of course, we will starve to death before we will . . . let whites and blacks go to school together."

Eighteen years later, in 1964, Senator Russell had not moved an inch. Earlier in March, before he began the filibuster, during a discussion about the bill on the Senate floor, Senator Russell had even proposed amending the legislation. He wanted it to include a commission that would round up Black people in the South, evict them from their homes, and resettle them in Northern states, to ensure that the proportion of Black people in each state would be the same. That way Black people would never have a majority in any state. "I favor inflicting on New York City, the city of Chicago, and other cities the same condition proposed to be inflicted by this bill on the people of the community of Winder, Georgia, where I live," he said. Desegregation was the *condition* he was saying the Civil Rights Act would *inflict* on his Georgia hometown.

On the morning of June 10, after seventy-five days of filibuster—the longest in history at the time—which culminated with Senator Robert Byrd of West Virginia holding the floor for the last fourteen hours, the Senate voted to end the filibuster.

Although final passage of the bill wouldn't come for another nine days, Martin, Ralph, and others went to the restaurant at the Monson Motor Lodge in St. Augustine the next day and attempted to enter for lunch. The owner, James Brock, who was also president of the Florida Hotel and Motel Association, blocked them. St. Augustine's Sherrif L. O. Davis had made special deputies of a group of businessmen on June 11. *The New York Times* reported that Brock was among the newly deputized men who were seen downtown that night, and Brock was spotted "carrying a shotgun, a billy stick, a pistol and a flashlight." The *Times* said during a twenty-minute conversation the next day outside the restaurant:

> Mr. Brock told Dr. King that he and his party of eight persons were not wanted. The two then began a polite debate of the civil rights issue.
>
> Dr. King asked if Mr. Brock understood the "humiliation our people have to go through." Mr. Brock said he would integrate his business if the substantial white citizens of the community asked him to or if he were served a Federal Court order.
>
> "You realize it would be detrimental to my business to serve you here," Mr. Brock said. "I have unfortunately had to arrest 84 persons here since Easter."
>
> Then he turned to the television cameras, smiled and said, "I would like to invite my many friends throughout the country to come to Monson's. We expect to remain segregated."

The night after Martin's arrest, the Ku Klux Klan marched through a Black neighborhood in St. Augustine, led by notorious Klansman J. B. Stoner. Before the march, the Klansmen had held a rally on the spot of the Old Slave Market downtown, and while waving a Confederate flag Stoner had told a group of three hundred Klansmen and sympathizers, "Tonight, we're going to find out whether white people have any rights. The coons have been parading around St. Augustine for a long time."

For good measure, Stoner also called Martin a "long-time associate of Communists."

All across the country, people were labeling our movement as Communist and saying it should be crushed. This wasn't just happening in St. Augustine, and it wasn't only from the KKK. As Freedom Summer was coming together, those accusations took on an even more dangerous potency. We were bringing about nine hundred mostly white college student volunteers to Mississippi to blanket the state with voter registration drives and open Freedom Schools, where Black children would learn about their history and gain literacy skills. The college students would also be staffing rural community centers that would provide essential services for Mississippi's most isolated people, who were almost exclusively Black and living in poverty.

We knew from previous smaller groups of students who had come to the South that the local and national press paid much more attention when white people worked with us. Reporters flocked to interview a white student from Stanford or Yale, and often ignored young Black SNCC workers who had been doing the same thing in the state for years.

By design, the Freedom Summer student volunteers could call more attention than we could previously to the vast inequities in the state. We also hoped that heightened attention would force the national Democratic Party to take notice and care about issues that affected Black people at its national convention in August.

But the students were going to be identified with Black folk, with King and the struggle, and with subsistence workers. They were going to be linked to SNCC, the NAACP, COFO, CORE, and the SCLC. As a consequence, they would be regarded as part of that phantom-like idea of us fomenting a Communist movement in America, and they would face immediate risks because of their associations with us. We had been living with the sometimes lethal threats, accusations, and degrading attitudes for years. But for these white, mostly non-Southern students, such an atmosphere was all new.

So we were quite aware that all the students needed support and orientation. Most had never been to the South. The screening process SNCC and CORE undertook had weeded out those who were not fit for the job, either because they underestimated the danger or held grandiose visions of being a savior of some sort. And no one under eighteen was allowed. The nine hundred or so who made it through had to be ready to be arrested. Anyone under twenty-one had to have signed permission from their parents. The students also had to pay their own way and have at least $500 bail money on hand.

For two weeks, from June 13 through June 27, the Freedom Summer student volunteers went through training on the campus of Western

College for Women, in Oxford, Ohio. The National Council of Churches funded the sessions. SNCC and CORE were the main organizers preparing the students for the work they were about to do. The volunteers were divided into two groups, each of which would complete a week-long session. Each day of the sessions had a theme. I was brought in to work with the students during the third day of the training, which focused on nonviolence.

I arrived at the campus on Tuesday, June 16, during the first week. That night, before my presentation the next day, we got word that the Ku Klux Klan had attacked parishioners and burned the Mt. Zion Methodist Church in Longdale, Mississippi, to the ground. The church had been the site of some of SNCC's and CORE's work in Neshoba County. Several of the SNCC and CORE workers taking part in the training sessions in Ohio that night had been organizing voter registration and setting up a Freedom School and a community center in that church just a few days before, including two CORE workers named James Chaney and Michael Schwerner.

Klansmen had beaten one male Mt. Zion parishioner and broken a woman's collarbone as they left the church that night. Then they used gasoline to set fire to the church. It was the latest in a rash of twenty Klan church burnings in Mississippi from the winter through the summer of 1964.

I held my workshop on nonviolence the next morning. A white graduate student in political science at Miami University, also in Oxford, Ohio, took very extensive notes. Ellen Barnes was writing her master's thesis on nonviolence, and was allowed to attend and observe the training sessions that week.

> Wednesday . . . was to be "nonviolence day." . . . Leonard Theater was packed when I arrived. As on the previous days there were several newsmen and photographers around. When Matthew Jones, one of the Freedom Singers, started the singing, the cameras really went into action. . . .
>
> When the singing was over, the first speaker of the day was introduced. He was Rev. James Lawson, a young Negro pastor from Memphis. Rev. Lawson was in his thirties and a member of Martin Luther King's Southern Christian Leadership Conference. He was well dressed, good looking, and had a very commanding speaking voice.

> He began to speak, and I immediately knew there would be some fireworks today.

I remember a youthful spirit among the group, no matter what their fears and anxieties might have been. Bringing in such large numbers of students for a whole summer to register voters and set up schools and community centers in the Deep South was something that had never been done in the United States. People were calling Freedom Summer a domestic Peace Corps.

I set about giving a methodical overview of the philosophy of nonviolence, but what I remember most was that the gathered students did not really want to hear about nonviolence as we practiced it in the movement. Looking back, I would come to realize that we were trying to teach them in one day everything that it had taken people months to learn during the Nashville Student Movement. So I think I lost the audience that day, and my presentation was a flop.

Ellen Barnes took note of the reaction to my talk during a ten-minute break before our question-and-answer session.

> Rev. Lawson had spoken powerfully and sincerely. There was no question in anyone's mind, I am certain, that this man had anything but the deepest and most final commitment on this question. However, watching the expressions on many faces during his talk I had noticed various reactions that promised a lively question period. Some faces had registered shock, others grew tense, still others suggested growing cynicism. This was the crucial area for each person in the room. They could learn about Mississippi, the white southerner, the role of law and so on, but they could not just "absorb" nonviolence. If they had not done so already, they were about to be faced with the necessity to make a commitment to nonviolence or go home. They were finding out that to many in the movement nonviolence meant more than just not hitting back. It was obvious that many were uncertain about the way they interpreted nonviolence, some had probably not really thought about it in Rev. Lawson's terms, others quite obviously had decided and disagreed.
>
> Under these circumstances the break was welcome. After ten minutes of stewing in the corridors and arguing in small groups the volunteers filed back in. There was no singing. By this time many

had worked up a healthy belligerence. Before the questions began, Rev. Lawson took a few minutes to clarify some points.

I am grateful that she was there to capture the atmosphere. Before I opened the floor to questions, she said I told the student volunteers that to make a commitment to the philosophy of nonviolence meant that they would be putting themselves at risk. "It is likely that at some time this summer you may have to face a mob of haters," I said. Then I gave them some practical suggestions about maintaining eye contact with hostile people, finding the leader of a crowd, and asking questions about why people were acting the way they were acting. I also told them that there would be times when it was best to retreat in order to fight again another day.

As they asked questions, a lot of the students challenged the concept of nonviolence, knowing so little about what it really meant in our movement. One question I got was about the nature of nonviolence. Ellen Barnes quoted me as saying, "Nonviolence is not passive. It is a positive force dedicated to change. It is not to be confused with submission or weakness."

Another questioner saw nonviolence as a practical tool, because it was working, but wasn't sold on the idea of an absolute commitment to nonviolence or, especially, to the religious terms I had used to illustrate it. At that moment I realized that these white students did not understand that they were coming into a Black movement.

I answered with that in mind: "I can't tell you what you must think, but I do think you are missing the point about the nature of the fight we are in. Right now, it is being fought on racial lines, but it could be fought on many others. The important thing to realize is that violence, injury, and hatred are a human problem, not a race problem. . . . If nonviolence is only employed because of its pragmatic virtues, then it is implied that there is a point at which you will be willing to switch to violence because now it is pragmatic. But violence is a force that has a deliberate intent to injure and intimidate someone. Its goal is destructive. We have dedicated ourselves and our struggle to the creation of a different order. We accept nonviolence because it has the power to move in a constructive and creative fashion, to persuade, to influence, to resolve conflict and bring change. . . . Violence does not bring peace."

The Washington Post reported on our session that day, too:

> Students and other volunteers here are not the beatnik crowd. There are a few bearded ones, but the overwhelming majority look like the clean-cut kid next door. They come from all over the country with large contingents from California, New York, Washington, D.C., Michigan and Wisconsin. . . .
>
> . . . The 200 trainees . . . were taught by about 80 . . . SNCC staffers. . . . The volunteers were about 7 to 1 white; ages ranged from 18 to 26, and men outnumber women 6 to 4. . . .
>
> Wednesday's meeting started with freedom songs and . . . Rev. James Lawson . . . talked about the components of nonviolence: faith and the ideas that . . . love is the law of life . . . people should have the moral courage not to be intimidated and . . . "love force" means a kind of love that is prepared to accept suffering.
>
> The students' questions, however, were practical: "What do you do in case a mob comes?" "What if there is police harassment?" . . . "Is there ever a place where violence is the only possibility?" Mr. Lawson's answer to the last question was no, but some in the audience disagreed.

After lunch, we spent the rest of the afternoon answering questions about nonviolence. John Lewis joined me for that session in his role as president of SNCC. Also joining us were Bob Zellner, a white Southerner who was a field secretary for SNCC, and Ivanhoe Donaldson, a Black field secretary for SNCC from the Bronx. There were still some vocal skeptics in the audience. Once again, I saw that the mostly white student crowd had been influenced heavily by being raised in the most violent and most militarized society in history. At that time, conversations on college campuses about revolutionary violence were in fashion. And these students were pretty enraptured with that violent talk.

In my opinion, some of those students were not the best additions to the movement. They had internalized too much white, liberal political theory, with romantic ideas of Marxism and revolutionary violence, which was not a solid, sustainable place for Black people in the South to be. When Black folk went to register to vote, they were risking their lives. They couldn't go to a county courthouse or voter registration office in Atlanta or Selma or Jackson with a weapon in their pockets for self-defense. Black people could not take a knife or gun with them to register, because a knife or a gun would be an excuse for the white power structures to kill them. So they did not carry weapons to defend themselves. They learned to use nonviolent defense. All the strategies to get Black folk involved in the political process from the very beginning, anywhere in the Southeastern part of the country, required that no one carry a gun or knife when registering to vote. In McComb, Mississippi, for example, Bob Moses insisted that people going to register had to leave their weapons at home. Even when you don't have a gun, white officials will say you do and use it as an excuse for harm, as had happened to Dr. Robert Hayling, whom Klansmen had assaulted in St. Augustine a few months before.

I think I did a poor job in conveying to those students the importance of the commitment to nonviolence in our movement. And because I was a minister, it stirred the students' skepticism of religion, and even their ridicule. But the whole week of training was an attempt to show them that they had to adjust to our movement. They had never experienced Black people organizing and leading them.

We were trying to incorporate these white students into a movement that was essentially a Black, Southern movement. A few months before the training session, SNCC had sent around a list of twenty problems their field staffers had identified when bringing white students into Mississippi. These students in the Ohio training sessions would have to understand the sorts of problems they could create, as much as they would need to know about the problems we were sending them to help remedy.

1. Fears (that Negroes have of being associated with an inter-racial group in Mississippi . . .)
2. Insecurities (skilled vs. unskilled—whites tend to have superior educational background and tend to get in command posts.)
3. Deep Feelings (past racial incidents that still are "bugging" people. Very deep, emotional, not easily gotten at by talking, etc.)
4. Growing up hating white people. Many people have grown up in isolated communities where the whites have killed their friends and relatives and have seen only whites beating or interrogating Negroes.
5. Role of whites in the Movement. . . . Question of where you want white people in the movement. Missionary attitudes are resented.

Other issues in the list included: "What does it mean for a white person to come down and work on projects . . . without grappling with their own feelings about Negroes?" and "Sometimes whites are an unnecessary risk" and "White reactions to Negroes feelings about whites."

These were challenges we had considered and tried to address. Above all, though, we knew it was most important for the trainees to understand the danger they were facing in Mississippi that summer. So despite their skepticism, we had to demand that the white volunteers learn to protect themselves nonviolently.

We could not tolerate a romantic notion of revolutionary violence in a nonviolent campaign. The idea of violence as a form of self-defense was Western European, white thinking and philosophy, and would not have helped in dismantling segregation in our country. In many communities where Black students worked to dismantle racism, they collaborated with the people who lived with them there. They didn't lead the campaign. The community did. Our training was an attempt to orient these students to that approach. It wasn't perfect. When I look back on it now, I see it as us doing the best we could at the time.

By the end of the day of nonviolence training, we had taken the students through a few scenarios and taught them the basics of how to respond to violence, both physical and verbal. Then, as a rebuttal to all I had said, Stokely Carmichael got up and cast doubt on the efficacy of nonviolence. The students responded to him positively, as Ellen Barnes described it:

> The opposition, in the person of Stokely Carmichael—a SNCC staff member—received equal time. He maintained that nonviolence had been successful in the South because the South had been unprepared and because there had been a hard core of well-disciplined workers. Now the movement is assuming a mass character and is losing the sympathy of the North as it moves closer to its doorstep. For these reasons the entire tenor of the movement is changing, growing more impatient, more militant, more difficult to control. . . . His point was that there were very practical reasons why the movement succeeded with nonviolence and equally practical reasons now why nonviolence was losing its hold. Success certainly was not due to any great transformation in the minds and hearts of men!
>
> The session seemed on the brink of returning to controversy again. Then Bob Moses rose. No human being could have been less dynamic, yet as he spoke—slowly, gently—a subtle and, I believe

permanent, change came over the room. . . . "In Mississippi we have two ground rules: 1.) No weapons are to be carried or kept in your room. 2.) If you feel tempted to retaliate, please leave."

Questions were resolved. The session ended.

The point I did not get across clearly enough to the students was that the ultimate goals of Freedom Summer—voting rights, full literacy, and self-determination for Black people in Mississippi—were in and of themselves some of the most evolved forms of nonviolent resistance. They had the power to dismantle structures of white supremacy without resorting to violence. Merely the idea of Black people voting and getting good educations and fair wages struck even more fear into the segregationists than a gun or a knife ever would. For all their bluster, the underlying fears of all the white people who opposed our movement was a belief that recognizing the humanity of everyone else was somehow a threat to their own humanity and right to live free. But our goals centered on the simple idea that—to quote Fannie Lou Hamer, from Ruleville, Mississippi, who was also mentoring students in Ohio that week, and who would become the face of the Mississippi Democratic Freedom Party—"Nobody's free until everybody's free."

After that Wednesday in Ohio, I headed back to Memphis, my family, and my congregation for the weekend. Martin had posted bond and left jail in St. Augustine on Monday, June 15. During his weekend in jail he had written to a rabbi named Israel Dresner, asking him to bring a group of rabbis to St. Augustine to demonstrate with the SCLC. Dresner and King had first met during the Albany campaign, in 1962. Dresner, from Brooklyn, New York, had been one of the early Freedom Riders into Florida in 1961. Martin knew he could count on his friend to stand with us. On Thursday, June 18, we planned to return to Monson's, the scene of Martin's recent arrest. He did not march or attend the earlier sit-ins on Thursday, because he was out on bond. But he was across the street observing what happened. *The New York Times* described the demonstration when about seventy demonstrators led by Fred Shuttlesworth and C. T. Vivian arrived at Monson's at noon. The manager, James Brock, once again met them outside the restaurant near the swimming pool.

> "This is private property and I will have to ask you to leave," Mr. Brock said.
>
> When the demonstrators refused to do so, he . . . pushed the leaders and one by one he pushed the rabbis. As one rabbi was pushed aside another would step forward to take his place.
>
> A crowd of white business men and townspeople stood by and shouted.

That's when five Black demonstrators who had been waiting in a car and two white men who were part of our campaign hurried into the hotel's swimming pool, effectively integrating it for the first time. Immediately, Mr. Brock, in a famous scene captured in photos, got two buckets of an acidic cleaner and dumped them into the pool. Because the acid was not harmful to their skin, our people stayed in the water and refused to leave. Next, a police officer jumped in to make them get out of the pool. Then, as the *Times* reported, "several other officers seized them, clubbed them and thoroughly roughed them up." In the end, all of our people who had gone into the pool and all the rabbis supporting us there were arrested, along with other demonstrators on the scene. They were added to the more than two hundred people already in the city's jail for participating in our sit-ins.

For those segregationists, St. Augustine was a last gasp, as they sought to prevent the inevitable. Their brutality was public enough to influence Congress to do away with the laws that had protected their conduct and kept the United States segregated for a century.

The next day, Friday, June 19, the Senate finally passed the Civil Rights Act of 1964, which outlawed segregation in public places and schools throughout the nation and made employment discrimination illegal. Only a single senator from the formerly Confederate states voted for the Act—Ralph Yarborough, a Democrat from Texas. He would be defeated for reelection in 1970.

The final bill was a watered-down version of the one that had passed in the House months before, because the Senate had weakened some requirements and enforcement powers. And it did not completely stop states from denying Black people the right to vote. Still, the bill was the first major legislative victory for our movement. It would not have happened without the sit-ins, the Freedom Ride, the March on Washington, our actions in Montgomery, Mississippi, Albany, Birmingham, and

St. Augustine, and countless other local campaigns of nonviolent direct action against segregation through the years.

My study since 1947 of Gandhi and nonviolent endeavors in the United States had convinced me by around 1951 that organized nonviolent campaigns would break the back of segregation in this country. I had always been convinced that our marches, boycotts, and strikes would put pressure on presidents and Congress to pass the legislation that would remedy it. These tactics are key to a nonviolent campaign: to push public officials, businesspeople, and church people, to get on the side of the angels, to leave the side of neutrality and of evil. A good movement accumulates power, then introduces a new form of power to the public agenda. It is of vital importance that at least one side insists on nonviolence. One side must not join with the wrongdoing, spiritually or physically, and must speak love above all, and act nonviolently—being arrested, if necessary. But very deftly that side must practice direct action, so that they drive a confrontation between the wrong and the new possibility.

Another component of a successful campaign is testing your wins to ensure that they are being implemented. We knew it would be a few weeks before the bill was signed and that we faced a long road before it was fully enacted. So we didn't let up.

Our St. Augustine campaign was part of what changed the momentum in Congress and helped get the Civil Rights Act passed in the Senate. Yet in the time between its passage and the president signing the bill, St. Augustine itself still had to deal with white terrorism and the intransigent white segregationists in positions of power. Our strategy was to begin testing the new order in light of the Civil Rights Act.

On Saturday, June 20, the day after the bill passed, Wyatt Tee Walker and Dorothy Cotton led one of the first of those tests—a wade-in at a whites-only beach in St. Augustine. They took a group of Black and white swimmers to a beach where integration had not been allowed, and they were attacked by segregationists. Dorothy Cotton suffered an injury to her ear that day. It affected her hearing for the rest of her life.

The New York Times was covering the St. Augustine campaign almost daily by then, and was particularly attentive to us on the day after the passage of the Civil Rights Act.

> Segregationists attacked an integrated group swimming at a public beach. . . . A group of whites waded into the surf and attacked the

> swimmers. . . . Holsted Manucy, the leader of a group of white toughs who have been harassing Negroes, was waiting in his car when the demonstrators arrived at the beach.
>
> By 2-way radio, he notified his men, called "Manucy's Raiders" by the townspeople, that the group had arrived. Within a few minutes several carloads of whites waving confederate flags arrived and poured out on the beach.
>
> They waded into the water and began beating some of the group, which numbered about 25.

Also on June 20, the students I had met with in Oxford, Ohio, finished their week-long training session and left for Mississippi. Some went on SNCC buses, and others went in cars. In one station wagon, CORE workers Mickey Schwerner and James Chaney took six of the students to Meridian, Mississippi. Schwerner, from suburban New York, and Chaney, who was from Meridian, had helped organize the Freedom School at Mt. Zion Methodist Church in Neshoba County, the church that Klansmen had burned down on June 16. One of the six volunteers leaving Ohio with them that day was a twenty-year-old college student from New York City named Andrew Goodman.

Soon after they arrived in Meridian, Schwerner, Chaney, and Goodman drove to nearby Longdale, Mississippi, in Neshoba County, to check out the KKK arsonists' damage at Mt. Zion Methodist Church. They left word with people in the CORE office in Meridian that they would call by four P.M., and if they didn't, someone should start looking for them. As they were leaving Longdale, James Chaney was driving. A sheriff's deputy pulled the vehicle over and claimed Chaney was speeding. All three men were arrested and taken to the Neshoba County jail in Philadelphia, Mississippi, where they were not allowed to make any phone calls. Since it was well past four P.M., the CORE office had begun calling all the jails in the area but could not find them. The sheriff released them around ten P.M. and told them to go back to Meridian. On the road back they were kidnapped by a gang of white men.

Chaney and Schwerner were experienced CORE workers in Mississippi, and were known among white supremacists in Neshoba County. The two men understood the importance of not traveling after dark and of keeping in touch with their home base. Both men had been trained extensively in nonviolent resistance. They had started their ride out of the county in daylight. The police had stopped them. They must have realized it wasn't over when they were sent home in darkness. I am sure they knew to leave as quickly as possible.

When white vigilantes shot at our car in rural Tennessee in 1963, I told my traveling companions that nonviolent direct action was meant to have witnesses, and this was not that kind of situation. So we drove away as fast as we could. I am sure that is what Schwerner and Chaney knew to do. This is why when no one could find them, it was obvious that something bad had happened, likely at the hands of the white terrorists who were in league with so many rural sheriffs, their deputies, and local police officers.

When I heard about their disappearance, I assumed they had encountered brutality of some sort. Two New York Jews and a Black man from Mississippi were not safe in that state, especially traveling together. I had just been with those three men in Ohio, warning of the danger, and three days later they were missing. The tragedy brewing in Mississippi was shadowing the triumph of the Civil Rights Act victory in Washington, D.C. Our movement put brave people in constant peril. But to see the dangers we had warned those students they might face become so horribly real again shook me up. It also demanded that I keep going. We all had to keep going.

By the following Tuesday night, June 23, I was back in Oxford, Ohio, to conduct another nonviolence session, this time with the second group of Freedom Summer volunteers. We had just received the news that Mickey Schwerner's station wagon had been found smoldering in a creek near Philadelphia, Mississippi. With that news, Bob Moses and Mickey's wife, Rita Schwerner, immediately left the training session and went to Mississippi. The disappearance haunted everyone and cast a pall over that second session.

In recent years, I have seen a report about that week from the Mississippi State Sovereignty Commission, dated Wednesday, June 24, 1964. We knew that the commission was spying on us. They were Mississippi's version of the CIA, an agency the white supremacists ran to keep track of any activism related to their state. They had sent infiltrators to Ohio for our training sessions. Their report began by giving times and dates, then went on to describe my presentation on nonviolence to the Freedom Summer volunteers. But most of the report was concerned with any information they could get about Martin. And since I had just been with him in St. Augustine on Monday and Tuesday before coming to Oxford Tuesday night, that was their main focus.

> The theme for this speech was non-violence. He stated the only way that the freedom summer would be a success would be for the students to remain non-violent. He told them that they were not going to Mississippi to make war, although it would be worse than a war, as they would be beaten by the police and local people.
>
> Reverend Lawson said that he had been in St. Augustine, Florida on Tuesday, June 23, where he had met Martin Luther King. He said he was reminded by King that the North and South are not together and that a house divided among itself cannot stand. King further stated that this would be a long hot summer in Mississippi for the white man and for the black man too. King said that as soon as he cleans up the St. Augustine, Florida situation he will be coming to Jackson to clean up things here.
>
> . . . Everyone in Oxford is very upset over the three missing workers. . . . They are very hurt but say that will not stop their plans.

Indeed, the second group left for Mississippi on Saturday, June 27. That group was going to set up the Freedom Schools and teach in them.

June ended with the SCLC announcing that it would be leaving St. Augustine on July 1. The city had agreed to our demands, including setting up a biracial committee to work on implementation of the Civil Rights Act in the city. Monson's was integrated, but soon thereafter the KKK firebombed it out of business.

On Thursday, July 2, Martin and others were on hand in Washington, D.C., when President Johnson signed the Civil Rights Act in a White House ceremony. A month later, on Tuesday, August 4, the bodies of Chaney, Goodman, and Schwerner were found buried in an earthen dam more than fourteen feet deep at Jolly Farm, the property of a KKK member. It was a lynching. It was police brutality. It was the worst of human cruelty. We had won some legal battles and had gotten laws changed. But as we had said all along, hearts and minds are not turned with laws alone.

A lot of Americans, including some Black people, were of the mind that the South was the problem when it came to racial injustices. But from the beginning, we knew that racism and segregation were national problems. And during the 1960s, most Americans were antagonistic to our movement. The Democratic Party never emphatically denounced segregation or economic inequality. Gradually, the Senate and the House Democrats voted for more and more of the changes we were promoting, like the 1964 Civil Rights Act, which also had support from some Republicans.

But the Democratic Party, congressional Democrats, and the White House did not embrace the vision of Freedom Summer or the Mississippi Freedom Democratic Party. At the Democratic convention in Atlantic City, New Jersey, in August, the Freedom Democratic Party asked to be seated as delegates from Mississippi. Fannie Lou Hamer spoke to the convention, but her forceful appeal didn't result in any Black delegates for Mississippi. The Democrats had the power to support and advance our vision, which could have propelled the nation forward. But the party suffered from a lack of character and the courage to make bold moves. Powerful donors to the Democratic Party were too afraid to take a stand against what was wrong. That inaction hurt our cause.

By the fall of 1964, I was getting more involved in Memphis politics, mostly because of my relationship to A. W. Willis, who was running to become the first Black member of the Tennessee legislature since Reconstruction, in the 1870s. He was a prominent member of my congregation, along with his wife and five children and his mother. His oldest son, Michael (Fombi), was one of The Memphis Thirteen—the Black first grade students who integrated the Memphis City Schools in 1961. He was also the lawyer for the church at the time, and he was part of the Shelby County Democratic Club, which was trying to organize the Black community in Memphis to become politically awake. When I came to Centenary, A.W. and his family were already active, visible people in the church. As his pastor, I was committed to his family. Then, in a very short time, A.W. and I became close friends, too. We were all delighted when he won the election in November 1964. A Black man would be in the legislature in Nashville after almost a century of only white people.

President Johnson would defeat Barry Goldwater that day, in a historic landslide. I believe that if the national Democratic Party had told the Mississippi Democratic Party to desegregate at their convention and seat delegates from the Mississippi Freedom Democratic Party, the election of Lyndon Johnson would not have been affected in any way. Even if, as a result, Johnson had lost Mississippi, he still would have won the election overwhelmingly, and the Democrats would have done what was right and seated a truly representative Mississippi delegation at the convention.

The year ended with Martin traveling to Oslo, Norway, to accept the Nobel Peace Prize. At that time, he was thirty-five years old and the youngest recipient in history.

Global recognition for our movement was important, but reaching our ultimate goal of a beloved community, one with economic and racial equity, was still distant. So we needed to keep building on our successes, step by step. In many places in America, and especially in the South, Black people were still not able to register to vote. As the new year began, our focus would be on securing the right to vote.

Malcolm X continued to move toward working together with Martin as he said he would when they met briefly in Washington, D.C., despite the fact that Malcolm was not going to dedicate himself fully to nonviolence. In early February 1965, Malcolm visited Selma, Alabama, where a voting rights campaign was gaining momentum. Martin had traveled to Selma to get the campaign off the ground, and was arrested soon thereafter. When Malcolm arrived, Martin was in the Selma jail. And so Malcolm visited with Coretta instead. They shared some time together, and he told her, "I didn't come to Selma to make his job difficult. I really did come thinking that I could make it easier. If the white people realize what the alternative is, perhaps they will be more willing to hear Dr. King."

Just two weeks later, on February 21, he was shot and killed in upper Manhattan while making a speech. Assassination was again stalking our movement. As we had done with the deaths of Medgar Evers and President Kennedy, we tried to channel the deep sadness we all felt into inspiring more of the work for justice to which Malcolm X and the rest of us had been devoting our lives.

On March 7, John Lewis and Hosea Williams organized a march for voting rights in the Selma campaign. But the event turned into a brutal police attack on peaceful protesters. As six hundred marchers made their way across the Edmund Pettus Bridge—the span that crosses the Alabama River in the center of Selma, named after a Confederate general and grand dragon of the Ku Klux Klan—Alabama state troopers viciously beat and tear-gassed them, and turned them back. John's head was bloodied, and many others also shed blood on the Edmund Pettus Bridge that day—a day that is now remembered as Bloody Sunday. Eight months after the president signed the Civil Rights Act, we still faced vicious police violence for the crime of walking—unarmed and nonviolently—in a public place, demanding our rights to be full participants in our country's democracy. The unspeakable acts of state violence continued in what had already been a horrendously violent decade. Bloody Sunday crystallized the urgent need for the federal government to ensure and protect voting rights in this country.

The day after Bloody Sunday, Martin gave a stirring sermon at Brown Chapel AME Church in Selma, saying, "Deep down in our nonviolent creed is the conviction that there are some things so dear, some things so precious, some things so eternally true that they are worth dying for."

The Selma voting rights campaign was happening just as the country was turning its full attention to the conduct of the Cold War in Southeast Asia. In the spring of 1965, President Johnson announced that the United States would escalate its military involvement in Vietnam. At the end of 1964, there had been 23,300 American soldiers, sailors, airmen, and marines in Southeast Asia. A year later, there would be 184,300 Americans in the war zone. In March 1965, Johnson began the U.S. military's first major campaign of bombing North Vietnam, called Operation Rolling Thunder. It would last until 1968.

In the nonviolent movement, we found it hard to reconcile the bombs our country was dropping on Vietnam with the bombings we had endured in Birmingham, Nashville, and so many other places in the South during our campaigns. The Fellowship of Reconciliation was particularly aggrieved with the escalation in Vietnam and established a group called the Clergymen's Emergency Committee for Vietnam. We co-signed a letter that was printed in an ad in the Sunday *New York Times* on April 4, 1965. The headline read: "2,500 Ministers, Priests and Rabbis Say: Mr. President: *In the Name of God,* STOP IT!"

We were all so concerned that this war would lead to ultimate destruction. My concerns for the future were also personal, because in April 1965 our second son, Morris, was born. Dorothy and I were thrilled to welcome him to the family, and John would soon adjust to having a new little brother. I took time to revel in the joy of Morris's arrival, and to be present as the dynamic in my family changed.

Yet my work never stopped. On May 12, I was part of a vigil at the Pentagon, held by the Interreligious Committee on Vietnam. I went home from that vigil feeling the pull of both our movement and movements for justice all over the world.

One morning later that month, I got a phone call from Martin at my office. He told me the International Fellowship of Reconciliation, FOR's umbrella organization, was sending a delegation of clergy members to Southeast Asia.

He said, "I feel this is not the time for me to be identified with such a campaign. I am fully in support of the trip. I would like to go, but I can't go because of where we are in the struggle."

Martin believed that going to Vietnam at that time would expose him to crippling criticism and would harm our movement. And then he said, "I want you to go in my stead. I would like to tell them I'm sending you."

His invitation astonished me. Martin had called on me to be a strategist, an adviser, and a counselor ever since 1958. And in 1965, we had been talking constantly about the Vietnam War and would continue to do so in coming years—on the phone, and face-to-face when we were together at a meeting or on a walk during a retreat. He was under a lot of pressure. William Sloane Coffin, the chaplain at Yale University, had organized an interfaith group against the Vietnam War with Rabbi Abraham Heschel, the outstanding prophet and teacher of Judaism in the United States, and Eugene Carson Blake, a Presbyterian minister who was the director of the National Council of the Churches of Christ in America. It was called Clergy and Laymen Concerned About Vietnam. Bill Coffin had been a Freedom Rider and had stood up in the movement at other times, too. He wanted Martin to come out publicly with them. All through the 1960s, interfaith pressure was building on King to join them in criticizing the Vietnam War. He declined.

The politics of the situation were too delicate. Lyndon Johnson had been doing good work in passing the 1964 Civil Rights Act, and would continue that by creating the Head Start and Medicare programs. Martin encouraged all of Johnson's Great Society plans, especially his War on Poverty. But we did not support Johnson's escalation of the war in Vietnam.

We both saw how U.S. foreign policy in 1964 and 1965 in Africa, Latin America, and Asia was very racist and centered on the interests of white people, the wealthy, and those who had military power. The United States went along with our French and British allies' attempts to preserve the French and British Empires, while claiming moral superiority for that endeavor. We were supposed to be the good guys. But we were not. We supported the restoration of Western European empires against the ideals of some quite notable people who—just as Thomas Jefferson and William Penn had—were fighting for independence, such as Kenneth Kaunda in Zambia, Kwame Nkrumah in Ghana, and Sarojini Naidu in India.

Still, I would tell Martin that as the icon and spokesperson for our direct action campaigns in our nonviolent movement in the United States, he had a special responsibility to speak at the right time, in the right place. But he had to make that decision in his own good time, and not according to other people or other forces. "You should not allow yourself to be pressured into speaking out on Vietnam until you are convinced that you cannot *not* speak up publicly," I told him. "Once you do, the issues around all of us will change. There will be people telling you that U.S. foreign policy is none of your business. People will be saying that you're mixing apples and elephants. As a symbol of our movement, you cannot move us to that stage until you are certain in your own heart, mind, and spirit that you have to speak out. Deep inside, you will know when and where that is to be. No one else can make that decision for you."

Of course, he understood that responsibility. One way he had handled it up to that point was through his wife, Coretta, who had become quite outspoken about the war, and had strong feelings about the link between the movement and the war. In the early 1960s, he had asked Coretta to speak instead of himself at some places. And she would criticize the Vietnam War. Martin had also told Jim Bevel, who was SCLC staff, that he should spend half his SCLC time on the peace movement. And now he was asking me to take his place on this trip.

I told Martin I would be honored to go, as long as my congregation backed me.

At Centenary the next Sunday, I informed my congregation about Martin's invitation. I explained that it meant I would be out of the city for three to five weeks, and that I was seriously considering doing it. After I spoke, I couldn't tell how they felt about it.

The following Sunday, however, I was deeply moved by their reaction. At the end of our eleven A.M. service, one of the staunchest members of our church, William Hunt, stood up and said, "Mr. Pastor, I want to put a motion before the congregation."

Hunt was a teacher, and he had been waiting to do this all morning. He usually sat with his wife, daughter, and two sons. That day, I had noticed, he was not with his family in their usual spot. He had taken a seat closer to the pulpit, toward the front of the church. When he stood up, I had no idea what he was going to say. But I'll never forget it—he called me "Mr. Pastor."

Then he said, "I want to make a motion that Reverend Lawson should go on this peace trip. And further, I want to make a motion that the congregation firmly supports him and backs this trip, and that we will all care for his family while he is gone."

With that, the whole congregation stood and clapped.

The moment brought me to tears.

In all my years of doing this work, I don't remember meeting a Black person who jumped on me about my work in the movement—not in Memphis or Shelbyville. I had all kinds of people in my congregations who would not do this kind of work themselves. I knew that. They could not do it and should not have been expected to do any more than they could. Nevertheless, they saw me as doing what needed to be done. And they bolstered me. I immediately told Martin I was ready to go.

I was about to travel into the middle of a war. Of course, it was not as if I hadn't been operating in the middle of a war for years in the South. And in the same vein as my revelation when I was a young boy that violence would not keep me safe, I knew as an adult that a military war would not be the ultimate resolution to conflicts that so many considered it to be. It was a theater where dueling sides put on special clothing and amassed equipment and machinery of death with real-life consequences. I had spent thirteen months in prison to demonstrate my objections to the inequities of the Selective Service draft. And I had been on the front lines of a movement that used nonviolent direct action against hate, injustice, and violence. We were as disciplined and committed as any military. But instead of a goal of destruction and domination, we entered into our battles with fierce love, so that soul force would prevail.

As ever, I took notes to remember the journey, starting on the day before I left.

> June 28th almost began too quietly to reflect either the restlessness I felt in moving out on a risky venture or the mood that prevailed as I thought of being away from my family for three weeks. But amid

> such thought, peace was also there—peace as an inner confidence and security which possessed me as I considered the "journey of reconciliation" to the war torn land of Vietnam. . . .
>
> I felt that God had made available to me a special opportunity to witness for peace. When God proposes, a person must answer "Yes." When you answer "Yes," no matter the risks, you can be sure to dwell in safety.
>
> . . . I left Memphis, Tuesday, June 29 at 8:35 via American flight #262. It was most difficult to leave my family. Dorothy and I have been telling John that I would be gone for a long time. The other night he came into my arms with a big hug and said, "Daddy, I miss you too very much."

Our group of clergy on the trip was to be an international team. From Europe came André Trocmé, the great French Protestant pastor and underground leader against the Nazi movement. And from Germany came Martin Niemöller, who was an anti-Nazi pastor during World War II and was one of the presidents of the World Council of Churches. He is perhaps most widely known for his famous poem about the Holocaust called "First They Came," which begins, "First they came for the Communists, and I did not speak out because I was not a Communist." It goes on to name all the groups the Nazis came for, and he didn't speak out, until they came for him. "And there was no one left to speak out for me."

The clergy from the United States included Bishop William Crittenden, the Episcopal bishop of northwestern Pennsylvania, and Monsignor Edward Murray, from the Roman Catholic Church in Boston. Alfred Hassler, the executive director of the Fellowship of Reconciliation, organized the trip and was the leader of our team. Then there was the president of Chicago Theological School, Howard Schomer, and his wife, Elsie Schomer, of the Women's International League for Peace and Freedom. We represented Roman Catholics, Jewish people, and Protestants. I was the only Black clergy member. And I was the only one representing the American South.

We flew from New York to Paris for a connecting flight to Rome, where we would stay the night. I read David Halberstam's book *The Making of a Quagmire,* which had just come out, based on his *New York Times* reporting in South Vietnam, for which he had won the 1964 Pulitzer Prize. I wrote about it in that journal I'd begun to keep.

> Spent the first leg from Kennedy to Paris reading David Halberstam's account of S. Vietnam. . . . JFK was unhappy about his reporting and even asked that he be brought home which the N.Y. Times refused to do. Book is good and hard. Relates our being in S. Vietnam, without knowing situation, to our South whose white leaders do not know Negro grievances, blame it on agitators.
>
> . . . A smooth flight over the ocean—followed by an hour at the Paris airport, another good flight to Rome. . . .
>
> What a shame, gross and indecent, to be so close to Michelangelo and Van Gogh, yet not have time to stop and say hello. Seems unreal to be so near to 2 of our greatest cities—Paris and Rome—yet be confined to an airport.
>
> We arrived in Bangkok at 10:00 AM, Thursday, July 1. Staying at the Viengtai Hotel—good facilities with air conditioning and a balcony. My only complaint so far is that Dorothy is not with me.

We spent the weekend in Thailand acclimating and getting prepared for our venture into Vietnam. We were going into a region where our country was dropping bombs. But for me, the potential for danger and the feeling that our government was on the wrong side was not new, after bombings in the American South, when the federal government would not send anyone to protect our people from the white terrorists trying to destroy us.

I could make a lot of the fact that we arrived in Vietnam on July 4, American Independence Day. But that wasn't really what I was thinking about at the time. I was eager to see as much as I could and talk to as many people as possible on all sides. In Saigon, we settled into the International Voluntary Services hostel, which was run by the State Department. Our government wanted us to see the upside of its war and the ways in which it believed it was helping the citizens of Vietnam.

The American embassy in Saigon worked hard to have us talk to a wide range of people. We met the prime minister at that time, Nguyễn Cao Kỳ, and other members of the South Vietnamese government. They took us into the villages to see some of the rehabilitation programs, the pacification programs, where former Viet Cong soldiers lived in compounds. That was the closest we got to any Vietnamese people who the Americans had considered to be the enemy. But we were aware that given their confinement, those men were not able to speak freely.

In Saigon, we met with people in labor and the military, and we talked to embassy workers, students, and European and American journalists. We met with a good number of the leaders of the Unified Buddhist Church and the very conservative Protestant churches, and with the Roman Catholic archbishop of South Vietnam, as well as Catholic priests.

A journalist for *Time* magazine, Frank McCulloch, told our delegation that the United States couldn't win. He said the United States could not stop North Vietnam, could not stop Ho Chi Minh. Ho had started the independence movement for Southeast Asia in the 1930s with his preliminary organizing in France. I had dinner with McCulloch one night, and what he said troubled me. He stated quite flatly that there was no possibility of the war ending soon.

I asked him, "Well, how do you think that could be averted?" I was searching for some hope.

He said, "If America sends in several thousands of troops quickly, we can stop an inevitable defeat."

I asked him, "And then do you think we can move on toward military victory?"

"Oh, no," he said. "The U.S. would have to send a million or more troops to Vietnam in order to win. And even then, the war would be long and very costly in terms of human life and money and our reputation in the world."

He added, "A half million soldiers from the United States are not going to win it. But in five years, a half million troops could prevent the Viet Cong from winning. And in about ten years we could reach a stalemate."

That was a shock to hear, in 1965. His view, of course, proved to be right. Except that the stalemate became a defeat.

In my notes, I wrote that we found the situation on the ground "more complex than what we have been told by our government. The other side is not all wrong. Our side is not all right." I wrote of the agony of the war, the suffering of the people, and the terror of the U.S. intervention. As I thought of the war escalating and our involvement deepening, the word "quagmire" in the title of David's book kept resonating:

> We are about to launch a major war in Asia of white men killing colored people. Such a war will not solve the problems of Vietnam. It will increase racial hatred and will make the white man of America more hated than ever before. Such a war could provoke China and the USSR thus bringing about World War III.

Some of the deepest connections many of us made were with leaders from the Unified Buddhist Church of Vietnam. We met in their pagoda with one Buddhist layman and three church leaders, including Thich Nhat Hanh, who had already written three books about peace and nonviolence. He told us, "The problem of Vietnam is not the problem of Vietnam anymore. It is an international problem. The Vietnamese people have lost hope and faith. Any government will need a long time before they win the trust of the people, since we have heard so many lies, and seen so many tricks. . . . People are not interested in any '-ism.' Most people are interested in being alive first of all."

Thich Nhat Hanh, who was in his late thirties at the time, was not on the side of either the Viet Cong in North Vietnam or the U.S.-supported regime in South Vietnam. He was cordial to our group and appreciated the fact that we had come to see for ourselves what was happening. And he was clear that the war before this one had been about the French Empire going home, and leaving the people of Southeast Asia to the task of governing themselves and discovering who they were. He clearly saw American involvement as an extension of the French and believed that it was destructive to the country and its people.

Martin had asked me to give his greetings to the Buddhist leaders. He asked me to tell them he recognized that our struggle in the United States was in unity with their struggle in Vietnam. And he specifically asked me to give his greetings to Thich Nhat Hanh. I took some time that afternoon at the pagoda to speak directly to him and told him, "Martin Luther King asked me to give you his best regards. He wanted to participate in this trip but felt we could not afford for him to do it at this point in our struggle. Still, he wanted me to let you know that he considers you a brother of faith, and that he is praying for you and for your movement."

I also told Nhat Hanh that I supported him. And I wanted him to know that in the United States there were critics of our government's policy in Vietnam. Clearly and quietly, he said, "I appreciate you being here. I am following the movement for Black people in the United States. We are united in the struggle for a faith that embraces all of the world, and all people."

Bringing Martin's greetings directly to the Buddhist resistance there was important to both me and to Martin. In fact, Martin had sent a cablegram to Alfred Hassler when we arrived in Vietnam, expressing his support for our trip. In it, he called our visit's purpose "conscience-seeking," and said the war must be stopped and negotiations must begin. "Guns and gasses," he said, were not the way to address our fear of Communism. Instead, he urged everyone concerned about its spread to come up with programs and policies that were so good for all people economically and in every other way, so that Democracy would be seen as the only system under which everyone can thrive.

On Wednesday, July 7, I left Saigon for Phnom Penh, Cambodia. The two Europeans in our delegation, André Trocmé and Martin Niemöller, had been there for a few days with unrealized hopes of getting into North Vietnam. We talked to a North Vietnamese trade mission team in Cambodia at that time. We also met with people from the Cambodian government and the Canadian International Control Commission, as well as Poles and Indians stationed in Cambodia.

We were told that Americans were not liked in Cambodia, which had decided to be neutral in the war, in part because of trade with China and North Vietnam. They spoke of how terrorism from the Viet Cong in North Vietnam and bombings from the Americans meant that the villagers whose homes were destroyed were victims of it all and were forgotten on both sides.

In my notes I summed up some of my feelings about what I was hearing and seeing.

1. We saw courage and conviction on both sides. . . . No side has all the truth. Both seem to operate from their bad sides. Both frozen in positions which can harm.
2. Almost depressed by the sheer complexity of the problems. More difficult than we have been told by our government, and more difficult than the government seems to recognize.
3. No military victory in sight for either side.
4. People are victims of 25 years of war. Gross suffering of the innocent and growing despair. Loss of self-confidence, division, no solidarity. War and Communism are both the enemies. No good can come of this war. The real enemies are war, violence, hatred, disease, poverty and ignorance.
5. Our suggestion: Stop the bombing as an act of good faith and an invitation to negotiations. . . . Have an international cease fire and develop a program for solving the real enemies.

Throughout the trip, as we heard from people on all sides, I made no friendly remarks concerning U.S. policy, colonialism, the dividing up of Vietnam, or the war. I opposed all of those things firmly and without reservation.

The fundamental issue in the war was not communism, as we were told in the States. It was decolonization. In North Vietnam, Ho Chi Minh was the president, and he was the founder of the Indochine Communist Party. He had led the fight for Vietnamese independence from the colonial French government. He supported the National Liberation Front (NLF) in South Vietnam, which was trying to oust the U.S. government regime and reunite Vietnam. Our government deemed the NLF the enemy. We had been told the reason for our involvement in Vietnam was to stop the spread of communism from the USSR and China. But it was clearly more complex on the ground and Vietnam had its own volition in the matter of its independence from colonizing nations. Repeatedly, people told us that Vietnam had already been at war for twenty-five years.

After World War II, many nations in Africa, Asia, and Latin America wanted independence. They said, "We do not want to be a British colony" or "We do not want to be a French colony." They said, "We want to be India," "We want to be Vietnam." But despite our own origins as a country throwing off colonial rule, the post–World War II United States never supported those struggling for independence and self-governing around the world. The trip confirmed my understanding that the only thing that would change our wars against decolonization was a fundamental change in United States mindset and policy.

We would demilitarize naturally if we made the kind of political, social, and revolutionary changes we had to make to live up to the true promise of the preambles to the Declaration of Independence and the Constitution. Becoming a truly democratic society would mean we would not be afraid of the world in which we lived. We would not need to have military bases on every continent.

Vietnam was the most dramatic example of the growing but mistaken notion at the time that if we don't stop "them" over there, they'll come here. That notion is why a large portion of our economy became a war economy, which was extremely profitable for investors but led to decimation of the planet and dissociation among the human family.

The American government hoped that our journey would bring back stories of the correctness of the U.S. involvement in Vietnam. Like me, all of the people in our delegation were opposed to the war in Southeast Asia and blamed the situation on the United States and France. As we met with people in Vietnam and Cambodia, we saw more clearly than before that in addition to being immoral, the Vietnam War was also bad policy.

We left Cambodia on Thursday, July 8, and arrived in Hong Kong late that night. The others in our delegation and I wrote a report detailing our findings. In it, we spoke of the complicated political and social aspects of the war for all sides. We called for an end to the violence and encouraged an understanding that Vietnam was a pawn in the larger Cold War, which saw everything in the binary terms of the United States and the West versus Soviet communism.

> We do not equate peace with the simple absence of military conflict; true peace is inseparable from justice. . . . We recognize that there are issues in Vietnam of justice, freedom and the need for social change, but we deplore the way in which powers have used and are using the villages of Vietnam as a testing ground for ideological positions such as "wars of national liberation" or "containment of Communism by military force."
>
> For too long we have lived within the narrow simplicities of nation against nation, ideology against ideology, race against race. Today we see the true enemies of man as what they have always been: injustice, poverty, disease, national pride and the abuse of power, and the hatred and war that are their creatures and creators. To be complacent about these is to deny humanity itself. To focus our attack on those evils rather than to fight within the family of man is to stand with the God of history.

We wanted our report to be a basis for a further dialogue. Instead, the Defense Department's reaction was to sponsor a smaller counter-trip of religious editors who they picked because they believed them to be more friendly to U.S. policy in Vietnam. That group was allowed to speak only to people the U.S. government sanctioned. They did indeed produce a more favorable report when they returned, justifying the U.S. presence in Vietnam.

When Johnson announced his escalation of American involvement in 1965, four hundred Americans had died in Vietnam. By the end of the war in 1975, fifty-eight thousand more would perish. At least two million

Vietnamese civilians from both sides—North and South Vietnam—would lose their lives in the war. In addition, more than a million North and South Vietnamese soldiers would die.

Our trip had increased my growing awareness of how war—a military approach to conflict—was obsolete and self-destructive. With the United States of America becoming more militarized in that period, its reckoning with segregation and racism was put on the back burner. This avoidance itself posed a far greater threat to democracy in the United States than the threat from abroad that the Vietnam War was meant to solve.

When I got back to Memphis from Vietnam, the manufactured hysteria about communism continued. The local John Birch Society said that my presence on the trip meant I was a dupe for communism. They claimed that I had gone to North Vietnam, which was false. In the 1960s, anti-communism in the United States was equivalent to white racism. Calling someone a Communist was just another way to call them a n——r.

Anti-communism projected all of our nation's problems on the outsider, the Communist, in the same way that the segregationist pretended that all our problems came from "outside agitators." Just as certain people in the power structure of America deliberately chose to make communism our enemy, so too did these same people make the Black person seeking full citizenship the enemy. Having an *other* to focus on relieved them of the responsibility to look at themselves. An epithet helps people ignore the real dangers of an authoritarian system, whether it be Communist, fascist, or segregationist.

The man who is starving doesn't care who feeds him. So if you are going to stop communism, you have to stop the appeal of communism. President Kennedy was absolutely correct in saying you have to try to help Latin America or Vietnam move in the direction of getting rid of its poverty, illiteracy, hunger, and disease. The idea behind communism is to establish a minimum level of health, work, income, food, clothing, and shelter below which no one falls. That was not always how it played out in practice, but that was its appeal. People in desperate circumstances don't cut fine lines between authoritarianism that comes from the United States or from Great Britain or Russia. Whoever speaks to those problems speaks the loudest to them. If you are going to stop communism, you have to stop the conditions that allow communism to sound like a good alternative to people.

For the most part, I ignored the accusations against me. I didn't ignore how such rhetoric does great harm. For instance, some people in the John Birch Society said that Chaney, Schwerner, and Goodman deserved to be killed because they were Communists. Others said King deserved to be killed, too. We lived with those threats on a daily basis.

A few weeks after I returned from Vietnam, President Johnson signed the Voting Rights Act into law, on August 6, 1965. Five days later, an incident of police brutality sparked six days of burning and looting in Watts, a Black neighborhood in Los Angeles—a signal that despite strides forward in policy, the underlying rage at injustice and racism was still festering, and continued to break through veneers of harmony all over the country, not only in the South.

Our strides against segregation and for voting rights had resulted in historic laws meant to break the institutional basis of our oppression. But the work was far from done. As we entered 1966, our agenda would expand to engage those chronic issues of economic justice and police brutality, as well as racial discrimination in education and housing.

THIRTEEN

With My Mind Stayed on Freedom

Martin Luther King Jr., Stokely Carmichael, Reverend Lawson, and others continued the Meredith March Against Fear, heading south on Highway 51 from the spot where James Meredith had been shot the day before in northern Mississippi, 1966. ERNEST WITHERS COLLECTION

Retaliation for all of the violence surrounding us had a certain allure—after the assassinations of JFK and Malcolm X, the murders of Addie Mae Collins, Denise McNair, Carole Robertson, and Cynthia Wesley in Birmingham and of James Chaney, Mickey Schwerner, and Andrew Goodman in Mississippi, the campaigns in St. Augustine and Selma, and the escalating war in Vietnam. The youngest people in our movement were becoming impatient with the idea of nonviolent direct action, even though it had gotten rid of segregation in many Southern cities and had delivered the Civil Rights Act of 1964 and the Voting Rights

Act of 1965. Martin felt the pressure. I felt it, too. So did Diane Nash and John Lewis and many of us who had made a commitment to nonviolence early on because we knew it as the most effective and sustainable way to dismantle systems that oppressed and killed people.

In May 1966, that pressure led to Stokely Carmichael's defeat of John Lewis in elections for the chairmanship of SNCC. *The New York Times* reported the change as a "major shift in its civil rights philosophy."

> Voted out of the committee chairmanship was John Lewis, a 26-year-old minister who believes in nonviolence as both a "way of life" and as a way of forcing concessions from the "white power structure" in the South.
>
> The new chairman is Stokely Carmichael, who at 24, is disillusioned with using nonviolent protest to force integration from reluctant white communities. Mr. Carmichael does not advocate violence, but neither does he believe in turning the other cheek.

John took losing that election hard. We had founded SNCC in the midst of the Nashville campaign. Two of its first three chairmen, Marion Barry, from 1960 to 1961, and then John, from 1963 to 1966, had been key in the Nashville student movement.

Stokely was at the founding meeting of SNCC in 1960 and had been in some of my workshops back then. He was a student at Howard University and a member of NAG, the Nonviolent Action Group, one of the few Black student groups above the Mason-Dixon Line that got involved in the sit-in movement. He became a field worker for SNCC in 1961, moved into the South, and worked in Alabama. He participated in the Freedom Ride on a train from New Orleans to Jackson on June 8, 1961. He and the other Black and white Freedom Riders were arrested as soon as they arrived at the Jackson train station, and taken to Parchman Prison, where we were together in the summer of 1961. I knew him through all this period. And when he and Dion Diamond came to Nashville and demonstrated with us as we were desegregating grocery stores in 1961, the Nashville Student Movement's central committee asked me to tell them to leave because they couldn't accept nonviolence.

Stokely was highly intelligent—well-read and curious. I always liked him and appreciated his presence. We became friends, and we remained friends after the movement, because we liked each other. He worked for

SNCC in Lowndes County, Alabama, for a time. That's where he coined the term "Black Panther." His work there was a long-term success because those counties organized themselves. And local people kept pushing.

But Stokely was mesmerized by and conditioned into the American way of violence. He had participated in one of the most significant periods of nonviolent social change in the history of the United States. Yet he remained tied to Western concepts of violence as the dominant form of power. Once he was elected head of SNCC, in 1966, I knew that organization had stepped away from nonviolence—the word I had insisted be in SNCC's name when we founded it.

Stokely and I had many conversations, through the years, about matters like Black pride and unity. We agreed that Black people couldn't wait for the white man to take the initiative. We agreed that Black people had to come together, organize, and proceed with direct action toward our goals, and that changing the laws was only part of the job. We agreed on the goal of using political, economic, and social direct action to break the system. But Stokely was never persuaded about nonviolence. Every time we talked about it, he said forthrightly, "I will go along with nonviolence because it is expedient and because it is working." He never tried to pretend that he endorsed it.

Only a few weeks after Stokely was elected chairman of SNCC, he got the chance to flex his muscles in his new role, and he used it to the fullest, for better or worse.

On Sunday, June 5, 1966, James Meredith, who had integrated the University of Mississippi under armed guard in 1962, started what he called his "March Against Fear" into Mississippi from Memphis. Meredith was thirty-two years old at the time and studying law at Columbia University. He was a loner and had not really been involved in our campaigns through the South. But he had campaigns of his own that aligned with the work we were doing. So I tried to support him.

I was out of town until late that first night, and so was not able to join the handful of people who marched with him that day from the Sheraton-Peabody Hotel, in downtown Memphis, to the Mississippi state line. I spent the next day in meetings at my church. When I was about to go home for the evening, a little after six P.M., a member came in to tell me that James Meredith had been shot on the highway near Hernando, Mississippi, about twenty-five miles from Memphis, and had been taken to a hospital in downtown Memphis. I went back to my office, and almost immediately the phone rang. It was Martin. He asked me to go to the hospital and see Meredith, and tell him we wanted him to get well, and to be back among us.

Martin and I talked on the phone and ended up agreeing on the idea of going to the spot where Meredith had been shot, the next day, and continuing the march. We felt we had to ask him in person if he was okay with us doing it. Martin wanted to come to Memphis that next morning, and asked me to find out how badly injured Meredith was and see if he could receive visitors. I rushed to Bowld Hospital, where James was still with the doctors. Of course, the hospital was segregated and served only Black patients. The police had already set up stringent security, so I wasn't able to get a message through to James. But I managed to communicate Martin's message to him through A. W. Willis, who was able to see him that night as his attorney, and tell him we were coming in the morning.

Next, I spoke to Dorothy. She was visiting her family in Charleston, Tennessee, with our sons John, who was four, and Morris, who was one. She was also pregnant with our third child, who was expected in November of that year. I told her what was happening and that Centenary would likely be the center of activity for a possible march.

Eventually, I got back to the church and called Martin. We arranged for his arrival, along with that of some SCLC people from Atlanta. That same night, Floyd McKissick, who had just become the executive director of CORE, called me to say he also wanted to join a march from the spot where Meredith was shot. I told him I would meet him at the airport, too.

On Tuesday morning, I picked up Floyd, Martin, Robert Green (education director for the SCLC), Bernard Lee (Martin's longtime assistant), and Ralph Abernathy. Luckily, I had my brown station wagon, which could fit them all, and we drove directly to the hospital. We got in to see James Meredith. A. W. Willis was already in the room. James was badly shaken, still suffering from shock, but able to talk. A white man from Memphis had shot him. Aubrey James Norvell, a forty-year-old unemployed hardware salesman, had hidden in the brush along Highway 51, waiting for Meredith. He used a shotgun to put sixty or seventy pellets in Meredith's body. Doctors were able to pull most of the pellets out. James was conscious during the procedure, done with local anesthesia.

When we arrived, we explained to James that there was no way we could allow him to get shot like that and ignore it. We all felt we had to respond. He asked a lot of questions, and he agreed with the need to respond, which surprised me, as he had always resisted being part of large campaigns or demonstrations. But he was brave, and seemed glad that Martin and Floyd had come, and glad the SCLC and CORE were supporting him. While we were there, Stokely showed up, too. He had been working in Arkansas and drove over when he heard what had happened. So the leaders of SNCC, SCLC, and CORE joined James in a discussion of how to proceed. After an hour of back and forth, everyone agreed that we had to take up the march that afternoon in Hernando, Mississippi.

Meredith would join the march at some later point, if and when he was able. And we would begin organizing and inviting people from around the country to come march with us right away. Martin held a brief press conference at the hospital. Then we went to my church to prepare and make some calls asking people to find their way to Memphis as quickly as they could. We got some food for everyone, and we left Centenary a while later in four or five cars, with about twenty of us headed to Hernando.

On the Sunday night before James had started his march, a reporter from the *Memphis Press-Scimitar* spoke with the white sheriff of DeSoto County, which is the first county over the Tennessee state line from Memphis into Mississippi. Hernando is the county seat of DeSoto County. The reporter asked the white sheriff, Walter Lee Meredith—who had the same last name as James—if he had planned any protection for James as he marched through the county that Monday. Less than twenty-four hours before James was shot there, Sheriff Meredith replied, "As far as we are concerned, he is like another nigger in the cotton fields. I anticipate no trouble. Though it looks like this guy wants to be killed. All he wants is publicity. Our job is to keep the traffic moving." Walter Lee Meredith's attitude was not an exception among Mississippi sheriffs.

So we were a little surprised when we got to the Mississippi state line on Highway 51 and the state police were everywhere. Although I didn't notice any DeSoto County sheriff's officers. There were also a number of reporters from local and national papers. We got out of our cars at the spot where James had been hit the day before and said a prayer. Then we began the walk on the highway, south toward Jackson, which was to be the ultimate destination of the march. We walked with arms locked together. Mississippi state troopers rode along beside us. A couple of them walked with us. One walked right in front of me. Bob Green and Floyd

McKissick were on the pavement of the highway, and the others, including Martin and Stokely, were on the shoulder as we walked forward.

Suddenly a few troopers got out of their cars and started shouting, "Get off the highway," and shoved Green and McKissick onto the shoulder. That jostled the five or six guys who had arms locked with them. I was already on the shoulder, about three or four feet ahead of them. Martin tried to talk to the officers. Everyone stopped. Then the state troopers told us, "Stay off the pavement." And one of the troopers told us, "Stop talking," and he pushed at Floyd again and at Cleve Sellers of SNCC. The fellows resisted but fell to the ground. Then Stokely acted as though he was going to go after the state troopers.

One of the troopers had stepped back toward where I was standing during this episode. I kept my gaze on him because he had turned pale and seemed dumbfounded. I tried to catch his eye. But he was watching the shoving. He didn't say anything, but he began to unbuckle his holster and just stood there shaking. He was trembling over his gun. That's how bad it was. We all stopped. Martin was behind me. When Stokely acted like he was going to lunge, he couldn't, because his arm was locked with Martin's. Martin held on to Stokely and wouldn't let him go. We were convinced that Stokely was planning to wrench himself free to try to tackle those guys. That would have put us in serious danger. These armed policemen were not going to take any of that from a Black man. That officer who was trembling had probably never been in a situation like that before: Negro men standing eyeball to eyeball with him and refusing to yield . . . he was thoroughly shaken. Yet Stokely wanted to charge him with his bare hands. Had he done so, the officer would probably have emptied his gun into us. He was backed by two other officers.

Afterward, we told Stokely that what he had tried to do was sheer stupidity. His position was "If anyone attacks me or pushes me, they are going to get pushed back." We said that was perfectly all right if you are only responsible for yourself. But it is not okay if you are in the midst of a nonviolent march and there are heavily armed policemen on the other side. Acting like you are going to attack them puts everyone in jeopardy. You can't pretend you can stop armed officers with your bare fists. It was not realistic. And it would have been a disaster. Stokely was backed by nothing but rage and rhetoric. I don't think he was an irrational man. But that would have been an irrational act.

In July 1966 I wrote an article about what we had begun calling the "Meredith March" for *Concern,* a magazine for Methodist college students. In it, I summed up that moment and the tone it set for the entire march:

> Here one of the burning disagreements of the March came to the surface and it remained throughout the demonstration. Carmichael and others, while committed to nonviolence as a tactic on the March, believe that violence is necessary, both to protect the Negro and fight segregation. Who dare blame them for believing that violence is more pragmatic? Is not that the stance of our land? All their lives they have heard, "The Russians only understand force," "A n——r needs whipping to keep him in his place," "You have to use force on some people." White America has no right to tell the Negro to remain nonviolent—not so long as we support war in Vietnam . . . and our massive military expenditure.
>
> The dissension over nonviolence has always been present. It becomes now more acute because of the deep dissatisfaction with the rate of serious change.

We managed to calm the situation and continue our walk along the side of the highway. *The Washington Post* reported some of our conversation as we marched on:

> For today, at least, there was a spirit of bantering exhilaration among Dr. King and the other leaders. Even after the shoving incident they joked with each other and teased Carmichael, who insists that he's not violent.
>
> "Stokely," Dr. King twitted, "if you'd been in my position, you'd have let someone get shot."
>
> "I couldn't fight," Carmichael answered. "I had my arms locked in yours."
>
> The Rev. James Lawson, the chief theoretician of nonviolent practice, said, "You see, Stokely, the difference between you and the military is that a soldier has singleness of purpose. When you get shoved, you get confused. If you're really not nonviolent, you ought to get a gun and be a guerrilla."
>
> Stokely laughed.

"Guerrilla warfare" was a common term then, because it was the style of fighting the Viet Cong were using against the United States in the Vietnam War. It involved smaller, mobile hit-and-run bands of fighters taking on larger, organized military troops.

As we continued down the highway, reporters covering the march asked Stokely about the idea of a split among the leaders of the movement when it came to nonviolence. He told them, "The problem isn't Dr. King or Mr. McKissick. It's the white racism in Mississippi." We always tried to steer the focus back to the issues we were trying to change, instead of going along with the obsessive interest in politics or differences of opinion within the movement. But concentrating on long-standing injustices often seemed beyond the grasp of many American news organizations.

Just before we got to Coldwater, Mississippi, we decided to end the march for the day. We all stood in an open field just off the highway, and I led us in a final prayer: "Pray that our feet may never turn back. We will see a thousand, yea ten thousands of feet marching toward Jackson, Mississippi, to end the days of moderation, when men can let a little bit of cruelty exist. We ask it in Thy name and for the sake of all mankind." Then Martin, Stokely, Floyd, and the rest of us linked hands and sang, "We Shall Overcome." Afterward, we got back in the cars and headed to my church in Memphis to continue planning.

By nighttime, more SCLC staff members had arrived, along with other leaders, including Roy Wilkins of the NAACP and Whitney Young of the Urban League. More than six hundred people attended a mass meeting that night at the church. Everyone spoke. Roy Wilkins told the local people in the crowd, "It is hard for you to remember that just a few miles south of here there is another country. We are going to show the people of Mississippi that they are part of the fifty states. This was a disgusting, revolting, cowardly act that happened to James Meredith, who was armed with nothing but his incredible courage."

Soon after the rally, Martin and the other leaders from out of town went to spend the night at the Lorraine Motel. An argument broke out around midnight as they met in Martin's room to discuss the march. Stokely had provoked Roy Wilkins and Whitney Young to the point where they both decided to leave and not participate in the march.

The next morning, I winced at a small piece in the local paper, reporting on how white business leaders worried that the shooting might affect

Memphis's image. It quoted a telegram that the head of the Memphis Chamber of Commerce had sent to James Meredith at the hospital, expressing regret from the business community for what had happened to him, while apparently holding the view that there had been no racial issues at play in Memphis that year, or any other. After asking him to view Memphis with "fairness to the community that has labored long and with unparalleled success to effect racial harmony second to no city in America," the message spoke of how the chamber hoped the city would be portrayed to the world, saying,

> This incident, while painful and tragic, by no means signifies any breakdown in reason that has prevailed here for years and which earned Memphis a well-deserved reputation nationally . . . as a peaceful and progressive community.

Needless to say, my feelings about Memphis's reputation did not echo those of the head of the city's chamber of commerce. But my focus was devoted to Centenary Methodist Church and our role in getting the march off to a successful start, as I described it in *Concern:*

> Centenary became a hectic place for the next two weeks. The March offices remained open night and day. Marchers slept on the floors. People throughout Memphis responded with their homes, cars, food, time, and dollars. Many of us marched. After a few days, most marchers slept in the field. Even then food and marchers moved through Centenary.
>
> How did members of Centenary take this sudden mission? While there were a few who fearfully opposed our involvement, the larger majority heartily endorsed The March as part of what the church must do. One layman said: "I can't think of a better thing for the church to be doing." Another remarked, "Something good will come out of this."

We were hastily trying to pull together the logistics for the fast-growing march. At first, everyone would return to Memphis at the end of each day of marching and sleep in local homes or at the Lorraine Motel. Our church operated a transportation group while the marching was still within a comfortable driving distance of Memphis. As we laid out the rest of the route through Mississippi, we sent some people ahead to make arrangements for the marchers. We rented tents, as well as trucks to carry all the equipment and supplies. People from all over the country were coming into the Memphis airport, and as soon as possible, we transferred them down to wherever the march was that day. If they arrived at night, we kept them overnight and cared for them, and we got them down to the march the next morning.

I marched for the first three or four days, to make certain we were doing our part well in organizing the 220-mile march to Jackson. And our church was working with the SCLC, CORE, and SNCC to plan the next steps. A couple of times, instead of returning to Memphis after the day's marching, I spent the night in a sleeping bag along the way.

From Wednesday, June 8, through Friday, June 10, we marched south, away from Memphis, along Highway 51 in Mississippi. We held mass meetings and rallies as we went, encouraging voter registration. In Senatobia, a fifty-eight-year-old sharecropper named Armistead Phipps joined the march. He had been active in the Mississippi Freedom Democratic Party. He kept the receipt from paying the poll tax in his wallet as a memento. His wife had urged him not to march, because he had high blood pressure and other health problems, which had forced him to stop farming. They were living in a three-room shack on $110 per month of income, from Social Security and disability payments from the state. But he was excited about the march. His wife told *Newsday* that he had said to her, "This is the greatest thing that has ever happened to our people in Mississippi. Now they won't be afraid to vote any more. I'll only march for a little. But I've got to be part of it."

Thursday, June 9, was scorching hot. Mr. Phipps listened to speeches from all the leaders on the march. And then he marched south with us into Senatobia. Martin was leading the way, and Mr. Phipps was waving to the crowds that had gathered, with some people joining in the marching. He walked past white people gathered too, waving Confederate flags and shouting, "Go home, n——rs." He would have heard one young white boy playing the song "Dixie" on his clarinet. But at some point, Mr. Phipps stumbled and fell to the ground. People stopped to help him, gave him some water. But his heart had given out, and he died.

The march stopped, and Martin gathered the press to make a statement. "We are deeply saddened," he said, "that one of our brothers, Armistead Phipps, has died of a heart attack. . . . This is Mississippi and his death means that he was probably underfed, overworked, and underpaid. . . . This is a man who was unafraid. . . . We will go on in the spirit that he went in, because he wanted to take a stand for freedom."

We continued. That weekend, both Martin and Stokely were in and out of the march. Martin had to travel to Chicago on June 10, because the SCLC had a campaign going on there, too. And Stokely had obligations at the SNCC offices in Atlanta for a few days. Others took up the leadership of the march. Fannie Lou Hamer led part of the time, as did Floyd McKissick and others from the SCLC, SNCC, and CORE. Martin returned that Sunday, June 12, and took time away from the march route to speak at Armistead Phipps's funeral in his hometown of Marks, Mississippi.

The march arrived in Grenada, Mississippi on Tuesday, June 14. When we got to the town square, the SCLC's Robert Green scaled a huge statue of Jefferson Davis, the president of the Confederacy, in the middle of the town square. Robert placed an American flag on the monument, over Davis's face. He said, "We're tired of seeing rebel flags." *The New York Times* reported, "The marchers cheered, while the white bystanders stared silently." Grenada had, the *Times* noted, "almost as many Negroes as whites in this county of 19,000." Before the march came through town, only 697 Black voters had registered to vote. After the march and the accompanying voter registration drive, that number doubled to about 1,400. That was the kind of result we were starting to get as we made our way through rural Mississippi. Southern sheriffs and the White Citizens' Council all over the state were noticing, too. But the national spotlight meant they couldn't act to intimidate Black people in the state as easily as they had always done, at least not while we were around.

Stokely returned to the march on the evening of Wednesday, June 15. I was there on Thursday morning to see what he did that day when we departed from Meredith's original route along Highway 51 to head southwest toward Greenwood, Mississippi. We had decided to march farther into the cotton-growing Delta region, where the legacy of enslavement and plantation culture meant we would reach a particularly high concentration of Black families who had been forced to live in poverty for generations.

Up to that time, a common chant in our movement had been for one person to say, "What do we want?" and everyone to shout back, "Freedom now!" At the mass meeting in Greenwood, Stokely and others in

SNCC had apparently planned it so that when he shouted, "What do we want?" some people would shout back the slogan "Black Power. Black Power. Black Power." Of course, the national press picked up on this and at every turn tried to make the rest of the march into a battle between nonviolence and Black Power. Later on, Stokely admitted that he joined the Meredith March primarily to get that Black Power slogan out into the open. He knew the press would be there if Martin was there. And he understood that the slogan would become known all across the country if he got it in the national press. He believed that Black people all around the country would take hold of it. And many did.

Even as we continued through rural Mississippi, with thousands attending mass meetings in the evenings in the towns where we stopped, the press obsessed about dynamics inside the movement—Black Power versus nonviolence—rather than with the issues the march was meant to address. We were bringing out Black people living in the deep poverty of rural Mississippi, and they were registering to vote for the first time. We were a multiracial group. In fact, at a few points along the way, white marchers slightly outnumbered Black marchers. But the focus from outside was rarely on the people whose lives our marching was meant to empower.

During the third week of the march, as we reached Yazoo City, some of us made a detour. Tuesday, June 21, was the two-year anniversary of the murders of James Chaney, Andrew Goodman, and Michael Schwerner. It felt right for a number of us to drive east to nearby Philadelphia, Mississippi, for a planned memorial. We convened at Mt. Nebo Missionary Baptist Church in Philadelphia, and then about 250 people marched to the Neshoba County courthouse steps, where Martin and others were to speak.

From the moment we left the church, we began seeing Philadelphia policemen stationed along our march route, a few at a time. It quickly became clear that the police were not there to protect us from the white people harassing us along the way, or from the angry white crowd that surrounded us when we got to the town square. The police were there to protect the white folks from us.

At times like that, the songs helped bolster us with the courage we needed to march on. We began to sing "Ain't Gonna Let Nobody Turn Me 'Round," and we headed into the heart of town.

Ain't gonna let nobody turn me 'round, turn me 'round, turn me 'round.
Ain't gonna let nobody turn me 'round.
I'm gonna keep on walking, keep on talking, marching up to freedom land.

As we came up a hill, a Ford Thunderbird started down the hill and charged right into the middle of the road, straight at us. We all scattered. As I jumped over to the side, away from the car barreling toward me, I saw a nearby police officer on the road's shoulder. It took me a second to realize that he had his bayonet pointed at me as I was running from the car. He was not shouting at or chasing the car that had just tried to ram into us. I looked around, and it was the same thing everywhere. Other cars began to barrel toward us, too, narrowly missing marchers. The police all had their bayonets and rifles pointed at us, while the cars veering toward us flew by freely. *The Washington Post* reported on the further violence that met us on our approach to the center of Philadelphia:

> A column of Negroes led by the Rev. Dr. Martin Luther King was attacked by screaming white toughs wielding hoes and axe-handles and flinging cherry bombs. . . . Angry local white men raced cars and trucks toward the Negro column. . . . One man was clubbed, and two television cameramen were manhandled and their equipment smashed.
>
> After a memorial service at the jail where the murdered three were held prisoner, the column moved toward the courthouse where a crowd of about 1000 whites clustered on the lawn.
>
> Deputy Sheriff Cecil Price, one of the 17 men facing Federal charges in connection with the 1964 slayings, stopped the march in front of the courthouse, where Mr. King spoke again. Referring to the murders of Chaney, Schwerner and Goodman, Mr. King said: "They'll have to learn to kill all of us."
>
> "We sure as hell will try," yelled a white, drawing laughter from the mob.
>
> "They don't understand this movement because they haven't learned to have love in their heart," Mr. King continued. "Mississippians, in trying to keep down the Negro, have kept Mississippi down. Anybody who is prejudiced is a slave, anybody who hates is a slave."

> "Why don't you go back to Africa?" jeered another white from the sidelines.
>
> Others tossed about 10 firecrackers or cherry bombs.

The New York Times noted that Deputy Price stood behind him as Martin spoke of the three slain men.

> "In this county Andrew Goodman, James Chaney and Mickey Schwerner were brutally murdered. I believe in my heart that the murderers are somewhere around me at this moment."
>
> Marchers murmured agreement.
>
> "They ought to search their hearts. . . ."
>
> The Negroes applauded. The whites hooted.
>
> "I am not afraid of any man," Dr. King said. "Whether he is in Mississippi or Michigan, whether he is in Birmingham or Boston. I am not afraid of any man." Perspiration glistened on his brow.
>
> Someone in the crowd of whites yelled: "Hey Luther! Thought you wasn't scared of anybody. Come up here alone and prove it."
>
> The Negro marchers sang, "We Shall Overcome." The whites yelled derisively.

When we left the town square and headed to the church, I was marching in the back of the group, where young white Mississippi men were swinging ax handles and sticks. My routine continued, of keeping watch over a march's rear, where there is sometimes trouble. The police back there were also acting tough toward us, and doing nothing to stop the harassment. Two or three young SNCC fellows wanted to have an encounter with them. But a few of us moved in to separate them from the taunting white guys again and again. We argued with the SNCC guys for a good part of the way back.

Their guiding principle was that you couldn't let yourself be pushed around. Again, we had to say, "Look. We have children and women here. And there are some very old people. Now, if you want to make an appointment with these guys afterward, well and good. But you are in a demonstration now, and you don't have a gun and that policeman has a bayonet and these children don't have any such protection. So, you'll put everyone in jeopardy." These guys were confusing self-defense with the responsibility you have when you are part of a public demonstration.

There are too many other ways to protect yourself and those around you. It makes no sense to assume that a big stick or a gun is your only recourse.

We managed to make it back to the Mt. Nebo church. That night, after we left Neshoba County and arrived back in Yazoo City, Martin gave a speech at a mass meeting in a park where the Meredith marchers had gathered with people from the town. A few SNCC people had talked to the crowd about arming themselves and fighting back against white terrorism. Having just been through yet another day of threats and insults, Martin spoke up for the way of nonviolence:

> Some people are telling us to be like our oppressor, who has a history of using Molotov cocktails, who has a history of dropping the atom bomb, who has a history of lynching Negroes. . . . Now people are telling me to stoop down to that level.
>
> I'm sick and tired of violence. I'm tired of the war in Vietnam. I'm tired of Molotov cocktails.

After the rally, Martin and the rest of us in the SCLC staff stayed in the Roman Catholic fellowship home parish at the St. Francis of Assisi church in Yazoo City. We met the next day with Stokely and Floyd and other members of SNCC and CORE.

Stokely was not repudiating nonviolent direct action. But at the same time, he was insisting there was such a thing as revolutionary violence—which, of course, Martin would not accept and I did not accept. Stokely and I had been debating this point for years, and we had more debates during this march, too. What the reporting missed was how much we all talked about issues and ideas as we marched. We were far more united than divided. But at every turn, reporters would quickly point to supposed rifts in our coalition, when in reality a functional unity continued throughout the three-week march. The March Against Fear gave us a chance to assess and explore the meaning of Black Power with one other.

I would not denounce Black Power, and neither would Martin—because we understood what it was about. Nonviolence understands clearly that the system is violent, especially when the structures of the system force people to live with torturous oppression. Nonviolence is anti-system, anti-evil, and anti-violence. That is why potential violence against a violent system is not something you denounce. It's also not something you embrace. But nonviolent direct action works to dismantle violent systems, and replace them with fair, strong, and beloved systems for the benefit of all. Those kinds of equitable systems rarely, if ever, are built from the rapaciousness of violence.

Nonviolence doesn't do damage to people. It doesn't destroy in order to rebuild. Nonviolence dismantles the wrong, and gives the right a far better chance of emerging. Nonviolence is more difficult to practice than violence. Yet nonviolence provides more lasting and sustainable relief to everyone.

At that meeting in Yazoo City, we reached a compromise. We would not use the "Freedom now" chant if they would not use the term "Black Power." It wasn't a solution for the long term. But it was a way to try to continue marching together through Mississippi without more diversion of the focus away from the issues of poverty and voting we were trying to bring to the forefront.

On Thursday, June 23, the march arrived in Canton, not far from Jackson. I had returned to my schedule in Memphis. A group had gone ahead of the rest of the march to put up tents in a schoolyard at a Black public elementary school in Canton, which had given us the okay to spend a few nights there. The police stopped them and said we couldn't put up our tents. When our people said they had permission from the school, they were arrested. The leadership of the march decided they would go to the school grounds and put their tents up for the night anyway. But the police swarmed in, accompanied by state troopers and tear gas. During that bloody encounter, people were beaten. Women and children were hit with clubs and gassed. This assault attracted national attention. Many white people in town and nationally commended the police for maintaining "law and order." But for Black people in the United States, and particularly Black people in Mississippi, law and order usually meant brutality and tyranny.

The next morning, when I heard about what had happened in Canton, I immediately drove down, as did other people from Memphis and the surrounding area. That afternoon, we had a meeting and decided to offer the city a compromise. We would go to the school grounds and hold a rally, but we would not put up any tents or camp there. Ralph Abernathy and Martin went to the city with our plan, and officials agreed that their officers wouldn't attack anyone who gathered. There was not much of a rally that night. Beforehand, the police had opened a fire hydrant to make the field at the school muddy.

Later that evening, I was at the Roman Catholic center, where we were headquartered. About five hundred of us were in the gym preparing for the next day, when the march was supposed to head out for the final leg to Jackson. Stokely had come back from the school site angry, accusing everyone of selling out. He took to the mic at the platform with a number of the SNCC fellows around him. He proceeded to harangue the leadership for failing to put the tents up in the schoolyard that night.

I had had it by then, and I challenged him. "Stokely," I said in front of everybody, "you are one of the leaders. So when you are talking about the leadership you are talking about yourself, because you were in on the strategy meeting. There were others of us prepared to go out in small numbers and set up the camp. But in the strategy meeting this afternoon you did not offer any alternative to the plan that was agreed."

I said, "It is your responsibility as a leader in the strategy session to have a plan for how we could have done it. But I heard no proposal from you." I continued: "So you are as much to blame as anyone else. If other leaders were not prepared to do it because they were scared, you should have suggested ways it could have been done." I had been at that meeting and also thought we should set up the tents. But when the group made a decision not to do it, I didn't have another option prepared, so I went along with their choice. I said to Stokely, "You should have, at least, if nothing else, come to some of us who were on the ground waiting for a decision and asked us what we wanted."

Of course, he was attacking Martin and Floyd primarily. But Martin was gone by then, because he had another commitment. He would, however, be coming back that next afternoon to join the group again. Stokely and some others who led SNCC often accused Martin of hogging the limelight and refusing to share it with SNCC. It was petty, childish kind of stuff, because the one thing you cannot say about Martin is that he was a selfish man. There is no way in the world to say that about him. If anything, he was generous to a fault. But they had accused him of taking the glory from SNCC—giving himself credit for it and garnering most of the financial contributions for the SCLC that came to the movement in the South. I thought it was unfair.

I didn't march the rest of the way to Jackson. I had to get back to my congregation and my family. The headquarters for the march had moved from Memphis to Jackson about a week before the end of the march, since that was where the marchers were going to finish up. Arrangements were made on that end for a rally at Tougaloo College on Saturday night, June 25. Celebrities performed, including Sammy Davis Jr. and James Brown. A crowd of more than ten thousand turned out. James Meredith was able to join the marchers on Sunday, the final day, as they walked into Jackson and ended their journey at the steps of the Mississippi state capitol.

As a result of the march, we registered voters and kicked off efforts in some rural communities, which then continued their own campaigns. The Black Power slogan became well known nationally, and it became Stokely's rallying cry. It also became the straw man of our movement and was vigorously attacked by the people already aligned against our goals. Across the country it stirred up hysteria. Because of that, few newspapers dealt with the actual issues we were addressing in our work. Instead, most outlets focused on that slogan: Black Power. And Stokely was the face of it. These white-run publications also tended immediately to equate Black Power with violence.

I discussed this in my article about the Meredith March for *Concern* magazine, in July 1966:

> My major quarrel with The March is that in spite of all the talk about "black power" and militancy, the leaders did not push toward turning the demonstration into radical direct action. Why did we not confront police brutality in Canton with civil disobedience? The townspeople were ready. Why did we not simply immobilize that city? The greater weapons of nonviolence have yet to be used in the civil rights movement. Marches are not enough to break the hold of racism on the economic, social, and political structures. . . .
>
> Somewhere along the line the civil rights movement will have to become revolutionary. So long as we do not, we not only open the door to impatience and bitterness, but we hasten the day when a new civil rights movement using violence aggressively will emerge.

When the SCLC embarked on its first campaign outside the South, in Chicago in 1966, violence was always lurking nearby. In the conversations in Atlanta and at retreats in 1965, I had voted against the SCLC going to Chicago. I always believed our task was in the South. Northern and Western places in the country could watch us, then adjust their work to their own situation. Chicago was so different from the South, a region we knew. It was a large, densely populated city, which was not the type of place we had worked in before. I didn't think we had sufficient energy, or time, or staff to deal with those unfamiliar circumstances. Martin King and I were talking a lot on the phone and in person then, and I often told him that I felt taking our movement to Chicago was an error. I never changed my mind about that. But once they decided to go, I didn't back away simply because I disagreed. A lot of times, I disagreed with a lot of people. And they disagreed with me. But we had a unity of purpose and came back together to do our best in the movement.

The SCLC had begun laying the groundwork for the Chicago campaign in the summer of 1965, after Albert Raby of the Coordinating Council of Community Organizations (CCCO), in Chicago, asked the SCLC to join them in their campaign. We decided to focus on fair housing in Chicago. Rents and mortgage rates were so much higher for Black people than for white people in large northern cities, and Chicago led the way in that inequity.

In late January 1966, Martin had moved into an apartment in a low-income neighborhood in Chicago called North Lawndale. He did it both to draw attention to the issue and to experience firsthand the challenges of living in what we called "the ghetto" back then. By the summer, SCLC staff members were working with CCCO and others. They planned a large freedom rally for June, but it was postponed when we took on the Meredith March in early June. Martin and others in the SCLC were splitting their time between Mississippi and Chicago all month. But in July, they were back in Chicago and ready to move ahead.

On July 10, 1966, more than thirty-five thousand people braved the blazing-hot sun to hear the speakers and music at the freedom rally in Soldier Field. "At the rally," United Press International reported, "Dr. King spurned the call for black separatism as unrealistic and said Negroes and whites were 'tied in a single garment of destiny.' . . . He said Negroes must be aggressively nonviolent and on guard against 'the tranquilizing drug of gradualism.'" Martin was making the appeal that fighting racism was everyone's responsibility, and he was addressing the impatience we all felt when we were continually told to wait.

During SCLC meetings in Chicago in 1966, a group of us, including Martin, talked about links between violence, racism, and poverty. And having achieved victories using nonviolent direct action against segregation and for voting rights in the South, the SCLC began shifting our emphasis in the mid-1960s toward economic equity. Chicago was one step in that direction.

Nashville student movement leaders had continued to dedicate themselves to our struggle through Birmingham, Selma, and into Chicago in 1966. James Bevel and Diane Nash were living in Chicago, Diane's hometown, and involved in the campaign. Bernard Lafayette was working on the campaign, too. But many in the SCLC and some of our volunteers in Chicago were feeling exhausted, overwhelmed, and having trouble getting the work done. It was what we would later call "burnout." Facing the raw-bone trauma of white resistance in Chicago wore them out. Martin saw people struggling. He discussed their fatigue at length with me, and we gave a lot of thought to how to care for them.

He asked me if I could fly up to Chicago for a few days every week to counsel some of our people, and I agreed. There was an office for me in the First Presbyterian Church, in the Woodlawn neighborhood on Chicago's South Side, where the SCLC had set up campaign headquarters. The church had a tradition of activism and resistance that dated to the nineteenth century, when it was part of the Underground Railroad. Staffers, local activists, and students who volunteered as office workers for the SCLC were invited to come in and talk with me.

That counseling was the same sort of pastoral care work I did with my congregations. In our sessions, some people would pour out stories of the turmoil they had internalized from the racism we were fighting in Chicago. Others did not open up as freely. Some had turned to things like alcohol and not sleeping to deal with the conflicts in their souls. Others were mostly interested in having a good time in their off-hours, and they had let their health and their work slide, especially as they faced more and more stressful situations in the campaign.

This movement work was new for all of us in the 1960s. We were all learning of its toll and how to deal with it together. I urged people to take breaks to process what was happening and to care for their bodies and their spirits and to sleep—to meditate, and reflect, and have conversations about the work they were doing. Being up against the hard wall of a segregated city and a barrage of racism was at the heart of the issues everyone was facing. A person cannot fight all the time. We all must nurture our minds and practice common sense in dangerous situations. That's what my workshops were designed to encourage.

In my counseling, I also helped our SCLC workers in Chicago develop new skills, like how to work alongside heavily burdened coworkers. And we fostered resiliency together. I tried to help them realize that they were a part of a much larger world, and that connection was critical to staying intact.

Sustaining this work takes cultivating a strong sense of yourself as someone dismantling the wrong you've experienced because of your minority status, or the wrong you've seen shackling other people. It requires you to strategize internally about how you can stop yourself from panicking. In the movement there is no room for panic. Instead, you strive to gain personal power by recognizing that your life is a mystery and a marvel, and that you live it one breath at a time. To cultivate that gift within yourself is a lifelong internal practice. Your homework never ends.

Some women staff members and volunteers who came in to talk were also dealing with men abusing or mistreating them. One woman who was still in college told me that some of the male staffers frequently came on to her. She tried to ignore them or brush it off, but that didn't work all the time. She was wondering what more she could do. Men harassing women at work was not yet something many people recognized or talked about back then. But, of course, it was a bigger issue for many women than many men ever realized. It was the result of what I call a false masculinity. It was sexism.

She and I talked about how she didn't have to accept that behavior. But I am afraid I didn't give her as much help as I would have done later in life, when I understood more about the nature of that kind of harassment. I might have spoken to the men doing the harassing about changing their treatment of women. We were in dangerous times, and each person's life was fragile. But for some, the only way they had ever learned to deal with fragility and vulnerability, in themselves and others, and with the various dangers and tensions in the work, was by taking their fears out on other people. That was especially true for some of the men, when dealing with women in Chicago.

James Bevel was one of the main people King had been concerned about when he asked me to come counsel people. I had known James since the Nashville campaign. But in Chicago, he avoided me. So I never was able to counsel him. We mostly encountered each other in staff meetings, talking about strategy. In some ways, James was a genius, when he was able to use his talents and energy constructively. But in other ways he was a peril for his family, and especially for women. He had an alcohol problem, and in Chicago it was evident to everyone. Diane carried the brunt of their troubles. They had two kids and were in the midst of a divorce. Diane was my friend as well as my colleague by that time, and so we talked a lot.

To do your best work in the movement you needed the discipline to treat people with the dignity you sought, and not to degrade or despise people. It takes training and preparation similar to that of an athlete. You have to prepare your body, prepare your mind, and prepare your spirit. When I was a coach in India, I taught the players the very same thing.

Many people in the movement didn't realize the importance of balancing their work with healthy physical activity every day. In my college years, I also figured out that in order to do the work, I had to block out the people working against me and respond instead to my own call from within and from God. So I spent time learning about Jesus—his heart, mind, and soul. Then I applied what I had learned about how he lived his life to the way I conducted myself in tense moments during the movement.

I shared another piece of advice with the people I counseled that I had found most useful in my internal work: learn to sing with others. Music is a great tool, not just as a conduit for processing our lives but also on a strategic, personal level, in the midst of conflict. Music feeds your spirit. Music was the opposite of the degrading racism we were standing against. Singing with others cultivated our sense of meaning and community.

For instance, during the Freedom Ride in 1961, in the jail in Jackson, Mississippi, and in Parchman Prison, when cellmates and I lifted up in song, it seemed as though we got a shot of something. *Woke up this morning with my mind (my mind it was) stayed on freedom.* Singing together with a common purpose gave us a sense that we were in the right place, on the right side. *We shall not, we shall not be moved. / Just like a tree planted by the water / we shall not be moved.* I had also endured thirteen months in federal prison, where the task of being a man and a child of God had been fortified by all kinds of music that helped me through.

I didn't go to many community events or marches in Chicago, because King wanted me to be the one who focused on the staff and not to have to take on anything else. I saw them working. I was in staff meetings and in the office. My energy was directed toward supporting them in their work and their lives. They knew my counseling was there for them. And a number of SCLC people, and especially some of the volunteers from Chicago, told me that I had helped them.

At the beginning of August 1966, Martin led another march, this one into Marquette Park, in an all-white Chicago neighborhood. A hostile white person from the malicious crowd that gathered threw a large rock at Martin. It hit him in the head, and he fell to his knees. Martin said afterward, "I have seen many demonstrations in the South but I have never seen anything so hostile and so hateful as I've seen here today." White Chicagoans were brutal in ways that equaled and even surpassed the worst of Mississippi. But we kept going. By the end of August, Mayor Richard Daley had agreed to some of our demands on housing. The SCLC stayed and continued the work, although Martin moved on to other places. I was in and out of Chicago through 1967, doing workshops on nonviolence for local people as our campaign there wound down.

FOURTEEN

These Two Americas

Reverend Lawson leading a workshop with nonviolence teacher and activist Ira Sandperl at an SCLC staff retreat, Penn Center, St. Helena Island, Beaufort County, South Carolina, 1966.

BOB FITCH ARCHIVE, STANFORD UNIVERSITY LIBRARY

As the SCLC looked to the future of the movement after Chicago, we affirmed that we would continue to focus on addressing poverty and its causes and remedies, since in the United States it disproportionately affected Black people. At the 1966 SCLC convention in August, Martin spoke of this deeper aim.

> Our continuing struggle grows out of the fact that there are still two Americas. One . . . is the habitat of men and women who have food and material necessities for their bodies, culture and education for their minds, freedom and dignity for their spirits. . . .
>
> But there is another America. . . . It is an America inhabited by millions of people who are poverty stricken aliens in an affluent so-

> ciety; too poor even to rise with the society; too impoverished by the ages to be able to ascend by using their own resources.
>
> So long as these two Americas exist, there must be a continuing struggle for human rights.

That divide was explicitly evident in Memphis, which perpetually maintained some of the nation's highest percentages of citizens living in poverty. And most of those citizens were Black. When I arrived in 1962, I became acutely aware of how the city of Memphis, in effect, enforced its workers' poverty, even though most people had jobs. Tennessee was a "right to work" state, meaning labor laws hamstrung unions, limiting their ability to recruit workers as members. Those laws were designed to have a chilling effect on any kind of union organizing where there was not yet an existing union.

A Black Memphis sanitation worker named Thomas Oliver Jones had been trying to organize a union among his co-workers since the early 1960s. I met T.O., as he preferred to be called, at NAACP meetings when I first moved to town. He would tell us about the problems of Memphis sanitation workers—who were all Black men. The pay was low. Many sanitation workers qualified for food stamps and welfare, even though they worked full-time. They were never promoted into management jobs, which were held exclusively by white men. They weren't provided with basic safety or hygiene measures on the job. No showers or toilets were available for them to use, even though their work exposed them to filth and bugs, and they would smell so bad when they got off work that bus drivers wouldn't allow them to ride city buses home. They had to work in all weather. If they did not come to work, they would not get paid, because they were contract workers, not staff employees like their white managers.

Most of the men had been born on plantations in Mississippi, Arkansas, or Tennessee, where they had worked as sharecroppers as children, picking the cotton that was the driver of Memphis's economy and the icon of its culture. The men and their wives came to Memphis for better opportunities. But the white men who ran the Memphis Public Works Department had also been born into plantation culture. So their treatment and mistreatment of the Black men were based on their upbringing, which taught them that Black people were something less than fully human. If a man got sick or hurt himself on the job, he had no health benefits, and if he couldn't work, that was his bad luck.

Until my time in Memphis, I had been fairly critical of unions, because I saw them as shortchanging the Black working man. I had also been critical of the labor movement, because I felt that it tended to forget the basis on which it was founded and therefore did not work to be a dynamic force for meaningful, creative social change. But in the 1960s, my views changed.

One of the largest early grants the SCLC received came from the AFL-CIO. Another labor union in New York also gave the SCLC money for our work—more than it had given any other civil rights organization because its officials liked what we were doing and knew it was going to empower people. But it wasn't a simple relationship. Traditionally, the labor union movement had been almost exclusively white. One of the first major Black unions was the Brotherhood of Sleeping Car Porters, founded in 1925 and led by A. Philip Randolph. He was a political activist and not a porter. So he was able to lead without the threat of losing his job, since management fired labor organizers so often. Sleeping car porters worked on the trains—shining shoes, waking up passengers at appointed times, and making beds. Their pay was based mainly on tips. And their hours were long. They worked for the Pullman Company, which was the largest employer of Black people in the country at the turn of the twentieth century and had made a point of hiring formerly enslaved men. The idea was that these porters would know how to provide superior service and not ask for much in return. But when they unionized, they exerted their collective power. Even though they never went on strike, through the years their union put enough pressure on the company to raise pay and improve working conditions for porters.

In 1963, T. O. Jones and a group of other sanitation workers in Memphis he had recruited formed their own union, called the Independent Workers Association (IWA). They held their first meeting in June 1963. About one hundred workers showed up and complained about old trucks with faulty wiring and bad brakes, and the lack of uniforms or showers where they could wash up after work. They also talked about how the metal tubs they were given to gather garbage from residents' backyards had holes in them. So when the men carried them from behind people's houses to the truck on the street, often balancing them on their heads, the garbage liquid and maggots dropped down onto them.

Around the same time, the Memphis police were also trying to organize a union. In reaction to all this union activity, Memphis police commissioner Claude Armour, along with Mayor Henry Loeb and others, began pushing for a city ordinance prohibiting any kind of union organizing among city employees. That's when Bill Ross, who was head of the Memphis Labor Council, asked me to testify before the county commission against the proposed ordinance, as part of a group of clergy, labor people, and others he had brought together. I told the commission that such an ordinance would be fundamentally wrong and would hurt the city. The ordinance never made it through the commission and into law. But the idea of outlawing unions among city employees did not die in 1963.

City leaders sent informants to infiltrate the sanitation workers' union and draw up a list of the instigators who were doing the organizing. Less than two weeks after that initial IWA meeting, thirty-three union supporters were fired from the sanitation department, including T. O. Jones. The sanitation department head said the men had been fired not for their participation in the union but because of their "inefficiency." Eventually, some of us in the clergy and the NAACP persuaded the city to hire the men back. But T. O. Jones decided not to stay on, and instead got into union organizing with full force. He knew he would be more able to operate if he didn't have the threat of losing his job at every turn.

In 1964, the American Federation of State, County and Municipal Employees (AFSCME) chartered the Memphis sanitation workers' union as Local 1733. The organizing workers in the sanitation department chose the number 33 as part of the name to honor the thirty-three men who had been fired for organizing in 1963. T. O. Jones was elected president of the union. And in 1965, along with other ministers, I again testified before the county commission about the men's needs and the importance of recognizing the union. But the county commission voted four to one against recognizing AFSCME as the negotiator for the thirteen hundred Memphis sanitation workers.

By August 1966, T. O. Jones, working with the AFSCME national office, had organized sanitation workers to go on strike against the city. But before they could strike, then-Mayor William Ingram and the commission issued an injunction against any city workers going on strike. The idea of making unions and strikes illegal was alive and well in the minds of white Memphis leaders. And just as injunctions had become a favorite instrument for blocking demonstrations during our campaigns across the South in the 1960s, so too were they used in Memphis to try to block labor organizing activity.

In September 1966, Martin came to Memphis for a Baptist convention. But he also convened a retreat, which I hosted, to discuss the morale of SCLC field staff members, who were still feeling the strain of their work. He had asked me to continue my counseling in Chicago after he left that city, and to expand it to counsel the staff in the South. I agreed, even though I was working on many fronts at that time, between the SCLC and my congregation and my political and community organizing in Memphis.

The happiest front of all of them was my family. In November 1966, our youngest son, Seth, was born. Dorothy and I were then raising three young sons—Seth the infant, Morris, who was one and a half, and John, who was five. Our kids were our joy and a reminder of the cycles of life. Dorothy and I had to pool and bolster our energy as much as we could to nurture our three energetic boys. And I had to find ways to split my time among all my commitments.

The SCLC had a full staff retreat in November 1966, at the Penn Center, in South Carolina. Throughout the movement, Martin would gather SCLC people and some invited guests at remote centers in the South. The two we visited most frequently were the Dorchester Academy, near Savannah, Georgia, and the Penn Center, on St. Helena Island in Beaufort County, South Carolina. During retreats, Martin was more relaxed than usual. He was able to let down his guard a little. We all could. And we would reflect, plan, and then balance out the work with some free time. When we met in the summer, it would usually be everybody from volunteers to executive staff. In the main sessions, all of us would discuss the issues together. And in between, Martin would have meetings and strategy sessions with the executive staff. But we also took advantage of being away from it all.

Generally, our meetings finished around four P.M. Then people would swim or play basketball or touch football. Martin loved to swim, and I did, too. Sometimes, Martin and I would take our long walks together and talk. In the mid-1960s, we also spent a lot of time on the phone with each other. By 1967, we were mostly concerned with Vietnam and the need to address poverty in the next stage of our movement.

On one of those afternoons after a meeting, a number of us agreed that we would meet in a nearby field to play touch football. I have never forgotten the moment when we were picking teams that day. Everyone was trying to divide up when very loudly, above it all, I heard Martin say,

"And Jim Lawson is going to be on my side. I want Jim Lawson on my side." We had played football before, so we knew what each other could do. He knew I was a good receiver and I knew he was a good passer. But I appreciated that he wanted me on his team, and we did win the game that day.

The Penn Center was a former Freedom School that Quakers from Pennsylvania had set up just after the Civil War to teach reading and writing to formerly enslaved people in the region. Frogmore was the name of the small town on St. Helena Island where the retreat center was located, and the area offered the best shrimp in the world. It was caught fresh each day and boiled in beer with corn, potatoes, and Old Bay seasoning into something called Frogmore stew. A place that sold it was walking distance from the retreat center. I would go with others, and sometimes I would even walk there by myself just to get some of that shrimp. It came out of the Gullah culture, which was preserved by enslaved Africans who were kidnapped and brought to South Carolina, one of the largest entry points for enslaved people in the United States.

During another retreat at the Penn Center in the mid-1960s, I witnessed an illustration of Martin's extraordinary listening skills that I will never forget. We all arrived at the retreat on Sunday night and Monday morning. As we gathered on the first day, we heard grumbling among the staff of about one hundred people. Some were saying that the SCLC offices were slow to get them their weekly stipends, which was how most of them paid for food and transportation. These were college students—most were working as our field people on voter registration, in community centers, and in Citizenship Schools scattered around the Southeast. They were also organizing locals to participate in the same work. Most of them had volunteered for a summer, but some of them had been with us longer. They came from Philadelphia, Chicago, and beyond.

The more they talked, the more they aired their pain and even trauma from the work itself. Because, again, it was not easy. It was dangerous. Many worked in rural places where they had to fend for themselves in a hostile community. The room at that retreat was full of emotion—weariness, anger, frustration, and even fear. It was useful for these people to talk to one another. But Martin King wasn't there as they commiserated.

He and Ralph Abernathy, as well as another staff member or two, sometimes stayed at a motel nearby. The rest of us stayed at the center itself. After stopping by on the first morning, Martin was not around for the rest of the afternoon or that evening. He had some sort of speaking engagement in Columbia, South Carolina, and left the retreat, which he should never have done. A lot of times during a retreat, Martin would leave to go raise funds in a nearby city. He couldn't resist it. He would preach, speak, and raise money. But those events usually didn't bring in substantial amounts. And I felt they weren't worth the time away. The retreat, I believed, should be a place for him to sit down and be quiet, and to play the sports he loved. He needed retreat time to recharge. We all did.

When the volunteers were voicing complaints, the fact that Martin had left that first day merely confirmed their feelings about him and the SCLC neglecting them. I pushed Martin to get back as soon as he could. I told him some of what we were hearing and how we needed him to come spend time with the volunteer staff. He agreed with me. And when he got back that second day, he had all the staff members sit in a big circle. Martin sat on an old couch among the group. I was nearby, to his right. Then Martin invited each person to talk about what concerned them. We went around the room. I listened, as Martin did, and when the last person in that retreat had spoken, Martin King went back around the whole oblong circle of about a hundred people and quietly repeated at least a sentence or two of what every single person had said. He would point to someone and say, "Now, I heard you saying this," and summarize what they had said. Then he would go on to the next person. He addressed each person separately, for forty-five or fifty minutes. It was extraordinary.

After that, he talked to them about how the SCLC would deal with what they were telling him and what he would do to help solve some of the problems, particularly the pay issue. Money was an eternal challenge for the SCLC. The retreats at the Penn Center were possible only because the Quakers, who owned it, would donate use of the place to us for free. Often other donors contributed to support a retreat devoted to a specific issue, with SCLC staff and invited guests coming together.

In the early 1960s, at a retreat on nonviolence, I had a part in reuniting Martin and Bayard Rustin. They had a falling-out in 1960 after the SCLC was getting pressure to fire Bayard because he was gay. His relative openness about it was considered bad for the movement. Bayard had offered to resign, thinking Martin would never accept that. But he did. And the two of them didn't speak for a few years. In 1962 and 1963, I moved, with Martin's consent, to try to bring Bayard back into a relationship with the SCLC. I simply insisted that he was one of the best minds in the country on nonviolence, strategizing, and organizing. I told Martin and others that since we were having staff retreats and workshops focused on his areas of expertise, he would be a valuable resource. We needed him. Martin agreed.

Our belief in nonviolence was not merely a tactic we used to spur desegregation in the South. We did not see the violence we were up against as only physical—as solely the fighting or guns we rejected in our movement. We viewed poverty as a form of violence used to suppress people. We viewed racism as a form of violence in words and deeds that harmed people. We saw how racism and poverty had become a dynamic duo in our nation—connected, related, and enforced throughout our history.

We didn't think the country would take well to the idea of our desegregation campaigns evolving into a larger movement in 1965 and 1966, addressing pernicious and ingrained social and economic injustice. But as 1967 dawned, we were broadening our scope in that direction anyway.

Martin and I continued to talk about Vietnam. We had both been critical of the war from the start, and we had both believed the Selective Service to be racist long before the war in Vietnam. Once the war began, unfortunately, we were proven right. Black men from all across the country were being killed at a higher rate in the Vietnam War than white men.

By 1967, Martin finally felt the time had come for him to make a major statement about Vietnam. Indeed, he had reached the point where he couldn't *not* speak out.

So when a large meeting of the interfaith Clergy and Laymen Concerned About Vietnam invited him to give a talk, he agreed. The speech was to take place at Riverside Church in New York City on April 4, 1967. Different people urged him not to do it, including the SCLC board of directors. I supported his decision to do it anyway, but it was not one he made lightly. In the end, he saw the speech as an act of conscience he could no longer deny.

He began the speech by talking about Black men who had grown up in poverty in the United States and were being disproportionately sent to fight the war in Vietnam:

> We were taking the Black young men who had been crippled by our society and sending them eight thousand miles away to guarantee liberties in Southeast Asia which they had not found in southwest Georgia and East Harlem. And so we have been repeatedly faced with the cruel irony of watching Negro and white boys on TV screens as they kill and die together for a nation that has been unable to seat them together in the same schools.

He said that our own government was "the greatest purveyor of violence in the world today." And he spoke of the wave of independence movements around the world, and particularly in Africa, throwing off European colonial rule. He said that getting on the right side of this moment called for a "radical revolution of values" in the nation.

> America, the richest and most powerful nation in the world, can well lead the way in this revolution of values. There is nothing except a tragic death wish to prevent us from reordering our priorities so that the pursuit of peace will take precedence over the pursuit of war.

He called for a stop to the bombing in Vietnam, reallocation of resources from war to social programs at home, resistance to the draft, and a total withdrawal of American troops—in short, an end to the Vietnam War.

> We still have a choice today: nonviolent coexistence or violent co-annihilation.

The speech drew much attention from the national press, and derogatory comments began hitting Martin from all sides. The speech even started a ruckus among many people in the movement, Black and white, who were upset that he had expanded his purview to include the war. Some said he was destroying the civil rights struggle. Black people by the hundreds argued that Vietnam was not related to the condition of the Negro, and that Martin King had no business mixing race with Vietnam. Some of his best friends started tearing him apart with criticism and saying he was reaching beyond his field. Martin had talked to me quite personally and at great length about the agony going on inside him. He said the pushback from everyone about his anti–Vietnam War views was the worst thing he ever had to withstand.

I think he had felt constricted not talking about the war when it weighed on him so greatly. Then he felt abandoned and alone when he did finally voice his views. I still believe he made the right move in speaking out when and how he did in 1967. And of course I told him that many times in the year that followed.

And it turned out he wasn't alone. Soon after Martin came out against the war, another Black luminary, champion boxer Muhammad Ali, refused induction into the United States military. I felt he inadvertently did me a great personal favor when he decided not to take the Selective Service oath of allegiance in 1967. Because that's basically what I had been charged with in 1951—violating the Selective Service Act. Ali validated the choice a young Jim Lawson had made sixteen years earlier.

Sometimes I would look back on my refusal to cooperate with the draft and laugh, amazed. I would ask myself, "Who did you think you were? How did you dare to take such positions?" Then I thought, "You had to be off your rocker." But when Muhammad Ali, who I greatly admired, refused to cooperate with the draft, I felt a new sense of pride at what I had done.

In July 1967, Newark, New Jersey, erupted with four days of uprising after two policemen, John DeSimone and Vito Pontrelli, viciously beat a Black cabdriver and trumpet player, John William Smith, during a traffic stop. In the end, twenty-six people were killed and fires virtually destroyed much of the city. It was one of the most intense of the series of uprisings all around the country during the summer of 1967, which came to be known as "the long, hot summer."

I was deep into my work in Memphis that summer. At Centenary, we provided space for people in the community to learn and grow beyond Sunday services. And we were especially attentive to the needs of the teenagers in our midst. We let them have parties in the basement of the church. And we even organized sex education classes, ensuring that teens had the information and counseling they needed to be safe—information that they were not getting anywhere else.

Our congregation was moving to a new, larger South Memphis location in 1967, a few blocks away from where it had been located for years. And Dorothy and I had a house full of young boys—John was almost six, Morris was two, and Seth was a few months old. When we got married, Dorothy and I made a rule that we were going to eat at least one meal together every day, no matter how hectic things got. Most of the time it was breakfast or supper. And once the kids came, I made sure I got home for supper whenever I wasn't out of town. Even on the worst of days, I would come home for dinner around six. I got a chance to visit, eat, and play with the kids. And we wouldn't rush dinner. So I had plenty of time. If I had to go back out after the meal, we still kept our dinner hour. During campaigns and movements, there were always meetings. Then there were church meetings, which couldn't be held during the day because people in the congregation worked. I tried to set after-dinner meetings for around seven-thirty P.M.

In the evenings, I was most deeply involved with a community organizing group I had co-founded to combat poverty in Memphis. It was called MAP-South (Memphis Area Project—South) and had grown out of President Johnson's War on Poverty, which had begun with legislation in 1964. Lyndon Johnson had made a pledge as a young teacher in East Texas to address the poverty he saw there, and it became a major issue at the start of his presidency. The Office of Economic Opportunity (OEO) was set up in 1964. President Johnson appointed Sargent Shriver as the director. He was the brother-in-law of John and Bobby Kennedy and had run the Peace Corps, which gave him experience with development work.

I had founded MAP-South with Autry Parker, a member of my congregation, in 1965, because we couldn't ignore the deep poverty all around us in Memphis. When the War on Poverty was initiated, 27.5 percent of all Memphis families earned less than $3,000 per year. At the time, if a family of four had an income at or below that level, the federal government designated them as living in poverty. The national poverty rate at the time was 21.4 percent. And it bears repeating: in Memphis as in much of the country, poverty primarily affected Black people. The poverty rate among all Memphis families who were not considered white was 58 percent in 1964.

Both Autry and I believed that people needed to be empowered so they could direct their own way out of such dire living conditions. The white Republican U.S. congressman for most of Memphis in 1965, Dan Kuykendall, didn't want any such thing as the Democratic president's anti-poverty program. So he did not go after the funding that came from the War on Poverty, because he swore we didn't have poverty in Memphis.

Autry and I saw that we would not get anything done by trying to work with those government officials who were in denial about poverty and openly hostile to people living in poverty. So we went around them, directly to the anti-poverty office in Washington, D.C. Sargent Shriver and the Johnson administration agreed that poverty money would bypass the local establishment and flow directly to our nonprofit. MAP-South was organized to address the needs of nine census tracts in South Memphis that had some of the highest levels of poverty in the city and the nation.

Memphis poverty was deep, prevalent, and vicious in a way I had not seen before in the United States. There had been nothing like it in the parts of Ohio where I grew up, or in Nashville. Not coincidentally, Memphis also had a much larger proportion of Black people than any other place I had lived. A majority of Black people in Memphis had been born into poverty, as a legacy of centuries of enslavement and then sharecropping in Memphis and the surrounding rural areas.

But while poverty in Memphis was much more visible and prevalent than I had ever experienced, to the white leadership of Memphis poverty apparently did not exist at all. Not only had Congressman Kuykendall often said that, but the entire white community, by and large, agreed that there was no poverty in Memphis. I was told early on that people who belonged to Memphis's many all-white, all-Christian country clubs—in particular, the very antebellum-minded Memphis Country Club—also said there was no poverty in Memphis. Of course, I wasn't allowed inside these country clubs because I was Black. But that's what I was told.

It takes an extraordinary level of arrogance and hypocrisy to profess to care about the city—as the white political establishment always did—while doing little to nothing to address the daily suffering of a large percentage of its citizens. It's especially infuriating when the distressing signs of poverty are so obvious as to be unavoidable. A lot of the housing in the Black neighborhoods of North and South Memphis were without indoor plumbing. Peeling lead paint hung from the walls in houses without heat or air-conditioning. The local wage rates didn't support the life of one human being living alone, much less a family. A Black Memphis woman working full-time in a white person's home doing cleaning and cooking was called a "maid." Her wages could be as little as $35 a week—less than a dollar an hour when the federal minimum wage was $1.40 an hour. If a woman worked full-time at $35 a week with no vacation, she would earn $1,820 per year, which was well below the poverty rate, especially if she was the only adult in a family and supporting children. But that kind of disparity was the way it had always been. In fact, the entire Memphis bus system was set up primarily to transport the Black women who worked as maids from their homes in North and South Memphis to East Memphis, where the white people lived.

Autry Parker had seen a lot more of this poverty than I had. He was a social worker, community organizer, and teacher in the Memphis City Schools district. His wife, Charlene, was also a teacher in one of the city's public schools, and they had both dealt with kids coming to school hungry and not having the clothes they needed. Autry was especially aware of the illiteracy that attended such poverty, much of which was imported from the surrounding areas, as Memphis was the migration point for people out of Mississippi, eastern Arkansas, and western Tennessee. We always remembered that this was the legacy from enslavement when it was against the law in those states to teach a Black person to read.

Autry and I had talked about this dire situation, starting from almost the moment I arrived in Memphis. Well before Johnson's War on Poverty began, in 1964, we saw the need to help local Black folk living in poverty take hold of their own circumstances. Black people have had to rely on our own communities and resources since our arrival in this country. With MAP-South, we set up the type of organization that our communities had been creating throughout much of the twentieth century. Saul Alinsky, in Chicago, had established such an organization in 1939. Called the Back of the Yards Neighborhood Council, it helped people living in poverty learn to organize themselves. He put community organizing on the map, having studied sociology in college, just as I had.

MAP-South was designed to grow from within the community it was serving. I was chair of the board, and Autry Parker was the executive director. He did the hiring and firing. And MAP-South became a kind of pioneer in Memphis and the South, as one of the first agencies founded on the idea of organizing communities from within to address the poverty engulfing them.

Our first step was to deploy people we called block workers or neighborhood aides. Each person was assigned to a street or a block, and would find out who lived there and learn something about their living conditions. We started with seventy-five block workers. A couple of white people from outside the community joined us, but it was mostly Black people. They went door to door and compiled a kind of inventory of who lived in each house. They talked to neighbors about their concerns, registered voters, and over time MAP-South became a force in the neighborhood.

Autry and I had always hoped to organize in South Memphis, and we knew we needed political support, but we wanted to work independently as much as possible, even independent of the NAACP and the Shelby County Democratic Club, the Black Democratic party group in town.

We aimed to steer clear of politics, but fairly soon into our work at MAP-South, politics found us anyway. Animosity toward us arose in official circles, mostly because we had been able to get started without the involvement of the local government. Armed with the information our block workers had gathered, we had started going to local government offices and advising them about the things we had seen. So city and county officials knew we were doing good work, even though for years they had never felt the need to do the same in Memphis. The money we had gotten from the OEO came directly to us from the federal government. When Representative Kuykendall learned of it, he suddenly said he needed oversight of that money. Our ability to bypass local officials and find ways to address our community's needs threatened their worldview, and their power. So, a few years in, the city and county, with Kuykendall's backing, succeeded in requiring us to present our budgets to them for approval, through their newly formed, white-run War on Poverty Committee of Memphis and Shelby County. The white power structures did not look favorably on a Black organization not needing their input or oversight.

Despite such roadblocks, in 1967, one of the biggest and most far-reaching results from MAP-South began. It came out of the home visits our block workers conducted. As they went from house to house, they found children with bloated stomachs, babies who looked as though they had been living in what, back then, was called a third-world country.

Just a mile away from many of these babies in need, St. Jude Children's Research Hospital had been founded in downtown Memphis. In 1962, the same year I moved to Memphis, entertainer Danny Thomas had established the hospital to fight childhood cancer. St. Jude treated all children, regardless of their family's ability to pay. And it did not turn away any child because of their race, either—a revolutionary move in a Deep South city still grappling with segregation.

The children with bloated stomachs were such a common sight in our work, we realized we had to do something more than merely count them. So we went to the medical director of St. Jude, Don Pinkel, and told him what we were seeing. Immediately, he told us to bring in every child we found with those symptoms. "Bring them," he said, "night or day, and we will treat them." The precise diagnosis the doctors gave for those children was "acute malnutrition." Instantly, we had a large volume of medical evidence about babies in Memphis who were slowly being starved to death.

The peaceful facade of prosperity that so many white people in Memphis enjoyed rested almost solely on the violent foundation of poverty under which they had always forced so many Black people in Memphis to live. White people ignoring the ways Black people suffered in that system was the solid framing that kept its cruel setup in place, for centuries.

The St. Jude doctors told us the babies were malnourished because their families were starving, too. Their prescription was simple: food, for the whole family.

We took as many babies as we could to St. Jude, and they fed them. And out of that came the MAP-South nutritional program. Fairly quickly, we set up an arrangement with the U.S. Department of Agriculture to send us surplus food by rail. We then passed that food on to the families. To store the food, we rented a warehouse and remodeled it as a distribution center. At one point during the program, we were feeding twenty-five hundred families a month.

A few months into the partnership, I was in St. Jude's parking lot when the medical director, Don Pinkel, spotted me and yelled, "Have you seen the first baby you brought in?" He told me that the malnourished boy was now a healthy child. He had recovered weight, and his bloated stomach had come back to normal. Dr. Pinkel was so excited. He urged me to go see the child. So I immediately did. No longer did the little boy have the sunken eyes and drawn face from his mistreatment in American society. He had the body weight and size of a well-nourished eleven-month-old baby. We were seeing that within weeks of getting proper feeding, these babies would turn around to enjoy great health.

As part of our program with St. Jude, we sent nurse practitioners around to people's houses, instead of making parents bring their kids to the hospital. Transportation was an issue, as was the time it took to go to an appointment. Home visits were particularly useful because, for instance, the symptoms of malnutrition can include skin issues, such as sores on a child's feet. The way to treat it was for parents to soak their children's feet three times a day. But when nurses went to the home where the child was living, they would see that the family didn't have running water in their house. And they didn't have a tub in which to soak the child's feet. So we brought them tubs and water to make sure the kids got the right treatment. A doctor could give people all the prescriptions in the world, but if they couldn't implement them, then they weren't getting the right help. That's why going to their homes was key to the success of the program.

MAP-South was exactly the right impetus for the Black community in Memphis to become more aware that the poverty put upon them was wrong, and there were things they could do to change the systems that entrapped them. We also persuaded the city and county that they needed to put Memphis's shameful poverty on their agenda and work to get rid of it. And we raised the consciousness of some white people in Memphis, too. But we never found much immunity to the political machinations fueled by many other white people's perception that we and our work were a threat to them. That played out most ferociously in 1967, when it came to two of our block workers, Coby Smith and Charles Cabbage.

I knew Coby Smith when he was a senior at Memphis's Manassas High School in 1963. He was the big man on campus. He was chair of the student government, head of the school's ROTC program, an honor student, and president of the senior class. Coby and I had extensive conversations then because some of us were trying to organize a boycott of all the high schools in an effort to protect Black students. The Memphis Board of Education was trying to fight desegregation in Black high schools, and we were organizing demonstrations against those efforts. Cody graduated and became one of the first Black students at an all-white private college called Southwestern at Memphis (now Rhodes College).

By the spring of 1967, Coby had left college and was exploring the idea of moving to Atlanta to work with SNCC. He had gone on the Meredith March with us the year before and was enamored of Stokely Carmichael. His hometown friend Charles Cabbage would be finishing up his degree at Morehouse College in 1967 and moving back to Memphis. Together they called me to talk about what was going on in the city and what could be done about the problems they saw.

I asked them if they would like to become neighborhood aides for MAP-South, working in the evenings on a part-time basis to organize young people. They were both interested. One of the weaknesses of MAP-South had been that the grassroots, door-to-door effort had not yet connected with young people. Most of the neighborhood aides were women who could not work at night or walk alone on the streets at any time because that was considered too dangerous for them. In South Memphis, one of the biggest groups experiencing poverty was young men between the ages of about sixteen and twenty-three. A quarter to a third of these folks were unemployed. To truly deal with problems of poverty, we had to find a way to reach this group. Quite a few of us had appealed to the city to try to get them jobs. But in the absence of opportunity, so many of these young men had simply given up.

I felt that Coby and Charles could probably help us connect with these young people and that, as well, we could learn some things from them. Quite readily, we hired them for evening work in the neighborhoods. But because of their supposed affiliations with SNCC, the white power structure had already turned Coby and Charles into villains trying to incite riots in Memphis. Then someone got wind that Coby and Charles were working as neighborhood aides for MAP-South. And the chair of the Memphis War on Poverty Committee asked us to fire them.

I said they were on our payroll in good faith, and we insisted that the committee's dictating who we hired and fired was way out of bounds. The issue got blown up, and we ended up having a hearing. We contacted two lawyers, Mike Cody and Lucius Burch, who talked at length with Coby and Charles. The War on Poverty Committee called them radicals, which we saw as race-based fearmongering. In August 1967, Coby Smith was quoted in *The Commercial Appeal:*

> "You can call this trial by rumor, or lynching by the press. . . . The reactionaries . . . are not concerned with the real question—that's those poor people out there and whether their needs will be met.
>
> "We can start with our congressman (Representative Dan Kuykendall), who wastes his time talking about Stokely Carmichael, and has not done one thing for the poor people of Memphis. And then

continue to our local officials, all-inclusive, who have turned their backs on the black community."

Disillusioned, Coby Smith and Charles Cabbage began to talk about a group they were organizing, which they called the Invaders. They were taking a line I didn't particularly like. Our disagreements were partly ideological and partly about methods. They were placing themselves in the militant category and claiming in part that King and others of us didn't know what was going on. To me, their militancy was mostly rhetorical, because they never actually organized to become violent. They just spoke of it and used it as a threat.

We did feel they used their position at MAP-South to propagandize in the neighborhood more than to organize the blocks for our work. We told them they had to stop. They had to follow our mission. Still, I supported them publicly, not because I necessarily agreed with their philosophy but because the War on Poverty Committee had no cause to try to dismiss them. If you are not going to work with all people in the community, then you are just playing games. You have to find a way for everyone to organize and work together constructively.

A major change in Memphis government was happening in the fall of 1967. Memphis switched from a commission-style government to a city council. Instead of general elections for all the commissioners, the city council was to be organized by single-member districts, which meant three Black members would be on the council, because three of the districts were composed of Black residents. It was the first time Black people had gained access to the power structure at that level. A major architect of that change was a white Republican attorney who served on the council, Lewis Donelson. But MAP-South's most constant and strongest political allies remained the Shelby County Democratic Club leadership: A. W. Willis, Ben Hooks, Russell Sugarmon, Jesse Turner, and a Jewish lawyer named Marvin Ratner. Willis, Sugarmon, and Ratner had started the first integrated law firm in Memphis. They were all part of the reform that catalyzed the movement in Memphis.

In the fall of 1967, in addition to pursuing election to the new city council, A. W. Willis ran to become the first Black mayor of Memphis. And the Shelby County Democratic Club urged me to run for the school board, because there were no Black members on the board of education and 40 percent of the student body was Black. In truth, I ran only because they asked me to, and particularly because A.W. and his wife, Anne, wanted me to. Dorothy thought it was a good idea as well. I would not have done it if Dorothy hadn't agreed.

I was running against the whole school board. Unlike the new city council, the school board was still elected citywide. That was one way Black people had been kept from elected office in the city. I chose to compete partly as a test case to see if white people would vote for a Black candidate, because I would need to win white votes to win. But I didn't run a very good campaign. My heart was not in it. I had no craving for serving on the board of education. I never saw myself as an elected or appointed official. And our campaign didn't have much money.

During the election, members of the segregationist John Birch Society again called me a Communist. They brought up my trip to Vietnam in 1965. They called me a Yankee from the North, since I was from Ohio. And they accused me of being subversive because I had gone to India and had studied Gandhism. They said I had imported it into America to undermine the government. If anything, I was using Gandhi's teachings to make our country and our government live up to its original promise. But that kind of nuance was lost on them.

At any rate, the election did not pan out. White folks did not vote for me. I lost, and A.W. lost. Henry Loeb was elected mayor again. It would be his second time in that office. He had resigned as mayor in 1963 to run his family laundry business. But he was back and would have to learn to operate with the new city council system, which gave the mayor more power but also gave Black citizens more of a voice.

I thought of myself as a person in the struggle who Martin could depend upon to be a teacher, counselor, mentor, and strategist. And I was a behind-the-scenes counselor to him, as well as a friend. The movement was quickly evolving, and in 1967, Martin and I had countless phone calls, plus many talks in person at retreats or board meetings or staff meetings to address ourselves to the future, analyzing where we were and where we wanted to go.

During our 1967 staff retreat at the Penn Center, the idea for the Poor People's Campaign emerged. Also, during that fall 1967 retreat, Martin and I agreed that as soon as the Poor People's Campaign was over, in 1968, we would declare a moratorium, in which the SCLC would take three to six months off with no demonstrations or campaigns. We would use the time to regroup and to strategize our next steps in the ongoing struggle. One of the things Martin kept saying to me at that retreat was "I expect you to join me at the SCLC full-time." Once again, he wanted me on his team. We planned to take the field together heading into a new decade.

Roy Wilkins had squelched the 1960 effort to have me join the staff. But in December 1967, things had evolved. Martin made his desires clear, and we finalized it between the two of us. Late one night we were joined by Ralph Abernathy, and we all agreed that I was to become more officially tied to the SCLC in 1968.

People have written about how King was tired and weary all the time. That wasn't true in my conversations with him in those final years. Maybe I didn't notice as much, because during the struggle you were always doing things when you were tired. You were walking when you were tired. You were going to bed only after you were way past tired. You were getting up and doing your work as a pastor when you were tired. Anyone who was active in the movement knew what it meant to be exhausted. And Martin King would live on three or four hours of sleep at night and then travel, and speak, and have meetings all day and night.

He was, I think, the best of us all.

PART THREE

1968

LOVE

The moment we choose to love, we begin to move against domination, against oppression. The moment we choose to love we begin to move towards freedom, to act in ways that liberate ourselves and others.

—BELL HOOKS

FIFTEEN

Beloved Community

Memphis police spraying Mace in the eyes of a sanitation striker during downtown march, February 23, 1968.
COMMERCIAL APPEAL VIA IMAGN

The period from 1967 to the start of 1968 was one of my most productive times. I was thirty-nine years old. My church had moved into a new building with more space, and we were expanding our ministry and outreach. MAP-South was going strong, addressing poverty in Memphis at its root. A small but dedicated anti-war movement was growing in the city. And Dorothy and I had a thriving family. Everywhere I looked in my life, I saw the fruits of my faith, convictions, and care. I had every reason to expect more of the same at the start of 1968. Instead, that year would become one of the most harrowing and demanding in my life—as a pastor, an organizer, a member of the nonviolent movement, and as Martin's friend.

When Martin was assassinated in April, he was in town supporting the thirteen hundred Black sanitation workers who had gone on strike against the city of Memphis. From my vantage point in the middle of it all, the Memphis sanitation strike will always stand as a defining moment in this country, and in my life. Those men called on us all to live up to who and what we said we were, as citizens and as a nation. They had as much courage, goodness, and valor as any of this country's most celebrated heroes, including Martin. And Martin knew that.

The sixty-five-day strike began in February. But what some thought were innocuous decisions made more than a decade earlier—by the man who would become mayor of Memphis and start his second term in January 1968—resulted in the tragedy that spurred the workers to walk off their jobs that winter.

Before Henry Loeb served as mayor for the first time in 1960, he was the city's commissioner of public works, a position that had him overseeing the sanitation department, from 1956 to 1959. One of his responsibilities in that role was buying equipment and vehicles for the workers to use. In 1957, he made a point of publicizing how he had purchased standard, factory-made trucks for the department, after loosening specifications so companies offering lower-end models could put in bids. Truck dealers had asked that the city require fewer special conditions to be met on the vehicles, and Loeb complied. That way, he reasoned, the city could save money by getting cut-rate trucks without modern safety features. Local papers reported Loeb and his staff believed those cheaper trucks would be "good enough" for the garbage collectors in their daily work. All of the people who picked up the garbage and most of the sanitation truck drivers were Black men. Instead of buying the safest and most current equipment, Loeb bought trucks that were already outdated before they were deployed, in the name of managing the taxpayers' money responsibly. It was part of his campaign to cut costs in all areas of the public works department's operations, so he could use those savings to fund massive street-paving and repair projects and sidewalk installations throughout the white middle- and upper-class neighborhoods of Midtown and East Memphis.

For instance, during his first three months in office, in 1956, his department installed ten miles of new sidewalks throughout subdivisions in those areas. Loeb's tenure also included paving more than 182 miles of streets in newly developed parts of the city. And in 1958, when the Memphis City Beautiful Commission—made up of socially elite, mostly unpaid white women—complained that in their neighborhoods, pieces of garbage had fallen from the tops of sanitation trucks as they made the rounds, the city immediately spent $7,000 on tarps for the men to put over the truck beds to contain the errant trash. A bulletin was issued to the drivers of the trucks warning that they could be arrested for any litter that spilled out onto the streets.

Loeb's responsiveness to the needs of his base constituency cemented his reputation among white Memphians as a man who got things done for the people. But he was a segregationist, a commander in Memphis's branch of the American Legion, and a wealthy businessman, so "the people" to whom he responded usually did not include the city's Black residents, who were also taxpayers, as were all of the sanitation workers. Loeb won his first mayor's race in 1959 largely because of the popularity he had gained among the white people of Memphis as public works commissioner. And he won again in 1967 without altering his worldview, even though—and partly because—change was erupting all around him in Memphis, and the world.

Six of those cheap garbage trucks Loeb had bought eleven years earlier were still on the road in February 1968 when faulty wiring in one of them unexpectedly triggered the garbage-crushing mechanism in the back of the truck. That grinder pulled two Black sanitation workers deep into the barrel where the trash was collected, and crushed them to death as they struggled to escape.

Thirty-year-old Robert Walker and thirty-six-year-old Echol Cole had been sheltering from heavy rain inside the back of the truck as it was heading to the county dump at the end of the day. There wasn't room inside the cabs of the trucks for all of the five-man crew. So three men, including the driver, would always sit inside the cab, and the other two men would ride outside the truck, standing on small platforms on either side of the back of the vehicle, hanging on as it rolled along.

Since there was nowhere else to protect themselves during stormy weather, Mr. Walker and Mr. Cole had sheltered just inside the barrel of the truck, a common practice among their colleagues on rainy days. The *Memphis Press-Scimitar* reported, "The two men usually ride . . . on the sides of the huge, barrel-like truck. But because of heavy rain, they got in the back next to the compressor. . . . The truck was full of trash and did not leave much space for the two men to stand without pushing against the compression unit."

The only eyewitness, a white woman who lived in the East Memphis neighborhood where the truck was collecting garbage, said she was at her kitchen table looking out her window when she saw what happened to one of the men: "He was standing there on the end of the truck, and suddenly it looked like the big thing just swallowed him. It looked like his raincoat got snagged in the thing and it pulled him in." She did not realize another man had already been crushed inside the barrel. The newspaper said the driver "came to a full stop when he heard the compression motors turn on." He jumped out and pressed the button on the side of the truck that stopped the motors, "but it was too late."

Charles Blackburn, director of public works, said that six trucks in the fleet, including the one that killed the men, were of the same type. They were taken off the road the next day, pending an investigation. All six were what was left of the cheapest fleet of trucks Henry Loeb could find to put into use in 1957. Three of those trucks, including the one that crushed the men inside the truck's barrel, had buttons on the outside of the vehicle that a man had to push to activate the motor that powered the trash compressor. Blackburn noted in the Saturday, February 3, *Commercial Appeal,* two days after the incident, that those three trucks were being held out of service while a full investigation was conducted into whether to re-deploy them. "The other three," Blackburn said, "are operated by a man standing outside the barrel and you have to hold the lever to operate them." Since those three trucks with levers instead of buttons could not be activated accidentally, he said, "they should be back on the route Monday."

To add to the cruel details of Mr. Walker's and Mr. Cole's deaths, the street where they were killed, Colonial Road, was among those paved and given sidewalks in 1957, with the money Henry Loeb saved by buying the cheaper trucks. In addition, Mayor Loeb and his family lived on Colonial Road, only a few blocks north of where the two men died.

Throughout the previous years, the sanitation workers' main complaints had centered on the safety and efficacy of the equipment the public works department supplied. Among the problems T. O. Jones heard about repeatedly when trying to organize the labor union were faulty brakes that still didn't work properly even after the department said they had been repaired, metal tubs for hauling the garbage that had holes in them, and lack of gear for bad weather. And the obsolete trucks, which workers had said should have been taken out of commission long before

1968, were particularly dangerous. Jones reported that the men working on the routes called their co-workers' deaths "a disgraceful sin."

On Saturday, February 3, Henry Loeb wrote identical condolence letters to the wives of both men saying, "I know over the city, and particularly in the ranks of city employees, I speak for many whose thoughts and prayers are with you."

The thirteen hundred Memphis sanitation workers who picked up the city's garbage in 1968 were not considered full employees, and so they did not receive health insurance or other benefits. When the men worked, they got paid. If they missed a day because of injury, illness, or bad weather, they did not get paid. They were given no vacation, no sick days, no personal leave. When it rained hard enough, the men were sent home, without pay, while their white managers and supervisors were still paid for a full day, because most of them received full city employee benefits. That's why, even though a heavy rain was falling during their ill-fated shift, the two men, along with everyone else on the trucks that day, had decided to keep working. Mr. Walker had five children, and his wife was pregnant with his sixth when he died. He also supported his mother. Mr. Cole had a wife. It was never mentioned publicly whether he had any kids. But legally, the families of Mr. Cole and Mr. Walker did not qualify for any compensation for the men's deaths.

The city was not even obligated to pay for their funeral expenses. Although that same Saturday, each family also got another letter, this one from Charles Blackburn, saying, "In addition to extending our sympathy, the City wants to pay $500.00 on the funeral expenses, if you need it." But that didn't cover the entire burial amount. So Mrs. Walker had to pay the rest of the funeral fees out of her husband's last paycheck.

Years later, one of Charles Walker's daughters said the family was told that her father was pulled into the truck barrel when he tried to reach for Echol Cole to help him escape, after Mr. Cole had been pulled into the crushing mechanism. Her family also was told that when the men's bodies were recovered, her father's hand was grasping Mr. Cole's hand.

The unnecessary deaths of Mr. Cole and Mr. Walker were a reflection of the abysmal, substandard conditions under which they had labored. The city certainly had not properly equipped the men to do their jobs. And most white residents and the white government of Memphis were not equipped for the reaction among Black workers and citizens following the deaths of Mr. Cole and Mr. Walker. The men who had to continue working on the trucks were afraid. The very same faulty equipment they had complained about for years had just killed two of their colleagues. The city seemed more concerned with getting the trucks back on the streets than with doing what it took to protect the sanitation workers from those trucks that could kill them. But the city made sure to appear to be generous, in giving the Cole and Walker families that bit of charity toward funeral expenses. Such superficial gestures were not going to appease the sanitation workers. As far as they were concerned, the days of the city not compensating them enough to support their families in their dangerous, unappreciated jobs were over.

Still, I don't think anyone outside of T. O. Jones's circle saw the strike coming. Within days, Jones and many of the men who had been fired for union organizing and then rehired in 1963 rallied most of the other thirteen hundred sanitation workers to go out on strike. They began to draw up their demands.

A union would strike only as a last resort. But the initial impetus to strike in Memphis in 1968 did not come from their union, the American Federation of State, County and Municipal Employees (AFSCME). It came from the sanitation workers themselves. AFSCME leadership in Washington was not sure such a strike was a good idea in the middle of winter. The steaming-hot Southern summer would have been a better choice if the men had wanted to pick an ideal time for a sanitation strike in Memphis. Garbage would fester in the heat, and the smell would radiate more revoltingly throughout the city. February was too cold for the garbage to decay to full effect, and public demonstrations in the frigid weather were a more difficult prospect, too. Strategy and planning were not what drove the men initially. The strike represented a hope, born from generations of pent-up anger, frustration, fear, and the courage brewing within each man and his family. When that faulty truck crushed Mr. Cole and Mr. Walker to death, their colleagues spontaneously came together, each deciding to advocate for his own life and livelihood.

On the morning of Monday, February 12, most of the thirteen hundred Memphis sanitation workers walked off their jobs. It was front-page news in the afternoon edition of the *Memphis Press-Scimitar*.

The paper reported that Loeb brought up "the 'illegality' of the strike as he talked with his department chiefs." The mayor referred to the injunction issued in 1966, the last time T. O. Jones and his men, under AFSCME, threatened to strike. Loeb said the ruling then still meant that "public works employees did not have the right to strike or picket the city."

The next day, the morning paper, the *Commercial Appeal,* led with tough words from Mayor Loeb calling the work stoppage illegal and saying, "Let no one make a mistake about it, the garbage is going to be picked up in Memphis. If the men do not return immediately, we will have no choice but to employ others to protect the public health."

The *Press-Scimitar,* which was the afternoon paper, had run an editorial the day the strike began saying, "Public employees have no moral right to strike against the public, whether present law forbids it or not."

The moral rights of sanitation workers were definitely at the heart of the sanitation strike in Memphis—except not in the way those local papers and the white community understood them to be. The idea that somehow these men didn't have a right to earn a living wage—that they could work full-time for pay that would keep them poor and unable to take care of themselves and their families—was embedded in the culture and thinking among Memphis's ruling class.

If I had been asked in 1968 how to start a campaign to eliminate poverty in the United States, I could not have come up with a better nonviolent strategy than to organize workers living in poverty and help them develop the unity and strength to fight indecent wages and working conditions.

The men in the sanitation department who gathered the garbage across Memphis were solid human beings. Most were family men who had been born on cotton plantations in Mississippi, Arkansas, or Tennessee. Their wives and siblings had also spent childhoods picking cotton in the Jim Crow South. And the men's parents and in-laws had lived their entire lives sharecropping on plantations.

Most Black sharecroppers were descendants of enslaved ancestors, some working on the very same land generations of their grandparents had worked without pay for centuries. They would farm the plantation, and the landowners were supposed to give them a share of the profits from the crops they produced. But sharecropping families had to pay the owners for so many of their necessities. The plantation store gave them credit against their profits, which they settled at the end of each year. They had to rent housing on the owners' land, which usually consisted of run-down shotgun shacks with no running water, electricity, or indoor toilets. In addition, the children of people who were sharecroppers would work in the fields year-round, too, missing school and never learning to read, further limiting opportunities for better work. They were caught in a system—a close cousin of enslavement—that kept them forever indebted to the landowners, so they could barely subsist and certainly could never get any of the profits their labor produced.

I didn't meet all of the Memphis sanitation workers, but I was in meetings and marches with many of them, and we spoke often. They were not only protesting bad wages. They were shaking off lifelong injustices.

For instance, Memphis sanitation worker Alvin Turner was born in 1934 on a plantation in Somerville, Tennessee. He went to work in the fields at the age of seven. He said, "My daddy gave me a cotton sack and he told me, 'Now you ain't out here to play, you out here to work.'"

Baxter Leach was born in 1939 on a plantation in Schlater, Mississippi. At nine years old, he went to work with his father in the fields. His wife, Jimmie Leach, was born in 1939 as well, on a plantation in Doddsville, Mississippi, and started working at age six picking cotton and gathering it in flour sacks all day.

Each year, the people working the land as sharecroppers piled up debts to the plantation owners for their food, housing, and other essential living expenses. As a result, after they settled up at the end of the year, the share they got of the profits from the crops they picked usually would not cover that debt. It was a trap.

"You would work a whole year," said Alvin Turner, "and at the end of that year, you wouldn't hardly get one hundred dollars. I feel I wasn't too far out of slavery."

While slavery was abolished legally in 1865, slavery by other names had yet to be abolished and dismantled in the United States in the mid-twentieth century. Our country had not made the full transition from embracing the practice of owning fellow human beings, paying them nothing for their work, and having unlimited power over them. Sharecropping inflicted harsh social and economic restrictions on people's lives. And violence enforced the status quo.

"When you met a white man and his wife on the street," Alvin Turner said, "you would have to get off the sidewalk, into the street, until they passed. You either did it, or you were subject to get beaten. I know several people who were beaten for no reason. I know one person who was lynched. They threw a rope around him, and hung him under the train tracks."

J. L. McClain was born in 1934 on a plantation in Cleveland, Mississippi, and went to work at age twelve, plowing cotton fields, chopping cotton, and picking cotton. "When it rained, I'd go to school, because I couldn't work. Maybe five or six times a month, I would go to school." Mr. McClain was one of the original thirty-three men the sanitation department had fired for joining the independent union that T. O. Jones created in Memphis in 1963. He was hired back a few weeks later.

Mr. Turner, Mr. and Mrs. Leach, and Mr. McClain all left the plantations when they came of age and headed to Memphis, to seek better living and working conditions. The promise of a municipal job in Memphis seemed like it would give them that opportunity. But many of the men and their families came to feel like they had just traded those inhuman conditions in the country for inhuman conditions in the city.

The job at the sanitation department was considered steady. But it surely wasn't a departure from their previous lives. The men called the public works department "the plantation." And they called the place they reported to work each day, where the trucks were parked and the supervisors worked, "the barn." Their jobs included venturing into residents' backyards with metal tubs the city gave them and pouring people's garbage from the metal garbage cans that were common at the time into the city-issued tubs and carrying those leaky tubs back to the truck. They encountered a menagerie of bugs and rodents along their routes, and liquid from the trash dripped down onto them all day. Of course, at the barn after work they couldn't use the showers, where Black men were not allowed. So they couldn't wash any of the day's filth off or change their clothes before leaving the job.

When they arrived home, they had to stand outside in their yard and run a hose over themselves to get the maggots and smells off their bodies, shoes, and clothes. Then they would go onto a back porch and take off some of their clothes and leave them outside before stepping inside to take a shower. Their wives often washed their clothes for them in washbasins because most of their homes did not have washing machines or dryers.

In the Memphis Public Works Department, there were no Black supervisors. A Black person couldn't get an office job in public works, in a city that was 40 percent Black. Their white supervisors and the white city fathers imposed upon the men and their wives and children a kind of torturous life they did not want. But because of their drive to care for themselves and their families, they kept their jobs, and did the best they could.

T. O. Jones was a worthy representative of the workers. My relationship with him was that of two men engaged in a common struggle. When I met him, a few years before 1968, I had told him I was in his corner for organizing labor and that if there were ever anything I could do to support him, he should not hesitate to call on me. I don't remember him asking for anything until the strike happened.

T.O. was a rugged, burly man of great mental strength who had spent a decade trying to organize a sanitation workers' union. That was not an easy thing to do in an anti-union state. But T.O. had a capacity to persevere, to not give up. He had a vision for how the men could improve their conditions and change the character of the job so they could make a living wage from it. Slowly, he persuaded most of his colleagues that unionizing would empower them.

From the very first days of the strike, Mayor Henry Loeb allowed himself to become a symbol of the worst of politics, segregation, states' rights, and white supremacy. Mayor Loeb didn't consider the men on strike as his equals in any way, shape, or form. And he clung to his strong conviction that city workers could not unionize.

On the second day of the strike, more than seven hundred sanitation strikers marched the five miles from the United Rubber Workers union hall, in North Memphis, to city hall, downtown. Leading them was Bill Lucy, an AFSCME official who had flown in from Washington, D.C., with other union leaders. A Black man born in Memphis, Lucy grew up in California, where he became a union organizer.

When the men reached city hall and began streaming into the city council chamber, it became clear that the room was too small to hold all of them. So arrangements were made to move to the city-owned Ellis Auditorium, a few blocks away. Both Mayor Loeb and the union leaders would be able to talk to the men there. Mayor Loeb stood up on the stage and spoke to them in the same polite but paternalistic tone he and most white Memphians always used with Black hired help.

"I urge you to go to work," he told the men. He wanted them back on their garbage-collecting routes before he would engage in any talks about changes to their job conditions. He thought he could bank on the trust he believed he inspired in sanitation workers, dating back to his time as head of the public works department. "I promise you that we're working on a raise and have been before this matter came up," he explained. "I say to you that I was with you four years and you know me. And when I tell you something you can believe it. We are working on a raise."

The men were not receptive to his talk, and most even laughed. He thought showing sympathy might win them over, so he said, "It's tragic for you. It's tragic for the city that this thing has come about."

Then he spoke to them as if their strike were simply a whim and he had only their best interests in mind: "I further say to you that the ones of you who say 'No,' if you don't feel like going back to work, this is your business. I think that you've lost quite a bit already, and I'd like to see you not lose any more."

All six foot five inches of Loeb stood tall at the microphone on the auditorium's stage, in front of the skeptical workers, proudly declaring how any of them could come in and talk to him at any time. He had, he said, an open-door policy. The workers laughed at him some more. A couple of them began to heckle him, saying it was no use going to talk to him because he wouldn't listen to them anyway. Not listening was part of Loeb's problem. He insisted that only when the men went back to work would he discuss their demands. But as P. J. Ciampa, field staff director of AFSCME, pointed out to reporters that day, no striking union had ever gone back to work before negotiations had resulted in an agreement.

Henry Loeb was personally affronted that as a former public works commissioner, overseer of the city's garbage workers, he had not been in on conversations with the workers before the strike. He felt that T. O. Jones should have talked to him first beforehand. But whenever Loeb did speak with T. O. Jones, he expected Jones to just listen. He did not expect Jones to have solutions that countered his. And he certainly didn't expect Jones to have viable ideas of his own.

Fundamentally, Loeb didn't see the sanitation workers as thirteen hundred human beings with the freedom and power to act independently of him, or the ability to stand up against him for their own worth. While he was outwardly friendly to the workers, he saw the strike as them showing unfriendliness toward him. He took it personally.

T. O. Jones strongly believed that a public works union would allow the men to improve their employment situation. But Loeb, like most white people in Memphis, didn't understand that coming together in community was the only sure way to solve the city's systemic problems, that being unafraid to bend in the direction of justice and dignity for all was the only way to resolution and even redemption. Instead, Loeb and his followers just wanted things to stay as they were.

Henry Loeb did not know how to be the mayor of a democratic government. He wasn't a Bull Connor type who strong-armed everyone. There wasn't that kind of leader in Memphis. Instead, the city's power base clung to a certain mannered but staunchly unyielding decorum. At first, the fact that Henry Loeb had grown up Jewish seemed incongruent with Memphis's tradition of white Christian rule. His grandfather Henry Loeb Sr. had immigrated to Memphis from Germany and had started a laundry business, which the mayor's father, William Loeb, had continued. The mayor, Henry Loeb III, had gone to Phillips Academy prep school in Massachusetts and graduated from Brown University. He was a patrol torpedo boat commander in World War II, and he was taught to emulate John F. Kennedy, who was also a PT boat captain. Still, Henry Loeb was deeply committed to preserving and defending the established order in Memphis, and that meant racial segregation first and foremost. He was never going to lead the city toward justice.

The cotton industry not only drove the region's economy, but also its culture. From the city's vantage point on the bluffs of the Mississippi River, it had grown into the cotton trading and distribution capital of the United States. The crop came up from Mississippi, and over from West Tennessee and eastern Arkansas, to Memphis. The white aristocracy of Memphis profited from cotton's sale and distribution, just as their ancestors had during enslavement. For many Black Memphians, even symbols of the cotton industry were enough to evoke menacing images of extreme racial oppression. Yet, as a constant reminder that cotton was king, a cotton boll icon anchored the base of the city's official seal—as it does to this day.

In 1968, there were still cotton fields within the Memphis city limits. But the most ostentatious display of the economic and social hold that cotton had on the city was the Memphis Cotton Carnival, an annual segregated celebration of the plantation South. Each year, a king of the Cotton Carnival was chosen. He was usually an older local businessman. A queen was also chosen. She was always a young college student of nineteen or twenty. The two were at the helm during a week of festivities, culminating in an extravagant parade downtown, which would often include floats celebrating cotton and flying multiple Confederate flags. The king and queen of the Cotton Carnival were seen as the royalty at the top of white Memphis society.

Not to completely ignore those at whose expense all that wealth was harvested, the white people of Memphis *let* Black people celebrate their role in the cotton economy separately, not as equals, in what was called the Cotton Makers Jubilee. After the week-long white carnival parades and balls were over, Black people were *allowed* to name their own king, queen, and princesses, and to have a modest parade, in the shadow of the major events the white people had staged a few days before. Segregation limited us not only economically, physically, and emotionally but also in the imaginations of white people who hoped to always dictate how we were to behave as citizens of our city and our nation. The many different fibers of plantation life, woven into the foundation and structure of Memphis, produced an enduring standard in the city of violence toward and neglect and mistreatment of Black people.

It was almost as if that standard had permeated the very land on which the city had originally been built—land swindled from Cherokee and Chickasaw nations in the nineteenth century and then cultivated with the labor of kidnapped and enslaved Africans. Andrew Jackson and two others from Nashville were the founders of Memphis, which they created in 1819 to be a distribution hub on the Mississippi River. Racism and segregation were elemental from the start of the white aristocracy—the make-believe kings and queens who reigned over parades, parties, people, and politics.

Henry Loeb answered to the soul of that segregation system. He didn't answer to himself. He had no vision of his own for the city. With his egotism and a shot of cottony aristocracy, he made himself emblematic of the Southern culture in which he'd grown up, as he tried to assimilate his Jewish heritage on both sides of his parents' families into white, Christian Memphis. He had to prove himself to the city's ruling class. The way Loeb eventually became the leader of that ruling class was by burying the part of him that didn't really belong. In 1951, Loeb married Mary Gregg, who one year earlier had been the queen of the Memphis Cotton Carnival. He took over his father's thriving laundry business, and within a few years, became public works commissioner, which led to his first term as mayor from 1960 to 1963. And in 1968 Loeb again took the helm of Memphis government. He had learned to embrace and reflect everything the constituents who put him in office cared about the most—so much so that on New Year's Day 1968, just before he began his second mayoral term, he converted from his family's Judaism to his wife's Episcopal faith.

The potential for Black political power in Memphis was greater than in a lot of other places in the Southeast, because Memphis was about 40 percent Black and so had a larger Black community than most other big cities. The new structure of the city government meant the 1968 city council was the first local political body in which Black people held elected positions of power in Memphis government. But the calcified white power structures shared only minimal authority with the three newly elected Black city council members. The mayor, the city council, Black and white citizens, and even the press had a long learning curve to understand how to act with three Black men suddenly holding seats in local government, when the city leadership had previously been exclusively white.

On Thursday, February 22, that learning curve showed itself. The chairman of the council's public works subcommittee, Fred Davis, one of the three Black council members, called a morning hearing to discuss the sanitation strike. Jerry Wurf, president of AFSCME, who was Jewish, and Jesse Epps, an AFSCME field representative, who was Black, were there, along with Jesse Turner, head of the Memphis NAACP, me, and a few other Black ministers. The council members questioned the union's legitimacy to represent the men, with Councilman Fred Davis saying he would like to hear from the men themselves. Jesse Epps, of AFSCME, told the council members, "These men don't feel comfortable coming to such plush surroundings. They are not equipped to come in here and speak. That's why they want to have some representatives to speak for them, and that's the union."

But since the council members insisted that they wanted to hear from some of the rank-and-file workers, a group of us got together with Jesse Epps and moved quickly to bring the men over to city hall. Jerry Wurf called AFSCME's Bill Lucy, who was at a meeting of the strikers in North Memphis, and asked him to invite the men to city hall. Once they started arriving and the council chambers filled up, Fred Davis and others began to say, “There are only so many seats here, they’re not going to all be able to come in. Some of them are going to have to wait outside.”

That’s when I, along with fellow Black ministers Ezekiel Bell and Harold Middlebrook, as well as a couple of others, immediately went to the door and invited the men to come on in anyway. We made it very clear to Fred Davis and his subcommittee and to other members of the council who were there that we weren’t going to stand for these insinuations that they were making about our integrity and the union’s ability to represent the men. We said, “You wanted to have them here, so we’ve called them. They’re here, and they’re all coming in. As many men as can get in, they’re getting in.” The men began to fill up the aisles and stood behind the seating in the back and on the sides of the wood-paneled chamber, which was designed to seat only about 425 people. Close to 700 men were inside.

Davis attempted to run the meeting but was continually heckled. He told us that he was a councilman but he was also a Negro, and therefore that meant “I’m with you, and I’m with the city council. I have to walk two sides of the street.”

I yelled out, “You can’t do it.” Others said the same thing. We told him he was either going to stand for justice or not.

Davis then said he still hadn’t heard from the men directly. This was the city council’s ploy to undermine the union’s authority to negotiate on the men’s behalf. Jesse Epps then asked the men questions, which they answered in unison.

“Did you walk out?”

“Yes.”

“Do you want a pay raise?”

“Yes.”

“Do you want dues checkoff?”

“Yes.”

“Do you want the union to bargain with the city and represent you?”

“Yes.”

Then union leaders said to the city council, “You can speak to T. O. Jones, you can speak to negotiators for the union, to the members of the strike committee, but we are not going to let you say we don’t speak for the men. That’s why they’ve elected us, exactly to speak for them.” The men cheered.

Davis and the rest of the council members present lost control of the meeting. They wanted to adjourn and meet again at the nearby Ellis Auditorium, as they had at the start of the strike. But we weren't sure they would show up. So we all decided it was better to stick it out in the council chambers and push for an agreement.

At one point, wives of the workers and other strike supporters brought in food. *The Commercial Appeal* described that moment: "The plush red-carpeted council chamber was jammed with strikers" when a group of people "bustled into the chamber with sacks and boxes containing 104 loaves of bread, 10 pounds of bologna and cheese, 9 pounds luncheon meat, 8 pounds of ham plus mayonnaise and mustard." Then "eight Negro women sliced up bologna on the city attorney's table for sandwiches." The fancy, long wooden table became a prep area, and "strikers waited patiently in their seats while the women prepared sandwiches, wrapped them in paper towels and went along the aisles passing them out." We were having a picnic inside city hall. "Union leaders," noted *The Commercial Appeal,* "said the money for the food came from passing the hat." As the meeting went on, "instant coffee was gulped down and strikers nodded approvingly as union leaders called for acceptance of the union contract."

The newspaper also pointed out how "the usually immaculate carpet of the chamber soon became spotted with bread crumbs and tiny pieces of paper." And outside the building, "142 officers sat jammed five to a car with motors running, awaiting orders from Mayor Henry Loeb."

After repeatedly trying to regain control of the crowd, Davis said he would either move the meeting to the city's Ellis Auditorium or adjourn it.

The crowd began to sing "We Shall Not Be Moved."

We shall not
We shall not be moved.
Just like a tree
Planted by the water
We shall not be moved.

T. O. Jones went up to the microphone and said, "We are here, and we are not moving until we get some satisfaction."

Jerry Wurf, in his role as the president of AFSCME, took to the mi-

Rev. James Morris Lawson Sr. and his five sons. Clockwise from top left: James Jr., Bill Lawson, John Lawson, Phillip Lawson, and Paul Lawson, 1930s. LAWSON FAMILY PHOTO

James Morris Lawson Sr. and Philane Cover Lawson. VANDERBILT LIBRARY

Washington High School, Massillon, Ohio, June 1946. VANDERBILT LIBRARY

Freshman year, Baldwin-Wallace College, 1947–1948.
VANDERBILT LIBRARY

At the typewriter table, Nagpur, India, 1955.
VANDERBILT LIBRARY

With the football team he coached, after a victory, Nagpur, India, 1955.
VANDERBILT LIBRARY

At work in the Fellowship of Reconciliation office, Nashville, 1960.
FELLOWSHIP OF RECONCILIATION ARCHIVES

Reading the Nashville Banner *with the headline "Liberals War on Compromise," as John Lewis sits nearby, 1960.*
BILL GOODMAN, *NASHVILLE BANNER* ARCHIVES, NASHVILLE PUBLIC LIBRARY

White men attacking sit-in demonstrators at Woolworth's lunch counter in downtown Nashville, February 27, 1960.
VIC COOLEY, *NASHVILLE BANNER* ARCHIVES, NASHVILLE PUBLIC LIBRARY

Matthew Walker Jr., Peggy Alexander, Diane Nash, and Stanley Hemphill successfully desegregating the Nashville lunch counter for the first time at Post House Restaurant in the Greyhound bus terminal, March 16, 1961.

GERALD HOLLY, NASHVILLE TENNESSEAN VIA IMAGN

Rev. Joseph Metz Rollins Jr. (center) speaks during a press conference at First Baptist Church; Ella Baker (left), Reverend Lawson (right), March 1, 1960.

ELDRED REANEY, NASHVILLE TENNESSEAN VIA IMAGN

With Dorothy Lawson at First Baptist Church, March 1, 1960.

PAUL SCHLEICHER, *NASHVILLE BANNER* ARCHIVES, NASHVILLE PUBLIC LIBRARY

Arrest at First Baptist Church, downtown Nashville. Dorothy Lawson (left) is behind Reverend Lawson's shoulder, March 4, 1960.

VIC COOLEY, *NASHVILLE BANNER* ARCHIVES, NASHVILLE PUBLIC LIBRARY

Silent march from Jefferson Street to Nashville City Hall on April 19, 1960, after terrorists bombed attorney Z. Alexander Looby's home that morning. First row: Rev. C. T. Vivian, Diane Nash, Bernard Lafayette; second row: Kenneth Frazier, Curtis Murphy, Rodney Powell; Reverend Lawson is marching behind them (holding a handkerchief to his forehead). JACK CORN, NASHVILLE TENNESSEAN VIA IMAGN

Rev. Andrew White (left) and Rev. C. T. Vivian and Nashville Student Movement leaders Diane Nash and Curtis Murphy (right) confront Nashville mayor Ben West (center) on the steps of city hall, April 19, 1960.
VIC COOLEY, *NASHVILLE BANNER* ARCHIVES, NASHVILLE PUBLIC LIBRARY

SCLC meeting at Atlanta University to discuss sit-in campaign, May 1960. Top row: Bernard Lee, Dave Forbes, Henry Thomas, Lonnie C. King Jr., James Lawson Jr.; middle row: Virginius Thornton, Rev. Wyatt Tee Walker, Martin Luther King Jr., Michael Penn; bottom row: Clarence Mitchell, Marion Barry.
HOWARD SOCHUREK, SHUTTERSTOCK

Studying at Boston University School of Theology after expulsion from Vanderbilt, June 7, 1960.
J. WALTER GREEN, ASSOCIATED PRESS

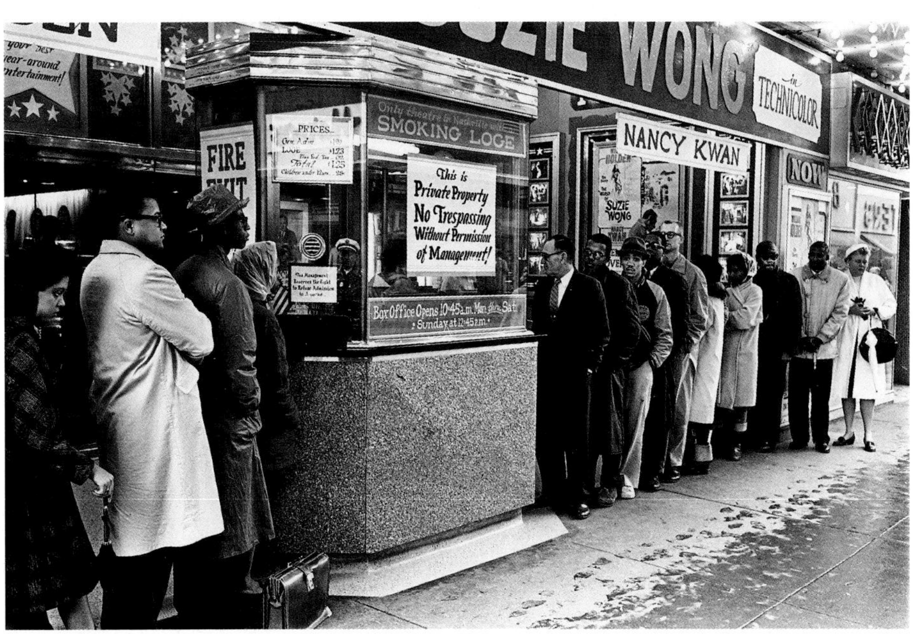

Tennessee Theater stand-in demonstration, downtown Nashville, February 21, 1961.
GERALD HOLLY, *NASHVILLE TENNESSEAN* VIA IMAGN

Desegregating the Montgomery Continental Trailways bus station lunch counter: Reverend Lawson drinking coffee, Martin Luther King's brother A. D. King (right), and Rev. C. T. Vivian (far right), before the Freedom Ride into Mississippi, May 24, 1961.
PAUL SCHUTZER, THE LIFE PICTURE COLLECTION, SHUTTERSTOCK

On the first bus headed to Jackson, Mississippi, from Montgomery, Alabama, on May 24, 1961. In front of Reverend Lawson are Joseph Carter (left), and Bernard Lafayette (right).
PAUL SCHUTZER, THE LIFE PICTURE COLLECTION, SHUTTERSTOCK

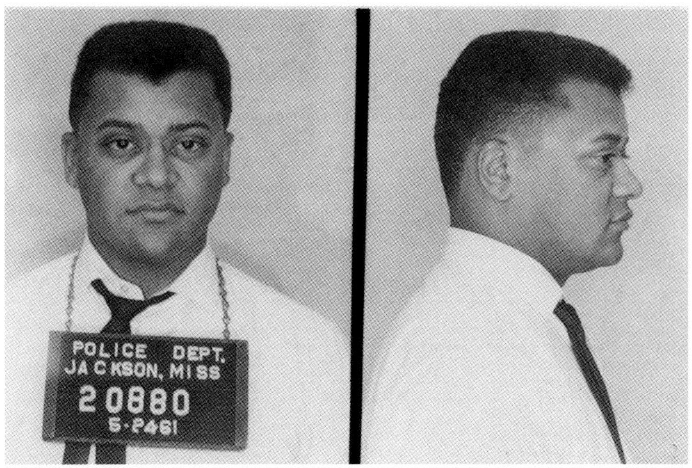

Freedom Ride police mug shot after arrest at Trailways bus station in Jackson, Mississippi, May 24, 1961.

MISSISSIPPI DEPARTMENT OF ARCHIVES AND HISTORY

Freedom Riders before meeting with Attorney General Robert F. Kennedy at the Justice Department, June 16, 1961. Left to right: Chuck McDew, Rev. Wyatt Tee Walker, Diane Nash, Lolis Elie, Reverend Lawson, Gordon Carey, and Charles Sherrod.

ED CLARK, THE LIFE PICTURE COLLECTION, SHUTTERSTOCK

SCLC annual conference, Clark Memorial Methodist Church, Nashville, September 1961, just after the Freedom Ride. The conference theme was "The Deep South in Social Revolution." Reverend Lawson was the keynote speaker.

DON FOSTER, *NASHVILLE BANNER* ARCHIVES, NASHVILLE PUBLIC LIBRARY

Martin Luther King Jr. speaks at rally in a St. Augustine, Florida, church before marching downtown, June 11, 1964. The sign on the podium reads "Dr. Martin Luther King is our leader."

ASSOCIATED PRESS

DO YOU NEED YOUR CAR WASHED, FLOORS CLEANED?

Do you need your car washed — floors cleaned? — If so, call the Youths Centenary Methodist Church, 878 Mississippi Blvd., they are sponsoring a "Quick Car Wash" from 9 a.m. to 3 p.m. Saturday, July 27 and Saturday, Aug. 3. The Youth organization has formed a "work pool" to raise money to send the church's youngsters to camp. Carry your car to 878 Mississippi Blvd. The wash will cost 75-cents. Also, if your lawn needs cutting, floors need waxing, yards need cleaning or windows need washing, call Mrs. Myrtle Donoho at WH 2-2398 or Mrs. Dorothy Lawson at WH 8-6994.

The Lawsons' black Volkswagen bug at Centenary Methodist Church car wash, Memphis, early 1960s.
TRI-STATE DEFENDER

Reverend Lawson, Dorothy Lawson, baby Morris, and John at home, Memphis, 1965.
LAWSON FAMILY PHOTO

Martin Luther King Jr., Stokely Carmichael, Bernard Lee (right), and Reverend Lawson (in profile) during the Meredith March Against Fear, 1966.
ERNEST WITHERS COLLECTION

Union organizer T. O. Jones (second from left) leading sanitation workers on a march downtown at the start of the Memphis sanitation strike, February 1968.
MEMPHIS PRESS-SCIMITAR, UNIVERSITY OF MEMPHIS LIBRARY

Reverend Lawson addresses Memphis city council and mayor during a contentious meeting with sanitation strikers at Ellis Auditorium downtown, February 1968.
UNIVERSITY OF MEMPHIS LIBRARY

Memphis police disrupt a peaceful march downtown with billy clubs and Mace spray, February 23, 1968.

TOM BARBER
MEMPHIS PRESS-SCIMITAR,
UNIVERSITY OF MEMPHIS LIBRARY
(TOP AND MIDDLE)

BOB WILLIAMS
COMMERCIAL APPEAL VIA IMAGN
(BOTTOM)

Degrading editorial cartoon outraged strike supporters the morning after police attacked peaceful sanitation strike marchers, February 24, 1968.

CAL ALLEY, COMMERCIAL APPEAL VIA IMAGN

Hambone cartoons

Left: February 1, 1968. Later that day, two sanitation workers were crushed to death in the trash compressor of a faulty truck, spurring 1,300 Black Memphis sanitation workers to go on strike.

Right: March 29, 1968. The day after Memphis police violence halted the march with Martin Luther King Jr., and officers maced Black sanitation workers inside Clayborn Temple, shot and killed unarmed Black teenager Larry Payne, and harassed and rounded up Black people in unjustified arrests throughout the night.

J. P. ALLEY/CAL ALLEY, COMMERCIAL APPEAL VIA IMAGN

Meeting with fellow ministers at Clayborn Temple during the strike, 1968.
UNIVERSITY OF MEMPHIS LIBRARY

Daily marches with sanitation strikers and supporters down Main Street, carrying early handmade signs with messages for Memphis mayor Henry Loeb, February 26, 1968.
EDWARD J. HARRIS, UNIVERSITY OF MEMPHIS LIBRARY

WILLIAM LEAPTROTT, *MEMPHIS PRESS-SCIMITAR*, UNIVERSITY OF MEMPHIS LIBRARY

Strikers carry stenciled signs, with trash piling up in the early days of the strike.

JIM SHEARIN, *COMMERCIAL APPEAL* VIA IMAGN

Six-year-old John Lawson (left) carries a stenciled "We Are Together" sign during a Saturday picket of downtown stores on Main Street in support of the strike, March 1968. Marching with him is Vasco Smith Jr. (center), the son of Maxine and Vasco Smith Sr. (Maxine was head of the Memphis NAACP and Vasco was head of the Shelby County Democratic Club.) Gerald Fanion Jr., the son of Gerald Fanion Sr. (director of the Shelby County Human Relations Commission) is at right.

ERNEST WITHERS, WITHERS COLLECTION

Strikers on daily march with printed "I Am A Man" signs, as National Guard patrols in tanks beside them.

MEMPHIS PRESS-SCIMITAR, UNIVERSITY OF MEMPHIS LIBRARY

Outside Clayborn Temple, waiting for Dr. King to arrive. Reverend Lawson (left, front of crowd, hand on forehead) is conferring with others. In back half of photo, rows of sanitation strikers are lined up, all carrying "I Am A Man" signs, March 28, 1968. UPI VIA GETTY

Memphis police with gas masks and billy clubs waiting for Dr. King and the marchers to arrive on Main Street, March 28, 1968. UNIVERSITY OF MEMPHIS LIBRARY

Policeman attacking teenagers on Beale Street; Larry Payne is at far right, in the light shirt.
JACK THORNELL, ASSOCIATED PRESS

Bernard Lee (in foreground) clears a path for Dr. King, Ralph Abernathy, and Rev. Henry Logan Starks, as Invader member Roy Turks (right) looks on, during tense march up Beale Street, just before Dr. King left the scene due to the police violence that also spurred Reverend Lawson to turn the marchers around and head back to Clayborn Temple.
SAM MELHORN, COMMERCIAL APPEAL VIA IMAGN

Police in gas masks use tear gas and billy clubs on retreating sanitation strikers and supporters outside and inside of Clayborn Temple, March 28, 1968.
MEMPHIS PRESS-SCIMITAR, UNIVERSITY OF MEMPHIS LIBRARY (LEFT); © COPYRIGHT RICHARD L. COPLEY (RIGHT)

Press conference after march was halted, Rivermont Hotel, downtown Memphis, March 28, 1968.
MEMPHIS PRESS-SCIMITAR, UNIVERSITY OF MEMPHIS LIBRARY

Reverend Lawson, Andrew Young, and lawyers Lucius Burch, Charlie Newman, and Mike Cody at Memphis federal courthouse to argue against the city's injunction, morning of April 4, 1968.
MEMPHIS PRESS-SCIMITAR, UNIVERSITY OF MEMPHIS LIBRARY

Lorraine Motel, inside Dr. King's room, 306, hours after the assassination, April 4, 1968. Left to right: Andrew Young (beside lamp), Bernard Lee, Hosea Williams, Ralph Abernathy, and Samuel "Billy" Kyles (on bed facing camera); Ben Hooks and James Bevel (in chairs next to them); Reverend Lawson (standing); Rev. T. Y. Rogers (in tan raincoat); and James Orange on bed next to Andrew Young (with backs to camera).
HENRY GROSKINSKY, THE LIFE PICTURE COLLECTION, SHUTTERSTOCK

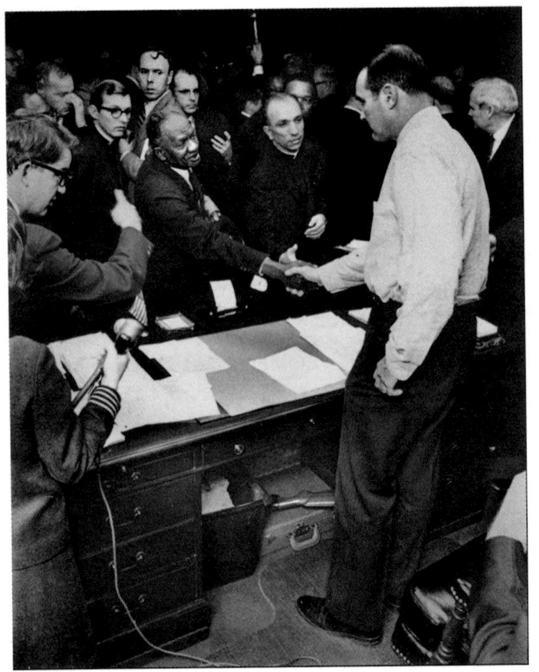

Reverend Lawson chose not to join the interfaith, interracial group of clergy that marched into Mayor Henry Loeb's office on April 5, 1968, to plead with him—unsuccessfully—to end the strike after King's assassination. The shotgun the mayor kept under his desk is visible in this photo. ROBERT WILLIAMS, *COMMERCIAL APPEAL* VIA IMAGN

Reverend Lawson with labor leaders during the Silent March, April 8, 1968: AFSCME's Jerry Wurf and T. O. Jones (second and third from left), United Auto Workers president Walter Reuther (to the right, directly over Reverend Lawson's shoulder). BILL PRESTON, *NASHVILLE TENNESSEAN* VIA IMAGN

Coretta King and family marching with Harry Belafonte (left, behind Reverend Lawson), James Bevel (to the left of Belafonte), and Ralph Abernathy (right of Mrs. King) on April 8, 1968. Andrew Young, Jesse Epps, and Bayard Rustin are farther right. Hosea Williams and H. Ralph Jackson are at right, in the foreground. Not in this photo but nearby Mrs. King during the march are Rosa Parks and Dr. Benjamin Spock. COMMERCIAL APPEAL VIA IMAGN

Silent March, Main Street, April 8, 1968. COMMERCIAL APPEAL VIA IMAGN

Coretta King speaking to the Silent March crowd on a raised platform in front of Memphis City Hall on April 8, 1968. Beside her (left to right) are Reverend Lawson, Harry Belafonte, and Yolanda, Martin III, and Dexter King. COMMERCIAL APPEAL VIA IMAGN

Silent March crowd listens to speakers on the raised platform above them in front of Memphis City Hall, April 8, 1968. ROBERT ABBOTT SENGSTACKE, GETTY IMAGES

The strike marches continued with armed National Guard troops overseeing, 1968.
CHARLIE KELLY, ASSOCIATED PRESS

Clayborn Temple, April 16, 1968, just after sanitation union members vote to accept a settlement agreement that ended the strike after sixty-five days. Left to right: Reverend Lawson, Rev. H. Ralph Jackson, AFSCME president Jerry Wurf, longtime local union leader T. O. Jones (far right, clapping). UPI VIA GETTY IMAGES

Eight-year-old John Lawson (in center of marchers) accompanied his parents to Memphis jail, where Reverend Lawson and others in the procession would serve time for Black Monday organizing and demonstrations, December 1969.
UNIVERSITY OF MEMPHIS LIBRARY

Seth Lawson, 1969.
VANDERBILT LIBRARY

Morris and Seth Lawson, March 1970. VANDERBILT LIBRARY

Co-chairs Reverend Lawson and Jean Fisher (at left of him) with campaign workers at Shirley Chisholm for President headquarters, Memphis 1972. ERNEST WITHERS COLLECTION

In Geneva, Switzerland, at the World Council of Churches conference, mid-1970s. JOHN TAYLOR, WCC VIA VANDERBILT LIBRARY

Anna Sandhu Ray displays ring and marriage certificate after Reverend Lawson performed the wedding ceremony for her and James Earl Ray, at Brushy Mountain State Penitentiary in Petros, Tennessee, October 13, 1978. JOE HOLLOWAY JR., ASSOCIATED PRESS

The Lawson family, late 1970s, Los Angeles: Seth, Reverend and Mrs. Lawson, John, and Morris, with Nandi Lawson the German shepherd.
LAWSON FAMILY PHOTO

Reverend Lawson with Rosa Parks at an ACLU dinner honoring her, December 1984.
HOLMAN UNITED METHODIST CHURCH

Bishop Desmond Tutu with the Lawsons at Holman United Methodist Church, 1990.
HOLMAN UNITED METHODIST CHURCH

At a demonstration against U.S. involvement in Central America, Los Angeles, 1980s. NARESHIMAH OSEI, VANDERBILT LIBRARY

Justice for Janitors march. SEIU local 399 leader Jim Zellers is talking with Reverend Lawson, Peter Olney, International Longshore and Warehouse Union (ILWU) leader (far left, in tie), early 1990s. SEIU

HERE Local 11 hotel workers dramatize their daily work with women making beds at a downtown Los Angeles intersection, 1993. Reverend Lawson was among those in the sit-in circle. After this photo was taken, police arrested the workers and supporters, including Reverend Lawson. UCLA LIBRARY

On the set of Lawson Live *with Bonnie Boswell and Jesse Jackson, 1996.* VANDERBILT LIBRARY

Delores Huerta, Rabbi Steven Jacobs, Reverend Lawson, and Rev. Jesse Jackson celebrating HERE Local 11's new contract with the University of Southern California, October 5, 1999.
LAWSON FAMILY PHOTO

Reverend Lawson, María Elena Durazo, and Kent Wong during class at UCLA, 2013.
SALVADOR "POCHO" SANCHEZ-STRAWBRIDGE, UCLA LABOR CENTER

Reverend Lawson, Dolores Huerta, and Kent Wong during a graduate seminar at UCLA, May 8, 2013. SALVADOR "POCHO" SANCHEZ-STRAWBRIDGE, UCLA LABOR CENTER

Representative John Lewis, Reverend Lawson, and John Lawson at Lewis's Washington, DC, office, 2018. KAREN HAYES, UBUNTU MOTION PICTURES

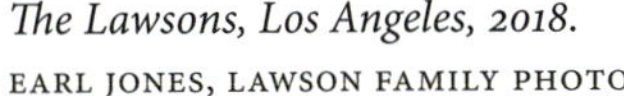

The Lawsons, Los Angeles, 2018. EARL JONES, LAWSON FAMILY PHOTO

Nancy Pelosi, John Lewis, and Reverend Lawson at the last Bloody Sunday commemoration that John Lewis attended before his death, Edmond Pettus Bridge, Selma, Alabama, March 2020. KENT WONG

Reverend Lawson reunites with Minnijean Brown-Trickey of the Little Rock Nine, Brown Chapel, Selma, March 2020. KENT WONG

Reverend Lawson and Senator Kamala Harris at Lannie's Bar-B-Q Spot, Selma, March 2020. KENT WONG

Opening of the UCLA James Lawson Jr. Worker Justice Center, 2021.
REED HUTCHINSON, UCLA LABOR CENTER

At Justice Center opening with María Elena Durazo. LAWSON FAMILY PHOTOS

Unite HERE Local 11 demonstration, Los Angeles, February 11, 2022.
GENARO MOLINA, GETTY IMAGES

With Tennessee Rep. Justin Jones—Vanderbilt Divinity graduate and one of the Tennessee Three—with Reps. Justin Pearson and Gloria Johnson—whom opposition colleagues temporarily forced from legislature, Nashville, 2023.
KAREN HAYES, UBUNTU MOTION PICTURES

Reverend Lawson speaking in support of hiring undocumented students in the University of California system on May 17, 2023—the last demonstration he attended. JAY L. CLENDENIN, *LOS ANGELES TIMES* VIA GETTY IMAGES

Christmas at Holman United Methodist Church, 2023. Surrounding Reverend and Mrs. Lawson are (from left) John Lawson, Devin Lawson, Cima Baker Lawson, Raven Lawson, James Charles Lawson, and Morris Lawson. LAWSON FAMILY PHOTO

crophone and spoke to the council about the union's commitment and the implications from some council members that the union had roped the men into a work stoppage. "There has been some attempt here today to distinguish between the union and the men," he said. "If we are to have peace and tranquility and to end this strike, you've got to understand that the men are the union and the union is the men."

He continued: "This strike can only go on so long as these men, these residents and workers for the city of Memphis, want it to go on. But I assure you of one thing, on behalf of the 375,000 members of our international union, that so long as they want help and they want support, by God, they're gonna get that help and that support." His voice rose as he spoke, and he pointed his finger at the council members. By the end, he was wagging his finger at them. Then he stepped away from the microphone, and every striker and supporter in the chamber erupted into loud and enthusiastic cheering and applause.

At around two-thirty P.M., Davis adjourned his subcommittee. We had decided to stay in place until we got agreements from the council. Our presence had turned into a sit-in at city hall, and we were willing to stay overnight if necessary.

Then Rev. Ezekiel Bell spoke. He mentioned the cotton and steamboat symbols on the city of Memphis seal, which hung prominently at the center of the council chamber. He said the steamboat had brought Black people down the river, and the cotton boll was symbolic of Black people having picked all that cotton during slavery—and yet many of them were still living in deep poverty. He talked of tearing down that seal.

For the rest of the afternoon, we negotiated with the council members behind the scenes as the sit-in continued. More people spoke to the crowd. The singing continued, with some verses that people made up.

We're waiting for the council
We shall not be moved.
We're waiting for the mayor
We shall not be moved.

I felt that Fred Davis made a mistake that day. When thirteen hundred Black workers are demanding justice, a Black politician can't sit in a council meeting and pretend that other Black people are not really representing the wishes of the workers. By doing that, he immediately identified himself with the white power structure, and not with the workers. He was operating under an old order, playing to the white politicians. He was being a city councilman first, a Black man second, and someone concerned for the plight of these workers third. But a main objective of the Black revolution and movement happening in the 1950s and 1960s was to upend that old form of politics. A Black politician couldn't be a cog in the old machinery. He had to be responsible to the needs of his own people, and the needs of his people living in poverty first of all. His real strength was not going to come from his ability to manipulate his constituents into accepting the old ways. His real power would materialize if he could be seen as the one who could get thirteen hundred folks down to the city auditorium. That's when the council was going to respect his strength.

Then, if his white colleagues attacked him, saying he was too sympathetic, let them. Instead, his white colleagues and the white press came to his defense, claiming that Black folks were not treating him right. That was the kiss of death in the Black community. Another Black councilman, J. O. Patterson, saw this clearly. That was why he came to almost every march and every mass meeting. He was out in the community all the time during the strike.

A few of us went back and forth with Fred behind the scenes that afternoon. We tried to make him understand why we were so rough with him. It wasn't anything personal, just simply that he had to decide who he was serving. The people of South Memphis had elected him, and they were Black, and some of them were sanitation workers.

At about five-thirty P.M., the subcommittee announced what it would recommend to the full council the next day: recognition of the union and a union dues checkoff—subtracting union dues from workers' paychecks. The subcommittee had gotten the full city council to agree to a meeting the next afternoon to hear the subcommittee members' recommendations, which was one of the things we were demanding. We had told them very clearly that we would not leave city hall until we had heard what they were going to recommend, and until we knew the city council would meet the next day to hear a full report from the subcommittee. Early Thursday evening, we were persuaded that the city council would meet the next day and that the subcommittee's report would be discussed. So, we decided to leave our sit-in.

By the time we left, Fred Davis was shaken, but he was in accord with us. The terms the subcommittee agreed to with the union and the rest of us who were representing the community were satisfactory for a settlement. The strike could end the following day if the city agreed to the recommendations.

But when we woke up the next morning to an editorial cartoon in *The Commercial Appeal,* we should have known the day would not go as we had envisioned when we had left the meeting the night before.

The cartoonist had drawn a rough, all-black silhouette of a large Black man wearing a hat and squatting on top of a metal garbage can with "CITY HALL SIT-IN" written on its side. The drawing insultingly evoked the persona of strike leader T. O. Jones. He was hunched forward, with his hands between his legs supporting his weight on the lid of the can. Strewn all around him were piles of garbage and overturned trash cans. Fumes were depicted rising up from the garbage and forming into letters, hovering in an arch over the man's head and spelling out the words "THREAT OF ANARCHY" in all capital letters. The headline above the cartoon read, "Beyond the Bounds of Tolerance."

The cartoonist was Cal Alley. He drew editorial cartoons for the morning paper, following in the steps of his father, who had held the job before him. But Cal Alley also carried on another repugnant family legacy. His father, J. P. Alley, had created a syndicated cartoon called *Hambone's Meditations,* which had been running consistently in *The Commercial Appeal* since 1916. It was wildly popular among white Memphians, and later among white people all across the country. Book collections of *Hambone's Meditations* cartoons were published. And when Cal Alley's father died, in 1934, he and his brother and their mother felt compelled to keep the racially insulting cartoon alive. So they began to create the panels themselves, without removing J. P. Alley's name, as a tribute to the beloved cartoon's original creator. The editor in chief of *The Commercial Appeal* in 1968, Frank Ahlgren, had been at the paper since the 1930s and was married to Elizabeth Alley—J. P. Alley's daughter and Cal Alley's sister.

Their Hambone was the quintessential, Jim Crow–era, demeaning caricature of a Black man. He was based on a real person, a formerly enslaved man who cleaned J. P. Alley's office when he worked in Greenwood, Mississippi. The story goes that Alley named the character Hambone because the first time he saw the man who cleaned his office the man was coming up the stairs chewing on a ham bone. White people who loved Hambone so dearly thought the portrayal was gentle and affectionate toward Black people. Hambone originally appeared, most days, in a single panel at the bottom right corner on the front page of the paper. Sometime before 1968, the paper moved the cartoon to the front page of the second section of the paper. Hambone would speak corny, folksy witticisms in a degrading dialect created by a white man, embodying the guileless, impotent, infantilized idea of Black people that most white people preferred to see, hear, and believe.

For example, on the day Mr. Cole and Mr. Walker were crushed to death in the sanitation truck, that morning's *Hambone's Mediations* panel had portrayed the familiar older, balding Black man in a white shirt with the sleeves rolled up, an oversized vest, loose-fitting striped pants, and big clownlike shoes. He also had a prominent nose and exaggerated lips. He was sitting on a stair stoop holding a corncob pipe, smiling, and saying, "HIT'S A GOOD THING DE LAWD DO LIF' UP DE MEEK, CA'SE SHO' AIN' NOBODY ELSE GWINE DO IT!!"

Hambone didn't appear in the paper the day after our sit-in. But Cal Alley's ugly editorial cartoon on the morning of Friday, February 23, was so large it took up more space than the lead editorial *The Commercial Appeal* ran beside it. In sync with the cartoon, the editorial writers berated the strikers and most of us who supported them—Black men who many readers no doubt perceived as very similar to Hambone himself.

> Memphis garbage strikers have turned an illegal walkout into anarchy and Mayor Henry Loeb is exactly right when he says, "We can't submit to this sort of thing!"
>
> The workers' conduct in taking over the City Council chamber at City Hall yesterday could widen the gulf between municipal government and the strikers. Threats were made, and there was a clear attempt to create fear in the public mind that violence might occur unless the administrative branch surrenders to union demands.
>
> . . . The City Council is the legislative branch of our government and the mayor is the administrative head, the man who must ultimately make the decisions in this strike.
>
> He is faced with an illegal strike, is representing the public, and through him the public is being pushed by scarcely veiled threats of "trouble" for Memphis. Mr. Loeb's stand is that we will maintain law

> and order and proceed through this situation in a lawful manner, and that is what this community wants.
>
> When the council deals with the problem today it should not be intimidated or stampeded into imprudent decisions by yesterday's belligerent show of force.

A short news brief a few pages later, headlined "Loeb Stand Backed," reported that the Memphis and Shelby County Young Republicans were backing what they called the mayor's "firm and fair stand" in the strike. A spokesman for the group said, "It is extremely unfortunate that the sanitation department workers have been used to their own detriment and for the union's purposes." The paper reported that the group had "passed a resolution calling on strike leaders to 'cease their unreasonable demands' and end the strike." The truth was beyond the imagination of those young people: that the men had had enough agency to go on strike of their own accord, and that the union had joined them hastily and only at the men's request.

Later that morning, the city council met in a closed executive committee meeting. That afternoon, a group of us—T. O. Jones, Jesse Epps, Jerry Wurf, Bill Lucy, Ezekiel Bell, Harold Middlebrook, and a few others—went to city hall for the public council meeting we had agreed to the night before. But police officers were at the doors, which were locked. They made it very clear that we were not allowed into the council chambers. The policemen were not smiling when they told us the meeting had been moved to the city auditorium. That set a different mood among us right away.

When we got to the auditorium, we were expecting to hear the public works subcommittee's report and to take part in a discussion afterward. We thought this might bring about the end of the strike. Instead, the head of the city council announced that they had rejected the subcommittee's recommendations during the closed executive session that morning. They did not ask for any presentations from any of us. We were not allowed to speak at all. The council chair read the resolution, the terms of which did not include a written contract with the union or a dues checkoff. Effectively, they would still not recognize AFSCME as the strikers' union negotiator. Further, the resolution said that Mayor Loeb, and not the council, was the only official with the authority to make decisions regarding the strike and the workers. The council approved the resolution by a vote of nine to four. All three Black councilmen voted against it, along with one right-wing white councilman who thought the resolution didn't go far enough in rebuking the union and the strikers.

Undoubtedly, after we left the subcommittee on Thursday evening, having agreed on the terms in the subcommittee's recommendations, Loeb took a look at them and went to work on the city council members behind the scenes. He convinced the majority of them to side with him against the union.

Fairly quickly after the new resolution was read to the men, the meeting was adjourned. T. O. Jones tried to get up and speak to the strikers as the council members were leaving. But the microphones had all been cut off and the city hall workers had been ordered not to turn them on again. So Jones and others walked up onto the stage to speak to the men without microphones. AFSCME's Jesse Epps, State Representative A. W. Willis, and the Memphis NAACP's Vasco Smith, as well as a few ministers, spoke about how disastrous and outrageous the city council's action was, calling it a betrayal of the promise they had made the night before to hear us out at their Friday meeting. About thirty minutes into the talking without microphones, all the lights in the auditorium were turned off, and we were told we had to leave or be arrested.

Some of us who were advocates and spokespeople decided to continue our meeting at Mason Temple, which was a couple of miles away. We were prepared to walk there in an orderly march that would start south down Main Street.

We instructed people to head outside, where we filled up the intersection outside Ellis Auditorium. Police officers were standing across the street, lined up with their arms intertwined and locked at the elbows to prevent anybody from marching through their ranks. They had clubs and guns. They stood in front of us saying, "You can't march."

I went right up to the front of the group and said to the police officers, "You know, this is not your fight. We are not opposing you. On the contrary. If this group of men is recognized, and their wages are increased, your wages will be increased, too. This is for all city workers. So don't let yourselves be used as tools." And I told some of the younger officers to relax. I said, "We are orderly, and things are under control. You don't have to be too harsh." I was trying to say to them, "Let's be human. We can get along. We are going to march downtown. It's going to be peaceful, so don't get excited about it."

A few of us had called the director of fire and police, Frank Holloman, and told him we had been shut out of the auditorium and the city council chambers. We had asked his permission for our large group of hundreds of workers to march down Main Street. We told Holloman we would walk without throwing stones or any other violence. Holloman gave us the go-ahead. He said we could march if we kept it peaceful.

At one point before we got underway, some officers began to jostle our men. Jerry Wurf, the AFSCME president, spoke to the commander, saying, "We just want to get them to a hall. . . . They've been treated very badly this afternoon and they are just upset. Just help us keep it peaceful." Once the police got the word from Holloman to allow our march, they backed off and let us make our way from the auditorium.

The march began with a festive spirit of shared purpose and resolve. We passed city hall and kept marching. But I was noticing police cars beginning to fan out from the side streets. Every car I saw had four or five officers in it. All of them were white. Their cars rolled up alongside us on the half of the street we weren't allowed to use. Some cops drove their cars right along the middle line of the street, close to the edge of where we were marching peacefully, causing people to have to move sideways into the crowd. The police proceeded to try to annoy us by veering just over the line, grazing people at the ends of the rows. It was clear they were deliberately trying to get some of the workers to put their hands on the cars. I tried to stop the police cars from continuing to push in on the marchers.

Then I went up and down the ranks, telling people, "Don't touch the police cars. Get away from them. They are trying to get you to touch them so they can attack you." A group of fellows directly behind me stopped and said to officers in a police car, "Get your car back and away from us." So I went over and said to the men, "Let's keep marching—they're trying to provoke us and let's not let them."

By the time we got to the big downtown department store called Goldsmith's, I was up ahead and didn't see what happened. But I heard later that just behind us, near Goldsmith's, a police car had run over the foot of one of our marchers, a woman named Gladys Carpenter. When the police cars had begun edging over the line and pushing the marchers toward the sidewalk, she had stepped to the end of a row to act as a buffer for the men, thinking an officer would never graze his car against a woman. But one did. She called out, saying the police had run over her foot. That's when the men reacted, trying to get the car off this Black woman's foot. Some of the men ran to her aid and lifted the car away from her foot, then put it right back down. That was all it took. The police officers in the car jumped out.

The car that ran over her foot was about two ranks behind me. I immediately went back to that car. I had just put my hand on it and on the nearest sanitation worker, to find out what the trouble was, when an officer hit me with Mace, spraying it on the side of my head. Then, lo and behold, from everywhere, nearby police officers poured out of their cars, wielding billy clubs and cans of Mace. I had seen the clubs, but I had not anticipated the Mace cans. And when the officers emerged from their cars, they all began to spray the caustic chemicals directly in marchers' faces up and down the rows. Farther up the line, the police were on the street or standing on their squad cars, spraying cans of Mace on everybody.

A cry went up in the crowd that they had this spray. That's when we realized the police had been trying to break us up all along. Officers ran after us, spraying as many people as they could in the face, calling us all kinds of names as they worked. And I saw police officers beating some of the men behind me with their billy clubs. It was an all-white police force attacking any Black people nearby—whether they were fellow city workers who had jobs in the sanitation department, or a Black clergy member wearing his clerical collar, or Black women marching in support of the strike. P. J. Ciampa of AFSCME was thoroughly maced, too—the only white person I saw getting sprayed. The police seemed to know who the leaders of the strike were, and they were targeting us along with the workers and their community supporters.

That first spray of Mace hit me fully on the side of my face, and then I turned and got another dose of it on the other side. It stung so badly I had to steer myself off toward the curb. I was trying to blink the stuff out of my eyes. I could still see well enough to be able to turn back, and when I did, I got a faceful of it. So I got three doses of Mace.

I never let the spray incapacitate me. My glasses stopped some of it, and the liquid rolled down my face and neck, and into my hair at the sides of my head. But some of it got into my eyes. I never closed my eyes, and I never touched the stuff in my eyes. Instead, I kept blinking rapidly to try to get the tears going. I pulled out a handkerchief and dabbed at the liquid on my face and neck.

I had never been sprayed with Mace before—hardly anyone in the country had. It was a relatively new police tool used for crowd control. In the Birmingham campaign and in the St. Augustine campaign and almost every campaign before Memphis, the cops had used tear gas, which I had experienced. They would throw it into a crowd inside a device kind of like a hand grenade. But if you held something over your face, most of the time you could keep functioning. You couldn't do that with Mace. It would blind you, temporarily. Mace stopped you from operating. It was in a little can that a police officer could have in his pack and spray directly in your face.

We were all trying to resist the attack. I tried to speak to the officers, but they were not hearing anyone in the frenzy they were creating. A lot of people fled the scene. The Mace broke up the march decisively, and there were only a few of us left on the sidewalk in front of Goldsmith's when the police violence stopped. Luckily, because I had never gotten blinded, I could keep walking, knowing where I was going. Some fifty or sixty of us rallied and continued to walk on to Mason Temple. We walked slowly, in twos and threes along the sidewalk, from Goldsmith's down Main Street to Beale Street, and down Beale to Danny Thomas Boulevard, over to Crump Boulevard, and on to Mason Temple.

The police walked along beside us.

It had become clear for the first time, during the city council hearing and then the meeting at the auditorium that afternoon, and with the police violence we encountered as we peacefully marched, that the dimensions of the sanitation strike went beyond the simple question of unionism in Memphis. Many of us had been saying from the very beginning that racism was part of the picture, as well as the poverty that grows out of racism in America. But our point was obvious after the city's actions during those two days.

When we finally arrived at Mason Temple, we called the fire and police director, Frank Holloman, and reported how the police taunted us and tried to goad us into being violent, and then they attacked us with cans of Mace. He said he had the field commanders on the phones the whole time, and they reported stone throwing and breaking of windows. I said none of that was done by the marchers. And I did not see anyone throwing any stones. I'm not sure Holloman knew that the field commanders let officers attack all of us.

We reconvened our meeting at Mason Temple. Community members and those of us who were advocates and spokespeople joined together in consensus that the Black community should organize and get behind this strike. Most of the folk there knew the strike was essential to begin shaking up the system of poverty imposed on Black people in Memphis. I did not take the stage during the meeting. I sat in the audience. I did hear them put my name on the list of a strategy committee. But I did not speak.

Pretty soon, I went home to Dorothy and the boys. The Mace still stung, and it had reddened parts of my face around my ears. Dorothy helped me take care of it. For days I had a severe rash all along my face, around my eyes, and into my ears. I eventually had to go to a doctor because of it, and he gave me some medicine to help heal it. Quite definitely the Mace was a poison. I think we made a real mistake in not suing the city and the police department, given all the cases of people who had rashes and other reactions from the copious spraying at that march.

At home that Friday night, I got a call from Rev. Harold Middlebrook, a young minister and ardent strike supporter. He said that after I left the meeting at Mason Temple, the group had unanimously elected me to be the chairman of the strategy committee they had formed that night in support of the strike. Harold told me they decided it made sense to select someone as chair who had hands-on experience in the movement. He said my reputation as an activist and a strategist in Nashville, on the Freedom Ride, in Birmingham and St. Augustine, and in countless other places made me their choice.

It was a big responsibility. Dorothy and I talked it over. We saw this as another campaign where we would be taking on an entire city. But unlike in Nashville, I had done it before and knew more about what worked and what didn't. And I knew whom to call when we needed support. So, Dorothy and I agreed it was another role I should embrace. We knew that, whatever may come, this was a time in our lives when we had to get involved, take some hits, and keep going.

I got the names of the other strategy committee members from Vasco Smith. He and his wife, Maxine, were on the committee, along with Rev. Harold Middlebrook, Rev. Henry Starks, Rev. H. Ralph Jackson, Rev. Malcolm Blackburn, T. O. Jones, and Jesse Epps of AFSCME. Vasco also told me that telegrams had been sent out that night to all the Black preachers in Memphis, inviting them to meet on Saturday afternoon and agree on what we would all say at our pulpits the next day.

The morning newspaper's front-page headline the day after the Friday macing march said, "Angry Sanitation Workers Clash Briefly with Police While Marching Downtown."

> Striking sanitation workers, marching down Main Street in an angry mood after a City Council session yesterday, turned on their escorting police officers near Main and Gayoso and began rocking a police emergency squad station wagon with five officers inside.
>
> Other police on the scene, using the new riot gas Mace and night sticks, quickly restored order as the 900 marchers scattered into Main Street stores.

The newspaper reporters did not say how many people got maced that day. Instead, they reported on people they saw as unruly sanitation workers who seemingly without provocation began to rock one of the cars, and how the police who were "escorting" us were merely doing some crowd control with their Mace cans.

> About 3:50 p.m. as the marchers reached the front of Goldsmith's . . . the strikers . . . suddenly began rocking the car violently.
>
> In seconds, the officers were out of their cars and on top of them, squirting Mace cans. Other officers waded into the crowd . . . with night sticks.
>
> . . . Most of the marchers were pushed onto the sidewalk in front of Goldsmith's and against plate glass show windows. The windows seemed to ripple with the pressure of the crowd, but none broke.
>
> Chief Bartholomew immediately accused T. O. Jones, a heavyset Negro, president of Local 1733 . . . who is leading the local strike, as the one who started rocking the police car.

Although the article mentioned the police car, it never gave an explanation for what might have caused the men to touch the car in the first place. Another description in the same article spoke of the marchers before the police violence started.

> The marchers did not appear to be in an ugly mood. They called out to Negroes on the sidewalk to join them and there was a good deal of joshing back and forth.
>
> The mood changed quickly as the police car started rocking.

> Officers started using the Mace quickly, many of them jumping onto the hoods and roofs of police cars and spraying the substance from small cans—they look like regular aerosol spray cans.
>
> . . . A moment later . . . officers started shouting, "Mace, Mace. . . ."
>
> P. J. Ciampa, the labor leader whose fiery arguments with Mayor Loeb were a feature of the first days of the strike, received a sample of the Mace from officers who saw him running south from the fracas.
>
> Philip A. Perel, who had just returned from the City Council session, watched from the window of his store, Perel and Lowenstein's, across the street from the action.
>
> "This is outrageous. They ought to put the whole bunch in jail."

Mr. Perel was a wealthy white businessman and member of the city council who opposed the strikers throughout, always voting with Mayor Loeb.

The paper went on to describe the aftermath of the police violence, but did not attribute it to the police. They attributed it to the sanitation workers. Police arrested six more men at the scene and charged them all with "night riding." That charge was both cynical and ironic. We were simply marching from one place to another and had gotten permission from the city to do so. The police and the newspapers put forth the idea that our peaceful march was violent. That narrative not only confirmed their long-held fears but justified their own violence in word and deed. We understood the motive. Night riders, however, were the white vigilantes who terrorized Black people just after the Civil War, and later in Black neighborhoods during the Jim Crow era. Many of the sanitation workers had experienced their terror in the streets of Memphis. In fact, the original night riders were terrorists against Black people. So night riding was not something Black people did.

Around six-thirty that evening, the police issued a warrant for the arrest of T. O. Jones, also on charges of night riding. The paper portrayed him as the ringleader in the rocking of the police car. The fire and police director, Frank Holloman, commented in the paper about the charges:

> "We were generous enough and eager to see them make their march peacefully, but the disturbance was started by Jones when he attempted to inflame the crowd into turning over a squad car."

The squad car was not turned over. The car had simply been lifted off Gladys Carpenter's foot. The fact that the police director implied that it had been turned over indicates the lie that had been spread among the officers. The article included two sentences near the end with the truth of what happened to her but dismissed it immediately, and erased Gladys Carpenter's existence in the process.

> Last night, union leaders claimed they rocked the police car because it had run over the toes of a Negro woman. However, persons at the scene said they saw no woman complaining at the time.

The afternoon paper that day joined in, running an editorial chastising the men and, especially, the union for rejecting the Friday afternoon city council resolution. It showed yet again how the idea that the men were being controlled by the union was taking hold among those who sided with Mayor Loeb. The paper spoke of "widespread sympathy" for the men in the community. But sympathy, like the charity that sometimes accompanied it, was the most that Black men living in poverty could expect. True equality and free agency for Black people were beyond the moral imaginations of most in the white community. In fact, the editorial warned the men that warm sentiments toward them among whites could fade fast: "The workers should take heed, lest they lose this sympathy. They should take advantage of it—not abuse it."

That same day, Saturday, February 24, an injunction was handed down preventing strike activity by local and national unions, specifically naming officials as well as many of the sanitation workers who were local union members named in the 1966 injunction, some of whom were also part of the original thirty-three men who had been fired for organizing union activities in 1963.

In 1968, it was an attempt to stop the strike and any demonstrations. We had faced many an injunction before in other campaigns around the South. We would face this one without flinching.

The local union had not come up with an organized strategy for continuing the strike. It was much more spontaneous when they started. Initially, they simply tried to bring workers into the union and unify them. With our community backing, their core group of supporters expanded and we were able to put together larger public demonstrations.

Early that Saturday morning, the strategy committee met downtown at the AME Minimum Salary Building, next door to Clayborn Temple AME Church. The building name came from the AME Church's focus on economic equality and fair wages for all. The strategy committee members were in accord on the next steps. Clearly, there was going to be an economic boycott of the downtown area, with daily marches and evening mass meetings at various churches around town. Given the coverage since the strike began, we also decided to call for a boycott of the two major newspapers.

Around one o'clock that afternoon, about 150 Black preachers showed up to hear the strategy committee plan. The ministers overwhelmingly endorsed everything we presented, and agreed that each would go to their pulpits the next morning and announce that they were supporting the strike and they expected their congregations to support it in every way, too. They would tell their church members to join a citywide economic boycott and to attend mass meetings, which would begin Monday night. And they began to take offerings to contribute to a relief fund for the strikers and their families. We also urged the ministers to attend the daily meetings of the workers when they could and to speak to the workers, giving their spiritual support and encouragement as the strike continued. We decided to call our group Community on the Move for Equality (COME) and would act as one under that name.

Late that Saturday afternoon, we held a press conference to announce COME and our support of the strike and to ask others in the community who supported the men to come together with us. I presented our objectives in front of local television cameras:

> The way in which these men have been treated thus far has galvanized Negroes and people of goodwill to their support. And we are moving from this moment . . . to see to it that their effort will not fail. But that instead, we will get more decency, more justice, more jobs for the poor people and for the Negroes who need them in Memphis.
>
> On Thursday and Friday of this past week, there were hundreds of us in the city hall chambers and in the march . . . yesterday—ministers as well as sanitation workers and other community people and leaders representing all walks of life—who were in the city hall and on the march because we were prepared then to go to jail if necessary.

I laid out five goals we had set for our campaign in Memphis that day:

1. Insist the city meet the fair demands of the workers.
2. Urge businesses and the city government to hire Black people for better and more important jobs.
3. Ask supporters to boycott all branch stores downtown, businesses owned by city councilmen, and businesses with the name Loeb on them.
4. Call on supporters to cancel subscriptions to the two daily papers, "until such time as Hambone illustrations and latent racism come out of the editorial pages, and Negroes are treated as people before God and before man."
5. We will hold night mass meetings at Clayborn Temple and begin demonstrations and marches.

The newspapers and city government officials generally tried to frame the strike as solely a labor issue. But I made it clear at the press conference that we saw the labor issue as a symptom of the larger problem of racial injustice.

> No matter how you dress it up in terms of whether or not a union can organize, it's still racism. For at the heart of racism is the idea that a man is not a man, that a person is not a person. And so the racism has been obvious, it seems to me, from the very beginning of this whole matter.

I spent the rest of the weekend finalizing the membership of the strategy committee. It included activists, ministers, and others from the community. One of the first people I invited to join was Charles Cabbage. He led the Invaders, the group of young Black activists he had formed with Coby Smith. I asked him to come help us organize among the young people, a similar thing I had asked of him and Coby when they were working with MAP-South. Most of the people on the strategy committee were male; one exception was Maxine Smith, executive director of the NAACP at the time.

Immediately, we began mobilizing community support for the strikers. The committee made plans to start the boycott downtown on Monday, along with a march through downtown. And we planned Monday's mass meeting at Clayborn Temple. One of the other clergymen on the committee became the chair for the subcommittee that planned the future mass meetings.

Many of the sanitation workers and many of their wives and families would come together with the community at those mass meetings for information and motivation. We would lay out the workers' issues, and what we had to do. We would talk about the need for negotiations with the city, which the city had refused.

The Memphis sanitation strike became the first big campaign in the South centered around working people. It became the first major strike that brought together workers, the union, and the Black community to dismantle the wrongs of enforced poverty, mistreatment of workers, and racism. And it proclaimed itself as a nonviolent strike. In fact, strikes were always a time-tested, effective, nonviolent means of seeking justice.

On Monday, February 26, at nine A.M., we gathered at Clayborn Temple for our first picket march. A few of us spoke, and then I talked about the rules of the march and presented some well-tested points, honed through all the marches I had been on, such as "Be peaceful and nonviolent. Ignore hecklers—pay them no attention." I instructed the marchers about what to do if they got arrested. "You do not have to say anything," I explained, "except to give your name, address and your age. You are entitled to ask for a lawyer. You are entitled to make a phone call. . . . A number of people—lawyers and your friends—will be on the outside working for you."

We set a pattern that week with a briefing session before we marched. I always talked during the briefing. We made announcements from the strategy committee and the leadership. Each day, different ministers from around the city would offer some essential spiritual inspiration. And then, Monday through Friday during the strike, the marchers would go out.

I made a point to walk with them every day. I would be upset if for some reason I wasn't able to join the men and their supporters on their daily march. We didn't talk much during the marches, because that would have interfered with the discipline. According to rules we'd worked out with police director Holloman when a few of us had met with him on that first Sunday night, we almost always marched single file on the sidewalk. We usually left the church and went up Beale Street to Main and north on Main to city hall. I think most days we simply walked around city hall and then headed back the same way to Clayborn Temple.

Some three hundred people joined that first morning march on Monday, February 26. We left Clayborn Temple around ten. There was no violence from the police or anyone else. I had asked Holloman in our meeting the day before to contact me before they made any moves to disperse our marches, so we could work together to keep it peaceful. We were exercising our First Amendment rights to protest. In the afternoon on Monday, we held another equally nonviolent march, with about 150 people taking the same route we did in the morning. Eventually, the afternoon marches were for the young people, timed for them to join after school.

The Memphis sanitation strikers were classic examples of Black men of dignity and purpose who had worked hard all their lives. Many were men of faith who knew inside their hearts, souls, and minds that they could stand and move peacefully together in a strike. I was not surprised by these men. My brother-in-law Bob Floyd, my sister Dorothy's husband, had come back from World War II and worked in steel plants in Ohio and Pennsylvania. Bob was such a good man. He had told me how the management gave the Black men the most dangerous work, closest to the furnaces, in Massillon, Canton, and Philadelphia. Through him, and through these men and many others, I repeatedly saw how the economic order was unjust and unfair to millions of Black workers.

In our first weeks of marching in Memphis, we held handmade signs. I wrote my own raggedy sign that said, "Only God Is King, Henry." I carried it every day during the first few weeks. Then I carried another handwritten sign that said, "King Henry, We Will Not Turn Back." I was delighted to start off my day marching. I knew the walk itself made me more muscular. I went steadily and joyfully and did not ever get tired. The march was part of the discipline that helped us persevere and ensure that the strike continued.

From day one of the strike, Autry Parker, the social worker and my parishioner who was my co-founder and the executive director at MAP-South, began establishing a relief program for the workers. We addressed how the men would keep their families fed and pay their bills throughout the strike. Because MAP-South was already set up and organized in the community, the union took us very seriously. When representatives from

AFSCME International came in to support the local union, they used the MAP-South infrastructure already in place to reach people who needed help. We had a fairly sizable volunteer base in Memphis, as well as paid block workers and other employees who could focus on relief work. We even had four social workers on staff by that time. Those neighborhoods in South Memphis where we had worked for a few years were where many of the strikers and their families lived too. I am fairly sure that at least some of the kids we found suffering from malnutrition in 1967 were children of sanitation workers. AFSCME organized the relief coming in from other places. And they administered the welfare fund that enabled them to support their union workers in different parts of the country who had to go on strike.

Early on in the strike, MAP-South secured use of an office at First Presbyterian Church, in downtown Memphis, which became what the union called the welfare office for the strikers. The men and their wives could come in and ask for what they needed. We were connecting with the workers daily. We used the church basement to store food and diapers and other necessities. And because the church was centrally located and on the daily march route, and the marches ran five days a week, it became a hub for giving help and keeping track of it.

By the end of February we had a well-organized effort that helped workers with their mortgages, and with food, medicine, and rent. Lots of congregations across the Black community raised money through special offerings every Sunday for the workers, and that money came to us and the union and we gave it to the men. I led Centenary in raising money for the strike and taking food to First Presbyterian. Food and help were also set up at Clayborn Temple, where we left for our marches each weekday, and at other strategically located churches around the city.

As the strike progressed, the strategy committee would meet at the Sheraton-Peabody Hotel, in downtown Memphis, for breakfast around seven each weekday. We were in a regular breakfast room right off the lobby. Waiters brought us our food, and all of the waiters were white. We worked hand in hand with the international union and with the local union leadership to strategize jointly and promote the strike. The regional man for AFSCME, Joe Paisley, was white. And Jerry Wurf was a faithful participant. When he was in town, he was always at that morning meeting.

Bill Lucy also attended the strategy meetings whenever he was in town. Bill was a thoughtful, sophisticated man, committed to unionization and to the AFSCME union. I met him when he came in during the first week of the strike as one of the union staff people who helped move the strike along. I would describe Bill as a fellow sojourner. I was pleased with all the international union staffers: Bill Lucy, Jesse Epps, and Jerry Wurf.

I was especially close with Jerry. We became intellectual and spiritual companions. In fact, Jerry Wurf took up a fight against the war in Vietnam, after our talks during the strike. I did not disengage from the antiwar effort during the strike. In fact, our criticisms of the war paralleled our criticisms of the city government. Poverty wages, unsanitary conditions, and sheer racism were all part of the Vietnam War. Those connections that Martin Luther King and I, as well as many other people, saw between Vietnam and the circumstances of the working poor in America were what Jerry Wurf and I talked about at the dinner table or the breakfast table from time to time.

My role in the Memphis strike, and Martin's role in the Poor People's Campaign, which he was planning for that year, were ones that pastors had rarely taken on—being identified with working people and, in Memphis, with working people who went on strike. The propaganda in the United States against unions was all negative. But in this strike, I was the chairman of the strategy committee—a Methodist minister and a well-known practitioner of nonviolence. I talked about it from my pulpit, because my congregations have always wanted me to talk about what was happening in the world around us. They wanted to be involved and aware. At a church conference once, I overheard a woman from my Memphis congregation saying, "Oh, that isn't new. Because Reverend Lawson keeps us informed about Vietnam." A lot of my ministry was letting what was happening in my life teach me and my congregations.

The greatest spiritual joy I found during the Memphis strike was in the spontaneous creation of a community whose goal was treating one another with dignity and grace and starting the work of justice in Memphis for unions, working people, and people living in poverty. When the men walked out on strike, they were not only forming a labor union. They were forming what became a beloved community. That is, they cared for one another and for one another's families. And as we backed them, they recognized in us a beloved community supporting them. In a civic way, we all acknowledged that first of all, we were human beings and we belonged to one another.

The fact that thirteen hundred men had walked off the job in a singular discipline of a sort that I suspect Memphis had never seen before transformed us all. I use the term "discipline" to mean they were all in step with one another. That kind of discipline always spoke to the men. It was initiated by T. O. Jones and his organizing, which convinced them that they deserved better working conditions, including wages. It also showed them, and both the Black community and the white community, that these men living in poverty still had power in their numbers. You don't have to hate anybody to go on strike. You simply have to want a little justice, a little more of what community represents.

When the police broke up that large march on February 23, they maced any number of preachers and other middle-class Black people. And all those people were only walking down the street having a good time during a march to support Black men and their families. When that Mace hit them, they didn't know what was happening. But it reminded them of the depth of the problem in a racist city. Because they were peaceful, enjoying themselves, in a good mood—and suddenly: BAM. Right away, some major middle-class Black people in Memphis had their minds changed. Rev. Ralph Jackson, for example, was a conservative who had tried to conform to the ways of white Memphis. He was thought of as a "responsible Negro leader." After getting maced, he said, "Thirty years of conservatism went down the drain." He became a powerful voice in the strike.

The clergy members who openly supported the strike were almost exclusively Black. The Memphis Ministers Association, which had desegregated its membership until just before I arrived in Memphis, supported the workers. In 1968, Rabbi James Wax was the president. I was vice president, but I was much too busy to go to meetings during the strike. Yet Temple Israel, Rabbi Wax's synagogue and the largest in the city, eventually supported the workers.

One of the people who was a bridge between Mayor Loeb, the union, and our community was a white Methodist minister, Frank McRae. He was a leader in the Methodist Conference in Memphis and Tennessee. He and Loeb were acquaintances, and Frank initiated conversations with Loeb. Frank also talked to the sanitation workers, to Rev. Henry Starks, to me, and to other Black leaders. When I arrived in Memphis, in 1962, Frank was my superintendent in the district of Memphis. So I knew him well. Those connections, in a close-knit town like Memphis, were the channels through which a lot of the negotiations were conducted.

Politically, the majority of the power in the white community in February 1968 was with Loeb. Knowing that, we continually tried to figure out how to force him to move beyond his hard line. We didn't consider the handful of progressive white people in Memphis to be a power group. And the white churches weren't going to help us. But the business community seemed to be the most obvious way through. Loeb was a business owner. He and his brother ran successful chains of Loeb's laundromats and barbeque restaurants in town, which were among the businesses we named in our boycott.

The business community in Memphis was not monolithic. Its members were divided. A few businesspeople worked with us to try to settle the strike in February 1968, and some establishments openly supported the workers. One was Dreifus Jewelers, owned by a Jewish family who spoke out for the workers during the strike. Some of the wealthiest businessmen in town wanted the strike ended, if only because they didn't want the disruption it caused. At first, Loeb didn't listen to them. A couple of them called me, and they talked to other Black leaders about the strike. But particularly after the February 23 macing, more of the business community put pressure on Loeb and the city council to deal with the workers and the union and get the strike ended. Jesse Epps of AFSCME was the key figure in those negotiating processes throughout the strike.

We tried to work with Loeb and the city council from the start. But Loeb was not a man of integrity, and most of the white members of the council were in his corner. On February 26, the Monday after the macing march, Loeb agreed to conditions that could settle the strike. Various negotiators—primarily from the business community, through direct conversations with Jesse Epps, Ralph Jackson, me, and others—came up with terms, and Loeb agreed to be on board. It would be announced that Tuesday or Wednesday, and the strike would end. But on Tuesday morning, February 27, the front-page headline in *The Commercial Appeal* had the word "compromise" in it: "Loeb May Offer Compromise Plan to Collect Dues." And the mayor blew his cool. The deal was off.

In the afternoon *Press-Scimitar* that Tuesday, Loeb was quoted saying he would never budge on rejecting the strikers' demand for the union dues checkoff and a signed contract. "The news of a 'compromise' this morning on these principles is news to me," he said. "My position is unchanged."

During the strike, I never spoke directly to Loeb. I felt that Rev. Henry Starks and Rev. Ralph Jackson represented the Black Memphis clergy better and could communicate with him more effectively than I could. And he would receive them better than he would me. So I concentrated on managing the boycott and the marches and on staying in touch with the workers in the union. During any campaign, I always looked at how I could best be deployed. Usually, being behind the scenes allowed me to do my work with less stress. In the Memphis strike, I marched every day and led the strategy committee meetings. I went to all the mass meetings. I might not have gone up on the platform. But I was there. You can't organize if you have to do everything. If you can't pick your niche and really focus on it while other people are working on other responsibilities, then you're in trouble.

If Loeb had called me directly and said, "I need to talk to you," I would've gone and talked to him. But he never did. I didn't expect him to do that, either. Loeb did not seem to know that one of the major tools in any standoff is talking to your opponents. Many problems the mayor faced could have been solved creatively and in surprising ways if he had simply tried to collaborate with those of us on the other side.

Even though we were boycotting the two local papers for their racist coverage and editorials, keeping up with them was a useful way to gauge what white Memphis was thinking and doing, or being told to think and do. On Wednesday, February 28, the morning after Loeb publicly reversed course on the agreement he had reached with us the night before, *The Commercial Appeal* used my name, along with those of other Black leaders, in an editorial written by its political editor—the person in charge of all of the coverage of politics. Entitled "How Race Politics Enters a Strike," the piece asked, in a somewhat bewildered tone, how "a labor problem" became a racial issue, and its explanation began by listing ways in which the Memphis strike had "all the necessary ingredients" for such a thing.

In the third week of the strike, the two daily newspapers were framing Negro leaders as particular villains, often blaming us even more so than the union. On that same Tuesday when Loeb publicly reversed course on our agreement, the *Press-Scimitar*'s afternoon editorial, entitled "What Memphis Needs Now," made "Negro ministers" into a derogatory term.

> The Press-Scimitar hopes, and believes, that the people of Memphis are not going to permit the sanitation men's strike and its sideshow, the Negro ministers' downtown marches, to disrupt the city's business and governmental operations.
>
> . . . It looks as if some hotheads who have been hankering for a racial clash in Memphis have decided the sanitation strike is their opportunity. It is regrettable that ministers, of all people, have been rallied to try to turn the labor controversy into *racial turmoil.*

In the same way that most segregationists would have said in 1968 that the Civil War was fought over states' rights and not slavery, Loeb and his supporters claimed the strike was a labor issue that had nothing to do with race. And the paper went on to mock my exact words from the previous Saturday's press conference announcing our goals.

> The fact that most of the Sanitation Department workers are Negroes is only incidental. The basic issue of the strike is that it is illegal for any public employees to strike against the public. It would have been just as illegal and as morally wrong for any other group of city employees to strike. . . .
>
> . . . The Negro ministers, in advocating a boycott, call for "many more jobs for Negroes and other poor people." Yet they are helping to keep 1300 Negro employees out of work—and out of pay—by supporting the illegal strike.
>
> And if the boycott they call for should by any chance be successful, it would endanger the jobs of many more "Negroes and other poor people," for hundreds of such persons are on the payrolls of the businesses which these ministers ask the public to boycott.

The last paragraph was in bold type and continued with the paper's urgings—aimed at the white community and reflecting the attitude most white Memphians had toward the strike. The last sentence of the boldfaced paragraph was a veiled threat toward Black strikers and their supporters:

> **And we urge Memphis people in general to go about their business, buy what they want to, where they want to, and not worry about the protest marches, should these be continued. The police are on the alert to protect all citizens.**

The phrase “all citizens” meant all white citizens. And that last sentence turned out to be a foreshadowing of what would happen during another major strike demonstration a month later, at the end of March 1968.

SIXTEEN

In This Rich Nation

Martin Luther King Jr. speaking to sanitation strikers at Mason Temple, March 18, 1968. Reverend Lawson is standing behind the pulpit to the right.
VERNON MATTHEWS, COMMERCIAL APPEAL VIA IMAGN

A lot of sanitation workers told me that at some point on the job, one or more of their supervisors in the public works department had called them "boy," or "n——r," or worse. The language reflected a deeper mindset within white Memphis—from white management in the sanitation department to white newspaper reporters and editors, and from Cotton Carnival royalty to the mayor of Memphis.

Racism in the United States aims to teach white people to believe that the natural order places their humanity above all others', and to teach Black people they are less than human. Enslavement robbed us of our sense of personhood, dignity, and freedom, while inflating white people's sense of entitlement. After enslavement, segregation's social-control system continued to make us believe we weren't worth much either, so that we would control ourselves—always deferring to white power and white standards of behavior. Such indoctrination was why one of Martin King's main teachings was an idea he called "somebodiness." He tried to impart a sense of dignity to Black people. You are somebody. Black revolution, Black pride, Black consciousness, Black manhood and womanhood were all part of counteracting the effects that endured after centuries of racism—helping Black people regain a sense that they are free, fully human, and endowed with inalienable rights.

The sanitation strike sparked a "somebodiness" catharsis among Black people in Memphis. Black Memphians across many sectors participated not simply in the marches but also in the economic boycott. Of course, we were not all of one mind. There was infighting and jockeying for position across the Black community. But never before had so many Black people in the city been involved in a campaign for ending injustice. We'd had demonstrations of one kind or another leading up to 1968, but none that truly confronted Black people in Memphis with themselves, and awakened them to the value of their own humanity.

A lot of people misinterpret the whole aim of the nonviolent movement in the South as appealing to the conscience of the white man. But in the workshops I conducted, I emphasized our need to organize and confront racial segregation as a prophetic word to Black people, as much as it was to white people. Because many Black people were still expecting change to come from the system, rather than change coming because we joined together and initiated it despite the system—because each of us decided *I am free* and began to act upon that freedom together.

In the 1950s and 1960s, our movement made white people increasingly aware that the targets of racism were no longer accepting American society as it had always been. That's when hysteria began to sweep the white community. A Black man who began to assert his dignity or a Black woman who began to express her feelings were not doing what they were supposed to be doing. Those Negroes who got out of their allotted place in society would be called "uppity" in the 1960s.

Yet the slurs did not crush us. In fact, perhaps the best response of all came about a month into the strike, in early March, when signs with the slogan "I AM A MAN" began to appear during our daily picket walks. The men had thought up the phrase—a simple call for the most basic respect we humans owe one another. And it boldly defied the entrenched social order in our feudal city of Memphis.

Mayor Loeb and his supporters seemed unable to understand the message "I AM A MAN." After all, they believed they had always taken care of their Negroes. Why would Negro workers betray their friendship, goodwill, and trust by standing up in this way, by going on strike? *Head on back to work,* they said, *and then we can talk about how we will take care of you some more, like we always have done, so thoughtfully and lovingly.* That was their stance. For Loeb in particular, appearing to capitulate to Negro workers in any way seemed to be a threat to his own manhood. And he was the kind of person who the more you pushed, the more stubborn he became.

But we were not backing down. The daily marches in the morning and the afternoon continued. A few times, usually on Saturdays, we would show community support for the strike and for resulting boycotts through picket walks in front of downtown department stores. That's when I brought my oldest son, John, who was six then, to march with us. Other people brought their kids to those marches, too. John always said marching was fun. He would carry a sign that read, "We Are Together."

On Tuesday, March 5, some three hundred sanitation strikers and many community members packed into the city council chambers yet again, in another attempt to settle the strike. Black council member J. O. Patterson was trying to introduce a resolution addressing some of the union's demands that the mayor had refused to settle. A few white council members objected to the resolution, and when discussion was opened to the public, Rev. Ezekiel Bell got up and spoke. We were all worked up, and he expressed much of the anger and frustration we were feeling.

> We didn't come down here to reason with you gentlemen. If you were reasonable, it would already be settled. . . . You are not reasonable people. . . . All these men . . . are asking is dignity and respect. You talk about whether it's the mayor's or the council's responsibility. If these men were white you would have already done something. I want you to know you have no backbone . . . and you are all going to hell.
>
> This is a racist town, this is a racist country. . . . You call our sons off to be killed to protect your way of life. They come back here and don't have a place to live.

One of the white council members interrupted Reverend Bell and asked him not to insult the members. While Reverend Bell was still talking, other council members abruptly moved to adjourn the meeting, without hearing from anyone else. All of the council members left the chamber except for the three Black members and one white member, Jerred Blanchard, who had become open to our point of view. From that day on, Blanchard began voting with the three Black members. "I quit rationalizing it as a labor matter," Blanchard would say years later, "and looked at it as . . . pure racism."

A few people spoke to the crowd even after most of the council members left. Then the assistant police chief, Henry Lux, announced that we had thirty minutes to leave the chamber or, he said, we would be arrested. Under the subheading "Obey Conscience," the afternoon paper reported on what I did next:

> Rev. James Lawson, pastor of Centenary Methodist Church, said Council has in the past made promises and not kept them, and he called for staying in the chamber.
>
> "I'm ready to be arrested," Lawson said. . . . "I'm here. I'm going to stay. You have to do what is in your own conscience. No one can make the decision for you. It is not dishonorable to go to jail for the right reason. . . ."
>
> . . . Some chanted: "We want jail, we want jail," and then "jail, jail, jail."

I got together with Rev. Henry Starks and Maxine Smith and other leaders in the chamber. We negotiated an arrangement with Assistant Chief Lux: all who were going to be arrested would file out of the chamber peacefully and follow the officers to the police station, a block away.

We told everyone that if they wanted to leave, they should do it. If they stayed, they would be arrested. Lux then got up and announced that everyone left in the chamber was under arrest on state and city charges of disorderly conduct, even though we would walk over to jail in such an orderly fashion. The *Press-Scimitar* described what happened next:

> The sit-in ended. Those arrested marched out two by two. They included two white ministers. There were a number of women. As they

marched out of City Hall through a cordon of police, they sang "Leaning On the Everlasting Arms."

That familiar hymn lifted our determined spirits.

> *What a fellowship, what a joy divine,*
> *leaning on the everlasting arms. . . .*
>
> . . . *Leaning, leaning, safe and secure from all alarms.*
> *Leaning, leaning, leaning on the everlasting arms.*
>
> *Oh how sweet to walk in this pilgrim way,*
> *leaning on the everlasting arms. . . .*
>
> . . . *What have I to dread, what have I to fear,*
> *leaning on the everlasting arms?*

The newspaper description of our arrest added one last detail:

> Before leaving the chamber room, however, the strikers and sympathizers picked up paper and other debris and left the room clean, at the suggestion of some of the ministers. When a similar sit-in was held in the chamber last month, the room was left littered with paper and debris.

Ultimately, 116 of us peacefully headed to the police station. Some of our student picketers who had been marching in front of Main Street stores that afternoon were waiting outside city hall. As we walked through the police gauntlet, the students cheered us on, singing "We Shall Overcome" and chanting, "Keep the faith, baby," and "Down with Loeb." We filed into the police station and everyone had a police photo taken. Our lawyers got us released without having to post bond. The police even complimented the ministers for how orderly the arrests had been. It was all part of our strategy, which had disarmed their hostility toward us and demonstrated how to express agitation without violence. The next day, we went to court and were given sixty days' probation. The judge said the charges would be dismissed automatically if there were no further incidents.

After we were arrested and released, on Tuesday night, most people went home, but I went over to a rally that was in progress at Clayborn Temple. Rev. Ralph Jackson spoke, and so did I. And a modified version of the Lord's Prayer was introduced, called the Sanitation Workers' Prayer.

Our Henry, who art in City Hall,
Hard-headed be thy name.
Thy kingdom C.O.M.E.,
OUR will be done,
In Memphis, as it is in heaven.

Give us this day our Dues Checkoff,
And forgive us our boycott,
As we forgive those who spray MACE
against us.

And lead us not into shame,
But deliver us from LOEB!

For OURS is the justice, jobs and dignity,
Forever and ever.
FREEDOM!

As the strike entered its fifth week, our marches continued. In *The Commercial Appeal* on March 12, the daily *Hambone's Meditations* cartoon was in its place at the right-hand, bottom corner of the front page of the paper's second section. Hambone was smoking his corncob pipe, sitting on a stair stoop talking about his wife: SOMETIME OLE 'OMAN KEEP ON ME TWELL HIT JES' SEEM LAK DE WUSS THING IN LIFE IS DAT "DEY'S ALLUZ HOPE"!!!

Above and around the cartoon an article ran with the headline "Negro Pastors Take Reins as Garbage Strike Leaders in Switch to Racial Pitch." It said union officials were less available to lead strike activities because the city kept taking the union to court for what the city always called an illegal strike. So, community leaders were stepping in to keep the momentum going.

The article mentioned how the NAACP and the Shelby County Democratic Club also backed the strike, and noted that their leaders had appeared at mass meetings to offer words of encouragement to the workers.

> But these leaders, unlike the ministers, seldom appear in downtown marches and they seldom stay around when some meetings at City Hall turn into sit-ins.
>
> . . . If the strike leadership is to be narrowed to one minister, he is the Rev. Mr. Lawson. Of the city's 300 Negro ministers, he says about 150 are active in the demonstrations.
>
> . . . The Rev. Mr. Lawson claims if Negro ministers drop the leadership ball, militants inclined toward violence will pick it up.
>
> The Rev. Malcolm Blackburn, strike leader and the only white minister in the AME Church, says some ministers find themselves pulled in opposite directions.
>
> "A lot of ministers are on a tightrope. We are trying to help the sanitation workers—normally a pretty mild-mannered group—assert their rights and on the other hand we are trying to hold down the young militants who want to tear the place up."

The group that most people viewed as representing young militants was the Invaders. But from my perspective, they weren't as militant as the movement was at that time. We invited the Invaders to support the strike, to join us and contribute to it. However, some of them, including Charles Cabbage and Coby Smith, would stand up in our public meetings and advocate for bits and pieces of violence in one form or another. Then Ralph Jackson or I would typically respond, "We can't go for that."

I understood their rage at the exploitation of Black people they saw all around them. I felt that rage myself. But again and again I would ask them to pay attention to where the expression of that rage was happening, and how it affected Black people. They were advocating for carrying guns, bombings, fires, and looting of businesses in neighborhoods where they lived, worked, and shopped. I would tell them, "The violence you might foster would destroy Black neighborhoods in North or South Memphis, while leaving white areas like East Memphis unscathed." Then, to get their attention, I would make a wild suggestion that I knew they would not carry out, to show them how their rage was misdirected and their strategy flawed. "So if you're going to do that, why don't you go out to East Memphis and do it? Don't do it where we live and work."

Of course I wasn't condoning violence of any kind, anywhere. They knew that. I was merely using my own wild rhetoric to ask them to think through theirs. I wanted them to realize the consequences of what they were suggesting when they called for violence. "If you're really radical," I'd say, "go out to those neighborhoods and do it." They never did. I tried to get them to see that vengeful violence was not the way to bring real change for us all. Yet nothing I said stopped them from continuing to use the rhetoric of violence.

Those kinds of statements I sometimes made, seemingly directing angry young Black men to bring violence to East Memphis, got me into trouble with a lot of white people. My point was tactical and strategic, though, not literal. The uprisings in Black communities in the mid-1960s, often called riots, had devastated many places where Black people lived. Violent destruction of our own neighborhoods was an unthoughtful strategy for the Black community. It caused us a great deal of harm. Lashing out might feel satisfying in the moment, but when you are violent, it is also yourself you are destroying. My statements were meant to point out the flawed strategy and to suggest where the understandable anger at injustice that fueled the unrest should be redirected. I was not literally encouraging anyone to go use violence in more privileged neighborhoods to express that anger.

We were able to confront the white power structure, nonviolently and creatively through the strike. But the Invaders did not support our commitment to nonviolence in all we did. Still, we did not need to focus on ideological battles among ourselves. We needed to concentrate on how to help bring the strikers' cause to an effective conclusion. Thirteen hundred men were on strike, and we had to care for them and their families. Eventually I simply said to both Coby and Charles, "If you have a better scheme, go ahead—no one is stopping you. But don't keep obstructing us. We are doing the best we know."

I think they saw me, in some ways, as a money guy, because they were always asking for money. And initially, I encouraged preachers to give them money just to help them get some things they said they wanted. But they kept coming back for more, and I finally stopped and told them we were not going to give them any more money. Especially during the strike, we needed all available funds to go to the sanitation workers.

Early on in the strategy committee meetings, we had discussed inviting national Black leaders to join us and put more pressure on the city. We made a list of people to call and ask to speak at our mass meetings. NAACP executive director Roy Wilkins was high on the list, as was Bayard Rustin. Then, if we really needed to step up pressure, we would ask Martin.

During the first month of the strike, I had rarely spoken to anyone outside Memphis, except Martin. I would call him at home. We spoke soon after the march in February where we got maced. He and I agreed that the Memphis strike was a part of our movement, and that he would want to join it soon. I told him then that he should not come immediately, no matter who called him. Strategically, I said, we had to get Roy Wilkins to speak first. "Because if you speak before Roy," I told Martin, "Roy won't come."

We waited, too, in hopes that we could settle the strike locally. But by the early weeks of March, with the intransigent mayor and city council, we had decided it was time to bring everyone in. Jesse Turner, the local NAACP president, was the national treasurer of the NAACP. So he asked Roy to come. AFSCME head Jerry Wurf had worked with Bayard Rustin in union organizing in New York and D.C., so he asked Bayard to speak. Both Roy and Bayard agreed, and it turned out they were scheduled for the same day—Thursday, March 14. That had not been the plan. We wanted to have each man here on different days, to spread their impact. But it was how things worked out.

The morning paper announced their arrival on Wednesday, March 13, with quotes from my announcement to the strikers on Tuesday:

> The Rev. James M. Lawson Jr., pastor of Centenary Methodist Church and now a key figure in the strike, made clear that this marked the beginning of an effort to bring in forces from outside the city.
>
> "This will be the first in a whole series of people coming in from all over the country to help you march and lead you on to victory," the Rev. Mr. Lawson told a brief rally in the lobby of City Hall.

During the city council meeting that day, Black council member J. O. Patterson tried yet again to introduce an ordinance in support of the strikers' demands. But nine of his ten white colleagues voted to table it. Again, Jerred Blanchard was the only white council member to vote with his Black fellow council members. That was when J. O. Patterson told his colleagues, "This city is reaching the point where racial strife and turmoil is not far off. . . . It is about time we on the City Council stop sitting here and waiting on the executive branch to make up its mind or change its mind on the subject."

The garbage had been piling up all over town. The city hired some workers to violate the strike and do the work, their trucks traveling with police escorts. Also, some volunteers organized in groups around town for a while to collect trash themselves and take it to the city dump. None of those efforts fully addressed the need, and pressure increased on the city, and on the men to return to work. But the men were determined and the growing support for their campaign, among Black Memphians and from people outside of the city, had strengthened their resolve. It was the right time for showing them and the city more of that outside help.

Just before Bayard's and Roy's speeches on Thursday night, the lead editorial in the March 14 afternoon paper expressed what most of white Memphis felt, advancing their cherished view that the city had no racial issues, and had been progressive on race up until the strike, and that local Black leaders had stirred the pot. The headline read: "To Our Civil Rights Visitors: Look First at City's Record."

> Two nationally known civil rights leaders will be in Memphis tonight to address a rally of Negro citizens concerning their future course of action in the strike of city sanitation workers. . . .
>
> For The Press-Scimitar's part, we welcome these widely recognized and experienced leaders with the confidence that they will fairly examine the strike from all sides and give us some constructive ideas as to how community relations can be restored to their former level.

The editorial went on to call the strike illegal and said the men should get back to work and then "rely on the city's pledge to negotiate on issues concerning working conditions." Then came their familiar pitch portraying Memphis as a bastion of racial harmony:

> The Press-Scimitar hopes Mr. Wilkins and Mr. Rustin will not forget that they are visiting the city with the best race relations record in the

> nation and this is the first occasion when leaders of national stature have been "called in" to take a hand in a local situation.
>
> Memphis is proud of its record, achieved through years of hard work and with the full co-operation of the Negro leadership. We prayerfully hope that nothing will happen to mar our good record.

Most white Memphians believed such boosterism with all their hearts. And at many points during the strike, it seemed they were more concerned with advertising their supposed stellar reputation on racial issues than they were with the well-being of the Black people—their fellow citizens—demanding the right to fulfill their own most basic needs.

That night, more than nine thousand people came out to Mason Temple to hear Roy and Bayard speak. I got up to introduce them. By then Roy and I had put aside the differences we had in the early 1960s, after I said publicly that I thought the NAACP was not doing enough and moving too slowly. Of course, Bayard and I were longtime friends and colleagues, and he was a mentor to me in the early days. I got the crowd going by talking about the strike and what it meant to us in Memphis:

> Our power has always been in ourselves and our people, and in our unity—in the courage that we have to say no to racism and injustice. So this is about our unity, our togetherness, and our being willing to face macing and marching and anything else, in order that out of that unity we will have a victory.

Then Roy spoke and commended the Black community in Memphis, and called out Henry Loeb and his supporters.

> I say the city of Memphis, Tennessee, ought to be ashamed of itself. If I were the mayor of this city, I would be ashamed. I wouldn't want these men to not be able to feed their families on the lousy pittance they are paid.

He compared the Memphis strike to the recently settled New York City sanitation strike, saying that in New York the settlement had brought an extra $425 per year to each worker. "No one expects Memphis to come up to New York's standards," he said, referring to the higher cost of living in New York, "but they do expect more than eight cents an hour," which was the raise Mayor Loeb had proposed since the strike began—up to about an extra $165 per year to each full-time worker. The men had rejected that offer and continued to ask for at least ten to fifteen cents more per hour instead. Roy Wilkins also criticized the mayor for saying his door was always open to any sanitation workers who wanted to talk to him about their jobs. He called for a more professional and systematic grievance policy and procedure. Then he got lots of applause when he spoke of the February 23 march.

> They squirted Mace on you. . . . I can't believe the mayor ordered that. I know enough about police. And I know a lot of bad policemen. But you give a policeman something to squirt, or shoot, or beat with, and he's gone man, he's gone.
>
> That Mace was invented to curb a riot, a mob, people running wild, people really tearing up the town, burning down the town. That Mace was not made for people who are marching down the street in an orderly fashion. . . .
>
> I came here to show you that even though I am far away in New York, that I understand what the problem is. I sympathize with you. I came down here to lend whatever aid and support I could. I didn't come down here to threaten anybody, but anybody who runs around picking on peaceful people is building for trouble.

Next, Bayard Rustin got up to speak. *The Commercial Appeal* reported on what he said and mentioned that he had organized the March on Washington, but didn't mention his pivotal role in also organizing the Montgomery bus boycott, which he brought up in his praise for our unity in the Memphis strike.

> Mr. Rustin, who in 1963 organized a march of more than a million persons in Washington, drew the loudest applause of the evening when he likened the sanitation strike to the 1955 Montgomery bus boycott and called the Memphis strike "one of the great struggles for emancipation of the black man today."
>
> "This becomes the symbol of the movement to get rid of poverty. The record here shows that in Memphis this fight is going to be won because the black people in this community and the trade unions stand together."

He said: "It is written that where there is justice, order will maintain it; where there is injustice, disorder is inevitable."

When Rustin got home from Memphis, he went on an educational channel and on the radio in New York City and the surrounding areas, asking for money for the workers in Memphis. He raised more than $80,000 for the men and their families. We had barrels coming in, full of bags of five-dollar bills from all over the East Coast. Both Roy and Bayard had encouraged us to keep going and let us know we were not alone in the Memphis struggle.

We wanted Martin to do the same thing. And we knew he would bring nationwide attention, because the real story of the men and the city was not getting out much beyond Memphis.

I started talking with Martin about when he might be able to come. In our first conversation, he told me he was at the point of exhaustion, and his doctor had ordered him to rest, saying he would drop if he did not take time off. Martin told me that he simply had to take the doctor's advice, particularly with the Poor People's Campaign ahead of him. So, he went off to Mexico for five or six days to rest in the sun. But he said he would definitely make it to Memphis when he got back, because he was deeply interested in what was going on in the strike.

While he was in Mexico, I remained in contact with Andy Young, Bernard Lee, and Martin's secretary, Dora McDonald. Somewhere in this period we pinned down Monday, March 18, as the date. When Martin returned, he had a number of other responsibilities he needed to take care of, including an SCLC executive committee meeting in Jackson, Mississippi, on that Monday and Tuesday. But he got the meeting moved to Memphis on Tuesday, so that on Monday night, he could speak to the sanitation workers and their supporters.

Martin and Andy were going to be in Los Angeles over that weekend before he came, and Andy gave me their hotel numbers. I talked to Andy at least once in Los Angeles about the whole context, because Andy was the person who briefed Martin and prepared him before he went into situations. I had told Andy about Mason Temple, where the mass meeting would be on Monday night, and its seating capacity of ten thousand.

On Sunday morning, March 17, 1968, Martin gave a sermon at Holman Methodist Church, in Los Angeles—the church where I would become pastor a few years later—entitled "The Meaning of Hope." Later that afternoon, I called Martin at his hotel in Los Angeles. I asked him, "Did Andy tell you that tomorrow night you'll be speaking to maybe ten thousand people in Mason Temple?" He said, "No. I didn't realize that." I told him how we were packing Mason Temple for some of our mass meetings. He knew the Church of God in Christ, and Bishop Charles Harrison Mason, the founder of that church, and that Mason Temple was their international headquarters. It was quite unusual in the South to have a building for mass meetings that could hold ten thousand people. I had been to a lot of mass meetings, in many of our major campaigns, and we never had access to a place as big as that.

I briefed Martin on the structure and intensity of our movement, and on recent events. We talked at length about the sanitation workers themselves, some of their problems and their main issues. Of course, I also told him about Mayor Loeb and his reaction to the strike, as well as about the reactions of other white leaders. We discussed the strike's relationship to the Poor People's Campaign and to nonviolence. Having worked closely with Martin and the SCLC over the years, I knew which concerns would be important to him as he came into this campaign.

As we ended the call, Martin didn't know the exact time he would be arriving, but assured me that I would be informed in plenty of time to be able to pick him up at the airport. He wanted me to pick him up. Then we asked after each other's families and he told me about his vacation before we hung up, aware that we would see each other the next day.

His flight arrived around seven on Monday night. Jesse Epps of AFSCME and I had gone by Mason Temple on our way to the airport, about an hour before the time of the mass meeting, and the place was already filled. The sheer fact that Martin was coming was major news for all of Memphis and was all over the radio and TV. We had promoted it on the Black radio stations, WDIA and WLOK, and in the city's two Black newspapers, the *Tri-State Defender* and the *Memphis World*. We had printed leaflets to pass around the union hall meetings, and at our mass meetings the week before. And we had teams of people on the phone calling residents of North Memphis and South Memphis, inviting them to come out.

As Jesse Epps and I drove to meet Martin and Andy, we decided to tease them. So we greeted them, and then Jesse, with a sad look, told Martin, "Jim was wrong."

Martin looked at me, and I nodded and looked away, kind of like I was too embarrassed to meet his eyes because I had been so wrong.

Jesse said, "Yeah. Jim said you would be speaking before probably ten thousand people." Martin nodded. So did Andy. Then Jesse said, "Well, we found out just tonight that was a mistake."

Martin said, "Is that right?"

I played along, nodding, looking disappointed.

Martin was quiet. We kept walking through the airport.

Jesse went on: "Yeah. You're not going to be speaking before ten thousand people tonight, Dr. King." They took in that news. Then, after a few more beats, Jesse added, "Because you are going to be speaking before fifteen thousand." We explained that we had to have loudspeakers set up in the parking lot of Mason Temple to handle the overflow of people who were already there to hear his talk.

Martin laughed, delighted. He talked in the car about how this was one of the most significant campaigns they had seen—when that many folk would come out to a single meeting. He was becoming aware of how crucial our Memphis effort was, and how key it was to his own work.

At Mason Temple, the crowd was electric. I said a few introductory words about Martin. He thanked me as he got up to speak, and he thanked the sanitation workers and their families. He said the strike and community support in Memphis were showing the world that "we are all tied in a single garment of destiny, and that if one black person suffers, if one black person is down, we are all down."

The whole place hung on his words as he spoke, interrupting his speech, entitled "All Labor Has Dignity," many times with cheers and applause. He said the sanitation workers and their families, and the Black community in Memphis, were "demanding that this city will respect the dignity of labor." He spoke of the job the sanitation workers did and its significance to society, calling them as important to everyone's well-being as doctors, because without them disease would run "rampant."

Then he gave one of the most stirring lines of the night when he told the crowd: "You are reminding, not only Memphis, but you are reminding the nation that it is a crime for people to live in this rich nation and receive starvation wages."

At that, everyone erupted in cheers and applause. Martin had expressed the heart of our work in the movement and, particularly, in the strike. It resonated far and wide.

He went on: "You are here tonight to demand that Memphis will do something about the conditions that our brothers face as they work day in and day out. . . . You are here to demand that Memphis will see the poor." He told the men on strike that their unity and determination were the keys to their strength, and urged them "to stick it out . . ." and "make Mayor Loeb and others say yes, even when they want to say no."

Coming in from the airport, we had talked about the kinds of things we saw as possible for the future, but Martin caught the mood of the movement and was able to respond to it quite spontaneously. I was sitting behind the speaker's rostrum as he spoke, with Jim Bevel, Andy Young, Bernard Lee, and Ralph Abernathy. In that moment, we all began to tell Andy that Martin ought to return to Memphis and lead a big march. Then Martin told the crowd that if things did not change, the people would need to stop working altogether and bring the city to a halt. He put forth that idea in his speech on the spur of the moment, fueled, I think, by the exuberant crowd. He said we should take a day when domestic workers and teachers do not go to work and students do not go to school.

That's when Andy asked for something to write on. I always carried a small notepad in my pocket. I pulled it out, Andy wrote on it, scribbling down our suggestion that Martin return and lead a march, and then tore the sheet of yellow paper off the pad. While Martin was speaking, Andy slid the note in front of him. I think Andy might even have written the date on that note, because he knew Martin's schedule and could suggest a date that would work best for him to come back. Martin had tours scheduled in Mississippi and Georgia that week, so Andy knew he could return to Memphis on Friday. Martin did not respond to the note immediately.

When he sat down after his speech, Andy and I quickly got in front of him, excitedly talking to him about coming back, and he was quite willing. We quickly agreed on the following Friday, March 22, and we decided that there would be a work stoppage that day, too. So Martin got back up and stood before the crowd to announce that he would return to Memphis and lead a march at the end of the week, on Friday, and that he wanted everyone to stay away from work and school that day. The already raucous crowd erupted with an ecstatic roar when he made the announcement. Everyone there caught the jubilant spirit of the moment.

The whole time Martin was speaking, I felt tremendous energy and warmth throughout the place. An authentic social movement was changing Memphis. I also felt something else: pride. The Mason Temple speech was our largest gathering of the movement anywhere in the South, which made it spectacular.

For me, one of the most important parts of Martin's language in that speech was how he talked about the sanitation workers, calling them "the sons and daughters of God," and "children of God." That was how I saw them, too, and how I tried to interact with them. We were standing with working people who were demanding better treatment, and it was an essential part of our decades of struggle. We could see newly unleashed energy in the faces as we looked out that night onto the buoyant *aliveness* in the sanctuary. Older people were having a good time. Young people were joining in. All of us were in it together. I know it strengthened the workers and their families, inwardly and outwardly.

Some people compared Martin to Jesus that night. It was a mystery, and a wonder, and an awesome thing. This kind of large, inspired event had happened only a few times before in the world. I had read of these gatherings in the journeys of some of the religions of the world. But I was a participant in this one. I had a hand in making it happen. So that was an exciting feeling. Dorothy was not there. She was home taking care of our three young boys. But we talked all during the day, and of course she shared in our delight.

After the speech, Martin and all the people on the SCLC executive committee stayed at the Lorraine Motel, downtown. It was the motel he always used when he was in Memphis. It was Black-owned and considered a safe place for him. Martin and Andy had their SCLC executive committee meeting the next day, then left for Mississippi and Georgia to tour some of the places they would be visiting on the Poor People's Campaign the following month. Their procession was to make its way from Marks, Mississippi, to Washington, D.C. They planned to start in Marks, the place where Martin had given the stirring eulogy for Armistead Phipps, the fifty-eight-year-old sharecropper who had died of a heart attack during the Meredith March in 1966.

In the days after Martin's Monday night speech, we were making preparations for the Memphis march and work stoppage that Friday. We had regular mass meetings each night, planning our strategy, talking to all the people involved in organizing it—including the police and the city—and getting the word out to the public. All the while, we continued our daily marches and the economic boycott of downtown businesses going on at that time. We marched on the Tuesday morning after Martin's speech. And we had a second march in the afternoon with young people. Harold Middlebrook, who was one of my colleagues at the SCLC and the pastor of a church just outside of Memphis, made that happen.

We began circulating leaflets throughout the community.

> Dr. Martin Luther King, Jr.
> and
> Community On the Move for Equality
> INVITE YOU
> To March for Justice and Jobs
> Friday, March 22, 1968
> 9:00 A.M.
> From Clayborn Temple A.M.E. Church
> 280 Hernando
>
> We ask you to stay away from work or school and walk with more than 10,000 people who want Memphis once and for all to learn that it must be a city for all people. A man is a man. God requires that a man be treated like a man.
>
> Memphis must do so in work, play, education, housing, by the police and in all other ways the rights of each man must be upheld. This will be a march of dignity. The only force we will use is soul-force which is peaceful, loving, courageous, yet militant.

On Wednesday, March 20, *The Commercial Appeal* published an editorial attacking Martin, the planned Poor People's Campaign, and our movement.

> Martin Luther King did nothing to hasten the settlement of the Memphis sanitation strike in his Monday night speech at Mason Temple. But he saw how many Negroes were aroused and quickly decided to attach himself to the local issue. He'll return to Memphis Friday to lead a march, which is usually good for a spot on the television broadcasts.
>
> . . . But there is no sign that his visit and words will get the garbage workers back on the city pay roll any time soon.

On Thursday, March 21, the day before the march, the afternoon paper, the *Press-Scimitar,* ran an editorial entitled "To Dr. King and His

Marchers," which started out listing all the ways the editors agreed with Dr. King's message and his call for an orderly march, for better jobs for Negroes, and for a better deal for the sanitation workers. But it shifted to a tone of warning, directed at Black Memphians:

> These goals all can be attained, but the white community cannot accomplish them alone. There must be a positive response from the Negro community . . . willingness and understanding . . . not "Burn, baby, burn!"
>
> Tomorrow, Dr. King may taunt Memphis with a cry of "Shame!" in an effort to bring about massive and overnight changes.
>
> We are not ashamed, Dr. King. We have not done all we have wanted to do, nor even what we should have done. But we're not ashamed.
>
> And if you don't watch out, Dr. King, you, and some of your fellow ministers here in Memphis just might undo what already has been accomplished.

At the same time that editorial was published, a group of us were meeting after one of our daily marches. Seated in the third-floor conference room of the Minimum Salary Building, next to Clayborn Temple, we were looking over our work and the plans for the next day's march with Martin when we noticed that it had begun to snow outside. We laughed among ourselves, saying, "Well, it can't last. It will probably stop shortly." Snow wasn't common in Memphis, and it was almost unheard of during the last weeks of March. But by the time we had finished the meeting, it was coming down in fairly big flakes. It continued snowing and became very thick by five-thirty or six P.M. as I went home to have dinner with my family.

We had scheduled a meeting of schoolteachers for that Thursday night at the Mt. Olive Cathedral CME Church. We were trying to enlist their support for the work stoppage the next day. We had been in general discussions with Black teachers, of all grades and in all schools, to help them make the decision to join us. We also wanted to show support for those teachers committed to our cause as they encouraged other colleagues to stand together with us all.

By seven-thirty, the time the meeting with the teachers was scheduled for that night, we already had four or five inches of snow. At first I thought, "Surely this will cancel the meeting for tonight. So what is the value of going?" But I went anyway. To my great surprise, I found about 150 teachers at the church, patiently waiting for us to brief them about their role in the next day's events. We heard many enthusiastic testimonials about their support for the sanitation workers and the need for our community to join together.

Having 150 Black schoolteachers getting involved in something as controversial as the sanitation strike was something that had never happened in Memphis. Black schoolteachers saying they were going to stay away from school themselves, and telling us they had been encouraging their students to stay away, too, was a major moment. Teachers represented the biggest segment of the Black middle class in Memphis, and they had ventured out in a freak snowstorm on the second day of spring to pledge their solidarity with the striking workers. We knew then and there that our Memphis movement had reached a zenith.

And the mass meeting that same snowy night drew five or six hundred people. I did not get over there, because I stayed with the teachers throughout that evening. But I heard it was also an inspired gathering. As the snow continued, the teachers' meeting ended at about eleven P.M. I did some last-minute checking with our key people, and then I headed on home, too. Because Memphis so rarely experienced snow, the city had no equipment to deal with it. So the roads were rough.

The snow continued all that night. I got up at about six the next morning and saw heaps of it. The radio said it was eighteen to twenty inches. I called Martin. He told me that the weather report in Atlanta had said the airport was fogged in and they couldn't take off. I told him, "Chances are we need to cancel today's march. But I need to make some spot checks with others before I definitely say we will call it off." He said, "You do that, and I will be sitting here at home and waiting, fogged in. So just let me know." By seven A.M., we agreed that we should not try to have the march in the deep snow. I called Martin back and told him, "We are canceling the march. On the bright side, we will have a perfect work stoppage today, because I am sure nobody is going anywhere with all this snow." We both had a laugh at that.

We couldn't lose our momentum. We needed to reschedule the march quickly. We hoped to make an announcement by that Sunday or Monday. Martin was committed to returning. For months before in our conversations, he had expressed his deep concern for addressing poverty, and doing so publicly, too, in his sermons and speeches. That's what motivated the Poor People's Campaign. He was wrestling with how to move toward direct action on the poverty question. He said to me during the strike, "What you are doing in Memphis is what I want to do—tie up the connections between economic justice and racism."

This is where a lot of people miss the meaning of Martin's last days, the meaning of his life, and what he was doing in the end. Those conversations not only cemented Martin's convictions but they bolstered me as I took on my role during the Memphis strike. Martin's deep support of the men and the strike gave us all courage. And for me, having a dear friend backing up my instincts and my leadership helped me carry on.

We were concentrating on the bread-and-butter economic issues. Before that, our movement couldn't even begin to tackle such issues. First, we had to get the "White Only" and "Colored Only" signs down, end segregation on public transportation, and work on eliminating voting rights restrictions. But by 1968, we were bringing the economic struggle to the foreground.

That snowy Friday, I announced at a press conference that the "citizens' march" was being postponed because of the weather. I spoke of our unwavering support for the sanitation workers and said that Dr. King would definitely come back to lead a march soon. Even though negotiations to settle the strike were escalating, they had failed so many times that no one was ever sure if any talks would work. So, as I said in my press briefing, we would continue with our plans for Dr. King to head up a march.

We did not have a regular march on that snowy Friday. But the next day, a Saturday, we did march. And during the week, we moved our morning marches to two in the afternoon, with the youth marches at four-thirty. The police had trouble with the youth marches because the young people held signs and yelled chants as they walked. The police asked us to stop them. But we explained that they were a vital part of our movement and pointed out that the students weren't breaking windows or destroying property. So they continued.

By Monday, March 25, we had rescheduled the march Martin would lead to Thursday, March 28. We had set the route of the march and announced it on new leaflets, along with instructions about where people should gather. The route of the march was the same as we followed in our regular daily marches: from Clayborn Temple to Beale Street, and then right onto Main Street and straight ahead to city hall, where we planned to have a rally. Then we would head back the same way and return to Clayborn Temple. We also handed out small flyers to everyone who marched with instructions about how to follow the discipline of nonviolence.

1. The only force we use is "soul-force" which is peaceful, loving, yet militant.
2. Follow the directions of the march marshals who are wearing yellow arm bands.
3. We will march in the streets.
4. Stay an arm's length from the row in front of you; do not crowd.
5. When the people in front of you stop, you stop.
6. At the City Hall we will stop for a few minutes and then Dr. King and other leaders will go back to the front and move on.
7. We will end the march at Clayborn Temple.
8. The march speaks for itself; no shouting—you may talk in quiet tones.
9. Remember that we have women and children in the march; do not crowd.
10. We have ambulances, doctors and nurses available for any emergency. Tell the nearest marshal.

We were ready for the biggest march yet of the six-week-old strike.

SEVENTEEN

A New Sense of Dignity and Justice

Reverend Lawson on bullhorn asking the last of the sanitation strike marchers to leave Beale Street and go back to Clayborn Temple, March 28, 1968.
UNIVERSITY OF MEMPHIS LIBRARY

The weather was beautiful, warm and bright, as I made my way to Clayborn Temple on Thursday morning, March 28. I knew it was going to be a great event because people were already beginning to gather. And as the morning progressed, people kept coming. We had planned it so marchers could congregate on different streets and then we would lead each group toward the march route. We reserved the area in front of the church for the workers and the ministers, so they could be at the head of the march. The sanitation workers all carried "I AM A MAN" signs, which we had printed for the march.

However, I did not like the fact that spectators who weren't part of the planned march were filling the sidewalks along the march route. They had come out to catch a glimpse of Martin. I tried to get the marshals to clear the sidewalks and ask people either to march in the street with us or leave. As an organizer, I was very uneasy about the sidewalks filled with people who nobody in our groups knew. If they were not participating in the march, they would not have made a commitment to our nonviolent approach and might cause trouble, either inadvertently or on purpose. I alerted the marshals a few times. Another troubling thing was that the police did not seem to have much of a presence before we commenced, to help us control any outside elements that might try to disrupt the march. But we did our best to keep in touch with the contacts we did have with the police, trying to ensure the safety of everyone who came out to join us—including my family. John was six years old, and he loved to march. He and Dorothy were toward the back of the march with Father Bill Greenspun of St. Patrick Catholic Church, so I didn't see them as we gathered.

The march was set to start at ten A.M. Martin's plane was running late. Either Andy Young or Hosea Williams had gotten in touch to tell us they would get there around ten forty-five. We had instructed them to come immediately to the scene of the march and be ready to go when they got there. I was as uptight as anyone about Martin getting there so late. Thousands of people had gathered, but we had promised everyone that Martin would be leading it, so we knew we had to wait until he was among us to start the march.

At about ten forty-five, Martin's car arrived at the intersection in front of Clayborn Temple, and pandemonium broke out. People in the march and on the sidewalks surged around his car. I didn't think it was wise to get going until the sidewalks had been cleared. I had originally wanted Martin to join the crowd after we had gotten the march underway, perhaps a couple of blocks down the route. Initially, he had agreed to this plan. But a couple of the SCLC staff people had said, "We have been in this kind of situation before. And we know there is a lot of excitement at the beginning. But if Martin goes ahead and joins at the start, the march will get itself straightened out and everything will be all right."

I yielded to them somewhat reluctantly. Ralph and Martin got out of the car. Some of our marshals tried to clear the way. But people wanted to get close to Martin. And in their exhilaration they ignored all instructions from anyone. At this point, the police were nowhere to be found and were not involved in helping monitor and control the crowd.

We proceeded from the church to nearby Beale Street, then started to march the three blocks up Beale to Main Street. The onlookers on the sidewalks were still there, not actively participating in the march but sometimes getting into the street and interrupting the flow of the marchers. Some people on the sidewalks who had come to watch were just pushed along with the crowd. Others on the sidewalks looked like they were waiting to cause trouble. I sent a couple of marshals from the front down along the side, asking them to try to get those folks off the sidewalks and to keep them away from store windows.

I was walking in front of Martin and others who were in the front rank, and I was behind a group of marshals who were about a half block or a block ahead of us. The assistant police chief, Henry Lux, was nearby, but not many of his officers were in sight. On our daily marches, there were always some policemen walking along with us. And policemen usually patrolled the streets pretty carefully. So I knew a lot of the officers, because we had worked together to keep the peace during the month of marches before this one.

As we got close to Main, I heard what sounded like a window breaking behind me. Later, some people would claim that marchers broke those first windows using the little one-inch-thick sticks on which the "I AM A MAN" signs were mounted. That simply was not true. Those sticks were too flimsy to break a window. The plate-glass store windows were pretty thick. A person would need a baseball bat or a heavy stone, or maybe the heel of a shoe if someone was strong enough to kick a window just right.

After I heard that window break behind me, we all heard more glass breaking. I asked Assistant Police Chief Lux to get me a bullhorn, which he did right away. We were still on Beale. Just before we got to Main Street, an officer brought me the bullhorn. I turned right at the corner of Beale and Main Street and saw that two blocks up, more people were breaking windows. They were not marchers. The police were making no effort to stop them from breaking windows and looting the stores. As we proceeded up the first block of Main, I saw looting on the east side of the street. I learned later that many police officers were waiting, grouped on the side streets. I did not see where they were at the time. I tried to use the bullhorn to talk to the people on the sidewalks, asking them to stop disrupting the march.

A few yards ahead of our marshals at the front ranks of the march, I then saw a phalanx of police, lined up in formation along Main Street, in rows of three, four, or more, wearing their gas masks. I said to myself, "The police are going to break up this march."

I went up to the marshals in the front of the march—Rev. Ralph Jackson was one of them—and I said, "I'm going to stop the march because the police officers look like they're about to do what they did February twenty-third, and break us up with Mace and billy clubs. So we're going to move it back to the church before they can start."

We got the first line of the march stopped in the street, and the marshals turned to face the rest of the marchers. With the bullhorn I told the other marchers to stop. Then I told Ralph Jackson and the marshals there, "I'm going to try to get King to leave the area. So you stand here, and you must be the last group that walks back down Main to Beale and then back to Clayborn Temple."

I then went directly to Martin and to Ralph Abernathy. Rev. Henry Starks was there, too. I said we had to take Dr. King out of harm's way. Martin balked. I said, "Martin, you have to leave here, because the police are lined up in riot gear blocking the street ahead. And I don't think they're going to move for us. They want to break up the march with Mace, tear gas, and billy clubs, and you will be one of their targets. They have attacked all of us like that before."

Henry Starks agreed with me: going forward with the march, he felt, could be a disaster. Immediately, a handful of people surrounded Abernathy and King, and they got off Main Street and onto a side street, out of the way. Reverend Starks told me they hailed a car on Front Street and the police escorted the car with Martin in it about a mile away to the Holiday Inn Rivermont. The police steered him to that luxury hotel because it was the closest downtown hotel that would have been accessible without having to cross streets closed down for the march. Also, the Rivermont, on a bluff overlooking the Mississippi River, was far enough away from the march to provide for Martin's safety.

I went back and told the front line of marshals that I was going to move down the middle of the street and tell everyone to turn around and march back to the church. I was not really listening to the window breaking at that point. I was concentrating on getting the march turned around. The guys doing the looting were jeopardizing the safety of the marchers, many of whom were women, children, and families who could not easily run from the police. Dorothy and John were there somewhere, too. If we kept moving ahead and the window breakers kept going, the police were going to take harsh action against everyone. And the streets would turn into a battleground.

I walked into the middle of the street with the bullhorn in my hand. "This is Reverend Lawson speaking," I said. "We are closing this march down. It has become unsafe. Please go back the way you came. Stay in the street, but turn around. Go to the church. Go to your cars. Go home. Let's leave the area."

As we moved back, young fellows were still busting windows and grabbing what they could along the way. I kept moving back and forth to get more people to turn the march around. Everyone in the march followed our instructions without hesitation. I stopped walking at the corner of Beale, near the church. I stayed at that intersection until the last rank of marchers and marshals reached the spot where I was. Then we went back to the church together. Once everyone was out of the street, I walked back up and down the street two or three times, trying with little success to urge some of the folks who were throwing stones at the police to give it up and go home.

Two and a half blocks west of the church I saw young men busting windows. I tried to get them to stop, but they didn't. There was an assumption that only young people took part in the looting that day. But I saw a number of folks who were not teenagers. I think most of us who were there would say that teenagers were a small minority of the trouble. It was mostly men between twenty and thirty. They were there to do some damage, to bust windows, loot, and throw things at the police. They used us as a cover.

I watched some guys bust a window at a liquor store and start looting it. In fact, I recognized a few of them. They were young adults, for the most part. None of these fellows had come that day to support the cause of the sanitation workers. Their violent actions and the violence of the police against them had the potential to discredit the strikers, King, and the nonviolent movement. However, I understood why these young Black men were doing what they were doing. Violence was the only option they could imagine for resisting, navigating, and surviving in the unwelcoming world around them, which treated them as second-class citizens.

When I was out on the street I could smell tear gas, and I could hear the shots of the tear gas guns as the police launched canisters into the crowd. I could hear more windows breaking. And I could hear shouts. I saw a couple of skirmishes with police officers. One of the ministers in the front rank, Rev. J. W. Williams, was a tall, elderly man—very distinguished-looking. He was standing in the middle of the road at the end of Beale Street, directing our folk back to the church. Calmly and with great dignity he helped us effect that turnaround. He stood right between the group doing the looting and our folk, where the danger would have been greatest if the police had started firing.

I headed back to the Minimum Salary Building, beside Clayborn Temple. At the moment I arrived, police began to hurl tear gas into the vestibule and sanctuary of Clayborn Temple, a place of worship full of sanitation workers, their families, and their community supporters. As the police escalated their assault on us, some of the people who had been breaking windows used the church for protection. They threw rocks and bottles at the police from the front and one side of the church, then ran into the church to get lost among the crowd of marchers.

I was with city council member Jerred Blanchard as this was happening. We got together in the Minimum Salary Building and called the head of the police, Frank Holloman, to tell him that his men were tear-gassing a church full of families. Holloman told us, "No tear gas is being used." As we had just run through a caustic cloud of tear gas, we let him know that he had bad information, and we told him that his officers were tear-gassing women and children and we wanted to get them out of there. His response, again, was that his men were under orders not to use gas. Then he said people were throwing rocks from inside the church. I told him those guys were not associated with our march. They were throwing things and running back into the church, using it as a cover. I said we would try to stop them but I wasn't sure how.

Eventually, the police stopped tear-gassing the people inside Clayborn Temple. But a lot of families had their first encounter with those police tactics that day. I left the church again and headed up Vance Avenue to where Dorothy had parked our car, in the lot of R. S. Lewis and Sons Funeral Home. The Lewis family were longtime parishioners at Centenary. On the way to the funeral home, I passed a group of guys breaking into a corner liquor store. I tried to dissuade them, but they kept going. I rushed on to the funeral home and was so relieved to find that Dorothy and John had already gone home. When Dorothy had seen the looting and police response starting, she had collected John and walked straight away from the crowd and back to the car, to drive home.

Just as I was heading back from the funeral home, I came upon some kids from the public housing project across the street throwing stones and attacking a white mail carrier in his truck on Vance Avenue. He had jumped out of the postal truck and started running, and they were chasing him. I caught up with him and pulled him into the funeral home while they threw stones at both of us. Neither of us was hurt. Reasoning with someone who is pelting you with stones is a risky proposition, but I simply tried to talk with these young people, and got some of them to stop what they were doing. "This doesn't do us any good," I told them. "The police have more weapons than you have, and better weapons. So this is not the way to fight back against the people who are keeping you down. This is not the way to show your manhood."

My own personal safety was secondary to my major concern for the march itself, and for the safety of the marchers. I stayed out there after most of our folks got back into the church building. At first, I was trying to slow down or stop what was going on in the streets. At one point, I did think about how it would have been a good time for some of those who had threatened my life in the past to try to do me in. In fact, some people had come up to me after the march turned around and said I shouldn't be out on the street for that very reason. But I had long since determined that violence would not be a reason to stop our movement completely, or to stop my work in the movement. It was only natural that the violence that was always lurking in our society would come to the forefront as we continued. The violence during this march, however, had been enough for me to call it off for that day. In Memphis we had never before had the level of violence that would push us to pause for long, or to stop the campaign and give up. Reaching our goals was the only end we saw.

I had never been in a march that needed to be turned around. I think the police didn't manage the situation well, even though we gave them all the information they needed about our plans. Holloman later told me they had certain groups of young people under surveillance, chiefly on Beale Street and Main Street, before the march got started. Why didn't they do more to stop them before they started breaking windows? When he insisted that no tear gas was being used, even though Jerred Blanchard and I knew better, I thought it was astonishing. His problem was that he was going by reports from the field. He didn't seem to consider any other way of getting to the truth except through those reports. That was his process, and he thought it led him to the truth. He was wrong.

During the strike I had a number of lengthy phone calls with Holloman. I actually had some hope for him in those first months. But I think that ultimately he saw his responsibility as protecting the professional officer first, even though there were a number of bad eggs on the force, those who caused much of the trouble. Holloman had been an FBI agent before he took over the Memphis police. And he believed that police officers and professional military men had to make quick, decisive shows of force. So he ensured that his officers on the scene had enough weapons and equipment to step in with might. Police officers learning to de-escalate tense situations nonviolently was not on the agenda back then, and would only rarely become a part of police culture well into the next century.

After a while, I gave up the role of trying to calm the people in the streets. I went back to the church and made sure the marchers there were able to leave and head home safely. Shortly thereafter, Mayor Loeb declared a curfew in the city for that night. And once most of the folk got out of Clayborn Temple and the Minimum Salary Building, I went home for a little while. I was able to see Dorothy and talk to her about the march and the violence. She told me she and John had been safe the whole time, which eased my mind. Somewhere along the line, I got the message that Dr. King was at the Rivermont, and I sent word that I was on my way.

I didn't think that the news that day could get any worse. But before I was able to head out to meet with Martin, I received at least three phone calls from people who had just seen a police officer kill a seventeen-year-old named Larry Payne at a housing project downtown. The callers told me that Payne had been unarmed and the policeman had shot him as he had his hands up, in the basement doorway of the housing project courtyard. It had happened in broad daylight and in front of many of the residents, including many young children. It was a devasting scene. Larry Payne's murder marked the third death at the hands of the city that happened as part of the strike, including the two sanitation workers crushed to death in the faulty garbage truck on February 1—the moment that sparked the start of the strike.

I needed to get to the Rivermont before the curfew to see how Martin was doing and talk with him about the march and its aftermath, and about the next steps. When I arrived at his room, he was lying on the bed. Andy Young and Ralph Abernathy were there, too. Martin was composed. Behind his calm, I knew he was upset. He saw the march as a disaster. His chief concern was that the march and the movement would have to go on. We didn't stop because of white violence, so we couldn't stop because of Black violence. We made that decision. And I made it clear from the very beginning that the next day the union and the community supporters would resume our daily marches, and we would be marching every day after that.

We discussed this march's implications for the Poor People's Campaign. Martin said he could see a lot of our critics now saying that we can't have nonviolent marches anymore and that we shouldn't go to Washington. For him, that was why we couldn't stop. We had to have a nonviolent march in Memphis. We couldn't let the scenes of violence in Memphis overtake our nonviolent movement, the sanitation strike, and our main message of justice for all. He had to return and we had to have a nonviolent march—in the same way we hadn't backed down when we faced violence during the Freedom Ride, or in the Birmingham or St. Augustine campaigns, or in the Bloody Sunday march across the Edmund Pettus Bridge in Selma. If there wasn't a peaceful march in Memphis, the criticism would grow so intense it would be almost impossible to have one in Washington with the Poor People's Campaign.

We knew we had to say something publicly that afternoon, so we shifted our attention to the immediate need for a press conference. We agreed that I would make the initial statement, and then Martin would make a statement. He would insist we should have another march, and he would announce that his staff would stay in town, helping us, to make certain that this time the march would be nonviolent.

The local press found out very quickly that King had gone to the Rivermont, and members of the media gathered outside. Hateful comments were already circulating about King having run away from the march like a scared rabbit. So without delay, we invited print, radio, and television reporters into a conference room at the hotel. I sat at a table between Martin and Ralph Abernathy, with Rev. Henry Starks and Rev. Ralph Jackson, Jesse Epps from the union, and King's aide Bernard Lee beside us. Some SCLC staffers and some of our COME people stood behind us.

As we had agreed, I spoke first, from notes I had made. I explained how earlier that morning we had more than twenty thousand people moving together in a massive march toward Main Street.

> There were women, children, people in wheelchairs, people from all walks of life across the Negro community. We began to see some of the younger people doing some minimum smashing of windows and looting, and doing some stone throwing. We, with bullhorns . . . got our march systematically to turn around and to move with dignity back to the church. We turned the march around.
>
> We want to make it very clear, however, that the issue is not a question of the violence today . . . or a question of Dr. King's presence here. But the issue is still the issue that was here last week in the city of Memphis, and that was here yesterday, and that is here today—namely justice, fairness for the sanitation workers, and a new sense of dignity and justice for the Black people and the poor people of this community. . . .
>
> Now, we saw . . . the violence by some of the young people—who are excellent students of this very sick society of ours, who . . . therefore cannot hear the message of nonviolence, the message of love and reconciliation. . . .
>
> We have insisted again and again that violent elements have been built into this city by racism, and that if the city would not listen, and somehow try to change injustice, then this violence would come to the foreground and that none of us would be capable of stopping it. We are now saying to the city, "Will you please listen? Will you please recognize that in the heart of our city there is massive cruelty and poverty and indignity, and that only if you remove it can you have order?"
>
> . . . We are planning, today, new marches, and new demonstrations, that we hope will stay . . . nonviolent. . . . Because we fear that if violence continues in our city it will become an excuse for the wholesale massacre of innocent people in our midst, including recognizable Black leadership of our city and nation.

Ralph Abernathy spoke next, saying that Martin Luther King would not be a part of any type of violent demonstration. He told of how we were able to persuade Dr. King to leave the march. And Ralph declared that Martin "did not run one step. He left in a dignified fashion. And it was only upon our insistence that he did leave. . . . He will not run. But none of us in the SCLC will participate in violent demonstrations."

Martin was asked whether threats of Stokely Carmichael and H. Rap Brown coming to town had stirred up young people. Brown was the head of SNCC at the time and had called for armed resistance to racism. Martin replied by trying to reframe the question.

> Carmichael and Brown are not the problem. They are products of the problem. They are rather angry fellows. But their anger is . . . derived from the continued existence of evil conditions within our society.
>
> And I would rather put my time and place my energy into getting rid of these conditions. Because as long as they are here, they're going to produce angry people. After all, Mr. Brown and Mr. Carmichael did not invent or bring slavery into being. They did not create slums. They did not create unemployment. They did not create segregated schools. And we've got to come to see that the causal basis for the riots taking place in our country can be traced to something much deeper than any particular individual.

Martin then said he would be in town longer than he had planned because of the way the march had unfolded. And I said the COME leadership and union members would be meeting the next morning at ten o'clock to continue strategizing for the sanitation workers and the movement. We would carry on our daily marches. And I called on the city to settle the strike.

Mayor Loeb's curfew went from seven P.M. to five A.M., and he had contacted the governor, who sent in four thousand National Guard troops.

Of all the news outlets in town, the *Tri-State Defender*, one of the two Black-owned Memphis weekly newspapers at the time, ran the most accurate coverage of the march and its aftermath, detailing the looting and the resulting police violence, under the banner headline, "Cops Wage War on Black Community."

> Memphis' Negro population has become a community under siege . . . many innocent Negroes have been beaten for no apparent reason.
>
> One Memphis youth has been senselessly slain by police. It is now impossible for Negroes to travel in their own community or sit

> on their own porches . . . without seeing heavily armed police, sheriff's men and fully armed national guardsmen.

The paper told of the march and the spectators who were only there to see Dr. King, and who rushed to him when he arrived, and it said the police did not appear to be addressing the looters. Instead, it said, they "dashed head long into the peaceful marchers and began to attack those people."

> The ministers then took emergency action. They dispersed themselves throughout the line and gave instruction to the marchers. The marchers conducted themselves very well being caught in the crossfire of police gas, guns and the looters' rocks and bottles. The ministers braved all of these things to get the marchers safely back to the Temple. Most of the looters got away. . . .
>
> . . . The police surrounded the Temple and shot tear gas in on the ministers, men, women, nuns and their students. As occupants of the church attempted to flee the police beat them with clubs and sprayed them with Mace.
>
> . . . A report came on the radio that police had invaded the NAACP office and had beaten Harold Whalum, president of Union Protective Life Insurance Co.
>
> . . . It was reported that the police had gone in a barbershop on Beale near Second beating the barbers and all their customers.

Across from the *Tri-State Defender* offices and a few blocks away from Clayborn Temple was a restaurant called the Big M Lounge. The paper said the entire newspaper staff saw police storm into the place around three P.M., hours after the disruptions, "dragging customers out and beating them unmercifully." A reporter and photographer saw a badly bloodied man who had been in the lounge. They suggested to the police that they take the injured man to the hospital. Immediately, ten officers "ran up, beat the man again and threw him in a police car. They cocked their guns and aimed at the reporter-photographer team and said, 'Move along niggers or we'll do the same thing to you.'"

Soon after the march, Jesse Turner, head of the local NAACP, sent a telegram to President Johnson asking for a federal investigation into the "numerous charges of brutality by officers of the Memphis Police Department."

Jesse Turner was also president of the Black-owned Tri-State Bank. Despite his suit and tie, police maced him that day too, along with one of the three Black city council members, Fred Davis, who was also wearing a suit. Davis had told the police he was a city council member before they maced him, poked him in the side with a billy club, and told him to "Move on." Turner said he also saw police officers viciously beat a young Black man unconscious, calling it "one of the most brutal attacks I ever saw."

Harassment and police violence continued through Thursday night. About three hundred people were arrested that Thursday afternoon and night, mostly young Black men. They were rounded up in our neighborhoods and hauled away. More than sixty were reported injured.

The next day, Martin met with members of the Invaders, who were being blamed for the looting. They wanted to see him to tell him they weren't part of the violence and to try to get his support for their organization. Martin talked about them at another press conference he and Ralph held at the Rivermont that Friday afternoon. Martin said he hadn't been part of organizing the march and did not know that locally there were ideological differences within the Black community in Memphis regarding violence and nonviolence. He said he usually saw those kinds of differences in Northern cities, but not in the South.

I had gotten wind of what Charles Cabbage and others in the Invaders had been saying to Martin. They strongly placed the blame for the violence on the Memphis preachers. I was told that I was mentioned specifically, as well as Ralph Jackson. They said we kept them out of the planning and organizing of the march. Martin would learn during the next few days that what they had told him that day was not entirely accurate.

While it is true that I argued with members of the Invaders who were sometimes at COME meetings, I did not exclude them. They simply weren't a constructive force and didn't bring ideas we could use, so I pushed them to do so. As chairman of the strategy committee, I had emphasized from the start that we should try to involve them. We talked to them almost every day, and they were encouraged to participate in the campaign. During the first days, when we started the daily marches, I also encouraged the ministers to raise money for them so they could continue to operate. As for the march, the Invaders had promised a certain number of marshals, but they did not show up.

The violence at the march tore Martin's staff people apart. They were more upset about it than he was. A number of them had not wanted Martin to travel to Memphis at all. They were aiming at the Poor People's Campaign, and they had his schedule and his plans lined up, and didn't at all like the idea of us changing his plans so he could come to Memphis. Andy Young tended to be far cooler-headed than some of the other staff people, even in the worst situations, which I appreciated. He and Martin understood perhaps best of all that backing the Memphis sanitation workers was essential and directly related to the goals of the Poor People's Campaign.

At Martin's press conference that Friday, he took some blame for not getting a better sense of the situation on the ground in Memphis. He certainly didn't blame me. Nonetheless, I also took some of the blame for what happened that day. I knew more about the situation in the city of Memphis than Martin's staff did. And I should not have accepted their analysis that if we got started with Martin there, instead of having him join us after a couple of blocks, the tension on the sidewalks would straighten itself out. I had not operated like that in the past, and I should have insisted we clear things up before we began.

We made two basic mistakes in the planning. One was that we did not work hard enough on training our marshals. For example, our marshals were very hesitant about what to do when the trouble began on the sidewalks. Those of us who were the chief marshals had to keep prompting and supervising the marshals at every point, saying out loud, "Marshals, get the sidewalks clear." We never should have had to do that. There should have been no hesitation at that point. But we had never had a march of that size, and we didn't foresee spectators milling about on the sidewalks. That was a weakness in our own planning and training.

The marshals should have known that clearing the path was a part of their responsibility. I am sure it was emphasized in the training sessions, but I think the marshals anticipated an easier time of it, because for six weeks all of our marches had been so well controlled. It was very apparent to me at the beginning of the big march that we had become weak and our marshal training was inadequate. I could have insisted that the march not go on. I could have had bullhorns up in front. And we could have said, "Dr. King is here but we are not letting him join the march until we know that the sidewalks are clear. It's not safe." And then we could have said that we were going to cancel the march unless we were able to proceed along the route with marchers lined up in the ranks we had organized.

After that march, we never took any chances again. We never started marches until all the sidewalks were cleared. And before at least two or three of the large marches that followed, we parked huge trucks on the streets as barriers at the starting points, to funnel everyone who was going to march through that entrance point.

The second major mistake we made was to attach the "I AM A MAN" signs to those sticks so that people could hold them more easily. We tried to correct that as fast as we could when we saw people taking the poster off the stick and a few young people waving the sticks around, as if they could use them as weapons. We had some of the marshals collect bundles of sticks that people had taken off and carry them into the church.

We did some investigating, and gathered a lot of pictures of people in the march and on the sidewalks. And it must be said that the people we saw starting the violence were not members of the Invaders. They had stayed away from the march that day, partly, I came to understand, because they did not believe nonviolence was the way to racial justice.

What our investigations did show was looting by guys who were fairly well known as small-time shoplifters and thieves in the Beale Street area. It became clear that these people planned their strategy for that day. I wouldn't say it was a formal group. But in those early moments, there was systematic looting of stores. Automobiles pulled up to certain stores on Beale Street and took everything out of the windows very quickly. So I don't think the problem was an ideological battle within the movement between violence and nonviolence. I believe some people used the march to commit property crimes. I also suspect other people or organizations opposed to our movement may deliberately have sent people there to incite trouble, so we could be discredited.

Martin left Memphis Friday night. I didn't talk to him that day or the next, because as chairman of the strategy committee, I was occupied with meetings from early in the day until two or three in the morning, to plan the logistics and next moves in the strike.

We met in a room at the Sheraton-Peabody Hotel, where Jerry Wurf and the other union leaders stayed during the strike. One of those nights at about two A.M., I left and went down the steps and through the lobby into the hotel parking lot. My car was isolated under a streetlamp. I drove a 1959 black Volkswagen bug convertible that Dorothy and I had bought before we had kids. It was the only car in the lot at that late hour, and I realized it could easily have been sabotaged, sitting there all by itself. I thought of the death threats I had received throughout the strike.

I approached the car fearfully. I walked around it, peered inside through the closed windows, and got down and looked under it. Seeing nothing suspicious, I unlocked the driver's door, inspected the front seat, and surveyed the entire interior of the car. I circled it again, trying to see what I hadn't seen the first time. I left the doors and windows open for a minute, and walked around the car double-checking, another time or two. Finally, I got in and started the engine, and made the drive home safely.

We all felt wary. Violence was stalking us again. Death threats were a regular feature for those of us in the movement. But for me they got worse during the strike. They mostly came through phone calls Dorothy answered at home or my secretary, Cheryl Johnson, answered at the church. She was a young woman from Memphis who was with me for the whole time I was at Centenary. Cheryl was a good, steady presence in my office. I know getting those calls was a hard thing for her to endure. The strike was a time in my life when I was most acutely afraid for myself, my congregation, and my family. Still, we all kept going because those thirteen hundred men—heroes who had endured so much themselves—deserved our utmost, unfailing support.

That weekend after the March 28 demonstration, a few other COME members and I met with police leaders Holloman and Lux at First Methodist Church in a give-and-take discussion about the march. We expressed our dismay at the brutality that had taken place, such as the murder of Larry Payne and the rounding up of young Black men after the march. It wasn't the most productive meeting. But Holloman gave some of us passes to be out in the community after the nighttime curfews.

The following week, Martin and his staff and I spoke on the phone several times, and we set Friday, April 5, as the date for King's next march in Memphis. When Martin King told me he was going to do something, I didn't question it. So I knew he was coming back to Memphis, even though I heard reports that some on his staff didn't want him to come. They saw participating in the Memphis scene as taking away from their longer-term priorities. I couldn't blame them for feeling that way. They found it difficult to justify the schedule changes. It wasn't any kind of ideological breech, as many writers and others outside the movement have tried to say ever since. Rarely was there a campaign without a lot of static. Martin was accustomed to people criticizing his moves. Direct action was such a new process for people, and everyone was experimenting together. So there were always going to be tensions and debates.

Right away, the local and national press jumped on what had happened at the march and said it showed that nonviolence was a farce and therefore our movement was also a farce. *The Commercial Appeal*'s editorial the morning after the march came with the headline "Moment of Truth." It spoke of how Memphis had to have law and order, and it praised the police for their restraint as violence erupted. And alongside the news articles about the chaotic day, there in his place at the bottom of the front page of the second section was Hambone, standing with one hand on his hip and one foot stuck out to the side, holding his pipe, and saying with a grin, "DON' MEK NO DIFF'UNCE WHUT KIN' O' FACE YOU'S GOT, HIT LOOK MO' BETTUH SMILIN'!!"

The headline of the afternoon paper's editorial used quotation marks to mock our nonviolent approach: "'Non-Violence' in Memphis." The piece began by asking the city, in a direct echo of the title of Martin's 1967 book, "Where do we go from here?" Then it also praised the police, perhaps unconsciously evoking the plantation past by using the word "masterly." And it turned the word "brutal" back on us, without ever mentioning the peaceful marchers of all ages who police officers beat, maced, and showered with tear gas in the church.

> Operating with efficiency under the direction of Police and Fire Director Frank Holloman, the policemen and firemen did a masterly job of protecting innocent citizens and property. There will be, inevitably, charges of police brutality. But it must be remembered that the police were dealing with a brutal situation.

The editorial went on to criticize me and other unnamed strike supporters:

> Now who was to blame? At this point, it would not be wise to accuse any individual or group. Let us say that yesterday's violence was the

explosion of hatreds long-smoldering in the hearts of young Negroes who have not learned to discipline their emotions.

But it must be said that the leadership of yesterday's march cannot dissociate itself from responsibility for the trouble. The Rev. James M. Lawson Jr. tried to do this in a statement he issued last night when he attributed the violence to individuals not connected with the march or with the movement sympathetic to the sanitation strikers. The Rev. Mr. Lawson and other leaders who take the same line know full well that the protest leaders had called on students to leave their schools to take up marching; mothers and children, too. Only a few days ago there was the call to "close down Memphis" in order to show solidarity of support for the strikers. No, the leadership cannot point the finger at others and say, "They were not in our crowd."

On Saturday, March 30, the vitriol did not let up. *The Commercial Appeal*'s morning editorial, entitled "King's Credibility Gap," was accompanied by a degrading drawing from Hambone's author, Cal Alley, of Martin standing in the middle of littered ground, wearing an awkward, loose-fitting suit and tie, with a bewildered, lost look on his face. He was staring straight ahead with big eyes and pursed lips. His oversized hands were contorted and pointing to his chest as he said, "WHO? ME?" The editorial unleashed the blame on Martin this time. It said his call during his speech on March 18 for a work and school stoppage had precipitated the violence on March 28.

Dr. King's pose as leader of a non-violent movement has been shattered. He now has the entire nation doubting his word when he insists that his April project—a shanty-town sit-in in the nation's capital—can be peaceful.

In short, Dr. King is suffering from one of those awesome credibility gaps.

Furthermore, he wrecked his reputation as a leader as he took off at his speed when violence occurred, instead of trying to use his persuasive prestige to stop it.

The white-run newspapers' coverage of our press conference after the march never mentioned the way Martin and I both repeatedly tried to direct the attention back to the sanitation workers and the poverty in which they were living. It never mentioned the way in which all of us in the Black community felt afraid for our lives when the police and the National Guard infiltrated our neighborhoods.

But an editorial in the *Tri-State Defender*, entitled, "Memphis Policing," caught the mood after the unprovoked police violence many Black people witnessed or experienced that day.

> Memphis police are receiving some half-baked praise for the so-called "restrained manner" in which they handled the disorders that occurred in the city. . . .
>
> . . . One citizen . . . said, "The Memphis Police Department was 'policing' Negroes not 'rioters.'"

Another editorial in the same weekly edition of the *Tri-State Defender* also called out the police:

> The Black people of Memphis resent the arrogant attitude of these "trigger happy cowboys" as they ride through peaceful communities, five and six in a car, waving their shotguns out the window and rudely spitting tobacco on streets where Negro women are standing.
>
> . . . Black people are tired . . . of the procrastinations of the city council; tired of Mayor Loeb's dictatorship; tired of miscarriage of justice in the courts; just plain tired.

Regardless of the facts of life for Black people in Memphis, the editorial stance of the white-run papers never seemed to alter or rest. That's not surprising, since there was hardly a Black person, if any, among their newsroom staffs. In fact, the mockery and vitriol continued to harden through the weekend. Perhaps the most cruel quip appeared as a subheading on Sunday, March 31, in a *Commercial Appeal* column that consisted of short anecdotes and news snippets that were meant to provide a lighter or humorous take on current events. The final, two-sentence piece in the column that day was about Martin leaving the march and had the subheadline "Chicken A La King."

On Monday, April 1, Dan Kuykendall, the Republican congressman from Memphis, spoke out against Martin on the floor of the United States

House of Representatives, with support from his two fellow Memphis representatives, both white Democrats. Kuykendall started with an insult: "Mr. Speaker: Last week an internationally known figure who by some unbelievable set of circumstances was at one time awarded a Nobel Peace Prize, came into Memphis, Tennessee, a city under stress." Then the congressman went on to blame Martin for the disrupted march, saying he had "tucked his tail like a scared puppy and ran." He also said of Martin, "In his afternoon press conference he blamed our local Negro leadership who stayed in the melee and desperately tried to restore order while he was cowering in a back alley several blocks away."

Kuykendall's selective account left out the fact that it was the local Negro leadership who had urged Martin to leave because we were concerned that he would be the main target of rogue police officers. The congressman then got to his main goal: a detailed defense of Memphis's reputation and how progressive the city had been in race relations. In closing, Representative Dan Kuykendall from Memphis ended his April 1, 1968, speech on the floor of the U.S. Congress with more insults for Martin, including what would prove in a few days to be an ominous quip about him avoiding gunshots:

> Call the roll of cities where King has taken his nonviolent demonstrations—in city after city there has been violence, the mob ran wild. There was burning and looting and people were killed. But King always manages to get away just before the shooting starts.

All over the country in the days that followed, editorial writers in national and local papers similarly seized on the march as a way to criticize Martin and nonviolence and to question the viability of the Poor People's Campaign. On Tuesday, April 2, *The Commercial Appeal* saw fit to republish a particularly virulent piece from *The Dallas Morning News* entitled "Memphis Blues" on its editorial page.

> Well, the headline-hunting high priest of nonviolent violence has done it again. This time, thanks to one of his press-agent protests, a local garbage strike has exploded into a full-fledged outbreak of racial violence, replete with looting, tear gas, mass arrests, dozens injured, one dead and a timely duck out by the marching militant himself, Martin Luther King.

> And this is in Memphis, noted throughout the nation for its progress in racial harmony and cooperation. . . . Presumably this is just a publicity warmup for the big Washington ruckus, so far as the Nobel Peace prizewinner is concerned.
>
> . . . King's road show came to Memphis Thursday, like a torchbearer sprinting into a powderhouse. And today there's a new version of the Memphis Blues that can be heard in the crackle of fires, the clatter of breaking glass and the rattle of gunfire.

Later that morning, we held a funeral for Larry Payne, the teenager a Memphis police officer shot and killed in a basement doorway that opened into the courtyard of his housing project. Police officers were chasing him as they believed he was a suspect in a looting of a nearby Sears store. They claimed he was carrying a knife and threatened the officer. But the many eyewitnesses at the scene said that he was unarmed. I was quoted in a *Press-Scimitar* article about the shooting, saying that we had statements on tape from fifteen witnesses, all affirming that Payne "had his hands raised when he was shot in the stomach with a shotgun, and that he didn't have a knife as police claimed."

The two white-run newspapers didn't cover Larry Payne's funeral at Clayborn Temple, which was attended by about five hundred people, including sanitation workers, ministers, activists, and many of his high school classmates. Martin had called Lizzie Payne, Larry Payne's mother, during the weekend and told her he would come see her when he returned to Memphis sometime in the next few days. The *Memphis World,* the other Black-run newspaper in town, covered the funeral and reported that during the service Mrs. Payne cried out, "They shot you down like a dog."

The *Tri-State Defender* reported most extensively on how eyewitnesses described Larry Payne's death:

> The cop ran up to the door and yelled "Come Out Nigger Or I'm Going To Shoot." The boy came out with his hands over his head, and pleaded with the cop not to shoot; without a word the cop shoved the gun in the youth's stomach and shot. Larry slid to the ground, dead with his mouth and eyes open. When Larry's mother arrived on the scene, she made an attempt to get to her son's body but the policeman who shot him pushed her back while cursing at her.

> She cried, "You Killed My Son! You Killed My Son!"
>
> The officer waved the gun in her face and said "If You Don't Get Back Nigger I'll Kill You." Some spectators said at this point the cop waved the gun in the mother's face and she fainted.

⸻

Despite the pain all around us, the white community seemed relatively untouched by these events in the days that followed. In East Memphis, where Mayor Loeb lived, life returned to the status quo—so much so that when *The New York Times* came to town to cover the aftermath of the march, the story's headline said, "Whites in Memphis Unshaken by Riot."

> The white leadership in Memphis, which has expressed pride in the city's racial climate for years, appeared largely unshaken in its conviction today despite a costly riot in the downtown area this week.
>
> "It's not bad at all," said Thomas W. Faires, president of the Memphis area Chamber of Commerce. "If the Negro ministers would tend to their ministering instead of trying to stir things up, we wouldn't have had this trouble.
>
> "Nothing can be done about this situation. It's going to take maybe 40 years before we make any real progress. You can't take these people and make the kind citizens out of them you'd like."
>
> . . . Much of the white leadership expressed satisfaction at the forceful manner in which the police and about 4,000 National Guard troops put down the Negro disorders that began on Thursday morning.
>
> "I think we'll come out of this mess with an improved image because of the careful handling of it by our law enforcement officers," declared George M. Houston, who is the president of Future Memphis, Inc.
>
> Wayne Pyeatt, executive vice president of the National Bank of Commerce, expressed the widely held view that racial problems were not serious here and that the mass of the Negro population was not badly frustrated. . . .
>
> Negro leaders have long been outraged by this sanguine attitude. One who rejected it today was Dr. Vasco A. Smith Jr., a dentist who is president of the Shelby County Democratic Club, the dominant Negro political organization.

> "It's a damn lie," said Dr. Smith, who also serves as vice president of the Memphis branch of the National Association for the Advancement of Colored People.

Vasco then spoke of the real problems we had in Memphis. The article caught the blindness—or willful ignorance—of so many white business leaders who headed up entities like the chamber of commerce and its offshoots and patrons. In Memphis, the chamber of commerce and other such groups persistently opposed living wages and access to opportunity because of what they called "the cost." They believed the only legitimate cost was the bare minimum they could do for everyone else, as they shaped, formed, and promoted a base of outsized wealth for a few people.

Out of all of President Johnson's Great Society legislation—the Civil Rights Act, the Voting Rights Act, the War on Poverty programs—the U.S. Chamber of Commerce opposed each of them. This country was born from the bloody conquest of Indigenous nations and the kidnapping of Black people from another continent into enslavement, which forced our ancestors to do hard labor without pay for 250 years. And this country originated from a spirituality that justified burning women at the stake as witches. Those three original sins were so foundational to the creation of the United States, and are such a part of who we are, that generations of Americans—including many economic leaders—have gone into deep denial, making them utterly blind to the harm they do.

The chamber's fixation on the wealth-gathering part of the economy, not on the salaries paid to working people, produced its value system, which promoted wealth for the already wealthy. Increased production of millionaires was an effect of the chamber's target goals for the economy in the 1960s. The ambition to produce, even at the expense of the workers who made it possible, blocked the chamber's executives' ability to see how the United States would be a much more stable place if everyone got a decent income. The chamber saw individuals, businesses, and nations that acquired more wealth than anyone else as the bastions of progress. Millionaires were revered as heroes. But that pro-wealthy stance usually prohibited the embrace of a more expansive standard for progress: that everyone in the wealthiest country on earth should be able to do all the things they needed to do for their families and themselves without an intense personal struggle. Sanitation workers should be revered as heroes.

As the city prepared for Martin's return, that *New York Times* article brought the focus back to the sanitation workers and the essence of their struggle, expressed in their simple, newly coined message, which was resonating through Memphis, and for Martin, and into the wider world:

> Much of the discontent, Negro leaders here said, concerns the general issue of their dignity. . . . Recent demonstrators have symbolized this feeling by carrying signs that read, "I am a man."

EIGHTEEN

Something Is Happening in Memphis

On the balcony of the Lorraine Motel, Rev. Ralph Abernathy, Martin Luther King Jr., Reverend Lawson, lawyers, and union leaders enter room 307 after receiving a restraining order barring King and his aides from leading a march in Memphis, April 3, 1968.

BARNEY SELLERS, COMMERCIAL APPEAL VIA IMAGN

We all lived the next two days hour-to-hour, even minute-to-minute. A breakthrough seemed possible. We believed Martin's return and the national attention it would bring could put enough pressure on the city to settle the strike. Finally, the sanitation workers would win. And we were committed to ensuring that Martin would lead a completely nonviolent march in Memphis sometime in the coming week. The organizing was moving along well, and we had a stellar legal team to address the hurdles we figured the city would try to put in our way. We started out with ardent determination and great hope.

WEDNESDAY, APRIL 3, 1968

7:00 A.M.: Sheraton-Peabody Hotel

The strike strategy committee met at our regular time and place for breakfast. We were still conducting marches each day, and the union was still trying to negotiate with the city. Staff members from the SCLC had been in town since the weekend, helping to plan the march, which we discussed moving from our original plan of later that week, on Friday, to the following Monday, April 8. A lot of people were coming in from out of town. Bayard Rustin and Victor Gotbaum, New York City's AFSCME leader, had been working with us to bring in union people and civil rights activists from around the country. But we suspected the city was about to file an injunction against a large march.

11:35 A.M.: Memphis Metropolitan Airport

Martin's plane was delayed because of a bomb threat in Atlanta. When he finally landed, he held a brief press conference at the airport.

He was asked about his plans while in Memphis.

> Martin: We will talk with the leadership of the community, Reverend Lawson, Reverend Jackson, and others, to determine our course of action. . . . At this time we are committed to having another massive demonstration. . . .
>
> Reporter: Dr. King, if there is a court injunction, would you obey it and not march?
>
> Martin: I'd have to cross that bridge when we come to it. I don't know exactly what we would do in that case. We have our legal advisers with us. And then, of course, we have our conscience to live with. And it's a question of whether we would go on, on the basis of what we think is a basic constitutional right.
>
> Reporter: What have your aides told you about the cooperation that has been arranged with the young people?
>
> Martin: They have been talking with various groups, and I have gotten some very encouraging reports from them. . . . These groups

have committed themselves to cooperation and committed themselves to following guidelines set forth of nonviolence. . . .

Reporter: How has the violence in the Memphis march affected your plans for the march to Washington?

Martin: Our plan in Washington is going on. Memphis will not in any way curtail it or deter it. We must spotlight the plight of the poor nationally.

11:45 A.M.: Federal Courthouse

As Martin was speaking to reporters at the airport, a temporary restraining order was approved in federal court. The city of Memphis filed it to stop out-of-towners from marching, meaning Martin and his staff would be arrested if they tried to march. The city's attorneys knew that a federal order would be harder for us to go against than the kinds of state injunctions we had faced in Birmingham and in Memphis in 1966 against T. O. Jones and other AFSCME organizers.

12:30 P.M.: Centenary Methodist Church

Martin, Andy, Ralph, and others arrived for a meeting of ministers in the fellowship hall of my church. Martin spoke briefly, urging strike supporters to stay the course.

We had known an injunction was coming since Sunday or Monday. So we had a chance to start planning to deal with it. I had been on the phone with Martin and Ralph and others about the possibility. We were all in agreement that we would have the march regardless of whether we could reverse the injunction or not. But we did fight it.

That morning, I had been on the phone with Lucius Burch, whose law firm had worked with us during the strike, asking him to represent Martin and COME (Community on the Move for Equality) in court. Burch also got calls from the ACLU in Atlanta, as well as the SCLC, asking him to represent Martin. The NAACP Legal Defense Fund, in New York, had already engaged attorneys Walter Bailey and Louis Lucas from A. W. Willis's firm. They had represented us that morning during the city's request for the restraining order. When Martin arrived, we told him to expect a visit at the church from federal marshals to issue that temporary restraining order against the march we were planning. It could become a permanent injunction at any time, and we knew we had to fight those efforts.

Not only were the U.S. marshals coming to the church to meet with Martin, so were the attorneys from Lucius Burch's law firm. But Martin and Ralph and Andy were hungry and headed to the Lorraine before anyone arrived.

1:30 P.M.: Lorraine Motel, Dining Room

Martin and Ralph went down to the hotel and ordered catfish. Three members of the Invaders talked to them while they ate. Some of the SCLC staff people who'd come in a few days before had been making a concerted effort to work with the Invaders and others. During the lunch, the federal marshals arrived, met with Martin in the courtyard of the motel, and served him and the five other SCLC staffers named in the restraining order.

2:30 P.M.: Lorraine Motel, Room 307

Lucius Burch arrived at the Lorraine with two younger attorneys, Mike Cody and Charlie Newman. I came over from the church, and we met with Martin, Andy, and a few other people in room 307, next door to the room Martin and Ralph were sharing—room 306. Then Lucius Burch filed a plea with the federal court that any injunction be set aside and the march be permitted. A hearing was set for the next morning, and it was decided rather quickly that Andy and I would be the witnesses at the hearing.

6:00 P.M.: 653 Alston Avenue, Memphis

I got home for my usual dinnertime with the family. Before supper, still in my suit and tie, I played basketball at the garage hoop with my sons, as I often did. Sometimes we would also play touch football in front of the house with some of the neighborhood boys. Then we cleaned up a little bit and sat down for dinner with Dorothy. I told her about my day, and that I would be testifying in the morning in federal court in our effort to have the city's order lifted. After dinner, even though a rainstorm was coming, I headed back to Mason Temple for a mass meeting with the sanitation workers and their families. Dorothy stayed home with the boys.

7:30 P.M.: Mason Temple

I got to the church before all the thunder and rain. Ralph told us that because the night was so bad, Martin thought people probably wouldn't show up. So he asked Ralph to take his place. But he said that if Ralph got there and it looked like he should come, to call him and he would head over.

Despite the weather, people came out. A few of us talked to the crowd as things got started. The killing and funeral of Larry Payne was on everyone's minds. So I spoke with the crowd about how the police had justified his shooting.

> They can talk all night long about . . . the fact that the police were fair and square. And that they were only doing their job. But if their job requires that they stick a shotgun in the midsection of a seventeen-year-old boy who has his hands over his head and is saying, "Don't shoot," then we need—

The ourburst after those words—*don't shoot*—was so loud and enveloping, I couldn't finish my sentence. Eventually I continued, saying it was "high time that we rid Memphis and this nation" of that kind of police work.

> Because we don't need it anymore. And this movement is going to insist that no matter what white citizens, or some white citizens, might say, we know what police brutality and harassment means. And we are through with it, and we want to see it end—once and for all.

The violence that occurred during the Memphis sanitation strike was almost entirely invoked, ignited, engineered, and perpetrated by the police. It did not come from the strikers at all, nor from the many people engaged in our nonviolent campaign. I don't even think it came from the so-called angry voices of the Invaders. And on March 28, the inability to police a few looters who took advantage of the situation turned into justifying tear-gassing families in a church, randomly rounding up hundreds of young Black men and boys from their own neighborhoods and hauling them to jail in paddy wagons, beating Black people who happened to be inside a nearby restaurant, and shooting and killing an unarmed teenage boy accused of robbery without any due process. I brought Larry Payne's murder up in that moment because I was describing the difficulty we continued to have with the structures of our society, bent in the direction of injustice and racism.

8:15 P.M.: Mason Temple

Fairly soon, we realized that the crowd that night still wanted to hear from Martin. I was one of the people who urged Ralph Abernathy to ask Martin to come on over. So he called him.

9:00 P.M.: Mason Temple

Martin arrived, and the place broke out in cheering. He stepped onto the platform and Ralph got up and gave him a splendid, twenty-eight-minute introduction. I told Ralph afterward how great it was. A few people joked that it was so long that it sounded like a eulogy.

Then Martin began to speak. He said he didn't expect such a turnout because of the storm warnings, but that everyone there was showing they were determined. "Something is happening in Memphis. Something is happening in our world."

Then he began preaching. He started off poetically, considering what period of human history he would choose if God said he could live during any era. He took the audience through milestones in history, from Egypt and biblical times to ancient Greece, Rome, and the Renaissance, and to Lincoln and the Emancipation Proclamation, and then to the Depression in the 1930s. But he said he would still pick the era we were in that night: "the second half of the twentieth century." He said he would choose our time because he saw God working right then all over the world, with people asking to be free, from the African independence movements to our movement in the U.S.

He mentioned the war going on and then talked about the importance of nonviolence. "It is no longer a choice between violence and nonviolence in this world," he said, "it's nonviolence or nonexistence."

A wonderful feeling filled the temple as he spoke. Outside, the thunder was rumbling, the lightning flashing, and the rain pouring down. But inside—even amid the great struggle and tension of the strike, with the windows flapping and echoing through the rafters from the tornado-level winds in the area—more than three thousand people in that church felt very much at home, with one another and in the universe.

Martin brought up the march that we turned around a few days before and the police response, saying the news media only wanted to talk about the violence. But he explained that we had to keep marching and putting the focus back on the sanitation workers:

> . . . And force everybody to see that there are thirteen hundred of God's children here suffering, sometimes going hungry, going through dark and dreary nights wondering how this thing is going to come out. That's the issue.

He spoke of the injunction and how we were going to court the next morning to fight against it.

In Mason Temple that night I felt a oneness, an enthusiasm, and great warmth. It was mystical. I basked in that feeling. At one point Martin even praised some of the clergy in Memphis.

> . . . I want to commend the preachers . . . these noble men: James Lawson, one who has been in this struggle for many years. He's been to jail for struggling. He's been kicked out of Vanderbilt University for this struggle. But he's still going on, fighting for the rights of his people.

I was touched that Martin mentioned me, and he also mentioned Ralph Jackson and Billy Kyles. But I was most pleased that he kept bringing the attention back around to the sanitation workers in Memphis, and how their fight was our fight, and how it fit into the larger movement.

At one point, someone came up to tell me there was a phone call for me, so I left the platform on the left side and walked up the long aisle to a phone on the wall in the back. It was strike business, but wasn't anything too important. I started to walk back to the stage, but the phone rang again, and again it was for me. This time, too, it was nothing particularly urgent. But I decided to stay in the back of the auditorium and watch from the staircase on the aisle near that phone, in case it rang again. I sat and listened from there to the storm outside and the rest of the speech.

Martin told the story of a fan letter he got from a white high school student in suburban New York City after he was stabbed at that Harlem department store in 1958. The doctors told him the knife was so close to vital arteries that if he had sneezed, he would have died. The teenage girl had read about that detail in *The New York Times* and wrote him to say, "I am so happy that you didn't sneeze." He picked up on her line, and used it to cycle through his work in our movement during the ten years since that incident. He said he was glad he didn't sneeze or he would not have been here to see the Freedom Ride; the Albany and Birmingham campaigns; the March on Washington; the Civil Rights Act; the Selma campaign; and then the Memphis sanitation strike.

Listening to Martin talk about the experience with the letter opener, and how he used it to set up the years that followed, I said to myself, "I have never heard him do that in public in quite that way." At staff meetings and on retreats we had talked about his nearly dying. Some of the pieces and parts of what he said I had heard before in other mass meetings. But he was weaving it all together in a way that was quite spontaneous and unique for him. It represented his genius when standing in front of a crowd.

Still, the word I would use to describe Martin that night was "placid." From the outside, the tensions and antipathies that were strongly churning on the inside did not show. He was not fidgety, or expressing nervous tension at all. Unless Martin talked to you quite personally, you would not know about the agony going on inside him.

The criticism we got after the violence at our last march affected him. He was concerned with it because it was undermining our nonviolent principles. Criticism did get to him. Not all of it. But when it threatened the movement, he was not immune. His decision to come to Memphis and his decision to come back again were not made lightly. I knew that. But I still marveled at how he was weaving together all the threads of our work and our world in his speech at Mason Temple that night.

Martin told of the plane from Atlanta being delayed that morning because of threats, since he was on board. He said he was told about more threats when he got to Memphis. He related that people were worried about "what would happen to me from some of our sick white brothers."

> . . . We've got some difficult days ahead. But it really doesn't matter with me now, because I've been to the mountaintop.
>
> . . . Like anybody, I would like to live a long life. Longevity has its place. But . . . I've seen the Promised Land. I may not get there with you. But I want you to know tonight, that we as a people will get to the Promised Land.
>
> So I'm happy, tonight. I'm not worried about anything. I'm not fearing any man. Mine eyes have seen the glory of the coming of the Lord.

I was not on the platform when the speech ended. As Martin King was talking, I was sitting on the steps, profoundly impressed and personally moved by the atmosphere of the night, and by the wonder of life. The rafters were still echoing, with more rain falling on that tin roof. But I had a very heartening feeling of being alive, and human, and of the community. Martin's speech engulfed me with a remarkable sense of kinship in the struggle during the last ten years, and at that very moment. I was enamored of it all. It was a momentous occasion in the midst of that sanitation strike. It was one of the most luminous, mystical moments in my life.

I wasn't as taken aback as some people were that King seemed to be anticipating his own death. Talk from staff members, followers, and others had been swirling in various planning meetings, fears that he might get shot down during the Poor People's Campaign. However, it was never what we talked about happening in Memphis.

10:30 P.M.: Minimum Salary Building

I went to a strategy committee meeting, which lasted until about midnight. I also consulted with the lawyers who had spent the evening working on our case. Then I went home.

THURSDAY, APRIL 4, 1968
7:00 A.M.: Sheraton-Peabody Hotel

The next morning, as usual, I met with our small group of organizers who held regular breakfast strategy meetings at the Peabody: Jesse Epps, Ralph Jackson, and a representative or two from the local union. We planned out the day to make certain things would be done properly. We discussed the temporary restraining order and how it could turn into a permanent injunction in court that day.

Of course, I had talked about that possibility with Martin King and Andy Young and several other people from the SCLC. Throughout the movement, we all had been in agreement that we would ignore injunctions against a march, though we would go to the court to try to get them set aside.

We believed the government and its police were not allowed to stop a peaceful assembly aimed at airing and correcting grievances. Instead, we saw the police as responsible for protecting such a peaceful assembly. We had a basic freedom of speech. If people came to our demonstration intending to break us up, it was the task of all of us to try to stop them. The country had too much to lose to say that peaceful assembly should be stopped, because you can't protest without any risk of threats or acts of violence.

I stayed at the Peabody, working, until it was time for me to get over to the court.

9:00 A.M.: Federal Courthouse

At the request of the lawyers, I arrived a little early. Lucius Burch had prepared our case, with the assistance of Mike Cody and Charlie Newman, and with Walter Bailey and Louis Lucas before them. All our lawyers were from Memphis. We pretty much knew what the city was going to do. Police Chief James C. MacDonald, Assistant Chief Lux, and Fire and Police Director Holloman were the witnesses for the city, and would testify that a march without violence was impossible and so there should not be any marches. Andy Young was representing the SCLC and Martin King, and I was the witness for the movement locally. John Spence, a local field representative of the U.S. Civil Rights Commission, was our third witness. We would argue that a nonviolent march was necessary to channel the anger that would likely turn into violence if not expressed publicly.

9:30 A.M.: Federal Courthouse, Judge Bailey Brown's Courtroom

The city presented its case first. Mayor Loeb sat in on the hearing at the start, but left after a while. All three police officials testified that the police could not prevent a large march from turning violent. Police Chief MacDonald said, "I don't think anybody can make a march next week without violence."

The judge posed a question to Holloman: If there were to be a march, would he rather have it led by Dr. King or some Negro leader not committed to nonviolence?

"If I had to make a choice," Holloman said, "between whether Mr. Rap Brown and Mr. Stokely Carmichael should lead a massive march in Memphis, or whether Dr. King and his associates lead a massive march, I would prefer a march led by Dr. King and his associates."

12:05 P.M.: Federal Courthouse

We stopped into the federal building snack bar to get a sandwich for lunch. Then we went back up to the courtroom to continue. I was to be the first witness for our side.

1:05 P.M.: Federal Courthouse, Judge Bailey Brown's Courtroom

Our attorneys had filed an answer to the city's injunction request. We had proposed some conditions on a march to take place on Monday, April 8, that would help make it nonviolent, including barring sticks of any kind on the signs, limits on the number of people per row as we marched, careful selection and training of the marshals, and constant communication between law enforcement and march organizers. But we had not proposed prohibiting participants under the age of eighteen.

Lucius Burch questioned me. After some preliminary discussion of my background, we got to the real issues at hand:

> Q: Tell us, for the record, and rather succinctly, what is the viewpoint of the Negro involved in the civil rights movement as to the value and the efficacy of demonstrations? What is the theory of demonstration itself?
>
> A: . . . The idea is that people . . . have to get a visible picture of the injustice, or of the truth, before they are willing to commit themselves to . . . changing it. So, a demonstration is essentially an effort to visualize the picture . . . to confront the community with the reality of what that visualization means. . . .
>
> Q: Now, in addition to the value of being able to communicate by demonstrations, do demonstrations have, in your opinion, value in furnishing an outlet for emotions that exist and . . . would otherwise be pent up in the community, and, if so, elaborate?
>
> A: Yes, very definitely. . . . When you have injustice, poverty and cruelty, you have . . . to give . . . people a legitimate and a hopeful way of changing that. . . . Demonstrations—mobilizing people and getting people to commit themselves to nonviolent direct action—gives them that hopeful means. And I think we have to say, also, that this has been the cost effective way of social change in this half of the twentieth century in the United States.
>
> Q: And do you draw that conclusion from your own experience . . . and from the writings and experiences of others?
>
> A: Very definitely.
>
> Q: Whether it is right or wrong, do you sincerely and conscientiously believe it?
>
> A: I know it. I believe it absolutely.

The questions turned to why we had brought in civil rights leaders from outside Memphis—such as Roy Wilkins, Bayard Rustin, and Martin Luther King Jr.—in March 1968 to speak at mass meetings of the sanitation strikers and their supporters. Then Burch asked me about Martin and nonviolence.

> Q: And what are the methods of accomplishing social change for which Dr. King is famous?
>
> A: Nonviolence. Soul Force.
>
> Q: Now, elaborate on that for us, please, if you will.
>
> A: . . . The way we think of it is that if a man . . . has courage and understanding . . . he uses these with his neighbor, and not hatred and violence. . . . Soul Force is the weaponry of the spirit.

Then he moved on to whether Dr. King had "a sincere and devout interest in preventing violence" if we held a march in Memphis on the following Monday.

> A: I am sure of it. . . . It is Dr. King's desire, as it is mine, that Memphis and people everywhere learn to put into application the high ideals that most of us confess concerning neighborliness, love, justice, understanding, and not just . . . on Monday, but every day of the week.
>
> Q: Now, Reverend Lawson, what, in your opinion, will occur in the community if Dr. King is either imprisoned or if he voluntarily absents himself from the march by reason of an order of Court?
>
> A: Well, I think . . . the City of Memphis is on trial as well as our country. . . . Many people of my own generation have lived in nothing but war. We don't know any other kind of life except wartime life, and this teaches us at least the efficacy of violence. And so you find strong forces and voices now who call out for violence as the only way of changing cruelty. Now, if we don't have alternative ways, if we don't show people that you can redress wrong in peaceful, active, vigorous, dynamic ways, that nonetheless are not violent, then you leave the gate open entirely to those forces that would prevail in other directions anyway.
>
> Q: And what do you think will happen if established nonviolent leaders are not permitted to lead the march that is scheduled for next Monday? What might, or could, happen?

A: There will be continued pushing against cruelty and injustice, and this can take any kind of form, including the violent forms. . . . Across the country in almost every city where there have been major riots, there have not been powerful and dynamic nonviolent movements.

Next, Assistant City Attorney Frierson Graves cross-examined me. His first line of questioning was about young people and violence and the idea of prohibiting young people from marching:

Q: . . . Would a restriction on any march that, say, no one under eighteen be permitted, would that be a reasonable and a valid restriction and tend to have a chance of less violence?

A: It would be a very unfortunate restriction. . . .

The young people of our nation and of the City of Memphis, as we well know, are very restive today, about themselves and about our society. Rightly or wrongly this is a matter of fact. Many young people who are Negroes feel very strongly that people like myself have been too slow in bringing about changes in our society, and that the normal ways of opening up equal opportunity, better education, housing and all have been totally inadequate.

They have been taught by the society to think in terms of violence and hate. Now, they have a persistent pressure. They want to do something. It is important that responsible leadership help them to discover creative ways of doing something. Young people in this city will march. They will do something regardless of my suggestions or not. If you restrict them from being in nonviolent marches and from being open to our admonitions and our teaching, then you leave them entirely to go at their own wills or to go to other forces in our day.

Q: Now, Reverend Lawson, to get back to my question—I want you to assume this: That we have a march that is nonviolent, or else we have no march, and the people will obey the law and will not have any violent actions or reactions. Now, is it better to have a march where there is a possibility of violence, or to have no march and people obeying the law and having no other violence? Now, just which of the two?

A: I would not accept either of them, and the point I would make again is, that if you restrict a march to people only over eighteen . . .

all you are going to do then is to build up the frustration itself of the young people. . . . It would only further leave them open to those elements that are trying to teach them that nonviolence and the idea of a nonviolent march is a lot of nonsense.

Mr. Graves's line of questioning then turned to violence itself.

Q: Now, also, in your proposed march, are you telling the Court that unless there is a march that there will be violence, and people will disobey the laws, have looting, fires, Molotov cocktails, et cetera?

A: No, I am saying something quite different from that. I am saying that the best defense against urban explosion in the midst of urban injustice is to have creative, vital, nonviolent movements, which include marches, because, then, this helps the angers and the frustrations and the fears of people to find legitimate expression and a means of changing their wrongs.

Eventually, Judge Brown, on behalf of the federal court, asked some questions.

Judge Bailey Brown: So, if you go encouraging children . . . not to go to school and come join the march, might not you be encouraging children who are not particularly wrought up about the social evils that you have described, but are simply out on a lark, and it is a good excuse to leave school and participate in a little excitement? Isn't that possible?

A: Yes, sir. I assure you that's possible.

Judge Bailey Brown: And, let me ask you one other question: It is generally true, is it not, that teenagers are more excitable and more impetuous as a general proposition than older people?

A: It's also true that teenagers tend to be more idealistic than older people. And it is also true that you have to try to somehow give them some resources that will help to feed that idealism in the right direction.

And may I say that one of my concerns as a pastor and citizen of this community and this country is this: . . . I see great evidence in our society that we are leaving our young people wide open to meaninglessness, to not being able to appropriate the many forces going on in our world—from technology to Communism. . . . I also see that . . . in the schools today there is not a bridge to somehow counteract all they see and hear. . . . As a pastor . . . I try to help them understand that they must learn to live by the ways of love and truth and justice. . . . I am giving them some very concrete guidelines by which they can move through these very difficult and transitional days through which we are going. . . .

. . . I have also found that some of our very best supporters in the movement are young people. They will do as we ask them to do. They will follow the nonviolent discipline, and those who have been identified with the marches from the beginning have not participated in any of the violence or the looting that has gone on in this city. . . . My own experience with young people is that they are a wonderful generation with whom to work—provided . . . you really try to challenge them in meaningful ways, both about themselves and about the world. If they think you are a phony and that you are playing "Mickey Mouse" with them, they will dismiss you in a moment's notice.

But, at least in the movement thus far in the City of Memphis, we have had a very wonderful experience with many young people. Some of these young people have been presidents of their classes, presidents of their student body, have won scholarships to the major colleges of this country, and are out marching every day, right now.

Judge Brown asked me directly about a possible march.

Judge Bailey Brown: Now, Reverend, of course, you have developed considerable recognition in this community as a nonviolent leader, and you have testified here that in your opinion a march could be carried out Monday. . . . That's your opinion, that that can be done?

A: Yes, sir, I believe that can be done.

Judge Bailey Brown: And you are willing to stake your reputation as a nonviolent leader . . . that it will be a peaceful march, is that right?

A: Yes, sir, I am.

With that, my part in the hearing ended. I had to leave at that point to speak at a local college. I heard that Andy was questioned next, and that he answered on behalf of Martin in the same way I'd answered the question about staking our reputations on a nonviolent march on Monday.

After the hearing, the lawyers were asked to regroup in the judge's chambers. He said he was inclined to rule in favor of a march with the conditions our lawyers had presented, which meant no age restrictions. Andy went back to the Lorraine sometime after four P.M. and told Martin about the day in court and the probability that the march could go forward without an injunction.

4:00 P.M.: Southwestern at Memphis

I spoke about the strike to a group of students at Southwestern, the small liberal arts college in Memphis where Coby Smith, one of the Invaders, had been one of the first Black students. Some of the students there had been active in the marches and supported the strike.

5:00 P.M.: Minimum Salary Building

I went back to the COME headquarters to make sure the day's plans were being carried out and to see if the afternoon march had taken place smoothly. It had. Our daily marches were not affected by the city's injunctions because for the past seven weeks of the strike, our smaller pickets and poster walks had all been nonviolent. And I heard then that it looked like the judge would overrule the injunction, so our Monday march was going to happen. All was well. We were moving along well. There was reason for much hope.

6:00 P.M.: 653 Alston Avenue, Memphis

As was my custom, I walked into the house for supper sometime around six. I kissed Dorothy, who was fixing dinner in the kitchen, and told her about my day in court. Our sons were watching television in an alcove near the kitchen. A few minutes later, I was almost ready to go outside and play basketball with them when Dorothy and I both heard over the television something about a shot.

In my peripheral hearing, I recognized Martin Luther King's name. Then I thought I heard "had been shot." I went to the television set and tried to see if I had heard right. The words appeared across the bottom of the screen, saying "Martin Luther King was shot." Then I heard the person on TV say it happened on the balcony of the Lorraine and he was being rushed to St. Joseph Hospital.

I choked up when I saw the words "King was shot." I stopped. Everything stopped. I went back to Dorothy, and we hugged each other. We talked. We hoped it was not happening. Dorothy cried. I held back tears. I stopped every tear. He wasn't dead. We wouldn't go to that thought. But I did think of Memphis, and of the sanitation workers, and of my parishioners. Violence had invaded our lives again. I had to cut it off, try to stop it. I had to do something.

I immediately said to Dorothy, "I need to get to the radio stations and let the Black community know, and call for the community to stand together, and go in the right direction." We decided she would call Jerry Fanion, a parishioner at Centenary and the director of the Tennessee Council on Human Relations, to ask him to meet me at WDIA. Dorothy and I agreed that with someone out there shooting, I probably shouldn't be going around alone any more than necessary. I told her I would try to stay in touch so she would know where I was. Then I jumped into the car and charged over to the radio station, which was downtown, right near the Sheraton-Peabody.

6:45 P.M.: WDIA Radio

I walked in and saw Gerald Hearn, the station's news director. We immediately taped my statement about the need for calm, the need for everyone to adhere to nonviolence. I said that as soon as we found out Dr. King's condition, we would let the listeners know. At that moment we knew only that he was wounded. We said he'd been shot but we didn't know how serious it was. We didn't say this on the air, but there had been reports that he had walked into the hospital holding a bloody towel up to his gunshot wound.

Gerald played the first statement on the radio. A few minutes later, we got the news over the teletype that Dr. King was dead. I didn't absorb it. I didn't want to think or feel. I could only do.

I made another tape. I again urged calm and asked everyone to stay in their homes. I said we should all honor Dr. King by seeking to live out what he had lived for and what he died for. I said we would go on with the struggle and announced that there would be a march tomorrow, Friday.

I talked briefly with Gerald, and we agreed that I should probably also go to the other Black radio station in town, WLOK, and make the same sort of statement for its listeners, too. Jerry Fanion had arrived at WDIA by then and could follow behind me in his car.

At first, when all I knew was that Martin had been shot, I tried to take it calmly and hoped that everything was okay. And then we learned of his death. At first, I took that calmly, too. I did almost break down when I got out of the radio station and into my car. I started to cry, but I stopped myself. I said, "There's a campaign going on. Martin King would expect me to see that it succeeded. And I'd better be sure that's going to happen. I will go do the work that has to be continued." And that's what I did.

My role in the strike locally meant my primary concern had to be with care for the movement. So I made the decision that my task could not be personal grief. I would not cry. I would not grieve at that moment. I did not exactly detach myself. But in various kinds of crisis situations, my own personal problems become secondary.

When I called Dorothy, she was crying. And she wanted to make sure I was safe. I assured her I was not alone. Jerry was with me. My own preoccupation at that moment had nothing to do with fear for my own life. People were beginning to wonder who had killed Martin. We heard reports about a Mustang car fleeing from the scene. But I didn't take time to speculate much. I had a fair degree of single-mindedness for the welfare of the struggle, and for keeping it going, even with the death of Martin King. I was very concerned that Black people in Memphis not be engaged in rioting and burning.

7:35 P.M.: WLOK Radio

I taped the same kind of message I had for WDIA, urging our community to adhere to Dr. King's nonviolent principles. Those two stations were the best way to reach the Black community in Memphis.

7:55 P.M.: St. Joseph Hospital

Jerry Fanion and I went to St. Joseph Hospital, thinking that Ralph Abernathy and others might be there. We saw a lot of police officers around. I didn't try to get in. But I found out that Ralph and others had gone to R. S. Lewis and Sons Funeral Home. I didn't go there. I knew that wasn't my task that night.

8:15 P.M.: Minimum Salary Building

I drove to COME headquarters, looking for Ralph Jackson. I didn't find him there. But I called Frank Holloman and told him I was going to move around to the television and radio stations. We agreed that this would help keep the city calm. A new curfew had been declared by that time. So he said he would give us a police escort and another pass to be out on the streets. I headed to the Lorraine. The streets were very quiet.

8:30 P.M.: Lorraine Hotel

At the Lorraine, people were milling around, and police officers were everywhere. I couldn't find any of the major members of the strategy committee, who I thought could appear on television with me. But Judge Ben Hooks was there. In 1963, he had been driving the night a group of us were chased out of Fayette County and shot at, and his windshield cracked. I persuaded Ben to accompany me to the television stations. We left our cars downtown and rode in a police cruiser. Jerry Fanion didn't come with us. First, we went out east to WHBQ, the ABC network affiliate.

9:00 P.M.: WHBQ-TV

At the TV station, we heard that President Johnson had made a statement, and so had Bobby Kennedy, who was running for president. One part of what Kennedy said at a campaign rally in Indianapolis that night, in reaction to Martin's death, particularly touched me: "What we need in the United States is . . . love and wisdom, and compassion toward one another, and a feeling of justice toward those who still suffer within our country, whether they be Black or white."

Ben and I made our statement on the air for the local audience. But Tom Jarriel, of ABC News, was at the station, reporting. He asked us to go on the air with him, live, nationally.

> Tom Jarriel: With me now here in Memphis are a couple of men who have been working hand in glove with Dr. King and his campaign here. These are two men who just last night I saw share the speakers' platform with Dr. King, and they were working for a common goal, and common purpose. They are the Reverend James Lawson of Memphis and Judge Ben Hooks of Memphis.
>
> Reverend Lawson, of course with the controversy that surrounded Dr. King, something like this could be expected. But no one ever really did. Did they?

I replied as best I could:

> This comes as a shock, even though his life was a life where threats of death were made almost every day. He could travel almost nowhere in this country without threats of death. This was a very common occurrence. I've had calls in my own home about death threats. I've had people come by, doing that in this city. But knowing this, and knowing that he had settled at least with God and was deeply committed to his work, it comes still as a great hurt that you cannot really describe.

Tom Jarriel then asked me what the reaction to Martin's death would be in the Negro community.

> We hope that the reaction will be that there will be a deeper commitment to the things for which Dr. King lived and worked—that this tragic death will not be a signal for violence and for hate and for fear. But rather that today more than ever before people will try somehow to do what we are attempting to do, which is to decide that we have got to turn the direction of our city and our land in such a way that the dream that Dr. King had for all people, here in Memphis and everywhere in this land and across the face of the earth, will somehow come to pass.
>
> It would be a compounding of this death if Negro people or white people around this country should despair and decide that now is the time to let loose an orgy of violence. This would not be a tribute to Dr. King, but it would be a denial of his life and work.

Jarriel mentioned the philosophy of nonviolence and then asked me about the speech at Mason Temple the night before, saying he thought Dr. King was in a pensive mood when he spoke. He considered that it might have foreshadowed what had just happened. I agreed with him:

> Somehow, maybe, God must have been speaking to him, because . . . it was a tremendous summary of his life's work and thought. I remember sitting at the back of the church and wondering what was moving him to make that kind of a statement on that night. It was appropriate, and powerful, and it certainly was a tribute to a firm life.

9:30 P.M.: WMC-TV

Next Ben and I went to the NBC affiliate in Midtown Memphis and recorded a statement.

10:00 P.M.: WREC-TV

We ended up downtown at the CBS affiliate and made statements for both the TV and the radio stations. The statement I made for the local CBS radio station was similar to others I had made that night.

> Dear Friends. I cannot in any way try to describe to you the pain and the shock that I feel for this very dreary moment in the life of this city, and in the life of this nation, and in my own personal life. It is a moment that I did not ever expect to live in.
>
> But one thing that we do want to say . . . is that Martin Luther King had his whole life committed to God's rule of love and truth, in the world and among the life of men. He died as he lived. As shocking as his death is, it would be more shocking and more tragic if we allowed his death to be a signal not for resurrection, and for loving, for understanding, but a signal for violence and hating.
>
> We urge all persons in the city of Memphis to stay in their homes tonight, to somehow not listen to rumors of any kind, but to rather get on their knees and pray to God that through this man's death, we may learn the ways of peace and truth, and that from his life we may take new hope in learning to live together.

10:45 P.M.: WMPS Radio and UPI Interview, Sheraton-Peabody Hotel

The longest interview I gave to any reporter that night was to Ray Sherman of Memphis's WMPS radio. The interview, which Ray did as a correspondent that night for United Press International, was recorded as we sat in the lobby of the Sheraton-Peabody Hotel.

He asked me about my relationship with Martin and when we met. I told him about first reading about Martin in the newspaper in India during the 1955 Montgomery bus boycott. Then I told of our meeting in person at Oberlin in 1957. Next, he asked me what Martin meant to Black people.

> I saw Dr. King as the voice for the voiceless . . . as the person who, more than any other person in the world today, symbolizes the long hope of man, that he could beat down the darker forces of his nature, the forces of cruelty, and hurt, and violence, and war—and that he could begin to lift up in practical ways, the deeper spiritual elements of his nature, love and truth, justice and peace. So for me, he was the prophet of this century, and the clearest voice that mankind, that the human race had, that life could be fairer and different.

Ray Sherman asked me how close Martin and I were in the movement.

> Well, I've been a consultant for SCLC since 1957. I've conducted workshops across the country. He has tendered invitations on a number of occasions for me to join his personal staff. I helped to plan certain of the major events, like Birmingham. I was active in the initiation of the Student Nonviolent Coordinating Committee, and he's often used me in various places around the country.

Then Ray asked, "Did he ever feel that he would be the victim of an assassin? Did he ever indicate that he feared this greatly?"

> The threat of death was something that came to his life almost daily, from the inception of the Montgomery boycott on December 5th, 1955. Probably no period of his life from that time on in the last thirteen years had been without the constant threat of death in his home or wherever he traveled—in the United States, that is. But Martin had reached a point, and in fact, he reached it during the Montgomery boycott in many respects, where he felt that if his life was to die in the midst of the struggle for social justice for his people and for all people, then he . . . had no fear of that kind of death.

I mentioned the threats to Martin's life that had been coming to my home phone, and said that of course he and Coretta had gotten those calls, and Fire and Police Director Holloman had gotten them to his home phone. In fact, Holloman had said in the court hearing earlier in the day that he had been receiving death threats for Martin and for me. Ray Sherman asked me about police protection.

> What precautions the police took, I really do not know. They say forty policemen were in the vicinity of the Lorraine Motel when Martin was killed. But if that's the case, this goes to show you that what we've got to fight in America is . . . the spirit . . . that encourages and permits violence, and hate, and assassination of people.

Then he asked: "Do you think that a person that would do something like this—pull the trigger on a sniper gun—is he a crazed man, or a racist, or what?" I simply said, "No." Then he asked if I would compare whoever did it to the man who shot James Meredith.

> Not necessarily. . . . When I hear the kinds of statements that have been made about Dr. King here in the city of Memphis, I know that these statements—even including the statements in our newspapers about him—are statements made by people who thought they were acting in their own best interest, even though what they said and what they wrote . . . were reflective of the kind of abuse and scorn and rejection of Dr. King that finally resulted in his death.

At that, Ray asked me, "Have you ever considered this thought? Do you think that Dr. King's own particular style of vernacular—for instance, his speech he made this Wednesday night and a week or so ago—do you think that his type of speech inflamed maybe the white race more, and it only built up the—or, rather, maybe let off the steam and the Negro hostility?"

> No . . . I think that if white people would ever listen to Dr. King's address from the beginning to end, they would be profoundly moved. . . . I've never heard Martin King speak a word of hatred or anger about anyone, or against anyone. And in the speeches he made here in Memphis, he lifted again and again the clear symbol of love and nonviolence.
>
> And that's the whole problem you see in our country today. So many white people just simply shut themselves off from these things. I experienced the same kind of thing constantly as well—not to the scale of Dr. King—but certainly here in Memphis. And I know who I am. I know what my life has been built on. I'm a father of three sons. I love my family very dearly. People who know me will tell you

> that I'm probably a very gentle, patient person who rarely expresses indignation or anger at people.
>
> And yet the attitude of most white people in this town about me is . . . that I'm a rabble-rouser, and a Red, and a man who's trying to burn the city down. This is because most of these people . . . never take the time either to sit down and listen to me, or to others like me. And so they act not really upon what I am, but upon the fears and the guilt feelings of their own hearts, which they project onto me.
>
> And the very same thing is the thing King experienced all his life. Here is a man who always sided with the underdog, who constantly tried to work for the people in poverty. I mean, this man could have been the president of any number of the finest universities of this country. . . . He could have long since left Atlanta, and gone to the outstanding pulpits of this country. . . . He's turned them down because of his deep commitment to trying to change social injustice.

In his final question, Ray Sherman asked me about the sanitation workers: "What about the commitment that Dr. King made in Memphis in connection with the problems of the Memphis Negro and sanitation workers? What will happen, say, even tomorrow?"

> Very likely tomorrow we will have our regular afternoon march anyway. I'm sure that knowing Martin as I did, that the one thing he would not want to happen would be what we've seen signs of in Memphis, and Miami, and Jackson, Mississippi—namely, looting and burning, and acts of violence against police and firemen. I'm sure that the one thing he would not want is for Negroes now to reject the voice, his voice, and to accept the violence of our society and proceed to imitate it.
>
> I think the one thing he would want of those of us who knew him well and loved him dearly and who saw him as our spokesman, as the person whom we tried to support and sustain, he would want from us the continued effort to, through nonviolence, help to change our society.
>
> And because I know that, therefore, I'm going to say to our strategy committee . . . and I'm going to say to the people in my parish, and the people in the city: we must not let the Memphis movement deteriorate into violence. On the contrary, we must press every en-

ergy we have and all the courage we have to see to it that through this nonviolent effort we will see the sanitation workers get justice.

After Midnight: Lorraine Motel, Room 306

The radio and TV statements and interviews ended, and I headed back to the Lorraine Motel. We all converged there at about the same time. Ralph Abernathy suggested we do some talking. So we sat up in Martin's room for a long while. Rev. Samuel "Billy" Kyles and Ben Hooks were there. Ralph Jackson was there. Andy Young was there. Hosea Williams was there. Jim Bevel was there. It was a small room. We sat on the bed and in a few chairs. I stood up for much of the time. We did some eating. But mostly it was rather serious talking, and evaluating of the whole event and what it meant, and deciding the next necessary steps. Those of us who were locally involved in the struggle made it clear that on Friday the sanitation men would march again and we would be with them.

There was a great sense of realization in the room that Martin had died for all of us. We compared it to the Crucifixion.

Quite a bit of talk went on about the fact that he had expected to be struck down one day. When we were in the midst of the Memphis situation, I didn't feel Martin was particularly anxious about death. I know he wanted to live—to continue to help the movement evolve, and move into the next decade. Of course, he was always aware that he could be shot down anytime. In fact, Coretta had said that on November 22, 1963, when we were all grieved by the assassination of John Kennedy, Martin told her it was going to happen to him one day, that he would be shot during this movement.

We definitely talked about our society, and about how Martin was killed and why. We knew it was the racism, the sickness of the society that killed him, no matter who pulled the trigger. A conspiracy was mentioned—the possibility that there was a plot and that others had planned it. That was very much a part of our conversation, but it really didn't dominate. One notable thing I realized later was that I do not recall a single word of recrimination that night toward whoever did this.

We did ask somberly, "What does this mean to us?" and "What does this mean to the SCLC?" and "How do we commit ourselves to the continuing struggle?" We knew Martin would have wanted us to consider those things.

We all were very clear in voicing our support for Ralph Abernathy, who we knew would succeed Martin as president of the SCLC. Sometime before 1968—foreseeing his own death—Martin King had the constitution of the SCLC changed to say that Ralph would succeed him in the SCLC leadership. He initiated the change for the continuity of the SCLC, and the board accepted it at his request. Ralph was Martin's choice. And in that room that night there was great unity. No one even thought of challenging it.

Ralph and I had been friends for almost as long as I had been friends with Martin. We all talked of Ralph's strength and contributions. Of course, Ralph also was solicitous of support. He realized the tough responsibility that was now going to be his.

Mostly though, we were mourning. Martin was dead. He had been struck down. We had a fellowship circle. We all prayed together. And we sang "We Shall Overcome" and some other songs. There were some tears. But I suspect a lot of our tears had already been shed. It was a very emotional meeting, yet people weren't breaking down in that room by the time we gathered.

I did not go to the funeral home. I did not see Martin's body at any point. I am not sure what time I got home. But I know I did not sleep at all that night.

NINETEEN

Of Infinite Worth

Reverend Lawson addressing the Memphis Cares rally at Crump Stadium, April 7, 1968. UNIVERSITY OF MEMPHIS LIBRARY

Martin was taken to R. S. Lewis and Sons Funeral Home, where Dorothy had parked our car when she and John joined the march downtown the week before. A large procession of Memphis mourners gathered at the funeral home, starting at dawn on Friday, April 5, filing in and out to pay their respects to Martin, who was essentially lying in state there. Coretta flew into Memphis with their children on a plane arranged by Bobby Kennedy and waited at the airport to accompany his body home to Atlanta.

In federal court that morning, the city agreed to the order issued in *City of Memphis v. Martin Luther King, Jr.*, which said a major march could proceed with the safety measures our lawyers had proposed. And the order included a nod to Martin.

> Dr. Martin Luther King, Jr. suffered his tragic death last evening and counsel were called back into conference this morning for further discussion. Counsel for the City stated that the City now joins with defendants in their proposal that the march be held and under the restrictions submitted to the Court by defendants.

We had won in court. Yet nothing felt like a victory. By nine A.M., I was calling key people, insisting that we were going to proceed with our regular march with the sanitation workers that day. It was unaffected by any court orders. On radio and TV the night before, I had stated that the campaign would continue, and that we would honor Dr. King by ensuring that this strike was successful.

Holloman, Lux, and the National Guard were trying to tell us that we could not march. The union and the workers met early. So did the volunteers. They all were committed to continuing. Much of my day was spent running between the phone and meetings with Holloman and Lux, and making it very clear to them that at around two P.M., we were stepping off no matter what, and if they didn't like it, they would simply have to arrest everybody. They said the city was so tense they couldn't manage it, and anything could happen. They had assumed we would not march. They mentioned King and the curfew and said they couldn't ensure our safety. Repeatedly, we told them none of that really mattered. We were engaged in a struggle for justice with these men, and continuing that struggle right away was paramount.

Our resolve brought out their prejudice and their fear of teenagers. For only that day and the next, we agreed not to have any marchers who were obvious teenagers. But we said that was unacceptable to us after the weekend. A couple of young people did get pulled out at the last moment. And they didn't like it. We didn't, either. But doing what we had to do so the men could march as usual was vital to us all. In between, we were planning for the big march coming that Monday. It had turned into a memorial march. We would not limit the age of any participants that day.

The Memphis Ministers Association, which had leaned toward supporting the strike but never spoken out fully and publicly, finally united that day at St. Mary's Episcopal Cathedral, downtown. I was the organization's vice president but had not been involved with them much during the strike because I was too busy, given my role in COME. Many of the white ministers felt much consternation about whether to support the strike. The ministers who openly supported the workers were almost exclusively Black. Rabbi James Wax's synagogue had eventually come around to supporting the workers. Yet that morning, many, but certainly not all, of the clergy members resolved to go to Mayor Loeb's office and implore him to settle the strike. We had a liturgy before marching. It was less than twenty-four hours since Martin's murder. I was still holding back tears, grief. I felt too unsettled to speak. Instead, when one of the other ministers saw that I was not in a state to say much on my own, he handed me a verse from Isaiah 53:3–12. I simply got up, and read it.

> He was despised and rejected of men; a man of sorrows and acquainted with grief: and we hid as it were our faces from him; he was despised, and we esteemed him not.
>
> But he was wounded for our transgressions; he was bruised for our inequities; the chastisement of our peace was upon him; and with his stripes we are healed.
>
> . . . He had done no violence, neither was any deceit in his mouth.
>
> . . . Because he hath poured out his soul unto death.

Then I sat down, saying nothing else.

The cathedral was located on Poplar Avenue, a major street connecting downtown to the white neighborhoods of Midtown and East Memphis. About 150 clergy members marched, two by two, on the sidewalk, heading a few blocks west to city hall and Mayor Loeb's office.

I did not join the march to the mayor's office, because I had so much else to do. Also, I still believed that Rev. Ralph Jackson and Rev. Henry Starks could represent us better in dealings with city officials than I could. I was still perceived in Memphis as a Northerner, a Yankee. So meeting with city officials didn't seem like an effective use of my time and energy. I had been in the same room as Henry Loeb only at a few public events, such as when he spoke to the sanitation workers in the city auditorium downtown at the start of the strike. I never met with him individually, shook his hand, or spoke to him directly. And I really did not want to be in his presence on that day, of all days. I wanted others to take the lead with him. And they did.

When the procession reached the mayor's office, the president of the ministers' association, Rabbi James Wax, spoke up, along with some of the white ministers, including Rev. John Aldridge and Rev. Baxton Bryant. Reverend Aldridge read a group statement urging Mayor Loeb to settle the strike without paternalism, and to give the sanitation workers the union recognition and dues checkoff they wanted and needed. Then Rabbi Wax spoke passionately, saying, "We came here today with a great deal of sadness in our hearts, but also a great deal of anger, sir. What has happened in our city is the result of injustice, oppression, and lack of human decency and concern. . . . I realize we live in a society of law and order. We must have laws. But I would remind you most respectfully, sir, that there are laws that are greater than the laws of Memphis and of Tennessee—the laws of God. And the laws of God are not subject to any Gallup Poll. . . . Let us not hide behind legal technicalities. Let us not wrap ourselves up in slogans. Let us do the will of God for the good of this city . . . that every person in this city can live with dignity and self-respect."

Mayor Loeb had grown up Jewish. Even though he had converted to his wife's Episcopal faith, it seemed like maybe a rabbi in his office speaking to him might have moved him. It didn't work. Even as my colleagues tried to appeal to his conscience in a spirit of peace and reconciliation, the trappings of war and violence surrounded Henry Loeb. Whenever I had seen Mayor Loeb on television giving statements from his office, there was always a large painting on the wall behind his desk of a PT boat, like the ones both he and President Kennedy had commanded during World War II. At the ministers' meeting that Friday, a newspaper photographer standing behind Mayor Loeb took a photo of him that revealed a large shotgun hidden under his desk, on top of his briefcase, while he was standing behind it, encircled on three sides by Memphis clergymen standing and facing him. But they could not see the mayor's weapon.

As a chorus of ministers appealed to the mayor, Loeb stood listening, then thanked them for coming. He spoke of his sorrow "in what happened yesterday," and said they were working "at getting together and going to talking . . . and . . . my heart is very much in getting this thing behind us as quickly as we can on a mutually fair basis." He also said he had a difference of opinion with them, but he respected them. In effect, he was dismissing them.

But Rev. Ralph Jackson was not done. He told the mayor, "We have come to petition you and the city for a recognition of the union and dues checkoff. . . . Mr. Mayor, this is the third time I've come to you pleading. If we had been able to get a hearing as ministers of the Black community, we never would have needed to send for King or anybody else. But you would not hear. You will not hear now."

As the meeting ended, two white clergy members also objected and began a sit-in at city hall then and there, led by Rev. Richard Moon, the Presbyterian campus chaplain at Memphis State University. Reverend Moon began a hunger strike as well, which ended up lasting for a few days. He was disappointed that the assassination and their meeting had not appeared to spur the mayor into urgent action. Reverend Moon was joined by Sister Adrian Marie Hofstetter. She told a reporter, "I'm here to ask the mayor and ask the people of Memphis that in God's name to please give the sanitation workers what they are asking for, so that we can in some way make up to the Negro community for the injustice that they've suffered for so many years at our hands."

Reverend Moon then said their demonstration in city hall was "only one more pressure brought to bear upon the city in order to let the mayor and the city council know that they do not have the support of the total white community in Memphis, Tennessee. They do have a majority support. But we are working in many ways right now to . . . bring part of the white community to its knees in repentance and to its feet for justice in our city."

Later on Friday, I was among those who met with Attorney General Ramsey Clark. President Johnson had sent him to Memphis. We met at the federal building and talked about the assassination, the strike, and the general situation in Memphis. Earlier, at the airport when he had arrived, he had met with Coretta, Ralph Abernathy, Andy Young, and Martin's brother, A. D. King, who had come into town on Wednesday night to see Martin. Clark said in a press conference late on Friday that he had then taken time in Memphis to speak with the governor and with Fire and Police Director Holloman, as well as other local officials, lawyers, and clergymen. He announced that the Justice Department had devoted all available resources in the area and in Washington, D.C., to the FBI's investigation of the assassination. "We have committed everything that could be reasonably and beneficially committed to the solution of this most tragic crime," he said. "We have reviewed with Director Holloman and with members of his staff the activities of his homicide squad and others here. And we are most hopeful that these efforts will consummate in an early solution, and apprehension and conviction of the individual responsible for this crime."

He also noted that there was more physical evidence than is usual in such an investigation, and that it had been delivered to an FBI lab in Washington. And he said they had no evidence that the killing was a widespread plot: "The evidence at this time indicates it was the act of a single individual."

Through the day, announcements were made about cancellations around Memphis in light of the curfew. The Miss Memphis beauty pageant scheduled for that Friday and Saturday was postponed, as were all official weekend pre–Cotton Carnival activities, including the king and queen's coronation ball, scheduled for Saturday night at the Holiday Inn Rivermont.

As it turned out, a prominent local architect named W. Jeter Eason had sent a letter to Loeb on Thursday, April 4, hours before the assassination, emblematic of the fears the white establishment had felt all along during the strike, but especially as the Cotton Carnival, scheduled for May, approached. Eason wrote, in part: "Regardless of what happens in the near future in regards to protest marches, I am terribly frightened over what might happen during Cotton Carnival. Suppose some militant 'Avengers' or other Black-Power advocates jump on the floats and 'integrate' the parades. Then, how many people from the sidelines will get in the fray? It could mean lots of old and young, boys and girls, might be hurt or killed."

We marched at two P.M. that Friday, nonviolently, as usual. The curfew went from seven P.M. to five A.M. each night. National Guard troops were everywhere. Memphis police monitored us throughout our daily marches, which remained peaceful. Much of the rest of my weekend was spent planning Monday's big memorial march. SCLC staff members were in town to help. Before the assassination, I had invited Bayard Rustin to join us in planning what was going to be this major march, with Martin leading. As chairman of the march locally, I asked him to work closely with us. Some SCLC people didn't like that, because Bayard and Martin had some disagreements, although those were worked out through the years. But Bayard was my friend, and he was too good a man not to call when we needed help. He remained one of my best counselors and advisers. I had been speaking to him throughout the strike anyway. He had communicated with other national unions to let them know what the strike in Memphis was about, and to get them to help provide relief for the sanitation workers. And wherever he could, he went on television and radio on the East Coast to talk about the strike.

On Friday night, April 5, I met with Jerry Wurf, Bayard Rustin, and a number of others in one of the rooms upstairs at the Sheraton-Peabody, to discuss the plans for the Monday march. Afterward, I went down to the lobby and met with John T. Fisher and Episcopal Bishop John Vander Horst from midnight until about two A.M. They were organizing a city-wide event for Sunday called Memphis Cares, meant to bring together Black and white Memphians in the aftermath of Martin's death. John T. (as everyone called him) and I had talked at length about race and Memphis and poverty a couple of times during the strike.

I had worked with a number of strong white associates across the country over the years. But I tended not to engage in this sort of organized white-Black conversation, because I saw a lot of talk with white people as too uncentered in any real understanding of Black life. I was already a part of a white-majority denomination. I had spent a lot of time working with white people within that fellowship. So I tried to use my energy in the movement working mainly within the Black community. On top of that, it was the height of the strike. Martin King had just been assassinated, and I was already running from early morning to the next early morning without a break. Consequently, I didn't particularly care about spending a lot of time talking to white folk in Memphis who suddenly wanted to have conversations about race.

But John T. was persistent. And he didn't share the usual criticism from white Memphians about my being anti-Memphis, or anti-human, or a Communist. John T. struck me as sincere, and I did see that his goals arose from his commitment to the same principles as mine. So I agreed to appear at the Sunday event and speak. I also gave him and Bishop Vander Horst the names of some Black people who could be involved and would probably endorse it.

John T. was a local car dealer and very much a part of the white establishment. He had grown up next door to Henry Loeb. He was raised a Methodist and served in the military in the late 1950s. His wife, Jean, had been crowned the 1958 Maid of Cotton, winning a beauty contest that was open to white women from all of the cotton-producing states. The winner served in the court of the king and queen during the Cotton Carnival and represented the cotton industry around the world during her reign. John T. and Jean met when he was her escort during a cotton-industry event while she was the Maid of Cotton. They married the following year.

The sanitation strike changed John T. and Jean. They began to see the ways in which the lifestyle they had been born into hurt the sanitation workers and contributed to the poverty that held Memphis back as a city. John T. was quite a successful businessman. But he was also a solid person of the church. His innermost compasses were rooted in Jesus of Nazareth, and in the Christian religion. Our deep faith helped bridge the gaps between us, and a genuine friendship developed. In those first months during and after the strike, John T. and Jean were just starting their journey of transformation, unlike most people in their social circle.

However, he almost blew it the next day, because someone called me that Saturday and said they heard Loeb was supporting Memphis Cares. I called John T. right away and said, "That destroys it for the Black community, so you need to get Loeb out of it." And John T. assured me that Loeb had nothing to do with it and would not be there. I was known in Memphis as the pastor of Centenary United Methodist Church, and I was also known as an activist who would constantly speak up. Many Loeb supporters would call me dangerous or irresponsible in the paper, or they'd say it behind my back, talking among themselves. But they would never come and talk to me. That was one of the things that drew me to John T. Fisher. He had heard all the talk and knew it well. But he had decided to visit me at my church anyway, in the first month of the strike. And we clicked almost from day one.

During most of the rest of the weekend, I was doing legwork for the Monday march and planning the continuation of the strike. AFSCME's Jesse Epps did a lot of legwork too, as did Bill Lucy and Jerry Wurf. We had extensive meetings with the police about the march. Then Bayard and I checked back with them to be sure the things on our checklists were getting done. A march of that size was a giant effort. For most of Saturday and Sunday we were consumed with arrangements—including coordinating the trucks we needed for crowd safety and equipment, ordering and placing mobile toilets, managing the news media from all over the world, designing and printing programs, arranging for the speaking platforms and sound systems, deciding on the order of the speakers, and printing the signs everyone would carry. Most of the black-and-white signs said either "I AM A MAN," "Union Justice Now!" or "Honor King: End Racism!"

At Centenary on Sunday, we had a communion service, because it was the first Sunday in April. It was also Palm Sunday. I was there and led the service, but I did not preach. Jim Bevel was in the city, so I asked him to preach. A number of us who had pulpits in Memphis invited SCLC people to preach from them that day. Introducing Jim, I said, "We have seen in the midst of our lives this week a crucifixion. We remember with gratitude the life of Martin Luther King Jr. May we the living be compelled . . . to have that spirit of love and truth that lived so well in him."

After church, I headed to Crump Stadium, in Midtown, to the Memphis Cares gathering. Nearly nine thousand people showed up—about 60 percent were white. A few white businesspeople spoke, along with a Black teacher, then Ben Hooks. I was one of the last to appear, and I spoke my mind:

> I decided to come this afternoon, after a great deal of hesitation. . . . As I understand our coming together this afternoon, it's not because we are only sorrowful, but because we know that the events that we have seen over the last few days in Memphis call us together. . . . We have witnessed a crucifixion in the city of Memphis just as surely as there was a crucifixion on a hill in Golgotha outside of Jerusalem two thousand years ago. Such a crucifixion horrifies our sensibilities. It shames us. It not only causes us to grieve, but it makes us deeply aware of our evil and sin, and soul-sick ways.
>
> But a crucifixion can only take place in a city which does not know the ways of peace, or the ways of justice. . . .
>
> . . . The death of Martin Luther King could be a sign . . . because . . . we have not really been willing to listen or to hear those men in our midst who have called for justice and peace. If this crucifixion is a sign from God, it may not only be a word of judgment, but . . . a word of healing . . . a call to repentance.
>
> Now, repentance is not illustrated by some of the things that I've heard over the last couple of days. I've heard some people say, as an example, "I'm only sorry that it happened in Memphis." . . . Or I've heard people laughing that this man, this human being like you and me, in the full prime of his life, is dead, shot down, executed in cold blood. That is not repentance.

> Repentance is not being concerned whether or not business moves away from Memphis. Repentance is not being concerned whether or not people outside of our city will have a good feeling about us. How can anyone have a good feeling about Memphis when one of the finest sons of this world of ours was shot down in her streets?
>
> But in the biblical word, there is another idea for repentance. . . . Change the direction of your life. Turn down a different road . . . move from racism to genuine brotherhood, from injustice to justice, from war and violence and killing and looting to peace and understanding.
>
> And to those . . . who . . . come here this afternoon in order to be able to say, "I was there and now all is well. I've made expiation for my guilt and for my sin," then our coming here is not healing.
>
> . . . We will only be judged by history and by eternity, by what happens to the least of those who are fellow citizens. . . . We must decide that we will have our eyes open—so that we can see cruelty in our midst, so that we can see that there are children being tortured by hunger and by the lack of opportunity here in the city of Memphis, so that we can see that there are men who would walk tall with dignity, but who are bent over by the slavery of poverty, so that we can see that there are women who are stripped of their personhood because there are not sufficient numbers of persons who do care. And you and I must go forth to repent, meaning that we must go forth with deeds that will somehow change the ignominious cruelty that still lives in the confines of Shelby County.

I think Memphis Cares permitted some white people to express their feelings, and at least to say, "We are really sorry for what took place in Memphis." Overall, it was a good thing. Whether it produced any tangible, long-term results is another question.

In between such gatherings through the whole weekend, as we continued to meet with the police and the National Guard to go over Monday's march point by point, Fire and Police Director Holloman told us he was going to march right up front as close to Mrs. King as he could. It was his decision, considering the threats against her that were coming in to him. He felt the closer he was to her, the safer she would be. I didn't say it then, but I believed that if there were any more guns around, they would not be aimed at Mrs. King. They would be aimed at me. I had been getting threats throughout the strike. And around three A.M. on the night before the memorial march, Dorothy and I got one of the many threatening calls we constantly would receive in the middle of the night. The caller said specifically, "When you hit Main Street and Poplar tomorrow, you will be cut down."

That Monday morning was dreary and cool with a possibility of rain. I positioned myself in the front of the march and worked the whole time to help the marshals coordinate with the police and keep the peace. We had handed out flyers beforehand with a message I had written to the marchers.

> Today we honor Dr. King for the great work he did for all people and particularly for his great love and sacrifice for us. How best can we honor him now? The answer is simply: we honor him by making sure that the Sanitation Workers win their rights nonviolently. . . . Each of you is on trial today. Not only Americans, but people from all over the world will be watching you on TV today. Therefore be considerate, polite and carry yourself with dignity.

A few of the Invaders were marshals and adhered to all our nonviolent principles. Coretta and the three oldest of their four children, Yolanda, Martin III, and Dexter, arrived a little late and joined the march in progress at Beale and Main Streets. Marching beside them were Harry Belafonte, Rosa Parks, Ralph and Juanita Abernathy, and Dr. Benjamin Spock. Countless other prominent celebrities and activists marched too, including Sidney Poitier Bill Cosby, Robert Culp, and Ossie Davis.

National guardsmen lined the route. Police helicopters flew overhead. Union leaders and members from all around the country marched. So did the sanitation workers and their families. Crowd estimates ranged from twenty thousand to more than forty thousand people. Everyone was mostly silent, by design. Sometimes, footsteps from the crowd were all anyone could hear, along with police helicopters circling overhead. In the end, the march went off without incident. Once we got to city hall, marchers gathered for speeches in front of the large platform set up in the big plaza outside the building. I was the emcee of the program. Union leaders, preachers, Harry Belafonte, and other national and local activists spoke.

Finally, Coretta rose to talk. It was the first time she had spoken publicly since Martin died. She said she came to Memphis because she felt

Martin would have wanted her to come. And she praised Martin as "a loving man, a man who was completely devoted to nonviolence. . . . We loved him dearly. The children loved him dearly. And we know that his spirit will never die." She said she and her family would carry on his work. Then she called Martin's death a crucifixion—one that she hoped would lead to resurrection and redemption. And she spoke to the sanitation workers:

> He was concerned that you have a decent income and protections that were due you. And this is why he came back to Memphis—to give his aid. We are concerned about not only the Negro poor, but the poor all over America and all over the world. Every man deserves a right to a job with an income that allows him to pursue liberty, life, and happiness. . . . We're going to continue his work to make all people truly free and to make every person feel that he is a human being. His campaign for the poor must go on.

She ended by saying, "How many men must die before we can really have a free and true and peaceful society? How long will it take? . . . I believe this nation can be transformed, into a society of love, of justice, peace, and brotherhood where all men can really be brothers."

Dorothy and I traveled to Martin's funeral in Atlanta on Tuesday, April 9. A number of Memphis people were there, and five busloads of sanitation workers and other supporters from Memphis came, too. The two of us and Ann and A. W. Willis flew down early that morning on a small private plane chartered by a Memphis businessman and stayed together as we moved from the funeral march to the services. The public ceremony was at Morehouse College, Martin's alma mater. Mahalia Jackson sang "Precious Lord, Take My Hand." Seconds before he was shot, Martin had asked a bandleader who was with them at the Lorraine Motel to play the song at a mass meeting later that night, where Martin was supposed to have given another speech.

While we were in Atlanta, John T. Fisher was at a Memphis Rotary Club lunch meeting speaking about Memphis Cares. He talked to the club members—who were almost exclusively white and male—about the previous few days. That morning, April 9, *The Commercial Appeal* had run an editorial about the memorial march and Memphis Cares entitled "Quiet March, Loud Talk," in which the editors called out me and Ben Hooks, without naming us, saying we were "strident speakers who went beyond the announced intent of the occasion" and that we were "preaching love but countenancing hate and racial polarization." John T. mentioned that editorial and then went on to tell the audience what he had learned from organizing the event, in discussion with me and other Black people in Memphis. In his gentle Southern accent, he described his feelings during the Memphis Cares event, and how he had evolved in the forty-eight hours since.

> This group . . . set out for a noble purpose. And we charged into there on a white horse. And I feel like I was lucky to get out with my hat on, because they did depart from what I thought we were going in to do. And I went home thinking I was going to be inspired, but I was anything but. The guidelines for this were for people to come of both races, and hopefully at the extreme polarities of this town, and listen. . . . And after that . . . stand up and make a commitment to yourself, to your fellow man, and in the eyes of God and say, "I am going to be involved in something."
>
> And I'll tell you what: about halfway through Ben Hooks's speech, I thought my stomach was going to turn inside out. Because he was saying things that I didn't like to hear. And I thought he was tramping on the rules that had been set down. But I was wrong. He did not. He stood up and did what we agreed to do. He spoke his mind, and I didn't like what he said. But he said the truth. He said what he believed, and I am glad that I was able to stay. Some didn't. Probably a hundred or two hundred people left.
>
> I never seriously physically considered leaving that platform up there, because there was too much at stake for that, but . . . I'll just share a little private thought with you. I became frightened up there. I wasn't frightened that somebody was going to hurt me.
>
> . . . What frightened me . . . was there were a couple of guys who had more resolve than I did. And they were going to change this world that I live in, and they were at work at it. While I'm out on Sycamore Grove selling cars, they're changing my world. They're changing the way I'm going to live tomorrow. I want to live tomorrow like I lived yesterday. . . . It made me uneasy. . . . Everybody I talked to shared my feelings at the time.

The other thing that sort of frightened me . . . was the fact that they no longer considered whether I cared about it or whether I liked it. . . . They had given up on that point. They were going along anyway.

And the third one that really got me was . . . that they just didn't need me—at least they didn't think so. And that was a tragedy, because I thought they needed me, and I didn't like to be told I wasn't needed anymore. . . .

. . . One thing that I learned while I was standing there on that platform is that I need those guys. If they're going to go to work like they're doing with the resolve that they've got, somebody better get with it and stop saying, "I'm gonna put Jim Lawson in the zoo, or behind the bars, or cut him off." Because he lives here, unless we want to destroy everything and run him off.

. . . In retrospect . . . the one thing that came out clear is that never one time did they mention taking anything away from me. The only thing they wanted were the things I had. That's all they wanted. There was never talk about taking this from me and giving it to him. All they wanted was the chance to do what I did. . . .

. . . James Lawson lives in this town, and Henry Loeb lives in this town. Unless one decides to leave here, they will both continue to live here. . . . The hope of this community lies in the involvement of all people, black and white, so we can go on without destruction.

Civic clubs in the white community were unnerved in those days after the assassination. The Kiwanis Club came out with a statement doubling down on support of Henry Loeb and his inflexible stance with the union. On Wednesday, April 10, Mayor Loeb spoke to another mostly white civic group, the Sertoma Club, at its luncheon in East Memphis. He never referred to Martin by name or called his death an assassination. One comment in particular showed his continuing tone deafness—although I believe his words played well with that audience:

In the first place, what came up is tragic. I'd like to say—and I know I speak for each of you—each of us, heart and prayers, are with Mrs. King and the King family.

Certainly we wish that incident had happened elsewhere—if it had to happen.

That same week, *Time* magazine's reporting on the assassination described Memphis in a way that seemed to draw more passionate condemnation from white Memphians than did the fact of Martin's killing itself.

> In causation and execution, the murder of Martin Luther King was both a symbol and a symptom of the nation's racial malaise. The proximate cause of his death was, ironically, a minor labor dispute in a Southern backwater: the two-month-old strike of 1,300 predominantly Negro garbage collectors in the decaying Mississippi river town of Memphis. The plight of the sanitation workers, caused by the refusal of Memphis' intransigent white Mayor Henry Loeb to meet their modest wage and compensation demands, first attracted and finally eradicated Dr. King, the conqueror of Montgomery, Birmingham and Selma.

On Wednesday, April 10, Memphis's U.S. congressman, Dan Kuykendall, announced that he had gotten in touch with the magazine, saying it had "plainly indicted Memphis for the killing." He said he had asked the magazine's editor for "a public apology for the immature and vicious insult." The hard feelings white Memphians had for *Time*'s description of Memphis as a "decaying Mississippi river town" would continue for decades. Later in 1968, the chamber of commerce would use the *Time* article to raise $4 million to hire a New York public relations firm to repair the city's image.

Through it all, the strike continued. After Martin's funeral, negotiations between the city and the union had resumed. But we felt they were going badly. Loeb was adamant about hanging on to his stubborn position. Therefore, we decided we had to increase our activity. We held almost daily strategy meetings. We started asking contacts around the country to go on television and radio to raise more money for the strikers' relief operation. We began to think in terms of extreme measures of civil disobedience. For instance, we were considering calling in volunteers to come in from around the country to pack the Memphis jail. And we devised plans to increase the demonstrations.

We continued our pressure with the boycott as Easter approached, and with the poster walks. Those were having an effect. As the curfew lifted, both papers ran stories about the impact of our boycott and the marches. *The Commercial Appeal* said merchants were warily trying to return to normal.

> The expected rush for Easter finery was crushed by an un-expected snow storm on March 21, followed by a riot and curfew on March 28 and another outbreak of violence after Dr. King's death. The boycott against downtown stores by the Negro community also helped turn Easter sales expectations downward.
>
> . . . "I'm afraid Easter is a flop this year. Hell, business is a flop right now," said the manager of a major department store. He estimated business was about 40 per cent below normal.

On Thursday, April 11, I spoke to a reporter at *The Commercial Appeal* about our continued support of the sanitation strikers in the Black community. We discussed the distrust of law enforcement among Black people in Memphis, as the hunt for Martin's killer continued.

> The Rev. Mr. Lawson also leveled a strong attack at local, state and national police officials in regard to the handling of racial violence and the investigation of the assassination of Dr. Martin Luther King in Memphis April 4.
>
> "There is a basic mistrust in the Negro community concerning the Memphis police, FBI and mayor's office. We do not feel that these agencies consider it in their self-interest to solve the crime."

On Friday, April 12, COME held a press conference announcing our continued support of the sanitation strikers, and I invoked the furor about the *Time* magazine article.

> We intend to keep the poster walks going, the boycotts going, the demonstrations going, because we know that this may well be the last chance that Memphis has to really change from being a decaying city on the Mississippi still filled with segregation and cruelty to become a city of good abode, which the name Memphis, of course, means.

I also brought up the issue of police brutality, which had been highlighted throughout the strike, and particularly in the aftermath of Larry Payne's murder. The police violence had continued throughout the seven P.M. to five A.M. curfews, which had finally been lifted on Wednesday,

April 10. I had spent time during the curfews bailing out parishioners who had been stopped when going home from their night jobs. *The Commercial Appeal* reported that I said, "Police brutality was probably the 'most sensitive issue' in the Negro community," noting that for Black people, the curfews were "repression in its worst form." I tried to explain further during the press conference:

> Even though many white people believe the curfew operation by the National Guard and Memphis police has been extremely effective, reports by Negroes are still coming in of beatings in their own homes, searches without search warrants, and people being stopped on the streets for no reason.
>
> . . . Now, all Negroes know, from business executives and doctors on down, how the poorer people have been harassed for decades.
>
> We want Memphis people to know the harassment we endured under the curfew. . . . At the very heart of our own concern is the recognition that we probably cannot expect protection of Negro people from brutality and from repression locally. Somehow we have got to gain the ear and the power outside of the city of Memphis. Because these matters have been taken again and again to city fathers without avail.

Rev. Billy Kyles and I told of several people who had been beaten but couldn't get ambulance service from the city, and of jammed telephone lines from the volume of phone calls being made, but the public utility would not send repair trucks into Negro neighborhoods to try to alleviate the problem. We mentioned that multiple Negro gas station operators recounted how police officers repeatedly harassed and threatened them—breaking their windows and beating their employees—if they were open even two minutes after the curfew began.

Frank Holloman responded by denying having heard of any incidents of police brutality and instead mentioned incidents of brutality against the police. He said the Memphis Police Department did not condone brutality.

We got through the Easter weekend and started back with our daily marches on Monday, April 15. Then on Tuesday, April 16, around twelve-thirty P.M., as we were meeting at Clayborn Temple before our daily march, the union leaders came back from negotiations. Something had changed. It felt like a breakthrough, but we had been disappointed so often before. Everyone in the church ready to march that day—the sanitation workers, union and community leaders, local activists, and clergy—all waited to hear what was happening.

Jerry Wurf got up and announced that the city had agreed to settle the strike.

Everyone seemed to breathe a collective sigh of relief, mixed with a lingering sadness too, as we waited to hear the settlement terms.

It was essentially what we had proposed in tandem with the city council way back in February. The win included a pay raise of fifteen cents per hour, with ten cents coming on May 1 and five cents more added by September 1. Also, the union won a dues checkoff through the credit union and recognition of AFSCME as the union authorized to negotiate on the behalf of workers. Other points had to do with grievance procedures and promotions.

The union men were asked to vote on ratifying the settlement. They approved it.

That's when the true celebration began—right then and there at Clayborn Temple. Great joy, happiness, and jubilant bedlam filled the same church where Memphis police officers had launched tear gas canisters into the sanctuary and sprayed Mace in the faces of the men and their families three weeks before. We were all jumping up and down and hugging each other, and doing a lot of singing and shouting, too.

Then T. O. Jones got up to speak. This man, who had started it all almost a decade earlier, had won. He and his fellow union members had stood up to a system that had taken so very much from them, their families, and their ancestors for generations. But as he tried to express his feelings, he was too choked up to say anything. T.O. then turned back to Jerry Wurf, and got himself over to his chair, where he sat for a minute, weeping bittersweet tears with a smile on his face.

The sanitation workers never wanted any of the violence. They didn't want anyone vandalizing their trucks, even though some strike supporters had suggested putting sand in the gas tanks to stop the trucks from running. The men did not think sabotage or violence would help their cause. They wanted to return to their jobs as quickly as they could, having made their witness and won the victory.

Yet we all knew what this victory had cost them, us, and the world. As one unnamed sanitation worker quoted in *The New York Times* said, referring to Martin, "We won. But we lost a good man along the way."

Many of us who had been strike supporters got up and spoke to the workers and their supporters. I was one of them.

> You have gained the right to stand on your own two feet and don't you let anybody turn you around. . . . The fact is that we were able to stand tall, and true, and together, and we have won this glorious victory, for you and for America. But we . . . have just begun. We want to get to the point where every poor family in this Shelby County can work together in an organization that will allow them to solve their own problems.

The local newspapers interviewed sanitation workers for the first, if not the only, time during the entire strike. *The Commercial Appeal* started by saying, "Mayor Henry Loeb's image didn't improve much among strikers yesterday." Then the article quoted a sanitation worker named Harvester Stokes, who called Mayor Loeb "a sick man." And another sanitation worker, Luby Finney, said, "Anytime a person has to go through this much to get 10 cents . . . I don't like him. We've got a union to fight for us now." Sanitation worker Sidney Robinson said, "It's been tough, oh man." And referring to the union he said, "They sure have fought for us, and I appreciate it."

At a rally that night, Ralph Abernathy came back to Memphis to speak, along with Martin's brother, A. D. King. Abernathy said the SCLC would not forget Memphis and announced that the Poor People's Campaign would come to Memphis on May 2 and would launch from the Lorraine Motel.

He called the strike settlement "a victory for teachers, janitors, maids and young students who stayed out of school every time we asked them." He praised the unity of our campaign and said it showed "Black power in its truest form. Black power is not violence, not separation from white folks, but the ability to make Loeb say 'Yes' when he wants to say 'No.'"

He also said the strike was a "significant and just breakthrough for labor and unions in the South. I'm convinced this victory will strengthen the unions of paid workers and inspire other unions to organize in the area."

T. O. Jones initiated the union and the strike in Memphis, and the men carried it through. They also woke up a large part of the organized labor movement, which began asserting itself around issues of better working environments and better wages for all workers. AFSCME itself expanded quite radically, and soon became one of the largest unions in the nation. After the Memphis strike, Jerry Wurf and Bill Lucy and that executive committee went all out in trying to organize.

In fact, a little more than a week after the sanitation strike was settled, janitors in the Memphis City Schools district, most of whom were Black, stayed off their jobs and threatened to strike. The school board quickly agreed to recognize AFSCME as representing them and other nonacademic school board employees. The janitors went back to work after only two days.

The Memphis sanitation strike was the first time the labor movement merged with the Martin Luther King–Rosa Parks movement. The strike forced labor to take a long look at what it had failed to do. Poverty among working people in the United States was a disgrace, and an all-white AFL-CIO had not fought for social and economic justice for all their people. The campaign in Memphis showed unions a better way forward in organizing workers.

In Memphis, the sanitation strike produced pay raises and better on-the-job conditions for all municipal employees, something they deserved. Many had worked for decades in unclean, dangerous conditions for woefully inadequate wages, making them extremely vulnerable. Even the Memphis police got a 10 percent pay raise after the strike, as I often reminded those officers assigned to patrol our marches and rallies. All employees of the city of Memphis began to recognize that the city government would be fair to them only if they had a common mind and approached the government with unity.

But the appreciation of what the strikers had accomplished did not make it to the inside of the mayor's office. Loeb and his people could not see that the strike benefited the whole community. They missed an opportunity. They mostly saw the strike as a threat—physically and to their established order, their way of life.

In the sanitation strike, we were dismantling the evil of racism and the social order it had fostered. You can't create new systems in a city, a company, or an institution without dismantling the old systems and the old ways of thinking about the place. As our movement went on, I realized we were not only integrating or desegregating. We were dismantling.

Our campaign in Memphis demonstrated that thirteen hundred ordinary Black men and their families could unite and demand change. And they did it in a bold fashion with a strike. They developed leadership among themselves, and they told Henry Loeb, the city, and the nation how and why their jobs were insufferable, and they demanded better.

I don't think we as a nation have learned the core lesson of the sanitation strike. These men, descended from formerly enslaved people, understood their situation. And once they realized that they could unite and do something about it, they went on strike to make change happen. All working people have that in them. If encouraged and supported, they can join in the task of making their work more effective and productive. Part of the failing of the democratic experiment in the United States so far is the continual push to keep working people at all levels from organizing for their own benefit and for the benefit of the jobs they do.

The strike also produced a catharsis among most Black people in Memphis. Their leadership had previously come chiefly from lawyers, who gravitated primarily to the political arena, rather than to the confrontation that activism required. These leaders tended to engage in political organization rather than grassroots direct action. But the strike involved mass participation on the part of all kinds of Black people, not simply in the marches but also in terms of the economic boycott. It helped radicalize people's thinking about themselves and their own power.

In 1968, Black citizens moved Memphis off its pedestal of doing nothing and allowing racism and poverty to prevail. Prior to the strike, racism was not on the city's public agenda. The nonviolent movement of America in the twentieth century changed that in city after city and town after town. In the Black community, we were astonished that the messiest job in Memphis, the garbage-removal job, was what caused white Memphis to stop seeing itself as a city of great racial progress, where cotton culture was king.

But in my opinion, the best outcome of the strike was that it harnessed the spirit of the thirteen hundred sanitation workers and their families, stirred their souls, and showed them and the world who they had always been: men and women of infinite worth.

After voting to end the strike, the men went back to work the next day, April 17. But our community action was not over. We immediately began to focus on the police brutality Black people had reported throughout the strike, especially since March 28, when police officers tear-gassed Clayborn Temple and killed Larry Payne. The Memphis NAACP asked the Justice Department to look into the many complaints we had all received and documented. The vilifying of our work also continued. In a letter to the editor in *The Commercial Appeal* on Sunday, April 21, under the headline "Doubt Cast on 'Brutality'"—the key word was set off in quotation marks—someone who gave only their initials, "J.W.T.," expressed what a significant number of white people felt.

> The Rev. James Lawson once again has forced himself upon the television audience of Memphis and the Mid-South, proclaiming the sanitation strike as only the beginning and promising action on police brutality charges.
>
> The Rev. Lawson's twisted interpretation of the recent life-saving curfew as an act of repression against the colored people of Memphis need only be examined by any right thinking human being. . . .
>
> Naturally, the aged, shop-worn charges of police brutality were aired again by the Rev. Mr. Lawson. However one must only look at the facts to see that the "so-called abused" were violating curfews or laws, which must be protected at all costs by our gallant, thankless, hard-working law enforcement officers.

In *The New York Times* that same Sunday, journalist Earl Caldwell wrote a story based on an interview he'd done with me a few days before. Earl was the only reporter on the scene when Martin was killed. He was staying in the Lorraine and raced out of his room, just below Martin's, when he heard the shot. He was photographed with police officers and others on the balcony beside Martin just afterward. It was the first time *The New York Times* had assigned a Black reporter to cover Martin. In fact, Earl was one of the first Black reporters at the paper.

His April 21 article was entitled "Negroes to Seek More in Memphis."

> Although the sanitationmen's strike has ended, Negroes here are determined to keep the pressure on this city in an effort to force greater racial change.
>
> . . . The Rev. James M. Lawson, pointing out that Negroes make up about 40 per cent of the city's population, said, "We want 40 per cent of the jobs and across the board in all categories."

> But he added that "the next case opened will be the police repression of black people in Memphis."
>
> . . . Like most other Negro leaders, Mr. Lawson called the strike settlement a "great victory" but said that it had been "written in the blood of Martin Luther King" and was not enough.
>
> "His death," Mr. Lawson said of the civil rights leader, assassinated April 4, "can only be compensated for by a new city."
>
> . . . With feelings still high over the shooting of Dr. King, Negro leaders believe that this is the time for an all-out drive against long-standing complaints.
>
> The unity among Negroes has also had an impact on the white community.

The article told of the talks we had that week with both the city council, on police brutality, and the chamber of commerce, on underemployment and unemployment in the Black community.

> Regarding the efforts to gain more jobs, Mr. Lawson said, "We have the troops now to move systematically from industry to industry." He explained that those industries that refused to alter their hiring practices would be subjected to economic boycott.
>
> On the issue of alleged police brutality, a drive is under way to document as many cases as possible. Special stations are being set up in Negro churches so that persons who were the victims of brutality or who witnessed such incidents can file complaints.

We continued our boycott against the two Memphis newspapers—both owned by Scripps-Howard—and began to picket outside their shared building. We gave out handbills listing our reasons for persisting. Among them were:

> They do not give impartial or full coverage to Negro News.
>
> They have kept poor "Hambone" out of the grave for half a century.
>
> They have no Negro reporters covering outstanding events in the city.
>
> Their Society pages are discriminatory.
>
> They designate race when crimes are committed by Negroes, but not by whites.

We also listed their attacks on Martin and said they helped to murder him in many ways:

> By assassinating the character of this great man in the April 2nd Editorial.
> By slanting the news regarding him for the past 2 years.
> By playing up derogatory remarks made in other racist newspapers.

Time magazine was also back in town to report on our boycott, and quoted me calling Memphis's two dailies "racist papers" that "attacked and vilified" Martin so often that they "share responsibility for his death."

The article's headline was "Newspapers: Hurt Pride in Memphis," and went on to say the editors of both papers found it "almost incomprehensible" that we were pointing out their culpability in what happened during the strike and in Martin's death. The editors seemed to think their coverage of Black Memphians and the strike was in line with what they saw as the papers' tradition of great journalism. *Time*'s reporting implied that the editors of both papers thought the fact that they each served on a city-run "biracial commission, which has tried to smooth the way for peaceful desegregation" was the best proof of their commitment to racial justice.

> The strike, however, caught the papers off guard. Memphis, as they boasted perhaps too often, had never had a serious racial disturbance. Partly because of this, the papers were rattled when it finally occurred.

The article said the papers portrayed the strike as a simple labor dispute, ignoring the fact that the sanitation workers who walked out were all Black men. That was how most of white Memphis chose to see the strike too. But *Time* went on to corroborate what we all suspected.

> They covered the strike with reasonable thoroughness but tended to play up acts of violence. They regularly attacked King, saying he had no business in Memphis. They ignored Negro militants leading the strike; for a while, the Commercial Appeal even banned Lawson's name from the paper. It also ran a tasteless cartoon showing a Negro striker perched on top of a garbage can from which fumes were pouring. . . .

Time mentioned our complaints about segregated classified ads, and the paper's practice of mentioning the race of Black people but not of white people who were charged with a crime. The article also told of us calling out Hambone, and described it as "a daily cartoon . . . in which a shambling old Negro delivers such bromides as 'Mos' folks, dey loses at de mouf whut dey teks in at de ears.'"

The article ended by surmising that the biggest effect from our boycott was the bruised egos of editors and reporters at both papers.

> Their pride has been hurt. The racial amity they thought they had achieved has dissolved. What seemed reasonably liberal yesterday is denounced as paternalistic today. But if the Memphis papers have been unfairly singled out for attack, the grievances are small enough to have been remedied long ago. The shame is that it took a bitter strike and an assassination to bring them to attention.

I had heard that the papers had intentionally restricted my name from being mentioned in some of their coverage of the strike. The *Time* article brought that out in the open. But we persevered.

Among the many repercussions of the loss of Martin King for the nonviolent movement was the fact that his presence during a local campaign immediately gave the people and issues involved an international platform. When Martin King was invited to come into a community, the whole world knew it. To get the leverage we needed in Memphis, we had to get news into *The New York Times, Time,* and other national publications, because *The Commercial Appeal* and the *Press-Scimitar* weren't willing to report fully on us. Once Martin King came to the community, it was news all around the world, and even *The Commercial Appeal* couldn't keep refusing to cover the issues or blackballing people like me. His presence was far more important to the movement than many people realized. Martin Luther King Jr. was a living symbol of the nonviolent movement, and any movement needs such an icon.

The business of seizing the momentum and focusing it on winning other gains for Black people, especially those living in poverty, was how I kept going despite the grief I felt. I didn't take much time in those first few months to feel the loss of Martin personally. I immersed myself in the work of continuing his legacy. And there were some small victories along the way.

Throughout the sanitation strike, I had also been involved with a major shift in the Methodist Church. Finally, in early May 1968, the church voted to eliminate segregation. The all-Black Central Jurisdiction would be folded into the larger white church and form the integrated United Methodist Church. In mid-May, we had our final meeting at my church of the all-Black Central Jurisdiction's West Tennessee and Western Kentucky Conference, which was to be merged into the existing, white Memphis Conference. I urged Black Methodists to see to it that we were active in shaping the new conferences, and not to allow the seventeen Black churches in our conference to be merely absorbed and assimilated into the white church and forgotten.

Another small but significant victory also came in early May: *The Commercial Appeal* announced that it had run its last Hambone cartoon. A series of letters to the editor after Martin's assassination had reflected the mood among more and more people that the cartoon had no place in our city. One said, "I want to criticize your publication of the loosely referred to 'cartoon' Hambone. I, and assuredly many others, have never appreciated this form of humor. I think under the present circumstances stopping the cartoon is imperative."

Our boycott of the papers always mentioned Hambone. And when the paper informed its readers that the cartoon was over, it did it with an article about Nona Alley, the widow of the panel's creator, J. P. Alley. She was the mother of Cal Alley, who had drawn Hambone for the past few decades and, of course, was the paper's current editorial cartoonist. She was also the mother-in-law of the paper's editor in chief. The headline read, "Hambone's Author Bows to Change."

> Today The Commercial Appeal and countless thousands of readers for more than a half century lose an old friend whose wit and wisdom mellowed the day. As with many other hallowed traditions, Hambone was not for the Computer-Space Age.

Nona Alley was then quoted describing what she thought of Hambone.

> The Negro of the South retains his racial originality, quaint thought, homely ways from which the white people of the South learned much. Jim Alley was able to transmit the unstudied humor inherent

in the Negro race to his well-loved feature, "Hambone's Meditations," with no malice in his heart, so that people all over the country recognized it as a compliment and as true art.

Some reporters at *The Commercial Appeal* who had gotten to know me used to talk to me privately or send me notes indicating that they had a sense of the wrong at their paper, and often they conveyed their thoughts with a sense of humor (although I wouldn't call it "unstudied humor"). Joseph Sweat, who wrote much of the coverage of the strike for the paper, mailed me the clipping about Nona Alley and the end of Hambone, accompanied by a short letter.

> Dear Rev. Lawson:
>
> I think a Computer-Space Age minister like you should have a copy of this death notice for your scrapbook. I suggested around the office that you likely would be happy to preach the funeral but no one seemed too interested.
>
> Onward,
> Joseph Sweat

Our monitoring of the newspapers despite our boycott continued after the strike ended. We kept our eye on the coverage, and particularly the editorial page and the letters to the editor. The papers always helped us keep track of what people opposing us and some surprising supporters were thinking and saying. There had been a few letters in April calling for Hambone to be discontinued, and there were a lot of letters and even an editorial in the other daily paper, mourning the end of Hambone when it was announced.

Plenty of letters throughout the strike and beyond attacked me and other strike supporters, directly or indirectly criticizing all aspects of our campaign. One that particularly stood out for its unique angle was a letter written a few weeks after the strike ended and signed only "White Memphian." It offered a post-strike assessment of Henry Loeb.

> So much has been said in these past days of the tragedy of Martin Luther King. But do we yet comprehend the tragedy of Henry Loeb—which is, in a larger sense, the tragedy of our city and of white America.

> Here is a man: A man blessed with all the virtues least appropriate to meet the crisis which was his (and our) Gethsemane.
>
> Here was a man who was "firm" when the crisis demanded flexibility. Here was a man who was "fair" when the crisis demanded generosity. Here was a man who was "courageous" when the crisis demanded compassion. Here was a man who said, "be proud again," when salvation for us all lay (and still lies) in humility.
>
> Here was a man who made his stand at the end of the first mile when the solution to our dilemma could have been found only by a leader willing to go (and to lead us) to the end of the second mile.
>
> Where is that man?

The gravity of the strike and the assassination were still fresh through the month of May. On May 16, a grand jury decided not to bring charges against Leslie Dean Jones, the officer who shot and killed Larry Payne on March 28. Fire and Police Director Holloman said Jones acted in self-defense, even though more than twenty eyewitnesses at the housing project said Larry Payne had his hands up and was unarmed. Jones claimed that Larry Payne had threatened him with a knife, even though none of the eyewitnesses saw it, and no fingerprints were found on a knife that the police later produced as evidence. The officer's word was all it took. The U.S. Justice Department declined the case as well, saying there was not enough evidence to pursue it. Leslie Dean Jones murdered Larry Payne, and then was sent back to work on the Memphis police force.

Gradually, a sense of calm began to return. Our boycott of the downtown businesses ended. And on May 28, we announced that we were dropping the newspaper boycott. The next day, I was quoted in *The Commercial Appeal* commenting on a new program dreamed up by the Memphis War on Poverty Committee, which had attempted at every turn to stand in the way of much of our MAP-South work in 1966 and 1967.

> One of the War on Poverty Committee's summer programs will see $9,000 spent to teach poor children how to use a bus, it was learned today.

> The program drew criticism from another War on Poverty leader, the Rev. James M. Lawson, chairman of the WOPC delegate agency, Map-South.
>
> Lawson laughed, "As I understand it, this money will be spent teaching black children how to ride a bus. I guess they will teach them how to get on a bus without walking into the door and the like."
>
> . . . Lawson said, "Most of these children know how to ride the bus already. That's the only form of transportation their families have. . . . It would seem far more important to me for summer programs to be focused around taking people into the poverty areas—not children out of them. I think we should utilize our community resources—like art students and music students going into the ghetto and teaching the children new and useful things."

In May, I even got back to spending more time with my own children. One day, I was playing with John, teasing him, saying, "I don't know what I am going to do with that John. He is just not right."

We were both laughing, and then I asked him, "What do you think I should do with you?"

Without missing a beat, six-year-old John replied, "You'll just have to get used to me."

What he meant, of course, was that I was just going to have to accept him and value him as he was.

TWENTY

Agitator Index

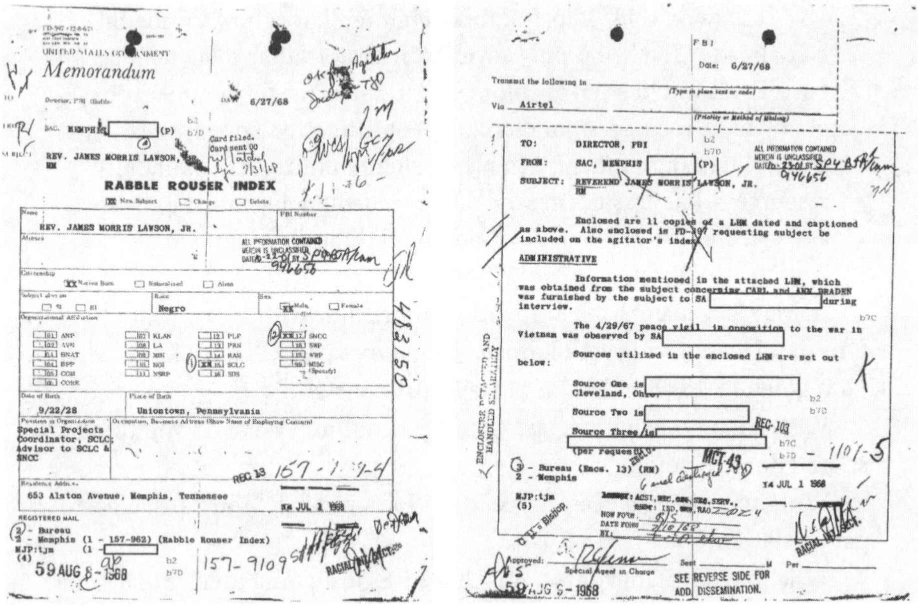

UNITED STATES GOVERNMENT

Memorandum

TO: Director, FBI

DATE: 6/27/68

FROM: SAC, MEMPHIS (P)

SUBJECT: REV. JAMES MORRIS LAWSON, JR.
RM

Card filed.
Card sent 00

RABBLE ROUSER INDEX

XX New Subject ☐ Change ☐ Delete

Name: REV. JAMES MORRIS LAWSON, JR.		FBI Number
Aliases		ALL INFORMATION CONTAINED HEREIN IS UNCLASSIFIED
Citizenship: XX Native Born ☐ Naturalized ☐ Alien		
Subject also on: ☐ SI ☐ RI	Race: Negro	Sex: XX Male ☐ Female
Organizational Affiliation: 01 ANP, 02 AVN, 03 BNAT, 04 BPP, 05 COM, 06 CORE, 07 KLAN, 08 LA, 09 MIN, 10 NOI, 11 NSRP, 12 PLP, 13 PRN, 14 RAM, XX 15 SCLC, 16 SDS, XX 17 SNCC, 18 SWP, 19 WWP, 99 MISC (Specify)		
Date of Birth: 9/22/28	Place of Birth: Uniontown, Pennsylvania	
Position in Organization: Special Projects Coordinator, SCLC; Advisor to SCLC & SNCC	Occupation, Business Address (Show Name of Employing Concern)	
Residence Address: 653 Alston Avenue, Memphis, Tennessee		

REC 13 157-...-4

JUL 1 1968

REGISTERED MAIL

2 - Bureau
2 - Memphis (1 - 157-962) (Rabble Rouser Index)
MJP:tjm (1 -)
(4)

59 AUG 8 - 1968

157-9109

RACIAL INT. SECT.

FBI

Date: 6/27/68

Transmit the following in ______ (Type in plain text or code)

Via Airtel (Priority or Method of Mailing)

TO: DIRECTOR, FBI

FROM: SAC, MEMPHIS (P)

SUBJECT: REVEREND JAMES MORRIS LAWSON, JR.
RM

ALL INFORMATION CONTAINED HEREIN IS UNCLASSIFIED

Enclosed are 11 copies of a LHM dated and captioned as above. Also enclosed is FD-397 requesting subject be included on the agitator's index.

ADMINISTRATIVE

Information mentioned in the attached LHM, which was obtained from the subject concerning CARL and ANN BRADEN was furnished by the subject to SA during interview.

The 4/29/67 peace vigil in opposition to the war in Vietnam was observed by SA

Sources utilized in the enclosed LHM are set out below:

Source One is
Cleveland, Ohio.

Source Two is

Source Three is

(per request)

3 - Bureau (Encs. 13) (RM)
2 - Memphis

MJP:tjm
(5)

REC 103

JUL 1 1968

ENCLOSURE DETACHED AND HANDLED SEPARATELY

Approved: Special Agent in Charge Sent ___ M Per ___

SEE REVERSE SIDE FOR ADD. DISSEMINATION.

59 AUG 9 - 1968

Reverend Lawson was added to the FBI's Agitator Index on June 27, 1968.

FBI RECORDS

For years, we had known that the FBI was watching us. During the movement, I saw the FBI as the enemy. And others felt the same way. It wasn't until decades later that we discovered the full extent of the bureau's surveillance. Its director and agents aggressively targeted Martin—the primary focus. And even though the rest of us weren't pursued with the same intensity, we were still monitored closely, as I found out when I eventually gained access to some of the files on me.

In an August 4, 1967, letter to all U.S. field offices, FBI director J. Edgar Hoover announced a new list of names the bureau's supervisors had created, instructing special agents to add to it.

> Rabble Rouser Index (Subversive Control)—Effective immediately in view of the widespread racial unrest the Bureau will maintain a Rabble Rouser Index. This Index will consist of the names, identifying data, and background information of individuals who are known rabble rousers and who have demonstrated by their actions and speeches that they have a propensity for fomenting racial disorder. . . .
>
> Very truly yours,
> John Edgar Hoover
> Director

In a November 28, 1967, memo to all FBI field agents, a "rabble rouser" was described more directly.

> Henceforth, the criteria for inclusion will be (1) agitators who have demonstrated by their actions and speeches that they have a propensity for fomenting disorder of a racial and/or security nature and (2) have attracted such attention, nationally or locally, as to be of significant interest with regard to the overall civil disturbance picture.
>
> A rabble rouser is defined as a person who tried to arouse people to violent action by appealing to their emotions, prejudices, et cetera; a demagogue.
>
> . . . This would include, for example, black nationalists, white supremacists, Puerto Rican nationalists, anti-Vietnam demonstration leaders and other extremists.

On March 21, 1968, a memo was sent saying the Rabble Rouser Index had been renamed, and going forward it would be called the Agitator Index.

And on March 28, 1968, the day of the march with Martin that the Memphis police violently disrupted, the special agent in charge of the Memphis bureau sent out a memo to other field offices about me, giving them biographical information he found pertinent, such as my arrest and prison term and my time in India. Also included were excerpts of informants' reports on my activities from years past, particularly in Memphis and during the sanitation strike. Finally, the memo included a list of all my long-distance phone calls in January and February of 1968, asking the pertinent offices to trace the names of the recipients of those calls to Ohio, New York, Mississippi, Tennessee, Nebraska, and D.C.

The memo also asked agents in the Washington, D.C., bureau to check the records of the passport division about a trip to Prague, Czechoslovakia, I had scheduled for the end of March 1968. That was a trip the Methodist Church was sponsoring, along with the National Council of Churches, to the All-Christian Peace Assembly, which in April was to bring together Christians from many countries around the world to discuss and plan for peace. I was supposed to leave on March 28 from New York. Because Czechoslovakia was a Communist country at the time, FBI suspicions were raised. Yet I would have been there at the height of the 1968 Prague student uprising, which loosened Soviet restrictions for a time and opened the country up to democratization, only to be repressed again in the fall of 1968. But the Memphis strike was consuming all my time in late March, so I had to cancel that trip a week or two before I was set to go.

At least 90 percent of anti-communism in the United States was really another form of racism. It projected all our nation's problems onto the outsider, the Communist. Any society as large as ours, and with as many historical forces operating within it, was bound to have some difficulties. Pretending all our problems were because of outsiders and Communists meant the American people did not have to examine themselves and could overlook so many core issues affecting the country—the very issues our movement was bringing to the forefront.

On April 17, 1968, the day after the sanitation strike was settled, the special agent in charge in Memphis, William Lawrence, sent a memo to J. Edgar Hoover with the subject line "James Morris Lawson, Jr. Racial Matters."

> A review of Bureau files indicated an investigation should be instituted on Lawson in accordance with the instructions in Section 87D of the Manual of Instructions for the purpose of considering Lawson for inclusion on the Agitator Index (formerly Rabble Rouser Index . . .) and/or Security Index. . . .
>
> . . . Lawson has been extremely active in racial matters in Memphis. He has made public inflammatory statements and has recently attacked local, state and national police officials in regard to the handling of racial violence and the investigation of the 4/4/68 assassination of Martin Luther King.

In May 1968, an odd report detailed a suitcase it said was sent to me at the Memphis Greyhound bus station from the American Friends Service Committee in care of the Southern Student Organizing Committee in Nashville. The report said the suitcase did not have my address on it. And I never received it. But an informant advised the bureau that in April this unlocked suitcase "was dropped from a storage shelf falling open," and that the informant was able to see that this suitcase contained a series of copies of pacifist, anti–Selective Service, conscientious objector, and anti–Vietnam War booklets and pamphlets. Then the report listed detailed descriptions, apparently cataloged by the informant, of thirty documents, with titles, authors, page counts, and descriptions. It included titles such as *The Christian Conscience and War, In Place of War: An Inquiry into Nonviolent National Defense,* and a twelve-page poem from 1966 called "To the Gallant Black Men Now Dead" by Vincent Harding, the great Black pastor, historian, and scholar and the first director of the King Center for Nonviolent Social Change, in Atlanta. Those books definitely would have interested me if I had ever received them. Instead, that suitcase full of them lives on only in the files of the FBI as evidence of my supposed subversive activity and associations.

On June 27, 1968, I was added to the Agitator Index, my inclusion justified by a separate, eighty-five-page report on any of my activities the FBI found notable, going back to 1949, when I was president of the Methodist Youth Fellowship of the Lexington Conference. That year, I served as co-chair of a meeting that called for an Ohio Bill of Rights. The agenda also urged support for a bill to enact fair employment practices in the state that had failed in the Ohio legislature. Of course, the FBI report also included federal records of my prison term.

While we took for granted the fact that there were informants all around us throughout the movement, I was especially aware of it in Memphis. In fact, one of the reasons I was wary of the Invaders was because we had gotten information that spies had infiltrated their ranks. Again, decades later, records and revelations from the people involved verified that many of our suspicions were true.

One particularly disturbing infiltrator was a young Black man from the Memphis Police Department who had embedded himself so fully in the Invaders that he was their transportation director. He is seen kneeling next to Martin in the famous photo on the balcony of the Lorraine Motel just after the shooting, in which everyone is pointing to where they thought the shot had originated. The tactics and methods the FBI and local police used against us were as invasive, underhanded, and unethical as we had always imagined. The very people and organizations charged with protecting and safeguarding our rights and liberties as citizens were betraying and undermining us at every turn.

Another memo verifying their vitriol toward us was sent to Director Hoover from the special agent in charge of the Charlotte, North Carolina, FBI office on the morning of April 4, 1968, just hours before Martin was murdered. It laid out a few of the ways agents felt empowered to execute their orders to undermine us. The subject of the memo was "Counterintelligence Program, Black Nationalist—Hate Groups, Racial Intelligence."

> This division feels that the Bureau might strike to eliminate the facade of civil rights and show the American public the true revolutionary plans and spirit of the Black Nationalist movement and its leaders, expose and discredit them in the eyes of responsible individuals and organizations who contribute financially to their activities as well as pay honorariums for personal appearances. It is felt that by educating state and local officials as well as the general public who are not privy to the knowledge in possession of the Bureau, these leaders could be isolated to influencing the small hard core group of revolutionaries.

The document then went on to name the means they could use, including "a Congressional Hearing; leaks to friendly news media; obtaining the mailing lists and bulk mailing permit numbers of the subversive organizations and counterfeiting literature damaging to the organization; fictitious letters to news media exposing their plans." Then the memo suggested eight ways to make direct attempts to disrupt the personal and official lives of targeted individuals. The first one said, "Intimate knowledge of the individual's daily activities is vital to implement an effective counterintelligence campaign, and therefore, mail, trash" and telephone wiretapping "should be considered in order to obtain leads. . . ." The list continued:

> (2) Prior to appearance of the individual at a campus or public function, fictitious letters should be circulated calling for extreme violence in the name of the subject or speaker.
>
> (3) Physical surveillance of the subject's motel room for immoral conduct. When such is detected, an anonymous phone to the local Police department and newspapers.

(4) Anonymous calls to the subject's wife alleging infidelity with his traveling companions and/or female co-workers.
(5) Selected personal appearances could be disrupted by anonymous bomb threats at the auditorium.
(6) When sufficient data is collected regarding subject's income, conferences should be had with IRS.
(7) The regulatory powers of local and state agencies should be utilized to police the minor transgressions of the subjects, such as building codes, permits, traffic violations, etc.
(8) The planting of stories that the subject's close "Lieutenants" are informants.

It wasn't only the FBI or local police seeking to sabotage our work. Some far-right-wing white supremacist groups sent out hate mail, including mass mailings of what were called "scandal sheets." One of the largest and most active was the John Birch Society, the national organization based in Massachusetts with state branches and chapters across the country. Its rules about discretion were similar to those of Alcoholics Anonymous: a member could not tell anyone outside the group who else was in the group. But it was okay for individuals to identify themselves as members to anyone. In the 1960s, Memphis had at least fifteen chapters, under the auspices of the state headquarters in Chattanooga. The chapters met at people's homes and were usually small groups with about fifteen members. Also, one of the country's many John Birch Society bookstores was located in downtown Memphis, called the Mid-South American Opinion Bookstore. It sold only books the national office published or sanctioned.

The John Birch Society was founded in 1958 by Robert Welch, a retired candy company executive whose firm created Junior Mints, Sugar Daddies, and many other popular candies. Another wealthy entrepreneur, Fred Koch, was also a founding member. Koch's sons later went on to lead the family business, Koch Industries, and heavily funded far-right-wing political causes into the twenty-first century. The John Birch Society was named after Rev. John Morrison Birch, a Baptist missionary and Office of Strategic Services field officer who was killed in 1945 in China by people his followers said were Communists. The John Birch Society's most fervent unifying principle was to subvert communism and undermine the Black liberation movement, which were the same thing in their minds. The books sold in their bookstores were anti-Communist and attacked our movement—particularly Martin. The group also funded billboards that implied that Martin was a Communist, a loaded slur at that time.

I largely ignored the Birch Society. I had encountered some of that group's tactics in the Nashville movement. The *Nashville Banner* had accused me of being a Communist and an agitator. Of course, they also had attacked me for going to Vietnam in 1965 and during my run for the Memphis school board. But those attacks were not as extensive and prolonged as the attacks on me in Memphis during and after the sanitation strike, starting in the late 1960s.

One of the most vicious came from Norman Saliba, a medical doctor and John Bircher in Forrest City, Arkansas. The town, about forty-five miles west of Memphis, was named in honor of Nathan Bedford Forrest, a slave trader, Confederate army general, and founding grand wizard of the Ku Klux Klan. On March 21, 1968, Dr. Saliba circulated a special edition of his, a newsletter called *The Voice of the Ridge*. The first page had the headline "Communism in Forrest City??? (Would You Believe in Memphis?)" The article attacked the sanitation strike, focusing on me and Bayard Rustin in particular.

It began with a warning that "Communists have infiltrated every aspect of our society" and noted "special involvement of ministerial and racial groups," cautioning "that the so-called 'civil rights movement' is almost completely dominated by Communists and is being used to bring about revolution and the destruction of our nation. . . . Forrest Citians may soon be ring-side spectators to a convincing drama in our neighbor to the east." The newsletter went on to say that Bayard Rustin had played a part in starting the sanitation strike, because he had spoken to the workers about unions. Then it laid out its version of the first month of the strike: "What began quietly enough as a grievance between workers and the City of Memphis quickly developed into a full-scale racial issue . . . nurtured by the presence of agitators and black racists, including Black Muslim representatives. Foremost in the picture, though, has been the ministerial profession, especially one Reverend James M. Lawson." The piece also took a passing swipe at Martin.

A Look at Some of the People Involved

The Communist affiliations of Martin Luther King are too clearly documented and too numerous to even list here. It should suffice to say that violence always follows Mr. Non-Violence as surely as night follows day. One need not linger too long on his purposes for being in Memphis. But what about Mr. Rustin and Reverend Lawson? Could their interests be similar? Let's review a few facts about them.

The next page listed nine points from our past that supposedly supported the idea that Bayard and I were leading a Communist takeover of Memphis. For Bayard, the points included an affiliation with a Communist student group in the 1930s, his co-founding of the SCLC, a trip to Russia in 1958, and his organizing of the March on Washington in 1963. The article also noted that he "was arrested and pleaded guilty to homosexual activity in 1953."

About me, the newsletter mentioned: my imprisonment for "refusing to register for the draft"; my time in India, where, it said, I "studied passive resistance"; my expulsion from Vanderbilt; my upcoming trip to Prague (which I canceled a few days later because of the strike); my trip to South Vietnam in 1965—although it claimed I "traveled to North Vietnam . . . sponsored by Rustin's Fellowship of Reconciliation Group" [*sic*]; a 1966 trip I took to Montevideo, Uruguay, for an international conference on nonviolence, which it said I made in Martin's place; and my affiliation with the ACLU. In addition, it questioned my relationships with other student and anti-war activists, all of whom it also called Communists.

Printed exactly one week before Martin's last march was disrupted and two weeks before Martin was assassinated in Memphis, the newsletter ended by saying, "We pray that violence does not occur but we feel that the public should know the type of men who would bring disorder now and economic ruin later to this city. . . . Need We Say More???"

A similar group in Memphis, called Enlighten People on Communism, or EPOC, took the information from Dr. Saliba's flyer, and made it their own on April 17, the day after the strike ended. That publication was sent to me a few times too, once again anonymously. It started with the headline "Communism in Memphis?" and then listed all the same information, adding, "Being a Negro does not grant Lawson immunity from criticism, nor does it make him a special target. Race has nothing to do with the utterances and actions which expose James M. Lawson."

Mike Cody, one of the lawyers who helped us in the injunction case, had been sent some of these publications, too. His law firm colleague David Caywood saw them as well and wrote me to say that it would be hard to stop these groups: "About all you can do is grit your teeth and bear it because you have become a public figure, and therefore, the libel and slander laws are greatly relaxed."

EPOC never came right out and said, "Lawson is a Communist." Its members said things like, "he is associated with Communist causes," or "he is a dupe of a Communist," or "he is a sympathizer." That was a way to play it safe. The kinds of cases where people had been charged with assassination of character, slander, or defamation were those in which a person directly called another person a Communist. Bringing a case for an indirect accusation was difficult.

The John Birch Society harmed the country greatly because it kept people from seeing the real dangers of an authoritarian system, whether it was Communist or fascist. They called so many people and things Communist that the label became a meaningless smoke screen.

Nonetheless, J. Edgar Hoover's FBI conducted an ongoing investigation into Communist influence in the SCLC in the 1960s. I didn't know even one Communist who was operating in the South at that time. I never met any, and I never heard of any associated with the SCLC. But if we are talking about anyone who was cooperative with some Communist front groups, that would have implicated all the American people. Because the Russians were our allies in World War II, as were the Chinese. We had a united front against Germany and Japan. Just about anyone in this country could have been accused of Communist associations, using that logic. Yet the suspicions of anyone trying to change this country continued from the FBI and racist groups. The special ridiculousness of the John Birch Society was its leaders and members even called President Eisenhower a Communist or a dupe, which was nonsense. Their influence in our culture perpetuated division, hate, and violence.

On Wednesday, June 5, Robert Kennedy was shot and killed, just after making a presidential campaign speech in Los Angeles. Another assassination. It left a hollow feeling inside me. Then on Saturday, June 8, James Earl Ray was caught and arrested at Heathrow Airport in London. In mid-April, the FBI had identified him as the main suspect in Martin's death, and he had been put on the Ten Most Wanted list. A grand jury had indicted him for first-degree murder in early May. And he was to be sent back to Memphis to stand trial.

That Sunday, June 9, I gave a sermon to my congregation.

Here we are again, sorrowing over the hurtful brutal death of one of our vital, young leaders.

. . . We are weary of weeping over fallen decent men.

. . . Robert Kennedy must be placed alongside his brother John and Martin Luther King as one of those men of the twentieth century who had dreams for a different world.

. . . I was impressed by him the first time I met him in August of 1961. He was Attorney General. I was chairman of the Freedom Ride committee. We met in his office to discuss what was happening in the South. He had his point view—a view with which I differed. But he listened, and he learned, and he grew in understanding.

He had the kingdom of this world offered to him. All he had to do was to wait quietly, stay away from championing the cause of the poor, be moderate for the Blacks and not demand full justice for them. Stay away from Harlem. Support the war. Certainly do not become a spokesman for the end of violence, for peace.

He did not choose that way. So in a nation bent upon swinging the club and the bomb, he was feared. In a society steeped in hatred, he was hated. In a land of wealth yet fostering poverty and cruelty, he, though a son of the land, possessed of some of the finest qualities of the land, he was an unwanted son.

. . . We are our brother's keeper. We are the keeper for Robert. We are the keeper for Sirhan Sirhan and James Earl Ray. No man is an island to himself. Every man is a part of every man. . . .

. . . Today . . . hatred takes a million forms in our midst. Young people hating LBJ because they disagree with his Vietnam policy and war. Anti-Communism which sows hate and suspicion of churches, politicians, leaders, ministers, educators, anyone who . . . dreams, or stands for convictions of brotherhood, or justice, or peace becomes a target of such hate.

. . . Hate has no limits. It is a virus for which doctors have no cure, except a loving heart.

Out of that hatred, we the American people nurse, tolerate, and encourage violence—all the way from paddling high school students thus teaching them not discipline which they need, but the effectiveness of violence, to burning down the huts of peasants, to shooting up the Black ghetto in Newark, or Detroit, or Memphis.

> . . . Three good and decent men cut down, may spell the beginning of the end. I believe it is a plot. Why not evil men cut down? Why men who champion righteousness for our nation? Blacks must not play into the hands of these who in killing such men would have us run to the streets . . . burning—then, in repressing us, would make our nation like a Nazi Germany.
>
> Three good men cut down, also God's bells, pealing out warning, appealing to our consciences:
>
> JFK, new leadership for this age
> MLK, love and nonviolence the only way
> RFK, lifting of the poor and needy, the first requirement
>
> . . . Our sick land can be healed. There is forgiveness available. Three good men loved us too much to hate or give up. God, through them, appeals to you and me: move into this age and work.

We have had such trouble in this country admitting that violence is a part of the American character. With all of the emphasis we placed on the American dream and American opportunity, we Americans have tended to create a veil of innocence. In spite of extremely vicious periods of our history—such as enslavement, the Civil War, the treatment of the Indigenous people, and even the treatment of our workers, with sixteen-hour workdays and child labor—we maintained a kind of willful-ignorance-is-bliss attitude, based on the idea that we have never had major problems in America.

Some in the South, for example, tried to pretend the Civil War was a nice thing and not a bloody reckoning with slavery. That facade underscores the importance of Black history and Black studies to the nation. Because a person or a nation cannot really build a future or deal with the present if they have a mythological idea of their past. If we hadn't admitted that we had a segregation system that exploited, brutalized, restricted, and excluded Black people, then we couldn't have dealt with how to make equal opportunity a reality.

The same moral blindness or insensitivity to our history was quite apparent to me after the assassinations of King and the Kennedys. We cannot understand meaningful social change purely through looking at the politics or economics of problems.

Where there is violence, there is always cruelty. When a social order depends on everyone going along and pretending the cruelty is not there with the violence, then the very act of people asking for meaningful change to the cruelty tends to bring latent violent reactions like racism to the surface. When Black people organized and got moving, white people who had latent prejudice and were not able to change increasingly found the courage to express their racism in public. It was an inevitable feature of change, and I saw it as a healthy one. Because as long as they pretended racism was not there, as long as they were afraid to express it, talk about it, and organize around it, then we were all in real trouble. Getting racism out in the open gave our society a chance to see it, and our institutions a chance to respond to it. They may have responded in the most fascist way in some cases. That was the real threat. But it was the chance we took.

I don't see any way, other than confrontation, to bring racism out of the shadows. And nonviolent confrontation is the only way to do it without imitating the cruelty of the racists. Confronting it causes real shock to a lot of people who did not see it before. I think there is a built-in apparatus in people that tends to insulate us from reality. You don't see what you don't want to see. On certain tough issues, like police brutality, there was always a massive sense on the part of white people that it was not really that bad, or that it didn't really go on, or that probably Black and Brown people instigated it, and, therefore, perhaps, we sort of deserved it. There is not the universal recognition that such brutality by the state violates the principles and the practice of our Constitution, and of human rights in general.

As long as we let poverty and racial injustice go along unchecked, it will inevitably reach proportions that lead to major explosions of tension. So in very real ways, those of us who actively tried to speed up the process of change were doing the nation a tremendous service, because the status quo would only lead to destruction of our nation, if not our whole world.

One local news outlet leader who saw the need for airing the issues we had raised during the strike was Mori Greiner, general manager of the NBC affiliate, WMC-TV. He and a friend and colleague of his, David Yellin, were persuaded during the strike that the station had to do something. David, a professor of film and television at Memphis State University, spearheaded the idea for a weekly show hosted and produced by Black people to talk about Black issues. No other show on television in Memphis was doing that every week. David and John Arnold, a Black advertising executive, worked together to organize it. David asked me and Ben Hooks to work with them to produce the show, which we called

The 40 Percent Speak. Ben and I were to alternate the hosting duties each week. In the announcement of the show, Mori told the papers there would be no restrictions placed on the show: "They may talk about whatever they want, our TV, the newspapers, charges of police brutality, housing, job opportunities, or whatever." The show began airing on June 28, and the first topic was "What Do We Want?"

The papers covered the show, reporting on our answers. I said, in part, "The Negro wants to feel most of all that he lives in a friendly society and not a hostile society." Ben Hooks said, "We want to feel that we are full-fledged, first-class American citizens." And my friend and parishioner Jerry Fanion said, "We want to walk the streets and not have to fear police problems. We want school systems that deal with all of our today problems."

The next week, I hosted an episode of the show focused on police brutality. We entitled it "We Accuse," meant as an echo of the famous letter from writer Émile Zola published on the front page of a French newspaper with the headline "J'Accuse . . . !" ("I Accuse . . . !"), calling out the government's anti-Semitic, wrongful imprisonment of a French Jewish soldier, Alfred Dreyfus, for being a spy, and the complicity of the French press in the whole incident. In English, "J'Accuse" came to mean any public denouncement of gross injustice and mistreatment of citizens, particularly from powerful government officials.

The *Press-Scimitar* television columnist, Mary Ann Lee, wrote an entire column about the program.

> From some 70 affidavits turned in to the NAACP office since April, plus other complaints made to the Civil Rights Commission and directly to the police department, three charges of police brutality were examined in detail last night on WMC-TV.
>
> The program, "The 40 Per Cent Speak," which made its debut a week ago last night, was entitled, "We Accuse." Next week a panel discussion will be built around the theme, "We Propose."
>
> . . . No half-hour program, showing but three cases, can ever fully describe a problem so complex or hope to heal the breach this one tackled, but this production . . . made a valuable and strong beginning.
>
> "We do not accuse all the Memphis police of being sadists," the Rev. Lawson said, but "the problem of law and order is related to the personal relationship of police to Black people."

We presented three cases of police beating and bloodying innocent Black people: a young deaf girl, a Vietnam War veteran who had won the Purple Heart, and two teenage brothers who were not in violation of any law.

A few days later, police director Holloman asked for and received equal time on WMC-TV to give his side of the story. He would say only that he didn't believe our stories showed firm evidence of police misconduct.

Having a platform on local television gave us the opportunity to show the whole city issues that affected Black people in Memphis. It was my first foray into exercising the power of the media to influence what the public sees and understands. Those who tell the story set the agenda. That desire to communicate was also why I had agreed to participate in a project that had begun just after Martin's assassination and was unique to Memphis in the movement: a multimedia documentation of the entire sanitation strike. A biracial group of local professors, journalists, and community activists formed the Memphis Search for Meaning Committee. My friends David, who co-produced *The 40 Percent Speak* with me, and his wife, Carol Lynn Yellin, were the directors of the project. They had moved to Memphis from New York City in 1964. She was a journalist and an editor at *Reader's Digest*. The group set about interviewing everyone and anyone involved in the strike. They took an interest in our campaign and said, "Let's create this archive for the future," so the story gets told from many different angles by the people who participated in it. It was absolutely singular.

The committee members were motivated by their observation that the local media, led by the two main local newspapers, were not covering the strike adequately. They believed that lack of information contributed to the strike starting and lasting, and ultimately to the assassination of Martin. So they gathered and preserved most of the film the TV news stations made during and after the strike, as well as recordings of radio interviews and reports. And they decided to create an oral history, beginning a month after the strike ended. Some 150 people involved from all sides were willing to speak into their microphones. Eventually they got a grant from the National Endowment for the Humanities, and Memphis State University gave them space to work and housed the archive in its library when they were done. The Yellins conducted the interviews, along with journalists Joan Beifuss, Bill Thomas, and other students and professors. They interviewed me eleven times between 1968 and 1972, about my life and especially about my role in the strike. It was an extraordinary affair and, I believe, one of the most important projects in which I ever participated. I know of no other community during the twenty-year period of the nonviolent movement of America where such a local group documented their city's campaign as immediately and thoroughly as they did in Memphis.

My first interview with them was in early July 1968. They talked to me right after a taping of *The 40 Percent Speak*, at the television station. That was probably the only way they could have caught me then, because I was trying to take a vacation that month, and I was on my way to serve as a delegate to the World Council of Churches General Assembly in Uppsala, Sweden. Martin King was originally going to be the keynote speaker at the event. James Baldwin ended up giving the keynote speech instead of him. I was already slated to go there, representing the United Methodist Church and the movement. So I spent much of the month overseas.

That month out of the country was when it really hit me that Martin was gone. I began to do some of my grieving in Sweden. It was the first time I cried about my loss. Martin Luther King Jr. was one of the finest human beings I've ever met—loving, gracious, gentle, strong, a highly talented man. That's why I don't think it was an accident that the people of Montgomery elected him to be the advocate of the Montgomery Improvement Association and the advocate of the bus boycott in 1955.

He and I shared a lot of sports and music passions. He was a good singer, and very athletic. So was I. We also both loved to eat all sorts of food—shrimp in South Carolina, soul food, the Black food we were raised on. He loved to play, and to dance. He was wonderful with his children, though he was away from them so much more than he wanted to be. But that was because of the demands upon him.

I can compare Martin to only maybe a couple dozen human beings across the history of humans so far. He was a normal human being but was selected to lead during a historic moment. I watched him make the changes he had to make to advocate for this new campaign of nonviolent direct action that went into the jaws of the enemy and say, "No. No more. We have to quit. Our country can be a better country than this, and we are better people."

I felt great loss, but not a sense of guilt about Martin's death. Because one of the realities that many of us faced—and Martin King more than anyone else—was that we expected to be killed at some time or another. Martin would say openly—in staff meetings, at staff retreats, and with personal friends—that he expected death during the movement. We all recognized that there were too many enemies around who wanted to get him. At the time Martin was assassinated, he was the most hated man in the United States.

After you get enough hate calls and threats of death, you do have to make a decision to carry on anyway, or not. I had to make that decision, too. You don't play games and ignore it. Otherwise, you would find it very difficult to keep working and maintain your sanity.

When I got back from abroad, in mid-August, the SCLC had its annual convention in Memphis. The organization usually chose a Southern city to host the annual meeting, one that had been particularly active during the year before. For better or worse, Memphis had been most active in 1968.

Time came to cover the convention, and didn't let up on critiquing the city and its leadership. "This steamy city on the Mississippi," the magazine noted, "still seethes in the residue of April's unlearned lessons, and the aloof attitude of Mayor Henry Loeb and other officials hardly helps." It went on to say the SCLC was convening "defiantly in the city where its founder was murdered," and then wondered about what would result given that Memphis police had what the magazine called a "traditional policy of heavy-handedness toward Negroes, which ranges from routine rudeness to blatant brutality." The article mentioned the more than fifty documented cases of police brutality that the U.S. Commission on Civil Rights collected during and after the strike, and it described a few of them.

One was Larry James Mitchell Holt, a twenty-four-year-old man who drove a red Dodge which ended up with a smashed fender after police pursued him.

> The car's glass was unbroken; yet it took 180 stitches to close gashes in Holt's face and head. Holt contends that the two cops dragged him from his car and beat him. The cops maintain that Holt's injuries came in the crash, but do not explain why no blood was found on the white upholstery of his car.

Another case *Time* mentioned was Robert Stewart, a twenty-one-year-old who was coming out of a grocery store when two police officers grabbed him and told him to get away from the area. He told them he was at the store to buy canned milk. One of the officers told him to stop "getting smart," and then the physical abuse began. Stewart and eight eyewitnesses said the two officers punched him and beat him with a billy club and a flashlight, while forcing him into their squad car.

Subsequent photos show Stewart's nose broken, eyes swollen nearly shut on a puffy face, the back of his head cratered by deep open wounds. Stewart received a probationary sentence for loitering and resisting arrest.

The article brought up how four police officers were fired in 1967 for brutality, noting that Mayor Loeb reinstated all of them when he came into office at the start of 1968.

> Such wrist-spanking discipline deepens Negro frustration. So does the chest-thumping of Fire and Police Director Frank Holloman, who recently promised an applauding white civic club that if Memphis' Negroes revert to "lawlessness," as he put it, "we'll knock them on their ass." There was further frustration when a bid by Negroes to prevent a sales-tax rise—partly to finance a 50-man increase in the police force—was defeated. The tax hike passed 3 to 2, which is roughly the ratio of whites to Negroes in Memphis.

Police brutality was not limited to Memphis, of course. In fact, just after the SCLC convention, during the national Democratic Convention in Chicago in late August, anti-war protests reached a peak. For days, police in riot gear and National Guard troops cracked down on demonstrators as well as journalists covering the turmoil, using billy clubs, Mace, and guns. Live national and international broadcasts from the convention transmitted the nonviolent demonstrations and the violent police response, as demonstrators chanted, "The whole world is watching."

The Commercial Appeal had finally hired its first Black columnist in May 1968—a month after the sanitation strike ended and a few weeks after Hambone was never to be seen in the paper again. Art Gilliam, a Yale graduate with an MBA from the University of Michigan, was a young executive at the Black-owned Universal Life Insurance Company in Memphis. He spent the summer of 1968 writing columns about the life of sanitation workers, fair housing, police brutality, poverty, and other topics that had not been covered from a Black perspective before in a major Memphis newspaper. He was, in effect, explaining Black people and Black life to white Memphians. On Monday, October 7, 1968 he wrote a column entitled "Blacks Face Life with Increasing Pride," in which he quoted me:

> The essence of black pride is that it allows American Negroes to face life without laboring under the scepter of an inferiority complex. As the Rev. Mr. Lawson explains: "Genuine pride comes when one accepts himself and the humanity of others and thereby refuses to let others reject his humanity."

A week or so after that column was published, I would need to remember those words as the city council met to consider funding requests for MAP-South. We had created many programs to empower people living in poverty in Black neighborhoods. Throughout North and South Memphis, we had a Black history course running, and a theater workshop in which students and professors at Memphis State University worked with thirteen- to twenty-one-year-olds teaching acting and theater production. The students then formed the Afro Theater Guild in the fall. Also, MAP-South had recently been recognized by the federal Office of Economic Opportunity as one of the top community action programs in the nation.

But when Memphis's War on Poverty Committee (WOPC) requested approval of financing applications to the federal government that would amount to $600,000, the biggest hurdle was our request for $8,400 in the committee's annual budget. Four white councilmen used our request as an opportunity to attack me, in a concerted effort to oust me as the board chair of MAP-South. I was a co-founder, and the board position was unpaid. Still, the council members and their backers tried.

On Monday, October 14, the city council's health, welfare, and institutions subcommittee called a special hearing to investigate MAP-South's activity. For two and a half hours council members questioned me and heard from several partners of MAP-South, all of whom spoke highly of our programs. Two Black councilmen, Fred Davis and Rev. James Netters, also defended the program. Meanwhile, the head of the Memphis

War on Poverty Committee, Herschel Feibelman, and three other white councilmen—Bill Todd, Bob James, and Lewis Donelson—derided me. Without quoting any of my words in the meeting, *The Commercial Appeal* reported:

> Several councilmen objected to the attitude of the MAP-South chairman, the Rev. James M. Lawson, and wanted him replaced.
>
> . . . Councilmen . . . are unhappy in part because the Rev. Mr. Lawson denounced the mayor and the council in a Saturday night television interview.
>
> "I don't believe as chairman of MAP-South he is an asset to the community," Mr. Todd said.
>
> Councilman James said many councilmen "like portions of these projects" but feel that personality conflict with the Rev. Mr. Lawson has caused "uncertainty and doubt" in the program.
>
> . . . Mr. Davis . . . defended MAP-South. . . . "To hear Mr. Todd speak," said Mr. Davis, "one would think that everything that has come out of the program has been bad. Some very fine contributions have come out of MAP-South."
>
> The Rev. Mr. Netters joined Mr. Davis in defense of the program. "I don't think Mr. (George) Wallace could have criticized this program as effectively as it has been criticized today.
>
> "We're trying to take personalities and kill all help for the poor people of this community."
>
> "The program has much to offer. It has a long way to go," said WOPC Chairman Herschel Feibelman. . . .
>
> . . . "It's difficult for me to understand why we can't do something about this group—the Rev. Mr. Lawson has outlived his usefulness," said Mr. Donelson. "We get a little tired of doling out the money and getting gratuitous insults."
>
> "There is absolutely nothing to criticize in MAP-South except the director," said Mr. Feibelman.

Other articles in both *The Commercial Appeal* and the *Press-Scimitar* also quoted the critical council members, as well as a few of our supporters. John T. Fisher said the city's new manpower commission, on which he served as chairman, planned to be working with MAP-South on placing unemployed and underemployed persons in fifteen hundred new jobs. A representative of the city's health department said working with

MAP-South had "increased three-fold the effectiveness" of a skin-testing program for tuberculosis: "I'm speaking for the tuberculosis section, and all we've seen is good." An administrator from St. Jude Children's Research Hospital praised their partnership with MAP-South. Their joint effort to address malnutrition had helped two hundred children and their families living in poverty, the administrator noted, adding, "The clinic has seen many starving children right here in Memphis."

The chair of the theater department at Memphis State, Keith Kennedy, said MAP-South's work with the university, placing six hundred high school students in university classes for the summer and exposing them to college life, was "the most significant thing Memphis State has done for this community." He noted that in the two years of the program, there had been only one dropout, and that many of the students had gone on to college, when without the program they likely might have never known they could do so.

But Councilman Wyeth Chandler, who would go on to become mayor a few years later, brought up my television interview that previous Saturday, saying, "I'm tired of hearing that we on the Council don't care anything about the poor and that we are a bunch of ruthless racists."

Another councilman, Billy Hyman, said, "This is what people are concerned about . . . that you take this man who wants to put the city in turmoil and put him in charge of MAP-South."

Despite my multiple responses to this criticism, I was quoted only once, in one article in the afternoon paper: "We are judged by whether we feed and clothe the poor. The only way we can eliminate poverty is to pull down the bars of prejudice and develop a climate of good will." The article then reported Councilman Hyman's response: "Referring to Lawson's leadership in the sanitation strike, Hyman said, 'Climate should come from some ministers as well.'"

The council members accused me of making statements about burning down the town, which was never something I said. The WOPC chair, Mr. Feibelman, remarked in reference to my resistance to the draft and my prison term, "I, myself, did not avoid the draft and served military duty." And councilman Lewis Donelson said, "If that man really wanted to help the community he would resign. I think we could say we could not approve the program unless he did so." The only woman on the council, Gwen Awsumb, said, "I do feel MAP-South is a good program basically but I show reticence to support it while it has its present chairman."

AFSCME's leader, Jerry Wurf, in an interview with the Memphis Search for Meaning Committee a few years later, said he believed many in the Memphis establishment reacted to me that way because I frightened them. "They feared Lawson," Wurf said, "because he was a totally moral man, and totally moral men you can't manipulate, and you can't buy, and you can't hustle. That's why they feared him, and that's why they hung this label of super-radical on him." Jerry was a good friend, and that was kind of him to say. But I didn't attempt to explain their behavior at the time. I merely tried to keep going despite it.

On Tuesday, October 15, 1968, the council decided to delay approval of funds for MAP-South.

My colleagues and many others were outraged. A group of Black ministers sent a letter to the members of the city council. They entitled it "A Pronouncement from the Elders, Religious, Civic and Community Leaders of the Black Community."

> Dear Elected Servants of the People:
>
> How long must we wait?
>
> For too long the white power structure in American cities and communities has presumed to hand pick the leaders of the Black Community.
>
> For too long the members of this white power structure have sat isolated and insulated from the crying needs of the Black Community, making cruel, thoughtless and vicious decisions which have adversely affected the lives and destinies of our people for this day and generations to come.
>
> . . . We are tired of being treated like second class citizens. We are fed up with postponements, delays, subterfuges, hypocrisy, false promises and intimidations.
>
> . . . Recent actions by our City Council give us . . . much cause for concern; and even more than that, it confirms our suspicions that we are being fed "the same old soup warmed over."

They called out the delay in MAP-South funding, reminding the council that this was the first time such funds had been requested from the city, because all of our funding since 1965 had come from federal sources. They said the hearing on Monday, October 14, and the city council meeting the next day consisted of "insinuations, intimidations, bullying, pressuring and threatening" of me.

> The Reverend James Lawson has been selected a leader of the Black Community by the Black people themselves. When he speaks, he speaks not only for himself but the rank and file of the Black people in Memphis.
>
> We denounce with all the vigor at our disposal the subtle intimidation directed toward the Reverend James Lawson and the MAP-South poverty program.
>
> We challenge you to stop applying "band-aids to cancer," healing the surface while the tissue continues to rot beneath.

The council considered MAP-South funding again on Tuesday, October 22. I was at the meeting but did not speak or talk to the press. The city council put forth a resolution granting the funding, but with an amendment attached, stipulating that no employees of MAP-South could use their time on the job to demonstrate or organize against the city, advocate for disobeying draft laws, or divert any of the money to encourage civil disobedience or demonstrations.

Rev. Ralph Jackson spoke to the council at the meeting, saying I had been slandered: "You are not going to pick the leaders of the Black community. . . . I say to you that there is never a night that goes by that Rev. Lawson and I don't receive threats and then this council makes such a statement that Rev. Lawson has outlived his usefulness to MAP-South. . . . You should know when you make a statement like that there are sick people out there who would misinterpret it; sick people like the ones who took three of the greatest leaders of this generation away by assassination."

In the end, the council approved the MAP-South funding, with the amendment. Four white men on the council voted against approval.

Through COME and MAP-South, I was still advocating against police brutality and for people living in poverty—the two areas Martin and I had agreed would be our focus as the movement continued.

As 1968 was ending, losing Martin had become my main sorrow. It would also prove to endure through the rest of my life as my ever-present spur.

I often keep notes of quotations that inspire me, from what I read, talks I hear, or movies I see. At the end of 1968, I wrote down on a note card the closing lines of Thornton Wilder's *The Bridge of San Luis Rey,* a novel about five random people who each simultaneously happened to be on a bridge when it collapsed unexpectedly, killing them all.

> There is a land of the living and a land of the dead and the bridge is love, the only survival, the only meaning.

Stubborn chance and immeasurable tragedy are part of life on earth. Yet we keep going.

PART FOUR

1969–2024

STILL GOING ON

I want to commend the preachers . . . these noble men: James Lawson, one who has been in this struggle for many years. He's been to jail for struggling. He's been kicked out of Vanderbilt University for this struggle. But he's still going on, fighting for the rights of his people.

—Martin Luther King Jr., April 3, 1968

TWENTY-ONE

On Resurrection Morning

Reverend Lawson marches with Dorothy and John Lawson on the way to turn himself in and serve time at the Memphis jail after the Black Monday campaign, December 1969. ERNEST WITHERS COLLECTION

Around seven A.M. on January 15, 1969—what would have been Martin's fortieth birthday—Dorothy answered a phone call to our home from a lady who said she was white but never gave her name. Right at the start of her long rant she told Dorothy, "Your husband has no business burying that colored boy in that cemetery. It is a white cemetery."

I was standing at the bathroom sink, getting ready for a funeral I was conducting later that morning for a thirty-year-old man from my congregation named Roy Mayes Jr. I had been visiting him in the hospital before he died, of alcohol poisoning. I began to shave, and that's when I heard our only phone ring and Dorothy going to answer it where it sat in the hallway. I could hear her voice in a long conversation but couldn't tell who was on the other end of the line. After about fifteen minutes, Dorothy suddenly broke out into huge laughter, like I had never heard from her before. She kept laughing uproariously and then talked a little more before I heard her hang up the phone.

She rushed into the bathroom to tell me what it had all been about. She said the woman had read Roy's obituary in the paper, which noted that the funeral would be conducted at Centenary and afterward the interment would take place at Forest Hill Cemetery, all of it presided over by me. She had found our home number in the phone book and called us to try to stop what she saw as a grievous violation of the way the world worked. Dorothy described how the woman went over the issue again and again. "For at least fifteen minutes," Dorothy said, "that woman admonished me about having his burial in that cemetery."

Dorothy had listened patiently. Then, well into the conversation, in a last-ditch effort to make us stop the burial the woman finally said, "Look, only white people are buried at Forest Hill. If your husband goes through with this and buries that colored boy beside white people, then I guarantee you that on resurrection morning all of those white people will wake up, see him lying there where he is not supposed to be, and will rush over and lynch that n——r."

Dorothy saw the hysterical humor and absurdity in what the woman was saying. Even death and resurrection couldn't stop her soul's imagination from spouting racism. We also saw the sadness in it all. The woman thought she had a right to say such things to my wife, because I happened to be the pastor who was going to bury one of the first Black people in that cemetery.

I lost count of the number of death warnings and hate calls we were getting on my office telephone at the church and at home. But that woman's call was the clearest illustration of how discombobulated some white people were back then. She showed us the kind of perversity that happens when, speaking theologically, people organize their lives around false gods, like racism.

Grief

After Martin's death, life was demanding that I deal with the aftermath of such a great loss. I kept reminding myself that I was still here on earth to carry out our shared vision. Just as I began to figure out how I—how all of us—would continue without him, I was stopped short again.

In March 1969, my mother had a massive stroke. She was seventy-three years old. I went home to Ohio to be with her on March 26. She was in a coma for several days and never recovered from it.

Philane Mae Cover Lawson died on April 3, 1969. I was at her side.

Death took my mother almost exactly one year after it came for Martin, my dear friend and spiritual brother.

My mother's journey from Jamaica to New York, to my father, and to all of us, was always guided by her steadfast inner compass and her innate spiritual sense of Christian love and grace. My mother was the pillar of my spiritual awakening, the one who launched me on my quest for a better way. I have missed her every day since that day she died, even as her spirit has forever stayed within me and helped guide me. The love she infused in me and in all of her children endured. It was a gift I have always cherished and tried to find within myself during both my darkest and my most joyous times.

From my mother's bedside in Cleveland, I traveled back to Memphis the next day to lead a march we had been planning for the first anniversary of Martin's death on Friday, April 4. Ralph Abernathy and Senator Ted Kennedy came to speak.

The following Sunday, Dorothy and I and the boys headed back to Cleveland for my mother's funeral, to be held on Tuesday, April 8. My brother Phil and I conducted the service. I had led many funerals by then as a pastor, but my own mother's was both an honor and one of the hardest.

When we arrived back in Memphis the next day, a long profile of me in the morning paper greeted us, written by a white reporter named Tom BeVier. It mentioned how my mother had died the day before I led the march on the first anniversary of Martin's death.

> Not even his mother's death in Cleveland, Ohio the afternoon before the march, hampered his almost indefatigable singleness of purpose.
>
> He said it was his mother who was the moving force in shaping the direction of his life.

Of course it is not entirely true that my mother's death did not hamper me. But my mother and Martin were my spiritual kin. For me, honoring them was related. The article also quoted me talking about how I felt right after Martin died: "My first reaction was great anguish. I'm not really over it. It's still quite painful to read things by him or about him."

The pain does not go away. But you do what you have to do to get through it. Martin's assassination and the heightened threats against me did prompt Dorothy and me to have a talk with our oldest son, John, who would be turning eight in the summer of 1969. I told him about the reasons I was speaking out: racism, discrimination against people living in poverty, and the importance of nonviolent demonstrations. We knew John had enjoyed the marches and demonstrations he already had attended. As gently as we could, we explained to him that there was a risk for me in my work of being hurt or killed. I thought it was important to say this. He was young, but he had seen what was going on around him and was starting to understand. Morris and Seth were still too young to comprehend it all.

Spread the Misery

In 1969, as Richard Nixon's administration took over from Lyndon Johnson's, the War on Poverty was de-emphasized. Consequently, in Memphis, we had to work harder to demonstrate to the white power brokers that the unmet needs of our fellow citizens living in poverty deeply affected our whole community and had to be addressed fully. That's when Jesse Epps of AFSCME, some fellow ministers, and I came up with what we called the "Spread the Misery" campaign.

There is a kind of blindness people have to develop and maintain in order to continue justifying their racism. It helps them dismiss or ignore the immorality of forcing certain people to live in chronic poverty in the richest nation on earth. But when some who have been blind to an evil, such as racism and its effects, suddenly have their eyes opened and can't deny what is happening, they go through a real shock. After 1968, in the United States of America, a number of white people were suffering from that sort of shock.

As the first step in our Spread the Misery campaign, at the end of May 1969, we transported approximately two hundred AFSCME members and their families from Black neighborhoods in South and North Memphis into a shopping center called Poplar Plaza, in the heart of the well-off white part of the city called East Memphis. The men and women entered stores and shopped without buying anything—trying on clothes, talking to shopworkers, taking their time but not actually making purchases. Then they left. The demonstration was meant to make their presence known and jar the residents of the area into paying attention to them. We handed out leaflets with the reasons for our action. The union was in negotiations with the city for better pay, full union recognition, and improved working conditions for city workers, many of whom still lived in poverty. The negotiated victory in the 1968 sanitation strike won basic concessions for union members, but the city was dragging its feet on implementing some of what was agreed, including looking like they might find a way out of giving the full pay raise. There was much more to do to lift many city workers out of poverty permanently. The leaflets warned of another possible sanitation or hospital strike if the union's demands weren't met by July 1.

The following weekend, we took more than four hundred people back to Poplar Plaza and to another, more exclusive shopping center about a mile farther east called Laurelwood, a couple of blocks from Mayor Loeb's home on Colonial Road. Some stores there closed down for the day. At a grocery store in Poplar Plaza, a few of our demonstrators filled carts and then left them in the aisles without paying. At department stores like Sears and pricier shops in Laurelwood, demonstrators tried on shoes and outfits but did not buy any of them.

By the end of the second weekend, the merchants' associations of both shopping centers were putting pressure on city officials and union leaders to stop the demonstrations. That's when Jesse Epps suggested that the union would like to invite some women from East Memphis to visit the homes of a few city workers to see the conditions in which the families were living.

A few days later, Jesse Epps met with about fifteen white women led by Jocelyn Wurzburg, a Republican precinct captain and the wife of a downtown businessman. Jesse asked the women to come on a bus tour and encouraged them to invite others. *The Commercial Appeal* spoke with Jocelyn Wurzburg about the idea but identified her by her husband's name, as was the style in newspapers at that time.

> "Mr. Epps told us he is trying to help the poor and the hungry and to fight racism and he thinks his union is the vehicle to do it.
>
> ". . . We're willing to listen because we're interested in the poor and the hungry and in eliminating racism," said Mrs. Richard Wurzburg.

Rev. Ralph Jackson, Rev. Henry Starks, Jesse Epps, other union leaders, and I rode on the buses with the East Memphis white women that Saturday. Ms. Wurzburg was quoted again in the paper: "Members of the sanitation department, their wives, and some of the women union members have been nice and invited all those on the tour into their homes. We're not going to look at people in a zoo, but are going as invited guests."

We had optimistically chartered two buses, which would have carried fifty or sixty women. It turned out that one hundred white women arrived that morning. We had to order another bus. The television news media also showed up like they had never shown up before for our demonstrations. Crews even came from Nashville to cover the tour.

At the first of the workers' houses, the women saw a structure with crumbling walls, and a single lightbulb hanging in a one-room home where the family slept, ate, and lived. Many of the houses did not have indoor bathrooms. There were holes in the floors and the walls. Flies infested the houses. The wives of the workers told of their children being bitten by rats inside their homes. There was raw sewage outside some of the houses.

It was the kind of poverty that most white Americans had never encountered, and had no idea existed in this country. It was similar to when Bobby Kennedy came to the Mississippi Delta in 1967 to visit families living in deep poverty and was shocked, along with most of the country, at the degree of deprivation. That Mississippi visit changed Kennedy and spurred him to begin emphasizing the push for economic justice.

When the women got back to East Memphis in the afternoon, they decided they would go before the city council the following week and report on what they had seen. During that city council meeting, the mostly white, male members spent a lot of time dismissively explaining to the women how the city worked, instead of listening to what the women were telling them about poverty in Memphis.

By the next week, the women had formed a group with both Black and white women from across the city called Concerned Women of

Memphis. They came back in full force to the council with a ten-point plan to avert another sanitation strike and to take action to address the poverty and neglect they had witnessed. Their well-researched proposal included ideas for feeding forty thousand schoolchildren who went hungry at lunch and through the day; reproductive planning resources; better housing for people currently living in poverty; and tax exemptions for people on fixed incomes. They also called for a minimum wage for domestic employees, for the city to pursue federal funding to alleviate poverty more vigorously, and for Black people to serve on the board of education. The council took note. And the women had found a cause that would continue.

Their work was one of the elements that helped avert another strike. The following week, the city and the union reached an agreement, a few days before the July 1 strike deadline. Salary increases and other improvements for workers were included in a three-year contract.

The Memphis press had hardly if ever reported on the depth and breadth of poverty in the city. It took our creative ideas for nonviolent direct action demonstrations to break through the lack of public understanding and show why workers were asking for more. We figured out dramatic ways to reach the handful of people living in comfort and power in the white community who would respond to our call and join our campaign for change. The attention followed them. Our power grew. But the work was not done.

Black Mondays

We knew we needed to focus on the Memphis public school system next, for the sake of all our children. But we had no representation in its administration. So I joined with the NAACP and others to bring a list of eighteen demands to the school board during the first weeks of the new school year, in the fall of 1969. The demands included a school lunch program to provide free meals to the forty thousand children in the system living below the poverty line, and the hiring of more Black teachers. In the four years leading up to 1969, 75 percent of the teachers hired were white. We asked that 75 percent of new teachers hired be Black and that 80 percent of newly hired administrative personnel be Black. Additionally, we asked that Black people be appointed to at least two positions on the school board, and that a Black assistant superintendent be hired.

The board of education did not respond to those demands, which meant we had to intensify our efforts. We started holding mass meetings at churches around town, including at Centenary.

As all this work was going on, AFSCME had embarked on a strike against a city hospital. Averting the strike during the summer did not mean the unmet needs for all city workers living in poverty had gone away that autumn. The NAACP also supported the hospital strike. It concerned all of us, so we formed the United Black Coalition, a coming together of Black ministers and activists to support workers and their fight for rights in both the hospitals and the schools. Our coalition with the NAACP was led by Rev. Ezekiel Bell, Maxine and Vasco Smith, and Miriam DeCosta-Sugarmon—who, in 1965, had become the first Black faculty member at Memphis State University. We began a series of demonstrations to bring attention to needed reforms in the Memphis school system. We called it the Black Monday campaign.

Our public demonstrations started on Monday, October 13, when more than sixty-two thousand Black Memphis City Schools students stayed home from school, boycotting the system that did not give them an equitable education. The boycotts continued every Monday through October and into November. During the fourth Monday, on November 3, almost two thousand city workers, including hospital workers, sanitation workers, and 660 Black city schoolteachers—some of whom had been having meetings at Centenary for a few months—did not report to work. And Ralph Abernathy joined us for the Memphis march.

After six weeks of demonstrations, on Friday, November 21, we agreed to end the Black Monday campaign when a group of us met with the school superintendent and the board. They assured us that there would be no repercussions to students, teachers, or staff members who had participated in the direct action campaigns and that the demands from our groups would be negotiated. They also agreed to appoint two Black advisers to the board while we worked out how school board positions would be opened to Black people. We were in the process of forming an SCLC branch in Memphis. So the NAACP and the SCLC both put their national support behind our efforts. That was part of why we felt the direct action campaign could be halted.

Then, in a flagrant show of bad faith, the city filed a $10 million lawsuit against the leaders of the United Black Coalition, the NAACP, and AFSCME, specifically naming individuals, including me. We were not afraid of the suit, but it was another obstacle put in our way. Still, the new SCLC branch would focus on the hospital strike, as well as school equity and the plague of police brutality. We issued a statement about using "fearless nonviolent activities" to pursue our goals. Fearlessness has always been a key component of nonviolent resistance.

By Tuesday, December 9, nineteen of us had been indicted for conspiracy to contribute to the delinquency of minors. Seventeen of the nineteen indicted met the next morning at Clayborn Temple. Ralph Abernathy was one of the indicted, but was in Atlanta and announced he would travel to Memphis soon to join us.

We held a press conference and then marched to the county jail, where we presented ourselves for arrest. It was a joyous march that reunited and reinvigorated our coalition. John and Dorothy marched with me. As we entered the jail building we sang, "Ain't Gonna Let No Grand Jury Turn Me 'Round." Nine of the group were released on $1 bonds. The remaining eight of us decided to stay in jail instead of posting the bond.

In jail we began to write letters, and we were able to have some visitors. I was thinking of my congregation a lot, and on Tuesday, December 16, I wrote them a letter to explain what I was doing and why:

> Since being here, I have been systematically reading the New Testament from cover to cover. My earliest decisions for Christ come back to me with overwhelming power.
>
> Jail for me is a time of repentance and renewal; self-examination and empowerment; re-evaluation of the ministries God has given me and prayer for fresh love and commitment.
>
> . . . My love stretches out to embrace each one of you.

On Wednesday, December 17, four of us were still in jail—two white ministers and two Black ministers. We wrote a letter to supporters listing a series of conditions we were protesting. We called out the board of education's racism, the city's continued failure to recognize the right of workers to organize unions, and "the growing police state mentality in Memphis," which, we noted, "still refuses to treat Blacks as persons." And we said, "We stay in jail to show Black and White People of Good will that justice will not come by itself. Our dreams of freedom and justice require risk and sacrifice." Nonviolence is not for the fainthearted.

On Thursday, December 18, the day before Ralph left for Memphis, he and Coretta King held a press conference in Atlanta in which she said the indictments of the nineteen Black leaders in Memphis were part of a nationwide repressive "reaction to the progress that has been made" by our movement. She and Ralph contended that the murder of Chicago Black Panther leader Fred Hampton two weeks before, on Thursday, December 4, 1969, was part of that reaction in the nation. Chicago police had raided Fred Hampton's apartment in the early morning and shot him to death in his bed while he was sleeping next to his pregnant wife, who survived. More than ninety shots were fired. Brutal police violence was as American as apple pie.

When Ralph arrived in Memphis the next day, he led a march to the jail and surrendered himself for arrest, saying he would fast during his time there, and told reporters he had come "armed only with truth and nonviolence" to "teach Memphis a lesson." We joined him in fasting and all five of us vowed to stay through the Christmas holiday.

Between the five of us, we got hundreds of letters of support and telegrams in jail. People from the clergy, friends, church and community members, and so many others wrote to tell us they appreciated what we were doing. The most heartfelt and touching letter for me came from my son John, who was in third grade at the time.

> Dear Dad,
>
> Thank you for the letter. Are you feeling well? How terrible is the food? The boys miss you and I do too. Let me see. Can you wear the blue jeans? One night Seth and I stayed up in bed for a long time. Are you going to come home? I miss you Meathead. Please do not miss Christmas next year. Do not miss Christmas Meathead.
>
> I love you. The boys love you. . . . Say hey to Mr. Blackburn. A big hug from Morris, Seth, mom, and me.
>
> Love, John

The next week, on the afternoon of Christmas Eve, John and Ezekiel Bell's son Fred, who was nine, led a march of more than one hundred people from Clayborn Temple to the county jailhouse steps. After the marchers gathered on the steps, the two boys briefly addressed them, then led a prayer for us in jail. By then both John and Fred had been with us on many marches. They were leading the day's demonstration because both of them were enrolled in Memphis public schools and we were staying in jail for the sake of all the city's school students.

Christmas Day came and we refused the turkey dinner the jailers offered us. Instead, we spent the day in reflection and prayer. In the evening, we got news that the union and the hospital had come to an agreement that would potentially end the strike. We decided to end our time in jail and announced that we would leave the next morning, at ten o'clock. Our lawyers paid our $1 bail and the newspapers covered our release.

One of the newspapers ended its account of the day with my response to a question about what we were going to do next. "On the lighter side, Lawson said he was looking forward to going home and sitting 'in a tub for 50 or 60 minutes and having a big Christmas dinner with my family.'"

Our 1969 Black Monday campaign set us up to achieve some of our objectives in coming years. Most notably, three Black people were elected to the school board in the fall of 1971, including NAACP executive secretary, Maxine Smith. Contentious battles about school busing marked that time. All-white, private, religious schools sprung up all over the South, mostly in the suburbs, such as Briarcrest Christian Academy in Memphis, one of the largest in the nation. They were known as the "segregation academies."

In the fall of 1972, all the court challenges to school busing for racial integration had played out in Memphis, twelve years after anti-busing advocates began bringing them in 1960, in the aftermath of the Supreme Court's 1954 *Brown v. Board of Education* ruling. School busing was to begin in the Memphis City Schools in January 1973, at the start of the second semester of the 1972–73 school year. The people in power could be said to have implemented a jarring and cynical approach to making the transition—shuffling children between schools in the middle of a school year. Our kids were able to stay in the same school during that time because not everyone was bused. But the white flight that characterized implementation of busing orders all over the country was in full force in Memphis early on. During the next few years, the majority of white families would find ways to abandon the Memphis school system, setting up a kind of de facto "separate but equal" dynamic all over again, mostly through the creation of several more private schools.

Larry Payne, Elton Hayes, Isaac Hayes, and the Invaders

As the nation's schools were changing, for better or worse, the connection between militarism and racism in the United States remained in place. Police brutality was still a seemingly unshakable fact of life for Black people living in Memphis in 1971. In April, the parents of Larry Payne lost a civil lawsuit in federal court against the city of Memphis for the killing of their son. He was the Black teenager who a white police officer shot in the stomach, point-blank, with a sawed-off twelve-gauge shotgun on Thursday, March 28, 1968—hours after the police had disrupted the last march Martin joined during the sanitation strike. The Payne family was defeated. Policing in the city stayed the same.

A few months later, on Friday, October 15, 1971, Memphis police officers reported that a standard car accident had resulted in the death of a passenger. But it turned out the officers were covering up their brutal beating of three Black teenagers during a traffic stop—lying about how they had killed seventeen-year-old Elton Hayes, another unarmed Black child. The two other unarmed Black teenage boys in the truck survived the attack. A reported twenty-three white police and sheriff's officers were on the scene when the boys were pulled from the truck and the attack commenced.

Once the abuse and the cover-ups finally were revealed weeks later, many Black teenagers around Memphis were outraged. They walked out of school, and some began vandalizing stores and other businesses. After a few hours into this uprising, Memphis musician Isaac Hayes—no relation to Elton Hayes—went to the areas where the violence was happening. Hayes drove up in a black Cadillac, got out, and spoke to residents and especially the young people, calling on everyone to stay calm. In other parts of town, another Memphis musician, Rufus Thomas, and others from the legendary soul music label Stax Records did the same. Yet the scattered violence continued for about a week.

Isaac Hayes had become famous nationally with the release of his albums *Hot Buttered Soul* in 1969 and *Black Moses* in 1971, and for his theme song for the 1971 movie *Shaft*. He went on to win an Academy Award in 1972 for the "Theme from *Shaft*," which he recorded at Stax Records in Memphis. The assassination of Martin in his hometown had spurred him to get more involved in the Black community in Memphis and beyond. Just after Elton Hayes was murdered, Hayes was quoted in the paper, saying of the police, "These officers are riding in the streets like it was duck hunting season and they were enjoying it. . . . They're tearing down everything we are building."

In the end, a jury of twelve white men did not convict even one of the police or sheriff's officers charged in the ruthless beatings of the two other boys in the car—George Barnes, who was fifteen, and Calvin McKissack, who was fourteen—or in the murder of Elton Hayes. The verdict was reached even though forensics investigators ruled that police had used billy clubs to forcefully strike Elton Hayes's head nine times, repeatedly crushing his skull. Two years after the murder, at the end of their trial in 1973, all the men who terrorized those three children and murdered one of them were acquitted. The police and sheriff departments rehired most of them, and three of the acquitted sheriff's officers were promoted immediately. Most white people still did not see police brutality as the centuries-long, systemic sickness it had always been. Violence had won again.

In December 1971, I wrote a letter to the editor of *The Commercial Appeal* criticizing press coverage of the murder, including the paper's use of the term "racial disorders" to refer to the uprising in the Black community after Elton Hayes's murder.

> You have, perhaps deliberately, encouraged many Memphians and helped many readers in our region to forget that a 17-year-old boy was brutally killed apparently by men who are employed as professional servants of our community.
>
> . . . There is a real "racial disorder" in Memphis. It is expressed in bad housing, poor schooling, imposed poverty wages, in forced unemployment and the use of police to control, abrasively, an already oppressed people.
>
> Racial disorder in Memphis is best expressed by the steady shoving of black people into a large inner city ghetto. . . . The perpetrators of this serious racial disorder are often well-intentioned people who sit in the councils of government, public boards and agencies and the large financial institutions of the city.

Black men, and particularly young Black men and boys, continued to be the primary targets of local and federal law enforcement, from the police to the FBI, as they continuously tracked and followed us all, and worked to undermine Black liberation in Memphis and the United States. Once again, some newspaper reporters, either knowingly or unknowingly, advanced the FBI's agenda through articles that portrayed young Black men—including those who were standing up to the oppression the best way they knew how—as dangerous criminals. Portrayals of them did not afford them any of the other dimensions of their lives or any sense of their humanity. The authorities routinely arrested members of the Invaders as well as many other young Black men, and kept them in jail indefinitely, accused of crimes for which others would avoid arrest or convictions.

Zealous FBI and Memphis police tracking had become an everyday reality. Their techniques included tapping our phones, photographing us in meetings and marches, following us and our families, planting informants, and more. I tried not to let it deter me. But these younger men did not have the same support as I did to keep working for justice despite the obstacles and distractions. While I did not appreciate many of the tactics the Invaders and others endorsed, which included the willingness to use violence, I tried to keep myself open to them, as a pastor and as a member of the community.

In January 1972, a news analysis article ran in *The Commercial Appeal* with the headline "The Attitudes of Blacks—Militants Are Changing Directions." Tom BeVier—the white reporter who had written the long 1969 profile of me in that paper that ran just after my mother's funeral—spoke to Black Memphians of different ages, including high school students. He quoted me in the article's mix of voices, saying I didn't see enough change in the structures of society for people living in poverty to move toward freedom. I said, "We have had a semblance of change but the hard core problems remain. . . . The mood in the streets is one of vast impatience. The young guys I talk to do not think there has been much change."

Catalyst for Change

That same year, when I heard that U.S. Representative Shirley Chisholm, a Democrat from New York, was running for president, I was all in. She had become the first Black woman elected to Congress in 1968, and in 1972 was still the only Black woman in Congress. I became co-chair of Volunteers for Chisholm in Memphis. One of the Chisholm campaign's slogans was “Catalyst for Change.” It was the first time a Black woman had run on a major party ticket for president of the United States. I enlisted my friend John T. Fisher’s wife, Jean, as my co-chair. At the event celebrating the opening of our headquarters we spoke of a “new coalition” for Chisholm.

We also recruited Memphis State University basketball star Larry Finch to serve as the chair of Youth for Chisholm. He was a hero in Memphis, after that year’s team had reached No. 19 in the national rankings, breaking into the top twenty for the first time in a decade. The next year they would go on to the NCAA finals against UCLA and lose in a heartbreaker. In March 1972, Finch was the biggest young celebrity in town. The 1972 election was the first one in which eighteen-year-olds were allowed to vote. The legislation had been passed the year before. So we knew we had to engage more teenage Memphians to vote for the first time. Finch organized a series of dances supporting Chisholm around town throughout that spring. Voting was an act of nonviolence, and eighteen to twenty-one-year-olds could finally take part in it.

The longest feature article on our campaign appeared in *The Commercial Appeal* in April, after Shirley Chisholm made her only campaign appearance in the city. But the article wasn’t exactly about the candidate. It was about the white former 1958 Maid of Cotton, Jean Fisher, and her unlikely support for Chisholm. “I am doing this,” Jean told the reporter, “because I think Shirley Chisholm has a lot to say that is important. . . . For a woman, and a woman who is also Black, to be running for president has got to be significant.” She went on to add that some of her former classmates from Vanderbilt University, where she had been a cheerleader and homecoming queen, didn’t understand why she was getting involved with Chisholm’s campaign. She said, “Ten years ago, I wasn’t aware of the problems. . . . Ten years ago I hadn’t studied the women’s rights movement. . . . And ten years ago was before Martin Luther King’s death.”

She related how King’s assassination caused her to become more aware. “I feel I was raised like most Americans,” she said. “I believed in the American dream that everybody has an equal chance. That’s what I learned as a Girl Scout and in Sunday school. But I learned that that dream isn’t being fulfilled as it should be for a number of people. I’m as guilty as anyone of looking and not seeing. . . . I do feel that a lot of women have been blocked from doing what they want simply because they are women. Getting involved in Shirley Chisholm's campaign was something I wanted to do. I think it's important."

We had hoped to get enough votes to send some delegates to the Democratic National Convention and have some leverage. But in the May 4 Tennessee Democratic presidential primary, right-wing Dixiecrat George Wallace won the state by so many votes that he got all the state's delegates.

Invitation to Los Angeles

Through the early 1970s, my work both within the church and in communities dedicated to social justice was expanding beyond the South more often, and beyond the United States. I was asked with increasing frequency to share teachings around the nation and the world about the work we had done in the South with Martin and the movement. During that same time, Bishop Charles Golden invited me to move from Memphis to the largest United Methodist church in Los Angeles, Holman United Methodist.

Golden had been bishop of the Nashville-Birmingham area when he had moved me from Nashville to Centenary in Memphis, in 1962. Since then, he had gone on to become a bishop of San Francisco in 1968, and by 1974 was the bishop of the United Methodist Church in Los Angeles. We had been close friends since my young adult years. He was originally from Mississippi, had served as a chaplain in World War II, and became a bishop in the Central Jurisdiction in 1960.

By 1974, when he asked me about moving to the West Coast, I had accomplished major tasks in Memphis. I had helped Centenary relocate to a site where it could expand and have the space it needed. I had involved the church in many of the pressing issues in the city. We had grown the congregation, and it was in a stable, thriving place.

Another factor that made it the right time for me to leave the South was that Martin was gone. In addition, more cities were joining in and desegregating themselves. There was not as much urgency for the kind of movement we had been waging. The nature of the work was shifting, and growing from being primarily in the South to all over the country.

And, finally, I had a high regard for the pastor at Holman United Methodist Church, Rev. Lanneau L. White. Black laypeople had established Holman in 1945, and it grew into a thriving and large congregation under his strong leadership. He told me he felt he had finished the work he could do, and that the congregation needed someone like me to succeed him. As much as we hated to leave Memphis, Dorothy and I decided it would be a good move for our family and for me. Dorothy was teaching high school in Memphis, but she felt she could teach in Los Angeles, too. John was in seventh grade. Morris was in third. And Seth was in first. It seemed better to move when they were young, rather than when they were in high school.

I accepted the appointment, telling Bishop Golden it was a very difficult decision because I'd had sixteen and a half good, productive years in Tennessee. The newspapers in Memphis announced the move in May 1974. There were all sorts of fond farewells. The Centenary congregation reacted to our departure with love and care. A big farewell event was organized at the convention center in June just before we left town. It felt like everyone I had ever known in Memphis came out to say goodbye. I was astonished. They had collected letters and telegrams from people all over Memphis and from around the country, including from people like Julian Bond and Shirley Chisholm, who both wrote letters wishing me well in L.A.

One notable letter in the bunch came from Tom BeVier, the reporter at the *Commercial Appeal* who had written about me for most of the time I was in Memphis. His farewell letter expressed admiration and said he often kept me in conversation longer than necessary because he liked hearing my opinions and appreciated our exchanges. He wrote that our conversations challenged his motives and affected the way he wrote about Black people, "but also about policemen, politicians and whites caught in the crunch of a changing social order. Things you have said about humanism, reconciliation and love have, I want to believe, had a great measure of influence. It is not overstating the case to say that I have often measured my performance by what I supposed you might think of it."

At the end of his kind, three-page letter he said, "Beyond all of the above, I have been flattered (and sometimes puzzled) by your trustfulness even though I am part of an organization whose performance in reporting the cause you have been most publicly involved in has been, at best, shoddy." People knew. Not everyone. But some people eventually saw what many of us had seen all along.

My time in the South forever shaped me, through all the extraordinary successes and devastating losses. From Little Rock to Nashville, from Birmingham and Montgomery to Jackson and St. Augustine, and in Memphis, our movement changed the course of this nation with steady, nonviolent, creative goodwill. We deliberately caused encounters, collisions with the evils of racism that surrounded us. We dramatized the intolerable hurt and cruelty of segregation and of enforced poverty—the glaring, intractable injustices for all to see—making them impossible to ignore. And we did it without ever imitating the viciousness and violence of those doing the hurting and hating, of those doing the assassinating.

I did not feel leaving the South was abandoning the movement work. Instead, I felt I would be carrying it with me, continuing it for the rest of my life, wherever I went.

TWENTY-TWO

Equal Protection

About four thousand people opposed to desegregation of the Los Angeles public school system attend an anti–school busing rally in Woodland Hills, 1978.

DEAN MUSGROVE, HERALD EXAMINER, L.A. PUBLIC LIBRARY

I am fairly sure my life will always be defined, first and foremost, by the work I did during my years in the South and with Martin. Rightly so. But throughout my time in Los Angeles during the late twentieth century and the early twenty-first century—where my family and I lived for decades longer than anywhere else—I confronted many of the same kinds of issues, patterns, and spheres of influence I had encountered in the South. Most people don't know this part of my story. But I would find that the LA-style power dynamics required applying once again the durable and effective nonviolence tactics and practices we had used to push the South to change. In L.A., I would learn and relearn the hard lessons of my own and this nation's experience.

Racism, segregated schools, and police brutality were ever present there, even if in somewhat different forms. I also encountered new sets of problems and challenges that echoed what I had seen before but with some less familiar dimensions. New immigrant workers were being mistreated in many of the same ways as the Memphis sanitation workers, while all non-white immigrants slowly but surely were being criminalized. A new labor union movement led by Black and Brown people and an immigrant rights movement would emerge in response. Also, an undocumented student movement would take hold. I was lucky to be able to share in those campaigns, using what I learned in the South to help new activists and everyday citizens, and continuing what I have always believed was my life's purpose.

In moving west to the state of California and the city of Los Angeles I thought I might encounter a more enlightened, more progressive, less oppressive place than I had seen during my time in the South. I assumed that L.A. would be different—somehow less of the same. It turned out that L.A. was different, but also somehow much of the same—and in several cases, even more so.

I stepped into my new role as pastor at Holman United Methodist Church, on West Adams Boulevard in a storied South Los Angeles neighborhood, in the summer of 1974. A few weeks later, Dorothy and I enrolled our three boys in the L.A. public schools. Almost immediately, we felt the reverberations of the city's long history of intentional racial segregation. Although we didn't realize it then, we were starting our new lives near the epicenter of one of the more famous local battles against segregation, waged by a few Black celebrities thirty years before we arrived.

In the early 1940s, actress Hattie McDaniel bought a large home in the stylish West Adams Heights neighborhood of Los Angeles, just a few blocks east of where Holman would later be located. In 1940, she had won an Oscar for her role in *Gone with the Wind,* as an enslaved woman known as Mammy, at the time of the Civil War. Soon after McDaniel moved in, she came up against her white neighbors. Even the fact that she had recently become the first Black person to win an Academy Award didn't shield her from their campaign to evict her and other Black homeowners from the neighborhood. The white residents had all signed covenants barring home sales to Black people when they bought their houses. In fact, the only Black people they allowed to reside in the neighborhood were the servants living in their homes. From the 1910s through the 1940s, many of the original white families in West Adams Heights had abandoned their mansions and moved to a newer wealthy enclave called Beverly Hills, farther to the west and north in Los Angeles. When some of those original owners had ignored the covenants and sold to Black buyers, prominent Black people had begun to move into West Adams Heights. The neighborhood soon got the nickname Sugar Hill, after the prominent Harlem community in New York City. The remaining white neighbors tried to stem the tide and keep their neighborhood white. In desperation, they formed a homeowners' association and took McDaniel, singer and actress Ethel Waters, and about fifty other Black neighbors to court to seize their homes, saying their presence violated the covenants.

The Black homeowners formed their own association and hired Loren Miller, a prominent Black lawyer. He argued that the neighborhood's racial covenants violated the California Constitution as well as the Fourteenth Amendment of the United States Constitution, which, among other things, forbids a state from denying "to any person within its jurisdiction the equal protection of the laws." A white Los Angeles Superior Court judge, Thurmond Clarke, agreed, saying, "It is time that members of the Negro race are accorded, without reservations and evasions, the full rights guaranteed them under the 14th amendment of the Federal Constitution. Judges have been avoiding the real issue too long. Certainly there was no discrimination against the Negro race when it came to calling upon its members to die on the battlefields in defense of this country in the war just ended." They had won. McDaniel and other Black residents remained in their stately homes.

A few years later, in 1948, when newly married musician and actor Nat King Cole and his wife, Maria, bought a home in the affluent, all-white, old-money neighborhood of Hancock Park, the covenants remained despite the Sugar Hill ruling. Hancock Park's covenants were even more explicit, saying homes could be sold only to white Christians. Knowing that homeowners there would likely honor the covenants, Cole's Black real estate agent got around them by hiring a light-skinned Black woman who could pass as white to stand in for him and the Coles during the purchase. She then signed the deed over to the Coles. Their new neighbors included the owners of Standard Oil, Shell Oil, and both Vons and Ralphs supermarkets. A group of Hancock Park residents—most of whom never identified themselves publicly—formed a neighborhood property owners' association in an effort to rid Hancock Park of the

Cole family. They offered the Coles bribes to buy back their home. They made threats to the seller's real estate agent.

Cole eventually called a press conference at the Hotel Watkins, on West Adams Boulevard, a few blocks away from where Hattie McDaniel lived. The prominent Black-owned hotel was where Cole had stayed in between his world tours, before buying the home. He told the press, "This is not an act of defiance. My bride and I like this house. I can afford it. And we would like to make it our home. I have always been a good citizen. I would like to meet all my new neighbors face to face and explain things to them." He told the Black newspaper the *Los Angeles Sentinel,* "I am an American citizen and I feel that I am entitled to the same rights as any other citizen. My wife and I like our home very much and we intend to stay there the same as any other American citizen would."

The neighborhood association met with him, but still filed an affidavit to forbid the Coles from moving in because they were not white Christians. Yet, a new Supreme Court ruling protected the Coles. In 1948, the court said that the kinds of local racial covenants against which Hattie McDaniel had fought a few years before were unenforceable. Loren Miller—the same Black Los Angeles lawyer who had won McDaniel's lawsuit—successfully argued the case before the Supreme Court, along with future Supreme Court Justice Thurgood Marshall. They based their argument on cases that had been brought in Missouri and Michigan.

In reaction to the ruling and to Cole's home purchase, the Los Angeles Realty Board campaigned for an amendment to the United States Constitution that would legalize racial restrictions on residential property—essentially trying to overturn the Fourteenth Amendment. That idea never took hold, even though Los Angeles had the largest realty board in the nation. So, L.A. realtors and white homeowners would continue to find less overt ways to keep housing segregated. The Coles moved into their new home in August 1948. During the following months and years, people put firecrackers in their bushes, fired a bullet through one of their home's windows, burned a cross in their front yard, and fatally poisoned their family dog. But they stayed.

When we got to Holman in 1974, the mystical course of our lives was placing us at a church in this neighborhood with that legacy—home to such important fights against injustice guided by the vision of another world where beloved community was possible. And sooner than we expected, we would join the convergence of people carrying the mantle of that vision across Los Angeles and the nation, both then and for decades to come.

We took the first step in that direction when we began to deal with the city's school system. Leaving Memphis, Dorothy and I had assumed the public schools in Los Angeles would be academically ahead of those in Memphis. So we spent some time in the summer of 1974 putting our teaching skills to work with our two younger boys—Morris, who was in fourth grade, and Seth, who was in second grade—making sure they were ready for more advanced classes in the L.A. public schools. It turned out that in spite of its reputation for good academics, our new neighborhood elementary school lagged significantly behind the elementary school all three boys had attended in Memphis. Ninety-nine percent of the students at Seth and Morris's new elementary school were Black. Both boys were unchallenged and found themselves far ahead of their classmates, with Morris doing things in the fourth grade that he had done early on in third grade at his Memphis school. He was also getting bullied and teased. We tried to tough it out for that first school year. Then, one day, Morris asked us to send him back to Memphis. "I know where I want to live," he said. "I'll arrange it. You just send me back and I'll go to school there."

We had to do something.

Los Angeles has the second-largest school system in the country after New York. In 1976, it encompassed 710 square miles in Los Angeles County, including the city of L.A. and ten other incorporated cities—serving almost six hundred thousand students in 665 schools. All people who were not seen as white were classified as minorities, and that cohort made up 63 percent of the student population in the system. Using the official breakdown from the time, white people made up 37 percent of students, 32 percent were Hispanic (the term was used for the diverse group of people whose ancestry tied them to Mexico, Central America, or South America), 24 percent were Black, and 7 percent were Asian American, Native American, or one or more of many other ethnicities. Among the multiple native non-English speakers in the L.A. public schools, 80 percent spoke Spanish. The remaining students spoke Korean, Chinese, Samoan, Filipino, Vietnamese, or one of dozens of other languages. At one school in South Los Angeles, for example, students spoke sixty-four different languages.

In 1963, the NAACP and the ACLU brought the original lawsuit to desegregate L.A. schools. It challenged a segregationist California law that said property taxes collected in each school zone could be used only in that school zone, and would not go to a general education fund for the entire school district. The law had kept the white, wealthy neighborhood schools white and wealthy, just as surely as it had kept underfunded schools underfunded in neighborhoods where many people lived in poverty. The lawsuit challenged the law's premise in one white school zone that bordered a school zone made up mostly of people of Mexican heritage. The two neighborhood schools were across the street from each other, and the white school had far more resources than the school across the street. Those property tax laws, along with the racial covenants, had cemented segregation in Los Angeles for decades.

Even as the housing covenants were weakened and then outlawed, another factor was emerging and reinforcing the city's racial divisions. The freeway system that was being built, from the 1940s through the 1970s, deliberately circumnavigated already established white neighborhoods like Beverly Hills, Brentwood, and Bel-Air. It was designed to encourage the creation of more all-white neighborhoods in the suburbs, while simultaneously displacing many minority communities. Notably, the path of Interstate 10, also known as the Santa Monica Freeway, cut right through the heart of Sugar Hill a few blocks north of West Adams Boulevard, destroying homes and a popular park, as well as the cohesion of the neighborhood itself.

By 1971, all of these racist tax, real estate, and transportation policies had created the housing patterns that led the United States Department of Health, Education, and Welfare to declare Los Angeles the most racially segregated public school system in the country. Only the year before, in 1970, the state court had finally issued a decision in the 1963 NAACP and ACLU lawsuit, and ordered the desegregation of the L.A. public schools. Years of appeals and delays followed. Some of those appeals argued that the L.A. school board had not deliberately enforced segregation and so did not need a remedy, and the appeals court agreed. No consideration was given to the way the school system had been complicit in the decades of segregation tactics that had formed the school system's foundation.

In 1975, at the end of our first school year in California, I spoke at a freedom march in South Central Los Angeles commemorating the twenty-first anniversary of *Brown v. Board of Education*. I said of the L.A.

district, "There is more segregation in these schools than exists in any of the schools in the southeast United States today." Such a statement was somewhat shocking to people who believed California was free of racism and that Southern schools were the same as they had been in the 1950s and early 1960s.

After our first year in California, we finally found an education option for the boys that suited our family, starting in the 1975–76 school year. It was a voluntary form of school busing, developed to try to address the court order as appeals were pending. Segregated minority schools were paired with segregated white schools in groups of two or three schools, and students could choose to attend one of their paired schools or their original neighborhood school. We were able to pick an elementary school for Morris and Seth in Brentwood and, eventually, a high school for John in Pacific Palisades, two affluent white neighborhoods. We drove Seth and Morris to and from their elementary school in Brentwood, and John rode a school bus to and from Pacific Palisades during high school.

The boys integrated those schools along with other mostly Black and Latino students. Of course, few if any white students from those schools opted to go to their paired schools in minority neighborhoods. All three of our boys had been in integrated schools their whole lives in Memphis. It was nothing new for them. In the long run, all three of them thrived during their years in L.A. public schools.

Yet real desegregation was a massive task in such a large school district. Navigating the vast distances in Los Angeles was a daunting challenge. Another obstacle was the same kind of opposition from white parents we had encountered in Memphis. White flight from Los Angeles escalated when the final desegregation order was issued.

I became part of the Citizens' Advisory Committee on Student Integration (CACSI), which the school board established in 1976. The school board was mostly white, as was CACSI. Many of the members of both groups lacked an understanding of the challenges non-white students and their families faced. Bringing attention to our needs was not always on the agenda. It wasn't until the 1978–79 school year that the court challenges were all settled and a busing plan finally went into effect.

But after one full year of busing, California voters approved the antibusing Proposition 1 in November of 1979, spawning yet another series of legal challenges. In 1981, the school board voted to end busing, thereby effectively re-segregating the schools, while promising to find other ways to satisfy the state court's order to desegregate. A plan emerged to continue the previous voluntary busing and add magnet schools that drew students from around the city.

By the time mandatory busing ended in L.A. three years later, the number of white public school students in the Los Angeles system had drastically declined, as had happened in Memphis and all around the country whenever busing plans went into effect. When white families fled to private schools or to insular public school systems in the suburbs, so few white students remained in the city's schools that many people felt the issue of racial desegregation had become moot. And soon, large numbers of white people had vacated not only the L.A. public school system, but the city itself.

TWENTY-THREE

Can We All Get Along?

Two weeks after the vicious police beating of Rodney King, Jesse Jackson, center, and Reverend Lawson, left, speak to journalists at a rally against LAPD police chief Daryl Gates, March 16, 1991. RICHARD PERRY, SYGMA VIA GETTY IMAGES

Just as the educational disparities in Los Angeles were no accident, neither was the rampant police brutality that I witnessed very soon after arriving. Challenging police misconduct and working to rectify educational disparities were a continuation of my work in Memphis and the South, but I also had a deeply personal reason for caring so much. Dorothy and I were raising our three Black sons in Los Angeles, and I was a pastor of a Black congregation. Segregated education was a direct threat to the futures of those we held near and dear, as was the way Black people were being overpoliced.

The Los Angeles Police Department (LAPD) had been a force in shoring up segregation in the city for decades. From 1950 to 1966, Chief William H. Parker had built a squad intent on heavily policing minorities and offering little to no protection for anyone who wasn't white. He rarely hired Black or Latino officers or promoted the few who were hired. He was said to favor recruiting white officers who came to Los Angeles from the South. Non-white officers who were already on the force were prohibited from having white partners. And his department never fully investigated or brought to justice the one hundred or more documented white supremacist incidents that occurred around the city during his tenure.

The new freeways cutting their way through Los Angeles helped Parker's police force keep the races separate. His men were known to harass or beat Black and Latino people who strayed too far past those infrastructure dividers into white communities, especially at night. He openly complained about Black people moving to L.A. during the Great Migration, saying white people didn't want them there. Parker also said publicly that Latinos had descended from the "wild tribes" of Mexico.

In 1965, in what were called the "Watts riots," the tactics his officers used escalated tensions to the point of causing more violence and deaths. During the six days of uprising—after a traffic stop in Watts, a Black neighborhood, in which the police became violent—Police Chief Parker compared Watts residents participating in the retaliatory violence to "monkeys in a zoo." By the second day of unrest, fourteen thousand California National Guardsmen had been called into Watts to work alongside Parker's police force. In the end, thirty-four people died, including twenty-five Black residents. Police or National Guard officers killed twenty-three of them. Almost thirty-five hundred people were arrested, and a thousand people were injured. Black L.A. residents were expressing pent-up rage at chronic overpolicing, enforced segregation, and lack of employment opportunities. They had had enough.

After Watts, the L.A. police only became more militarized. In 1969, 350 LAPD officers were deployed to serve warrants on the Black Panthers' headquarters in South Central Los Angeles. A new unit of the LAPD called the Special Weapons and Tactics (SWAT) unit carried out the early morning raid. The officers used explosives, tanks, and other military weapons and procedures. The thirteen people inside the Black Panthers' headquarters building included five teenagers and three women. They tried to fight back with the weapons they had on hand. Six of the Panthers were wounded, along with four officers. Eventually the people in the building surrendered. No one was killed.

The raid was part of an experiment to see if the military-style SWAT unit would be effective in suppressing uprisings like the one in Watts four years earlier. A rising star in the LAPD named Daryl Gates, who went on to become the police chief in 1978, was involved in creating the SWAT unit. Although it was known by its acronym, Gates came up with the original full name: the "Special Weapons Assault Team." Some in the police department suggested adjusting that full name to "Special Weapons and Tactics," to be less revealing of its intent, pointing out that Gates's name for the unit might be too provocative in the community. With such open hostility from the police department, we had to remain vigilant. The assault on the Black Panthers' headquarters marked one of our first encounters with Gates, but it would not be our last.

Near the start of Gates's tenure as chief, in January 1979, police officers shot and killed a thirty-nine-year-old Black woman named Eula Love inside her own home in South Central Los Angeles. That was when several local ministers and I organized a group of more than two hundred clergy members called the Gathering. One of the first things we did was to call out Chief Gates for the LAPD's use of excessive force in the Eula Love case. We also documented the LAPD's terrible history of excessive force toward Black and Brown people, and we campaigned for civilian oversight of the police department. We didn't succeed then. As with school busing, the entrenched powers aligned against us continued to win. But our campaigning didn't stop.

In the spring of 1979, John graduated from Palisades High School and decided to go to Oberlin College, in Ohio, where I had been studying when Martin and I first met in person. Morris and Seth were still in junior high, in Brentwood, and would go to Palisades High School in the next few years. Dorothy was teaching English at Orville Wright Junior High, a public school near where we lived in the southern part of Los Angeles, and where John had gone to school when we first arrived.

I was always deeply engaged with my congregation. My weeks were filled with sermons, funerals, weddings, hospital visits, counseling parishioners, and the administration of the church. I loved being at Holman and felt grateful for all I was able to do there. Holman had some interesting members, including Sugar Ray Robinson. When he retired from boxing, he moved to L.A. and lived in a second-floor apartment in West Adams Heights, a few blocks from Holman. He and his wife were doing good work to help local kids through their foundation. Growing up, our whole family would sit at the radio and listen to Joe Louis fights and then to Sugar Ray Robinson fights. I was delighted years later when I became his pastor. It was astonishing to spend time with one of my childhood heroes, even as his health declined. He died in 1989, and I was a co-officient at his funeral service.

In 1983, Morris decided to enroll at a small school in North Carolina called Pfeiffer College. It was affiliated with the Methodist Church and located just outside Charlotte. He studied psychology and writing. John graduated from Oberlin in 1983 with a degree in sociology and continued on to Howard Law School in the fall of 1983. The last of our three boys, Seth, went off to college at the University of Colorado at Boulder in 1985 to study psychology and sociology.

When the boys were gone from the house, our dog companions were there to keep Dorothy and me in good company. We'd had dogs for years, starting with our first one in Memphis when John was a toddler and told us he wanted a puppy for his birthday. We went to what used to be called the dog pound in Memphis, where he selected a small collie-shepherd mix. She was about twenty pounds, beige-brown all over, with a waggy tail. We named her Cindy. Then in 1968, our friend John T. Fisher gave us one of the puppies from his German shepherd's litter. That's when we began having larger dogs. We called the German shepherd Nandi, a South African Zulu name.

A veterinarian in the congregation at Holman had become our good friend. And of course we took our dogs to him. One day, he introduced us to a beautiful, large rottweiler somebody had abandoned at his office. We decided we would take that dog and we named him Zorro. By then Cindy had died, so we had two dogs, Nandi and Zorro.

I fell in love with rottweilers. Seth did, too. They are big, but also very gentle and loving, and are wonderful companions. Seth stayed in Boulder after college, working as a chef, and got a rottweiler for himself and named her Mama. She then had a litter, and he sent us one of the puppies. Morris named him Zorro II. At one point, we had three rottweilers all together in our house, and Seth also had two or three rottweilers in his apartment, and he would walk and run them even in the heaviest Colorado snow. He was particularly good with them, and they were extremely well-trained. Dogs win you over and become a steadfast part of your family. I know they also can be mistreated and misused in society, as I would come to see a few years later when I challenged Daryl Gates's police force's techniques in court.

═

The LAPD's practices were on glaring display in March of 1991 when four white L.A. police officers brutally beat a twenty-five-year-old Black man named Rodney King, whom they had pulled over for a traffic stop off the 210 freeway in Los Angeles. As the assault was happening, a resident in a nearby apartment complex walked out onto his balcony and used his new video camera to record four officers mercilessly kicking and beating King as twenty-three other officers stood by watching the assault. King's skull was fractured, his teeth and bones broken, and his brain was permanently damaged. The video was released, and the world saw what some of us had been saying for years: the LAPD was brutal beyond any bounds, racist to its core, and its leader, Daryl Gates, should be fired.

At that time, I was the lead plaintiff in a lawsuit the ACLU and NAACP Legal Defense Fund were bringing against the LAPD and Chief Daryl Gates for their abusive use of police dogs on minority citizens. The mean spirit that drove lynching in the United States had not yet ended. In many ways, our society seemed more violent than ever before. I saw the escalation as a natural result of America's reflexive use of military force all over the world to impose our will. Our continually violent culture also springs from our failure to teach American children that violence is wrong in all its forms and show them how they can use active, sustainable nonviolence techniques to address conflicts and change society without such cruelty, domination, and destruction.

In 1991, I started another stint hosting a television show. What began as a venture of Methodist Church outreach became a weekly national live call-in cable TV show called *Lawson Live* and later *Jim Lawson Live* on the national Odyssey Network. I initially hosted it by myself, but as the show evolved, a wonderful journalist and friend, Bonnie Boswell—niece of Whitney Young, executive director of the Urban League in the 1960s—became my co-host.

One of our first programs examined police brutality, a subject I had examined twenty-three years earlier on the TV program I hosted in Memphis.

In April 1992, the four police officers seen on video brutalizing Rodney King stood trial in Simi Valley, California, a suburb of Los Angeles where many LAPD officers lived, and the place where many people who had opposed school busing had moved when they'd left L.A. to escape public school integration in the 1970s. The officers' defense attorneys had succeeded in having the trial moved out of Los Angeles, arguing that it would be impossible for the defendants to get a fair trial in the city. In Simi Valley, we would soon discover, it was impossible to get a fair trial on behalf of anyone the police had abused. The trial ended on April 29, 1992, when the jury—nine of its members were white, one was Latino, one was biracial, and one was Asian—found all four officers not guilty of their savage beating of Rodney King which the entire world had witnessed.

South Central Los Angeles erupted in a rage that spilled over into the outskirts of West Los Angeles. The uprising lasted for five days, resulting in more than fifty deaths, including ten people who L.A. police officers or national guardsmen shot and killed. Two thousand injuries were reported, and about six thousand people accused of looting were arrested. L.A. was under curfew. Smoke could be seen rising from buildings all over South Central and nearby neighborhoods for days. On the third day of the uprising, Rodney King, terribly shaken and trying to process the injustice of the verdict, did his part to call for an end to the destruction and violence. Speaking with his lawyer by his side, in a shaky voice, he asked, "Can we all get along?"

I have dedicated my life to nonviolence, and reject any impulse to violence and destruction, always. But I believe we can't be blind to despair. Even as we condemn violence in all its forms, we must also understand it. Just as we strive to become scholars of state violence so that we might best oppose it, we must also understand the violence of frustration at oppression and neglect, so that we might find better alternatives to it.

In my sermon at Holman the following Sunday, I asked everyone to recognize that we are all in this together. To answer the question Rodney King asked, I said we all had to work harder to find ways to get along with each other. We cannot be uninvolved, because the people who looted and the people who saw them as less than human are all part of humankind. And while humankind got us to this moment, humankind can also change it from here on out.

> We can be engaged in healing the wounds, feeding the hungry, lifting up the need of the people. And . . . we will continue to work for justice. . . . We will also continue to work that the criminal justice system will be changed, so that the poor and the young, and the people of color can gain justice in our midst.

Los Angeles was traumatized. No one could say they didn't see the pain. And by July 1992, we had successfully compelled Daryl Gates to resign as chief of police. Yet within a few more months, the collective concern had dissipated. White Los Angeles moved on. Once again, we were left with the same system of policing. So, we kept pressing the issues.

In November 1992, I was deposed in *Lawson v. Gates,* the class action lawsuit the NAACP Legal Defense Fund, the ACLU, and I had brought a few years earlier about the LAPD's illegal use of police dogs. In the deposition, I explained my point of view, with our lawyer, the NAACP's Constance Rice, by my side. First, we outlined my longtime work on police violence in Memphis, which had included making presentations to the police force and the chief of police. I also mentioned that I had conducted workshops on violence and nonviolent ways of handling conflicts with the International Association of Chiefs of Police, through the Methodist Church. I told of my work in Los Angeles, in particular on the Eula Love case. I said I had long felt that police officers using excessive force obstructed democratic values and prevented the police from dealing with the root causes of crime.

Then we talked about the training of police dogs, and I was asked if I had dogs myself. I said I had two great rottweilers and a wonderful German shepherd, adding that I loved dogs. "And," I remarked, "I protest the use of dogs. . . . To condition them to bite and to be used in this fashion, it seems to me, is a shameful misuse of the dogs."

The defendants' attorney asked if I believed in employing police service dogs. I said I could see good use for their special scent-sniffing skills and in patrolling with officers in the community.

Q: Do you think there are situations where it would be appropriate to have a police service dog bite a suspect?
A: No.
Q: Under no circumstances?
A: I don't think so.

I mentioned Luis Fernandez, a nineteen-year-old man I had visited with when we announced our case. He had been stopped in his car, taken out, handcuffed, and laid on his stomach on the shoulder of the freeway. Then a handler released a police dog, and it started to bite at him. He began to cry out for someone to stop the dog. He was already on the ground, flat on his belly, and handcuffed. He cried something like, "Oh God, help me."

The handler said, "Who is God?" Pointing to a deputy, he asked, "Is he God?" He pointed to another officer: "Is he God?" Then he pointed to himself and said, "I'm God."

As a preacher, I told the lawyers, I found it shameful to hear that kind of hard-heartedness, the officer declaring himself to be God while a dog was chewing on another human being, a teenager, and he had the power to stop it but he didn't.

"The other problem that we're dealing with," I said, "is . . . the philosophy of police officers . . . that there's a war out here. It's between them and us. So officers go into many of these situations with their fears, rather than with an understanding" of the circumstances under which the human beings they are confronting are living.

A few minutes later, the defense lawyer asked me about my attitude toward the police.

Q: Are you anti-LAPD?
A: Of course not. . . . I have police officers in my congregation and I count them as my friends. I am persuaded that we must have law enforcement. But law enforcement must be a servant of the people and a servant of the best ideals of the democratic society.

The case dragged on before we finally settled it in 1995. Additional cases against the LAPD regarding the force's abusive use of dogs were also settled at that time. Fifty-four people in our case who had suffered dog attacks—most of them Black or Latino—divided a $3.6 million settlement from the city of Los Angeles. The settlement also came with extensive policy changes in the procedures surrounding the use of police dogs.

My son John was a public defender in L.A. as this case was moving forward. I was proud of him and his legal career as he joined in the work of defending some of the most vulnerable in our society. Our links into the life of L.A. and the quest for justice there became even clearer when John was in law school at Howard in the mid-1980s, and met one of his greatest friends, a fellow law student who had also grown up in Los Angeles named Michael Miller.

It turned out, Michael was the grandson of Loren Miller, the lawyer for Hattie McDaniel who won the 1945 case in Los Angeles Superior Court against racial covenants in the city, and then got them outlawed throughout the nation in the case before the U.S. Supreme Court in 1948. Loren Miller's son and Michael's father was Loren Miller Jr., who became a superior court judge in L.A. John used to go over to their house and talk to him a lot, about the law and being a judge and their family's legacy.

Michael Miller and John were in each other's weddings in the 1990s, and a few years later John went on to become a superior court judge himself, just as Loren Miller Jr. had been. Our family's relationship to Loren Miller Sr.'s whole family was strengthened by our shared commitment to standing up to racism and brutality in all its guises. And L.A. was teaching me that the challenges of that quest went beyond the ongoing reckoning that still needed to be done between Black and white people in this nation.

When the chaos of discord and pain swirled around during such times as the L.A. uprising, I could always find my own refuge and renewal in one of the most peaceful places in the world for me: the sanctuary at Holman United Methodist Church.

I was connected to Holman even before I became its pastor. Earlier—when the great Lanneau L. White led Holman—I had been a guest preacher there. And so had Martin. In fact, Martin was in Los Angeles about to preach at Holman as I was calling him from Memphis to make the final arrangements for his first speech supporting the striking sanitation workers on Monday, March 18, 1968. The day before, on Sunday, March 17, Martin had given a sermon in the packed sanctuary at Holman entitled “The Meaning of Hope.” He began by talking about Holman itself. “As I walked in,” Martin said, “I could not help but be deeply moved by the magnificent beauty of the sanctuary.” Then he thanked the congregation for its consistent support of the SCLC and all of its work in social justice.

During the week and sometimes on Sundays, I would go to Holman's sanctuary by myself for the kind of solitude that prayer requires. The space is welcoming, vibrant, and airy, yet sacred. A mid-century modern architect with Swedish roots designed it in 1958. The Southern California sunshine filters in almost year-round through the glass windows that form the two side walls, from the floor halfway up to the high ceilings. Miniature stained-glass-window insets dot the upper white portions of the side walls. The front of the sanctuary is an artful mix of wood and metal. The church organ's huge silver pipes are mounted on the front wall. Behind the pulpit hangs a sort of curtain of small wooden blocks strung together, with different colors on each side of each block so that the curtains of color can be changed—from blue, to yellow, to green, purple, or red—according to the liturgical seasons.

The Black families who founded Holman in 1945 held great hopes of dismantling the systems in our society that blindly mistreat so many people. At Holman, I became even more deeply engaged in political action than I had been in Tennessee. Robert Kennedy and Edward Kennedy spoke in that sanctuary. Bishop Desmond Tutu and Jesse Jackson preached there. And most Sundays for twenty-five years, I preached in Holman's sanctuary, where I also conducted countless baptisms, weddings, and funerals—services of life, love, and death.

In March 1968, Martin told the Holman congregation, “It is midnight in race relations in our country.” Years later, I finally heard an audio recording a church member had made of Martin's entire sermon at Holman that day, just three weeks before he was killed.

> Hope is necessary for life. . . . The loss of hope makes you irrational. You can't see the truth. . . . Anger becomes your program.
>
> . . . I'm angry about racism still existing in our society . . . I'm tired of it, really. And I guess I would be extremely irrational and bitter if I didn't have a faith that tells me that all life hinges on moral foundations . . . and they're just as abiding as the physical laws. . . .

> . . . There is a law of love in the universe. There is a law of justice in the universe. It's silent. It's inexorable, invisible, but it's there. . . .
>
> Hope is a refusal to give up. It is medicinal. . . . It frees you from give-up-itis. . . . There are some difficult days ahead in our struggle for justice, and yet I'm not going to yield to the politics of despair. I'm determined to keep hope alive.

The voices of all those who took Holman's pulpit before and during my time there echoed for me through that sanctuary. But hearing the recording of Martin preaching there, and knowing it had been one of his last sermons ever, I felt as if his essence had been resonating through that place ever since, and between the two of us, animating my time as pastor at Holman, and affirming my course.

TWENTY-FOUR

The Tragedy Would Be Compounded

Reverend Lawson with James Earl Ray after testifying at his parole hearing, Nashville, Tennessee, May 26, 1994. ASSOCIATED PRESS

No matter how much I necessarily focused on my family, congregation, and social justice work in Los Angeles, thoughts of that awful April evening in Memphis would sometimes pull me away from the moment. I made more and more peace with my grief at losing Martin as the years passed. But I kept coming back to lingering questions around the circumstances of his murder. I wasn't the only one. Coretta King and her family couldn't accept the official explanation of what happened either.

Skepticism about the story of a lone assassin and no government involvement had haunted us and this nation ever since 1968.

Martin's family and some of his friends and associates agreed that the only way to move beyond our doubts was for the accused assassin, James Earl Ray, to get the full trial that never happened. Then, the records of the FBI's role in it all could be accessed and scrutinized under oath. An opposite of haunting is release. That was what we were after—release from our concern that the story of Martin's assassination would forever be incomplete and would leave this country and those of us close to that moment with a permanent, nagging sense of suspicion, uncertainty, and distrust.

Our drive to try to find out led me to one of the most surprising relationships I have ever developed—with the man in prison for Martin's murder. Not only would I conclude that he had been falsely accused and wrongly imprisoned, but James Earl Ray and I would become friends. Some people didn't understand our relationship. And many didn't agree with my insistence on his innocence, including my son John. But for me, it all sprang from the decision I made when I served time in prison myself: I would never see or treat anyone else as less than a human being worthy of care and concern.

Rekindled interest in James Earl Ray's story reached a feverish pitch in the years just before and after he died, in 1998. But our improbable alignment had its real beginnings twenty years earlier, in the summer of 1978.

One evening, Dorothy, the boys, and I were at home in Los Angeles having dinner together when the phone rang. Back then, there were no cellphones or caller ID. Everybody only had landlines—one number for everyone living together, with corded extensions throughout the house. You answered calls even during family meals because it might be something important. I got up from the dining room table and went to the nearest phone, which hung on the wall in the kitchen. The caller was James Earl Ray's girlfriend, Anna Sandhu. I had met her a few months before when I first visited Ray at Brushy Mountain State Penitentiary, in eastern Tennessee, where he was serving his ninety-nine-year sentence for Martin's murder. I had also seen her in Washington, D.C., a few weeks earlier, in August 1978, when Ray testified before the House Select Committee on Assassinations, which was investigating the murders of John F. Kennedy and of Martin.

After our hellos, Anna got right to the point: "James and I want to be married. And we want you to perform the ceremony." Both of those pieces of news surprised me. I didn't know if I wanted to do it. We talked a little bit about their decision.

She and James met when she was the sketch artist hired to draw him during a trial for his 1977 escape from a Tennessee prison. A local television station in Knoxville, near the prison, hired her again to sketch him during an interview for a documentary about him. She and James connected and began writing letters. She lived in Knoxville and visited him in prison a few times, and she said that, as unlikely as it seemed, they fell in love. She was thirty-two and James was fifty.

The request to perform their wedding was a lot to absorb. I told her I would think about it. We chatted for another minute, and then the call ended.

I walked back to the dinner table and told my family about it all. Everybody was a little stunned. Then I put the question to them: "Should I perform James Earl Ray's marriage ceremony in prison?"

John, who was seventeen at the time, spoke right up, even with food in his mouth. He said, "If you believe that stuff you preach all the time, you'll do it."

The entire dinner table fell silent. We all recognized the truth in his words. There was not much else to debate. It was a significant family moment that resonated for us all. What could I say? I aimed to carry out my ministry in the spirit of Martin, and I believe Martin King would have done it, too. Dorothy, Seth, Morris, John, and I agreed: I had to continue talking to James Earl Ray, go visit him in the Tennessee prison again, and officiate at his wedding there.

James Earl Ray was named as the suspect in Martin's assassination a few weeks after it happened, in 1968. Two months later, Ray was captured in England, brought back to the United States, and put in the Shelby County jail in Memphis. Prosecutors accused Ray of carrying out the murder on his own, and he was held in Memphis during the nine months before the trial date. In March 1969, as the trial was about to begin, Ray pleaded guilty to the murder, which meant there was no need for a trial, and he was sentenced. He recanted a few days later, saying his lawyer had coerced the confession and he wanted a trial. But the state had the plea, and they weren't turning back.

By the time I had moved to Los Angeles, in the mid-1970s, doubts had multiplied about the official story of the assassination and the conclusion that James Earl Ray did it, and that he acted alone. From March through

May of 1977, members of the House Select Committee on Assassinations held a series of five interviews with Ray in prison. However, on June 10, 1977, Ray and six other prisoners climbed a wall at Brushy Mountain State Penitentiary and escaped into the thick woods. Three days later, on June 13, 1977, he and five of his fellow inmates were captured eight and a half miles away. The sixth escapee was brought in a few days later.

When Ray and Anna Sandhu decided to marry, Anna spoke to *People* magazine in a question-and-answer article about their courtship. She said the spark between them began when the TV reporter working on the documentary asked some questions that she said it was obvious Ray would never answer, such as if he intended to escape again and where he would go.

> James and I were smiling at each other because the questions were so silly. Later he sat down beside me. He has the most direct gaze of any man I've ever known. . . . James will look right into your eyes and won't flinch. The first thing he said to me was "Do you know anything about Picasso?"
>
> Later . . . he said, "I'm not proud of what I'm accused of." People think James is unfeeling and they don't take the time to get to know him. But I go to court a lot and I read people's faces. I feel their pain and I know what they're going through. I felt this with James. It was just as though I could read his mind.

She said James wrote beautiful love letters, and when she visited him in prison she brought him a book of Carl Sandburg's poetry. They decided to get married a few months later. At first, James didn't want to marry her because, she said, he was afraid people would ridicule her or hurt her. She disagreed:

> This may not be the easiest road to take, but at least I know it's the right one. I can tell that James' love is sincere. He's not a saint, and I've even called him a penny-ante crook. But that was because I didn't want people to say, "She's a nut. She's fantasizing. Prisons must be her thing." I'm not like that.

In 1977, Ray's new lawyer, Mark Lane, began a push to get him the trial he never had. I was all for it. Lane had served in the New York state legislature in the early 1960s, had been a Freedom Rider in 1961, and had been the vice-presidential pick of third-party candidate Dick Gregory in 1968. Lee Harvey Oswald's family engaged Lane to defend Oswald's name before the Warren Commission, the official panel that would investigate the Kennedy assassination. Lane suspected that the federal government had played a role in the Kennedy assassination and, later, in Martin's assassination.

I first met Ray when I visited him with Mark at Brushy Mountain. My initial impression was that Ray was a white, Southern-bred man who grew up without much education or many privileges or opportunities in life. He had very few skills for real work and freely talked to me about his life of crime. My second impression was that if he was the assassin, racism had not been his motive. That perception of him became a sticking point for me in the whole official explanation of his motivation for the shooting.

When we talked in his cellblock, I felt a man-to-man, human bond with him. He was, I think, an unfortunate man who never really got to experience much joy. In my earliest visits in 1977, I simply tried to befriend him. My motivation was simple. I did not see it as something apart from the love of God or the love of Jesus. I had a fair amount of experience with jails and prison, and I knew that everyone behind those walls had their own stories that explained why they were there. I did not make a judgment on their legal status of guilty or not guilty. Instead, I saw them as children of God, just as I was.

Most Black people were not satisfied at all with the official version of Martin's murder. They tended to feel there was much that hadn't been revealed, and that Ray was the patsy and may not have been the trigger man. If he was involved, they believed, he was part of a team. He couldn't have pulled it off by himself. He must have been paid to do it. There are too many unanswered questions that were not pursued because there was no trial. I have always believed that reopening the Ray case to get to the truth would have done no harm.

On March 15, 1978, the House Select Committee on Assassinations interviewed me. The committee members asked me about the sanitation workers' strike and founding COME in Memphis to support the strike. They asked about inviting Martin to Memphis and his appearances there in 1968, including the march we turned around on Beale Street. My interview was mostly informational for them. I had nothing to hide. They already knew what my testimony would be, because the United States government had been following me and spying on me for most of my adult life, although it had never found what it had hoped to find. I was not a Communist, and I was not a threat to this country. Racism, poverty, and abuse of power were and are the real threats to this country.

I stayed involved with Ray's quest to take his case to trial. On August 1, 1978, Jesse Jackson made plans to go to Brushy Mountain State Penitentiary and meet Ray. Mark Lane and I went with him, along with Dr. Alvin Poussaint, a Harvard psychiatry professor. We had a two-and-a-half-hour meeting with Ray inside the prison on August 10. After the meeting Jesse was quoted at a press conference saying, "I have profound doubt that he killed Dr. King. . . . I am convinced that he was involved but was not alone. We have a moral obligation to go way beyond the realm of superficial investigation that has permeated this case." Jesse went on to say, "I think Mr. Ray should be taken back to court so we can find out all the forces involved in Dr. King's murder. . . . The FBI seems to have a better motive for wanting Dr. King dead than Mr. Ray."

About a week after Jesse's visit to Brushy Mountain, Ray was transported under heavy security to a federal prison near Washington, D.C., to testify in person before the House Select Committee on Assassinations. On Wednesday, August 16, Ray spoke to the committee in open hearings. I was there along with Anna Sandhu and others. Mark Lane sat at the table with Ray, as his lawyer. Ray read from a thirty-eight-page statement, saying that he did not kill Dr. King and that his lawyer at the time had coerced his confession. Ray told the committee, "I did not shoot Martin Luther King, Jr."

That summer, I was quoted in *SCLC,* the Southern Christian Leadership Conference's magazine, talking about when I had been approached in Memphis during the aftermath of Martin's assassination and the investigation: "Back at the very beginning the FBI came to me and asked me to tell the Black community to accept its investigation. I declined the offer. I don't know of any Black people in Memphis who believe that, if James Earl Ray did it, he did it alone. Ray's guilty plea was made under duress and pressure."

At the end of August 1978, I got a letter from Chauncey Eskridge, Martin's lawyer and the lawyer for the SCLC at the time of Martin's death. He was in the courtyard of the Lorraine Motel when Martin was killed and witnessed the assassination. He had read what I said in the SCLC magazine and disagreed with my conclusions about Ray's role. He said he was present in the Memphis courtroom when Ray pleaded guilty in 1969 and had always believed he was guilty. He ended by saying, "Sorry, but I do not agree with you but still have great affection for you."

I was taking a controversial stand, and I knew it. Chauncey Eskridge would not be the only person I respected who disagreed with me on this.

James Earl Ray and Anna Sandhu Ray married on October 13, 1978. I performed the ceremony in a room inside the prison. Only a few people were present. The couple was not allowed to have conjugal visits. So they were never alone. Anna told *People* she believed they would be, once he had a trial and was released from prison.

> I don't think James killed Martin Luther King. I'm sure he was a part of it in some way, but it was without knowledge of what was going on. I'm sure that James thought he was smuggling guns or something like that. I know that James would never be party to a murder because, as he said, he could have gotten the same kind of money by robbing a supermarket. I know a lot more about this than I'm telling you now, but I know James is innocent.

In 1979, the House Select Committee on Assassinations released its report on the killing of Martin. It concluded once again that James Earl Ray had shot Martin. It said there might have been co-conspirators, but they were probably St. Louis businessmen who had put a bounty on Martin's head and hired James through his brothers, John and Jerry.

Dorothy, Morris, and Seth generally shared my view on James Earl Ray. But John and I never saw eye to eye. He did think there was something more than the official story. But he said the lawyer in him couldn't believe Ray had no part in the killing. He didn't subscribe to my view of the case. Yet we were able to discuss why we disagreed.

John would tell me that he saw it as a case built on conjecture. "Look, Dad," he would say. "I understand you have a natural bias, and a sense of paranoia with the FBI. For a large part of your life, they were digging through your trash, talking to your friends, wiretapping your phones. They were after you and sent you to federal prison when you objected to the draft in college. They followed you everywhere and put informants all around you in the 1960s and 1970s. The mightiest government in the free world was watching your every move, looking to get something on you. I get why you can't believe what they say happened."

Through the 1980s and into the 1990s, I remained determined to support independent investigations while trying to get the trial for Ray that never was. I firmly believed that a trial would air all the theories, give us a chance to review the most secret FBI files, and allow the lawyers to question under oath the people we believed knew more than they were saying.

In May 1994, I attended Ray's parole hearing and testified on his behalf. So did Hosea Williams, a longtime movement leader who had witnessed the assassination at the Lorraine. Anna Sandhu Ray also was there. She and Ray had divorced the year before, and by then she had experienced a change of heart about his claims of innocence. At the hearing, she repeated allegations she had made in the press that Ray had once told her during a phone call that he did kill Martin Luther King.

Ray was not given parole. Hosea and I were criticized for standing with him. In *The Washington Post,* Courtland Milloy, who was Black and a longtime journalist, wrote a column entitled "No Sympathy for a Murderer," decrying Ray's parole request.

> And if that wasn't shocking enough, the Rev. James M. Lawson, a civil rights leader, showed up at the hearing to speak on Ray's behalf. . . .
>
> . . . With a news photographer capturing the obscene moment for all the world to see, Lawson walked over to Ray and affectionately shook the gunman's hand.
>
> What is wrong with our people? How many ways can we come up with to make ourselves look totally stupid?

Milloy went on to lay out evidence that he believed proved that Ray was the shooter, including his guilty plea and the conclusion of the House Select Committee on Assassinations.

> Lately, however, there have been a steady parade of black civil rights activists acting as if Ray has been as wronged as Nelson Mandela. . . .
>
> . . . I could understand Williams and Lawson showing some compassion if Ray, having confessed, had expressed great remorse and sorrow. You could shake his hand on the way to the gas chamber.

> But to offer a hand of support to an unrepentant sinner? Come on, Rev. Lawson. Sometimes we bend over backward so far to appear forgiving that we end up kissing our own behinds.

My determination was not swayed. Ray brought on another lawyer, William Pepper, who began the push for a new trial in a Memphis court in the mid-1990s. Ray was diagnosed with fatal liver disease in 1996, the result of long-term hepatitis C, which he may have contracted after a blood transfusion when he was stabbed in prison in 1981. The only hope was a liver transplant, which he was unlikely to get. The goal of a new trial took on more urgency, as we did not want the truth to die with Ray.

In February 1997, the King family came out publicly for the first time in calling for a new trial for Ray. I was with Coretta when she took the stand in a Memphis courtroom during a hearing on a motion to have the rifle that was said to have killed Martin tested. She said, "We call for the trial that never happened," explaining that if Ray was never able to tell his story and be questioned about what he knows in court "the tragedy would be compounded."

The petition was denied but was subject to an appeal. About a month after that Memphis hearing, I accompanied Martin and Coretta's second son, Dexter King, along with William Pepper, to the Nashville prison for sick and disabled inmates where Ray was being held. We met in a conference room there, with cameras and reporters witnessing the encounter. After about fifteen minutes of the two men talking, Dexter King, who was thirty-six years old, said to James Earl Ray, who was sixty-nine and in a wheelchair, "I just want to ask you, for the record, did you kill my father?"

And Ray replied, "No, no, I didn't. No."

Dexter then said, "Well, as awkward as this may seem, I want you to know that I believe you and my family believes you, and we are going to do everything in our power to try and make sure that justice will prevail."

Through the spring and summer of 1997, the bid to test the gun continued and was successful. At the end of the summer, the tests were ruled inconclusive. And by the end of 1997, Ray was getting sicker. He was in and out of a coma.

In April 1998, almost exactly thirty years after Martin was killed, I spent an afternoon with Ray in prison praying with him. He was weak but coherent, and told me he wanted me to conduct his funeral service, and I agreed to do it. Ray died a few days later, on April 23, 1998. He was seventy years old. I would turn seventy that September. And Martin would have turned seventy the following January, had he lived. The three of us had been the same age.

On May 29, 1998, I officiated at James Earl Ray's memorial service at a Black church in Nashville. Ray's two brothers, John and Jerry, were there, along with Martin's nephew Isaac Farris Jr., the son of Christine Farris, Martin's sister. Ray's last lawyer, William Pepper, delivered the eulogy.

In 1999, the Kings filed a wrongful death civil suit in a Memphis court and won. But it didn't change many people's minds. There were complaints that our evidence was not sufficient and would not have exonerated Ray in a criminal court.

While my son John still disagreed with me on Ray's innocence, he continued telling me he understood my belief in it. He said, "Everyone is bewildered that you were there with James Earl Ray until he died. And for me, too, it was a difficult relationship to wrap my head around, Dad. But those of us who know who you are recognize you are a minister. And what better example is there of ministering to those in need than to deal with the assassin who murdered your best spiritual friend."

The Justice Department conducted one last inquiry into Martin's killing and released its report in July 2000, dismissing the civil trial findings and agreeing with all the previous government reports that Ray was King's killer. The Kings were dismayed but not surprised. I felt the same way. We remained convinced that James Earl Ray was not the one who killed Martin.

TWENTY-FIVE

Unidos Venceremos

Hotel workers from HERE Local 11 union stage a "wake-up call" demonstration at the Wilshire Hyatt Hotel, Los Angeles, 1989.

MICHAEL HAERING, HERALD EXAMINER, L.A. PUBLIC LIBRARY

I was coming into my sixties and still finding that my work was in demand—teaching and counseling people interested in using nonviolent direct action. In fact, one of the most significant moments in my deepening involvement in Los Angeles happened in 1985, when a group of young activists contacted me and asked me to meet with them and advise them on being more effective at advancing social change movements in the city. I agreed to meet, and we began getting together monthly at my church. We became known as the Holman Group. My relationships and shared goals with everyone in the group set me on a course for more decades of activism—working on some of the same economic justice issues that Martin, as our leader, was hoping to address had he lived on into his forties, fifties, sixties, and beyond.

I didn't know it then, but much like in Nashville when we turned out so many leaders in the nonviolent movement, members of the Holman Group would go on to shape Los Angeles, the state of California, and the nation for decades to come.

It included Karen Bass, who was a physician's assistant and community organizer at the time and would become Speaker of the California State Assembly, a U.S. congressperson, chair of the Congressional Black Caucus, and in 2022 the first woman mayor of L.A. Also in the Holman Group was Antonio Villaraigosa, a union organizer at the time who became Speaker of the California State Assembly and the mayor of L.A. from 2005 to 2013. Gilbert Cedillo was part of the group. He was a legal advocate and became general manager of the Service Employees International Union (SEIU) and was later elected as a state representative, a state senator, and an L.A. City Council member. Anthony Thigpenn, a community organizer who spearheaded major initiatives to uplift South Los Angeles, was in the group, along with Michele Prichard, who became the director of a progressive community foundation in the city.

Holman Group member María Elena Durazo was a labor organizer at the time, who went on to become the first Latina leader of a major Los Angeles union when she was elected president of the Hotel Employees and Restaurant Employees union (HERE) in 1989. Later, she was elected to the California State Senate, where she sponsored groundbreaking bills. María Elena and I fostered important social and economic justice causes together for decades, which cemented our abiding friendship.

In my work with the Holman Group I also got to know Kent Wong, who was a lawyer with SEIU when we met and would later become the head of the UCLA Labor Center and the founding president of the Asian Pacific American Labor Alliance. Kent and I formed a deep friendship, and during the next four decades taught and worked together on major issues.

What began as an informal group meeting once a month in the mid-1980s ended up in the late 1980s and 1990s enacting the nonviolence strategies and philosophy we had honed in our Holman Group sessions. Soon, we were at the forefront of an emerging, more diverse, and more equitable labor movement. The seeds had been sown. There was work to be done.

A raucous, piercing racket shook guests from the quiet luxury of the Wilshire Hyatt Hotel on Normandie Avenue in Los Angeles at six-thirty on a spring morning in 1989. If they went to their windows, they saw union members from the HERE Local 11 union gathered outside, blowing airhorns, shouting through megaphones, and banging on drums. The Hyatt employees who worked as maids, busboys, and bellhops carried signs that read, "We Deserve Dignity," "Don't Insult Us," and "Unidos Venceremos!" ("United We Will Win!") The union members were conducting a special kind of "wake-up call" demonstration, as they had named it, aimed at pressuring the Hyatt management into a fair and equitable contract. By the terms of the company's proposed contract, workers would have had to work ten days straight, without a day off or overtime compensation.

The mostly Latino members of HERE Local 11 had begun to use some of the same methods of nonviolent direct action we had used in the South, led by María Elena Durazo. About two months later, she was elected as the union's new president after a protracted two-year battle within the leadership ranks. She wanted to continue building nonviolent direct action campaigns within the union. I will never forget the day in late spring of 1989 when she asked for my help. I was in my office at Holman. María Elena called and said, "As the new president of HERE Local 11, I am inviting you to come and do a major workshop for my executive committee and organizers on nonviolent direct action. Because you helped organize the sanitation strike in Memphis, I want you to teach nonviolent struggle, methodology, and resistance to our union."

I was elated. Here was a union saying we're going to organize around nonviolent tactics and a fierce commitment to getting rid of injustice. I said yes immediately.

The wake-up call was an example of what we referred to as a "street drama," a tactic we strategized about further in our first training sessions. These kinds of demonstrations gave union members a chance to get creative—using their imaginations to find ways of calling attention to the value of their work. Some dramas also would be used to educate the city—the onlookers—about the nature of the jobs they did or would illustrate some of the obstacles workers in Los Angeles faced.

A few weeks after the wake-up call, the union held another variation of the street drama demonstration. Hyatt was taking its time in negotiations and didn't seem willing to concede much to their workers. So I joined with union members and supporters on one particular day, and we booked all the restaurant reservations for the busy lunchtime at another Hyatt hotel in Los Angeles. We showed up at the appointed time and filled every table in the place. We were seated but did not order any food. We only asked for water and sat quietly. Soon we made it known that we were members and supporters of HERE Local 11 and we would not be moved. We were there to get the attention of Hyatt by depriving the hotel of a potentially lucrative lunch day. The management called the police. We got up to be arrested in the nonviolent way I had helped prepare everyone to practice, but we made sure to leave tips for our servers at every table. We called the demonstration a "water-in," a variation on our sit-ins in the 1960s.

María Elena's election as HERE Local 11's union leader had unseated the deeply entrenched white male leadership that had come before her, in a union with mostly non-white members. María Elena's parents had immigrated to California from Mexico to become "migrant farmworkers." She told me they moved around from crop to crop to crop and from town to town to town a few times a year in the 1950s and 1960s. They lived in tents or in flatbed trucks, because they usually didn't make enough money to afford rent for an apartment or home. She and her ten brothers and sisters had all worked side by side in the fields picking grapes, strawberries, and peaches. They were her father's crew. Her parents had an unwavering work ethic. And the growers took full advantage of them, and many others like them.

When María Elena was a small child, with her entire family working, they still did not make enough to put a roof over their heads, or to buy the food they needed. When they lived in a tent near San Jose and her infant little brother fell ill, they were unable to get him to the doctor, and he died. She said her anger at the injustices she and her family experienced when she was growing up, coupled with the love of her family and, especially, her parents, led her to become an activist.

In high school, her older brother was a student activist at California State University, Fresno. He introduced her to the Chicano Movement, which had risen up from the Central Valley of California in the mid-1960s. César Chávez and Dolores Huerta were its leaders, standing up for the rights of Mexican farmworkers, the ones who lived in the deepest poverty. During that campaign, two unions merged to form the United Farm Workers union (UFW). Chávez and Huerta organized the UFW to be nonviolent, because they had studied Gandhi and had watched what we had done in the South. They knew violence hadn't worked for farmworkers in the past, and saw nonviolence as the most proven, effective way for them to succeed.

Before I ever met them in Los Angeles in the 1980s, I knew of their nonviolence campaigns and had supported them in Memphis during their national grape boycott in 1965. I led boycotts at local grocery stores and encouraged my Memphis congregation not to buy grapes, in support of the farmworkers' movement. Years later, when I met Dolores Huerta and began working with her, I found out that she had been at our silent march in Memphis on April 8, 1968, four days after Martin's assassination. Our two movements observed, inspired, and learned from each other.

María Elena's experiences and grounding in social change work are what spurred her to include recent immigrants in the union. She and other organizers knew they would infuse the whole labor movement with new energy and power. María Elena's blunt invitation asking me to teach her people nonviolence—the history of the struggle and of unionism in the United States and in Los Angeles—marked the start of a decades-long relationship I had with Local 11. Little by little, I worked with her and the union to cultivate the most important elements of building a nonviolent movement.

First, she brought together her new executive committee and several field organizers. In a one-day workshop, we went through the basic elements of a nonviolent philosophy, nonviolent history, and nonviolent strategy and tactics. I drew from the workshops I had done with Martin and the Little Rock Nine and the Southern Christian Leadership Conference, and in the Nashville and Birmingham campaigns. I talked to the union's leaders about their connections to an ancient tradition of resistance, even including Jesus as a practitioner of nonviolence. I described to them how I had personally found ways to fight racism from studying Jesus of Nazareth. I saw Jesus as a radical social activist, and I explained how his strategic thinking about facing the enemy was as relevant to our lives as it had been to the people of his time.

The organizers and executive board of HERE Local 11 developed a good sense of what it meant to engage in nonviolent struggle. All of their street dramas went off like clockwork. Everyone was highly disciplined. They started it when they said they would start it. They ended it when they said they would end it.

The demonstrations also helped the union members launch a whole series of organizing efforts, and the union grew by a factor of ten. Often that kind of fast growth can bring on internal conflicts. I never saw any major campaigns in which any conflict among members or community supporters took precedence over the campaign. There was much more of a spirit of unity around organizing for economic justice.

Seeing the care, attention, compassion, and love that Local 11 epitomized again and again—whether in a workshop or on the front line during a demonstration—was one of the most moving experiences of my life. As we engaged further, I watched Local 11 become a beloved community. I marveled at how the lessons of Nashville, Birmingham, St. Augustine, and especially Memphis had endured and evolved into action in Los Angeles. The injustices were still going on. So were our campaigns to dismantle them.

Social justice work unfolds that way. We don't often solve a problem and never face it again. It usually comes back in a more covert, insidious form, as the late twentieth century and early twenty-first century have shown us. It's the relationships we forge and the victories we share along the way that help sustain us through those inevitable setbacks and regressions we encounter. Between María Elena, her staff, the unionized workers, and me, an unbreakable kinship had formed.

As I had affirmed in Nashville and Memphis and throughout the South, ordinary human beings whose common agenda is uplifting our families, our friends, and our neighbors don't need to adopt language or actions that despise and degrade other people to achieve our goals. Instead, we need to concentrate on connection and collaboration—seeing one another as sisters and brothers. In L.A., that process and its continuous practice would once again produce effective sustainable changes.

Historically, business and political leaders always opposed unionization of the Los Angeles workforce. In the late 1980s and especially in the 1990s, the labor movement we were building there began to grow and become a multicultural political force that challenged them as never before.

In 1990, Kent Wong, aware of the work I had been doing with HERE Local 11, invited me to hold workshops on nonviolent direct action for SEIU members. This training would be part of the union's national campaign called Justice for Janitors. The SEIU's local leader, Mike Garcia, was trying to negotiate with a major national landlord in Century City, a part of Los Angeles near Beverly Hills with high-rise office towers where many of the tenants were Hollywood executives.

The landlord had fired the Black janitors who had worked there for years and begun outsourcing janitorial work to companies that hired immigrants they could pay less and give fewer, if any, benefits. But the newly hired immigrant janitors joined SEIU, despite the outsourcing firm's objections, and went on strike in Century City. The janitors belonging to SEIU realized that a very public strike with daily direct action would get attention.

On June 15, 1990, Justice for Janitors held a peaceful demonstration outside the office complex to call attention to their cause. Soon around one hundred Los Angeles police officers arrived and viciously attacked them, beating and severely injuring many of the strikers. A pregnant woman was hurt so badly she miscarried. All of this happened in full view of print reporters and news cameras. Outrage at the graphic, unprovoked brutality was widespread and immediate. If any companies thought that violently putting down workers was a viable way to solve labor issues, they were proven terribly wrong that day. Prominent tenants in Century City buildings, including some in the film industry, pressured their landlords to get the strike settled. In short order, the outsourcer signed a union contract, with a wage increase of $2 per hour and full family health coverage. The union had found strength in its unity. The janitors won their fight.

Justice for Janitors became a model for organizing security guards, who were mostly Black men, and then for organizing home healthcare workers, who were mostly Latina, Asian, and Black women. In the late 1980s and through the 1990s, Ophelia McFadden was the founder of the home healthcare workers' union, which she grew to seventy-four thousand members. In 1999, they succeeded in their eleven-year push for better wages and working conditions, as well as more funds from the state for the care of the infirm and elderly. I was out picketing on the street with them a couple of times.

I often say that I was arrested far more in L.A. than during my entire time in the South. In November and December of 1989, for example, I was arrested four times during our weekly Wednesday morning nonviolent, inter-religious demonstrations against American involvement in Central America. It being L.A., celebrities were often on the front lines with us, and we all got arrested together.

At various times, as I remember it, both Seth and Morris asked if they could be arrested with me too. They would claim years later that they didn't ask. With some amusement they recounted that I would have them drive me, and as we parked the car I would casually mention to them that we might get arrested. But as I remember it, they were young adults who volunteered to go to jail. John never did get arrested with us. He was in law school and then began working as an L.A. public defender in the late 1980s.

Once, Morris and I were arrested with Ed Asner, Martin Sheen, and Jackson Browne. When we were all in the jail cell, Jackson Browne had his guitar and played some music for us. That was quite a moment. We were released a few hours later.

During the 1990s, Los Angeles experienced a rapid growth in unions, especially among immigrants. Many other unions around the city and the country were inspired by the example of what was happening with groups like HERE Local 11—the small, mostly Latino union that used nonviolent resistance creatively and with deep respect for the humanity of the opponent, even if the opponents did not always respect them. In hotel after hotel across the city, fearful workers had been transformed into fearless nonviolent practitioners.

Activists and union members have told me many times that a sense of fearlessness is something which must be practiced before it becomes a part of you. Then it can end up serving you in other parts of your life, too. I was grateful for my own practice of fearlessness when a major earthquake struck Southern California on Monday, January 17, 1994. At four-thirty A.M., we were woken up when the whole house was shaking back and forth for many seconds. Dorothy and I held hands across the bed. I was rather astonished to find that I felt no fear, not even the adrenaline kind of fear in the moment. When it was over, Dorothy and I went back to sleep. A few minutes later, someone banged at my door. I put on some pants and rushed downstairs to answer it. There was my dear friend Mort, a church member, with a flashlight in his hand because the lights had all gone out. He said, "Reverend, just checking to see if you are okay. Everything all right?" I told him we were fine and thanked him for coming by. After that, we stayed awake for all the aftershocks.

When I reflected on it, I was amazed how in that very dreadful moment we felt no fear. I know it wasn't recklessness. I came to see it as a spiritual experience. In that moment of danger, I was embraced at the depth of my being with the sensibility that God was near. God was available. God was still my security. Across the years, I've gone into a variety of experiences where there was danger, without anxiety or fear. I've lived my whole life with a profound sense that God is my refuge and strength, my stronghold. And I have always maintained a confidence that I will see the goodness of God in the land of the living.

My nonviolence practice has guided me through, as I have helped pass its lessons on to my congregations, to my friends, family, and neighbors, to labor union members in Memphis, Los Angeles, and all around the nation, and to so many others. In turn, the bonds of care and activism I have seen formed from it have bolstered my belief in the power and promise of the beloved community.

In 1996, I co-founded Clergy and Laity United for Economic Justice (CLUE) in Los Angeles. The goal was to bring together a wide range of people in the faith community to work with labor on economic justice campaigns, such as the push for a living wage for underpaid service workers.

One of the campaigns in which CLUE worked with HERE Local 11 was against the labor policies of the University of Southern California, one of the largest private employers in the city. In 1996, the university began to outsource janitorial and food service work to subcontractors who hired people as independent contractors, much like what happened in Century City a few years before. The university's goal was to stop dealing with unions, and stop paying benefits to employees, most of whom were Black and Latino and lived in the neighborhoods around the campus. Janitors and food service workers were losing their jobs. If the outsourcers rehired them, it would be at lower wages and without healthcare, employment security, or union representation. The workers organized through Local 11 and stood up to the university in what turned out to be a four-year battle.

When the workers began to demonstrate on campus in 1996, the university got an injunction to prevent the union from assembling there. So, we organized larger community demonstrations just outside the university's perimeter. When student groups who supported the workers tried to take part in those actions, USC's administration placed stricter regulations on student demonstrations. USC's president Steven Sample held firm against a union contract. We continued the pressure and held vigils, held strikes, and fasted. Many USC students got the kind of firsthand view of union organizing during the course of our campaign that they never would have had studying such campaigning in class.

Two years later, CLUE and HERE Local 11 conducted a creative demonstration at the 1998 USC graduation. The commencement speaker, comedian Bill Cosby, was to receive an honorary PhD that day. Just outside the site of the ceremony, we staged an alternate commencement for what we called the University of Justice. Thirty-nine janitors, food service workers, and union leaders dressed in caps and gowns and sat down in the street blocking traffic near intersections on Figueroa Street by the official campus graduation site. Each worker was to be conferred a degree in justice for exemplifying the struggle for equity and equality in the city of Los Angeles. The university was mistreating those workers and trying to bust their union, but the more than three hundred union workers had bravely stood their ground.

Of course, everyone was arrested for blocking the intersection. As the members of Local 11 were taken away and put in the police bus, one by one, I handed each of them a diploma of justice. Their arrests signified the final step to graduation. Then María Elena and I and others were arrested too.

USC and the union finally reached an agreement in 1999 on a five-year contract that fortified the union workers' job security and benefits.

In 2004, I was still quite involved with HERE Local 11 and María Elena Durazo's work there, when we staged one of the most creative nonviolent street dramas I have ever seen.

We blocked off a busy intersection in downtown Los Angeles and Local 11 members demonstrated the kind of work they did each day in hotels and restaurants around the city. Union members set up a circle of beds in the street. Maids arrived in housekeeper uniforms, and one woman, Rose Rivera, went around the circle making the beds, the way she did during every shift at her job. Cooks were cooking food. Waiters were serving it to people in the street.

We were bringing the hidden economy behind L.A. tourism into the open. Instead of holding a news conference, union members simply passed out a one-page message to the onlookers to educate them about what they were doing. Then one by one we got arrested.

TWENTY-SIX

Inalienable Rights

Reverend Lawson teaching immigrant student activists from around the United States about nonviolent resistance during the Dream Summer program at UCLA, 2011.

SALVADOR "POCHO" SANDRIDGE-STRAWBRIDGE, UCLA LABOR CENTER

As I got nearer to my seventies, I began to experience several full-circle moments of reconciliation in my own life. The first two happened in places where my fearlessness had once frightened the people in charge.

In 1994, the then president of Baldwin-Wallace College, Dr. Neal Malicky, brought me back to be the commencement speaker at graduation. The college also gave me an honorary PhD in divinity. In my address, I told the students about the importance of having a vision for their lives and advised them, "As you move from graduation to your next arena, ignore career-making. Go for your calling. Career accentuates success. A calling pushes values. A career pursues money. A calling strives to make a difference."

At one point during the weekend, Dr. Malicky asked me if there was anything he could do for me. I thought about it and replied, "Put me back in the class of 1951." When I was arrested with only a few weeks left in my senior year, the president at the time and the other faculty members who disliked me would not grant my degree. Coming back in the fall of 1952 for a semester to get my degree meant I was always considered to be part of the class of 1952. He granted my request. In all the alumni materials I got after that conversation, I was listed in the class of 1951.

Then two years later, in 1996, Vanderbilt Divinity School brought me back to campus to give me its first ever Divinity School Distinguished Alumni Award. The dean of the divinity school at the time, Joseph Hough, arranged a meeting between me and Harvie Branscomb, who had been chancellor of the university in 1960. Thirty-six years after those early days of the sit-ins, I went to Branscomb's Nashville home to see the man who had kicked me out of the university. He had never talked to me in 1960. If he had, I think we could have settled things without so much turmoil.

He was 101 years old when we visited as two men who once had been cast as adversaries. We had a very pleasant exchange. I felt no animosity in the man, and I had none toward him. He had come to recognize he was wrong in 1960, and let me know he had evolved. It was his way of apologizing. Sometimes people need a few decades of distance to reconsider events with the kind of impact our sit-in campaign had.

In the mid-1990s, I got a call from David Halberstam, the journalist who had covered our movement in Nashville for the *Tennessean* newspaper in 1960. He was writing a book about that time and wanted me to sit down with him for a series of interviews. He had been such an important figure in our lives, and we trusted him. I could think of no one better to write our story. He also asked to interview my son John, who was working as a public defender in Los Angeles. Even though John was very young during our early years in Tennessee, David knew he would have some insights and memories to share. So I embarked on another project to document a part of the movement. David's book came out in 1998. It was called *The Children,* and it was one of the most accurate and detailed studies of any campaign in the King movement.

In 2001, I attended my fiftieth college reunion at Baldwin-Wallace I had never gone to a class reunion before, since I had officially been listed in the class of 1951 for only a few years. I knew some of my classmates thought I didn't do the right thing when it came to resisting the draft in

1951. My friends told me there was that kind of talk after I left campus and was arrested, stood trial, and was sent to prison.

At the reunion in 2001, fifty years later, an extraordinary thing happened. One of our classmates was a guy named Arthur Worth Collins. He went by the name Bud Collins, and for fifty years he wrote for *The Boston Globe*, becoming one of the most respected sports columnists in the country. He covered professional tennis for many years on NBC Sports and later on ESPN. I had seen him on TV a few times, calling matches at Wimbledon and the U.S. Open, and remembered him from college. He couldn't make it to that fiftieth reunion because he was in Paris covering the French Open. So he sent an audio message for us. To my great surprise, near the end of his joyful reminiscences of Baldwin-Wallace and calling out some of our classmates from college, he spent a few sentences talking about me.

> There's a guy I hope is there, and I'd like to greet him, named Jim Lawson. He was president of our freshman class. And Jim didn't leave a very good impression with a lot of us guys in 1951, because we were headed for the Korean War. And Jim Lawson, who later became a marvelous aide to Martin Luther King, said, "I'm not going to war."
>
> . . . And those of us who did go and put on a uniform, well, we didn't think much of that. But, on reflection over time, Jim Lawson was a very brave man. He followed his conscience. I'm certainly proud that he was one of my classmates.

I was stunned that he would say that in such a setting, because there were any number of people like Bud at BW. And I was touched he was being respectful to me in front of them.

Those reckonings with people who had once expelled, rejected, or scorned me and my convictions reinforced my belief that people and institutions can change. It usually isn't fast enough, and it often isn't fully enough. But maintaining hope for transformations can drive change in unexpected places.

The Methodist Church has a mandatory retirement age of seventy-two, and while I never thought I would make it to forty, somehow, I had kept on pastoring into my seventies. Yet, as the new century was beginning, I had to retire as a pastor. I didn't want to do it, but the time had come. I had gotten my preacher's license when I graduated from high school in 1947, and in college I had my first congregation in Canton, Ohio. I was ordained as a deacon in 1952 and as an elder in 1960, and became a pastor in Shelbyville, Tennessee in 1960. I went to Centenary in Memphis in 1962 and was there for twelve years. Then I spent twenty-five years as pastor of Holman in L.A.

For my retirement, the congregation at Holman held a gala celebration dinner at the Regent Beverly Wilshire Hotel on Saturday, June 12, 1999. There was music, dancing, dinner, and tributes from friends and colleagues. The hosts of the evening were KNBC anchorwoman Bonnie Boswell—who had been my co-host for ten years on the 1990s cable television show *Lawson, Live*—along with actor and activist Mike Farrell. Speakers included C. T. Vivian, María Elena Durazo, Rabbi Steven Jacobs, State Senator Tom Hayden, Mark Lane, Congresswoman Maxine Waters, the leaders of the ACLU and FOR, and others. California Governor Gray Davis and California's First Lady Sharon Davis were in attendance. My sons spoke.

And then Dorothy spoke.

> Governor and Mrs. Davis, family, Holman-ites, and friends—thank you. We are truly honored and humbled by your presence this evening. As I revel in the wonderful words, the dance, the magnificent music that we have experienced this evening, I can only say, life is beautiful, indeed.
>
> We have heard many wonderful tributes in recognition of my husband's extraordinary journey and work. I thank you. He has been called or characterized as a prophet, a priest, a peacemaker, a civil rights advocate, and even a mystic. I can attest to the validity of such characterizations.
>
> However, I cherish him, most of all, as a wonderful and caring father, as a loving and supportive partner—one who seeks daily to make his inner and outward life one.
>
> So, deep beneath the words, deep beneath the accolades, I know there is a Godly man of integrity, of courage, who really believes thy Kingdom can come on earth, as it is in Heaven. Again, I thank you.

Retirement from the church meant I would be stepping into the new century as a pastor emeritus of Holman. Retiring also meant I would no longer lead the congregation, and retirement also meant a reduction in my almost-daily, solitary prayers in that sanctuary. With retirement, Dorothy and I moved out of the Holman parsonage where we had raised our boys. We ended up buying a home in nearby Baldwin Hills, a fine neighborhood and strong community.

In many ways, my spiritual and political path opened up when I retired, as I was able to spend more time engaged in advocacy work, widening my focus to include women's rights, LGBTQ rights, and immigrants' rights in the twenty-first century. For instance, in 2000, I wrote an opinion piece about abortion rights for the *Los Angeles Times* with my friend and colleague, United Methodist pastor Rev. Ignacio Castuera. The headline was "We Should Trust Women to Do the Choosing." To me, abortion is not only about healthcare. It also represents the autonomy of human beings who give birth. At the heart of the debate is whether a woman is a full human being. That's it. If she is, then let her run her own journey. Let her manage her own life. She's more than her body. She has the right to make decisions that allow her to live as she needs and wants to live.

I had always been a teacher in the movement and afterward in my ongoing workshops on nonviolence. So it was a natural step for me to take up teaching after I retired from the church. In 2001, Harvard Divinity School invited me to be the Luce Lecturer on Urban Ministry. I taught two courses that semester. One was called "Nonviolence: An Unexplored Human Option"; the other was the "Urban Ministry Seminar."

Then, in 2002, my friend Kent Wong invited me to co-teach a course with him at UCLA, where he had been hired in 1991 to teach labor studies and Asian American studies and to be the director of its Labor Center. The course we began teaching together was called "Nonviolence and Social Movements."

Many of the students Kent and I taught had immigrated as children from Mexico, Central America, or South America with their parents, or their parents had immigrated and they were born in the United States. I was inspired about the future as I watched them learn to advocate for their own issues, even though many of our students and their families lived with a fear of capricious U.S. politicians.

Working with those students opened my eyes to the harsh conditions they and their families had to contend with, both here and in the countries they had left, and to the fact that their lives deserved more attention than they were getting.

In 2003, María Elena Durazo's fertile mind came up with the idea for an Immigrant Workers Freedom Ride, inspired by our Freedom Ride in 1961. I was thrilled when she asked me to join in on the planning and it ended up becoming a major national event. María Elena was the national chair, and many major unions and immigrants' rights and religious organizations got involved.

In September of 2003, eighteen buses carrying more than nine hundred riders set out from ten cities, heading toward Washington, D.C., and continuing on to New York City. The idea was to make stops in towns and cities along the way where the riders would meet with community groups and advocate for safe working conditions for immigrants all over the United States. Buses launched from Seattle, Portland, San Francisco, and Los Angeles on the West Coast; from Las Vegas, Houston, Chicago, and Minneapolis in the middle of the country; and from Miami and Boston on the East Coast. The bus from Houston stopped in Montgomery, Alabama, where Freedom Riders had been mercilessly beaten in the bus station in 1961, and in Anniston, Alabama, where a 1961 Freedom Ride bus was set on fire. The Las Vegas bus stopped in Memphis, at the Lorraine Motel, where Martin was shot, which by then had become the National Civil Rights Museum.

In Los Angeles, we had a big send-off rally a few days before the bus left. I was quoted in a *Los Angeles Times* column by Frank del Olmo, saying that in 1961 "we were trying to expose outdated Jim Crow laws. . . . Now we are trying to expose outdated immigration laws." Del Olmo wrote:

> Four decades after the original freedom rides, Lawson points out, it is easy to forget that they "were just an early step in a long struggle to dismantle a system of American apartheid. In fact, that struggle continued well into the 1970s, and in some areas continues to this very day," he said. "I see the same model here. . . . The freedom rides are just a beginning, not an end."
>
> Coming from almost anyone else, such a lofty idealism might be discounted. But I'm not about to underestimate a Freedom Rider.

On Tuesday, September 23, more than eighty riders boarded two buses from Los Angeles to head east. Before they departed, I gave the riders a kind of pep talk. Everyone on the buses had been in the nonviolence training sessions I had conducted with María Elena and others in the weeks leading up to the ride. We had talked about how to handle hecklers at rallies and government authorities boarding the bus. We had role-played ways to react nonviolently. But I also felt the need to tend to their spirits. I remembered how it felt to be on such a bus, riding into uncertain territory.

I started by encouraging them to let this ride wake them up "to the beauty and wonder of being alive. Learn the struggle. Find your own voice in concert" with everyone else on these buses. I urged them to "discover each other as companions in the journey now and ongoing. Be a community since you seek to help change us all."

I didn't join the riders on the bus out of Los Angeles, on their way to Palm Springs and Phoenix. I was scheduled to join them and other riders at points along the route. Seth came with me on those journeys. Traveling with me to my speeches and appearances was what my boys did from time to time once they became adults. Seth and I flew to Tucson, Arizona, the next afternoon to meet up with the Los Angeles riders. I spoke at a rally there, and we spent the night. The next morning we boarded the buses with the riders for a day, and headed to Nogales, Arizona, and Lordsburg and Las Cruces, New Mexico. In Nogales, we stopped and held a vigil, remembering the 147 reported deaths of immigrants crossing the Arizona desert that year. The riders each took a cross bearing the name and date of death of one of the people who had died. Some of those names on the crosses were children. The riders were to carry those crosses across the country to Washington, D.C., and into their rallies and meetings with members of Congress.

We arrived in El Paso on Thursday afternoon, where we met with people at a farmworkers support center. Both Nogales and El Paso were as close to the southern U.S. border as any of the freedom ride buses were traveling. Many riders had legal status, but some were undocumented, which meant they were risking arrest and deportation, especially in these border areas where checkpoints were common. For some riders the experience of being so near the border brought up painful memories. There were immigrants on the buses from more than fifty countries in Latin America, Africa, Asia, and the Middle East.

They told us about their brutal working conditions and poverty pay in the United States. Some said they had to collect fifty large buckets of chilies each to earn just $38 for the more than eight hours of work it took. One of our spokespeople, Hilda Delgado, was quoted in an article that mentioned those conditions, calling them "the kind of exploitation and slavery that people here are subject to."

The two L.A. buses were stopped, and some riders were questioned in Texas on the day after Seth and I had been on the bus with them. But all the riders engaged in nonviolent civil disobedience, peacefully resisting the questions and remaining calm and united, as we had practiced in the trainings. Their solidarity worked. No one was arrested and they were allowed to continue on the Freedom Ride.

The buses from Los Angeles traveled east through Texas and up into Tennessee. They stopped in Memphis and then in Nashville, where Seth and I met them again on Monday, September 29. The day before, I had spoken at a rally in Milwaukee, addressing riders on the buses that had left from Minneapolis. Hundreds of immigrant workers in Nashville showed up to a march and held a rally across from the Country Music Hall of Fame. We were in the same part of downtown where our Nashville Student Movement had conducted the sit-ins at Woolworth's and other nearby lunch counters in 1960. I was able to draw parallels between the immigrant movement and the Nashville Student Movement when I spoke at the rally. "Like the civil rights movement," I told the crowd, "the plight of immigrant workers is about denial of human rights. . . . We must remember that Black Americans will not achieve full human rights if immigrant workers do not achieve them."

I also pointed out that the nation's immigration system was untenable, and I criticized President George W. Bush and the nation's "$800 billion war machine," which was partly to blame for the immigration crisis.

One young man came up to me afterward and asked for some words for his soul. I said, "Grow into the inward power of nonviolence, of compassion, of nonviolent struggle, and you will find a life of adventure that is astonishing." Then we embraced, and laughed, and kept on going.

On Wednesday, October 1, the eighteen buses converged in Washington, D.C., for rallies. John Lewis, who had become an eminent congressman, spoke to the riders about the Freedom Ride in 1961 and the importance of this new campaign. John and I had maintained a deep, close friendship through the years. And even though he had become a celebrated insider, he would never lose the impulse to take to the streets and demonstrate against injustice. The next day, groups of riders met with various members of Congress. Then on Friday, October 3, the riders headed to Liberty State Park in New Jersey and, with the Statue of Liberty in sight, held another rally. Nearby, anti-immigration groups staged a small counter-rally, led by a right-wing radio host and attended by neo-Nazi groups.

Seth and I arrived in New York City on Friday night and went to the culminating rally of the Immigrant Workers Freedom Ride in Queens, New York, on Saturday, October 4. Approximately one hundred thousand people showed up through the afternoon at Flushing Meadows Corona Park to hear and see speakers, musicians, and politicians celebrating the mix of people and rallying for the rights of all. I was the closing speaker, and I told the crowd:

> No human being in the sight of God is illegal. No human being in the sight of God is undocumented. . . .
>
> Every boy and every girl, and every man and every woman, no matter what country, what creed, what language, what culture, what color—every man and every woman has a right to jobs with dignity, safety at work, families being united and to be able to support themselves and sustain themselves.

The full circle moments continued in 2005, when Vanderbilt University honored me with its Distinguished Alumni Award (not to be confused with the similarly named honor I received from Vanderbilt's divinity school a decade earlier). And in 2006, I was invited back to the campus to teach as a distinguished professor. For three years I taught a course called "The Nonviolent Struggle," in which we studied nonviolent movements of the twentieth and twenty-first centuries. I included Gandhi's fight for India's independence from the United Kingdom, our movement for Black freedom in the 1950s and '60s, the women's movement from suffrage to equal rights, and the labor movement of the twentieth century. During that time, Dorothy and I rented an apartment in Nashville and went back and forth between that home and Los Angeles, where Morris lived in the house.

Dorothy and I took some excellent trips around then, to places where we had deep connections. In 2008, I was the featured speaker at the 146th Emancipation Festival in Owen Sound, Ontario, which, along with the area called the Queen's Bush, was the northernmost terminus of the Underground Railroad. The festival had been held ever since it was started in 1862, during the American Civil War, to celebrate the Slavery Abolition Act, which Britain passed on August 1, 1834. My great-grandfather was among those called a pioneer in the Queen's Bush.

During the visit we also had a family reunion and got to know more of our Canadian cousins. John and his wife, Cima, came, along with their children, Raven and Devin, who were young at the time. We got a chance to see the place where my father, grandparents, and great-grandparents lived and to meet the relatives who were also descended from my great-grandfather.

In reconnecting with my Black Canadian ancestors, I came to see how seriously I have taken the lessons and love of my father and mother and tried to emulate them. One seemingly trivial way that manifests is in how I dress. Sometimes I laugh to myself because in public I usually wear a tie, a button-down shirt, and a jacket. When I'm getting dressed, I often think, "I'm honoring my parents and my ancestors." I was taught that wearing those clothes was a sign of respect for others, and I've never thought that was bad teaching. I enjoy it because I feel it connects me to the people who came before me. They put me in a position to dress well. I have never found a reason to rebel against it.

Soon after that trip to Canada, Dorothy and I went even deeper into our heritage. On our fiftieth wedding anniversary, in 2009, our sons gave us a trip to Ghana, which we had always been told was the homeland of my great-grandfather Dangerfield Lawson. The story we grew up hearing was that his people had been kidnapped in Ghana and forced onto crowded, inhumane ships that brought them to the United States and a life of enslavement.

When I was in Ghana in 1956, I had visited the departure places. I don't remember them making as much of an impression on me as they did when Dorothy and I went back in 2009. We saw the dark dungeons where people were tortured, and where they stayed before being sent to the United States. We walked through the narrow passageways in the walls of Elmina Castle and in Cape Coast Castle in Ghana, where we felt the gravity of the "Door of No Return." Once you went through that door, you were never coming back to Africa, much less Ghana. When I visited those places in 1956 there wasn't much there. By 2009, it had become much more of a tourist site—a moneymaking device for Ghana, owned and maintained by the state.

I'm as deeply rooted in the United States of America, or even more so, than many people who immigrated here from Europe. Some people think that's not so, because our country has permitted racism to grow up and be preserved here. So, at times, my country has tried to define me, to classify me as less than a human being or to say I don't belong here. When I moved to the South, people hurled "Yankee, go home" at me.

In the face of such ill regard, I remain absolutely committed to the incredible ideals in the Declaration of Independence and the preamble to the U.S. Constitution. This country was organized around those extraordinary documents, and I have spent my life trying to help it live up to its visionary principles. Yet, our country has not done enough to help people see the infinite potential for human thriving in those documents.

By the people. For the people. Of the people. We hold these truths to be self-evident.

For me, that is scripture, and poetry. It is quite sacred. Martin, Rosa Parks, Ella Baker, and so many others were the founding fathers and mothers of what this country must become. Our movement's goal was always to urge the nation to live up to the ideals written into our founding documents. Our country's hope is in finally realizing the promise of its original vision. I see no other way for the nation to survive.

While I taught at UCLA with Kent Wong, I also began teaching a course called "Nonviolent Struggles, Civil Rights and Social Change" at California State University, Northridge.

Putting a lot of energy into nurturing the youngest generation kept me moving forward with the work I had done all my life. I was determined to help launch twenty-first-century students toward fulfilling their potential and finding their own meaning in life. Many undocumented student leaders enrolled in my classes. I was excited to be among them as a new undocumented youth movement was emerging in the 2010s, focused on reforming the broken American immigration system.

I felt particular connections to these students, since I, too, am the son of immigrants to the United States. My father, a second-generation immigrant in Canada, came to the United States and met my mother, a Jamaican immigrant. Immigration was a personal issue to me as well as a cause for action.

One of the first major slogans the students within the immigrant youth movement created was "Undocumented and Unafraid," a radical expression of personal and social empowerment. In some of the meetings with immigrant students at the start, I pushed hard the message I had pushed on the Immigrant Workers Freedom Ride: that in the sight of God, no human being is illegal. No human being is undocumented. Every human being needs to be acknowledged as having full human rights. You can and will build a movement to claim your inalienable rights.

LGBTQ+ immigrant students voiced their particular challenges within the larger movement, and coined the term "undocuqueer." Students involved in that campaign told me they had drawn great inspiration from my friend Bayard Rustin and his work for full equality and justice for all.

I saw students begin to say to themselves, "I am undocumented. That's not my fault. It's the fault of the systems in place. But I'm no longer going to be invisible." "Undocumented and Unafraid" was their bold and audacious personal affirmation: "According to society, I'm undocumented. But according to my vision of life, I am a human being. And I'm not afraid." It reminded me of the Memphis sanitation workers who found their individual and collective power and declared simply, radically: I am a man.

A major policy proposal the immigrant youth movement rallied around was the DREAM Act. The acronym stood for Development, Relief, and Education for Alien Minors. It was first introduced in Congress in 2001 and provided a path to U.S. citizenship for the children of people who came to this country to work, mostly on farms and in private homes. Exploiting these workers and their families is a prime example of the continuing unjust and abusive system upon which this country's wealth has always been built. In 2001, the DREAM Act did not pass. But the idea of it sparked young immigrants, in particular, to become active in organizing for their own rights.

Another step we took to support their efforts came when Kent Wong and the UCLA Labor Center worked with the United We Dream national network of immigrant students and created an internship program for immigrant student leaders from all over the country, called Dream Summer 2011. For ten weeks, students met and worked in social justice, labor, and community organizations around Los Angeles. During a three-day retreat at the start of the summer, the student leaders went through workshops on the law, social issues, and nonviolent direct action. I taught a workshop on nonviolence. Throughout the internship they were provided the space to connect with one another and with other professionals, allies, and groups working on immigration issues all over the country.

One genius tactic of their undocumented student movement was staging relatively small demonstrations that took place in many parts of the country. There were no big parade-like marches. For instance, the first civil disobedience act the undocumented students led was in 2010, in Arizona, which is a very anti-immigrant state. The students successfully staged a sit-in at Senator John McCain's office, risking arrest and deportation. In another instance, they held a small but powerful hunger strike. Those kinds of focused, smaller actions exerted pressure strategically, which educated the public, chipped away at opposition, and led to changes.

In 2012, just as the second year of Dream Summer was underway, the Obama administration announced a program called DACA, Deferred Action for Childhood Arrivals. It meant that children of undocumented immigrants could apply for work and education authorization for two years, with renewal possible. The immigrant student movement had a part in advocating for DACA and finally got to feel what it is like to enjoy a first big victory.

For many, many years I have said that the United States will not change without large, united, sustained, strategic nonviolent campaigns. Even with election victories, politicians run into the filibuster and leadership without motivation or imagination. We need nonviolent campaigns—such as those of the immigrant student movement—to tell the system that we are still living in the wrong, and to demand that people and institutions transform and become what is right.

TWENTY-SEVEN

Plantation Capitalism

A cotton field in Clarksdale, Mississippi, 2015. Artist Ruddy Roye created this photo, entitled Don't Shoot, *as the Black Lives Matter movement was gaining momentum across the nation.* RUDDY ROYE PHOTOGRAPHY

Racism has driven our economic and social order from the start of this nation. Rather than being adamant as a society that no one should live in poverty and no babies anywhere should die, racism is used to justify poverty and infant mortality among certain groups of people. And a vital part of racism is keeping the people who benefit from those unjust systems unaware of the costs those systems impose on the people they exploit. Then, if the exploited people ask for more or band together to stand up against the unjust system, the people who benefit learn to call the exploited people asking for more "lazy," or "freeloaders," or "radicals."

For instance, we have folk in the United States who care deeply about their own well-being but not about the families in Mississippi, a state with the highest infant mortality rate in the country, for babies of both Black and white mothers. We tolerate those deaths. In political discussions we pretend those working parents living in poverty in Mississippi aren't even there or don't matter. Tolerating, accomodating, and perpetuating such cruel inattention has long been our default position. The number of babies who die in our nation, along with our ability to ignore their deaths, is a practical measurement of our humanity.

The infant mortality rate in any state is a better barometer of our health as a nation than any other measure. Such an inexcusable wrong anywhere in our country is an undeniable warning sign of our overall, weakened well-being. Why shouldn't the president of the United States be telling the American people at least once a year that the infant mortality rate in Mississippi is evil? Why does the political scene abide such suffering in the richest country on earth?

Allowing evil to exist without remedy through so many generations, we have let callous leadership believe that there is no consequence to their malign neglect. This reflexive cruelty built into the U.S. economic system is what I call "plantation capitalism." I came up with the term in the early 2000s to describe the oppressive economic system I see in the United States. Our nation hails equality, but we don't practice it. That mindset goads us into becoming extremely hypocritical and fortifies the belief that our hypocrisy is right and normal.

I got the idea for the term from the Memphis sanitation strikers in 1968—when they called the city's public works department "the plantation," and the place where their trucks left for work each day "the barn." Most of those men and their wives were born into sharecropping and had descended from enslaved ancestors. When they left the plantations to come to the city and find better work, it didn't take long to realize they were caught again in a similar kind of unfair and brutal system. The men and their families understood full well who and what were exploiting them.

Once they saw they had the collective power to do something about the injustice, they went on strike to make necessary change happen. Their nonviolent direct action defied centuries of plantation capitalism.

We make choices as people, as communities, and as nations either to do good or do harm in the world. Violence in its very nature is about doing harm. I have lived all of my life in a country that glorified violence. Exploiting some people's labor for the benefit of others is one form of that violence. It has been enforced through the the omnipresent cycle of police violence against Black people in the United States from as far back as the first slave patrols and citizen militias. Every time we as a nation have had a chance to alter that pattern, we have failed.

Starting in 2012, this country got yet another few years' worth of chances to find a better way. Mostly, we missed the opportunity. But a new movement began to emerge, even as the forces against it gained power.

In a gated community in Sanford, Florida, neighborhood watch captain George Zimmerman shot and killed a seventeen-year-old named Trayvon Martin in 2012, a child armed with nothing but Skittles.

In 2014, Darren Wilson, a Ferguson, Missouri, police officer, shot Michael Brown, an eighteen-year-old, on his way back from a convenience store. Michael Brown was unarmed and just blocks from his home in a St. Louis suburb.

Each time I heard stories like those, I immediately thought of Larry Payne in Memphis in 1968. I remembered how a police officer shot him, a few yards away from his mother's apartment. Witnesses then had reported that Payne was unarmed and had his hands over his head, saying, "Don't shoot." It happened a few blocks from where, a few hours before, we had turned Martin Luther King's last march around, because of the threat of violence the Memphis police posed to us.

Wilson killing Michael Brown in 2014 triggered a national uprising. In Ferguson and throughout the nation for the next several days, peaceful protests in the streets were met with police in riot gear. Everyone marching was subjected to the kind of military equipment designed for warfare between nations, the kind of disproportionate firepower Daryl Gates and his SWAT teams began amassing after the Watts uprising. All around the nation, more protests were met with more militarized police reactions.

In the process, a resistance movement that had started in the aftermath of Trayvon Martin's death emerged as the nation reacted to Michael Brown's murder. Three Black women took a chant, "Black Lives Matter," and made it into the name of one of the major organizing forces behind what became the Movement for Black Lives. The language, feelings, and urges that produce violence are invisible. But these women, as well as the mothers of the people police murdered, demanded that killing Trayvon

Martin and Michael Brown not be invisible. Their great strength was their challenge to unaccountable police authority, clearly demonstrating that those murders were not true law enforcement. Murdering those children was brutal terrorism and unacceptable in any community.

The Movement for Black Lives was highly effective at putting police violence on the agenda, and in showing how American policing is not a democratic force for justice in our society. We did not succeed in communicating that message in the twentieth century.

The Movement for Black Lives did in the 2010s—effectively pushing this nation to consider how we can enforce justice, equality, and liberty, without the horrendous, often deadly, violence policing has always employed, chiefly against Black people and Brown people. The police in a democratic society must become more nonviolent. They must become more aware of economic inequality and social justice, and less sexist and homophobic.

The Movement for Black Lives also adopted a deeply spiritual, moral, and ethical strategy. It surrounded every family touched by a killing with a loving, caring, grieving community. It has practiced what can be called "good grief"—not getting sick from grief but, rather, talking about it and expressing it, building a compassionate circle around the hurt family that helps them grieve publicly, ultimately inspiring them to join the ongoing struggle. That generous support is one of the most powerful forms of ministry in a public movement. It can prevent families from becoming paralyzed in grief, and give them a new path to personal transformation.

In St. Louis, one minor demonstration stood out to me because it was an example of smaller groups of people creatively expressing anger at our policing system, and thereby helping to sustain a movement. And my favorite movement song was at the center of it.

On October 6, 2014, the St. Louis Symphony was about to begin its performance, when two audience members stood up and began singing, *Justice for Mike Brown / Is justice for us all* to the tune of "Which Side Are You On?"

Then two more stood up from the other side of the concert hall and joined them. Then a few more in the back and in the balcony stood up. *Which side are you on, friend? / Which side are you on?* As they sang, they unfurled banners from the upper level that said, "Requiem for Mike Brown 1996–2014" and "Racism Lives Here," with an arrow pointing to a drawing of the Gateway Arch and the city skyline. They were met with some applause and a few stares. The musicians and conductor watched with respect. The mostly white demonstrators ended with chants of "Black Lives Matter" as they walked out of the concert hall.

Yet the familiar cycle was not overcome. In November 2014, a St. Louis grand jury decided not to indict Darren Wilson for shooting Michael Brown. In March 2015, the U.S. Department of Justice investigation cleared Wilson of civil rights violations in the killing. Frustration with the legal system grew as the trend of police killing Black boys and men was exposed more publicly than it ever had been all over the country.

Just before Michael Brown was killed, a white NYPD officer in Staten Island named Daniel Pantaleo put a forty-three-year-old father and grandfather named Eric Garner, who was Black, in an illegal chokehold on the ground for selling cigarettes illegally on the sidewalk. Garner died of suffocation. As usual, a grand jury decided not to indict Pantaleo.

Two days after Michael Brown's death, the Los Angeles police shot and killed a twenty-five-year-old Black man on August 11, 2014. His name was Ezell Ford, and he was mentally ill and unarmed.

On November 22, 2014, Cleveland police shot and killed Tamir Rice, a twelve-year-old Black child who was playing with a toy gun in a local park.

On April 4, 2015, police in North Charleston, South Carolina, shot fifty-year-old Walter Scott five times in the back, killing him, as Scott, who was Black, was running away after being questioned for having a broken brake light.

Those killings and others reinforced the abiding idea that no Black man was safe from police officers in the United States. The lynching of Black life runs throughout American history. In my life alone, I have seen it again and again—whether it was Emmett Till, Larry Payne, Elton Hayes, Eula Love, Trayvon Martin, Michael Brown, Tamir Rice, or so many others. This country seems incredibly immune to recognizing racism as an ideology, and a structure, and a way of life in the United States.

As with George Zimmerman, it is not only police in this nation who violently act out that way of life. On June 17, 2015, a twenty-one-year-old white supremacist named Dylann Roof killed nine people and injured one at a Wednesday night Bible study at Mother Emanuel AME Church in Charleston, South Carolina. He picked the church, founded in 1816, specifically because it has a rich history of promoting Black empowerment, human rights, and justice—from the anti-slavery movement to the Civil Rights Movement to Black Lives Matter.

The horrific mass murder at Mother Emanuel led to national questioning of the power inherent in racist symbols and monuments throughout the South and, later, across the rest of the country. Large, small, and solo acts of nonviolent resistance popped up all over. Most notably, activist Bree Newsome climbed a flagpole at the South Carolina capitol building on June 27, 2015, and pulled down the Confederate flag flying there. Soon thereafter, the state removed the flag forever. Concerted strategic, nonviolent demonstrations forced many cities and states, during the next few years, to remove the ubiquitous monuments to failed Confederate war heroes.

In 2016, the country elected Donald Trump as president.

From my perspective, that moment was a consequence of long-dormant but never-vanished opposition to the changes we had begun to make in the 1960s and '70s, which reemerged, as ugly as ever, despite the progress we were starting to make again in the 2010s.

I've witnessed the evolution of that bigotry. I saw it when William Buckley of Yale, *National Review,* and the *Firing Line* television show—a wealthy Catholic conservative—said in the mid-1960s that in the struggle between Martin Luther King and white civilization, the conservative movement has to identify itself with white civilization. Then, in the last part of the twentieth century the Southern segregationists morphed into the Southern conservatives. The Dixiecrats became Republicans. For many white people, private academies took the place of public schools. And conservatism became a mixture of the worst forces in human life: male chauvinism, white superiority, violence, and plantation capitalism. It is a combination that was able to triumph—from Nixon to Reagan to the Bushes to Trump.

Donald Trump has lived his whole life in the pursuit of control and domination of others. He has an emptiness—a vast hole in his soul. He really may not know how to love life or himself. Donald Trump was a rich young man with an affinity for the *Playboy* and *Penthouse* magazines' ethos of objectifying women, and worse. He was caught up in a wave of American culture where human sexuality was commodified, thing-afied. To ignore that part of his life is to miss who Trump has always been. To dismiss it is to overlook the kind of disease infecting his core.

Black people who had been watching Trump early on saw the civil rights suits against him and his father for not renting to Black people. And later we saw his vicious campaign against the five teenage Black and Brown teenagers who were falsely accused in 1989 of assaulting a woman in Central Park. He took out full-page ads in four New York newspapers, including *The New York Times,* implicitly calling for the death penalty for the teens, with some of the headlines saying "Bring Back the Death Penalty. Bring Back Our Police!" DNA evidence later proved they had not committed the assault and had been pressured to confess. Then the man who actually assaulted the woman came forward and confessed. But Trump never relented. As late as 2019, he kept trying to justify himself, saying they had pleaded guilty, and he maintained this argument even after the DNA tests and the real perpetrator had exonerated them. In 2011, we watched as Trump mounted a whole racist campaign, saying Barack Obama was not born in Hawaii but in Kenya and so could not be president. In that same era, there was his television career on a reality show where he was the capitalist bully boss who glorified viciously humiliating and firing people.

Those areas of his life, as well as his rampant mistreatment of women, were on full display in the public eye for decades leading up to the 2016 election. So a vote for that kind of man showed the serious disease infecting many people in our country. Electing him was a gargantuan spiritual and intellectual error. He embodied evils this country has always tolerated. Voting him into office showed that about sixty-three million Americans had such an extremely loose connection to our founding documents that they could vote for a tyrant.

I felt then and I still feel that unless we the people can push one of the parties to become the party of the Constitution and the Declaration of Independence, we're in the most serious trouble. But the Democratic Party kept refusing to employ bold, courageous politics at the national level. Its leaders simply did not step out front on important issues.

In 2017, white supremacists marched in Charlottesville, Virginia, where the city council had just voted to take down a huge statue of Robert E. Lee, the leader of the Confederate army. They marched across the University of Virginia campus, which Thomas Jefferson built, to the Lee statue in the center of a public park. They carried tiki torches and chanted, "Jews will not replace us." These were the people who had been hiding in the dark corners of our nation for decades. Donald Trump encouraged their emergence, and made them feel safe to reveal their hatred in public—proudly. Nonviolent countermarchers organized against them. On the second day of their demonstrations, the far-right extremists had set an atmosphere that became violent. A white man deliberately drove his car into a peaceful countermarch and killed a young woman who had come out to join those standing up against the bigotry.

That Charlottesville moment put organized white nationalism on the front pages again. It surfaced the Nazi Party and other white extremists in our country. All the forces of spiritual wickedness—from those that had introduced enslavement to the continent in 1619, participated in the execution of women accused of being witches in New England in 1692 and 1693, and carried out lynchings in the nineteenth and twentieth centuries—came to a head in the Trump era, when his forces employed and promoted racist terror.

What I hoped for, envisioning our future in the face of Trump, was that the movements for the greater good would not get trapped in the conventional politics of the United States, defined as only the Left or the Right. With at least 340 million people in the United States, and more than eight billion people on earth, there are far more options to represent humans than merely left or right.

Dividing us into the Left and the Right is what plantation capitalism wants. Because clear division means the imaginative powers of God contained in the billions of people on earth will not break forth. Instead, a few people will profit the most when our collective power stays in the bottle, with a heavy lid on top.

Predictably, Trump and his people began calling Black Lives Matter and some parts of the Democratic Party "socialist" and "Communist." If anyone proposes childcare programs, Head Start programs, or other ways of building an infrastructure for four- and five-year-olds, the conventional pushback is to call them Communists or socialists. Once that label sticks, sizable numbers of people will support doing nothing for children in poverty or for middle-class children who also need child-development programs beyond what their parents can offer or afford. Of course, this same kind of misdirection and mislabeling were what Martin endured. And so did I. More than fifty years later, it was still happening.

On January 6, 2021, I was watching news coverage from my Los Angeles home when Trump-inspired white supremacist groups broke into the U.S. Capitol, using violence in the name of patriotism. I watched the lethal, rudderless sabotage on display as they climbed the walls of the Capitol building and broke into the halls of Congress. I began to think about where their rage originated. The people driving that moment were not patriots. They were not shaped by "We hold these truths to be self-evident," that all people are created equal. They were not shaped by the aspiration to form a more perfect Union, establish justice, and ensure domestic tranquility. And they were not shaped by the Christian religion most of them claimed to practice.

Hearing reporters describing them as "storming the Capitol" and "invading Washington, D.C.," took me back almost sixty years to that spring morning in Birmingham, Alabama, at the height of our campaign against racial segregation there in 1963. I heard echoes from our Good Friday strategy meeting in Martin's room at the Gaston Motel, when he and Ralph decided to march—violating the city's injunction and knowing they would be arrested. Everyone in the room was angry at the federal government's lack of response to the relentless white terrorism we had been experiencing in Birmingham. Hosea Williams. James Bevel. People were speaking up in that room.

"Why isn't the national government doing more to combat the brutal forces against us?"

"We have to do more—take some action."

"We should storm the Capitol."

"Let's go invade Washington. Let's put a million people around the walls of Washington, D.C., and refuse to move until changes begin."

Instead of following those first impulses, we chose an alternate path: nonviolent direct action. We channeled the seeds of rage from that moment into organizing the massive, peaceful 1963 March on Washington, where Martin made his "I Have a Dream" speech and invoked our founding documents.

In 2021, former President Trump and his followers channeled their wrath into a violent, hate-filled insurrection. Five people died. Many more were injured. Watching it all on that day reminded me how the white supremacist rage that forged America had not been fully transformed in my lifetime.

I have been convinced that from the time of desegregation in the 1950s we were not involved in an integration campaign. We were involved in a dismantling campaign. We were trying to rid this nation of some of the old structures that perpetrate an evil economy—one that wants cheap or free labor from working people, working families, while it also promotes massive wealth gathering for a small group of people.

I consider it violence when a college kid sets out to become a billionaire before he's thirty, like the founder of Facebook, Mark Zuckerberg. I see such a goal as doing infinite damage to a person's humanity. But it is celebrated in our culture. The billionaires are conferred the status of heroes or kings.

The United States still embraces the idea that it is all right to declare itself a democracy but run an economy that creates poverty, keeps it in place, and doesn't address it. I remember hearing at least one president say in a television news conference something to the effect of, "Poor people are poor because of bad choices."

No. People are living in poverty in the United States because of the morally bankrupt economic system that created slavery and even embraced it for more than two hundred years. And then our economic system has continued to allow greed, power, and exploitation to demonize a whole community of people who work hard but remain entrapped in poverty. At the same time, our society keeps debating whether or not governments should use public taxes for the benefit of all people.

No society should be debating whether public dollars can be used to make sure no baby dies in the first year of life. No society should debate whether anyone can have access to healthcare or public education. No society should empower its police to subject whole groups to relentless harassment, danger, or death. And no society should prevent people from having their basic needs and wants fulfilled because of their race, religion, gender, or any other made-up way of marginalizing them.

As a strategist, I know evil is temporary. Despite its inhumane damage and cruelty, its demise is inevitable. As a man who has lived almost a full century, I know love is what endures.

TWENTY-EIGHT

With Liberty and Justice for All

Los Angeles City Hall, October 26, 2021.

IRFAN KHAN, LOS ANGELES TIMES VIA GETTY IMAGES

On the fiftieth anniversary of the 1968 sanitation strike and Martin's assassination in Memphis, the city held a major commemoration, with a week of events and panel discussions. On April 4, 2018, I marched with surviving sanitation workers, along with Martin's son Martin Luther King III and his daughter, Yolanda Renee King, who was nine years old and Martin Luther King Jr.'s only grandchild. I was delighted to see her and thought of my own grandchildren—John and Cima's daughter, Raven, and son, Devin, and Seth's son, James—and how rich they have made my life. Of course, I also felt sorrow that my friend Martin didn't get to meet his granddaughter and she didn't get to meet him. But mostly, I felt part of the continuum of our vision, our quest for justice.

Late that April afternoon, a large crowd assembled at the Lorraine Motel, which had become the National Civil Rights Museum. I spoke on the balcony outside room 306, where Martin was killed. A few minutes later, at 6:01 P.M., the moment it happened fifty years before, we bowed our heads as bells rang out.

I will never fully get over the loss of Martin. And fifty years later, I didn't think the city of Memphis or the nation would get over it fully anytime soon, either.

Later that night, John Lewis and I appeared together to talk about the movement and our roles in it. A half century later, one of my dearest lifelong friends and I were carrying on the work.

I had a small moment of reckoning during my visit, when someone gave me *The Commercial Appeal*'s retrospective on its coverage of the sanitation workers in the 1960s, and of me. The headline of the article was "Memphis Sanitation Strike Met with Hostility, Misunderstanding from Media."

The reporter who had written about me the most, Tom BeVier, was quoted in the article saying, "There was just no appetite (among editors) for the sorts of stories that should have been done." He said reporters knew their editors did not see the sanitation strikers' lives as worthy of much attention. "Given the views of top management," BeVier believed that "writing profiles humanizing the strikers" would not go over well with his editors. As BeVier put it: "You knew intuitively . . . nobody was going to be very enthusiastic about such stories."

Then BeVier added to what I had heard all along and what *Time* magazine reported in 1968:

> The newspaper maintained a "hands-off approach" to Lawson even though he quickly emerged as a dominant force in the strike, BeVier said.
>
> "Things that he said kept getting cut from stories, and it bothered the hell out of me."

Apparently, BeVier and a like-minded editor had to go to unusual measures to ensure that the 1969 story about me even made it into the paper.

> Eventually, BeVier solicited help from metro editor Angus McEachran in getting a profile of Lawson published. The two did little to notify other staff members about the story, and they waited until a certain copy editor—described by BeVier as an overt racist—had gone home for the day before filing the story.

Back in California in 2018, former San Francisco mayor and California lieutenant governor Gavin Newsom was running for governor. After he won the Democratic primary, we had a breakfast meeting while he was in the midst of campaigning. *The New Yorker* mentioned our meeting in a lengthy profile of Newsom by Tad Friend, a staff writer who followed him through his campaign.

> In September, he sent me a long text after a breakfast with the Reverend James Lawson, a civil-rights leader who met with Bobby Kennedy. He wrote that Lawson "hit me hard saying what was missing was 'a sense of urgency' a declaration to a 'cause' . . . 'passion' / 'vision.' " He made Newsom realize that "this campaign is not about a campaign for governor, resplendent w dozens of policy ideas," but is a crusade to address "poverty, particularly childhood poverty."
>
> Lawson, he told me, had provided the narrative he'd been seeking. As Newsom put it in his subsequent ads, urging prenatal nurse visits and pre-kindergarten for all, "Renewing the California Dream? It starts with ending child poverty." More important, Lawson had reminded him what it was all about: "He asked me—it was almost spiritual—what my purpose in life was: '*Why are you here?*'" The question hit Newsom so hard that he couldn't muster an answer.

More reckonings followed, including ones with myself. In September 2018, I turned ninety years old. Since the age of four, I had been fighting, resisting, and trying to learn about the structures and ideology of racism. I was still committed to continuing the work. As I looked back at my ninety-year journey, I felt a kind of inward confidence and contentedness flooding into my present. But I realized I was not going to live to see the job be done.

Being in my nineties did not stop me from working. But my family kept more of a watch on both me and Dorothy than ever before. We were living in Baldwin Hills, and I was still teaching and doing some traveling. A family member always went with me on my trips—one of my sons or one of my grandchildren. Also, Dorothy began to have some health issues. But the biggest blow ever to both of us and our family came in October 2019, when our youngest son, Seth, died unexpectedly. He was at home where he lived with Kari, the mother of his son, my grandson James Charles. When Kari and James were both out, Seth apparently had some sort of heart issue. We were never sure exactly what it was. But when Kari came home, she found him and called 911. It was terribly sad. James was only eleven. Seth was fifty-two.

My brother Phil conducted the funeral at Holman. Seth had grown up in that church, so, of course, the sanctuary was full. Losing a son is a wrenching pain that defies reason. I was supposed to go before him. Dorothy and I were deeply heartbroken. So were John and Morris. They lost their little brother. Our whole family will carry the loss of Seth for the rest of our lives.

In 1952, when my brother John died in a plane crash in the mountains of Southern California, it didn't make sense, either. I thought of my parents, and how what I was feeling about Seth must be what they felt losing their son John back then. Eventually, trying to find reasons gives way to pure grief. I knew grief. I knew I would need to take time to find my way again.

In early March 2020, I traveled to Alabama with Kent Wong. He had invited me and key leaders of the Los Angeles labor movement to Montgomery and Selma to visit the Equal Justice Initiative (EJI) and its Legacy Museum in Montgomery and meet with founder and lawyer Bryan Stevenson, well known for his fight against mass incarceration and excessive punishment in the United States. He and his staff work to end these practices, and the museum traces their history from slavery to Jim Crow and segregation to the drug wars and police brutality of the late twentieth and early twenty-first centuries. EJI's work is seeking racial justice, eliminating poverty, and educating the public about our past. In addition to its museum, EJI built the National Memorial for Peace and Justice on a hilltop overlooking Montgomery, which it describes as "the nation's first comprehensive memorial dedicated to the legacy of Black Americans who were enslaved, terrorized by lynching, humiliated by racial segregation, and presumed guilty and dangerous." EJI's stated intention is to remember the "more than 4,400 Black people killed in racial terror lynchings between 1877 and 1950" in the United States. More than 800 steel monuments carrying their names hang down—one for each county where lynchings happened. It is a moving memorial to our enslaved ancestors and those who lived and died under Jim Crow.

Bryan Stevenson and I had a discussion session for our delegation and the entire staff of EJI, in which we talked about a range of topics, including our great-grandparents who were enslaved. I spoke about how nonviolent resistance has always been a key to Black liberation.

> Lawson: I maintain that the first level of resistance on the part of many slaves was this formation of an indomitable spirit inside that said, "I know who I am and what I'm about." Some of the museums I have seen have belittled or ignored . . . the escape through the Underground Railroad. . . . But that was a major form of resistance under circumstances that you and I can never really understand.

Then we talked about violence.

> Stevenson: I think it's worth reflecting on the difference between power and violence. . . . We are persuaded that for us to succeed, we're going to have to demonstrate a power that is greater than violence . . . because usually violence leads to more violence.
>
> Lawson: Violence's greatest power is . . . to impose suffering structurally, and thereby dominate, control, and manage. . . . The prison system is primarily structural violence. . . . But violence does not have the power to heal and reconcile and to build a new community. That has to be done from a different source, a different character.
>
> . . . Violence is . . . an abuse of power. Nonviolence seeks to recover the use of power so that it enables and empowers life. But it is a lonely and longer struggle.

In Montgomery we also visited the Freedom Rides Museum at the old Montgomery Greyhound bus station, where white supremacists viciously attacked John Lewis and other Freedom Riders, beating them until they were unconscious. The director of the museum, Dorothy Walker, greeted me warmly in front of a photo of me and others in the Nashville Student Movement. She emphasized how we were integral to the continuation of the Freedom Ride.

The next day we went to the First Baptist Church of Montgomery, where Ralph Abernathy had been pastor. His daughters welcomed me back. Historian and journalist Jon Meacham then moderated a panel with Ralph's daughters, me, and another good friend from the Nashville movement, Bernard Lafayette, who rode on that first bus into Jackson with me. Introducing my Los Angeles friends and colleagues to the South and to some of the Southern movement people was an amazing meeting of two worlds of mine.

After Montgomery, Kent and I traveled to Selma, Alabama, where we joined in John Lewis's annual pilgrimage across the Edmund Pettus Bridge in commemoration of Bloody Sunday. In 1965, billy-club-wielding Alabama policemen beat voting rights marchers, including John Lewis, as they tried to cross that bridge. It was fifty-five years later, and John was battling for his life. He had late-stage pancreatic cancer. But he wanted to be a part of the event, organized by his Faith and Politics Institute, one more time. A delegation of about twenty members of Congress marched with John. I marched beside him and Speaker of the House Nancy Pelosi, along with Senator Kamala Harris, who had recently dropped out of the 2020 race for president. When we got to the end of the bridge, John spoke. The first thing he said was "I'm so honored to be here with my friend, my mentor, and my brother Jim Lawson." Our bond was never to be broken, not even in the face of death.

Afterward, we went to Brown AME Chapel, the hub of the movement in Selma in the 1950s and 1960s. Nancy Pelosi and Senator Cory Booker were among the speakers. And I spoke. I urged the politicians to live up to our founding documents: "Where there is no vision, a people perish. With liberty and justice for all, the people flourish."

When the talks and fellowship were over, Speaker Pelosi and I said our goodbyes, and she invited me to address the congressional Democratic caucus in Washington, D.C. I agreed, and we planned to work out the dates for it in the following few weeks. I also got to see and speak to Minnijean Brown-Trickey, one of the Little Rock Nine. We hugged, and she teared up as we remembered the time I had spent with her and her classmates in 1958. It was such a joy to reconnect. Then I went into the minister's office in the church, where John had been resting. He was clearly not feeling well. But we had a brief, private visit, and I promised him I would go to see him in either Atlanta or D.C. I was going to be there for him in the end. I told Kent that visiting John would be a top priority in the next month or two.

I was invited to a lunch for the congressional delegation. But Kent and I had to get back to Montgomery to catch our flight home to Los Angeles. So we went to get a quick meal at Lannie's Bar-B-Q Spot in Selma instead.

In a small brick building, on a tiny street near Brown Chapel, Lannie's has been serving not only barbecue but fried chicken and all the soul food classics since the early 1940s. It was a favorite spot for movement people in the 1950s and 1960s.

Just after we ordered, Kamala Harris walked in the door with some of her staff. We both had the same idea of getting an authentic Southern meal before we headed out. She and I had known each other for years. She had come to Holman a few times during various political campaigns across California. Also, it turned out her father and my mother were both from Brown's Town, in St. Ann Parish in Jamaica. She came right over to me and sat down at our booth, and we talked. We ended up having lunch together. She was not yet the vice-presidential pick, but she confided that she was about to endorse Joe Biden. We discussed the Democratic Party, and I told her I thought its leaders could do more to support social and economic justice. We had a good visit. As we left, I said I would see her when I came to Washington to speak to the Democratic caucus in the next few months. When we got in the car, I told Kent, "You know, she might be our next vice president."

Of course, the plans to visit Washington, D.C., never materialized. Because just a week or so later, the COVID-19 pandemic began. That trip to Alabama turned out to be the last time I would ever see John Lewis.

A couple of months into the pandemic, in May 2020, Minneapolis police murdered a forty-six-year-old man named George Floyd outside a grocery store. One officer, Derek Chauvin, knelt on Floyd's neck, pinning him to the pavement beside his car for more than nine minutes, causing him to suffocate.

A video of Floyd's killing again put the issue of law enforcement and government institutions brutalizing and killing Black people into the consciousness of our whole country. I remembered how a video of the Rodney King beating in 1991 had done the same thing. A nation that calls itself a place of liberty and justice for all had never been anything of the sort. Being a Black person in the United States still was not safe.

In July of that awful year, John Lewis died of pancreatic cancer. I was so grateful we had a little time together during the trip to Selma, just before the pandemic. But I was having a hard time understanding how I had outlived John. He was more than ten years younger than I was. At

Holman, I was still officiating funerals, often of much younger people whose families had been in the church for so long that they wanted me to conduct their funerals. As it turned out, our other great friend and colleague C. T. Vivian died on the same day as John. He was ninety-five years old, just a few years ahead of me.

Soon after John's death, his assistant called to tell me that John had asked that I speak at his funeral, which was set to be held at Martin's church, Ebenezer Baptist Church, in Atlanta, on Thursday, July 30, 2020. There was no question of whether I would go or not, even with the pandemic, and no vaccine yet. We decided Morris would come with me. He and I put on our masks and flew to Atlanta. As we arrived at the church on the morning of the ceremony, everyone had on masks. We entered the church and greeted a few people. I said hello to Andy Young. Morris knows his children, so we visited with them briefly, too. Then we sat down.

More than fifty members of Congress attended, as did three former presidents. John was famous and beloved enough that his entire funeral was broadcast live on all the major television stations and streamed online. I spoke about an hour and a half into the service, after former Presidents George W. Bush and Bill Clinton and Speaker of the House Nancy Pelosi and before former President Obama. I started with a poem called "Meaning" by Czeslaw Milosz, a Polish American poet. Then I talked about meeting John and how he got involved in the movement.

> As I moved to Nashville, Tennessee . . . in . . . came people like Kelly Miller Smith and Andrew White and Johnetta Hayes and Helen Roberts and Delores Wilkerson—and John Lewis—and Diane Nash, C. T. Vivian, Marion Barry, Jim Bevel, Bernard Lafayette, Pauline Knight, Angeline Butler. How all of us gathered . . . in the same city at the same time, I count as being providential. We did not plan it. We were all led there.
>
> . . . John saw the malignancy of racism in Troy, Alabama. There formed in him a sensibility that he had to do something about it. . . . He was convinced that he was called, indeed, to do whatever he could do, get in good trouble, but stop the horror that so many folk lived through. . . .
>
> John was not alone. Martin King had the same experience as a boy. I had the same experience from age four in the streets of Massillon, Ohio. Matthew McCollom, a pastor whose name you don't know,

in South Carolina had the same experience. C. T. Vivian had the same experience. I maintain that many of us had no choice to do what we tried to do, primarily because at an early age we recognized the wrong under which we were forced to live, and we swore to God that, by God's grace, we would do whatever God called us to do in order to put on the table of the nation's agenda: This must end. Black lives matter.

. . . The forces of spiritual wickedness are strong in our land because of our history. We have not created them. John Lewis did not create them. We inherited them. But it's our task to see those spiritual forces. I've named them racism, sexism, violence, plantation capitalism. Those poisons still dominate far too many of us. . . . Do not let our own hearts drink any of that poison. Instead, drink the truth of the life force. If we would honor and celebrate John Lewis's life, let us then recommit our souls, our minds, our hearts, our bodies, our strength to the continuing journey to dismantle the wrong in our midst and to allow a space for the new Earth and new heaven to emerge.

John's spirit would keep on influencing our political leadership beyond that day.

Reaching my nineties seemed to bring on yet more full-circle moments in my life, mostly in the form of lifetime achievement awards and things named in my honor. You know you've reached old age when that's happening.

In March 2021, I received the Chairman's Award at the NAACP Image Awards. It's a lifetime achievement award for people who have created change. I had been involved with the NAACP since I was a teenager and went door-to-door in Massillon during the 1940s trying to raise money for the local chapter. Then, in 1960, I had publicly criticized the organization as bourgeois and the chair, Roy Wilkins, had threatened Martin with withdrawing his support for the SCLC if they hired me. In Memphis, I was on the board of the local NAACP, and in Los Angeles, I worked closely with the national NAACP and the national NAACP Legal Defense Fund. I never used to care about recognition and awards. But it did feel good to get the honor.

In December 2021, UCLA renamed its downtown Labor Center

building next to MacArthur Park the UCLA James Lawson Jr. Worker Justice Center. The building was a hub for the labor movement in Los Angeles starting in the 1980s. It is where we had pivotal meetings, and the park is where we staged demonstrations and began marches to city hall. Kent Wong made the renaming happen, saying it was to honor my longtime involvement in the labor movement.

In April 2022, Vanderbilt University launched the James Lawson Institute for the Research and Study of Nonviolent Movements. I traveled with Morris to the ceremonies around the opening. I also got to meet with students and adults who were opening a new public school in Nashville named after me.

I have always believed that students should learn nonviolent philosophy and methods. Nonviolence allows people to be enmeshed in the most profound public issues without animosity and without fear, even when they have differing views. It teaches people to recognize and operate on the premise that there is always a creative solution to be found that will strengthen human life, not destroy or oppress human beings. So it was heartening in June 2023, when my friend María Elena Durazo, who had become a state senator, introduced a resolution to provide a nonviolence curriculum for California public high schools. She named it the Rev. James Lawson Jr./Dolores Huerta Nonviolence Education Project. The California legislature approved the resolution unanimously. It meant all teachers across the state would have the opportunity to teach nonviolence to their students.

Dorothy and I celebrated sixty-four years of marriage in the summer of 2023, and I turned ninety-five in September. Both Dorothy and I had some health issues, but we were able to attend a large celebration that Holman Church organized for my birthday. People spoke. There was music, and so many important friends and colleagues joined us. My grandson Devin helped me to the pulpit to thank everyone. It was a glorious moment. As I have said, I never thought I would make it past the age of forty.

And in January 2024, the city of Los Angeles renamed the part of West Adams Boulevard around Holman United Methodist Church the “Rev. James Lawson Mile.” For me, it was more than a mere ceremonial gesture. A mile could be seen as embodying my entire life—encompassing both my heritage and my legacy.

Before I got there, that mile was being paved for me. When Hattie McDaniel hired Loren Miller to fight the wicked racial covenants her neighbors were using against her, she was paving that mile for me to walk, just a few blocks from her West Adams Heights home.

And when Martin gave one of his last sermons at Holman in March 1968, just before he came to Memphis to support the sanitation workers, he was paving that mile for me and for us all.

Fifty-six years later, in 2024, I got to speak to those gathered at the street-naming ceremony. "I am deeply grateful," I said. "My wife and I are very glad that this is happening, though this surprised us. As we started out sixty-five years ago, we did not anticipate this—we expected jail, we expected mobs, and we expected the loss of dear friends and colleagues in the struggle."

I preached one more time on that spot, that mile, lifting up the better way my mother had imagined, and had set me on my lifelong trek to find. "Nonviolence is the only way," I told the people assembled there. "Compassion is the only way. Justice is the only way. The end of sexism, racism, and violence represent the only way forward." Then I asked everyone at the ceremony to recommit "to the nonviolent revolutions in the United States that will change you and change the world."

My great-grandfather also forged and paved that mile, when he had his own revolution from within, which propelled him to venture out onto the path of freedom and justice that my grandparents, my parents, my brothers and sisters, Dorothy and I, our children and grandchildren, and everyone to come after us continue to pursue.

For we each must discover our own mile, and join the great visible and invisible community of human beings who seek a country and a world that do not yet exist.

AFTERWORD

A Family Tribute

by John C. Lawson

Rev. James Morris Lawson Jr. died on June 9, 2024, after a short illness. He was ninety-five.

Dorothy Wood Lawson, his wife of sixty-four years, died two months later, on August 25, 2024, at the age of eighty-nine.

John Clifford Lawson II, their oldest son, wrote this remembrance.

Imagine the day in the late 1950s. My mother, Dorothy Wood, a young woman from rural Tennessee, meets Jim Lawson. And he tells her, "I have been to prison for refusing to join the draft" and "I recently returned from India as a missionary studying Gandhi." He goes on to say, "I plan on being involved in the civil rights movement and will be putting my life on the line for equality and justice for Black Americans. I plan on protesting, marching, and going to jail if need be. And I expect my life to be threatened and put in danger."

Then he asks, "Can we go out on a date?"

And she says, "Yes."

I sometimes marvel at how Mom had the courage to fall in love with and marry a man like James Morris Lawson Jr. But very soon after they got together, our strong, loving mother was out marching with him, and later they were bringing me and eventually my two younger brothers along, too.

My family and I were overwhelmed by the prayers, condolences, love, generosity, and mutual sense of loss that countless people expressed at the passing of my father, who I affectionately called Dad, Father, Pop, and Old Man. The terms were interchangeable at any given moment, but all were used with equal love and respect for the man who raised me to be the person I am today.

So many spoke beautifully about James Lawson's passion for fairness and dignity for all human beings, his love of people, and his lifelong friendships. Stories flowed about how his actions or words have moved people to resist the forces of violence, racism, sexism, discrimination, and plantation capitalism. Others also mentioned his love of ministry and his lifelong quest to walk in the footsteps of Jesus and obey God. I would be remiss if I did not add that with all the organizing, preaching, teaching, marching, speaking, and going to jail, he still found the time and had the same passion for being a great husband and father.

My family and I also were humbled and grateful for the outpouring of love and praise for the life of my mother, Dorothy Dolores Wood Lawson, who brought me and my brothers into this world, and encouraged and nurtured us throughout her life. She was the one her children and grandchildren could always depend upon, and whose opinion all of us valued the most. She could be thoughtfully honest, or she could be bitingly sarcastic—but in an unselfish manner, constantly looking out for our best interests.

My father often said that all his life's work and any achievements along the way were because his partner, our mom, was there by his side. My parents cared for each other, appreciated each other's points of view, were deeply committed to serving God, and worked hard together to love and raise three knucklehead boys.

There were many times when Seth, Morris, or I deserved to be placed over their knees, but my parents never spanked us. We did get in trouble, and there were consequences for bad behavior. But they sincerely believed and practiced the principle that there is a better way to raise children than with any forms of violence—physical, emotional, or verbal.

My dad taught each of his sons how to swim, ride a bike, play ping-pong, wrestle, throw a baseball and a football, and shoot basketball. When we were teenagers living at the Holman Church parsonage, we put a basketball goal over the garage door. The driveway was just big enough for two-on-two games. When he could get home early, Dad would change clothes and we would play. Soon enough, all the boys our age in the neighborhood would come and play at our house. At least a couple times a week, Dad would join one of his sons playing against any two of the neighbors. We had home-court advantage and usually won.

My mother stayed on Dad about getting his hair cut. She would try to enlist her sons to "tell your father he needs his hair cut." Dad would respond by telling us to remind her he was letting his hair grow, so he could look like Frederick Douglass. She would laugh, and quickly tell him that he had lost his mind.

My father exposed us to the beauty of America's landscape—driving us on vacations in the old station wagon to visit national monuments and parks. He loved to laugh, make jokes, and play harmless pranks on all of us. And he took us to the movies.

I will clue you in on a secret. For such a peace-loving man, his absolute favorite movies were cowboy westerns. Until his last days, every time I walked in the door to visit and he had the TV on, he would be watching some old shoot-'em-up, bad-guy-versus-good-guy, cowboy-versus-Indian movie. I would often ask, "Haven't you seen this movie at least ten times?" The answer would usually be "Yes."

Then, after asking how I was doing, he would begin his diatribe: "You know, John, this movie is an example of the brainwashing and racism perpetrated by Hollywood and the denial of this country to recognize how it massacred and mistreated Indigenous people, and still does, even now. That harm continued when we were kidnapped and brought over to be enslaved. It shows how we must keep up the work to heal this nation and fight against the forces that want—"

"Pop! Stop!" I would demand when he went on one of those rants. Next, I would ask him the most obvious question: "Then why are you watching this movie?"

His response would always be "'Cause it's entertaining."

My father made a point of bringing each one of his sons at an early age, individually and jointly, to his meetings and rallies, and to visit and pray with the sick in the hospital or at their homes. He wanted us to know and experience the life he was living outside our home. He wanted us to see what it meant to be kind and loving to a neighbor. So when Dad would be away—gone to some meeting, the hospital, a march, or off to jail again—we were not disappointed. When he occasionally missed a piano recital or our football games, there were no feelings of abandonment or anger. We knew he wanted to be there. We understood that our father was out doing the good work of helping people—the work that God had called him to do.

Dad taught us what it meant to be brave without balling your fist. He taught us how to be humble and laugh. He instilled in us the idea that we were to love and respect all people, no matter their status in life.

My father was a great, good man.

At ninety-five years old, he would still sit at the dining room table surrounded by books, newspapers, and one of his well-worn Bibles, with a concerned look on his face.

I would ask him, "Dad, what's wrong?"

He would say, "I am trying to figure out how best I can serve God and what kind of movement we can start."

And even on the day before he died, he was still paying attention to student demonstrations on campuses across the country, telling us he needed to get out there and help them build a new, nonviolent student movement, one that he was sure was going to change the world.

Reverend James Morris Lawson Jr. devoted his entire life to creating the beloved community. My family and I hope his story continues to inspire future generations to organize, march, and teach with love, and to find the bravery needed for deploying the full and awesome power of nonviolence against any forces seeking to crush liberty, justice, and equality for all.

Acknowledgments

Reverend Lawson, 1968.
UNIVERSITY OF MEMPHIS LIBRARY

From the Lawson Family

James Morris Lawson Jr. often spoke with immense gratitude of all the people who shaped his journey. He did not get to write his own acknowledgments before he died. So, to all those both named and unnamed here, we thank you on his behalf.

First and foremost, we know our father would thank Dorothy Dolores Lawson, his devoted, faithful companion and soulmate for sixty-four years of marriage. He would often say that Dorothy was the foundation of all his work in the struggle for justice and equality. Their bond is best illustrated by one of the many letters he penned to her:

> Your presence has formed and shaped my being and doing. You are the only person who could have been my choice to love. We could not have lived as we have lived without you. I feel very lucky and very blessed to have walked with you. You, my Love, have been and remain the lovely, enduring, loving presence of my journey without whom I could not be or become Jim Lawson and with whom I am linked eternally.

We are thankful for the many friends who contributed to the creation of this book. To dear friends such as Rev. Louis Chase; Elton and Gloria Bailey; Earl and Dr. Josephine Isabel-Jones; John and Cheryl Sweeney; the Wilburn family; and Giselle Fontaine; who stood by JML and our family in the joyous moments and the chaos—your companionship meant the world. This book could not have been possible without the support and contributions of Karen Hayes and Kent Wong. Karen has been a steadfast chronicler of JML's life and a dedicated friend to him through many years of their work together both on the documentary film she produced about his life and at Holman Church. Kent Wong was a friend like no other—a partner in the labor movement, a colleague in courses taught at UCLA, and a companion always willing to drive JML to eat his Peking duck, which he loved so much. He greatly cherished your camaraderie, for which we will forever be grateful.

We also thank so many of JML's trusted friends, colleagues, and supporters, who have stood with him and our family through the years, including: Dr. Louis Outlaw; Senator María Elena Durazo; Karen Bass; Bonnie Boswell; Mark Ridley-Thomas; Lee Saunders; Rabbi Steven B. Jacobs; Rev. Sandra K. Olewine; Bishop Escobedo-Frank; Rev. Mark Matheny; the family of John T. and Jean Fisher; the family of A. W. and Ann Willis; SCLC; Los Angeles Urban League; NAACP; FOR; ACLU; CLUE; AFSCME; Unite HERE; SEIU; AFL-CIO; Marian Wright Edleman; Diane Nash; Dolores Huerta; Andrew Young; Jesse Jackson; and Bernard Lafayette.

We are thankful for Centenary United Methodist Church. The congregation welcomed this man of God when he was appointed pastor there in 1962. During the turbulent times of the Memphis sanitation strike, the many members and families of Centenary surrounded the pastor and our family with love and support. The members of this church willingly opened the doors to striking sanitation workers, attorneys, and labor leaders who were all engaged in the cause of battling racism and pursuing fair labor protections. Centenary was also where teenagers, whether they were members of the church or not, got their first experience of beloved community.

We thank Rev. Victor Cyrus-Franklin, and the clergy and members of Holman United Methodist Church for their love and continued support of James M. Lawson Jr. and our family. After his move to Los Angeles, Holman became the foundation for his spiritual and community activism, which were inextricably linked. During the difficult time of the passing of our parents and grandparents, our Holman family provided material and moral support.

We are indebted to Vanderbilt University for collecting and archiving the writings, interviews, photographs, and newspaper articles about Rev. James M. Lawson Jr. Much of the firsthand account written and visualized throughout this book would not be possible without Vanderbilt's archivists. We also thank the James M. Lawson Institute; Phillis Sheppard; the Vanderbilt Divinity School; and Chancellor Daniel Diermeier. And we are grateful to the Nashville Public Library for preserving and presenting the history of the movement in the city and JML's role in it.

We are grateful as well to the University of Memphis Library for preserving the history of the movement in Memphis, and to the National Civil Rights Museum and Clayborn Temple for honoring JML's role in the sanitation strike and the ongoing fight for justice in Memphis.

We are thankful to Penguin Random House and in particular our editors Jamia Wilson and Mark Warren, who recognized that James M. Lawson Jr. was a significant figure in American history whose life journey needed to be told. They have been supportive and steadfast in making this endeavor come true. And thanks to our agent Jennifer Gates at Aevitas Creative Management for championing this book from the very beginning and all the way through.

An incredibly special and heartfelt thanks to Emily Yellin, the collaborator who worked tirelessly with James M. Lawson Jr. in creating this memoir. She spent countless hours interviewing, researching, and writing the life of the man we so greatly admired. JML entrusted Emily with this immense undertaking and valued her input and guidance. We are indebted to her for her commitment and care in telling his story.

To his contemporaries in the fight for justice and fellow freedom fighters—those known and unknown, the ones who have gone to glory and the ones yet to come—we know of the struggle you face and the enduring spirit that compels you to push on. We implore you to continue to fight the good fight. Your voices, actions, and commitment to liberation for all are just as necessary today as they were in the 1960s.

And lastly, to the reader: We hope this book serves as both a window and a mirror. It aims to give insight into the life and work of someone who never stopped striving for a more tolerant, loving, and just society. We hope you saw not only the essence of the man, but also the circumstances through which he persisted. In reading this book, please reflect on your own life and how the lessons and teachings of JML can encourage you to organize and use the power of nonviolence to resist the forces of racism, sexism, and plantation capitalism.

These pages honor not just JML's words, but his heart. May this memoir serve as a testament to a life lived deeply, and a voice that resonates forevermore.

From Emily Yellin

One day, in the summer of 2020, I called Rev. Lawson and asked him if he was interested in publishing a memoir of his life, and I offered to work with him on it. After consulting with his family, he agreed, to my great delight. We decided to have regular phone interviews a few days a week, every week, for as long as it took. Neither of us understood just how long that would be.

From September of 2020 to May of 2024, we would talk and talk and talk on the phone—he was in Los Angeles and I was in Memphis. We also met in person several times at Holman United Methodist Church in Los Angeles and talked some more. In those sessions in the lounge of the church, he would recount parts of his life for hours at a time, remembering with remarkable clarity things that had happened sixty or seventy years before. At first, I would ask him if he needed a break. I had a daughterly concern since he was in his nineties. He would always say, "No, let's keep going." Soon, I began to admit that I was the one who needed a break, to get some water or stretch my legs. We would take five minutes, and then we would talk some more.

I am deeply indebted to Rev. Lawson for giving me the honor of those sessions and the chance to help write about his amazing life. And I am especially grateful to his entire family, for always welcoming me in and supporting this major endeavor. I have known the Lawsons just about my whole life. My parents and Rev. and Mrs. Lawson became friends soon after our family moved from New York to Memphis in the mid-1960s. Rev. Lawson and my father were both outsiders from the North with immigrant parents, and were happy to find kindred spirits in that turbulent time and place. John and I were in school together from first through sixth grade at Memphis State Campus School, and Rev. Lawson was a first-grade class parent during the sanitation strike in 1968.

Twenty-four years later, I was living in L.A. during the 1992 uprising in reaction to the acquittals of the police officers who beat Rodney King. I will never forget sitting in a parking lot in Marina del Rey during my lunch break from work and hearing Rev. Lawson on KCRW radio the day after the most intense looting and burning in the city. He compared that moment to the day after Dr. King's assassination in Memphis. I had not heard his voice for years, but I felt he was talking directly to me.

Then in 1996, I had moved back to Memphis and was covering the South for *The New York Times,* when James Earl Ray was trying to get a new trial. Suddenly, I found myself reporting on the entire effort by the King family, Ray's lawyers, and Rev. Lawson from 1996 through 1999, and even writing the news story about Ray's 1998 funeral in Nashville, which Rev. Lawson officiated.

In 2017, I produced a series of video stories about the lives of the 1968 Memphis sanitation strikers and their families for *The Root*. Rev. Lawson was the only person we interviewed for that project who wasn't one of the workers or their family members. He was so integral to the story and was able to give us such nuanced background, that he ended up in almost every episode of the ten-part series.

Writing this book with Rev. Lawson has felt like something I was always meant to do. Rev. Lawson called it providential that we were working together. I joked it was a secular parable teaching everyone to be nice to all your kid's friends, and your friends' kids, because you never know which one will help you write your memoir one day. This book was born of love on both of our parts, and a shared conviction to liberty and justice for all.

The last thing Rev. Lawson said to me in May 2024 when I visited him in the hospital two weeks before he died was, "Emily, you have had a very unique role in my family's life." The last thing I said to him was, "I love you."

In the course of creating this memoir, we visited and worked with several libraries where parts of Rev. Lawson's life were documented. Great thanks to all the archivists who helped us gather those pieces. First is Vanderbilt University Library, where Rev. Lawson's papers are archived with great care. Special thanks to Molly Dohrmann; Zach Johnson; Mary McSparran; Brynna Farris-McManus; Philip Nagy; Katie Grant; Tim Gollins; Celia Walker; and Teresa Gray.

At the University of Memphis Library Special Collections we are forever grateful to Brigitte Billeaudeaux; Gerald Chaudron; Ed Frank; Grace Neeley; and Michelle Duerr.

At UCLA, thanks to Tobias Higbie, Caroline Luce, Reed Hutchinson, Salvador "Pocho" Sanchez-Strawbridge, and Lisa Monahan; at UCLA Library Special Collections thanks to Maxwell Zupke, Simon Elliott, and Neil Hodge; at University of California Press thanks to Niels Hooper and Naja Pulliam Collins.

Special thanks to: Vicki Russo at Swarthmore College Peace Collection; Megan O'Connor at Wright State University Libraries; Elliott Robinson, Kathleen Feduccia, and Laura Scott at the Nashville Public Library, Special Collections; Brad Spurlock at Hamilton Lane Library; Jeremy Farmer at the National Archives and Records Administration; Wayne Dowdy at the Memphis Public Library; and Christine Adolph, Christina Rice, and Lucia Odono at the Los Angeles Public Library.

Many thanks for invaluable photo assistance from: Autumn Smith at the SCLC; Connor Scanlon at the Ernest Withers Collection; Kim Reis, Drew Cuthbertson, Ariel Weintraub, and Deb Dadlani at Imagn; Matthew Lutts and Mark Humphrey at AP; Angel Simonetti at Getty Images; and Susan Smith at the Fellowship of Reconciliation.

Sincere thanks to the extraordinary Darren Walker and his colleagues Jeffrey Hernandez and Juliet Mureriwa at the Ford Foundation for their vital support of this project when it mattered most.

Four people read all or parts of this book and their notes saved us many times. Thank you for your generous and frank feedback: Leanne Kleinmann, Louis T. Outlaw, Raquel Baker, and Kent Wong.

Karen Hayes and Kent Wong were essential to making this book. Without their input and generosity, and their dedication to documenting Rev. Lawson's story, this account would not have been complete. So many others were also there for us giving support, historical context, and valuable information during the creation of this book, including: Rev. Kenneth Walden; Ryan Jones; David Dennis Sr. and Jr.; Joan Browning; Lesley Younge; Gail McMurray; Tom BeVier; Bettye Fountenot; Marc Perrusquia; Amari Lloyd; Anasa Troutman; Brooke Sarden; Laura Kebede-Twumasi; Otis Sanford; Tom Jones; Rev. Keith Caldwell; John Dear; Tom and Mary Beckner; Ron Borod; Alyssa Wolf; Lorin Vincent; Paul August Smith; Churchill Roberts; Dory Lerner; Daphene McFerren; Eric Robertson; Tseday Betry; Faith Morris; Russ Wigginton; Andrew Jehl Mathewes; Jericka Webster; Kashif Graham; Mark Matheny; Rev. Mark Thompson; Jessie Jones; Johnny Mosley; Michael Honey; Bertha Looney; Aram Goudsouzian; Charles McKinney; Charles Hughes; Shimica Gaskins; John Beifuss; Joan Beifuss; Bill Thomas; Susan McCue; Richard Copley; and Henry Kaufman.

Deep thanks to the friends who supported me during the writing process, including Raquel Baker; Merry Mariano; Duffy-Marie Arnoult; Suzanne Bonefas; Jerica Burgette; Ellen Klyce; Val Gutwirth; Neil Kramer; Garner Chandler; Laura Goodman-Bryan; Alison Markell Wetter; Jill Weiner; Ebet Roberts; Dorian Spears; David Lebson; Junius Harris; Tiffany Monet Scott; Deniene Harrison; Maria Speidel; Anthony Curran; Kelly Fisher; Suzannah Fisher Ragen; Anna and Shawn Kelly; Susan Dynerman; Juju Bushman; Kathleen Hall; Nancy Knight; Bill and Susan Remijan; Kelly and Rory Gardner; Frank and Carol Fourmy; Harriet Alterowitz; Anne Cumberland; Sandy Ainger; Lurene and Chris Kelly; Georgene and Sal Cachola; Kirsten West Savali; Baxter and Jimmie Leach and family; Christie Watts Kelly; Eddie Felsenthal and the class of 1959; Elizabeth Hart; Alvin and Helen Turner and family; Janann Sherman; Ann and Jim Utterback; Beverly Bond; JL McClain; Ozell and Florence Ueal and family; Laura Testino; Henry Proegler; Michael Flamini; Rosalyn Nichols; Jocie Wurzburg; Rosalyn Willis; Roz Withers; Vasco "Smitty" Smith III; Sonia Walker; Tony Horne; and Yoshi James.

Mary Jehl Kenner read every first draft of every chapter in this book, and every second draft, too. We would not have gotten it done without her excellent feedback, her empathetic hand-holding, and her wry humor. If you ever want to write a book, get yourself a Mary.

Lue Palmer expertly handled all the photo research and permissions and was an asset to the writing and editing process. Their persistence, patience, and kindness made a complicated process manageable and even fun. The Canada-Jamaica connection was uncanny, too.

Random House was the ideal publisher for this book. From the very first meeting the care, understanding, and support they gave was a rare thing in publishing and in our world today. For that, I am grateful to Andy Ward; Tom Perry; Alison Rich; Ben Greenberg; London King; Milena Brown; Matthew Martin; Dennis Ambrose; Bonnie Thompson; Taylor Teague; Greg Mollica; Simon Sullivan; Miriam Khanukaev; Chayenne Skeete; Darryl Oliver; and Monica Brown.

Mark Warren and Jamia Wilson were the perfect editing team for this book. Without Mark, this book would not exist. He grasped the importance, value, and need for Rev. Lawson's story from the very first moment he heard about the idea, and gave his heart and soul to the entire editing process. His expert vision and guidance brought a rigor mixed with compassion to the process that few editors possess. Mark also won a Pulitzer for his own writing while he was at it. I am forever grateful the universe brought us together. Jamia's insights and encouragement are just what every writer wants, and few ever get. She not only nurtured the best from Rev. Lawson's and my collaboration, but she was an advocate for the truth and emotion throughout the narrative. If I ever felt some kind of fear or frustration during the writing, she was able to talk me through it and get me back on track with the same love and care she gave the manuscript. I have never had two editors on a book before. It was the best combination. Team Lawson forever.

As always, a heartfelt thank you to my wonderful agent Jennifer Gates at Aevitas Creative Management. No matter what was happening, she was there for us at every twist and turn, offering guidance, support, and great advocacy for securing this book's place in the world. Also, we got to laugh a lot, which helped in both good and not as good times.

I want to thank my two dogs, Gus Yellin and Layla Yellin, trusted coworkers who slept through a lot of the writing, but were always ready for a walking break, or a lunch, dinner, or breakfast break, and who shored me up whenever I needed it. Shout-outs also to JoJo, Susie, Ruby, Otis, Zelda, and Oona.

Darius B Williams is my dear friend, supporter, and brain manager day in and day out, since before the idea for this book even came into being. I would not have made it through the whole thing without his kindness, love, and bolstering. I am grateful I always get to celebrate all the joys along the way—big, medium, and small—with him.

I thank the Lawson family with all my heart. The love and care they gave me during this five-year process was the foundation of every word in this book. Dorothy Wood Lawson graciously expressed confidence in me that propelled me forward if mine ever faltered. John, Morris, Cima, Raven, Devin, and James have been nothing but kind, supportive, and fun as we have navigated the ups and downs. Thank you especially to John and Morris for making your dad accessible to me while he was here and for answering my endless, detailed questions after he was gone about your family history, your lives, and his.

And to my own family, I am always supremely grateful for your love, support, and cheers: Tom, Doug, Peyto, Chloe and Jeremy, Isabel and Ephraim, Cole and Lara, and Susan. Mom and Dad would be so proud of you all. I sure am. And to my dear sisters-in-law Shari, Mary Jean, and Linda, thank you for all your love and encouragement. And thank you to all my cousins on both sides, on earth and those who are no longer here. And to the next gen (so far): Ezra and Athena, onward.

Finally, I want to thank my parents, David and Carol Lynn Yellin. There are sentences in this book that were based partly on responses to Dad's interviews with Rev. Lawson in 1968 and partly on responses to my interviews in the 2020s. If not for their work and dedication to justice and equality, and to documenting its history, I would not have had the grounding needed to do this work. I know they are always with me, but on this book I felt it more strongly than ever, which makes me one of the luckiest of writers and daughters.

Notes

Foreword: An Exemplar for Our Time: James Lawson, Saintliness, and Nonviolence

xviii **"where the claims of the non-ego are concerned":** William James, *The Varieties of Religious Experience* (New York: Library of America Paperback Classics, 1990), pp. 249–250.

xx **"on the just and on the unjust":** James, *The Varieties of Religious Experience,* pp. 255–56.

xx **"the bloodstained self":** James Baldwin, "To Crush a Serpent," *The Cross of Redemption: Uncollected Writings,* ed. Randall Kenan (New York: Vintage, 2011), p. 204. Baldwin wrote, "those ladders to fire—the burning of the witch, the heretic, the Jew, the nigger, the faggot—have always failed to redeem, or even to change in any way whatever, the mob. They merely epiphanize and force their connection on the only plain on which the mob can meet: the charred bones connects its members and give them reason to speak to one another, for the charred bones are the sum total of their individual self-hatred, eternalized."

xx **transformed by spiritual emotion:** James, *The Varieties of Religious Experience,* pp. 334–341.

xx **"a leaven of righteousness in the world":** James, *The Varieties of Religious Experience,* p. 340.

Part One: RESISTANCE

TWO: I Shall Always Love You

Note: Some of this chapter is based in part on interviews with Reverend Lawson by writer Diane Lefer.

THREE: Concealed Battle

40 **Aug. 28, 1947 . . . "a Christian Example":** James M. Lawson Jr. Papers, Special Collections, Vanderbilt University Library.

46 **"There is a Spirit":** *The Works of James Nayler (1618–1660)*, 4 vols. (Farmington, ME: Quaker Heritage Press, 2003–09).

FOUR: Unimaginable Warfare

58 **"America makes an atomic" . . . "actions and institutions":** James M. Lawson Jr. Papers, box 15, folder 30, Special Collections, Vanderbilt University Library.

62 **but the judge rejected our logic:** *The United States of America v. James Morris Lawson* (National Archives Identifier 280949914); Criminal Case Files, 1912–1996, U.S. District Court for the Eastern (Cleveland) Division of the Northern District of Ohio; Records of District Courts of the United States, Record Group 21; National Archives at Chicago.

FIVE: Troublemakers

Note: Journal entries and letters in this chapter are from James M. Lawson Jr. Papers, Special Collections, Vanderbilt University Library. My letters to Carol Hamilton are at Vanderbilt Library because, in a very kind gesture that I knew nothing about, Carol gave those letters to the library because she knew that my papers were being archived there.

PART TWO: AGITATION

SEVEN: Nashville Symphony

124 **In early March 1958, Glenn and I:** These conferences were mentioned in *The Columbia Record,* March 20, 1958; *The State,* March 20 and 21, 1958.

126 **"continuous mass meetings and workshops":** James M. Lawson Jr. Papers, box 95, folder 33, Special Collections, Vanderbilt University Library.

132 **On July 22, she wrote:** Lawson Papers, box 21, folder 23.

135 **On November 3 . . . "want such leadership":** Lawson Papers, box 11, folder 9.

136 **I wrote Oral Roberts:** Lawson Papers, box 93, folder 3.

EIGHT: Let My People Go

149 ***"Let my people go":*** "Go Down, Moses," United Methodist Hymnal No. 448.

153 **We settled on a name:** James M. Lawson Jr. Papers, box 21, folder 26, Special Collections, Vanderbilt University Library.

NINE: The Myth Has Exploded

159 **Back in Nashville:** James M. Lawson Jr. Papers, box 10, folder 32, Special Collections, Vanderbilt University Library.

160 **The day after the first sit-in:** *Nashville Tennessean,* February 14, 1960.

160 **The following Thursday, February 18:** *Nashville Tennessean,* February 19, 1960.
161 **Back in Nashville, on Saturday:** *Nashville Tennessean,* February 21, 1960.
162 **But in Richmond, Virginia:** *Richmond News Leader,* February 22, 1960.
163 **Downtown merchants pressed:** Lawson Papers, box 10, folder 32.
164 **Instead of arriving:** Lawson Papers, box 10, folder 32.
166 **Young white men entered:** Lawson Papers, box 10, folder 32.
166 **But soon, our observers:** Lawson Papers, box 10, folder 32.
167 **At that, the mayor exclaimed:** Lawson Papers, box 10, folder 32.
168 **One specific newspaper that ran:** *Nashville Banner* editorial, March 1, 1960.
169 **The dean of the divinity school:** Lawson Papers, box 21, folder 30.
169 **But my statement . . . "temporary or otherwise":** *Nashville Banner* editorial, March 2, 1960.
170 **The *Banner* had published . . . destructive foreign influences back to America:** *Nashville Banner,* March 1, 1960.
170 **"His departure for other fields":** *Nashville Banner,* March 2, 1960.
174 **By the end of March, the biracial committee . . . "A revelation":** David Halberstam, "A Good City Gone Ugly," *The Reporter,* March 31, 1960.
178 **Halberstam's *Reporter* article . . . "over in a minute":** Halberstam, "A Good City Gone Ugly."
180 **My talk got a lot . . . "a redeemed society":** Lawson Papers, box 10, folder 8.
181 **The speech reached:** *New York Times,* April 17, 1960.
182 **On Easter Sunday, April 17:** Lawson Papers, box 99, folder 24.
182 **Martin and Doug had been:** *New York Times,* April 17, 1960.
183 **The Easter season boycott . . . "their present policy":** *New York Times,* April 18, 1960.
185 **But C.T. began with:** Tennessee Virtual Archive, statement delivered to Mayor Ben West, April 19, 1960.
186 **As C.T. ended:** *Nashville Tennessean,* April 20, 1960.
186 **After a few more words . . . "INTEGRATE COUNTERS—MAYOR":** *Nashville Tennessean,* April 20, 1960.
187 **About an hour later:** *Nashville Tennessean,* April 21, 1960.

TEN: Such Starry-Eyed Men

190 ***Time* described . . . "notes on tactics":** "Central Africa: The Visitors," *Time,* April 25, 1960.
190 **That day in Nashville:** *Nashville Tennessean,* May 4, 1960.
193 **Dorothy and I also continued:** James M. Lawson Jr. Papers, box 21, folder 20, Special Collections, Vanderbilt University Library.
194 **The sit-in movement:** Martin Luther King Jr., "Debate with James J. Kilpatrick on 'The Nation's Future,'" November 26, 1960, Martin Luther King, Jr. Research and Education Institute, Stanford University.
195 **All of the Nashville theaters:** *Nashville Tennessean,* February 3, 1961.
195 **The next day we went back:** *Nashville Tennessean,* February 5, 1961.
196 **Each of the next:** *Nashville Tennessean,* February 23, 1961.

196 **We stood quietly:** *Nashville Tennessean,* February 23, 1961.

196 **As we left:** *Nashville Tennessean,* February 23, 1961.

197 **On Friday, February 24:** *Nashville Tennessean,* February 25, 1961.

198 **Sometime in the spring:** *Student Voice,* March, 1961.

200 **So Rock Hill was known:** "Albert Bigelow: Brief Life of an Ardent Pacifist, 1906–1993," *Harvard Magazine,* July–August 2013.

202 **Upon their arrival at the Birmingham:** Lawson Papers, box 103, folder 7.

202 **Just before the violence:** Lawson Papers, box 103, folder 7.

204 **Early on the morning . . . could always get through:** Raymond Arsenault, *Freedom Riders: 1961 and the Struggle for Racial Justice* (New York: Oxford University Press, 2006).

205 **At the jail, they were separated:** John Lewis, *Walking with the Wind* (New York: Simon & Schuster, 1998).

207 **Once it was over, most:** Arsenault, *Freedom Riders.*

208 **On Tuesday, May 23, 1961:** WSB-TV (television station, Atlanta, GA), "WSB-TV newsfilm clip of a press conference during which Alabama governor John Patterson condemns the Freedom Riders," Montgomery, AL, May 23, 1961, WSB-TV Newsfilm Collection, Civil Rights Digital Library.

209 **A few hours after the governor:** WSB-TV (television station, Atlanta, GA), "Series of WSB-TV newsfilm clips of a press conference with comments by Dr. Martin Luther King, Jr., about the Freedom Ride," Montgomery, AL, May 23, 1961, WSB-TV Newsfilm Collection, Civil Rights Digital Library.

209 **Seven of the twelve:** FBI, via FBI Records: The Vault, Freedom Riders, Section 2, Complete; Arsenault, *Freedom Riders.*

210 **I spoke to an Associated Press:** Associated Press via the *Clarion-Ledger* in Jackson, MS, July 16, 1961.

211 **Claude Sitton, one of the . . . "freedom's mainline":** *New York Times,* May 28, 1961.

213 **On the television news:** Arsenault, *Freedom Riders.*

215 **In a report from . . . "call from God":** FBI, via FBI Records: The Vault, Freedom Riders, Section 2, Complete.

218 **As the days went on . . . "provocative action in the South":** *New York Times,* May 28, 1961.

219 **A Gallup Poll of public:** Gallup Poll (AIPO), May 28–June 2, 1961, Roper Center for Public Opinion Research, via crmvet.org. Note: The poll adds up to 101 percent, presumably because of rounding up.

220 **David Halberstam reported . . . "two Southern Senators":** *New York Times,* June 20, 1961.

223 **But it was working:** *New York Times,* September 23, 1961.

223 **Although an editorial . . . "this nation stands":** *New York Times* editorial, September 24, 1961.

223 **A few days after . . . "world cannot ignore":** Lawson Papers, box 96, folder 33.

ELEVEN: Which Side Are You On?

226 **Some of the original lyrics:** Guy Carawan and Candie Carawan, ed., *Sing for Freedom: The Story of the Civil Rights Movement Through Its Songs* (Montgomery, AL: NewSouth Books, 2007).

227 **In the Albany campaign . . . some freedom songs:** Carawan and Carawan, *Sing for Freedom.*

230 **In April 1962, Diane . . . "I have made mine":** Diane Nash Bevel, SNCC statement, April 30, 1962, via crmvet.org.

232 **"Which Side Are You On?":** Tom Maxwell, "A History of American Protest Music: Which Side Are You On?," *Longreads,* August 29, 2018.

232 **Even though Memphis . . . "capital city of Mississippi":** James M. Lawson Jr. Papers, box 93, folder 7, Special Collections, Vanderbilt University Library.

235 **Of course, the state of Alabama . . . "Segregation forever":** "The Inaugural Address of Governor George C. Wallace," January 14, 1963, Montgomery, AL, AL.com.

235 **As white Birmingham . . . "most thoroughly segregated city in the South":** Martin Luther King Jr., *Why We Can't Wait* (1963; repr.; New York: Signet Classics, 2000).

238 **On April 3, 1963 . . . "in her larger destiny":** Fred L. Shuttlesworth and Nelson H. Smith, ACMHR, "Birmingham Manifesto," April 3, 1963, via crmvet.org.

238 **That morning, Martin . . . "not victory":** King, *Why We Can't Wait.*

240 **On Palm Sunday, April 7:** Lawson Papers, box 124, folder 18.

240 **As the situation developed . . . "in eight days":** *New York Times,* April 12, 1963.

241 **"Come all you northern liberals":** Carawan and Carawan, *Sing for Freedom.*

242 **Among my handwritten notes . . . "under the water":** Lawson Papers, box 124, folder 18.

244 **Martin wrote about . . . "a court order":** King, *Why We Can't Wait.*

244 **A few days later, on April 16 . . . "at a lunch counter":** King, *Why We Can't Wait.*

246 **On Wednesday, April 24 . . . and other details:** Diane McWhorter, *Carry Me Home: Birmingham Alabama: The Climactic Battle of the Civil Rights Revolution* (New York: Simon & Schuster, 2001).

247 **By eight A.M. that Thursday . . . Birmingham campaign:** *New York Times,* May 3, 1963.

247 ***Jet* magazine covered . . . "on her again":** *Jet,* May 2, 1963.

249 **There were definitely costs . . . outlawed segregation:** "Mass Action in Durham (May)," Civil Rights Movement History 1963 (January–June), via crmvet.org.

250 **In Danville, Virginia . . . throughout 1963:** "Danville, VA, Movement (May–Aug)," Civil Rights Movement History 1963 (January–June), via crmvet.org.

250 **The students and the Tougaloo . . . any more demonstrations:** Lawson Papers, box 96, folder 23.

251 **I was back . . . right to vote:** John F. Kennedy, "Televised Address to the Nation on Civil Rights," June 11, 1963, John F. Kennedy Presidential Library and Museum.

253 **Eventually, I would . . . "demonstration 'workshops'":** A report from the Memphis field office of the FBI in July 1963, courtesy of journalist Marc Perrusquia.

255 **Ben Hooks turned . . . the front seat:** *Duty of the Hour,* documentary produced by the Benjamin L. Hooks Institute for Social Change, University of Memphis.

258 **Born out of . . . "justice is bankrupt":** NPR, transcript of Martin Luther King Jr.'s "I Have a Dream" speech.

260 **Two days after . . . "this mortal moment":** Lawson Papers, box 62, folder 27.

TWELVE: Quagmires

264 **Black response to . . . registered voters:** Bruce Hartford, "Mississippi Freedom Summer 1964," 2014, via crmvet.org.

265 **One day in late . . . "from now on":** *Washington Post,* January 14, 2018.

268 **The June 6, 1964 . . . "Ku Klux Klan":** *New York Times,* June 6, 1964.

268 **set on fire:** *New York Times,* June 9, 1964.

269 **The House had . . . "school together":** *Congressional Record,* 79th Cong., vol. 92, part 1, Senate, January 25, 1946. (Note: This quotation from Senator Russell on the Senate floor has been cited in more recent news reports as being said in 1964. But Russell said it in 1946, according to the *Congressional Record.*)

269 **Eighteen years later . . . Georgia hometown:** *Congressional Record,* 88th Cong., vol. 110, part 5, Senate, March 16, 1964.

269 **On the morning . . . "to remain segregated":** *New York Times,* June 12, 1964.

270 **"long-time associate of Communists":** *New York Times,* June 13, 1964.

272 **Ellen Barnes was writing . . . "some points":** Ellen L. Barnes, "Mississippi Volunteers," 1964, Freedom Summer Digital Collection, Lucile Montgomery Papers, Wisconsin Historical Society.

274 ***The Washington Post* reported . . . "audience disagreed":** *Washington Post,* June 21, 1964.

276 **We were trying . . . "about whites":** James M. Lawson Jr. Papers, box 97, folder 20, Special Collections, Vanderbilt University Library.

277 **By the end . . . "session ended":** Barnes, "Mississippi Volunteers."

278 **After that Wednesday . . . in our sit-ins:** *New York Times,* June 19, 1964.

280 ***The New York Times* was covering . . . "about 25":** *New York Times*, June 21, 1964.

282 **In recent years . . . "their plans":** Mississippi Department of Archives and History, Sovereignty Commission Online, Oxford, OH, June 24, 1964.

286 **"Deep down in our":** Martin Luther King Jr. speech, Brown Chapel AME Church, March 8, 1965, video of speech via the King Center, Atlanta, GA.

286 **In the nonviolent . . . "STOP IT!":** Ad in *New York Times,* April 4, 1965.

289 **As ever . . . "too very much":** Lawson Papers, box 95, folder 26.

290 **The clergy from the United . . . American South:** Swarthmore College Peace Collection, Fellowship of Reconciliation (U.S.) Records, Vietnam: Clergy trip to Saigon, 1965.

290 **We flew from . . . "not with me":** Lawson Papers, box 95, folder 26.

292 **A journalist for . . . "a stalemate":** Lawson Papers, box 95, folder 26.

292 **In my notes . . . "World War III":** Lawson Papers, box 95, folder 26.

293 **Some of the deepest . . . "first of all":** Lawson Papers, box 95, folder 26.

293 **destructive to the country and its people:** Mary Hershberger, *Traveling to Vietnam: American Peace Activists and the War* (Syracuse University Press, 1998). This book informed the telling of the entire journey with facts and insights not in Reverend Lawson's journal.

293 **Bringing Martin's greetings . . . everyone can thrive:** Lawson Papers, box 95, folder 26.

294 **In my notes . . . "real enemies":** Lawson Papers, box 132, folder 17.

296 **We left Cambodia . . . "God of history":** Lawson Papers, box 95, folder 26.

THIRTEEN: With My Mind Stayed on Freedom

300 **In May 1966, that pressure . . . "the other cheek":** *New York Times,* May 22, 1966.

302 **Martin and I talked . . . coming in the morning:** James Lawson, "The Meredith March . . . and Tomorrow," *Concern,* July 15, 1966.

303 **On the Sunday night . . . "the traffic moving":** *Memphis Press-Scimitar,* June 7, 1966.

304 **One of the troopers . . . two other officers:** Lawson, "The Meredith March."

305 **I wrote an article . . . "of serious change":** Lawson, "The Meredith March."

305 ***The Washington Post* reported . . . "Stokely laughed":** *Washington Post,* June 8, 1966.

306 **Just before we got . . . continue planning:** *Southern Courier,* June 11–12, 1966.

306 **By nighttime . . . "incredible courage":** *Commercial Appeal,* June 8, 1966.

306 **The next morning . . . "progressive community":** *Commercial Appeal,* June 8, 1966.

307 **Needless to say . . . "out of this":** Lawson, "The Meredith March."

308 **From Wednesday . . . "part of it":** Aram Goudsouzian, *Down to the Crossroads: Civil Rights, Black Power, and the Meredith March Against Fear* (Farrar, Straus and Giroux, 2014); *Newsday,* June 10, 1966.

308 **Thursday, June 9 . . . he died:** Goudsouzian, *Down to the Crossroads; Newsday,* June 10, 1966.

308 **The march stopped . . . "for freedom":** Goudsouzian, *Down to the Crossroads; Newsday,* June 10, 1966.

309 **The march arrived . . . "of 19,000":** *New York Times,* June 15, 1966.

309 **Before the march . . . rural Mississippi:** *New York Times,* June 15, 1966; *Southern Courier,* June 18–19, 1966.

310 **At times like . . . "*freedom land*":** Guy Carawan and Candie Carawan, ed., *Sing for Freedom: The Story of the Civil Rights Movement Through Its Songs* (Montgomery, AL: NewSouth Books, 2007).

311 **As we came up . . . "cherry bombs":** *Washington Post,* June 22, 1966.

312 ***The New York Times* noted . . . "yelled derisively":** *New York Times,* June 22, 1966.

313 **We managed to . . . "Molotov cocktails":** *New York Times,* June 22, 1966.

316 **I discussed this . . . "will emerge":** Lawson, "The Meredith March."

317 **On July 10, 1966 . . . to wait:** UPI via *Pittsburgh Press,* July 11, 1966.

321 **At the beginning . . . "here today":** *Chicago Tribune,* August 6, 1966.

FOURTEEN: These Two Americas

322 **As the SCLC . . . "human rights":** Martin Luther King Jr., "President's Annual Report," speech, SCLC convention, Jackson, MS, August 10, 1966, via crmvet.org.

324 **One of the largest . . . for porters:** Library of Congress, "Brotherhood of Sleeping Car Porters Union Formed," research guide.

325 **City leaders sent . . . at every turn:** Michael K. Honey, *Going Down Jericho Road: The Memphis Strike, Martin Luther King's Last Campaign* (W. W. Norton, 2007).

329 **He began the speech . . . "violent coannihilation":** Martin Luther King Jr., "Beyond Vietnam: A Time to Break Silence," speech, Riverside Church, New York, NY, April 4, 1967, via crmvet.org.

332 **I had founded . . . in 1964:** *Memphis Press-Scimitar,* March 16, 1964.

338 **I asked them . . . were unemployed:** Elena Delavega, *The Poverty Report: Memphis Since MLK,* National Civil Rights Museum, 2018.

338 **I said they . . . "the black community":** *Commercial Appeal,* August, 10, 1967.

PART THREE: LOVE

FIFTEEN: Beloved Community

346 **Before Henry Loeb . . . East Memphis:** *Memphis Press-Scimitar,* August 5, 1957; *Commercial Appeal,* August 6, 1957; *Commercial Appeal,* January 2, 1957; *Memphis Press-Scimitar,* January 2, 1957.

346 **For instance, during . . . the streets:** *Memphis Press-Scimitar,* April 12, 1956; *Commercial Appeal,* January 2, 1957; *Memphis Press-Scimitar,* April 15, 1958.

347 **Loeb's responsiveness . . . the world:** Mantri Sivananda, "Henry Loeb III as Public Works Commissioner, 1956–1959," *West Tennessee Historical Society Papers* 54 (2000).

347 **Six of those . . . to escape:** *Commercial Appeal,* February 2, 1968; *Commercial Appeal,* February 3, 1968; *Memphis Press-Scimitar,* February 2, 1968.

347 **Since there was nowhere . . . "too late":** *Memphis Press-Scimitar,* February 2, 1968.

348 **Charles Blackburn, director . . . "route Monday":** *Commercial Appeal,* February 2, 1968; *Commercial Appeal,* February 3, 1968; *Memphis Press-Scimitar,* February 2, 1968.

348 **To add to . . . men died:** *Commercial Appeal,* December 18, 1956.

348 **Throughout the previous . . . "disgraceful sin":** Memphis Search for Meaning Committee (MSM), interview with T. O. Jones by David Yellin and Joan Beifuss, January 30, 1970, University of Memphis Library Special Collections.

349 **"prayers are with you":** Letter from Mayor Henry Loeb to Mrs. Robert Walker, February 3, 1968, Civil Rights Collection, Digital Archive of Memphis Public Libraries.

349 **husband's last paycheck:** "Two Sanitation Workers Killed," Sanitation Strike Exhibit, 2018, Digital Archive of Memphis Public Libraries; letter from Charles B. Blackburn to Mrs. Robert Walker, February 3, 1968, Civil Rights Collection, Digital Archive of Memphis Public Libraries.

349 **Mr. Cole's hand:** Interview with Ruth Walker, *1300 Men: Memphis Strike '68,* episode 3, "Crushed" (*The Root* and Striking Voices, 2018).

351 **"picket the city":** *Memphis Press-Scimitar,* February 12, 1968.

351 **"the public health":** *Commercial Appeal,* February 13, 1968.

351 **"forbids it or not":** *Memphis Press-Scimitar,* February 12, 1968.

352 **For instance . . . working conditions:** *1300 Men: Memphis Strike '68,* (*The Root* and Striking Voices, 2018).

354 **On the second day . . . "lose any more":** MSM film archives, February 13, 1968.

360 **At one point . . . "orders from Mayor Henry Loeb":** *Commercial Appeal,* February 23, 1968.

360 **After repeatedly trying . . . "is the men":** *Memphis Press-Scimitar,* February 22, 1968.

361 **"This strike can" . . . and applause:** MSM film archives, February 22, 1968.

361 **Then Rev. Ezekiel Bell . . . that seal:** "Strikers Hold Sit-in at City Hall," Sanitation Strike Exhibit, 2018, Digital Archive of Memphis Public Libraries; MSM, interview with Ezekiel Bell, University of Memphis Library Special Collections.

363 **But when we woke . . . "Bounds of Tolerance":** *Commercial Appeal,* February 23, 1968.

363 **The cartoonist was . . . and believe:** "J. P. Alley—Cal Alley . . . Editorials and Hambone," Historic-Memphis website.

364 **For example, on . . . "GWINE DO IT!!":** *Commercial Appeal,* February 1, 1968.

364 **Hambone didn't appear . . . "show of force":** *Commercial Appeal,* February 23, 1968.

365 **A short news . . . men's request:** *Commercial Appeal,* February 23, 1968.

367 **The march began . . . right back down:** MSM, interview with Gladys Carpenter by David Yellin and Joan Beifuss, September 11, 1968, University of Memphis Library Special Collections; interview with J. L. McClain, *1300 Men: Memphis Strike '68* (*The Root* and Striking Voices, 2018).

371 **The morning newspaper's . . . "at the time":** *Commercial Appeal,* February 24, 1968.

373 **The afternoon paper . . . "not abuse it":** *Memphis Press-Scimitar,* February 24, 1968.

374 **Late that Saturday . . . "and marches":** MSM film archives, February 24, 1968.

375 **The newspapers and city . . . "whole matter":** MSM film archives, February 24, 1968.

376 **On Monday, February 26 . . . "working for you":** *Memphis Press-Scimitar,* February 26, 1968.

381 **We tried to work . . . deal was off:** *Commercial Appeal,* February 27, 1968.

382 **"position is unchanged":** *Memphis Press-Scimitar,* February 27, 1968.

382 **Even though we . . . such a thing:** *Commercial Appeal,* February 28, 1968.

382 **In the third week . . . "all citizens":** *Memphis Press-Scimitar,* February 27, 1968.

SIXTEEN: In This Rich Nation

387 **On Tuesday, March 5 . . . "place to live":** *Memphis Press-Scimitar,* March 6, 1968; *Commercial Appeal,* March 6, 1968.

388 **One of the white . . . "pure racism":** Emily Yellin, "The Sanitation Strike, the Assassination and Memphis in 1968," APM Reports, 1998.
388 **A few people . . . "jail, jail, jail":** *Memphis Press-Scimitar,* March 6, 1968.
388 **We told everyone . . . "*everlasting arms*":** "Leaning on the Everlasting Arms," United Methodist Hymnal No. 133, 1887.
389 **"paper and debris":** *Memphis Press-Scimitar,* March 6, 1968.
389 **Ultimately, 116 of us . . . further incidents:** *Memphis Press-Scimitar,* March 6, 1968; *Commercial Appeal,* March 6, 1968.
390 **After we were arrested . . . "*FREEDOM*":** James M. Lawson Jr. Papers, box 118, folder 9, Special Collections, Vanderbilt University Library; COME mentioned in the rewritten prayer was the community group started at a meeting of ministers on February 24, 1968, to support the strikers.
390 **Above and around . . . "the place up":** *Commercial Appeal,* March 12, 1968.
393 **The morning paper . . . "on to victory":** *Commercial Appeal,* March 13, 1968.
393 **During the city council . . . "on the subject":** *Commercial Appeal,* March 13, 1968.
394 **Just before Bayard's . . . "our good record":** *Memphis Press-Scimitar,* March 14, 1968.
395 **That night, more . . . "have a victory":** Memphis Search for Meaning Committee (MSM) film archives, March 14, 1968, University of Memphis Library Special Collections.
395 **Then Roy spoke . . . "building for trouble":** MSM film archives, March 14, 1968.
396 **Next, Bayard Rustin got up . . . "is inevitable":** *Commercial Appeal,* March 15, 1968.
399 **At Mason Temple . . . "want to say no":** Martin Luther King Jr., "All Labor Has Dignity," speech, Mason Temple, Memphis, TN, March 18, 1968.
402 **We began circulating . . . "yet militant":** Lawson Papers, box 118, folder 9.
402 **On Wednesday, March 20 . . . "any time soon":** *Commercial Appeal,* March 20, 1968.
402 **On Thursday, March 21 . . . "has been accomplished":** *Memphis Press-Scimitar,* March 21, 1968.
405 **That snowy Friday . . . head up a march:** MSM film archives, March 22, 1968.
405 **By Monday, March 25 . . . "nearest marshal":** Lawson Papers, box 118, folder 9.

SEVENTEEN: A New Sense of Dignity and Justice

415 **The local press . . . "city and nation":** Memphis Search for Meaning Committee (MSM) film archives, March 28, 1968, University of Memphis Library Special Collections.
417 **"in violent demonstrations":** MSM film archives, March 28, 1968.
417 **Martin was asked . . . "particular individual":** MSM film archives, March 28, 1968.
417 **Of all the news outlets . . . "same thing to you":** *Tri-State Defender,* April 6, 1968.
418 **"the Memphis Police Department":** *Memphis Press-Scimitar,* March 30, 1968.
419 **Jesse Turner was . . . "attacks I ever saw":** *Memphis Press-Scimitar,* March 29, 1968; *Memphis World,* April 6, 1968; Joan Turner Beifuss, *At the River I Stand* (B&W Books, 1985).

423 **Right away, the . . . "BETTUH SMILIN'!!":** *Commercial Appeal,* March 29, 1968.

423 **The headline of . . . "in our crowd":** *Memphis Press-Scimitar,* March 29, 1968.

424 **On Saturday, March 30 . . . "to stop it":** *Commercial Appeal,* March 30, 1968.

425 **But an editorial . . . "just plain tired":** *Tri-State Defender,* April 6, 1968.

425 **Regardless of the facts . . . "Chicken A La King":** *Commercial Appeal,* March 31, 1968.

425 **On Monday, April 1 . . . "shooting starts":** *Memphis World,* April 6, 1968.

426 **All over the country . . . "of gunfire":** *Commercial Appeal,* April 2, 1968.

427 **Later that morning . . . "police claimed":** *Memphis Press-Scimitar,* March 30, 1968.

427 **The two white-run . . . "like a dog":** *Memphis World,* April 6, 1968; Michael K. Honey, *Going Down Jericho Road: The Memphis Strike, Martin Luther King's Last Campaign* (W. W. Norton, 2007).

427 **The *Tri-State Defender* reported . . . "she fainted":** *Tri-State Defender,* April 6, 1968.

428 **Despite the pain . . . "of Colored People":** *New York Times,* March 31, 1968.

429 **As the city prepared . . . "I am a man":** *New York Times,* March 31, 1968.

EIGHTEEN: Something Is Happening in Memphis

432 **Martin's plane . . . "forth of nonviolence":** Memphis Search for Meaning Committee (MSM) film archives, April 3, 1968, University of Memphis Library Special Collections.

433 **"the poor nationally":** *Memphis Press-Scimitar,* April 3, 1968.

434 **I got to the church . . . "once and for all":** MSM film archives, April 3, 1968.

436 **Martin arrived, and . . . "of the Lord":** Martin Luther King Jr., "I've Been to the Mountaintop," speech, Mason Temple, Memphis, TN, April 3, 1968.

440 **"If I had . . . and his associates":** *City of Memphis v. Martin Luther King, Jr. et al.,* U.S. District Court for the Western District of Tennessee, Western Division, April 4, 1968; *Commercial Appeal,* April 5, 1968.

441 **Our attorneys had . . . "Yes, sir, I am":** *City of Memphis v. Martin Luther King, Jr. et al.,* U.S. District Court for the Western District of Tennessee, Western Division, April 4, 1968.

449 **At the TV station . . . "Black or white":** Robert F. Kennedy, "Statement on Assassination of Martin Luther King, Jr., Indianapolis, Indiana, April 4, 1968," Robert F. Kennedy Speeches, John F. Kennedy Presidential Library and Museum.

449 **Ben and I made . . . "a firm life":** MSM recordings, Poppy Karchmer, "Home Recordings of T.V. Coverage," April 4–8, 1968.

451 **We ended up . . . "live together":** MSM recordings, "WREC Post-Assassination Statements," April 4, 1968.

451 **The longest interview . . . "get justice":** MSM recordings, "WMPS Radio On-the-Spot Newscasts," April 5, 1968. Ray Sherman's reports also aired on United Press International radio in the aftermath of the assassination. In the interview that night, Reverend Lawson said he had been consulting with SCLC since 1957. He knew Martin Luther King and others who were involved in starting the SCLC in 1957. Reverend Lawson came South in 1958 and began working in person with them then.

NINETEEN: Of Infinite Worth

457 **In federal court . . . "by defendants":** *City of Memphis v. Martin Luther King, Jr. et al.,* opinion and temporary injunction, April 5, 1968; James M. Lawson Jr. Papers, box 118, folder 15, Special Collections, Vanderbilt University Library.

460 **When the procession . . . "and self-respect":** Memphis Search for Meaning Committee (MSM) film archives, April 5, 1968, University of Memphis Library Special Collections; Joan Turner Beifuss, *At the River I Stand* (B&W Books, 1985).

460 **As a chorus of ministers appealed . . . dismissing them:** MSM film archives, April 5, 1968.

461 **As the meeting . . . "at our hands":** MSM film archives, April 5, 1968.

461 **Reverend Moon then . . . "in our city":** MSM film archives, April 5, 1968.

461 **Later on Friday . . . "a single individual":** MSM film archives, April 5, 1968.

462 **Through the day . . . Holiday Inn Rivermont:** *Commercial Appeal,* April 6, 1968.

462 **As it turned . . . "hurt or killed":** John Branston, "Reign Check," *Memphis Magazine,* April 1, 2008; Papers of Henry Loeb III, Memphis Public Libraries.

465 **At Centenary . . . "well in him":** *Commercial Appeal,* April 8, 1968.

465 **After church . . . "of Shelby County":** MSM recordings, WMPS live radio broadcast of Memphis Cares, April 7, 1968.

467 **That Monday morning . . . "with dignity":** Michael K. Honey, *Going Down Jericho Road: The Memphis Strike, Martin Luther King's Last Campaign* (W. W. Norton, 2007).

467 **Finally, Coretta rose . . . "be brothers":** MSM recordings, WMPS live radio broadcast of Memphis Cares, April 7, 1968; *New York Times,* April 9, 1968.

468 **While we were . . . "racial polarization":** *Commercial Appeal,* April 9, 1968.

469 **John T. mentioned . . . "without destruction":** MSM film archives, April 9, 1968; *Commercial Appeal,* April 10, 1968.

470 **Civic clubs in . . . "to happen":** MSM film archives, April 10, 1968.

471 **That same week . . . "Birmingham and Selma":** *Time,* April 12, 1968.

471 **On Wednesday, April 10 . . . city's image:** *Memphis Press-Scimitar,* April 10, 1968; *Commercial Appeal,* July 14, 1968.

471 **We continued our . . . "below normal":** *Commercial Appeal,* April 10, 1968.

472 **On Thursday, April 11 . . . "solve the crime":** *Commercial Appeal,* April 12, 1968.

472 **On Friday, April 12 . . . "of course, means":** MSM film archives, April 12, 1968.

472 **I also brought . . . "without avail":** MSM film archives, April 12, 1968; *Commercial Appeal,* April 13, 1968; *Memphis Press-Scimitar,* April 12, 1968.

473 **Rev. Billy Kyles . . . condone brutality:** *Memphis Press-Scimitar,* April 12, 1968.

474 **The sanitation workers never . . . "man along the way":** *New York Times,* April 17, 1968.

475 **Many of us . . . "their own problems":** *Commercial Appeal,* April 17, 1968; *New York Times,* April 17, 1968.

475 **The local newspapers . . . "I appreciate it":** *Commercial Appeal,* April 17, 1968.

475 **At a rally . . . "in the area":** *Commercial Appeal,* April 17, 1968; *Memphis Press-Scimitar,* April 17, 1968; *New York Times,* April 17, 1968.

476 **In fact, a little . . . only two days:** *New York Times,* May 1, 1968.

477 **After voting . . . "enforcement officers":** *Commercial Appeal,* April 21, 1968.
478 **In *The New York Times* that same . . . "file complaints":** *New York Times,* April 21, 1968.
479 **We gave out handbills . . . "racist newspapers":** Lawson Papers, box 118, folder 9.
480 ***Time* magazine was also . . . "them to attention":** *Time,* April 26, 1968.
482 **Throughout the sanitation . . . church and forgotten:** *Commercial Appeal,* May 17, 1968.
482 **Another small but . . . "cartoon is imperative":** Dr. Thomas Walters, letter to editor, *Commercial Appeal,* April 21, 1968.
482 **Our boycott of . . . "as true art":** *Commercial Appeal,* May 1, 1968.
483 **Some reporters at . . . "Joseph Sweat":** Lawson Papers, box 27, folder 4.
483 **Plenty of letters . . . "that man?":** *Commercial Appeal,* April 28, 1968.
484 **The gravity of . . . Memphis police force:** *Commercial Appeal,* May 17, 1968.
484 **Gradually, a sense . . . "useful things":** *Memphis Press-Scimitar,* May 29, 1968.
485 **In May, I even . . . as he was:** Lawson Papers, box 28, folder 10.

TWENTY: Agitator Index

486 **In an August 4, 1967, letter . . . "other extremists":** FBI Case File Number 157-HQ-7782, "Rabble-Rouser Index."
487 **On March 21, 1968 . . . set to go:** FBI documents, Memo to J. Edgar Hoover, the Weisberg Archives, Hood College, March 28, 1968.
488 **On April 17, 1968 . . . "assassination of Martin Luther King":** FBI documents, Freedom of Information Act request, James Morris Lawson, Jr., 2002.
488 **In May 1968 . . . records of my prison term:** FBI documents, Freedom of Information Act request, James Morris Lawson Jr., 2002.
489 **The tactics and methods . . . "are informants":** "Black Extremists, Part 2"; FBI Records: The Vault.
491 **It wasn't only the FBI . . . published or sanctioned:** *Commercial Appeal,* November 15, 1965.
492 **One of the most vicious . . . "Need We Say More???":** James M. Lawson Jr. Papers, box 117, folder 20, and box 118, folder 10, Special Collections, Vanderbilt University Library.
493 **A similar group . . . "expose James M. Lawson":** Lawson Papers, box 118, folder 10.
493 **Mike Cody, one . . . "are greatly relaxed":** Lawson Papers, box 117, folder 20, and box 118, folder 10.
495 **That Sunday, June 9 . . . "age and work":** Lawson Papers, box 28, folder 23.
497 **One local news . . . "What Do We Want?":** *Memphis Press-Scimitar,* June 3, 1968; *Commercial Appeal,* June 29, 1968.
498 **The papers covered . . . "our today problems":** *Commercial Appeal,* June 29, 1968.
498 **The next week, I . . . of any law:** *Memphis Press-Scimitar,* July 6, 1968.
499 **A few days later . . . of police misconduct:** *Commercial Appeal,* July 9, 1968.
501 ***Time* came to cover . . . "Negroes in Memphis":** *Time,* August 16, 1968.
502 ***The Commercial Appeal* had . . . "reject his humanity":** *Commercial Appeal,* October 7, 1968.

503 **A week or so after . . . in the fall:** *Memphis Press-Scimitar,* July 23, 1968; *Commercial Appeal,* October 9, 1968.

503 **Also, MAP-South . . . in the nation:** *Memphis Press-Scimitar,* October 12, 1968.

503 **On Monday, October 14 . . . "said Mr. Feibelman":** *Commercial Appeal,* October 16, 1968.

504 **Other articles in . . . "here in Memphis":** *Commercial Appeal,* October 15, 1968; *Memphis Press-Scimitar,* October 15, 1968.

505 **But Councilman Wyeth Chandler . . . "ruthless racists":** *Commercial Appeal,* October 15, 1968; *Memphis Press-Scimitar,* October 15, 1968.

505 **Another councilman, Billy . . . "of MAP-South":** *Commercial Appeal,* October 15, 1968.

505 **Despite my multiple responses . . . "ministers as well":** *Memphis Press-Scimitar,* October 15, 1968.

505 **The council members . . . for MAP-South:** *Memphis Press-Scimitar,* October 16, 1968.

506 **AFSCME's leader Jerry Wurf:** Memphis Search for Meaning Committee (MSM), interview with Jerry Wurf by David Yellin and Carol Lynn Yellin, Washington, DC, February 3, 1972, University of Memphis Library Special Collections.

506 **My colleagues and . . . "to rot beneath":** Lawson Papers, box 120, folder 5.

507 **The council considered . . . "away by assassination":** *Memphis Press-Scimitar,* October 23, 1968.

507 **voted against approval:** *Commercial Appeal,* October 23, 1968; *Memphis Press-Scimitar,* October 23, 1968.

PART FOUR: STILL GOING ON

TWENTY-ONE: On Resurrection Morning

512 **I was standing at . . . "in that cemetery":** Roy Mayes Jr. obituary, *Commercial Appeal,* January 14, 1969.

513 **When we arrived back . . . "or about him":** *Commercial Appeal,* April 9, 1969.

515 **By the end of . . . "Mrs. Richard Wurzburg":** *Commercial Appeal,* June 13, 1969.

516 **Rev. Ralph Jackson . . . "as invited guests":** *Memphis Press-Scimitar,* June 13, 1969.

516 **By the next week . . . board of education:** *Memphis Press-Scimitar,* June 19, 1969.

517 **We knew we needed . . . be hired:** *Commercial Appeal,* September 29, 1969.

518 **As all this work . . . Black Monday campaign:** *Memphis Press-Scimitar,* October 13, 1969.

518 **on Monday, October 13 . . . equitable education:** *Memphis Press-Scimitar,* October 13, 1969.

518 **Then, in a flagrant . . . our goals:** *Commercial Appeal,* November 25, 1969.

519 **By Tuesday, December 9 . . . posting the bond:** *Memphis Press-Scimitar,* December 10, 1969; *Commercial Appeal,* December 11, 1969.

519 **In jail we . . . "one of you":** James M. Lawson Jr. Papers, box 120, folder 12, Special Collections, Vanderbilt University Library.

519 **On Wednesday, December 17 . . . "Blacks as persons":** *Tri-State Defender,* December 20, 1969.

519 **"We stay in jail . . . risk and sacrifice":** Lawson Papers, box 120, folder 12.

519 **On Thursday, December 18 . . . shots were fired:** Alicia Maynard, "The Assassination of Fred Hampton," Digital Chicago, Lake Forest College and the Chicago History Museum, 2019.

520 **When Ralph arrived . . . Christmas holiday:** *Commercial Appeal,* December 19, 1969.

520 **Between the five of us . . . we were doing:** Lawson Papers, box 120, folder 14.

521 **Christmas Day came . . . "with my family":** *Memphis Press-Scimitar,* December 26, 1969.

522 **A few months later . . . attack commenced:** *Commercial Appeal,* October 18, 1971.

522 **Isaac Hayes had . . . "we are building":** *Commercial Appeal,* October 22, 1971.

523 **In the end . . . had always been:** Smart City Memphis, "Elton Hayes Killed 50 Years Ago, Part 4: The Verdict," October 22, 2021.

523 **In December 1971 . . . "of the city":** *Commercial Appeal,* December 26, 1971.

524 **In January 1972 . . . "been much change":** *Commercial Appeal,* January 16, 1972.

524 **when I heard . . . throughout that spring:** *Commercial Appeal,* March 31, 1972.

525 **The longest feature . . . "it's important":** *Commercial Appeal,* April 29, 1972.

526 **We had hoped . . . state's delegates:** *Memphis Press-Scimitar,* May 5, 1972; *New York Times,* March 2, 1972.

527 **One notable letter . . . "at best, shoddy":** Lawson Papers, letter from *Commercial Appeal* reporter, box 139.

TWENTY-TWO: Equal Protection

530 **In the early 1940s . . . their stately homes:** Hadley Meares, "The Thrill of Sugar Hill," Curbed Los Angeles, February 22, 2018; "Beneath the Santa Monica Freeway Lies the Erasure of Sugar Hill," National Public Radio, May 4, 2021; *Los Angeles Times,* December 7, 1945.

531 **A few years later . . . "American citizen would":** *Los Angeles Sentinel,* August 5, 1948.

532 **The neighborhood association . . . they stayed:** "When Nat King Cole Moved In," Curbed Los Angeles, December 20, 2018; *Daily News* (Los Angeles), August 11, 1948; *Pasadena Independent,* August 3, 1948.

533 **Los Angeles has the second-largest . . . different languages:** "A Generation Deprived: Los Angeles School Desegregation; A Report of the United States Commission on Civil Rights," May 1977; *Teach Our Children,* KABC-TV, Los Angeles, 1979.

534 **By 1971, all of these . . . delays followed:** "A Generation Deprived: Los Angeles School Desegregation."

534 **In 1975, at the end . . . and early 1960s:** *Los Angeles Times,* May 18, 1975.

TWENTY-THREE: Can We All Get Along?

538 **The Los Angeles Police Department . . . "wild tribes" of Mexico:** *Los Angeles Times,* August 11, 2020; Jasmyne Cannick, *Is This Really Who the L.A.P.D. Wants to Name Its New Building After?,* YouTube, April 12, 2009.

538 **In 1965, in what . . . had had enough:** *Los Angeles Times,* August 11, 2005.

538 **After Watts, the L.A. police . . . in the community:** *Los Angeles Times,* August 11, 2020; *Salon,* October 21, 2017; *Los Angeles Times,* December 8, 2019; *Los Angeles Times,* July 29, 2015.

541 **At that time, I . . . all its forms:** *Los Angeles Times,* January 11, 1992.

542 **In April 1992 . . . world had witnessed:** Anjuli Sastry Krbechek and Karen Grigsby Bates, "When LA Erupted in Anger," National Public Radio, April 26, 2017.

542 **South Central Los Angeles erupted . . . of looting were arrested:** Krbechek and Bates, "When LA Erupted in Anger."

542 **On the third day . . . "all get along?":** Krbechek and Bates, "When LA Erupted in Anger."

542 **In my sermon . . . "in our midst":** James M. Lawson Jr. Papers, box 62, folder 14, Special Collections, Vanderbilt University Library.

543 **In November 1992 . . . "democratic society":** Lawson Papers, "Deposition of Reverend Dr. James M. Lawson," *Lawson v. Gates,* November 19, 1992, box 3, folder 16.

544 **The case dragged . . . of police dogs:** Lawson Papers, press release on settlement of *Lawson v. Gates,* ACLU, NAACP Legal Defense Fund, Law offices of Litt & Marquez, Mann & Cook, March 30, 1995, box 128, folder 17.

546 **In March 1968, Martin . . . "keep hope alive":** Martin Luther King Jr., "The Meaning of Hope," sermon at Holman United Methodist Church, March 17, 1968, Holman UMC on SoundCloud.

TWENTY-FOUR: The Tragedy Would Be Compounded

Note: Some of this chapter draws from video interviews of Reverend Lawson conducted by documentary filmmaker Karen Hayes. Other parts of the chapter are partially based on an online video interview with Reverend James Lawson, Nashville, TN, United Methodist Communications, posted January 12, 2017.

551 **When Ray and Anna . . . "I'm not like that":** *People,* October 30, 1978.

553 **I stayed involved . . . "permeated this case":** *Commercial Appeal,* August 11, 1978.

553 **Jesse went on . . . "dead than Mr. Ray":** *The Tennessean,* August 11, 1978.

553 **That summer, I was quoted . . . "duress and pressure":** *SCLC* magazine, July–August 1978.

553 **At the end of August 1978 . . . "affection for you":** James M. Lawson Jr. Papers, box 122, folder 1, Special Collections, Vanderbilt University Library.

554 **Anna told *People* . . . "James is innocent":** *People,* October 30, 1978; *Washington Post,* October 13, 1978.

555 **In May 1994 . . . "our own behinds":** *Washington Post,* May 31, 1994.

556 **In February 1997 . . . "would be compounded":** *New York Times,* February 21, 1997.

556 **The petition was denied . . . "justice will prevail":** *New York Times,* March 28, 1997.

556 **out of a coma:** *New York Times,* March 28, 1998.

TWENTY-FIVE: Unidos Venceremos

Note: Some of this chapter draws from video interviews of Reverend Lawson conducted by documentary filmmaker Karen Hayes, and from recordings of classes Reverend Lawson taught with Kent Wong at UCLA.

564 **On June 15, 1990 . . . picketing:** Patricia Ford, "Ophelia McFadden," in *SEIU: African American Leaders in Labor*, SEIU, 2015.

567 **Two years later, CLUE . . . workers' job security and benefits:** Caitlin Parker, "Hotel Workers Transform the Labor Movement," chapter in *Nonviolence and Social Movements: The Teachings of Rev. James M. Lawson Jr.*, edited by Kent Wong, Ana Luz González, and Rev. James M. Lawson Jr., UCLA Center for Labor Research and Education, 2016.

TWENTY-SIX: Inalienable Rights

568 **In 1994, the then president:** James M. Lawson Jr. Papers, box 56, folder 19, Special Collections, Vanderbilt University Library.

569 **Then two years later . . . sit-in campaign had:** *Vanderbilt Magazine*, Fall 2002.

570 **At the reunion in 2001 . . . "of my classmates":** Lawson Papers, "Bud Collins's Class of 1951 Message to His Classmates for Their 50th Reunion," 2001, box 15, folder 31.

571 **For my retirement . . . "I thank you":** Lawson Papers, box 8, folder 22.

573 **In Los Angeles, we had . . . "a Freedom Rider":** *Los Angeles Times*, September 21, 2003.

574 **I started by . . . with members of Congress:** *Arizona Republic*, September 27, 2003; "Los Angeles Freedom Riders," Immigrant Workers Freedom Ride Documentary Project, executive producer David Koff, UCLA Archive Research & Study Center, 2003.

575 **They told us:** Associated Press via *The Monitor*, McAllen, TX, September 27, 2003.

575 **The buses from Los Angeles . . . "do not achieve them":** United Methodist Church News Service, Nashville, September 30, 2003.

575 **I also pointed out . . . the immigration crisis:** United Methodist Church News Service, Nashville, September 30, 2003.

575 **One young man . . . kept on going:** "Los Angeles Freedom Riders."

575 **On Wednesday, October . . . by neo-Nazi groups:** *Los Angeles Times*, October 5, 2003.

TWENTY-EIGHT: With Liberty and Justice for All

592 **I had a small . . . "filing the story":** *Commercial Appeal*, March 18, 2018.

593 **Back in California . . . muster an answer:** "Gavin Newsom, the Next Head of the California Resistance," *The New Yorker*, October 29, 2018.

594 **In early March 2020 . . . under Jim Crow:** Equal Justice Initiative, eji.org.

595 **Bryan Stevenson and I . . . "and longer struggle":** Rev. James M. Lawson Jr. with Michael K. Honey and Kent Wong, *Revolutionary Nonviolence: Organizing for Freedom* (Oakland: University of California Press, 2022).

References

Source Books

At the River I Stand, Joan Beifuss, B&W Books, Memphis, TN, 1985

Carry Me Home: Birmingham Alabama: The Climactic Battle of the Civil Rights Revolution, Diane McWhorter, Simon & Schuster, New York, 2001

Down to the Crossroads: Civil Rights, Black Power, and the Meredith March Against Fear, Aram Goudsouzian, Farrar, Straus and Giroux, New York, 2014

Freedom Riders: 1961 and the Struggle for Racial Justice, Raymond Arsenault, Oxford University Press, New York, 2006

Going Down Jericho Road: The Memphis Strike, Martin Luther King's Last Campaign, Michael K. Honey, W. W. Norton & Company, New York, 2007

Nonviolence and Social Movements: The Teachings of Rev. James M. Lawson Jr., edited by Kent Wong, Ana Luz González, and Rev. James M. Lawson Jr., UCLA Center for Labor Research and Education, Los Angeles, 2016

Revolutionary Nonviolence: Organizing for Freedom, Rev. James M. Lawson Jr. with Michael K. Honey and Kent Wong, University of California Press, Oakland, CA, 2022

Sing for Freedom: The Story of the Civil Rights Movement Through Its Songs, edited by Guy and Candie Carawan, New South Books, Montgomery, AL, 2007

The Works of James Nayler (1618–1660), Quaker Heritage Press, Farmington, ME

Traveling to Vietnam: American Peace Activists and the War, Mary Hershberger, Syracuse University Press, 1998

Walking with the Wind: A Memoir of the Movement, John Lewis, Simon & Schuster, New York, 1998

Why We Can't Wait, Martin Luther King, Jr., Signet Classics, New York, 1963

Books Consulted

A Force More Powerful: A Century of Nonviolent Conflict, Peter Ackerman and Jack Duvall, St. Martin's Press, New York, 2000

A Spy in Canaan: How the FBI Used a Famous Photographer to Infiltrate the Civil Rights Movement, Marc Perrusquia, Melville House Publishing, Brooklyn, NY, 2017

Ali: A Life, Jonathan Eig, Houghton Mifflin Harcourt, Boston, 2017

An American Death: The True Story of the Assassination of Dr. Martin Luther King, Jr., and the Greatest Manhunt of Our Time, Gerold Frank, Doubleday & Company, Garden City, NY, 1972

An Unseen Light: Black Struggles for Freedom in Memphis, Tennessee, edited by Aram Goudsouzian and Charles W. McKinney Jr., the University Press of Kentucky, Lexington, KY, 2018

At Canaan's Edge: America in the King Years 1965–68, Taylor Branch, Simon & Schuster, New York, 2006

Autobiography: The Story of My Experiments with Truth, Mohandas K. Gandhi, Public Affairs Press, Washington, D.C., 1948

Bearing the Cross: Martin Luther King, Jr., and the Southern Christian Leadership Conference, David J. Garrow, William Morrow and Company, New York, 1986

Black Power in the Bluff City: African American Youth and Student Activism in Memphis, 1965–1975, Shirletta J. Kinchen, the University of Tennessee Press, Knoxville, TN, 2016

Field Guide to Christian Nonviolence, David C. Cramer and Myles Werntz, Baker Publishing Group, Grand Rapids, MI, 2022

Freedom's Daughters: The Unsung Heroines of the Civil Rights Movement from 1830 to 1970, Lynne Olson, Scribner, New York, 2001

From Boss Crump to Prince Willie: How Race Changed Memphis Politics, Otis Sanford, the University of Tennessee Press, Knoxville, TN, 2017

From Rights to Lives: The Evolution of the Black Freedom Struggle, edited by Françoise N. Hamlin and Charles W. McKinney Jr., Vanderbilt University Press, Nashville, TN, 2024

Jesus and Nonviolence: A Third Way, Walter Wink, Fortress Press, Minneapolis, MN, 2003

Killing the Dream: James Earl Ray and the Assassination of Martin Luther King, Jr., Gerald Posner, Random House, New York, 1998

King: A Life, Jonathan Eig, Farrar, Straus and Giroux, New York, 2023

Nonviolence Before King: The Politics of Being and the Black Freedom Struggle, Anthony C. Siracusa, University of North Carolina Press, Chapel Hill, NC, 2021

Parting the Waters: America in the King Years 1954–63, Taylor Branch, Simon & Schuster, New York, 1988

Pillar of Fire: America in the King Years 1963–65, Taylor Branch, Simon & Schuster, New York, 1998

Stride Toward Freedom, Martin Luther King, Jr., Harper & Brothers Publishers, New York, 1958

Tender Warriors, Dorothy Sterling with Donald Gross, Hill and Wang, New York, 1958

The Autobiography of Malcom X, Malcolm X with Alex Haley, Random House, New York, 1964

The Autobiography of Martin Luther King, Jr., edited by Clayborne Carson, Little Brown Book Group, London, 1998

The Children, David Halberstam, Random House, New York, 1998

The FBI and Martin Luther King, Jr., David J. Garrow, Penguin Books, 1981

The Movement Made Us: A Father, A Son, and the Legacy of a Freedom Ride, David J. Dennis Jr. with David J. Dennis Sr., HarperCollins, New York, 2022

The Race Beat: The Press, the Civil Rights Struggle, and the Awakening of a Nation, Gene Roberts and Hank Klibanoff, Knopf, New York, 2006

The War on Poverty: A New Grassroots History, 1964–1980, edited by Annelise Orleck and Lisa Gayle Hazirjian, the University of Georgia Press, Athens, GA, 2011

Waging a Good War: A Military History of the Civil Rights Movement, 1954–1968, Thomas E. Ricks, Farrar, Straus and Giroux, New York, 2022

Warriors Don't Cry: A Searing Memoir of the Battle to Integrate Little Rock's Central High, Melba Pattillo Beals, Pocket Books, New York, 1994

We Are Not Afraid: The Story of Goodman, Schwerner, and Chaney and the Civil Rights Campaign for Mississippi, Seth Cagin and Philip Dray, Macmillan, New York, 1988

Photo Credits

Many of the photo attributions inside the book were abbreviated. Here are the full credits for those photos.

- Photos attributed to Vanderbilt Library: courtesy of James M. Lawson Jr. Papers, Special Collections and University Archives, Vanderbilt University Library
- Photos attributed to University of Memphis Library: courtesy of Special Collections Department, University of Memphis Libraries, Memphis Search for Meaning Committee Collection, University of Memphis
- Photos attributed to *Memphis Press-Scimitar:* courtesy of Special Collections Department, University of Memphis Libraries, University of Memphis
- Photos attributed to *Herald Examiner,* L.A. Public Library: courtesy of *Herald Examiner* Photo Collection, Los Angeles Public Library Special Collections
- Photos attributed to UCLA Library: courtesy of Los Angeles Alliance for a New Economy (LAANE) Collection, UCLA Library Special Collections
- Photos attributed to *Nashville Banner,* Nashville Public Library: courtesy of *Nashville Banner* Archives, Special Collections Division, Nashville Public Library
- Photos attributed to Associated Press: courtesy of AP Images
- Photos attributed to *Commercial Appeal* and *The Nashville Tennessean:* courtesy of © USA TODAY NETWORK via Imagn Images
- Photos attributed to Ernest Withers Collection: © Dr. Ernest C. Withers, Sr. courtesy of Withers Archive Enterprises
- Photo attributed to National Archives: courtesy of the National Archives and Records Administration at Chicago
- Photo attributed to SCLC: courtesy of the Southern Christian Leadership Conference Archives (via Lawson Papers, Vanderbilt Library)
- Photo attributed to Bob Fitch Archive: courtesy of the Bob Fitch Photography Archive, Stanford University Library Special Collections
- Photo attributed to *SEIU*: courtesy of Service Employees International Union, Local 721

Index

About the Authors

Rev. James Lawson Jr. was a Methodist pastor, a teacher, a strategist, and a father, grandfather, and husband. He was integral to the Civil Rights Movement and key to ongoing campaigns for labor, gender, and immigrant rights. He taught the strategic, philosophical, and spiritual components of nonviolent direct action to generations of students and organizers, and inspired countless people worldwide to join in creating the beloved community.

Emily Yellin is a journalist, author, and producer. She is a longtime contributor to *The New York Times* and has written two other books. She also produced a ten-part video series, *1,300 Men: Memphis Strike '68,* for *The Root.* She met Reverend Lawson when she was five, while attending elementary school in Memphis with his eldest son, John.